THE INDEX LIBRARY

General Editor
Peter Spufford, M.A., Ph.D., Litt.D., F.S.A., F.R.Hist.S.

BEDFORDSHIRE PROBATE RECORDS

PART I: A - KIMNOT

ISSUED BY
THE BRITISH RECORD SOCIETY
[104]

THE INDEX LIBRARY

INDEX OF BEDFORDSHIRE PROBATE RECORDS 1484-1858

PART I: A - KIMNOT

Compiled by
Alan F. Cirket

Edited by
Joan Stuart and Peggy Wells

With an Introduction by
Christopher Pickford, F.S.A.

Issued to Subscribers by
THE BRITISH RECORD SOCIETY, LONDON
1993

Published by the British Record Society
c/o Patric Dickinson
The College of Arms
Queen Victoria Street
LONDON EC4V 4BT

ISBN Part I 0 901505 33 1
ISBN Part II 0 901505 34 X
ISBN for the set 0 901505 35 8

Camera copy by Moira Coleman Secretarial Services, Halesworth, Suffolk
Printed by Parchment (Oxford) Ltd., Oxford

CONTENTS PART I

Supplementary indexes to Places and to Trades and Conditions will appear at the end of Part II.

BEDFORDSHIRE
The HISTORIC PARISHES (c1880)

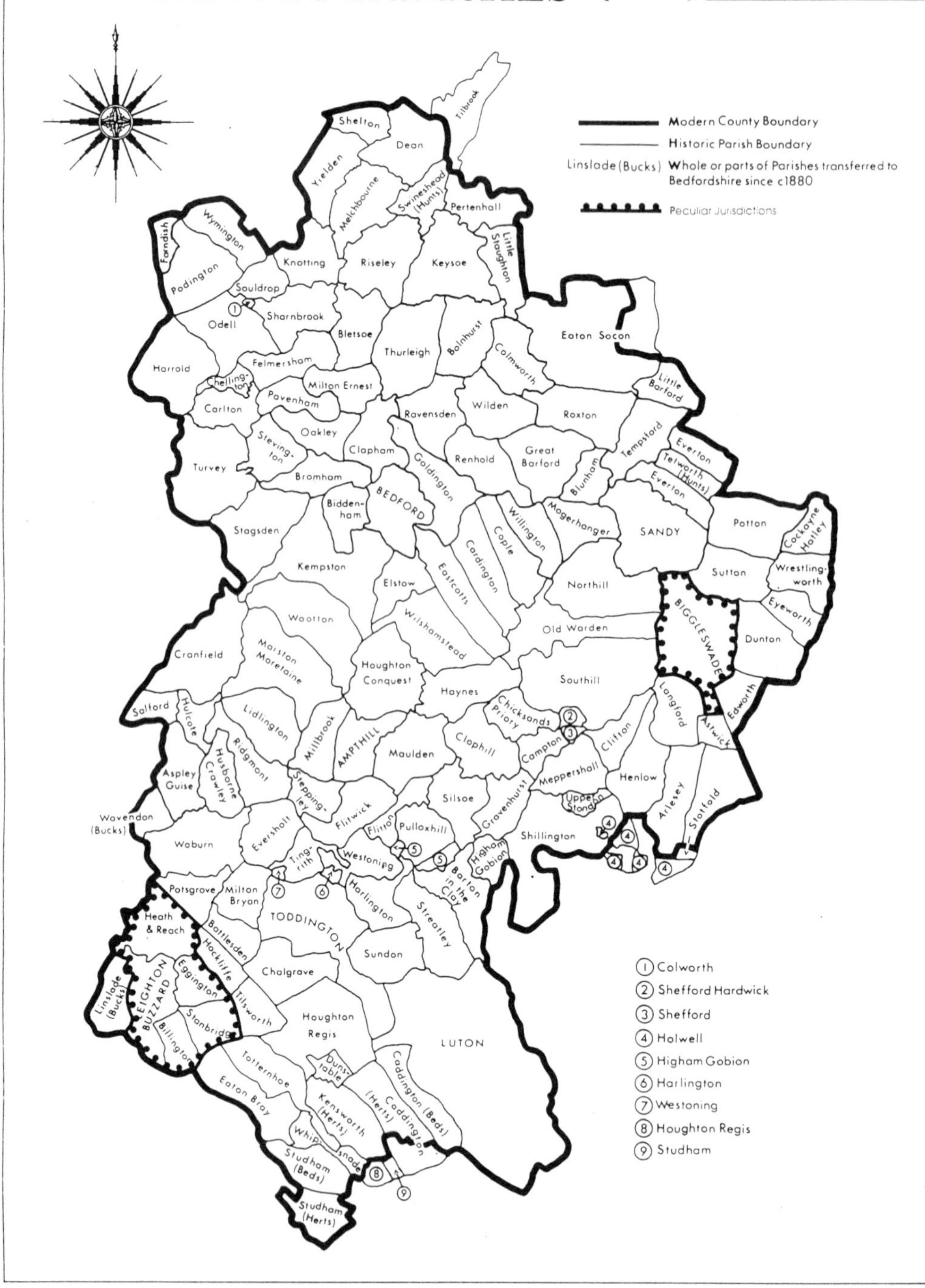

MAP 1

INTRODUCTION

As probate jurisdictions go, those covering the administrative County of Bedford are relatively straightforward. Originally in the great mediaeval Diocese of Lincoln, the archdeaconry of Bedford covered more or less the same area as the County. Probate matters were effectively delegated to the archdeaconry court from an early date, and there are very few Bedfordshire wills among the Lincoln probate material. The archdeaconry was transferred first to the Diocese of Ely in 1837, and then in 1914 (some time after the closure of the ecclesiastical courts in 1858) to St. Albans (established in 1877).

Within the County there were two Peculiars with probate jurisdiction, at Biggleswade and Leighton Buzzard (shown on map 1). The latter included the dependent chapelries of Billington, Eggington, Heath and Reach, and Stanbridge (*see* map 3). Peculiar status was also claimed at Woburn (1), but testamentary matters were always dealt with in the archdeaconry court.

Other exceptions are those parishes which have been added to or removed from the Archdeaconry and County (shown on map 2). These include

Place and present County	Location of records
Caddington, Beds.	Partly in Herts. until 1897. Probate records at BRO. An area of the Hertfordshire part now forms the parish of Markyate.
Eaton Socon, Cambs.	Historically in Beds., and still in the Diocese of St. Albans and Archdeaconry of Bedford. Probate records at BRO.
Everton, Beds. & Hunts.	In Archdeaconry of Huntingdon. The present parish includes Tetworth which was historically in Huntingdonshire. Probate records chiefly at Cambridgeshire CRO (Huntingdon branch). Some Everton probate material at Bedford.
Holwell, Herts.	Originally in Bedfordshire and in the Archdeaconry of Bedford. Transferred to Herts. in 1897. Probate records at BRO.
Kensworth, Beds.	Originally in Herts. Transferred to Beds. in 1897. Probate records in Huntingdon (Hitchin Division) at Herts. RO.

---

(1) For Woburn Peculiar, *see* Dorothy Owen, "The exempt jurisdiction of Woburn" in *Miscellanea* BHRS. Vol. 49 (1970) pp. 122-134.

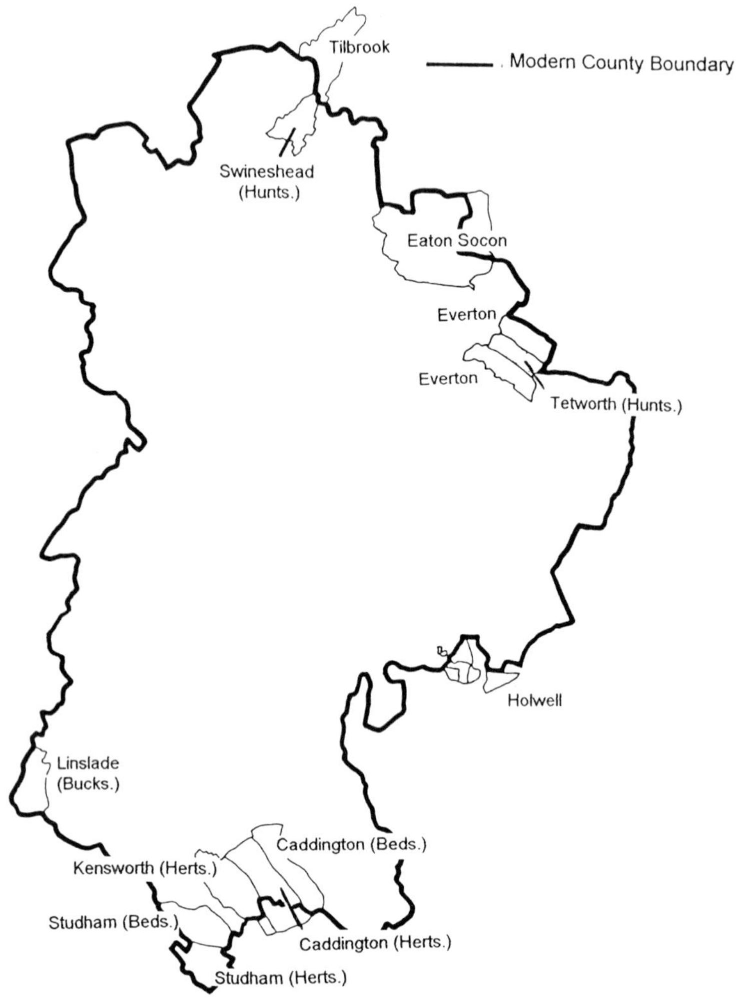

Boundary changes affecting probate jurisdiction

MAP 2

Linslade, Beds.	Originally in Bucks. Transferred to Beds. in 1965. Still in Oxford Diocese. Wills proved in Archdeaconry of Buckingham, and now at Bucks. RO.
Markyate	Originally in Caddington, Herts. Probate material with Bedfordshire records.
Studham	Partly in Herts., but wholly in Bedford Archdeaconry. Probate records at BRO.
Swineshead, Hunts.	In Archdeaconry of Huntingdon. Probate records at Cambridgeshire CRO (Huntingdon branch).
Tilbrook, Beds.	Originally in Bedfordshire and in the Archdeaconry of Bedford. Probate records at BRO.

THE COURTS

In addition to the local courts whose records are indexed in this volume, the courts of higher jurisdiction will have been involved with the wills of Bedfordshire people. The following notes will help researchers who are seeking the wills of people whose names do not occur in this index (2).

OTHER JURISDICTIONS

ARCHBISHOPS' REGISTERS

The records of the higher courts include those at Lambeth Palace Library. These comprise the records of the Court of Arches - a court of appeal for the Province of Canterbury - and wills from the Archiepiscopal registers. An index of the wills for the period c. 1350 to 1600 was published by J. Challoner C. Smith in 1919 (3).

Some Bedfordshire wills from the Lambeth material have been published by BHRS. These are contained in F.A. Page-Turner's edition of "The Bedfordshire Wills and Administrations proved at Lambeth Palace..." (4), and "Some Bedfordshire Wills at Lambeth..." by Mrs Hilary Jenkinson and G. Herbert Fowler (5).

---

(2) For further information on probate generally, *see* A.J. Camp, *Wills and their whereabouts* (4th ed. 1974); J.S.W. Gibson, *Wills and Where to Find them* (1974); J.S.W. Gibson, *A Simplified Guide to Probate Jurisdictions* (Federation of Family History Societies, 3rd ed. 1985); E. McLaughlin, *Wills before 1858* (Federation of Family History Societies, 3rd ed. 1989).

(3) *Index to wills recorded in the Archiepiscopal Registers at Lambeth Palace*, by J. Challoner Smith (1919) - later reprinted, with an additional index of admons. c.1350-1600, in *The Genealogist*.

(4) BHRS Vol. 2 (1914) pp. 3-59. This includes lists and abstracts of thirteen Lambeth wills 1379-1603 and three Lambeth administrations 1463-1486.

(5) BHRS Vol. 14 (1931) pp. 79-113. This includes lists with abstracts of twenty Lincoln wills 1319-1533.

PROVINCIAL: PREROGATIVE COURT OF CANTERBURY

Bedfordshire falls within the Province of Canterbury. Many wills for people who lived in the County were proved in the Prerogative Court of Canterbury (PCC) which has superior jurisdiction. The records of this Court are held in the Public Record Office (PRO) (6).

Indexes to the PCC wills and administrations have been published by the British Record Society, the Society of Genealogists and others. The following lists - in chronological order by coverage and not by date of publication - describe the volumes published to date (1993) (7):

Wills

1383-1558	PCC wills Vol. I (A-J) and II (K-Z) - *Index Library* vols. 10-11 (1893, 1895)
1558-1583	PCC wills Vol. III - *Index Library* vol. 18 (1898)
1584-1604	PCC wills Vol. IV - *Index Library* vol. 25 (1901)
1605-1619	PCC wills Vol. V - *Index Library* vol. 43 (1912)
1620-1629	PCC wills Vol. VI - *Index Library* vol. 44 (1912) (8)
1630-1655	*Sentences and Complete Index Nominum* 1630-1639 ed. J. and G.F. Matthews (1907) and *Abstracts of Probate Acts* 1630-1655 (7 vols) (1903-1914)
1653-1656	PCC wills Vol. VII - *Index Library* vol. 54 (1925)
1657-1660	PCC wills Vol. VIII - *Index Library* vol. 61 (1936)
1661-1670	*Wills, Sentences and Probate Acts*, ed. J.H. Morrison (1935)
1671-1675	PCC wills Vol. IX - *Index Library* vol. 67 (1942)
1676-1685	PCC wills Vol. X - *Index Library* vol. 71 (1948)
1686-1693	PCC wills Vol. XI - *Index Library* vol. 77 (1958)
1694-1700	PCC wills Vol. XII - *Index Library* vol. 80 (1960)
1701-1750*	[contemporary manuscript indexes at PRO only]
1750-1800	*An Index to Wills Proved in the Prerogative Court of Canterbury*, ed. Anthony J. Camp (Society of Genealogists, 1976-1993) - Vol. 1 (surnames A-BH), Vol. 2 (Bi-Ce), Vol. 3 (Ch.-G.), Vol. 4 (H-M), Vol. 5 (N-Sh), and Vol. 6 (Si-Z)
1801-1852*	[contemporary manuscript indexes at PRO only]
1853-1858	*Calendars of Grants of Probate* (16 vols) (contemporary)

---

(6) Chiefly in PRO class PROB 10 (original wills 1484-1858) and PROB 11 (registered wills 1384-1858), but *see* Amanda Bevan and Andrea Duncan *Tracing your Ancestors in the Public Record Office* (4th ed., 1990) pp. 65-73 for a general guide to the records of the Prerogative Court of Canterbury and other probate material at the PRO.

(7) For earlier lists with fuller bibliographical details and information on unpublished indexes, see J.S.W. Gibson *A Simplified Guide to Probate Jurisdictions* (Federation of Family History Societies, 3rd ed. 1985) p. 3 and Bevan and Duncan *op. cit.* pp. 72-3.

(8) For 1620-1624 see also *Abstract of Probates and Sentences in the Prerogative Court of Canterbury 1620-1624* ed. J. and G.F. Matthews (1911). This contains additional references to *Index Library* vol. 44.

Admons.

1559-1580	*Administrations in the Prerogative Court of Canterbury* (2 vols) ed. R.M. Glencross (1912-1917)
1581-1595	PCC admons. Vol. III - *Index Library* vol. 76 (1954)
1596-1608	PCC admons. Vol. IV - *Index Library* vol. 81 (1964)
1609-1619	PCC admons. Vol. V - *Index Library* vol. 83 (1968)
1620-1630	*Letters of Administration* ed. J.H. Morrison (1935)
1631-1648	PCC admons. Vol. VI - *Index Library* vol. 100 (1986)
1649-1654	PCC admons. Vol. I - *Index Library* vol. 68 (1944)
1655-1660	PCC admons. Vol. II part 1 (A-F), Vol. II part 2 (G-Q), and Vol. II part 3 (R-Z) - *Index Library* vols. 72, 74 and 75 (1949-1953)
1661-1852*	[contemporary manuscript indexes at PRO only] (9)
1853-1858	*Calendars of Grants of Probate* (16 vols) (contemporary) (10)

The County Record Office has copies of most PCC wills for Bedfordshire people up to 1700 (11), and has card indexes by name and place. Copies of some of the PCC inventories (12) have also been obtained and indexed.

A selection of the earliest PCC wills for the County has been edited by Margaret McGregor in *Bedfordshire Wills proved in the Prerogative Court of Canterbury 1383-1548* (13). Further Bedfordshire PCC wills were abstracted by F.A. Blaydes in *Genealogia Bedfordiensis 1538-1700* (1890). Others were published by the same editor in *Beds. Notes and Queries* (14). Blaydes also produced *An Index of early Bedfordshire Wills and Administrations 1411-1712* (15), and *A Calendar of Some Bedfordshire Wills* (16). The latter contains a list of Archdeaconry, PCC and other wills, with references to published abstracts in various learned journals etc. - unfortunately only up to 1893 when the booklet was published.

---

(9) A series of volumes covering the period from the Restoration to the end of the seventeenth century is in active preparation (September 1992).

(10) BRO has microfiche copies of these.

(11) BRO ref: FAC 1/... - followed by full PRO reference (e.g. PROB 11/...).

(12) From PRO class PROB 2, 3, 4/1-2989, and 5 (A-Z).

(13) BHRS Vol. 58 (1979).

(14) For *Beds. Notes and Queries*, *see* note 34.

(15) Manuscript index held by the Society of Genealogists, n.d. [c.1890]. It is a list of PCC wills, with some abstracts. BRO has a typescript copy made by Mrs J.M. Howe in 1986 (searchroom library class 120).

(16) F.A. Blaydes, *A Calendar of Some Bedfordshire Wills*, (Bedford, 1893).

DIOCESAN: CONSISTORY COURT OF LINCOLN

Records in this court refer mainly to Lincolnshire, as court records of the bishop's commissary were generally kept with the archdeaconry records. However, some wills for Bedfordshire people up to 1837 occur in the Lincoln material. Indexes to the PCC wills and administrations have been published by the British Record Society, and many of these have been cross-referenced in the BRO card index. The Lincoln index volumes published to date (1993) are as follows:

Wills: calendars published by the Lincoln Record Society

1271-1526	Lincoln wills Vol. I, ed. C.W. Foster *Lincoln Record Society* Vol. 5 (1914)
1505-1530	Lincoln wills Vol. II, ed. C.W. Foster *Lincoln Record Society* Vol. 10 (1918)
1530-1532	Lincoln wills Vol. III, ed. C.W. Foster *Lincoln Record Society* Vol. 24 (19130)

Wills: lists published in the Index Library (British Record Society)

1320-1600	Lincoln wills Vol. I - *Index Library* vol. 28 (1902)
1601-1652	Lincoln wills Vol. II - *Index Library* vol. 41 (1910)
Various	Lincoln wills (misc.) (17) - *Index ibrary* vol. 57 (1930)
1660-1700	Lincoln wills and inventories Vol. V - *Index Library* vol. 101 (1992)

Admons.

15409-1659	Lincoln admons. Vol. III - *Index Library* vol. 52 (also issued as *Lincoln Record Society* vol. 16)

Further material will be found in the *Abstract of all the Wills and Administrations recorded in the Episcopal Registers of the old Diocese of Lincoln* by Alfred Gibbons (Lincoln, 1888). This abstract, however, fails to identify places by County and it is impossible to separate Bedfordshire places from those with similar names in other parts of the Diocese - e.g. Barton, Carlton, Marston, Sutton and Weston.

Some Bedfordshire wills proved at Lincoln have been published in *Some Bedfordshire Wills at Lambeth and Lincoln* by Mrs Hilary Jenkinson and G. Herbert Fowler (18).

---

(17) This volume lists the 13 stray wills for Biggleswade Peculiar 1639-1740 then at Lincoln, but since amalgamated with the main series at BRO.

(18) BHRS Vol. 14 (1931) pp. 79-113. This includes lists with abstracts of twenty Lincoln wills 1319-1533.

DIOCESAN: CONSISTORY COURT OF ELY

From 1837 to 1858 Bedfordshire fell within the probate jurisdiction of the Ely Consistory Court, although as in earlier times the majority of wills were proved in the archdeacon's court. The Ely Records are at the Cambridge University Library (19). An index to the probate record of the Ely Consistory Court is forthcoming (20).

ARCHDEACONRY OF HUNTINGDON

Like its Bedfordshire counterpart, the Archdeaconry of Huntingdon shared its boundaries with those of the administrative county. Correctly speaking, the records are those of the Commissary Court of the Bishop of Lincoln and of the Archdeacon in the Archdeaconry of Huntingdon. The wills are now at the Huntingdon branch of the Cambridgeshire Record Office. They include some material for the Hitchin Division (see below). An index of wills 1479-1652 and admons. 1559-1614 has been published by the British Record Society in *Index Library* vol. 42 (21).

The parish of Everton, partly in Bedfordshire and partly (with Tetworth) in Huntingdonshire, falls within the area of this Court. However, Jeremy Gibson states that there are no references to Everton in the published index of Huntingdon wills up to 1652 (22). The probate records for Swineshead, transferred to Bedfordshire in exchange for Tilbrook in 1896, will also be found among the Huntingdon Archdeaconry probate records.

Some Bedfordshire wills proved at Huntingdon have been published by BHRS (23).

---

(19) For details, *see* Dorothy M. Owen (compiler) *Catalogue of the Records of the Bishop & Archdeacon of Ely* (1968) p. 28 etc. These were transferred to the Cambridgeshire Record Office in 1989.

(20) The "Index to the Probate Records of the Consistory Court of Ely (1449-1858)" in three volumes is to be published in 1993-5. The Ely volume already published - *Index Library* vol. 88 (1976) - covers the probate records of the archdeaconry court 1513-1857 and not those of the Consistory Court.

(21) "Calendars of Huntingdonshire wills 1479-1652", comp. W.M. Noble, *Index Library* vol. 42 (1911).

(22) J.S.W. Gibson *Wills and where to find them* (1974) p. 8.

(23) "The Bedfordshire Wills and Administrations proved at Lambeth Palace and in the Archdeaconry of Huntingdon" ed. F.A. Fowler, BHRS Vol. 2 (1914) pp. 3-59. This includes lists and abstracts seven Huntingdon wills 1525-1627.

ARCHDEACONRY OF HUNTINGDON, HITCHIN DIVISION

The Hitchin division covers that part of Hertfordshire which was originally in the Diocese of Lincoln, including until 1845 the parish of Kensworth which since 1897 has been in Bedfordshire. Some probate material for the Hitchin division is to be found with the records of the archdeaconry of Huntingdon (see above). Some Biggleswade wills found in the records of the Hitchin Division were transferred from Herts. RO to Bedford in 1974.

PECULIAR COURT OF AYLESBURY, BUCKS.

Some wills for the Leighton Buzzard area - 1712-1798 - were proved in the peculiar court of Aylesbury. Both Aylesbury and Leighton Buzzard were prebendaries of Lincoln Cathedral - *see* Gibson (1974) p. 15.

POST-1858 WILLS

Ecclesiastical probate jurisdiction was abolished in 1858, and a civil probvate registry was established. The new arrangements came into effect on 11 January 1858. England was divided up into probate districts, each with a registry, and copies of all wills were submitted annually to the Principal Probate Registry in London. Bedford did not have its own probate registry, the nearest being that at Northampton to which the pre-1858 wills were transferred. Registered copies of Bedfordshire wills proved at Northampton since 1858 are held at the Northamptonshire Record Office (24).

There are no official copies of post-1858 wills at the Bedfordshire Record Office, although office copies and drafts often occur among privately deposited papers. There is a full name index of all wills in private collections - from the fourteenth century to recent times - in the Record Office searchroom.

The County Record Office also holds an incomplete set of the printed Calendars of Probate for the whole country, published annually by the Probate Registry. The series covers the period 1901 to 1935 (25). Microfiche copies of the whole series from 1858 to 1935, with the printed calendars of PCC wills for 1853-1857, have recently been obtained.

---

(24) These do not necessarily include all Bedfordshire wills, as there was no requirement that wills for a given area should be proved in a particular registry.

(25) BRO ref: prob/Cal 1-35.

BEDFORDSHIRE PROBATE RECORDS

ARCHDEACONRY OF BEDFORD

The Records (26)
These records were originally kept in the Archdeacon's court at St. Paul's, Bedford. They were transferred to Northampton in 1857-8, and subsequently to Birmingham. They were deposited in the Bedfordshire Record Office in 1950. They were microfilmed (with the card index) by the Genealogical Society of Utah in 1954 (27).

Will registers (BRO reference ABP/R
The registered wills begin in 1484. There are 56 volumes (28). The oldest volumes were kept haphazardly, and bear more than one sequence of lettering or numbering. Three of the volumes include acts of the Archdeacon's court and other extraneous matter. The first of these, which has sporadic proceedings of the Archdeacon's courts for 1496-1500 has been left in place with the registers (ref: ABP/R 1). The other two (registers 7 and 10) contained duplicate will entries and court proceedings for 1539-40 and 1544-5 respectively, and were removed from the series and placed with the main court records (refs. ABC 1-2).

Among the probate records at Lincolnshire Archives Office there are three further registers which include Bedford material with that of other Archdeaconries for various dates between 1516 and 1678 (29).

With the early registers, more than one book covers the same period. The wills were not registered in strict date order, and some were not entered at all. Sometimes the entries are duplicates, as shown in the following table:

---

(26) This section is based mainly on Alan Cirket's introduction in the BRO catalogues.

(27) BRO ref. MIC 41-43 (3 reels). These films were made in 1954.

(28) BRO refs: ABP/R 1-65 (with gaps in the series for missing volumes). Some of the registers are bound together. The BRO list gives full details of coverage, format, and condition.

(29) They are as follows:-
- F. Wills proved before T. Reyner, Bishop's commissary, in Bedford [an entire section, much decayed, ff. 166-187] 1549-50.
- J. Wills, with some inventories, proved before the Bishop and vicar-general, 1516-1550, 1660-1678.
- K. Wills, with inventories, proved before John Belley, vicar-general, 1591-8.

	Not duplicates		Duplicates
Date	Register (ABP/R)	Date	Register (ABP/R)
1515-21	1-2	1537-45	5, 6, 11 (main registers) 8, 9, ABC 1-2 (copies)
1558	13-15		
1559	13-16		
1560	14-16		
1561	14, 16		
1565	16-17		
1566	16-17		
1584	20-21		
1586	20-22		
1587	21-23		
1588	22-23		
1589	21-23		
1590	21-24		
1591	21, 24		

Registers are lacking for the years 1552-4, 1571-5, 1623-37, and 1641-1703.

The later registers after 1704, with one exception, formed a continuous series with letter sequence. Extraneous matter is limited to register 43 which contains a list of induction mandates 1552-1746, and register 53 which originally included applications for registration of Nonconformist meeting-houses (30). The binding of the registers was in a bad state when the volumes were deposited, and in rebinding the large registers have been divided into two.

The modern card index gives separate references for each registered will and original document up to 1655. From 1704 the numbering for original wills and registered copies is the same.

The early registered wills in the first volume (31) have been published by the Bedfordshire Historical Record Society (BHRS). Abstracts of the wills in the two following volumes have also been prepared for possible future publication (32).

---

(30) Detached at the time of rebinding, and now classed at BRO ref: ABN 1/1.

(31) "English Wills 1498-1526", ed. A.F. Cirket in BHRS Vol. 37 (1957) pp. 1-82. *Bedfordshire Wills 1480-1519*, edited by Patricia Bell, BHRS Vol. 45 (1966). The date 1480 refers to when John Crowche of Caddington made his will. It was proved in 1500.

(32) Abstracts of ABP/R 2 and ABP/R 3 prepared by John and Isobel Thompson. Reference copies are available in the BRO searchroom library (class 120).

Various Bedfordshire wills (33) - including some from the Archdeaconry Court Records as well as others from the Prerogative Court of Canterbury - were published by F.A. Blaydes in the three volumes of *Bedfordshire Notes and Queries* (34).

<u>Wills (BRO ref: ABP/W)</u>
There are 23,695 wills altogether (35). The earliest surviving original will is dated 1536. There are only 17 from then until 1548. The numbers then increase so that by about 1560 and certainly by 1600, the majority of wills proved in the court seem to have survived. From 1600 to 1730 about 100 wills were proved annually. By 1760-1770 the number fell to 60 or 70 a year, declining further by 1800 to around 50, but by 1857 the level of business had slightly recovered to 60 or so a year.

Until about 1600 the documents seem to be copies, the executors keeping the original will. Later the wills are signed and sealed, and probate copies were issued to the executors.

Wills before 1700 seem to have had more than one previous numbering system. Because of this, a new sequence was made and written on the wills in red ink when the records were at the Northampton Probate Registry in the nineteenth century. This system usually covers two or more years (e.g. 1556-9 numbered as 1-400; 1560 begins 1-n again). Even in this there are gaps, perhaps because of a bundle going missing since the documents were marked, and sometimes for other reasons. An overall index (index 3) (36) made at Northampton in about 1880 accompanied this re-numbering. After 1700 there is usually only one number on a will, and this corresponds to the contemporary index (37). Original wills and registered copies bear identical numbers.

The BRO card index is the main means of reference to the wills, and it forms the basis for the index published here. There is no separate list of the wills in bundle order.

---

(33) These are identified as records of the District Probate Court, then held at Northampton.

(34) *Bedfordshire Notes and Queries* (3 vols.) (1886-1893), edited by F.A. Blaydes. The principal references to wills are Vol. I pp. 342, 363-377; Vol. II pp. 3-13, 53-5, 137-9, 182-91, 219, 222-5, 233-8, 242-3, 267, 318-21, 347-51; and Vol. III pp. 23-30, 49-60, 73-84, 118-9, 158-60, 187-8, 211-8, 243-4, 278-81, 285, 296-305, 327-9.

(35) But see note 75 *re* discrepancies in published numbers.

(36) BRO ref: ABP/IX 3. In at least one year there is a gap in this index, indicating that the original wills were by then already missing.

(37) BRO ref: ABP/IX 2. Each year has its own set of numbers.

Administrations (BRO ref: ABP/AR and ABP/A)
Records of administrations are incomplete, and there is a total gap for the years 1692-1700. The main series of administrations covers the period 1700-1857. There are 5377 documents (35). In addition to these papers, there are registers for the years 1670-1692, and 1818-1857 (38). A caveat book among the Archdeaconry records contains an incomplete register of administrations for 1558-1662 (39).

As with the wills, the BRO card index is the main means of reference to the administrations.

Probate inventories (BRO ref: ABP 4 etc.)
When the probate records were transferred to Northampton in 1858, some 166 probate inventories were left behind with the other Archdeaconry records. These were deposited at the Record Office in 1922. Other inventories were removed with the probate records and reached the Record Office in 1950. Fourteen for 1587-1618 (40) had been stitched at the head into a roll. Others for 1610-1634 and 1806-1832 (41) were in bundles. All three categories are stored together in the Record Office as ABP 4/1-290 and are listed in the catalogue in alphabetical order by name, with the reference to the relevant will number where known. Some cannot be linked to surviving wills. There is an earlier partial list with the records (42).

Other inventories, of which there are 105 covering the period 1605-1832, had never been detached from the wills or administrations they originally accompanied. These are listed in the Record Office subject index under "HOUSEHOLD, Inventories, Archdeaconry and Peculiars".

It will be noted that the survival rate of inventories is generally poor. This can be partially accounted for by a tradition which suggests that some of the inventories were at one time used to kindle the fire in the Archdeacon's registry.

---

(38) BRO refs: ABP/AR 1-2. The volume for 1670-1690 is set out by deaneries, and within the deaneries by years.

(39) BRO ref: ABC 24.

(40) BRO refs. ABP 4/167-80.

(41) BRO ref: ABP 4/181-290.

(42) BRO ref: ABP 4/02.

Most of the early surviving inventories have been published by the Bedfordshire Historical Record Society (BHRS). Those for c.1562-1591 were edited by C.E. Freeman (43), and those for 1617-1619 by F.G. Emmison (44). Some further inventories have been calendared for possible future publication.

All the surviving probate inventories are cross-referenced or listed in this edition of the index.

Means of reference (BRO ref: ABP/IX etc.)

All earlier indexes to the probate records have been superseded by the main Bedfordshire Record Office card index prepared in 1950-1953 by Alan Cirket. The present edition is based on that index. However, information on the contemporary indexes and other means of reference may be useful to researchers.

Many wills registers up to 1700 have indexes at the front or rear.

For those which had none, indexes were made in the Northampton office. These are now stored with the registers (46). There are also three index volumes:

BRO reference	Description	
ABP/IX/1	Index no. 1 Apparently made in the seventeenth century and much corrected in red ink when index 3 was made; it gives names only for wills from 1536, and for admons. from 1670.	1536-1700
ABP/IX 2	Index no. 2 A contemporary index, giving names only for wills and admons. to 1719, and names and places thereafter. It can be used for wills or registered copies. It also includes a place index to c.1560.	1701-1857
ABP/IX 3	Index no. 3 Made in the Northampton Probate registry in about 1880. It gives names only, and only for wills, and it is of uneven accuracy.	1536-1700

(43) "Elizabethan Inventories", ed. C.E. Freeman, in BHRS Vol. 32 (1952) pp. 92-107. This edition includes some other inventories of the period.

(44) "Jacobean Household Inventories" edited by F.G. Emmison in BHRS Vol. 20 (1938) pp. 1-143.

(45) Calendars of ABP 4/181-199 in CRT 150/18 at BRO.

(46) Boxed with BRO ref: ABP/R 34-36.

The present card index was completed between 1950 and 1953 by BRO staff and microfilmed in 1954 - to good effect, as this has made it possible to replace index cards that have become misplaced or lost over nearly forty years of use. Publication by the British Record Society was first considered in 1959.

Other papers

Where related papers survive, they will normally be found with their relevant will or administration. For a number of disputed cases, though, there will be additional material in the Archdeacon's court books (ref: ABC) and court papers (ref: ABCP) (47). Frequently the Archdeacon's visitation was used as a means of coercing people to get wills proved, and the citation *quorum nomina* lists testators, sometimes with their parishes (48).

Correspondence about probate jurisdiction and Stamp Office returns will be found in ABP 1-3, where old bundle labels are also listed. Some of these refer to individual testators (49).

BIGGLESWADE PECULIAR

The Rectory of Biggleswade was attached to a prebendary of Lincoln Cathedral by 1132 when, together with the manor, it was granted to the Bishop of Lincoln (50).

---

(47) The main references to testamentary cases in the surviving court papers are in BRO ref: ABCP 156, 199, 205, 214, 248, 269, 295, 297, 299, 306, 308, 317, 327-8, 330, 332, 340, 346-7, 355, 359, 362-3, 373.

(48) For instance one of 1770 (ref: ABCP 327).

(49) The monitions to transmit wills to the Prerogative Court of Canterbury (BRO ref: ABP 1) include papers for Blandina Marshe of Charterhouse Square London, 1737; Benjamin Palmer of Bedford, 1820; William Strange of Silsoe, 1821; Edward Sutton of South Mills, Blunham, 1824; James Readman of Ridgmont, 1825; John Burrows of Clophill, 1826; Mary Gascoyen of Podington, 2816; Thomas Crawley of Little Bramingham, Luton, 1827; William Newell junior of Pavenham, carpenter, 1828; James Coleman of Luton, Bricklayer, 1832; Thomas Hill of Pertenhall, woolcomber, 1833; John Freeman of Toddington, miller, 1834; William Gregory of Luton, farmer, 1840; Ann Green of Broom, Southill, widow, 1841; Thomas Street of Renhold, farmer, 1841; Thomas Attlee of Westoning, farmer, 1846; John Laurence of Luton, 1850; and William Harbett of Toddington, gent., 1851. These papers also include letters relating to the wills of Ann Hunt and Thomas Allbone of Biggleswade proved in the Archdeacon's court in 1823, and a letter of 1823 asking whether letters of administration may be granted to Ann Bates (a married daughter of Charlotte Norris) for her mother without the concurrence of her husband who was overseas on military service.

(50) *VCH* II (1908) p. 214. For the later history *see also* unpublished article on "The Peculiar of Biggleswade in the Eighteenth Century" by Canon W.A. Pemberton at BRO, ref: CRT 130 BIG 68.

Biggleswade thus became a peculiar with probate jurisdiction. Jeremy Gibson states that there is no Biggleswade material in the records at Lincoln (51). There are some 95 Biggleswade wills and 48 admons. among those proved in the Archdeacon's Court. The records of the Peculiar court were transferred to Northampton in 1858 (52), and were deposted in the County Record Office in August 1950. Some further material from Lincoln and Hertford was added to the deposit in March 1956 and November 1974 respectively. The original means of reference, now superseded by the County Record Office card index, was a manuscript index of wills and administrations 1712-1857 (53). In addition to the wills and admons., there are a few papers regarding probate cases (54).

Register (BRO ref: PBwP/R 1)
This is a will register, containing seventeen wills, for the period 1540 to 1559. It contains fourteen pages only.

Wills (BRO ref: PBwP/W
There are 175 wills covering the period 1713 to 1857, with single strays for 1575 (actually an inventory only) and 1639. The series includes ten wills for 1639-1740, listed with the Lincoln wills by Canon C.W. Foster but transferred to Bedford in March 1956 and since amalgamated with the main series of Biggleswade Peculiar wills at the CRO (55). Five additional wills (three with inventories) from the records of the Archdeaconry of Huntingdon, Hitchin Division, wsere transferred from Hertfordshire Record Office in November 1974 (56).

---

(51) Gibson (1974) p.7.

(52) The records include a receipted schedule of documents of the Peculiar Court of Biggleswade sent to Northampton Probate Registry dated 5 March 1858 (BRO ref: PBwP/V 17).

(53) BRO ref: PBwP/V 18.

(54) These include intimations in the effects of deceased persons 1749, 1773-4 and 1793 (BRO ref: PBwP/V 5-9), and copies of Acts of Court 1736, 1749 and 1774 (PBwP/V 10-15). The Archdeaconry Court records include papers concerning Biggleswade testamentary casses in 1823 (ref: ABP/W 1).

(55) Listed by C.W. Foster in "Calendars of Wills and Administrations at Lincoln" Vol. 4, *Index Library* vol. 57 (1930) p. 367. They are BRO refs: PBwP/A1734/7a, 1736/7b, 1737/7c and PBwP/W 1639/1b, 1734/32a-d, 1737/32e, 1739/32f, and 1740/32g-i.

(56) These are PBwP/W 1714/2a*, 1714/3a-b, 1715/3c*, and 1721/9a*. Those with asterisks have inventories.

Admons. (BRO ref: PBwP/A)
The main series of admons. covers the period 1712 to 1755. There are 81 documents, including three stray admons. 1734-1737 received from Lincoln in 1956 (see note 17).

Inventories (BRO ref: PBwP/W and A - i.e. with probates)
There are 45 inventories among the probate records of the Peculiar court, all filed with their respective wills and admons. One Biggleswade inventory of 1575 was found loose (57), and is included in Freeman's edition of Elizabethan probate inventories (58).

LEIGHTON BUZZARD PECULIAR
The church at Leighton Buzzard was attached to the royal manor of Leighton, and at the time of Domesday in 1086 it was held by Remigius, Bishop of Lincoln. During the episcopate of Hugh of Wells, Bishop of Lincoln from 1209 to 1235, Leighton became a prebend of Lincoln Cathedral 59). From this came its position as a peculiar with probate jurisdiction. The peculiar included the chapelries of Billington, Eggington, Heath & Reach and Stanbridge.

Leighton Buzzard Peculiar

According to Jeremy Gibson, the Lincoln probate material includes only one will (1634) and one admon. (1638) for Leighton and its chapelries (60). The records of the Archdeacon's court include 173 wills and 43 admons. for Leighton Buzzard, and others for the chapelries. These are Billington (37 wills and 3 admons.), Eggington (30 wills and 3 admons.), Heath & Reach (35 wills and 4 admons.) and Stanbridge (32 wills and 1 admon.).

Some probate material for Leighton Buzzard for 1712 to 1798 will be found with the records of Aylesbury peculiar at Buckinghamshire Record Office. Further wills for Leighton Buzzard 1736-1857 have also been found in the Court of Probate of the Archdeaconry of Northampton (61).

---

(57) Received from Somerset House on 1 June 1950. BRO ref: PBwP/W 1575/1a.
(58) "Elizabethan Inventories", ed. C.E. Freeman, in BHRS Vol. 32 (1952) pp. 92-107. No. 2 is the inventory of John Ratchford the younger of Biggleswade, husbandman, 12 April 1575.
(59) *VCH* III (1912) p. 414.
(60) Gibson (1974) p. 8.
(61) Notes by the Genealogical Society of Utah on "Pre 1858 English Probate Jurisdictions: Bedfordshire" (1967).

The Records
The records of the Leighton Buzzard Peculiar Court were deposited at the County Record Office with the other probate material in 1950. Some additional records were received from the Bodleian Library in 1959 (62). They had been transferred to Northampton in 1858 (63). The original means of reference, superseded by the County Record Office card index, included indexed register volumes, a register of administrations 1739-1842 (64), and a list of wills proved in Leighton Peculiar 1816-1821 (65).

In addition to the original probate records, the County Record Office has facsimile copies of a number of wills and admons. dating from the years 1700 to 1779. These were taken from two mixed registers for the Peculiars in Oxfordshire and Buckinghamshire (66) and from original documents then at the Principal Probate Registry. They are listed in alphabetical order by surname in the BRO list. An original will of Elizabeth Howe of Heath, 1826, survives among the Richmond collection of Prebendal Court papers received from private custody (67).

In addition to the wills and admons., the records of the Peculiar include some other testamentary material. There is a commission to prove a will dated 1818, two proxies of renunciation 1819 and 1823, and a bundle of affidavits of executors 1816-1846 (68). There are further testamentary papers and accounts for 1811-1841 in the Richmond collection (69).

---

(62) Gibson (1974) p. 8 observes that these records still appear in the Bodleian Library indexes, which are now at the Oxfordshire County Record Office.

(63) There is a draft schedule of wills received by the District Registrar at Northampton from Leighton Peculiar in 1858 (BRO ref: PLBP/W/V 4.).

(64) BRO ref: PLBP/AR 1.

(65) BRO ref: PLBP/W/V 3.

(66) BRO ref: FAC 9/1-96, from the registers for 1701-9 and 1712-1779. When these copies were obtained in 1951 these volumes were at the Principal Probate Registry. They were subsequently deposited in the Bodleian Library, and have since been transferred (with the Oxford Diocesan and probate material) to the Oxfordshire County Record Office.

(67) BRO ref: RI 3/6825.

(68) BRO ref: PLBP/W/V 1-2, 5. The affidavits were formerly catalogued as ABPV 2/106-225.

(69) BRO ref: RI 3/6826-7.

Will registers (BRO ref: PLBP/WR 1-4)
There are four will registers, each with contemporary indexes, covering the years 1537-1554, 1736-1795, 1797-1818, and 1819-1846. The cover of the first volume is a fragment of a manuscript relating to the burning of two Fraticelli at Avignon in 1354 (70). It has now been detached and is stored separately (70).

Wills (BRO ref: PLBP/W)
There are about 309 original wills for the period 1718 to 1846. They were stored in four bundles, which included ten probate inventories for the years 1806-1846 (72). The series includes five wills 1718-1741 which were transferred from the Bodleian Library in 1959, and of which the County Record Office had already obtained photocopies(73).

Admons. (BRO refs: PLBP/A and ABP/AR)
The records include a register of admons. for 1739-1842, and about 114 original letters of administration (most with their accompanying bonds) for 1712-1846. Among them are fourteen admons. for 1712-1779 transferred from the Bodleian Library in 1959 (74).

Inventories
There are very few inventories, and those that survive are stored with their respective wills and admons. They include one of 1840 with the admons., and ten of 1806-1846 with the wills.

Bedfordshire wills and administrations - statistical summary
The number of probate documents (administrations and wills) for each parish and named settlement (e.g. Biscot and Markyate) is shown in the following table. This includes wills for unspecified places - e.g. "Barford", "Eaton" and "Houghton" - and out-County material.

---

(70) See "A Bedford Fragment and the Burning of two Fraticelli at Avignon in 1354" by D.W. Whitfield in BHRS Vol. 38 (1958) pp. 1-11.
(71) BRO ref: PLBP/WR 1a.
(72) The references of the wills in each bundle are 1) PLBP/W 1718-9/0a - 1762/50 (55 wills), 2) PLBP/W 1766/1 - 1795/102 (102 wills), 3) PLBP/W 1797/1 - 1818/68 (68 wills), and 4) PLBP/W 1818/1 - 1846/90 (90 wills).
(73) These wills (with their photocopy references in brackets) are PLBP/W 1718-9/oa (Fac 9/76), 1734/0b (Fac 9/77), 1736/4a and b (Fac 9/79 and 78), and 1741/19a (Fac 9/81).
(74) These (with their photocopy references in brackets) are PLBP/A 1712/0a (Fac 9/76), 1733/0b (Fac 9/84), 1737/0c (Fac 9/67, 85), 1741/1a (Fac 9/69, 88), 1741/1b (Fac 9/68, 86), 1741/1c (Fac 9/87), 1751/20a (Fac 9/89), 1753/21a (Fac 9/70, 90), 1758/36a (Fac 9/71, 91), 1764/47a, 1770/24a, 1773/32a, 1778/48a, 1779/53a.

Parish	Admons.	Wills	Parish	Admons.	Wills
Ampthill	120	349	Eversholt	73	284
Arlesey	34	167	Everton	5	14
Aspley Guise	32	150	Eyeworth	15	58
Astwick	9	22	Farndish	29	
Barford [unspecified]		69	Felmersham	42	181
Barford, Great	55	119	Flitton	39	142
Barford, Little	8	45	Flitwick	38	181
Barton le Cley	47	223	Goldington	39	113
Battlesden	8	44	Gravenhurst	4	11
Bedford	303	1053	Gravenhurst, Lower	13	72
" St. Cuthbert	17	49	Gravenhurst, Upper	2	24
" St. John	13	45	Harlington	35	161
" St. Mary	55	129	Harrold	46	178
" St. Paul	103	268	Hatley, Cockayne	5	26
" St. Peter Dunstable		5	Haynes	37	140
" St. Peter [de Merton]	21	84	Heath and Reach	11	62
Biddenham	23	125	Henlow	59	218
Biggleswade	128	283	Higham Gobion	6	18
Billington	11	59	Hockliffe	24	140
Biscot		14	Holwell	8	31
Bletsoe	29	119	Houghton [unspecified]		8
Blunham	61	248	Houghton Conquest	44	183
Bolnhurst	13	122	Houghton Regis	64	387
Bromham	20	113	Hulcote	11	49
Caddington	10	148	Hyde		29
Campton	13	77	Husborne Crawley	25	223
Cardington	86	443	Kempston	127	488
Carlton	36	141	Keysoe	51	216
Chalgrave	42	224	Knotting	5	43
Chellington	12	60	Langford	32	215
Chicksands	4	24	Leagrave	11	52
Clapham	17	72	Leighton Buzzard	159	415
Clifton	29	137	Lidlington	332	58
Clophill	46	199	Limbury	4	29
Colmworth	33	182	Luton	207	742
Cople	46	162	Markyate	9	109
Cranfield	89	418	Marston Moretaine	67	375
Dean	32	179	Maulden	61	274
Dunstable	105	406	Melchbourne	14	98
Dunton	27	149	Meppershall	20	87
Eaton [unspecified]		139	Millbrook	27	112
Eaton Bray	40	232	Milton Bryan	21	124
Eaton Socon	149	577	Milton Ernest	23	124
Edworth	5	35	Mogerhanger	17	88
Eggington	4	40	Northill	74	245
Elstow	39	251	Oakley	29	180

Parish	Admons.	Wills
Odell	36	146
Pavenham	501	
Pertenhall	20	111
Podington	27	127
Potsgrove	12	44
Potton	85	383
Pulloxhill	28	153
Ravensden	23	112
Renhold	27	125
Ridgmont	31	149
Riseley	57	244
Roxton	40	238
Salford	19	93
Sandy	122	472
Sharnbrook	30	172
Shefford	70	171
Shefford Hardwick		
- "Hardwick"	1	9
Shelton	4	65
Shillington	80	423
Silsoe	25	124
Souldrop	11	51
Southill	74	261
Stagsden	40	232
Stanbridge	8	66
Staughton, Little	25	154
Steppingley	17	73
Stevington	41	208
Stondon	2	19
Stopsley	2	80
Stotfold	40	179
Streatley	16	78
Studham	23	102
Sundon	31	133
Sutton	16	137

Parish	Admons.	Wills
Tempsford	55	198
Thurleigh	62	180
Tilbrook	32	144
Tilsworth	10	99
Tingrith	14	63
Toddington	106	464
Totternhoe	29	181
Turvey	45	191
Warden, Old	35	131
Westoning	31	156
Whipsnade	10	32
Wilden	38	186
Willington	25	90
Wilstead	59	278
Woburn	82	314
Wootton	68	302
Wrestlingworth	31	89
Wymington	11	75
Yielden	23	77
Buckinghamshire	3	46
Cambridgeshire	1	8
Devon	1	1
Essex		1
Hertfordshire	5	38
Huntingdonshire	12	24
Kent		3
Lincolnshire	1	1
London	1	10
Middlesex	3	5
Northamptonshire	3	17
Nottinghamshire	1	2
Oxfordshire		3
Rutland		1
Suffolk	1	
Yorkshire		1
East Indies	1	
Totals (75)	5,841	23,931

(75) These totals, calculated by computer, differ slightly from those previously given in the Bedfordshire Record Office catalogues and guides. They include the total number of administrations and wills in the records of the Archdeaconry and Peculiar courts.

British Record Society index - scope, conventions, etc.
This index covers all wills and admons. proved in the courts of the Archdeaconry of Bedford, the Peculiar of Biggleswade, and the Peculiar of Leighton Buzzard. It includes papers mentioned in the contemporary index but no longer extant, and finding references for wills found in bundles for years other than that in which they were proved (e.g. a will proved in 1635 may have a note "bundle 1638"). Also included are the stray items for Leighton Buzzard Peculiar of which BRO has facsimile copies (*see* above).

With the aim of making the index as comprehensive as possible, the inclusion of cross references to wills elsewhere and to those in private collections was seriously considered. Ultimately, however, it was decided that these should be excluded, partly because of cost, partly because of editorial complexity, partly to avoid confusion for the user, and partly because information on many of these wills is already available from volumes in the *Index Library* series and other publications. As has already been mentioned, this information is also available from the BRO card indexes.

The editorial conventions for the testamentary records in this index are as follows:

1. BRO reference prefixes are omitted for ABP wills and admons.
    Will only - just date/number, e.g. 1745/36
    Register only - R - [date], [register number], [folio number - "f" omitted, but "d" always given], e.g. R1523: 2/23 or R 1560: 15/104d
    Admon. - A [date/number], e.g. 1703/37
    Admon. register only - AR 1703: 3/203

2. BRO reference prefixes for the peculiars of Biggleswade (Bw) and Leighton Buzzard (LB) have been retained, in shortened form:

    Biggleswade (Bw)
    Registered wills - prefix BwR [date], [register number], [folio number], e.g. BwR 1540: 1/1d
    Wills - prefix Bw, date/number, e.g. Bw 1726/21
    Admons. - prefix BwA, date/number, e.g. BwA 1749/14

    Leighton Buzzard (LB)
    Registered wills - prefix LBR [date], [register number], [folio number], e.g. LBR 1545: 1/11
    Wills - prefix LB, date/number, e.g. LB 1745/15
    Admons. - prefix LBA, date/number, e.g. LBA 1803/35
    Admon. registers - LBAR 1803: 1/62
    Facsimile copies - Fac., date: 9/n if will; and Fac., A date: 9/n if admon; e.g. Fac. 1756 9/39 and Fac. A 1731 9/29.

3. Where registered copies **AND** original wills exist in any given series (i.e. Archdeaconry or Peculiar), only the original is noted.

4. Inventories have been cross referenced to the main entries where possible, and listed separately as necessary. The conventions are:

Archdeaconry Inventories

Separate inventories (without wills or admons) - I 4/[no]...
Inventories filed with wills or admons. - "I" added after reference.

Peculiar inventories

Biggleswade and Leighton Buzzard - mainly with wills, and denoted only by "I" after reference.

Acknowledgements

The thanks of the Society and of the County Record Office are due to a large number of people whose contributions have made possible the publication of this index. These can only be expressed adequately by recounting the events along the way.

The probate records were deposited in the Bedfordshire Record Office in August 1950. They were collected from the Birmingham Probate Registry in a County Council van by Alan Cirket and Freddie Stitt (later County Archivist in Staffordshire). The card index of names, places and occupations was compiled between 1950 and 1953 mainly by Alan Cirket, assisted by various helpers including Peter Renouf, Freddie Stitt and Joan Sinar. The actual typing of cards was done by Alan Cirket. On completion, the index was microfilmed by the Genealogical Society of Utah.

Miss Joyce Godber, as County Archivist from 1945 to 1968, was responsible for securing the deposit of the wills in 1950. She oversaw the indexing, and it was under her auspices, and those of Marc Fitch as Chairman of the British Record Society, that the process of preparing the index for publication began in July 1959.

Patricia Bell, County Archivist 1968-1986, re-activated the project in 1970. Work began on typing the index from the cards and from the microfilm, and continued until a draft index for surnames A to H had been completed. Those who helped with the work included Fiona Reynolds (pre-1970), Andrea Burnage (from Feb. 1972), Leona Parkinson (Aug. 1970 to Feb. 1972), Sheila Holgate, Mrs Fisher (1974), and Debbie Radusin (1975). At that stage work was abandoned. Following an approach from the Society in 1984, work again re-started and I inherited the still unfinished task from Patricia Bell in 1986.

It has not been a straightforward job. It is never easy to take forward a job someone else has begun, and breaks in continuity have caused a number of problems. It may well have been easier, given advances in technology, to have made a fresh start but on the whole it was felt that too much had been done for this to be justifiable. Fortunately, willing volunteers were at hand to take on the challenge and see the work through to completion. Without the hard work of our editors - Joan Stuart and Peggy Wells - this index would not have been published.

Initially, they re-checked and corrected the typescript version of the index for surnames A-H. Using print-outs of the cards kindly supplied by Dr F.G. Emmison, they then checked the remainder of the will index, sorting out any problems as they arose. They also checked the index cards for the admons., and for the wills and admons. of the Peculiars. Alan Hunter kindly cross referenced the probate inventories. When the index had been word-processed, Joan and Peggy checked the copy for the entire volume.

Special thanks are due to Moira Coleman, for patiently persevering with what has been a frustratingly awkward job, coping with poor copy, working from separate sets of papers to amalgamate entries, and carefully fine-tuning the final copy.

Those who have been involved on behalf of the Society include Marc Fitch, the Hon. Guy Strutt, Dr Peter Spufford, and lastly Mrs Nesta Evans.

Given the complexity of the task, it is inevitable that some errors will remain. For these, the joint compilers must accept responsibility and offer their apologies.

Lastly, the British Record Society gratefully acknowledges a grant made towards the cost of publication by the Whitbread Trust. Thanks are also due to Dr F.G. Emmison for a generous personal contribution and for assigning his royalties on sales of copies of the volumes in the *Bedfordshire Parish Registers Series* towards the project. The cost of producing the maps - prepared by the drawing office, Beds. County Planning Department - has been borne by the Bedfordshire County Record Office.

Bedford - June 1993

Christopher J. Pickford, FSA
(County Archivist)

List of Abbreviations

A	Admon.
ABP 1	Archdeaconry of Bedford Probate Records (general papers re jurisdiction over wills, 21 items)
admons.	Letters of Administration
AR	Admon register (followed by date, register no. and folio no.)
bach.	bachelor
BHRS	Bedfordshire Historical Record Society
BRO	Bedfordshire Record Office
BRS	British Record Society
Bw	Biggleswade Peculiar
carp.	carpenter
d.	*dorso* (for folio numbers or registers)
Fac.	Facsimile (BRO reference for copies)
FFHS	Federation of Family History Societies
gent.	gentleman
husb.	husbandman
I	Inventory
jun.	junior
lab.	labourer
LB	Leighton Buzzard Peculiar
PCC	Prerogative Court of Canterbury
R	Register of wills or admons. (followed by date, register no., and folio no.
RO	Record Office (so BRO is Bedfordshire Record Office)
sen.	senior
spins.	spinster
wid.	widow
yeo.	yeoman

ABARTON, Jn., Carlton, yeo. 1576/25
ABBAT see ABBOT
ABBESS, ABBISS, ABES, Edm., Eyeworth, husb. 1711/76
Jerman, Eyeworth, husb. 1695/4
Jn., sen., Over Caldecote, Northill. 1650/88
Jn., Upper Caldecote, Northill, yeo. 1671/42
Jn., Eaton Socon, yeo. A 1749/19.
Jn., Hill, Old Warden. 1698/77
Lawr., Nether Caldecote, Northill, husb. 1604/48
Robt., Northill, husb. 1634-5/130
Thos., Cople, husb. 1593/81
Thos., Eyeworth, yeo. 1698/80
Thos., Nether Gravenhurst, clerk. 1698/96
Thos., Hill, Warden. 1698/169
Thos., Northwood End, Haynes. 1702/21
Wm., Caldecote, Northill, husb. 1643/62
Wm., Cockayne Hatley, yeo. 1682-3/116
Wm., Cardington, bach. AR 1682-3: 1/208
Wm., Eyeworth, yeo. A 1707/19
Wm., Eaton Socon, yeo. A 1743/39
Wm., Lidlington, yeo. 1773/45
ABBOT, ABBAT, ABBOTT, ABBOTTS
Ann, Poddington, wid. 1627/180
Dan, Bletsoe, lab. 1619/257, I 4/94
David, Bedford St. Paul, cabinet maker and broker. 1843/54
Dorothy, Milbrook, wid. 1622/77
Edmund, Maulden. R 1558: 14/59
Edw., Bedford St. Mary, innholder. A 1806/3
Eliz., Carlton, wid. 1640/15
Fra., Pertenhall, gent. 1811/23
Geo., Tilbrook, husb. A 1707-8/16
Harry, Kempston. 1557/310
Hen., Husbourne Crawley. R 1523?: 2/23
Hen., Lidlington, weaver. 1719/50
Jane, Podington, wid. 1625/147
Jane, Stratton, Biggleswade, wid. Bw 1726/21
Joan, Husborne Crawley, wid. 1613/188
Jn., Podington. R 1538: 5/14d
Jn., Husborne Crawley, yeo. 1661/366
Jn., Bedford, lab. 1694/27
alias Phillips, Jn., Bedford, butcher. 1706-7/37
alias Phillips, Jn., Bedford, butcher. 1726/13
Jn., Pulloxhill, yeo. 1790/16
Jn., Pulloxhill, farmer. 1791/12
Jn., Turvey, victualler. 1832/45

ABBOT, ABBAT, ABBOTT, ABBOTTS continued
Jn., sen., Flitwick, farmer. 1847/22
Jonathan, Pulloxhill. A 1783/19
Jos., Millbrook, yeo. A 1740/18
Mahanaim, senr., Goldington, Castle Mills, miller. 1781/39
Margt., Tempsford, wid. 1632/26
Mary, Flitton, wid., formerly Purser. 1854/6
Mary, Leighton Buzzard, wid. LB 1844/87
Nicholas, Husborne Crawley. 1559/167
Nicholas, Husborne Crawley, bricklayer. 1648/129
Peter, Houghton Regis. 1599/156
Ric., Chellington. 1619/196, I 4/133
Robt., Hinwick, Podington, lab. 1616/63
Robt., Tempsford, yeo. 1627-8/218
Robt., Steppingley, esq. A 1731/1
Sarah, Flitwick, Ruxox Farm, wid. 1856/40
Simon, Bedford, victualler. A 1720-1/53
Thos., Pulloxhill, farmer. A 1844/2
Wm., Hinwick, Podington, sen., husb. 1582-3/66
Wm., Sutton, lab. 1676/180
alias Phillips, Wm., Bedford, butcher. 1695/23
Wm., Husborne Crawley, yeo. 1704/21
Wm., Luton, husbn. 1721/30
see also Phillips
ABERRY
Jos., Totternhoe, yeo. 1723/41
see also Aubrey; and Wright
ABES, see Abbess
ABINGTON, Thos., Caddington. 1561/62
ABLE, ABELL, Jos., Sandy, dyer. AR 1680-1: 1/111d
ABLESTONE, Jn., Harrold, gent. 1726/7
Sarah, Harrold, wid. 1727/76
ABNEY see Halfpenny
ABOLNO (alias Miller), Robt., Riseley, yeo. 1623/176
Thos., Riseley, yeo. 1584-5/255
ABORROWE, Chris., Bedford St Paul, tiler. 1597-8/23
Ric., Bedford. 1606/43
ABRAHAM, HABRAHAM, Sir Thos of "Babenham", Felmersham. R 1509: 1/54d
Sarah, Cranfield, wid. 1720-21/101
Robt., Harrold. AR 1676: 1/40
Jn., Kempston, dairyman. A 1737-8/3
ABURNEY, Jn., Harlington, labr. 1593-4/1
see also Halfpenny
ACE, Robt., Little Barford. R1536: 4/55d
ACHURCH (see also Archurch), Jn., Bedford, distiller. A1752/12

ACOCK see Alcock
ACWORTH, Alex., Bedford St. Paul. 1639-40/153
Barnard, Bedford, barber. 1579-80/120
Geo., Toddington. R 1530: 3/28d
ADAM(S), Agnes, Husborne Crawley. 1614-15/17
Alice, Cople. 1603/127
Ann Sanders Shaw, Toddington. A 1837/9
Clement, Potton, bach. 1692/50
Geo., Caldecote, Northill. AR 1686: 1/126d
Hen., Lt. Barford, yeo. 1805/23
Humph., Toddington, yeo. 1799/39
Jas., Brogborough Park, Ridgmont, farmer. 1821/33
Jas., Potton, fuller. 1719/78
alias Barker, Joan, Wootton Underwood, wid. 1618/100
Jane, Crosshall, Eaton Socon. 1778/3
Jn., Aspley Guise, yeo. 1602/27
Jn., Sandy. 1613-14/134
Jn., Biddenham, yeo. 1632-3/5
Jn., senr., Lidlington. 1661/287
Jn., Toddington, whitesmith. 1731/7
Jn., senr., Lt. Barford, yeo. 1735/39
Jn., Bletsoe Castle, wheelwright. 1756/17
Jn., Crosshall, Eaton Socon, innholder. 1775/11
Jn., Woburn, yeo. 1787/49
Jn., Brogborough, Ridgmont, yeo. 1793/11
Jn., Cardington, farmer. R 1799/11
Jn., Leighton Buzzard, carp. LB 1821/8, I
Jos., Shefford, brewer. 1836/17
Lawrence, Cople, husb. 1600-1/70
Luce, Sandy, wid. 1614/30; R1614:31/16
Martha, Shefford, wid. 1837/33
Mary, Weald, Eynesbury, Hunts., wid. 1682/92
Mary, Cardington, wid. A 1723-4/38
Mary, Flitton, wid. 1785/25
Nich., Cople, husb. 1629/110
Ric., Turvey. 1583/115
Ric., Lidlington, gunsmith. 1718/4
Robert, Barford, yeo. 1611-12/181
Robt., Woburn, yeo. 1731/24
Robt., Woburn, husb. 1789/17
Susan, Potton, wid. 1724/91
Thos., Wootton. R 1536-7: 4/76
Thos., Stevington, lab. 1579/180
Thos., Lt. Barford, blacksmith. 1790/18
Wm., Tempsford, yeo. 1630/88

ADAM(S) continued
Wm., Stopsley, yeo. 1662/78
Wm., Sewell, Houghton Regis, husb. 1673/58
Wm., Tempsford, yeo. 1674/78
Wm., Dunstable, tailor. 1699/7
Wm., Harlington, butcher. 1704/81
Wm., Eversholt, dairyman. A 1747/8
Wm., Cranfield. 1749/24
Wm., junr., East End, Flitwick, weaver. 1750/13
Wm., Lidlington, dairyman. A 1793/6
ADCOCK(S), Jn., Thurleigh, dairyman. A 1704/24
Thos., Biggleswade, tailor. 1569-70/137
ADDER, Wm., Pavenham, husb. 1586/140
ADDINGTON, Ann, Tempsford, wid. 1792/17
Eliz., Bedford. A 1829/9
Eliz., Bedford, spins. 1851/21
Jos., Bedford, P/IX2. A 1812/15
Luke, Bletsoe, yeo. A 1729-30/71
Luke, Tempsford, yeo. 1775/21
Mary, Kempston, wid. 1626/86
Mary, Riseley, spins. AR 1681: 1/73
Peter, Chawston, Roxton, farmer. 1784/14
Silv., Goldington, gent. 1766/47
Silvester, Melchbourne, yeo. 1651/27
Silvester, Bushmead, Eaton Socon. AR 1687: 1/80d
Thos., Pertenhall, weaver. 1716/31
Thos., Tempsford, yeo. 1769/2
Thos., Tempsford, yeo. A 1782/22
ADE, see also Adye, Geo., of Lidlington. 1552/315
Harry, Lidlington. 1556/127
ADEANE, Thos., Melchbourne. R 1537: 4/88
Wm., Luton, maltman. 1555/83
see also Adowne; see also Haydon
ADENDES, Henry, Eaton. 1593-4/6
see also Hadden; see also Adowne
ADEY, see Adye
ADHOW, Wm., Haynes. 1539: 5/36d
ADKINS, Alice, Girtford, Sandy, spins. 1715/3
Ann, Biddenham, spins. A 1727/27
Eliz., Biddenham, wid. 1715/52
Eliz., Sandy. 1705/48
Geo., Westoning, husb. 1692/47
Geo., Marston. 1726/69
Hen., senr., Girtford, Sandy, bricklayer. 1705/47
Hen., Girtford, Sandy, mason. 1725/84

ADKINS continued
Hugh, Bedford St. Paul. 1614-15/20
Jas., senr., Cranfield, dairyman. 1739/69
Jas., Maulden, yeo. 1761/33
Jn., Girtford, Sandy, mason. 1660-1/132
Jn., Girtford, Sandy, yeo. 1693/152
Jn., Girtford, Sandy, bach. 1718-19/58
Jn., Goodman, Aspley Guise, yeo. 1857/11
Martha, Cranfield, spins. A 1808/10
Ric., Leighton Buzzard. LBA 1803/53
Thos, senr., Girtford, Sandy, bricklayer. 1648-9/97
Thos., Biddenham, farmer. A 1714-15/41
Thos., Eversholt, lab. A 1761/15
Wm., Potton, basketmaker. AR 1682: 1/117d
Wm., Marston, lab. 1742/50
see also Atkins
ADKINSON, see Atkinson
ADNATT, ADNUTES, Thos. (no parish given). 1617/282
Wm., Keysoe, lab. 1593/79
ADNUTES, see Adnatt
ADOWNE, Annes, Studham, wid. 1592/47
alias Clothier, Robt., Whipsnade, husb. 1587-8/117
alias Clothier, Robt., Caddington, lab. 1606/28
Robt., Clophill. R 1536: 4/58
see also Adeane, Addendes, Hadden, Hayden
ADYE, ADEY, ADY, Edm., Tempsford. 1630/55
Joan, Langford. 1628/68
Thos., Tempsford, farmer. A 1715/21
Wm., Arlesey, yeo. 1723-4/2
see also Ade
AGER, Eliz., Bedford. 1787/1
see also Hagar
AGGLETS, AGLETT, Ric., Astwick. 1560/211
Simon, Broom, Southill, husb. 1560/217
AGGS, Jn., Blunham. 1723-4/87
see also Haggas
AGNUSDEI, AUGGUS DAY, ANGLESDAY, John, Marston. R 1536-7: 4/80d
Renold, Wroxhill, Marston. R 1539: 6/6
Ric., Cranfield, husb. R 1533: 3/94d
AGUTTERS, AGUTTER, Chas., Oakley, yeo. A 1788/15
Chas., Podington, victualler. A 1853/10
Jonathan, Oakley, farmer. 1760/62
Jos., senr., Oakley, parish clerk. 1832/18
Robt., Salford, yeo. A 1846/13
Robt. O., Salford, yeo. A 1832/12 (limited admon.)

AILEWARD, see Ayleward
AINSWORTH, Ralph., Tempsford, farmer. 1714/15
Ralph, Tempsford, husb. 1731/73
Thos., Potton, blacksmith. 1663/69
Thos., Potton, shepherd. 1723/18
alias Cooke, Wm., Hockliffe, Chalgrave, innholder. 1588/103
Wm., Potton, yeo. 1730/42
AKERS, Geo., Sandy, lab. A 1752/3.
AKINS, see Atkins
ALBANY, ALBAN, ALBON(EY), AL(LI)BONE, AUBORN, ELBOURNE
Abr., Warden, yeo. 1669/21
Abr., Haynes. AR 1682: 1/207
Abr., Shefford, innholder. A 1712/29
Abr., Henlow. A 1785/28
Annise, Stanford, Southill. 1559/164
Dan., Turvey, farmer. 1790/34
Edw., Cople, yeo. A 1730/4
Edw., Bedford St. Mary, barber. 1749/38
Eliz., Wilshamstead, wid. 1630/3
Hen., Bedford, innholder. 1582/83
Hugh, Stanford, Southill, yeo. 1631-2/141
Jas., Clifton, carpenter. 1692/57
Jn., Bedford St. Paul. R 1527-8: 2/74d
Jn., Wilshamstead. 1557/371
Jn. senr., Wilshamstead. 1604/45
Jn., Stanford, Southill, yeo. 1613-14/14
Jn., Wilshamstead, yeo. 1626/77, 78
Jn., Stanford, Southill, gent. 1697/147
Mary, Bedford St. Paul, spins. AR 1685: 1/28d
Mary, Bedford, spins. 1685/103
Math., Thurleigh, weaver. c.1670/236
Ric., Thurleigh, weaver. 1649-50/77
Thos., Stanford, Southill, bach. 1621/175
Thos., Bedford St. Paul, gent. 1634-5/177
Thos., Holme Mills, Southill, weaver. 1639/39
Thos., Southill, pumpmaker. 1724-5/100
Thos., Meppershall, yeo. 1788/30
Thos., Biggleswade, lab. A 1822/16
Thos., Biggleswade. BwA 1823/66 (also correspondence in A.B.P.1)
Walt., Sandy. 1617/296
Wm., Henlow, shearman. 1588/90
Wm., Stanford, Southill, husb. 1590/170
Wm., (Old index Docket mislaid). A 1709/34
Wm., Turvey, husbn. 1748/20
Wm., Stotfold, lab. 1848/5

ALBRIGHT, Eliz., Aspley Guise, wid. 1703/44
Hugh, Leagrave, husb. 1683/56
Jas., Woburn, oatmealmaker. 1699/39
Jas., Woburn. A 1711-12/57
Nat., Woburn, warrener. 1722/35
Thos., Luton, yeo. 1725/4
Wm., Dunstable, yeo. 1559/192
ALCOCK, AUCOKE, AWCOCK, HALCOCK, ACOCK
Edw., Bolnhurst, yeo. 1648/113
Eliz., Bolnhurst, wid. 1587/113
Fra., Bolnhurst, wid. 1632/63
Joan, Chawston, Roxton. 1609-10/118
Jn., Thurleigh. R 1541: 6/97d
Nath., Keysoe, yeo. 1707/26
Nath., Bolnhurst, yeo. A 1722/4
Nath., Keysoe, farmer. A 1724/44
Ric., Bolnhurst, husb. 1619-20/241 I 4/49
Robt., Bolnhurst, husb. 1627/203
Simon, Bedford St. Mary, mercer. 1636-7/60
Simon, Keysoe, husb. 1703/47
Stephen, Duloe, Eaton Socon, lab. I 1619: 4/67
Thos., Bolnhurst. 1563/84
Walter, Bolnhurst, husb. R 1501: 1/27
Walter, Thurleigh. R 1559: 15/59
Wm., Pertenhall, clerk. 1557/357
Wm., Ravensden. 1588/99
see also Harcock
ALDERMAN, Geo., Bedford, gent. 1795/14
Thos., Keysoe, yeo. 1637/134
Thos., Bedford St. Peter. 1711-12/92
ALDIN, Jn., Leighton Buzzard. AR 1682: 1/162d
ALDRIDGE, ALDRYCHE, Edw., Westoning, butcher. 1846/12
Joan, Sandy, wid. 1557/257
John, Melchbourne, husb. 1572/52
Wm., Sandy. R 1514: 1/180
Wm., Ampthill. A 1714/12
ALEE, ALEY, alias Cook, Jas., Dunstable, wheelwright. 1684-5/103
Jane, Caddington. 1685/10
alias Cook, Jn., Thrales End, Luton, husb. 1687/45
Robt., Dunstable. R 1518: 2/85
see also Hailey, Hale
ALEXANDER, Nich., Kempston, gent. 1590/161
ALFORD, Rebecca, Westoning, wid. 1706-7/82
Wm., Westoning, clothier. A 1704/8

ALFORD continued
see also Halford
ALIGHT, Alice, of Goldington. R 1505?: 1/89
John, of Goldington. R 1505: 1/89
ALKINS, Wm., senr., Milton Ernest, late husb. 1557/291
ALLBONE, see Albany
ALLCOCK, see Alcock
ALLEN, ALEN, ALYN, ALLIN, ALLYN
Adam, Ampthill. AR 1670: 1/186
Alice, Kempston. R 1498: 1/148d
Alice, Cotton End, Cardington. 1617/318
Ann, Millbrook, wid. 1824/31
Anne, Houghton Conquest, wid. 1719-20/8
Annes, Eaton. 1588/94
Barth., Biddenham. R 1550: 12/120d
Ben., Harrold, farmer. A 1736-7/30
Ben., Bedford St. Mary, fellmonger and parchment maker. 1788/11
Edm., Eaton Bray. R 1551: 12/167d
Edm., Wootton, schoolmaster. 1667/51
Edw., Bolnhurst, lab. 1643/142
Edw. senr., Ampthill, currier. 1738/56
Edw., Eversholt, yeo. 1746/32
Edw., Stopsley, yeo. 1834/21
Eleanor, Ion, Over Gravenhurst, wid. 1702/64
Eliz., Bedford St. Mary. A 1816/8
Eliz., Eversholt, wid. 1556/148
Eliz., Kempston, wid. 1636-7/118
Eliz., Blunham, wid. 1691-2/126
Fra., Biddenham, mason. 1657/51
Fra., Felmersham. AR 1683: 1/44d
Fra., Houghton Conquest, husb. A 1719-20/36
Fra., Houghton Conquest, husb. A 1719-20/38
Fra., Ravensden, yeo. 1844/6
Geo., Leighton Buzzard, lab. 1607/127
Geo., Flitwick, yeo. 1721-2/67
Geo., Elstow, tailor. A 1730/8
Geo., Bedford, victualler. 1788/29
Geo., Harrold, shoemaker. 1810/51
Geo., Harrold, shoe manufacturer, farmer, maltster and common brewer. 1838/36
Helen, Bedford St. Mary, wid. R 1558: 14/54d
alias Atwood, Hen., Houghton Conquest, husb. R 1537: 4/95
Honour, Girtford, Sandy, wid. 1786/42
Hugh, Eaton Bray, husb. R 1548: 12/31d
Jas., Wyboston, Eaton Socon. 1582/90

ALLEN, ALEN, ALYN, ALLIN, ALLYN continued
Jas., Kempston, blacksmith. 1657-8/39
Jas., Stagsden, yeo. 1719/70
Jas., Bedford, innholder. 1723/45
Jas., Stagsden, husb. A 1763/17
Jas., senr., Stagsden, husb. and farmer. 1763/23
Jas., Stagsden, yeo. 1773/18
Jas., Melchbourne, grazier. 1795/44
Jas., South Mills, Blunham, yeo. 1803/29
Jas., Blunham, farmer. A 1815/5
Jn., Lidlington. R 1520: 2/121
alias Stacey, Jn., Tebworth, Chalgrave. R 1541: 6/86d & 8/13
Jn., Eaton. 1547/12
Jn., Bedford St. Mary, smith. R 1557: 13/70
Jn., Thurleigh. 1614/90
Jn., Silsoe, innkeeper. 1615/215
Jn., Kempston. 1626/89
Jn., Wootton, blacksmith. 1660/179
Jn., Cranfield, yeo. 1668-9/189
Jn., Sutton. 1670/138
Jn., Samshill, Westoning, yeo. 1679-80/103
Jn., Houghton Park, Ampthill, gardener. 1688/28
Jn., Stevington, yeo. 1691-2/134
Jn., Stagsden, yeo. 1711/86
Jn., senr., Silsoe, innkeeper. 1716/23
Jn., Riseley, cordwainer. 1718/47
Jn., Harrold, farmer. A 1754/22
Jn., Souldrop, lab. 1765/42
Jn., Girtford, Sandy, yeo. A 1782/28
Jn., Barton, carpenter. 1819/34
Jn., Barton, carpenter. 1840/14
Jn., Kempston, yeo. 1847/56
Jos., Girtford, Sandy, yeo. A1789/9
Mary, Tilbrook, wid. 1689/61
Mary, Stagsden, wid. 1714/81
Mary, Leighton Buzzard, wid. LB 1755/25
Mary, Stagsden, wid. 1784/52
Mary, Bedford St. Mary, wid. A 1804/13
Math., Flitwick. 1645-6/61
Math., Flitwick, husb. 1716/70
Math., Barton. A 1830/1
Math., Barton, carpenter. 1847/44
Moses, (old index only, bundle missing). A 1718/35
Nich., Sandy. 1618/150
Nich., Carlton, lab. 1702/24

ALLEN, ALEN, ALYN, ALLIN, ALLYN continued
Phill., Flitton. AR 1679-80: 1/203
Phoebe, Ampthill, wid. 1670/172
Ric., Cranfield. 1559/148
Ric., Stotfold. 1624/69
Ric., Girtford, Sandy, gardener. 1629/71
Ric., Kempston, blacksmith. 1639/33
Ric., Stagsden, lab. 1662/54
Ric., Pavenham. 1670/149
Ric., Cardington. 1712-13/31
Robt., Clapham, husb. R 1546: 11/143d
Robt., Eversholt. 1580/231
Robt., Barton, lab. 1584/249
Robt., Stagsden. 1600/41
Robt., Tilbrook, husb. 1609/157
Robt. alias Atwood, Kempston, lab. 1633/123
Rog., Eaton. R 1520: 2/16d
Roger, Kempston, husb. R 1564-5: 16/128
Sam., Biggleswade. AR 1676: 1/105
Sam., Biggleswade, grocer. 1676/153
Sam., Bedford. A 1742/8
Sarah, Bedford, wid. A 1746/22
Steph., Stagsden. AR 1671: 1/36
Stev., Stagsden, husb., 1671/76
Thos., Ridgmont. 1547: 12/17
Thos., Carlton, husb. R 1551: 12/162
Thos., Cranfield, husb. 1557/254
Thos., Woburn, shoemaker. 1576/35
Thos., Bedford St. Mary, (no date, 17th century). I 4/198
Thos., Kempston, lab. 1600-1/72
Thos. Allen "at Vine", Carlton, husb. 1608/67
Thos., Sharpenhoe, Streatley, husb. 1613-14/139
Thos., Moggerhanger, gent. 1626-7/30
Thos., Bourne End, Wooton, husb. 1640/72
Thos., Eaton, weaver. 1642-3/15
Thos., Felmersham. AR 1670: 1/35 186d
Thos., Kempston, husb. 1711/9
Thos., Langford. 1721/55
Thos., Dean, farmer. A 1736-7/28
Thos., Houghton Regis, victualler. 1749/5
Thos., Sandy, Beeston, yeo. 1763/36
Thos., Felmersham. A 1769/3
Thos., Beeston, Sandy. A 1771/8
Thos., Harrold, yeo. 1784/57
Thos., Millbrook, yeo. 1805/26

ALLEN, ALEN, ALYN, ALLIN, ALLYN continued
Thos., Bedford, carpenter. 1808/20
Thos., South Mills, Blunham, farmer. 1838/48
Wm., Carlton. R 1528: 2/139
Wm., Eaton Socon, husb. R 1559-60/15/61
Wm., Eaton, husb. 1562/104
Wm., Kempston, yeo. 1575/73
Wm., senr., Carlton, husb. 1582/61
Wm., senr., Sandy, yeo. 1614/172, I
Wm., senr., Girtford, Sandy, yeo. 1615/224
Wm., Carlton, lab. 1639/115
Wm., Carlton, husb. 1652-3/80
Wm., Lidlington, lab. 1663/49
Wm., Girtford, Sandy. AR 1673: 1/97
Wm., Stagsden. 1683-4/125
Wm., Stagsden, dairyman. 1686/10
Wm., Tilbrook. AR 1688: 1/82
Wm., Blunham. AR 1688: 1/130
Wm., Blunham, bach. 1688/8
Wm., Tilbrook, yeo. 1688/68
Wm., Sharnbrook. AR 1692: 1/51
Wm., Kempston, blacksmith. 1694/13
Wm., Chalton, Toddington, lab. 1700-1/144
Wm., Stagsden, husb. A 1711/16
Wm., Kempston, blacksmith. 1731/52
Wm., Leighton Buzzard, currier. LB 1741/12
Wm., Everton, maltster. A 1776/18
Wm., Biddenham, shepherd. 1798/34
Wm., Potton, Vicarage Farm, farmer. 1842/1
Wm., Puckeridge Lodge, Offley, Herts., lab. 1857/26
ALLINGHAM, Fra., Luton, baker. 1851/29
Hen., Tilbrooke, husb. I 1619: 4/148
Jas., Luton. 1851/30
Mary, Luton, Church St., wid. 1851/28
see also Ellingham
ALLINSON, Wm., Sundon, bach. R 1540: 6/57
ALLISON, Ann, Bedford, wid. 1840/20
Edm., Nether Staploe, Eaton Socon, lab. 1671/68
Edw., Bedford, innholder. 1814/25
Hannah, Bedford St. Peter, wid. 1818/3
Jas., Bedford, yeo. 1777/34
Jn., Tempsford, lab. 1669/59
Mary, Bedford St. Cuthbert, wid. A1811/2
Mary, Bedford St. Cuthbert, wid. of Geo. 1811/4
Ric., Dunstable, innholder. 1586-7/146

ALLISON continued
Robt., Bedford St. Paul. A1771/7
Thos., Eaton Socon, lab. 1691/96
Wm., Steppingley, bach. R 1677-8: 1/198d
Wm., Bedford, cordwainer. A 1840/1
ALLMAN, Peter, Bedford St. Paul, baker. 1625/189
Wm., Bedford, gent. 1610-11/177
see also Holman
ALLOWAY, Jn., Woburn, tailor. 1711/26
see also Holloway
ALLPIN, Jos., ?Ravensden or Gravenhurst. A 1774/4
ALLWAY, see Alway
ALLWINCKLE, Math., Millbrook. A 1719/6
ALSOP, Ann, Bedford, wid. A 1711/2
Arthur, Tilbrook, lab. 1719/101
Jn., Eaton Socon, gent. A 1727-8/40
ALSTON, Jn., old index only, bundle missing. A 1718/30
Sarah, Pavenham, wid. 1714/104
Vere Jn., Odell, clerk. 1762/38
Wm., Pavenham, esq. 1709/1
Wm., Pavenham, gent. 1715/49
ALTROP, Jos., Tempsford, farmer. A 1757/8
ALWAY, ALLWAY, HALWAY, Jas., Eaton Bray. A 1853/14
Jn., printed B.N.Q. ii 318. 1543
Ric., Sandy. 1639/105
Ric., Woburn, yeo. 1684/70
ALWEN, Alice, wid., Harlington. R 1548: 12/22d
alias Carpenter, Jn., jnr., Harlington, husb. R 1544-5: 11/36
alias Carpenter, Jn., Harlington, husb. R 1545: 11/67
AMBER, Thos., Wyboston, Eaton Socon. 1573/132
AMBRIDGE, Ann, Wootton, wid. 1761/5
Fra., Houghton Conquest. 1772/22
Fra., Kempston, maltster. 1784/32
Jas., Aspley Guise. 1657-8/261
Jas., senr., Aspley Guise, yeo. 1708-9/39
Jas., Kempston Hardwick, husb. 1746/1
Jas., Kempston, farmer. 1773/4
Jn., Cranfield, husb. 1760/36
Jn., Cranfield, publican. 1816/1
Jn., Salford, yeo. 1817/21
Ric., Kempston. A 1755/3
Ric., Cranfield, yeo. 1824/20
Thos., Cranfield, yeo. 1825/28
Wm., Kempston, farmer. 1773/16
Wm., Cranfield, gent. 1822/12, I 4/244

AMBRIDGE continued
see also Ramridge
AMBROSE, Jonas, Caddington, husb. 1782/5
Robt., Potton, vict. A 1706/7
AMERICK, Robt., senr., Dunstable. R 1545: 11/92
AMERY, AMERE, EMERY, Jn., Dunstable. 1623/141
Robt., Biddenham, husb. 1622-3/5
Wm., Bedford. R 1527-8: 2/72
AMES, AMEAS, AMIAS, AMIS, AMSE, Ann, Northill, wid. 1751/13
Edw., Leighton Buzzard, gent. 1606/26
Eliz., Dunstable, wid. 1590-1/139
Eliz. Horbuckle, Bedford St. Paul, wid. 1824/26
Jn., senr., Southill, husb. 1619-20/174, I 4/19
Jn., Stagsden. 1659/96
Jn., Odell, baker. 1737/20
Jn., Odell, baker. A 1777/15
Jn., Bedford St. Paul, shopkeeper. A 1810/18
Ric., Dunstable, gent. 1589-90/110
Robt., Northill, vintner. 1729-30/123
Thos., Kempston. R 1500: 1/20
see also Amps, Annis
AMISDAINE, Agnes, Leighton Buzzard, wid. 1572-3/67
AMOWR, Thos., Carlton. R 1516: 1/178d
AMPS, AMPES, Edm., Campton. 1575/89
Jn., Wingfield, Chalgrave. R 1558-9: 11/72
Jn., senr., Kempston. 1635-6/134
Jn., Kempston. R 1675: 1/11
Jn., Bedford, apothecary. 1691/95
Jn., Felmersham, lab. A 1752/10
Mary, Sundon. 1713-14/77
Thos., Sundon. R 1545: 11/72
Thos., Kempston, husb. 1582/86
Thos., senr., Sundon, husb. 1617/184
Wm., Campton. 1592-3/63
see also Ames, Annis, Hems
AMYS, see Ames
ANABLE, ANNABAL, Cath., Markyate Street, wid. 1801/31
Eliz., Dunstable, wid. 1835/1
Jn., Markyate St., victualler. 1801/10
ANDER, Jn., Houghton Regis. 1565/8
ANDERUS, see Andrews
ANDERSON, Eliz., Eyeworth, wid. A 1763/19
Mary, Clifton, wid. 1857/28

ANDREW, ANDREWS, ANDERUS, Alice, Houghton Regis, wid. 1682/81
Edm., Eggington. 1558/29
Edm., Eaton Bray, lab. 1672/160
Eliz., Eaton Socon, wid. 1618/51
Eliz., Elstow, spins. 1625-6/130
Eliz., Wrestlingworth, wid. 1630/60
Eliz., Elstow, wid. A 1702-3/21
Ellen, Elstow, wid. 1618/83
Fra., jnr., Eversholt, spins. 1700/96
alias Tyler, Geo., Tingrith, yeo. 1624-5/19
Grace, Elstow, lacemaker. 1665/73
Hannah, Milton Brian, spins. 1662/82
Jn., Stanbridge, husb. 1582/277
Jn., Barton, husb. 1602/14
Jn., Bedford St. John. 1632/65
Jn., Eggington, yeo. 1638/53
Jn., Caddington, yeo. 1686/61
Jn., senr., Caddington, yeo. 1762/58
Mary, Markyate St., wid. (bundle 1679) 1678/20
Mary, Leighton Buzzard, spins. 1749/31
Mary, Caddington. R 1678 1/156
Mary, Marston, spins. A 1735/2
Oliver, Harlington, husb. 1558/281
Ric., senr., Eggington. 1601/130
Ric., Houghton Regis, draper. 1623/191
Ric., Eaton Socon, carpenter. 1631/201
Ric., Eaton Socon, carpenter. 1633/159
Ric., Eggington, yeo. (bundle 1638) 1636/157
Ric., Houghton Regis, tailor. 1678/93
Ric., Eggington, gent. 1683/6
Ric., Cardington, victualler. 1687-8/73
Ric., Elstow, ale-draper. 1725/64
Ric., Eversholt. A1700/4
Robt., Leighton Buzzard. 1558/227
Robt., Caddington. R 1677: 1/153
Thos., Leighton Buzzard. 1558/27
Thos., Markyate Street, yeo. 1606/20
Thos., Dunstable, chandler. 1633/136
Thos., Felmersham, shoemaker. 1667-8/98
Thos., Henlow, millwright. 1696-7/145
Wm., Clipstone, Leighton Buzzard, husb. LB R 1545: 1/14
Wm., Clipstone, Leighton Buzzard, husb. 1576-7/224
Wm., Eggington. 1599/167
Wm., Wrestlingworth, husb. 1617/174
Wm., Bedford St. Paul, ironmonger. 1630/133

To all British Record Society subscribers

The Society sends you its latest volume, **104**, *Index of Bedfordshire Probate Records 1484-1845, Part I: A - Kimnott*, compiled by Alan F. Cirket, edited by Joan Stuart and Peggy Wells, with an introduction by Christopher Pickford.

Please note that volume **103**, the first part of an index to the Consistory Court of Ely, has been overtaken at a late stage of production, and will be issued to subscribers within the next few months. You have *not* missed a volume.

November 1993.

ANDREW, ANDREWS, ANDERUS continued
Wm., Houghton Regis, yeo. 1639/111
Wm., Marston, lab. 1733/30
ANGEL, ANGELLES, ANGLE(S), Alice, Moggerhanger, wid. 1566/76
Edw., Tilsworth, husb. 1727/42
Hen., Little Staughton, victualler. 1820/6
Jas., Chalton, Blunham. A 1771/39
Jas., Chalton, Blunham. 1771/69
Jn., Moggerhanger, husb. 1610/74
Rog., Cople, yeo. 1605/138
Thos., Moggerhanger. 1610/50
Wm., Sandy, farmer. 1689-90/88
Wm., Sewell, Houghton Regis, husb. 1708/19
see also Angold
ANGER, Jn., Colmworth, yeo. 1679/75
Jn., Colmworth, Chandlers End, yeo. 1683/14
Jos., Colmworth, gent. 1688/17
see also Hangar
ANGLESDAY, see Agnusdei
ANGLESEY, Alice, Marston. R 1540: 6/35
ANGLISEY, Thos., Bolnhurst, gent. 1622/67
ANGOLD, Jn., Tempsford. R 1540-1: 6/65; see also Angel
ANNICO, Agnes, Wilden, wid. 1639/98
Eliz., Willington. 1614/25
alias Lewis, Jn., Elstow, yeo. 1694/77
Jn., Thurleigh, yeo. 1661/355
Jn., Gastlings, Southill, yeo. 1710/3
Jn., Elstow, lab. 1749/9
Peter, Cople. 1630/96
alias Lewis, Wm., Cople, husb. 1679/54
ANNIS, Isabell, Kempston, wid. 1599-1600/173
Jn., Kempston, husb. 1599/169
Jn., Odell, miller. 1768/35
see also Amps
ANSELL, Bennett, Shillington, lab. AR 1672: 1/95d
Fra., Streatley. 1737/27
Joan, (no parish given), wid. 1609-10/105
Jn., Luton, innholder. 1590/142
Nich., Cadwell, Holwell, gent. 1723/31
Ric., Cadwell, Holwell, gent. 1726/58
Thos. senr., Great Barford, gent. 1591/110
Thos., Barford, esq. 1623/99
Thos., Pulloxhill, lab. 1802/4
Wm., Shillington. R 1537: 4/92d
Wm., Harrowden, Cardington. 1684-5/119

ANSELL continued
Wm., Pegsdon, Shillington, yeo. 1827/1
see also Anstill, Aunsell
ANSTEY, ANSTEE, Allen, Markyate Street, innholder. 1605/146
Ben., Houghton Regis, yeo. 1799/3
Grace, Stagsden. R 1546: 11/217
Jn., Biddenham. R 1541: 6/94 & 8/15
Jn., Biddenham. R 1546: 11/230d
Jn., Chalton, Toddington, yeo. A 1841/3
Jos., Houghton Regis, yeo. 1804/11
Wm., Dunstable, straw hat manufacturer. A 1803/7
ANSTILL, alias Clarke, Dorothy, Marston, wid. 1587/175
alias Barber, Eliz., Toddington, wid. 1609/160
see also Ansell and Aunsell
ANTHONY, Crosley alias Anthony see Crowsley
Eliz., Potsgrove, wid. 1733/29
alias Crosley, Thos., senr., Toddington. 1617/176
Thos., Leighton Buzzard, peruke maker. LB 1817/64
APHILLIP, Morgan, Dunstable. R 1547: 11/249d
see also Phillip, Phillips
APJENKIN, see Jenkin alias Gough
APOULTON, Nich., Toddington, fletcher. 1612/22
see also Poulton and Appleton
APPERLEY, Judith, Potton, wid. 1795/43
APPLETON, see Apoulton
APTHORPE, Clement, Biggleswade. AR 1692: 1/135
Dor., Everton, wid. 1680/72
see also Thorpe
ARCH, Jn., Thurleigh, farmer. 1738/86
Jos., Keysoe, carpenter. 1795/46
Sam., Bedford St. Mary, innholder. 1799/51
ARCHBOLD, Jn., Husborne Crawley, baker. 1660/172
Jn., Woburn, baker. 1676-7/174
Jn., Woburn, baker. AR 1676-7: 1/196d
Mary, Woburn, wid. 1682/72
ARCHER, ARCHARDE, Ann. Ampthill, wid. of Thos. of Houghton Conquest. 1638/49
Ann. Clifton, wid. A 1776/5
Dor., Bletsoe, wid. 1703-4/68
Eliz., Houghton Conquest, wid. 1560/226
Essex, Bletsoe, innholder. A 1731/2
Geo., Eaton Socon, baker. 1833/22
Hen., (Lidlington). R 1541 6/71 & 8/6
Jn., Lidlington. R 1518: 2/80
Jn., Lidlington. 1584/180

ARCHER, ARCHARDE continued
Math., Clifton, yeo. 1755/22
Math., Clifton, yeo. 1805/24
Rebeccah, Ampthill, wid. 1685/90
Ric., Eyeworth. R 1547: 12/10d
Ric., Lidlington, yeo. 1617-18/221
Thos., Lidlington. R 1523: 2/56
Thos., Houghton Conquest, (clerk) parson of. 1630/129
Timothy, S.T.P. Meppershall. AR 1672: 1/96
Wm., Lidlington, yeo. 1584/244
Wm., Lidlington, yeo. 1617-18/168
Wm., Lidlington, yeo. 1619-20/226, I 4/40
Wm., Roxton, baker. A 1839/8
ARCHURCH, Nich., Cranfield. (Old index only, admon missing). A 1726/18
see also Achurch
ARDEN, ARDIN, Francis, Haynes, husb. 1611-12/137
Thos., Stagsden. 1608/71
Thos., Haynes, dairyman. 1624/90
Thos., Potton, lab. 1685/74
Wm., Pavenham, freemason. 1619-20/222, 223, I 4/20
see also Harden, Harding, Hardon
ARDLEY, Thos., Shillington, yeo. 1676/99
ARDS, ARDYS, Anthony, Elstow, gent. 1553/260
Thos., Renhold, gent. 1607. 1594/95
ARGENT, Jonathan, sen., Kempston, yeo. 1683/70
ARGIENT, see Argent
ARMFIELD, Margt., Marston. AR 1678: 1/200
Robt., Marston, weaver. AR 1671-2 1/188d
ARMITAGE, see Hermitage
ARMOUR, Ric., Clifton, wheelwright. 1830/27
Thos., Henlow, carpenter. 1857/16
Wm., Stanford, Southill, carpenter. 1836/45
see also Harmer
ARMS, Jn., Tempsford. 1671/29
Jn., Tempsford. AR 1671: 1/93d
ARMSDEN, Nath., Potsgrove, dairyman. A 1731/40
ARMSTRONG, Chas., Houghton Conquest, gent. 1781/36
Fra., Ampthill, wid. 1758/40
Geo., Hockliffe, farmer. 1838/44
Jn., Houghton Conquest, farmer. 1843/24
Jn., Bedford, lab. A 1723/32
Sarah, Wootton, wid. 1836/46
Thos., Ampthill, esq. 1748/19
Thos., Wootton, farmer. 1853/55
Wm., Wilshamstead, farmer. 1845/56

ARMSTRONG continued
Wm., Battlesdon, farmer. 1850/28
ARNALD, see Arnold
ARNE, Dan., sen., Thurleigh, yeo. 1721/60
Tim., Stagsden, victualler. 1755/47
ARNOLD, ARNALD, Alice, Pulloxhill, wid. 1809/10
Edw., Houghton Conquest. R 1545: 11/116d
Edw., (?Lower) Gravenhurst. 1622-3/16
Edw., Shillington, yeo. 1637/89
Edw., Wootton. AR 1676: 1/12d
Frances, Bedford. 1855/30
Jas., Clophill. 1798/40
Joan, Pegsdon, Shillington, wid. 1648-9/103
Job, Woburn, yeo. 1797/10
Job, Woburn, yeo. 1799/21
Jn., Eversholt. R 1558: 14/48d
Jn., Shillington, yeo. 1601-2/141
alias Cooper, Jn., Toddington, lab. 1610-11/14
Jn., Shillington, carpenter. 1626/63
Jn., Wootton, lab. 1705/69
Jn., Arlesey, husb. 1714/37
Jn., Arlesey, dairyman. A 1771/19
Jn., Tilbrook, lab. A 1839/11
Jos., Upper Gravenhurst, lab. AR 1670: 1/91d
Jos., Cross Hall, Eaton Socon, miller. A 1802/12
Lawr., Holwell, lab. 1629/148
Margt., Ampthill, wid. 1722/46
Martha, Ampthill, spins. 1723/34
Mary, Melchbourne, wid. 1606/32
Math., Shillington. R 1523: 2/9d
Mich., Bedford, clerk. 1742/84
Ric., Maulden. 1601/95
Ric., Arlesey. 1725/19
Robt., Lower Gravenhurst, lab. 1622/82
alias Cooper, Robt., Cranfield, yeo. 1634/114
Robt., Ampthill, yeo. 1827/32
Sam., Cotton End, Cardington, farmer. 1790/31
alias Cooper, Sarah, Bedford, wid. 1662/106
Thos., Shillington. 1570/2
Thos., Southill, victualler. 1828/40
Thos., Melchbourne, husb. 1584-5/254
Thos., Ampthill, yeo. 1612/24
alias Cooper, Thos., Bedford, gent. 1658-9/209
Thos., Ampthill, esq. 1696/80
Thos., Ampthill, gent. 1718/51

ARNOLD, ARNALD continued
Thos., Shillington, lab. 1718-19/75
Wm., Elstow. R 1526: 1/248d
Wm., Shillington, lab. 1631/168
Wm., Upper Gravenhurst, lab. 1678/128
Wm., Over Gravenhurst, bach. 1682/36
Wm., Husborne Crawley, farmer. 1775/34
Wm., senr., Cainhoe Park, Clophill, farmer. 1796/2
Wm., Pulloxhill, farmer. 1799/50
Wm., Henlow, yeo. 1831/45
Wm., Luton, boot & shoemaker. 1840/15
Wm., Upper Gravenhurst, gent. 1853/51
Wm., Wootton, farmer. AR 1681-2: 1/20d
ARNOTT, Ric., Houghton Regis, gent. 1725/75
ARRIS, Jas., Sharnbrook. 1837/16
Jn., Tingrith. 1570/8
alias Stephen, Thos., Pottsgrove, lab. 1630/4
see also Harris
ARROWSMITH, Jn., Hockliffe, dealer in hardware. R 1770/12 (reg. only)
Jos., Bedford St. John, clerk. AR ?1689: 1/33
Tim., sen., Hockliffe, staymaker. 1754/13
Tim., sen., Hockliffe, yeo. 1791/2
Tim., Hockliffe. A 1823/2
ARTHUR, alias Bouskell, Arthur (see under Bouskell)
alias Buskin, Benj., Bedford St. Cuthbert, pipemaker. 1759/38
alias Bonskin, Jos., Bedford, barber. A 1723-4/36
alias Bouskell, Rebeccah, Bedford, wid. 1724/39
Robt., (old index only, bundle missing). A 1717/6
Wm., Biddenham. 1679/57
ASABEE, ASBEE, see Ashby
ASAM, Thos., Ampthill, gardener. 1853/22
Wm., Bedford. 1810/17
see also Askam, Axham
ASBY, ASBE, ASSBEE, Ann., Aspley Guise, wid. 1833/43
Eliz., Leighton Buzzard. LB A 1815/70
Ric., Luton. R 1531: 3/44
see also Ashby
ASHBOLT, Eliz., Wilshamstead, wid. 1678/121
Jn., Hawnes Grange, Haynes, yeo. 1672/133
Jn., Great Barford, yeo. A 1702/18
Jos., Little Staughton, lab. 1702/51
Prudence, Keysoe, wid. 1752/5
Sam., Wilshamstead, yeo. 1678/101
Sam., Wilshamstead, husb. 1679/9
Thos., Wilshamstead, yeo. 1678-9/144

ASHBOLT continued
Thos., Tempsford, lab. A 1724/16
Wm., Norwood End, Haynes, lab. 1702-3/47
ASHBOURNE, ASHBURN, Jn., Pavenham, blacksmith. 1753/16
Wm., Pavenham. c.1660/247
Wm., Pavenham. 1720/31
Wm., Pavenham, blacksmith. A 1737/42
ASHBY, ASABEE, ASBEE, Andrew, Meppershall, gardener. 1828/20
Edw., Luton, weaver. 1619/180; I 4/162
Fra., Goldington. 1619/235; I 4/56
Geo., Millbrook, lab. 1601/80
Hen., Sundon, lab. 1626-7/28
Jn., Sundon. 1661/387
Jn., Upper Sundon, yeo. 1678/133
Jn., Sundon, husb. 1681/59
Jn., Houghton Conquest, carpenter. 1708/79
Jn., Dunstable, yeo. 1711/93
Jn., Someries, Luton, yeo. 1739/30
Jn., Milton Bryan, yeo. 1772/14
Jn., Leighton Buzzard. LB 1797/4
Jn., Totternhoe, shepherd. A 1721/24
Jn., Maulden, husb. A 1822/14
Jn., Tho., Aspley Guise. A 1854/3
Mary, Shillington, wid. 1629/85
Ric., Cranfield, lab. 1669-70/99
Ric., Toddington, shoemaker. 1856/12
Robt., senr., Milton Bryan, yeo. 1802/27
Robt., Leighton Buzzard, lab. LB 1758/34
Ruth, Luton, spins. 1840/32
Ruth, Pulloxhill. A 1803/8
Sam., Ampthill, draper. 1813/29
Thos., Shillington, bricklayer. 1629/85
Thos., Sundon. AR 1683: 1/165d
Wm., Milton Bryan, shepherd. 1728/2
Wm., Meppershall, gardener. 1853/23
ASHCROFT, Alice, Husborne Crawley, wid. of Rich. A 1703-4/20
ASHFORD, Ric., Langford. 1587-8/98
Robt., Langford, husb. 1564/41
Wm., Langford. 1715-16/88
Wm., Langford, lab. 1756/21
ASHMORE, Thos., Potton, yeo. A 1856/4
ASHPOLE, Ann, Pavenham, wid. 1849/40
Jn., Markyate St., miller. 1782/17
Pen., Husborne Crawley, wid. A 1704/38
Ric., Sharnbrook, husb. 1759/4

ASHPOLE continued
Ric., Pavenham, butcher. 1846/6
ASHTON, Ann, Millbrook, wid. 1706/38
Dale, Shillington, yeo. 1830/42
Edm., Millbrook, husb. 1706/25
alias Benson, Geo., Turvey, yeo. 1608-9/96
Geo., Shillington, yeo. 1639/42
Geo., Pavenham, yeo. 1657/5
Geo., Shillington, carpenter. 1688/59
Geo., Shillington. AR 1674: 1/100
alias Benson, Hen., Pavenham. 1617-18/213
alias Benson, Hen., Turvey, yeo. 1646/100
alias Benson, Jn., Pavenham. AR 1675: 1/39d
alias Benson, Jn., Pavenham, lab. A 1724/17
Ric., Shillington. 1660
Susannah, Stevington, spins. 1749/13
Thos., Shillington. 1612-13/56
Thos., Shillington, yeo. 1644/88
alias Benson, Thos., Stevington, yeo. 1679/64
Thos., sen., Shillington, yeo. 1680-1/107
Thos., Shillington, yeo. 1707/55
Thos., Shillington. A 1737/38
Wm., Bedford St. Cuthbert. 1676-7/178
alias Benson, Wm., Bedford St. Cuthbert. AR 1676-7: 1/13
Wm., Pavenham. AR 1677-8: 1/41
see also Aston, Haston, Astin
(Benson alias Ashton, see also under Benson)
ASHURST, Jas., Arlesey, clerk. AR 1679-80: 1/109d
Mary, Arlesey, wid. 1688/40
ASHWELL, Agnes, sen., Leighton Buzzard, wid. LB 1741/18
Alice, Totternhoe, wid. 1553/160
Ann, Leighton Buzzard, wid. 1678/106
Anne, sen., Leighton Buzzard, wid. Fac. 1737: 9/80
Edw., sen., Leighton Buzzard, ironmonger. Fac. 1708: 0/27
Eliz., old index only, bundle missing. A 1718/32
Eliz., Eaton Bray. A 1854/8
Isabell, Totternhoe, wid. R 1546: 11/188d
Jas., sen. Eaton Bray, yeo. 1667-8/8
Jas., Eaton Bray, yeo. 1687/61
Jas., Eaton Bray. gent. A 1704/34
Jn., Totternhoe. R 1545-6: 11/120d
Jn., Eaton Bray, bach. 1712-13/28
Jn., Leighton Buzzard, gent. 1742/102
Jn., Tempsford, farmer. 1842/5
Jn., jun. Leighton Buzzard, yeo. A 1817/8

ASHWELL continued
Ric., Eaton Bray, yeo. 1720/1
Ric., Eaton Bray, farmer. 1795/51
Ric., sen. Moor End, Eaton Bray, yeo. 1802/1
Sam., sen., Henlow. 1834/33
Thos., Totternhoe. R 1532: 3/64
Thos., Eaton Bray. 1843/29
Thos., Leighton Buzzard, scrivenor. LB 1738/8
Wm., Totternhoe. R 1545: 11/55d
Wm., Totternhoe. 1558/37
Wm., Totternhoe, yeo. 1635/1
Wm., Eaton Bray, yeo. 1720/38
ASKEW, Ann, Northill P/IX2. A 1812/3
Fanny, Stagsden, spins. A 1849/3
Jn., Nether Dean, yeo. 1725-6/86
Jn., Dean, farmer. 1783/8
see also Esgor
ASKHAM, Robt., Hatch, Northill, yeo. 1806/34
Wm., Shelton, yeo. 1809/24
see also Asam, Axham
ASLIN, ASLYN, Jn., Chaul End, Caddington, yeo. 1788/15
Jn., Caddington. 1823/41
Thos., Luton. AR 1675: 1/150d
ASLOWE, ATSLOW, Jn., Marston. R 1532: 3/75d
Wm., sen., Eversholt. 1536/1
Wm., Eversholt. 1559?/271
see also Slow
ASPELAND, ASPLAND, Joan, Riseley, wid. AR 1685: 1/78d
Jn., Riseley, lab. AR 1679: 1/69d
Oliver, no parish given, miller. I 1619: 4/90
Thos., Bletsoe. 1642/20
Wm., Riseley, lab. 1684-5/94
Wm., Riseley, lab. AR 1685: 1/78
ASPIN, (alias Jas., see under James)
Ann, Sharnbrook, wid. 1725/67
ASPINALL, Agnes Caroline, Bedford St. Peter, spins. 1854/31
Eliz., Elstow, spins. 1850/18
Jas., vicar of Kempston. 1816/10
Mary, Bedford, wid. 1770/40a
Thos., Blunham, yeo. 1730/4
ASPITAL, Hen., Thurleigh, blacksmith. 1708/60
Hen., Northill, Ickwell, blacksmith. A 1768/1
Thos., sen., Keysoe, blacksmith. 1752/39
ASPLAND, see Aspeland
ASPOODE, see Aspud

ASPREY, Steph., Ampthill, hempspinner. 1820/7
ASPUD, ASPOODE, Thos., Eaton Socon. 1644/99
ASTELL, Clark alias Astell, see Clark
Cath., Harlington, spins. 1760/46
see also Axtell
ASTIN, Dan., Clophill, hempdresser. AR 1680: 1/204
Edw., Holwell, Shillington, weaver. 1676/105
Helen, Wilshamstead, wid. 1641/148
Jn., Wilshamstead, yeo. 1641/124
Jn., Beadlow, Clophill, dairyman. 1669-70/119
Nich., Wilshamstead. R 1548 12/13d
Ric., Shillington, bach. 1660-1/81
Thos., Shefford. AR 1685: 1/24
Thos., Shefford. 1685/35
Wm., Felmersham, lab. 1627-8/220
Wm., Wilshamstead, husb. 1650/118
Wm., (Wilshamstead). R 1540: 6/44
see also Ashton, Asteling, Astling, Aston, Austin, Haston
ASTELING, see Astin
ASTLING, see Astin
ASTON, see Astin; see also Ashton
ASTNEY, Mich., Toddington, gent. 1679-80/98
ASTRY, ASTREY, Wm., Maulden, gent. 1771/14
ASTWOOD, Ann, Wootton, wid. 1707/79
Luke, Potton, yeo. 1703/14
Luke, Potton, cutler. R 1755/20
Luke, Potton. 1838/43
Sam, Honeydon, Eaton Socon, yeo. 1760/49
ATHALL, Wm., Tempsford. R 1545: 11/96d
ATHEY, Thos., Easton Maudit, Northants., husb. (Note on back states "lived atSharnbrook viii or ix years and died there"). 1645/2
Wm., Harrold, butcher. c.1674/133
ATKINS, ATKYN, Anne, Colmworth, wid. 1576-7/13
Bartholomew, Potton. R 1500:1/15d-16
Dan., Eaton Bray. 1684/44
Dorcas, Eaton, wid. 1678/91
Eliz., Sundon, wid. A 1727/22
Esther, Eaton Bray, wid. 1717/12
Geo., Cardington. 1602/21
Hannah, Stanbridge, wid. LB A 1773/25
Hen., Wilden, yeo. 1718/48
Hen., Westoning, bach. A 1764/6
Jn., Studham. R 1550: 12/91d
Jn., Wilden, lab. 1663/2
Jn., Biggleswade, tailor. Bw 1726/23

ATKINS, ATKYN continued
Jn., Toddington, P/IX 2 Admon missing. A 1783/14
Mary, Carlton, wid. 1687/93
Ric., Yielden, lab. 1571/61
Ric., Eaton, carpenter. 1623/188
Ric., sen., Eaton Bray, yeo. 1705/1
Ric., sen. Eaton Bray, scrivener. 1722/2
Ric., Eaton Bray, gent. 1731/100
Robt., Colmworth. 1558/3
Thos., Eaton Bray. R 1541: 6/9
Thos., Girtford, Sandy, bricklayer. 1665/52
Thos., Dunton, lab. 1716/36
Thos., Nether Stondon, Shillington, 1720/30
Thos., Girtford, Sandy, yeo. 1737/58
Thos., Eversholt, lab. 1761/16
Walt., Wilden, parson of Wilden. 1579-80/123
Wm., Toddington. R 1547-8: 12/21d
Wm., Leighton Buzzard, yeo. 1747/4
see also Adkins
ATKINSON, ADKYNSON, Alex., Potton, gent. 1699-1700/73
Ann, Potton, wid. R ?1673-4: 1/98
Cath., Potton, wid. 1715/51
Chris., Dean, clerk. 1777/20
Jn., Ampthill. R 1545: 11/79
Jn., Ridgmont, Segenhoe, husb. 1617/190
Jn., Potton. R 1672: 1/95
Kath., Potton, wid., (inventory & papers). A 1722 also 1715/51
Len., Barford, husb. 1617/257
Ric., Potton, husb. R 1520-1: 2/173
Ric., Potton, grocer. 1709/38
Sarah, Potton. 1703/59
Thos., Eynesbury, Hunts., yeo. 1830/22
Wm., Studham. R 1508: 1/166d
Wm., vicar of Potton. R 1537: 5/4
ATPOUND, Thos., Maulden. R 1521-2: 2/104d
ATSLOW, see Aslowe and Slow
ATTACK, Dan., Bedford, gent. 1854/1
Eliz., Bedford, wid. 1827/53
ATTERBERRY, ATTERBURY, Eliz., Bedford, spins. 1834/16
Geo., sen., Chalgrave, yeo. 1758/22
Ric., Houghton Conquest, husb. 1761/37
Ric., Marston. A 1811/14
Sam., Bedford, gent. 1834/7
Sam., Cople, wheelwright. 1847/5
Sarah, Chalgrave, wid. A 1766/32

ATTERBERRY, ATTERBURY continued
Thos., Wilshamstead, lab. 1590-1/165
Wm., Chalgrave, yeo. A 1714/35
Wm., Wootton (P/IX 2 Admon missing). A 1783/15
ATTERTON, Eliz., Warden. 1601/117
Eliz., Ampthill, wid. A 1721/30
Isaac, Willington, husb. 1756/2
Jn., Warden, yeo. 1598/86
Jn., Nether Caldecote, Northill, yeo. 1738/61
Jn., Pavenham, farmer. A 1762/12
Judith, Hatch, Northill, wid. 1661/393
Mary, Lower Caldecote, Northill. R 1682: 1/119d
Mary, Biggleswade, wid. R 1685-6: 1/126
Nath., Willington, farmer. A 1744/1
Robt., Holme, Biggleswade, lab. 1639/4
Thos., Nether Caldecote, Northill, yeo. 1662/95
Wm., Clophill, yeo. 1621/142
Wm., Hatch, Northill, yeo. 1656/32
Wm., Ampthill. R 1691: 1/219d
ATTLEE, Thos., Toddington, carrier. 1790/35
Thos., Westoning, farmer & grocer. R 1845/25
(Monition to transmit to P.C.C., A.B.P. 1/1846)
see also Hatley
ATTYEO, Ric., Beeston, Sandy, yeo. 1636/34
ATWELL, Ann, Eggington, wid. 1618-19/28
Eliz., Heath, spins. LB 1814/59
Martha, Husborne Crawley, wid. 1715-16/79
Nich., Cople, lab. 1601-2/113
Thos., sen., Eggington, yeo. 1682/66
Wm., Eggington, husb. 1598-9/146
Wm., Battlesden, dairyman. 1764/1
see also Oatwell, Wells
ATWOOD, AWOOD, Allen alias Atwood see under Allen
Eliz., Luton, wid. 1624-5/3
Eliz., Duloe, Eaton Socon, wid. 1728-9/93
Fra., Eaton Ford, Eaton Socon, yeo. 1733/32
Gamaliel, Goldington, lab. 1694/48
alias Allen, John, Kempston. R 1533-4: 3/121d
Jn., Dunstable. R 1581: 1/233
Jn., Silsoe, glazier. 1566/65
Jn., Luton, yeo. 1623-4/151
Jn., Chiltern Green, Hyde, husb. 1678/138
Jn., Little Staughton, yeo. 1692/29
Joseph, Little Staughton, tailor. 1667/75
Nich., Little Staughton, yeo. 1623/143

ATWOOD, AWOOD continued
Ric., Luton. R 1537: 5/1
Ric., sen., Toddington, Herne, horse dealer. 1806/38
Robt., Marston, tailor. 1628/36
Smith alias Atwood see under Smith
Thos., Keysoe. 1566/80
Thos., Little Staughton. 1584/265
Thos., Budna, Northill, lab. 1669/88
Thos., Eaton Socon, yeo. 1698/149
Thos., Little Staughton, yeo. 1702-3/46
Thos., Wootton, husb. 1706/32
Thos., Eaton Socon, yeo. A 1728/26
Thos., Eaton Socon. A 1737/23
Wm., sen., Harlington, yeo. 1559/185
Wm., Marston. 1638-9/94
Wm., Toddington, farmer. 1846/39
AUBENY, see Halfpenny
AUBORN, see Albany
AUBREY, AUBERRY, AWBERY, Nich., Langford, lab. 1632/106
Thos., Potton, husb. R 1534: 4/15
Wm., Potton. 1593/73
see also Aberry
AUD(E)LEY, AWDIE, HAWDLEY, Anne, Houghton Conquest, wid. 1599/165
Edw., Langford. 1613/166
Eliz., Kempston, wid. 1660/155
Hen., Stotfold, lab. 1638/50
alias Hoye, Jn., Bolnhurst, husb. 1603/109
Jn., Renhold, lab. 1618/165
Jn., sen., Husborne Crawley, yeo. 1657/49
Jn., Husborne Crawley, yeo. 1658-9/17
Mary, Kempston. R 1674: 1/9d 194
Math., no parish given. 1610/85
Robt., Henlow. R 1545: 11/96
Thos., Henlow. 1553/280
Thos., Stotfold, yeo. 1613/193
Thos., Grayes Inn, Middx. (property in Wilshamstead and Houghton Conquest. 1630/21
Wm., Stanford, Southill, yeo. 1625/201
AUDY, AWDIE, see Audley
AUGER, AUGAR, Alice, Lidlington. 1705/82
Wm., Lidlington. R 1683 1/208
Wm., Millbrook, tailor. 1751/4
Wm., Lidlington, tailor. A 1755/4
AUGGUSDAY, see Agnusdei
AULABY, Thos. "at Dunstable". R 1525: 2/76d

AUNSELL, Thos., Luton, husb. 1592-3/6
see also Ansell, Anstill
AUSTIN, AUSTEN, AWSTEN, AWSTYNE, Anne, Potton, wid. 1728/15
Barnard, Stanbridge. 1568/44
Edw., Potton. AR 1681: 1/112
alias Pake, Geo., Stagsden, dairyman. 1718/5
Hen., Over Dean, lab. 1755/38
Humphrey, Wilden, lab. 1599/75
Jas., Sutton. A 1700/26
Jn., Campton, tailor. AR 1683: 1/119d
alias Peak, Jn., Cardington, lab. 1719/51
Jn., Bedford. A 1729/63
Jn., Melchbourne. 1806/5
Jn., sen., late Kimbolton now Eaton Socon, Ford End, yeo. 1808/31
Jn., Keysoe, yeo. 1823/38
Jn., Podington, carpenter. A 1831/5
Jonathan, Marston. A 1750/17
Louisa, Podington, yeo. A 1806/20
Mary, Podington, wid. 1825/21
Odell alias Austin see Odell
Oliver, Henlow, victualler. 1651/121
Phoebe, Meppershall, wid. 1672-3/180
Ric., Haynes, yeo. 1639/67
Ric., Meppershall, lab. 1664-5/69
Ric., Potton, baker. 1717/11
Ric., Potton, old index only, bundle missing. A 1745/1
Ric., Ampthill, grocer. 1752/46
Robt., Stanbridge. 1552/311
Robt., Tilsworth, husb. 1621/171
Robt., Potton, barber. 1626/111, I 4/195
Sabee, Potton, wid. 1646/111
Sam., Toddington, mealman. 1715/54
Sam., Ampthill, grocer. 1741/20
Sam., Aspley Guise, wheelwright. A 1742/9
Thos., Tilsworth, lab. 1607/132
Thos., Aspley Guise, carpenter. 1718-19/82
Thos., Henlow. 1721-2/78
Thos., Podington, farmer. 1815/21
Thos., Wymington. A 1837/5
Wm., Sundon. AR 1679: 1/157
Wm., Biddenham, bach. A 1702/12
Wm., Potton, baker. 1717/19
AVEERIS, Geo., Warden, lab. 1604/49
AVERELL, Eliz., Cardington, spins. 1640/7
Wm., Cardington, husb. 1618/152

AVERY, Jn., jun., Sewell, Houghton Regis, husb. 1687/87
Jn., Totternhoe, lab. 1698/160
Wm., Eversholt, yeo. 1662/18
Wm., Dunstable, maltster. 1740/60
AVISE, see Ames, Amps, Annis
AWALLEY, Alice, Millbrook, wid. 1613-14/152
Jas., Millbrook, yeo. 1601-2/148
Margy., Millbrook, wid. 1608/21
Walley alias Awalley see under Walley
AWCOCK, see Alcock
AWDEY, AWDIE, see Audley
AWMONT, Edw., Felmersham, lab. 1599/15;
see also Hammond
AWOOD, see Atwood
AXHAM, Fra., Wootton, lab. 1804/21
Wm., Eversholt. A 1830/7
see also Asam, Askham
AXTELL, Ann, Leighton Buzzard, wid. LB 1736/3
Anne, Leigton Buzzard, wid. Fac. 1736: 9/79
Sam, Houghton Regis, grocer & rag merchant. 1851/44
see also Astell
AYLEMER, see Elmer
AYLEWARD, AILEWARD, Wm., Luton, gent. 1728/74
AYLSTON, see Hailstone
AYNSHAM, see Ensame, Eynsham
AYRE, AYRES, ARES, AEIRS, EARE, Ann, Beeston, Sandy, wid. A 1762/6
Edw., Bedford, sawyer. 1843/25
Emma, late Shefford, now of Bedford. 1855/34
Geo., Ridgmont, yeo. 1829/32
Isaac, Girtford, Sandy. 1741/28
Jacob, Roxton, yeo. 1764/41
Jacob, Roxton, farmer. 1820/15
Jn., Beeston, Sandy. AR 1674: 1/100
Jn., Sandy, yeo. A 1747/16
Jn., sen. Cockayne Hatley, farmer. 1790/3
Jn., Blunham, yeo. A 1793/7
Jn., Tempsford, farmer. A 1819/4
Joan, Beeston, Sandy, wid. 1647/65
Robt., Beeston, Sandy, farmer. 1838/19
Sellis, Beeston, Sandy, yeo. 1830/25
Stephen, Tingrith, husb. 1561/150
Thos., Kempston, husb. 1607/109
Thos., Beeston, Sandy, jun. 1611/3
Thos., Beeston, Sandy, jun. 1611-12/135
Thos., Beeston, Sandy, yeo. 1639/43

AYRE, AYRES, ARES, AEIRS, EARE continued
Thos., Roxton, yeo. A 1793/8
Thos., sen., Sandy, yeo. 1804/18
Thos., Blunham, farmer. 1804/35
Wm., Kempston, yeo. 1626/87
Wm., Goldington, lab. 1728/46
see also Eyre, Hare, Hares

B

BABINGTON, Eliz., Marston, wid. 1683/1
Eliz., Bedford, wid. 1696/105
Jn., Wootton, yeo. 1655-6/190
Mary, Turvey, wid. 1668/157
Ric., Turvey, yeo. 1684/36
Thos., Luton, yeo. 1835/1
Wm., Wootton, gent. 1685-6/99
BABBINGTON, Geo., Turvey, bach. AR 1675: 1/39
Ric., Turvey. AR 1684: 1/46d
BACCHUS, Edw., Harlington, miller. A 1737/35
Jas., Studham. A 1784/8
Susann., Harlington, wid. 1753/12
Thos., Shillington, husb. 1752/55
see also Backhouse; see also Bacon
BACHELOR, see Batchelor
BACK, Hen., Bedford, gent. 1749-50/27
BACKER, see Baker
BACKHOUSE, Jn., Leighton Buzzard. LB 1774/38
Mary, Shillington, wid. 1754/57
Wm., rector of Chellington. R 1558: 14/60
see also Bacchus
BACON, Grace, Shillington, wid. 1697/68
Isabell, Bedford St. Mary, wid. 1675/7
Peter, Shillington, maltster. 1727/55
Thos., Shillington, bricklayer. 1626/62
Thos., senr., Shillington, bricklayer. 1677/32
Thos., Lidlington. A 1705-6/64
Thos., Shillington, maltster. 1717/52
Thos., Shillington, maltster. A 1753/15
Wm., Shillington, bricklayer. 1680-1/98
see also Bacchus
BADCOCK, Heritage, Cardington. AR 1689-90: 1/33
BADSWORTH, Pattenson alias Badsworth see Pattenson
BADWIN, see Baldwin

BAILEY, BAYLIE, BAYLY, Abr., Dean, carpenter. 1752/29
Alice, Bedford, wid. 1701-2/82
Ann, Ampthill, wid. AR 1675: 1/194d
Arthur, Flitwick, carpenter. 1641/220
Eleanor, Bedford St. Cuthbert. A 1840/9
Eliz., Steppingley, wid. 1560/235
Hen., Husborne Crawley. 1610/111
Hen., Hockliffe, yeo. A 1830/3
Jas., Bedford, innholder & alderman. 1751/2
Jas., Bedford, carrier. 1801/26
Jas., Bedford, woolstapler. 1802/9
Jas., Bedford St. Paul, servant to Dr. Brereton. 1834/13
Jas., Biggleswade, victualler. Bw 1775/61
Jn., Bedford. R 1558: 14/50
Jn., Radwell, Felmersham, lab. 1582-3/67
Jn., Milton Brian, lab. 1614/66
Jn., Pavenham, matmaker. 1689-90/81
Jn., Luton, husb. 1709/7
Jn., Maulden, lab. A 1722/11
Jn., Thorncote, Northill, farmer. A 1775/8
Martha, Bedford St. Mary, wid. A 1769/30
Martha, Bedford, wid. 1799/12
Mary, Wilshamstead, wid. 1662/23
Ric., Ampthill, plumber. 1675/67
Ric., Ampthill. AR 1675: 1/194d
Ric., Thorncote, Northill, farmer. 1782/56
Ric., Girtford, Sandy, farmer. 1810/5
Thos., Westoning, miller. 1567-8/118
alias Gibbons, Thos., Tilsworth, lab. 1582-3/120
Thos., Ridgmont (Segenhoe), milner (miller). 1598-9/107
Thos., Ridgmont. AR 1672: 1/189, 202
Thos., Flitwick, lab. 1673/25
Thos., Shefford. 1721-2/77
Thos., Shefford, gent. A 1723/33
Tim., Ampthill, yeo. 1654/188
Wm., Ampthill, baker. 1716/46
Wm., Stotfold, miller. A 1722/22
Wm., Dunstable, yeo. A 1760/21
Wm., Bedford, carrier. 1779/33
Wm., Oakley, farmer. 1790/39
Wm., Bedford St. Peter. A 1804/1
Wm., Houghton Regis, victualler. 1804/40
Wm., Bedford, surgeon. 1855/38
BAINES, Hugh, Tempsford, yeo. 1606/46
Jas., Sandy, blacksmith. 1804/48

BAINES continued
Jn., Sutton, cordwainer. 1695/2
Jn., Sandy, blacksmith. 1714/99
Jn., Sandy, blacksmith. 1757/4
Mary, Bedford, wid. 1730-1/2
Matthew, Tempsford, husb. 1616-17/27
Sam, Sandy, wheelwright. 1780/2
Simon, Chawston, Roxton. 1582/107
Stephen (no parish given). 1662/50
Wm., Tempsford, yeo. 1624/50
Wm., Sandy, blacksmith. A 1721/18
Wm., sen., Sandy, blacksmith. 1777/19
Wm., Sandy, blacksmith. 1790/13
see also Banes, Baynes, Bayes
BAINTON, Ric., Milton Ernest, lab. 1661/314
BAKER, BACAR, Tredway, alias Baker, see under Tredway
Andrew, Maulden, bricklayer. 1712/70
Ann., Wootton, wid. 1691/116
Edw., Cranfield, husb. 1565-6/58
Eliz., Eversholt, wid. 1631/228
Eliz., Cranfield, spins. 1713/28
Eliz., Cranfield, wid. 1715/55
Eliz., Ridgmont, wid. 1772/29
Eliza, Kempston. A 1855/11
Frances, Tilbrook, wid. 1843/37
Geo., sen. Dunstable, shoemaker. 1579/146
Geo., sen., (?Harlington). 1643/56
Geo., Cranfield, gent. 1669/27
Geo., Leighton Buzzard, stocking seller. AR 1682: 1/162d
Geo., Cranfield, grocer. A 1704/2
Geo., Cranfield, yeo. A 1721/25
Geo., Ridgmont, grocer. 1722/47
Geo., Ridgmont, grocer. A 1727/18
Geo., Cranfield, yeo. 1744/21
Hannah, Tilbrook, wid. A 1823/12
Hannah, (?Tilbrook). A 1827/14
Hen., Sundon. R 1533: 3/96
Hen., Marston Pillinge, Marston, yeo. 1685/51
Hen., Sundon, wheeler. 1695/21
Hen., Tilbrook, farmer. 1819/25
James., Houghton Conquest, yeo. A 1780/19
James., sen. Gt. Barford, licensed victualler. 1848/10
Jn., Streatley. R 1533: 3/90d
Jn., Leighton Buzzard. 1562/94
Jn., Sundon, yeo. 1563/98

BAKER, BACAR continued
alias Thrape, Jn., Temspford, yeo. 1594-5/96
Jn., Maulden, yeo. 1639-40/154
Jn., Cardington, dairyman. 1640-1/87
Jn., Warden, butcher. 1693/148
Jn., Sharnbrook, farmer. A 1740-1/20
Jn., Tilbrook, victualler. 1787/5
Jn., Stanford Southill, carpenter. 1797/13
Joel, Cranfield, yeo. 1693/154
Jos., Houghton Regis. AR 1672: 1/143
Jos., Warden, farmer. A 1746/29
Margt., Stagsden, wid. 1636-7/63
Martha, Sundon, wid. 1701/14
Martha, Bedford St. Paul, wid. 1723/24
Mary, Cranfield, wid. A 1747/10
Mary, Bedford St. Mary, wid. A 1855/24
Matthias, Tilbrook, victualler and farmer. 1807/33
Mich., Cranfield, husb. 1562/237
Mich., Cranfield. 1608-9/13
Nich., Luton, lab. 1566/136
Rebecca, Tilbrook. A 1833/4
Ric., Radwell, Felmersham. 1619/253, I 4/99
Ric., Cranfield, yeo. A 1707/3
Ric., Pulloxhill, yeo. 1633/128
Ric., Oakley. 1684-5/61
Robt., Cranfield. 1580/225
Robt., Wharley, Cranfield. 1628/42
Robt., Shelton, Marston, lab. 1658/151
Robt., Houghton Conquest, How End, yeo. 1735/4
Robt., Brogborough, Ridgmont, yeo. 1794/41
Robt., Houghton Conquest, How End, farmer. A 1803/10
Robt., Marston Park, farmer. 1836/20
Sar., Tilsworth, old index only, bundle missing. A 1745/2
Sar., Gt. Barford, wid. 1807/19
Susan, Cranfield. 1612/96
Thos., Cranfield. R 1544: 11/26d
Thos., Cranfield, yeo. 1657/203
Thos., sen., Maulden, bricklayer. 1669-70/118
Thos., Battlesden, clerk. 1701/2
Thos., jun., Cranfield. 1708/7
Thos., sen., Cranfield, gent. 1710/38
Thos., Marston, grocer. A 1729/32
Thos., Bolnhurst, clerk. 1749/25
Thos., Cranfield, yeo. 1754/1
Walt., Harlington. AR 1676: 1/195d

BAKER, BACAR continued
Wm., Cranfield, husb. R 1533: 3/91d
Wm., Eaton, (bundle 1572). 1575/89
Wm., sen., Cranfield. 1621/172
Wm., Dunstable, shoemaker. 1641-2/201
Wm., Warden, weaver. 1660/206
Wm., Clifton, yeo. 1662/110
Wm., Eversholt, yeo. 1671/47
Wm., Clifton. 1719-20/91
Wm., Cranfield, yeo. 1723/1
Wm., Northwood End, Haynes, yeo. 1734/55
Wm., Dunstable, lab. 1787/24
Wm., Tilbrook, shepherd. 1837/9
Wm., Tilbrook, shepherd. A 1837/16
Wm., Toddington, victualler and plumber. 1847/14
see also Barker
BALDOCK, BAUDOKE, BOLDUCK, Ann, Arlesey, spins. 1610-11/55
Anne, Stotfold, wid. 1641/125
Dan., Arlesey, yeo. 1661/280
Dan., Arlesey, yeo. 1720/126
Edm., Arlesey. 1603/90
Geo., Stotfold, shepherd. 1635-6/36
Jn., Arlesey. 1577-8/75
Jn., Haynes, yeo. 1640-1/95
Jn., Henlow, lab. 1661/282
Jn., Stotfold, lab. 1670-1/166
Jn., Henlow, husb. 1692/26
Jn., Arlesey, farmer. 1767/45
Joan, Arlesey, wid. 1555/129
Joan, Arlesey, wid. 1612/28
Jos., Beeston Sandy, gardener. 1801/29
Margt., Arlesey, wid. 1637/99
Mary, Oakley, wid. 1799/15
Mich., sen. Arlesey, yeo. 1620/105
Mich., Arlesey, husb. 1627/186
Mich., Arlesey. AR 1684: 1/121d
Peter, Arlesey, lab. 1686/22
Ric., Potsgrove, husb. R 1558: 13/148
Ric., Arlesey, lab. 1623-4/137
Ric., Haynes. 1638/64
Ric., Arlesey, yeo. 1665-6/9
Ric., Arlesey, yeo. 1721/84
Ric., Oakley, miller. 1785/34
Thos., sen. Arlesey, husb. R 1540: 6/40d

BALDOCK, BAUDOKE, BOLDUCK continued
Thos., Arlesey, husb. 1554-7/176
Thos., Stotfold, yeo. 1611-2/140
Thos., Henlow, yeo. 1622/70
Thos., Stotfold, lab. 1623/148
Thos., Stotfold, lab. 1664/33
Wm., Arlesey. R 1540: 6/41d
Wm., Tilsworth, husb. 1615/144
Wm., Arlesey, husb. 1705/27
Wm., Wyboston Moor, Eaton Socon, victualler. 1729/74
Wm., Tempsford, P/IX2 admon missing. A 1782/1
BALDREY, BALDERY, BAULDRY, Eliz., Luton, wid. 1752/41
Eliz., Luton, spins. A 1758/19
Hugh, Eaton Bray, butcher. 1666/290
Jn., Eaton Bray. AR 1685: 1/169
Jn., Bidwell, Houghton Regis, weaver. 1714/79
Judith, Eaton Bray. 1717/25
Ric., Eggington. 1682/75
Robt., Houghton Regis, yeo. 1682/63
Robt., Luton, baker. 1739/50
Wm., Houghton Regis, weaver. 1686-7/88
Wm., Houghton Regis, weaver. AR 1686-7: 1/173
Wm., Eaton Bray, butcher. 1698/120
Wm., Luton, bach. A 1743/38
see also Bawdrey
BALDWIN, BADWINE, BAWDWYN, BAWDWYNE, Hen., Harrowden, Cardington, husb. 1617/280
Jn., Harrowden, Cardington, husb. R 1548: 12/30
Jn., sen., Cardington. 1563/83
Jn., Harrowden, Cardington. 1582-3/118
Jn., Ampthill, innholder. A1734-5/17
Phinnina, Elstow, wid. 1665/40
Ric., Flitwick, yeo. 1637-8/162
Wm., (Cardington). R 1539: 5/36
Wm., Harrowden, Cardington. 1564/45
BALES, BAYLES, Daniel, Tillbrook, husb. 1597/38
Jn., Tilbrook, lab. 1586/85
Mary, Ford End, Eaton Socon, wid. 1661/232
BALET, BALEIT, John, chaplain of Wyboston. R 1529: 3/10d
BALL, BALLA, BALLS, BOOL, Agnes, Dean, wid. R 1532: 3/56d
Alice, Pulloxhill, wid. 1600/50
Ann, Ampthill, wid. 1774/5
Ben., Sandy, yeo. A 1802/3
Chris., Sandy, wid. 1780/50
Edw., Girtford, yeo. 1777/4

BALL, BALLA, BALLS, BOOL continued
Eliz., Turvey. 1609/123
Eliz., Odell, "Widdow". 1661-2/260
Gerrard, , Dunton. 1627/158
Grizzell, Potton, wid. 1669/83
Jn., Dunton. R 1505-6?: 1/78d
Jn., Turvey. R 1520-1: 2/169d
Jn., "the town of Woburn Chapel in the parish of Birchmore". R 1535: 4/20
Jn., Woburn, yeo. 1581/16
Jn., (Turvey). 1605/124
Jn., Dunton. 1606/71
Jn., Millhoe, Dunton. 1624-5/6
Jn., Greenfield, Pulloxhill, yeo. 1675/46
Jn., Hockliffe, butcher. 1720/71
Jn., sen., Tilsworth, butcher. 1725/75
Jn., Tilsworth, butcher. 1761/36
Jn., Milton Ernest, farmer & cornfactor. 1856/5
Jn., Wilshamstead, lab. A 1714/6
Jn., Stotfold, victualler. A 1725/16
Joan, Barton, wid. 1585/37
Joan, Woburn, wid. 1587/116
Joan, Limbury, wid. 1587/121
Joan, Eversholt, wid. 1630-1/130
Jos., sen., Tebworth, Chalgrave, farmer. 1774/32
Jos., Wilshamstead, farmer. 1804/46
Judith, Tebworth, Chalgrave, wid. 1731/75
Mary, Tilsworth, wife of Jn. 1761/26
Mary, Ampthill, wid. A 1735/26
Mary, Tilsworth. A 1762/17
Ric., Turvey. R 1520: 2/165
Ric., Thurleigh, dairyman. AR 1682: 1/73d
Robt., St. Neots, Hunts., mercer. 1610/92
Robt., Marston. 1612-13/63
Robt., Pavenham, lab. 1657-8/84
Robt., Ampthill. 1723/65
Robt., Ampthill, gardener. 1743/42
Robt., Stratford, Sandy, gardener. AR 1671-2: 1/93d
Steph., Turvey. 1529: 3/16d
Steven, Pulloxhill, tailor. 1590/180
Thos., Odell. 1575/110
Thos., Eversholt. 1614/162
Thos., sen., Odell. 1649/64
Thos., Odell, yeo. 1667-8/110
Thos., husb. 1704-5/80
Thos., sen. Bolnhurst, husb. 1706/23

BALL, BALLA, BALLS, BOOL
Thos., Bolnhurst, husb. 1706/71
Thos., Wilshamstead, yeo. 1820/11
Thos., sen. Girtford, Sandy, gardener. 1837/26
Wm., Bedford St. Paul. R 1505: 1/90
Wm., Podington. R 1544: 11/47
Wm., Turvey. 1557/252
Wm., Willington, yeo. 1609-10/125
Wm., Tebworth, Chalgrave, butcher. 1731/76
Wm., Tilsworth, yeo. A 1818/13
BALLAND, Wm., Meppershall. R 1551: 12/158d
BALLARD, Anthony, Elstow, yeo. 1606-7/86, I
Sam., Cotton End, Cardington, yeo. 1695-6/63
Sam., Bedford, gent. 1758/21
Thos., Milton Bryant. R 1512: 1/109
Thos., Bedford St. Paul, baker. 1589/65
Wm., Elstow, husb. 1556/121
Wm., Kempston, yeo. 1674/121
BALLS, see Ball
BALSTON, Jn., Odell. 1668/158
BAMFORD, Bamforth alias Bamford, see under Bamforth
Eliz., Bedford, wid. 1723/27
Hannah, Bedford, wid. 1728/8
Jn., Bedford, innholder. 1717/10
Robt., Lt. Barford, clerk. 1720/82
Wm., Podington, clerk. A 1734/5
BAMFORTH, alias Bamford, Amy, Bedford, spins. 1704/86
Eliz., Bedford?, wid. 1615/154
Jn., Bedford (St. Paul), gent. 1630-1/119.
Jn., Bletsoe, gent. 1675/95
Peter, Bedford (St. Paul), gent. 1626/70
Robt., sen., Bedford, gent. 1664/6
Wm., Bedford, alderman. 1692/49
BANDY, Eliz., Cranfield, wid. 1712-13/59
Jn., Cranfield, victualler. 1708/43
Jn., Lidlington, yeo. 1719/43
Jn., Podington, tailor. 1724/90
Ric., Potsgrove. R 1533: 3/90
Ric., Potsgrove. 1559-60/197
Robt., Wootton, lab. 1692/51
see also Bendy, Bundy
BANES, see Baines
BANKS, Eliz., Bedford, wife of Wm., innholder. 1762/52
Jane, Wyboston, Eaton Socon, wid. 1826/41
Jeremiah, Eaton Socon, yeo. 1820/25

BANKS continued
Mary, Biggleswade, wid. Bw 1841/153
Thos., sen., Stotfold, yeo. 1841/33
Wm., Eaton Socon, carpenter. 1647/25
Wm., sen., Castle Mills, Goldington, yeo. A 1784/20
BANNISTER, Fra., Bedford St. Paul, doctor of physic. 1655-6/8
Fra., Bedford St. Paul, doctor of physic (copy of 1655-6/8 very badly mutilated in bundle 1670/250)
Fra., Bedford, Dr. of Medicine. R 1670: 1/1d
Judith, Woodside, Caddington, wid. 1741/22
Ric., Caddington, Woodside, lab. 1738/14
Wm., Tilbrooke, husb. 1628/54
Wm., Tilbrooke, lab. 1668-9/181
Wm., Pertenhall, lab. 1677/16
BANWELL, Jn., Milton Brian, farmer. 1818/27
Jn., Milton Brian, farmer. 1825/8
Judith, nee Turney, Milton Brian. A 1802/8
see also Barnwell
BARACLE, Robt., Over Gravenhurst. I 1619-20: 4/35
BARASE, John, Stanbridge, cordwainer. Fac. 1708: 9/31
BARBAR, see Barber
BARBER, BARBAR, BARBOURE, Anstill alias Barber see Anstill; Momford alias Barber, see Momford
Abr., Felmersham, yeo. 1690/6
Abr., Pulloxhill, yeo. 1708/44
Abr., Keysoe, yeo. 1737/35
Alice, Biggleswade, Holme, wid. 1638/205
Ann, Dunton, wid. A 1721/20
(or? Barker) alias Enterduce (Enterdewce), Bartholomew, Kempston, butcher. 1617/337, I 4/87
Bartholomew, Potton, yeo. 1635/15
Bartholomew, sen., Shillington "toy" (?tawer). 1748/51
Edw., Shillington. 1614-15/2
Eliz., Dunton, wid. 1695/37
Eliz., Eyeworth. 1705/71
Hannah, Broom, Southill, wid. 1813/23
Isaac, Felmersham. 1749-50/62
Isaac, Thurleigh, schoolmaster. A 1759/24
Isaac, Souldrop. A 1814/6
Jas., Dunton, carpenter. 1698-9/173
Jane, Dunton, wid. AR 1680: 1/11d
Jane, Felmersham, wid. 1729/24
Joan, (Luton). 1582/74
Jn., Houghton Regis. R 1533: 3/117
Jn., Stevington. R 1544: 11/33

BARBER, BARBAR, BARBOURE continued
Jn., Dunton. R 1549: 12/63d
Jn., Gravenhurst. 1553/155
Jn., Dunton, husb. 1591/21
Jn., Southill, yeo. 1614/49
Jn., Dunton, lab. 1638/117
Jn., Dunton. 1662/93
Jn., Meppershall, gardener. 1720-21/109
Jn., Old Warden, yeo. 1730-1/3
Jn., Southill, farmer. 1730-1/9
Jn., Moggerhanger, bricklayer. 1738/50
Jn., trooper in Gen. Wade's Reg., late of Blunham. A 1746/17
Jn., sen., Broom, Southill, gent. 1807/3
Margt., Houghton Regis. R 1546: 11/164
Margt., Lidlington, wid. 1668/153
Mary, Luton, wid. 1632/109
Mary, Elstow, wid. 1666/123
Mary, Ampthill, wid. 1726/17
Mary, Moggerhanger, wid. 1743/56
Mary, Felmersham, spins. A 1748-9/23
Michael, Luton, yeo. 1590/179
Nich., Southill, yeo. 1641/207
Phyllis, (?Luton). 1558/256
Ralph, Southill. AR 1687: 1/129d
Ralph, Shefford, baker. 1706/47
(alias Grigge, Ric., yeo. 1607-8/164)
Ric., Potton, brazier. 1689/23
Roger, Eversholt. R 1557: 13/104d
Roger, Higham Gobion. 1570/18
Sam., Biggleswade, shoemaker. Bw1827/134
Sam., Dean, farmer, 1842/17.
Thos., Dunton. R 1509: 1/57
Thos., Dunton. R 1517/8: 1/177 203d
Thos., Houghton Regis. R 1535-6: 4/48
Thos., Houghton Regis. 1563/93
Thos., Luton, yeo. 1606/55
Thos., jun. Southill, yeo. 1616/59
Thos., Southill. 1618/184
Thos., Westoning, yeo. 1620/59
Thos., Luton, maltster. 1622/55
Thos., Pavenham. 1622/69
Thos., Langford, lab. 1649/63
Thos., (Langford). 1670/239
Thos., Wootton, yeo. 1681-2/97
Thos., Southill, yeo. A 1702-3/22

BARBER, BARBAR, BARBOURE continued
Thos., Langford, yeo. A 1719/21
Thos., Thorncote, Northill. 1725/65
Thos., Keysoe, yeo. 1736/40
Thos., Ickwell, Northill. 1755/44
Thos., Felmersham, yeo. 1756/34
Thos., Old Warden, yeo. 1799/17
Thos., Shillington, collarmaker. A 1753/21
Thos., Sandy, (P/IX2 admon missing). A 1783/26
Thos., Ridgmont, baker. A 1828/8
Wm., Gastling, Southill. R 1534: 4/11
Wm., Segenhoe, Ridgmont, yeo. 1573/44
Wm., Clifton, husb. 1606/38
Wm., Felmersham, yeo. 1614/24
Wm., Dunton. 1633/180
Wm., Dunton, yeo. 1637-8/1
Wm., Luton, victualler. 1638/54
Wm., Broome, Southill, yeo. 1649/55
Wm., Lidlington, gent. 1665/61
Wm., Shefford. AR 1674: 1/100
Wm., Broome, Southill, husb. 1677/31
Wm., Over Caldecote, Northill, yeo. 1682/85
Wm., jun., Dunton. 1684/41
Wm., sen., Dunton, yeo. 1688/69
Wm., Shefford, currier. 1695/31
Wm., Broom, Southill, yeo. 1710/10
Wm., Warden, yeo. A 1716/26
Wm., Broom, Southill, farmer. 1757/39
Wm., Shefford, collarmaker. A 1761/7
Wm., Langford, yeo. A 1779/1
Wm., Sandy, bricklayer. 1781/17
BARCOCK, BARCOKE, Agnes, Basmead, Eaton Socon, wid. 1567-8/101
Edw., Chawston, Roxton. 1576/6
Jeffrey, Nether Staploe, Eaton Socon. 1616/58
Jn., sen., Oakley. R 1544-5: 11/60
Jn., Chawston, Roxton, yeo. 1612/229
Jn., Eaton Socon, wheelwright. 1766/6
Jn., Gt. Barford, shopkeeper. 1843/44
Ric., Eaton Socon, farmer. AR 1680: 1/71
Ric., Eaton Socon. AR 1689: 1/82d
Ric., Eaton Socon, yeo. 1692/13
Ric., Eaton Socon, wheelwright. 1795/25
Thos., Tempsford, husb. 1593/69
Wm., Eaton Socon, husb., (Wyboston). 1561-2/139
Wm., Tempsford, yeo. 1616/143

BARCOCK, BARCOKE continued
see also Buckoke
BARCOLE, Robt., Harrold, baker. 1621/156
BARDOLPH, Jn., Bedford, alderman. A 1739/32
Mary, Pertenhall. 1660-1/101
BARENGER, see Barringer
BARFOOT, Jn., Lidlington. A 1741/13
Wm., Marston, dairyman. A 1703/29
BARFOOTE, Eliz., Millbrook, wid. of Ric., cordwainer. 1731/18
Jn., Haynes, warrener. 1620/65
Margt., Salford, wid. 1679/14
Ric., Lidlington, lab. 1670/165
Ric., Millbrook, cordwainer. 1725/56
Wm., Salford, husb. 1645/10
BARFORD, Jn., vicar of Chalgrave. R 1539: 5/30d
Jn., Barton, yeo. 1834/4
Sarah, Abbots Langley, Herts. A 1822/3
Thos., Hockliffe (cert. of removal only). 1773/11
Wm., Riseley. R 1539-40: 6/9
Wm., Millow, Dunton. 1624/63
BARGE, Robt., Milton Brian. R 1538: 5/20
BARGOINE, see Burgoyne
BARIGE, Robt., Kempston. 1564/3
Robt., Kempston. 1564/52
BARINGER, see Barringer
BARINGHAM, BARRINGAM, Cresses, Chellington, wid. 1627/182
Ric., Honeydon, Eaton Socon. AR 1690: 1/83d
Robt., Odell. R 1531: 3/48
Thos., Tilbrook, weaver. 1634/106
Thos., Pavenham. A 1740/4
Wm., Lit. Staughton, yeo. 1817/5
BARKER, Adams, alias Barker, see Adams; Merryweather, alias Barker, see Merryweather
Ann, Potton, wid. 1693-4/118
Ann, Bedford St. Paul's, wid. 1753/35
Ann, Bedford, wid. 1817/15
Ann, Bedford, wid. 1846/47
Arthur, Sutton, husb. 1609/185
(or Barber alias Enterduce), Bartholomew, Kempston, butcher. 1617, 337, I 4/81
Edw., Toddington. 1847/10
Eliz., Bedford, spins. 1695/36
Eliz., Bedford, wid. 1780/46
Eliz., Biggleswade, wid. 1821/40
Eliz., Sandy, wid. 1842/49

BARKER continued
Faith, Wootton, wid. 1670/174
Fra., Ampthill, lab. 1748/22
Fra., Bedford St. Cuthbert's, spins. A 1835/8
Hannah, Favenham, wid. A 1802/6
Jeremiah, Newmill End, Luton, yeo. 1718/38
Jeremiah, sen. New Mill End, Luton, yeo. 1752/12
Jn., (Eaton Socon?), priest. R 1547: 12/3d
Jn., Marston. 1670/170
Jn., Kempston, yeo. 1673/66
Jn., Kempston, yeo. 1694/49
Jn., Luton, carp.. 1744/6
Jn., Bedford St. Mary, woolsorter. 1748-9/61
Jn., Bedford, mealman. 1770/55
Jn., sen., Biggleswade, yeo. Bw1810/107
Jn., Sandy, tailor. 1811/28
Jn., Bedford, brewer. 1815/40
Jn., Kempston, lab. 1823/24
Jos., Kempston, tailor. 1729/62
Jos., Kempston, hempdresser. A 1758/2
Jos., Bedford, butcher. A 1781/28
Jos., Bedford, mealman. 1785/17
Jos., Goldington, gent. 1834/14
Math., Kempston, tailor. 1684/89
Math., Kempston, baker. A 1779/2
Reinold, Wootton, tailor. 1649/2
Ric., Bedford St. Paul, grocer. R 1680-1: 1/18d
Ric., Bedford, grocer. 1696-7/147
Ric., Stagsden, farmer. A 1847/6
Robt., Hockliffe in Chalgrave (sic), yeo. 1713/26
Roger, Elstow, yeo. 1644/136
Sam., Bedford, gent. 1741-2/69
Susanna, Luton, wid. A 1741/21
Susannah, Kempston, wid. 1694/50
Susannah, Bedford, wid. 1785/41
Thos., Wootton, yeo. 1639/51
Thos., Kempston, miller. 1747-8/54
Thos., Bedford, baker. 1754/51
Thos., Bedford St. Paul's, baker. A 1806/14
Thos., Sandy, tailor. A 1827/5
Wm., Bedford, yeo. 1553/167
Wm., Cople, yeo. 1640/116
Wm., New Mill End, Luton, carp. 1651/4
Wm., Wootton, yeo. 1658/37
Wm., Luton, farmer. A 1729/4

BARKER continued
Wm., Luton, maltster. 1729/69
Wm., Clapham, farmer. A 1738-9/9
Wm., Biggleswade, victualler. Bw A 1806/50
Wm., Cardington, victualler. A 1808/16
see also Baker
BARLEY, Wm., Woburn, brewer. 1624-5/25
BARN, BARNES, Smith alias Barnes, see Smith
Abraham, Harlington. 1649/61
Ann, Salford, wid. 1719/52
Ann, Lidlington. A 1779/3
Dan., Riseley, dairyman. 1683-4/115
Edm., Riseley, lab. 1605/106
Edw., Dunstable, coachman & bach.. AR 1670-1: 1/141
Edw., Dunstable, yeo. 1709/92
Eliz., Sandy. 1552/320
Fra., Woburn, waggoner. AR 1684: 1/211
Fra., Lidlington, lab. 1833/9
Geo., Thurleigh, yeo. 1854/18
Isabel, Wilshamstead. 1617/155
Jas., Biggleswade, publican. Bw A 1803/45
Jn., Cranfield, husb. R 1558: 14/38
Jn., Woburn, draper. 1593/88
Jn., Odell. 1609-10/126
Jn., Poddington, yeo. 1623-4/101
Jn., Salford, tailor. 1663/110
Jn., Maulden, lab. AR 1671-2: 1/188d
Jn., Bletsoe, yeo. 1774/6
Jn., Barton, carpenter. 1781/25
Jn., Bletsoe, (P/IX2 admon. missing). A 1783/2
Jn., Bedford, victualler. 1805/13
Jos., Woburn, grocer. 1797/20
Kath., Maulden, wid. 1589-90/104
Mary, Bedford St. Cuthbert's, wid. 1753/19
Mich., Milton Brian, lab. 1664/30
Ralph, Clophill, gardener. 1678-9/136
Ric., Toddington. 1556/90
Ric., Potters End, Eversholt. 1628/10
Ric., Harlington, (bundle 1660). 1659/190a
Ric., Harlington. 1682/71
Ric., Harlington. AR 1682: 1/207
Robt., Markyate St., Studham. 1559/143
Robt., Eaton Bray, husb. 1658-9/239
Sam., Knotting, grazier. 1787/42
Sam., Bedford, sadler. 1853/41

BARN, BARNES continued
Thos., (Lidlington), yeo. 1577/65
Thos., Wilshamstead, carpenter. 1616/89
Thos., Maulden, yeo. 1618/161
Thos., Poddington, yeo. 1628-9/19
Thos., Felmersham, millwright. 1647/46
Thos., junr., Wingfield, Chalgrave, yeo. 1658-9/112
Thos., Riseley, tailor. 1687/92
Thos., Shefford, painter. 1796/24
Thos., Southill, farmer. 1826/13
Wm., Flitwick. R 1540: 6/54d; 8/1
Wm., Broom, Southill. 1609/186
Wm., Shelton, yeo. 1671/70
Wm., Greenfield, Pulloxhill, lab. 1690/8
Wm., Salford, lab. 1692/31
Wm., Stanbridge, husb. Fac. 1702: 9/5
Wm., senr., Thurleigh, farmer. 1811/34, I 4/216
BARNARD, BERNARD, Cripsey, alias Barnard see Cripsey
Eliz., Chawston Roxton, wid. 1759/2
Jn., Westoning, husb. 1559/174
Jn., Chawston, Roxton, yeo. 1707/19
Jn., Chawston, Roxton, yeo. 1747/14
Jn., Maulden, gent. AR 1680: 1/204d
Martha, Maulden, wid. AR 1682-3: 1/208d
alias Crispley, Mary, Houghton Conquest. 1614/67
Robt., Silsoe, collar maker. 1801/16
Thos., Pulloxhill, yeo. 1733/7
Wm., Silsoe, collarmaker. 1825/32, I 4/259
see also Barnet
BARNARDISTON, Margt., Yielden, wid. of Jn., gent. 1664-5/87
Robt., Ickwell Bury, Northill, esq. 1631-2/230.
Sigismond, Cotton End, Cardington, gent. 1621/130
BARNES, see Barn
BARNET, BARNATT, BARNETT, Anne, Colmworth, wid. 1660-1/61
alias Cripsey, Geo., Flitwick, yeo. 1677/2
alias Cripsey, Geo., Flitwick. AR 1677-8: 1/199
alias Cripsey, Hen., Westoning, yeo. 1684/31
Ric., Colmworth, husb. 1658/225
Robt., Shillington, dairyman. A 1705/52
Wm., Luton, yeo. 1785/12
see also Barnard
BARNEWELL, see Barnwell
BARNGAM, see Barnham

BARNHAM, BARNGAM, BARNIAM, BARNJAM, BARNSUM, Chris., Pertenhall, weaver. 1664/51
Edw., Harrold, lab. (bundle 1618). 1617/60
Eliz., (?Odell). 1610-11/41
Geo., Odell, lab. 1611/35
Thos., Odell. 1644/91
BARNIAM, see Barnham
BARNJAM, see Barnham
BARNSUM, see Barnham
BARNWELL, BARNEWELL, BERNEWELL, Ambridge, Husborne Crawley, farmer, carter, etc. 1832/10
Eliz., Wilshamstead. 1616/88
Jane, of "Salveshope", wid. 1553/278
Jn., Husborne Crawley, husb. 1559-60/203
Jn., sen., Husborne Crawley, husb. 1561/185
Jn., Cranfield, lab. 1615/173
Jn., Husborne Crawley. AR 1683: 1/209
Jn., Husborne Crawley, yeo. 1735/47
Jn., sen., Husborne Crawley, farmer. 1810/34
Jn., Husborne Crawley, victualler. 1827/34
Jn., Husborne Crawley, victualler. A1842/40
Joshua, Ridgmont. AR 1679: 1/202
Ric., sen., Ridgmont. 1721/5
Ric., Wilshamstead, husb. 1625/202
Ric., Ridgmont, husb. 1665/37
Robt., Segenhoe, Ridgmont. R 1500: 1/11d
Thos., Tingrith, lab. 1622-3/15
Wm., Eversholt. R1533: 3/103d
Wm., Ridgmont. R 1548-9: 12/48d
Wm., Husborne Crawley, husb. 1557/373
Wm., Ridgmont. 1647/39
see also Banwell
BARON, ?Robt., Lidlington, yeo. 1660/170
BARR, BAYRE, Ann, Blunham. A 1719/10
Christ., Blunham, husb. 1652/62
Fra., Southill. 1679/70
Geo., Wilden. 1658/18,19
Geo., Wilden, lab. 1658/222
Jn., Thurleigh. R 1546: 11/213
Jn., Moggerhanger, tailor. AR 1687: 1/129d
Jn., (no parish). 1717/9
Oliver, Shefford. AR 1690: 1/133d
Ric., sen., Northill, carpenter. 1727/12
Ric., Northill, carpenter. A 1761/1
Thos., Shillington, Apsley End, lab. 1763/13

BARR, BAYRE continued
Thos., Nether Dean. R 1520: 2/53
Wm., Creakers, Gt. Barford. 1557/245
Wm., Renhold, lab. 1592/38
Wm., Moggerhanger, tailor. AR 1673?: 1/97d
BARRACLE, Edw., Luton. 1591-2/94
Isabel, Leighton Buzzard, wid. 1592/32
Thos., Leighton Buzzard. 1592/80
Wm., Leighton Buzzard. 1585/150
BARREFF, Thos., Wyboston. R 1541: 6/79
Wm., Wyboston. R 1547-8: 12/20
Wm., Staploe. 1558/253
BARRETT, BARAT, Ann, Carlton, wid. 1729-30/110
Edm., Luton, bricklayer. 1813/30
Edw., Sharnbrook, tailor. 1669/58
Eliz., Salford. 1734/16
Eliz., Clophill, wid. A 1825/3
Geo., Cranfield, blacksmith. 1657/129
Geo., Melchbourne, lab. 1695/26
Geo., Old Warden, Honour, cordwainer. 1850/27
Gregory, Melchbourne. 1660-1/187
Jn., Maulden, cook. 1630/14
Jn., Cranfield. 1644/102
Jn., Cranfield, lab. 1662/21
Jn., Haynes, blacksmith. 1709-10/78
Jn., Salford, blacksmith. A 1711/12
Jn., Salford, blacksmith. 1711/16
Jn., Turvey Lodge, farmer. 1795/42
Jn., Langley St., Luton, bricklayer. 1846/41
Joan, Cranfield. AR 1673: 1/191d
Jonas, Carlton, lab. 1712/13
Mary, Sharnbrook, wid. AR 1672: 1/36d, 92d
Mary, Turvey Lodge, wid. 1809/2
Ric., Stagsden. 1561/58
Ric., Eaton, lab. 1564/38
Ric., Melchbourne. 1680-1/102
Ric., form. Heath and Reach, now Northampton plait dealer. LB 1837/64
Robt., Wootton, husb. 1605-6/81
Robt., Cranfield, weaver. 1677/1
Robt., Kempston, late husb. 1772/37
Sam., Luton, bricklayer. 1848/33
Thos., Stagsden. 1558/145
Thos., Salford, blacksmith. 1696/118
Thos., Biggleswade, wheelwright. 1760/36
Thos., Salford, blacksmith. A 1798/6

BARRETT, BARAT continued
Wm., Bedford St. Mary, lab. 1770/50
BARRICK, alias Barwick, Jn., Clophill, horse dealer. 1825/4
Thos., Over Gravenhurst, yeo. 1715/70
Thos., Cranfield, victualler. 1717/86
see also Barwicke
BARRINGER, BARENGER, Hen., Renhold, farmer. 1779/8
Jn., sen., Odell. 1548/13
Jn., Odell, ploughwright. 1572/80
Jn., Sharnbrook, matmaker. 1798/9
Leah, Goldington, wid. A 1815/4
Ric., Pavenham, yeo. 1660/139
Robt., Turvey, yeo. 1650-1/124
Rochel, Stevington, wid. 1661/381
?Thos., Sharnbrook, husb. 1553/249
Thos., sen., Stevington, yeo. 1624-5/108
Thos., Kempston, lab. 1667/42
Thos., Carlton, tailor. AR 1688-9: 1/49d
Thos., Bedford, tailor. A 1742/23
Thos., Goldington, farmer. 1811/40
Wm., Odell. 1660-1/118
Wm., Ravensden, farmer. 1822/28
BARRINGHAM, see Baringham
BARRY, Jn., Renhold, lab. 1617/156
BARTLE, Thos., Cockayne Hatley, shepherd. 1706/28
BARTLETT, Jn., Wootton. 1564/201
Sam., Squire, Biggleswade, hair-dresser. Bw 1837/148
Sam., Squire, Biggleswade, hair-dresser. Bw 1853/162
BARTON, Anthony, Luton, grocer. 1779/30
Edw., Studham, husb. A 1726/22
Geo., Samshill, Westoning, husb. 1704/59
Jn., tailor, Studham. 1707/8
Jn., sen., Eversholt, yeo. 1723/51
Jos., Eversholt, butcher. A 1740/15
Nich., clerk, late minister of Stevington. 1608/64
Ric., Bedford St. Paul. R 1512: 1/197
Robt., Luton, farmer. 1823/29
Thos., Luton. 1783/27
Wm., Wymington, husb. R 1536: 4/72
BARTRAM, BARTRUM, Eliz., wife of Thos., Woburn. 1761/22
Eliz., Wootton. A 1801/7
Jn., Bedford St. Paul, tailor. 1679/27
Jn., Wilden. 1725/29
Jn., Lidlington. 1756/25
Lewis, Stagsden, grazier. 1664/61

BARTRAM, BARTRUM continued
Lewis, Wootton, yeo. 1746-7/45
Lewis, Kempston, yeo. 1814/29
Lewis, Wootton, yeo. A 1790/4
Ric., Stagsden. 1630-1/109
Ric., Stagsden. 1680-1/109
Wm., Stagsden, lab. 1622/52
Wm., sen., Stagsden. 1642/41
Wm., sen., Wootton, yeo. 1727/3
Wm., Kempston. A1806/4
BARWICK, Ann, Wymington, spins. 1851/17
BARWICKE, Alice, Cranfield, wid. 1689-90/83
Ann, Maulden, wid. (affidavit). A 1834
Anne, Cranfield, spins. 1721/106
Jn., Cranfield, lab. 1677/21
Jn., Cranfield, matmaker. A 1711/61
Jn., Maulden, yeo. 1845/31
Mary, Cranfield, spins. A 1720/4
Ric., Cranfield, lab. 1661/302
Robt., Wymington, lab. 1688/42
Thos., Tilbrooke, husb. 1564-5/220
Wm., Cranfield, carpenter. 1670/212
see also Barrick
BARWORTH, Eliz., wid., Woburn. 1557/378
Jn., Campton. R 1539: 5/35d
BASELEY, BASLEY, BAZLEY, Ann, Dunstable, wid. 1711-12/83
Eliz., Pavenham, wid. 1826/19, I 4/264
Jn., sen., Clapham, yeo. 1799/33
Margt., Caddington, wid. 1589/110
Simon, Cranfield, yeo. 1662/24
Simon, Cranfield, yeo. 1673/64
Simon, farmer, Pavenham. 1800/1
Thos., Eaton Socon. 1638-9/118
Thos., Ravensden, yeo. 1837/28
Wm., Pavenham, blacksmith. 1784/28
BASKERVILLE, BASKERFIELD, Eliz., Bedford, spins. 1743/40
Hen., Bedford, currier. 1762/32
Jn., Bedford, cordwainer. 1719/100
Mary, Wootton, wid. AR 1685: 1/26
Miles, Bedford, sadler. 1742/62
Ric., Wootton, grocer. 1659/111
Robt., Shefford, currier. A 1815/9
Thos., Tempsford, cordwainer. 1736/30
Wm., Woburn, lab. 1638/72
Wm., Woburn, grocer and tallow chandler. 1753/10

BASLEY, see Baseley
BASS, BASSE, Ambrose, Cranfield, yeo. 1782/47
Ann, Pertenhall, wid. 1781/18
Edw., Cardington, lab. 1669/65
Edw., Bedford Houghton (Conquest), husb. 1701-2/80
Edw., Dean, Nether, blacksmith. 1720/65
Edw., Yielden, blacksmith. A 1742-3/48
Eleanor, Podington, wid. 1691/65
Eliz., Stagsden, baker & spins. 1854/16
Geo., Cranfield. 1750/19
Godfrey, Elstow, matmaker. 1628/30
Humph., Sharnbrook. 1529: 3/15d
Jn., (old index only, bundle missing). A 1717/30
Jn., Pertenhall, farmer. A 1721-2/55
Jn., Pertenhall, butcher. A 1764/3
Jn., Pertenhall, butcher. 1764/11
Jn., Marston, dairyman. 1765/34
Jn., Bedford St. Mary, plumber & glazier. A 1826/5
Joel, Cranfield, yeo. 1741/18
Joel, Stagsden, yeo. 1804/52
Jos., Ampthill, woollen draper. AR 1681: 1/205d
Josiah, Pertenhall. AR 1683: 1/76
Martin, Lidlington, grocer. 1680/76
Mary, Ampthill, wid. 1836/27
Mary, Kempston, wid. 1744-5/48
Morton, Biggleswade, victualler. 1691/102
Ric., Bedford, innkeeper. 1843/19
Ric., Podington, husb. 1686/52
Ric., Cranfield, matmaker . 1693/155
Sarah, Kempston, wid. 1715/5
Simon, Sharnbrook. 1510: 1/173d
Simon, Pertenhall, yeo. 1642-3/14
Simon, Bedford St. Paul, schoolmaster. 1714-15/49
Simon, Pertenhall, shoemaker. 1737/37
Thos., Kempston, yeo. 1691/66
Thos., Kempston, yeo. 1721/49
Thos., Kempston, yeo. 1742-3/95
Thos., Wootton, yeo. 1811/2
Thos., Bedford, plumber and glazier. 1825/12
Walt., Potton, hatter. 1620/90
Wm., Sharnbrook. R 1506?: 1/95
Wm., Eaton Socon, Staploe, yeo. 1628/37
Wm., Pertenhall, gent. 1658-9/226
Wm., Cranfield. 1711/100
Wm., Gt. Barford. 1714/12

BASS, BASSE continued
Wm., Wootton, parish clerk. 1753/28
BASSELL, Thos., Shillington. 1608/60
BASSETT, Jn., Cranfield, matmaker. 1686/53
Jn., Marston, husb. 1707/88
Jos., Eaton Socon, clerk. 1718/7
Susan, (old index only, bundle missing). A 1718/13
Susannah, Keysoe, wid. A 1724-5/38
Thos., Blunham, 'The Salutation', victualler/innholder. 1820/14, I 4/239
BASSINGER, Wm., Kempston, grazier. AR 1670-1/2
BASTERFIELD, Marg., Marston, wid. 1608/30
Math., Sharnbrook. AR 1680-1: 1/42d
Math., Cranfield, lab. 1732/66
Robt., Marston, Wroxhill, yeo. 1647/36
Thos., Marston. R 1532: 3/72
Thos., Marston, husb. 1645/112
Thos., Cranfield, tailor. 1669/89
Thos., Leighton Buzzard, gent. 1715/67
Wm., Bedford, locksmith. 1610-11/169
Wm., sen., Wootton Shelton, yeo. 1658/162
Wm., Pertenhall, yeo. 1668/122
BASTING, Thos., Haynes, yeo. 1649-50/33
BASTON, Jas., Dunstable, maltster. A 1803/6
BASWELL, Hugh, Tebworth, Chalgrave, husb. 1683/21
BATCHELOR, BACHELER, BACHELDOR, BACHELOR, Eliz., Ampthill, wid.
Eliz., Eggington, late Drayton Beauchamp, Bucks., wid. 1840/75
Emerton, Cardington. AR 1670: 1/1
Hen., Eaton. 1552/305
Jn., Ridgmont, grazier. A 1740-1/2
Jos., Lidlington, yeo. 1804/50
Odell alias Batchelor, see Odell
Robt., Chawston, Roxton. 1582/63, 73
Robt., Lidlington, yeo. 1792/11
Robt., Lidlington, yeo. shopkeeper & schoolmaster. 1817/22
Sam., Ampthill, carpenter. 1810/29
Susannah, Dunstable, wid. 1845/35
Thos., Mogerhanger. AR 1679-80: 1/203
Thos., Lidlington, farmer. 1838/26
Wm., Tilbrook. R 1542: 6/129
BATE, see BATES
BATEMAN, BAYTEMAN, Edm., Dunstable. R 1545-6: 11/125d
Edm., Markyate Street, glazier. 1780/36
Ric., Dunstable. R 1542: 6/116
Robt., Husborne Crawley, blacksmith. 1760/37
Thos., sen., Husborne Crawley, blacksmith. 1808/24

BATEMAN, BAYTEMAN continued
Thos., Husborne Crawley, blacksmith. 1841/10
BATES, BATE, BEATS, Edw., Southill. AR 1685: 1/125d
Edw., Toddington, lab. AR 1686-7: 1/173
Edw., Luton, husb. A 1742/13
Joan, Cardington, wid. 1604-5/10
Jn., Priv. Marine on H.M.S. Blake. LB 1830/46
Jos., Shelton, farmer . 1802/7
Mary, Heath and Reach, spins. LB A 1830/91
Ralph, Flitwick, clerk, vicar of Flitwick. 1619/207, I 4/143
Robt., Girtford, Sandy. 1567/99
Robt., Chellington, wheelwright. 1665-6/86a
Thos., Cotton End, Cardington, tailor. 1628/55
Thos., Dunstable. AR 1684: 1/166d
Thos., Luton, yeo. A 1729/30
Wm., Harrold. 1593/19
Wm., Eaton Socon, weaver. 1606/54
Wm., Eversholt, Folbigg, yeo. 1845/27
BATH, BATHE, Mary, Studham, wid. 1684/18
Matilda, Henlow. R 1500: 1/16d
Thos., Henlow. R 1532: 3/67d
Wm., Studham. 1684/110
Wm., Studham. AR 1684: 1/166d
BATTAMS, Jas., Totternhoe, yeo. 1818/13
BATTISON, Ann, Bedford, spins. A 1795/8
Eliz., Bedford, wid. of Thos. 1751/47
Jas., Milton Ernest, husb. 1694/43
Jas., Milton Ernest, farmer. A 1732/9
Jn., Bedford St. Paul, bach. 1685/47
Jn., Bedford St. Paul, bach. AR 1685: 1/28
Thos., Wootton. 1626/58
Thos., sen., Bedford, maltster. 1675/15
Thos., Biddenham. 1681/62
Thos., Elstow. AR 1686: 1/29
Thos., Elstow, yeo. 1694/89
Thos., sen., Bedford. 1724/61
Thos., Bedford, coal merchant. 1732/73
Thos., Milton Ernest, yeo. A 1743/22
Wm., Ampthill, an out-pensioner of Chelsea Hospital. 1834/44
BAUDOCE, see Baldock
BAULDRY, see Bawdry & Baldrey
BAVINE, Jn., Cranfield, grazier & dairyman. 1730/65
See also Bevan
BAVISTER, Grace, Eaton Socon. AR 1681: 1/73d
BAWBY, Hen., Marston, husb. 1586-7/135

BAWDIN, see Baldwin
BAWDREY, BAWDRY, Thos., Markyate. R 1557: 13/102d
Thos., Stanbridge. 1558/35
Wm., Stanbridge, husb. 1601/90
see also Baldrey
BAWDWIN, see Baldwin
BAWSWELL, see Boswell
BAXTER, Chas., Potton, yeo. 1781/21
Eliz., Colmworth [Sharnbrook], wid. 1838/34
Crashe alias Baxter see under Crash
alias Crashe, Hen., Bedford St. Mary, baker. 1605/119
Jn., Potton, (priest). 1556/204
Mich., Bedford, barber. 1635/64
Ric., Little Staughton, farmer. 1782/11
Wm., Eaton Socon, yeo. 1703/63
Wm., Colmworth, [Sharnbrook], farmer. 1827/21
BAYES, Agnes, Tempsford, wid. 1609/169
alias Harding, Ann, wid of Chris., Lt. Barford. AR 1686: 1/127d
Cheeseman, Sharnbrooke, mason. 1650/84
Fra., Podington, (Hinwick). 1663/27
Jn., Sutton. 1550/9
Jn., Stagsden, mason. 1695/50
Jn., Sharnbrook, gardener. A 1731/33
Lydia, Tempsford. 1703/62
Margaret, Podington, Hinwick. 1682/56
Silvester, Dunton, husb. 1617/323
Thos., Elstow, yeo. AR 1670-1: 1/4
Thos., Tempsford. 1692-3/70
Thos., Stagsden, mason. 1721/34
Wm., sen., Sharnbrook, mason. 1703/33
see also Baines
BAYFORTH, Wm., "of Wrestlingworth and of Hatley Port". 1561/63
BAYLES, see Bales
BAYLISS, Nath., Woburn, stone mason & victualler. 1768/37
BAYMAN, Fra., Northill, weaver. ?1679/80
BAYNARD, Hannah, Leighton Buzzard, wife of Jn. AR 1677: 1/198
BAYNES, see Baines
BAYNTON, see Bainton
BAYRE, see Barr
BAYS, Jas., (Stevington). R 1529: 3/11
John, Oakley. R 1505: 1/83
Wm., Oakley. R 1534: 4/10
Wm., Tempsford. R 1546: 11/142
BAZELEY, BAZLEY, see Baseley
BEADLES, Thos., Thurleigh, clerk. A 1748/20; A 1748/26; see also Bedels

BEALE, Edw., Ridgmont. 1630-1/123
Jn., Houghton Conquest, lab. AR 1672: 1/6
Jn., Thurleigh. 1736-7/55
Ric., Bolnhurst, Blacklands House, husb. 1734/53
Sam., Bletsoe, Park Farm, farmer. 1845/14
Sophia, Bletsoe Park, wid. 1854/26
Thos., Wilden, farmer . 1839/41
Wm., Wootton, lab. 1622/72
Wm.,Houghton Conquest, How End, husb. 1638-9/105
Wm., Houghton Conquest. AR 1691: 1/34d
Wm., Flitwick, Denel End, yeo. 1738/5
Wm., Flitwick . A 1747/7
Wm., Lidlington, husb. 1749/4
Wm., sen., Toddington, Herne, dairyman. 1804/28
Wm., Pulloxhill, gent. 1809/18
BEAMOND, BEMAN, BEMOND, BEMUND, BEOMOND
Richard, Maulden, carpenter. 1559?/14
Thos., Northill. 1608/52
Wm., Studham. R 1543: 6/159d & 9/13
Wm., Pulloxhill, yeo. 1592/2
Wm., Bedford St. Mary, Cauldwell, husb. 1625/192
See also Beaumont.
BEAN, Hen., Sandy, gardener. 1799/30
Jane, Biggleswade, wid. Bw 1763/39
Jn., Hockliffe. 1610/87
Jn., Luton, innholder. A 1763/25
Simon, Biggleswade, hog dealer. Bw A 1761/22, I
Wm., Harlington, husb. 1587-8/103
Wm., Bedford St. Mary, wheelwright. A 1723-4/35
Wm., Harlington. A (1822)
Wm., Sandy, Beeston, gardener. 1826/47
BEAR, Jn., Yielden, husb. 1604/32
Thos., Yielden. 1613/211
BEARD, Eliz., Bedford, wid. A 1850/9
Eliz., Bedford, spins. A 1851/4
Hen., Gt. Barford. AR 1683-4: 1/76d
Jn., Stevington, lab. 1661/324
Josh., Haynes now Bedford St. Paul, baker and mealman. 1836/38
Martha, Barford, wid. 1622-3/13
Ric., Stevington. AR 1670-1: 1/36
Sam., Haynes. 1834/37
alias Farmer, Thos., sen., Sutton, gent. 1617-18/312, I 4/5
Thos., Roxton, blacksmith. 1796/6
Thos., Salford, yeo. 1806/30
Thos., Wilden, farmer & blacksmith. 1837/53

BEARD continued
Wm., Stevington, fisherman. 1651/28
Wm., Houghton Regis, Thorne, yeo. 1677-8/65
Wm., Marston, lab. A 1772/1
BEART, Thos., Westoning, gent. 1661/391
BEASLEY, BEESLEY, Geoff., Houghton Regis, yeo. 1695/24
Jas., Cranfield, blacksmith. 1819/18
Thos., Keysoe, carpenter. 1714/9
BEATS, see Bates
BEAUCHAMP, BECHAM, BECHAME, Joan, Bedford, wid. 1558/4
John, Eaton. 1553/292
Ric., Bedford, shoemaker. 1558/25
Ric., Houghton Conquest, husb. 1711/45
Thos., Sundon, bachelor. 1593-4/5
BEAUMONT, BEMONTE, Ben., Westoning, Sampshill, husb. 1719/13
Ben., Westoning, yeo. 1734/17
Charity, Bedford, wid. 1745/42
Edw., Studham, yeo. 1669/9
Edw., Biggleswade, maltster. 1683/64
Eliz., Biggleswade, wid. 1727/91
Eliz., Leighton Buzzard. LB A 1810/63
Fran., Whipsnade, yeo. 1700/141
Hen., Bletsoe, yeo. 1626-7/18
Hen., Flitton, North End. 1681/72
Hen., Flitton, Greenfield, husb. 1709/37
Hen., Flitton, Ward End, farmer. 1718/50
Hen., Pulloxhill, gent. 1719/11
Hen., Millbrook, minor. A 1723/9
Hen., Eversholt, gent. 1731/51
Jemima, Silsoe, wid. 1772/28
Jn., Flitton, Worthy End, yeo. 1611/147
Jn., Whipsnade, yeo. 1636-7/61
Jn., Southill, yeo. 1686/35
Jn., Woburn, apothecary. 1692/53
Jn., M.A., Bedford, practitioner in physic. 1697/40
Jn., Woburn, apothecary. 1698/112
Jn., Flitton, Ward End, husb. 1703/29
Jn., Bedford, chirurgeon. 1703/73
Jn., Edworth, yeo. 1704/53
Jn., Biggleswade, grocer. 1710/75
Jn., Henlow, yeo. 1716/76
Jn., Langford, Scrups, yeo. 1727/26
Jn., Bedford, apoth. A 1742/38
Jn., Leighton Buzzard, yeo. 1790/21

BECKETT continued
Sara, Bedford St. Paul, wid. 1625/183
Simon, Turvey, gent. 1604-5/4
Simon, sen., Bedford, brewer, alderman. 1651/36
Simon, sen., Bedford, alderman. 1675-6/69
Simon, Bedford St. Leonard, gent., alderman. 1684/11
Simon, Bedford, brewer . 1711/55
Thos., Eaton Socon, Wyboston, farmer. 1757/7
Wm., Bedford, alderman . 1713/1
BECKLEY, Chris., Potsgrove, yeo. 1676/114
Robert, Luton, yeo. 1729/20
Thos., Eaton, husb. 1625-6/129
Wm., Woburn, blacksmith. 1683/40
Wm., Potsgrove . AR 1689: 1/176
BECKWITH, Jn., Steppingley. 1573/116
BEDCOTT, BEDCOT, Cath., Lidlington. AR 1674-5: 1/92, 192d
Eliz., Lidlington, wid. 1661/367
Fra., Lidlington. 1612/71
Fra., Lidlington. 1640/31
Fra., Leighton Buzzard, tallow chandler. 1746/24
Jn., senr., Lidlington, yeo. R 1540-1: 6/77
Jn., Marston Pillinge, yeo. 1649/46
Jn., Lidlington, yeo. 1655/14
Jn., senr., Lidlington, yeo. 1680/19
Kath., Marston, Pillinge, wid. 1603/114
Mary, Lidlington, wid. 1692-3/58
Ric., Lidlington, husb. 1566-9/62
Ric., Lidlington, yeo. 1644/95
Ric., Goldington, clerk. 1676/155
Ric., Wilshamstead, yeo. A 1736/31
Sarah, Marston, wid. 1699/25
Thos., Ampthill, baker. 1728/7
Wm., Lidlington. 1602/67
Wm., Lidlington, Battlesden End, yeo. 1649/47
Wm., Lidlington, yeo. 1658/117
Wm., Marston, gent. 1686-7/87
Wm., Wilshamstead, yeo. 1743-4/80
BEDDING, Jn., Lidlington, shepherd. 1627/190
Wm., Elstow, weaver. 1632/88
BEDELS, Ellen, Kempston, wid. 1614-15/16
alias Tanner, Jn., Bedford St. Peter, tanner. 1616-17/10
Math., Kempston, yeo. 1607/148
Rebecca, Bedford, spins.. A 1734/10
see also Beadles

BEDFORD (Dawson alias Bedford, see under Dawson)
Barnard, senr., Markyate Street, tailor. 1825/31
Hen., Luton, carpenter. 1740/44
Isaac, Clifton, Rector. 1662/3
Isaac, Clifton, clerk. 1672/135
Jn., Leighton Buzzard, tailor. LB 1823/23
(Pemberton, Henlow, index only, admon missing. A 1726/26)
Sam., Southill, clerk. A 1752/4
Wm., Dunstable. R 1683: 1/165
Wm., Bedford, clerk. A 1817/9
BEECH, BECHE, Agnes, Luton, wid. 1610/113
Alice, Luton, wid. AR 1682: 1/163
Chris., Bedford, fellmonger. 1644/93
Jn., Bedford St. Mary, (mentions St. Mary or St. Peter, Dunstable), glover. 1619/202, I 4/153
Jn., Clophill, grocer; also limited admon. 1766/16
Jn., Ampthill, gardener & shopkeeper. 1823/15
Jn., Clophill, grocer. A 1766/9
May, Wilshamstead, wid. 1716/60
Ric., Ampthill, pipemaker. A 1705-6/17
Ruth., Wilshamstead, wid. 1683/13
Sarah, Caddington Woodside, wid. 1750-1/67
Thos., Wilshamstead, yeo. 1671/75
Thos., Wilshamstead, yeo. 1684/22
Wm., Luton. R 1548: 12/29
Wm., senr., Luton, maltster. 1606/47
Wm., Wilshamstead, yeo. 1667/83
Wm., Luton, Newmill End, yeo. 1682/51
Wm., Luton, Newmill End, AR 1682: 1/164
Wm., Potton, woolstapler. A 1727/25
BEECHAM, see Beauchamp
BEECHENER, see Bichener
BEEGRAVE, see Bygrave
BEELY, Wm., senr., Woburn, gent. R 1591: 21/58d
BEER, BERE, John, Shelton. R 1534: 4/1d
Ric., Yielden. R 1532: 3/63d
Thos., Yielden. R 1558: 14/84d
BEESLEY, see Beasley
BEESTON, BEYSTONE, Jn., Chalgrave. 1558/16
BEETON, BETUN, Joan, Langford. R 1546: 11/242
BEILCHE, Ric., Chalgrave, Tebworth. 1610-11/17
BELCHER, BELLSHAR, Hen., Oakley, husb. 1742/72
Jn., Felmersham, Radwell. AR 1690: 1/50d
Wm., Dean. A 1805/5

BELL, Adery, late Brooks, Elton, Hunts. A 1789/4
Alex., Cardington, husb. R 1547: 12/15
Alice, Bedford St. Mary, wid. 1598-9/105
Fra., Henlow, roper. A 1705/25
Fra., (old index only, bundle missing). A 1717/4
Fra., Henlow, ropemaker. 1760/12
Hen., Maulden, yeo. 1632/36
Isaac., Upper Dean, miller. 1754/53
Jas., Tilbrook. 1707/57
Jas., Dean, miller. A 1741/17
Jn., (old index only, bundle missing). A 1717/28
Jn., Eaton Socon, innholder. A 1735/27
Jn., Shillington, yeo. 1783/34
Jn., Dean, lab. 1788/13
Jn., Dean, yeo. 1834/28
Jos., Eaton Socon. 1723/48
Jos., Eaton Socon, roper. A 1731-2/7
Ric., Bedford St. Mary, baker. 1597-8/32
Ric., Bedford St. Mary. AR: 1686-7 1/31
Robt., Leighton Buzzard. AR: 1679 1/155d
Robt., Bedford, esq. 1685/127
Robt., Bedford, esq. 1734/50
Sam., Henlow, yeo. A 1782/20
Susannah, Henlow, mercer. 1719-20/94
Thos., Souldrop. 1555/192
Thos., Stotfold, lab. 1626/81
Wm., Odell. R 1544: 11/48d
Wm., Northill, Caldecote, yeo. 1850/19
BELLAINE, see Blane
BELLAMY, Eliz., Roxton, wid. 1613/182
Robt., Roxton, Colesden, lab. 1639/104
BELLDAM, Jn., Bedford, shoemaker. 1846/30
BELLFIELD, BELFELDE, Hen., Studham. A 1700/3
Jn., Studham, gent. 1591/23
Wm., Studham, gent. 1559-60/205
Wm., Studham, gent. 1604-5/5
BELLGROVE, Ann, Leighton Buzzard, wid. LBA 1819/78
Robt., Leighton Buzzard, yeo. (see also will). LBA 1819/
Robt., Leighton Buzzard, Over End Green, yeo. (see also admon.) LB 1819/2
BELLINGHAM, Lewis, Turvey. AR 1683: 1/45
Ric., Sharnbrook. 1632/61
Thos., Turvey. 1664/16
BELLMAN, Jn., sen., Potton, worsted manufacturer. 1812/8
BELNIAM (?Bellman), Wm., Potton. 1560?/209
BEMAN, see Beamond

BEMOND, see Beamond
BEMUND, see Beamond
BENBOW, Thos., Turvey. 1844/11
BENDS, Jn., Warden. 1593-4
BENDY, BENDEE, Wm., Maulden, carp. 1823/10
see also Bandy
BENFORD, BENTFORD, Wm., Sutton, maltster. 1638/134
BENHAM, Wm., Luton, Copt Hall, husb. 1708/48
Wm., sen., Sundon, yeo. 1743-4/73
Wm., Sundon, yeo. 1763/4
BENNELL, Chris., Toddington, maltster. 1709/9
Chris., Milbrook, yeo. 1761/21
Chris., Ampthill, grazier. 1803/9
Eliz., Toddington, wid. 1712/52
Hen., Dunstable, yeo. 1570-1/33
Jos., Houghton Conquest. A 1835/5
Sam., Kempston, husb. A 1831/3
Susannah, Ampthill. 1810/39
Wm., Dunstable, yeo. 1607/124
BENNETT, BENET, BENNET, BENYT, Alice, Potton, wid. 1632/29
Ann, Kempston, wid. 1735-6/54
Ann, Bedford, wid. 1794/2
Chris., Cardington, Cotton End, husb. 1604/1a
Eliz., Kempston, wid. 1740/32
Eliz., Eaton Socon, wid. 1754/9
Eliz., Wootton, wid. 1777/17
Eliz., now Milton Ernest, late Tempsford, wid. of Sam. 1842/21
Hen., Sharpenhoe, Streatley, lab. 1683/60
Hen., Ampthill, tailor. 1729/22
Jn., Potton. R 1521: 2/81
Jn., Potton. R 1538: 5/13d
Jn., sen., Blunham, Chalton. 1554/190
Jn., Arlesey, husb. R 1559: 13/158
Jn., sen., Riseley, yeo. 1642/8
Jn., Wilshamstead, cordwainer. 1662-3/60a
Jn., Eaton Socon, gent. 1737/21
Jn., Bedford St. Paul, grazier. 1769/30
Jn., Leighton Buzzard, cordwainer. 1827
Jn., Leighton Buzzard, cordwainer (register only). LBR: 1827/40
Jn., Aspley Guise, Salford Ford. 1853/30
Jos., Wootton. A 1748/8
Jos., sen., Wilshamstead, husb. 1851/3
Margt., Blunham. 1558/79
Mary, Riseley, wid. 1613/175
Math., Stotfold, shepherd. 1688-9/73

BENNETT continued
Matt., sen., Stotfold, yeo. 1771/3
Ric., Wilden. R 1506: 1/80
Ric., Pavenham, husb. 1589/120
Ric., Cranfield. AR 1677-8: 1/199
Robt., Felmersham. 1566/69
Robt., Kempston, grocer. 1735/27
Sarah, Riseley, wid. (bundle 1660). 1662-3/250
Simon, Mogerhanger. R 1538: 5/21, 25d
Stephen, Riseley. 1659/203
Thos., Warden, husb. 1602/41
Thos., Silsoe, lab. 1621/176
Thos., Keysoe, yeo. 1629/111
Thos., Wilshamstead, tailor. 1707/48
Thos., Turvey, yeo. 1766/52
Thos., Husborne Crawley, yeo. 1820/42
Walt., Keysoe. 1630/24
Walt., Keysoe. 1660/137
Wm., Colmworth. 1616/48
Wm., Milton Brian, husb. 1667-8/4
Wm., Cranfield, yeo. 1670/183
Wm., Stotfold, ar 1687-8: 1/129d
Wm., Caddington, tailor. 1698/176
Wm., Caddington, lab., A 1728/18
Wm., Aspley Guise, husb. A 1729/17
Wm., Stotfold, weaver. 1791/24
Wm., Eaton Bray, yeo. 1846/24
BENSON, Chris., Studham. AR 1690: 1/177d
Edw., Potton, lab. 1744/39
Eliz., Stagsden, wid. R 1770/31
Hen., Turvey, husb. 1601/106
Jas,, Goldington, Putnoe. 1700-1/136
Jn., Little Staughton, yeo. A 1723/3
Jos., Ravensden, dairyman. 1725/71
Mary, Bedford St. Paul, wid. 1715/37
Mary, Potton, wid. 1744/38
Phillip, Bedford St. Paul. A 1772/20
Thos., sen., Stagsden, farmer. 1747/64
Thos., Bedford St. Paul, gardener. 1754/39
see also Binson alias Ashton
BENSTONE, Wm., Bedford St. Paul. 1553/266
BENTFORD, see Benford
BENTHAM, Eliz., Rattlesden, wid. AR 1682: 1/162d
BENTLEY, Edm., Haddenham, Bucks. R 1542: 6/141d & 9/2
Edw., Astwick, farmer. A 1736/34

BENTLEY continued
Hugh, Warden, Warden Street, dairyman. 1625/200
Jas., Stotfold, yeo. A 1789/11
Jn., Warden. 1587/104
Jn., Stotfold, shepherd. 1749/21
Jn., Astwick, yeo. 1761/37
Jn., Shillington, Pegsden, yeo. 1787/32
Mary, Elstow, wid. 1632/52
Mary, Bedford St. John, wid. 1714/82
Mary, Biggleswade, Sunderland, spins. Bw 1777/66
Thos., Stotfold, shepherd. 1711/21
Thos., Dunstable, yeo. R 1547: 11/250
Wm., Bedford St. John, lab. 1711/38
BENTON, Adary, Bedford, wid. 1754/36
Jn., Marston Pillinge, lab. 1685/93
Jn., Marston. R 1686: 1/215d
Thos., Milton Ernest, lab. 1625-6/119
Wm., Felmersham, Radwell, yeo. 1738-9/31
BEOMOND, see Beamond
BERECROFT, Joan, wid. of Rob., Elstow
BERKLEY, Robt., Colmworth, gent. 1689/10
BERNARD, see Barnard
BERNERS, Ric., Pertenhall, gent. 1704/40
BERNEWELL, see Barnwell
BERRELL, BERRILL, Chas., Elstow, shopkeeper. A 1841/6
Jn., Marston Moretaine, husb. 1557/237
Jos., Bedford, farmer. 1842/41
Mary, Bedford St. Mary, wid. 1855/35
Thos., Goldington, bricklayer. 1811/30
Wm., Bedford, victualler. A 1742/20
Wm., sen., Bedford, builder. 1831/51
Wm., Bedford, builder. 1843/30
BERRIDGE, Clement, Bedford, Clement, currier. 1663-4/85.
Clement, Bedford. A 1670-1/1
Isabell, Riseley, wid. 1669-70/103
BERRIMAN, Jn., Luton, Thrales End. AR 1675: 1/150d
Mary, Luton, Thrales End, wid. 1679/34
BERRY, BERY, BURY, Alice, Felmersham, Moore End, wid. 1578/109
Alice, Lt. Barford, wid. 1710/50
Audrey, Felmersham, Radwell, wid. 1736/31
Dan., Felmersham, gent. A 1777/14
Edw., Henlow, yeo. 1669-70/107
Eliner, Felmersham. 1618/46
Eliz., (no parish given). 1634/5/88

BERRY, BERY, BURY continued
Eliz., Elstow, wid. 1719/87
Eliz., Felmersham, wid. A 1724/1
Emma, Thurleigh, wid. 1620/93
Geo., Clifton, yeo. 1630/49
Geo., Henlow, yeo. 1700/99
Hen., Henlow. 1614-15/19
Jn., Felmersham, Radwell, husb. 1557/348
Jn., Moore End, Felmersham, husb. 1557/351
Jn., Clifton, yeo. 1590-1/125
Jn., Felmersham, Radwell, yeo. 1603/131
Jn., Henlow, yeo. 1683-4/104
Jn., Lt. Barford. 1705/6
Jn., Elstow, lab. 1714/36
Jn., Henlow, yeo. 1715/56
Jn., Husborne Crawley, yeo. 1726/55
Jn., Marston, husb. 1740/40
Jn., Felmersham, gent. 1748/41
Jn., Wootton, yeo. 1780/12
Lionel, Eversholt, yeo. 1777/12
Martha, Felmersham, Radwell, wid. 1692-3/75
Martha, Felmersham, spins. 1745/33
Mary, Felmersham, wid. 1664/55
Mary, Felmersham, spins. 1748/47
Ric., Felmersham, Moore End, husb. 1593/77
Ric., Felmersham, Moor End, husb. 1615-16/132
Ric., sen., Henlow, yeo. 1671/51
Ric., Henlow, husb. 1680-1/103
Ric., Bedford, carpenter. 1726/24
Robt., Bedford, innkeeper. 1630/85
Robt., Sandy, Girtford. 1659/87
Robt., jun., Felmersham, Moore End, gent. 1661/382
Robt., Felmersham, Moor End, yeo. 1663/35
Rose, Felmersham, wid. 1614/91
Sam., Lt. Barford, yeo. 1695/7
Sam., Wootton. yeo. 1695/45
Sarah, Wootton, wid. 1710/52
Thos., Clifton (?). 1556/201
Thos., Melchbourne, husb. 1590/140
Thos., Felmersham, Radwell. 1679-80/111
Thos., Stotfold, yeo. 1718/39
Thos., Wootton, yeo. 1721/94
Thos., Felmersham, Radwell, gent. A 1730/44
Thos., Wootton, brickmaker. 1771/66
Wm., Felmersham, Moore End, husb. 1593/77

BERRY, BERY, BURY continued
Wm., Oakley, yeo. 1656/208
Wm., Wootton, butcher. A 1739-40/7
Wm., Biggleswade, farmer. BwA 1760/20
Wm., Wilshamstead, husb. 1765/37
Wm., Wootton, husb. A 1816/4
see also Wright alias Berry
BERRYMAN, see Berriman
BERSEY, see Birdsey
BERWICK, see Barrick, Barwicke
BEST, Ann, Ampthill, spins. 1729/61
Bart., Willington, gent. 1748/25
Bart., sen., Ravensden, yeo. 1761/34
Eliz., Willington, A 1759/3
Jn., Ampthill, maltster. 1727/16
Jn., Pulloxhill, dairyman. 1791/26
Joan, Potton. R 1500: 1/22
Ric., Willington. A 1770/8
Thos., Woburn, innholder. A 1711-12/58
Thos., Wilden, yeo. 1737/39
BESTOWE, Anne, Flitwick. 1664/90
Ric., Flitwick, yeo. 1667/67
BETHERY, see Bithrey
BETT, BETTS, Alice, Maulden, wid. 1609-10/98
Chas., Maulden, gardener. 1720/8
Chas., Maulden, farmer. A 1766/11
Edw., Gt. Barford, maltster. 1709-10/61
Eleanor, Gt. Barford. 1717-18/78
Eliz., Maulden, spins. 1752/43
Eliz., Maulden, wid. 1752/72
Esther, Stevington, wid. 1723-4/75
Fra., Holcote, lab. 1618-19/11
Fra., Langford, yeo. (bundle 1668). 1666/136
Freelove, Bedford, spins. (bundle 1713). 1712/67
Jn., sen., Maulden. 1559/306
Jn., Maulden, husb. 1635/12
Jn., Willington, clerk. 1745/31
Jn., Maulden, schoolmaster. 1745/32
Jn., Harrold, lab. 1784/12
Joan, Mogerhanger, wid. 1597/50
Math., Potton, draper. 1828/44
Nicephorous, Stevington, mason. 1713/54
Ric., Maulden, lab. 1597-8/16
Robt., Bedford. 1680-1/111
Thos., Harrold, husb. A 1729/27

BETT, BETTS continued
Wm., Eaton Socon, maltster. 1696-7/153
Wm., sen., Maulden, yeo. 1706/54
Wm., Flitwick, yeo. 1744/1
BETTERIDGE, Jos., Bedford, cordwainer. 1702/25
BETTLE(S), Eusabey, Sharnbrook. 1745/41
Geo., Cranfield, husb. 1782/52
Wm., Sharnbrook, yeo. 1745/2
Wm., Over Dean. 1768/25
BETTLEY, Thos., Totternhoe, husb. 1728/65
BEVAN, Betsy, Ampthill, wid. 1833/32
Jas., Chicksands. 1730-1/104
Jas., Biggleswade, Holme, yeo. 1754/29
Jn., Gravenhurst. 1830/29
Jos., Ridgmont, yeo. 1783/15
see also Bavine
BEVERLEY, Robt.,Melchbourne, clerk. A 1703/15
BEYSTONE, see Beeston
BIBBY, BYBY, Bryan, Bedford. R 1545: 11/56d
Thos., Cardington, farmer. A 1767/31
BICHENER, BECHNER, BEECHENER, Hen., Steppingley, blacksmith. A 1816/3
Jn., Turvey. R 1527: 2/52d
Ric., Wootton. R 1518: 2/43d
Robt., Steppingley, yeo. 1797/35
BICKERSTAFF, BIGGERSTAFFE, Edw., Henlow. 1633/130
Eliz., Henlow, wid. 1637/125
Geo., Wilden, lab. 1640/35
Thos., Henlow, tailor. 1798/32
BICKERTON, Ann, Luton, wid. 1709/75
BICKNALL, see Bechenol
BIDKIN, Jn., Elstow, shepherd. 1631/140
Robt., Elstow, shepherd. 1623/156
BIGG, BIGGE, BIGGS, Abraham, Toddington, Chalton, yeo. 1624-5/14
Abr., sen., Lidlington, yeo. 1661-2/248
Abr., Lidlington, yeo. 1729/54
Abr., Henlow, wheelwright. 1834/42
Abr., Toddington. AR 1674: 1/148
Abr., Lidlington. A 1784/26
Alice, wid., Ayot St. Lawrence, Herts. 1616/147
Alice, Husborne Crawley, wid. 1762/27
Ann, Lidlington, wid. 1768/50
Ann, Lidlington. A 1779/4
Edw., Dunstable, lab. 1726-7/106
Edw., Lidlington, yeo. 1758/25

BIGG, BIGGE, BIGGS continued
Edw., Wootton, yeo. 1848/39
Eliz., Luton, Whitehill, spins. 1733/60
Francis, Stopsley (bundle 1597). 1596/13
Fra., Toddington, Chalton, yeo. 1616-17/24.
Fra., Luton, wid. 1630-1/124
Fra., Stopsley, Falconds Hall, yeo. 1664/52
Geo., Houghton Regis, yeo. 1753/43
Helen, Lidlington, wid. 1633/131
Jas., Ampthill, plumber & glazier. 1767/25
Jn., Sundon. 1589-90/16
Jn., Eaton Socon, Ford End, husb. 1647/64
Jn., Wilshamstead, yeo. 1662/52
Jn., Kempston, yeo. 1720/36
Jn., Marston, yeo. 1818/48
Jn. Barratt, Bromham, miller. 1842/15
Jn., Luton, auctioneer, ironfounder & wood turner. 1850/35
Marg., Eaton Socon, wid. 1676/140
Mary, Barton, wid. 1682/45
Mary, Cranfield, wid. 1846/28
Mary, Luton, wid. A 1851/15
Mich., Ampthill, glazier & plumber. 1761/38
Mordecai, Houghton Regis, yeo. 1716/87
Oliv., Eaton Socon, tailor. 1680/30
Phillip, Sundon, yeo. 1589-90/14
Phillip, Sundon, husb. 1590/145
Ric., sen., Stopsley, yeo. 1597/34
Ric., Lidlington, Westwood End. 1627/156
Robt., Totternhoe. 1593-4/25
Robt., Luton, bach. AR 1681: 1/160d
Robt., Eaton Socon, Duloe, lab. 1728/101
Robt., Limbury. AR 1682: 1/164
late Saul, Marston, Usley. A 1813/8
Thos., Gravenhurst (Lower). R 1550: 12/106d
Thos., Eaton Socon, yeo. 1577/60
Thos., Sundon. 1618/82
Thos., Wilshamstead, yeo. 1657/102
Thos., Shillington. 1688/34
Thos., Luton, yeo. 1693/149
Thos., Ampthill, cordwainer. A 1744/6
Thos., Lidlington, yeo. 1749/49
Wm., Stopsley, yeo. 1602/8
Wm., Lt. Billington. 1681/42
Wm., Luton, husb. 1683/93
Wm., Ampthill, widower. 1790/17

BIGG, BIGGE, BIGGS continued
Wm., Bromham, miller. 1799/29
Wm., Marston, blacksmith. 1840/17
BIGGERSTAFFE, see Bickerstaff
BIGGINS, Jas., Silsoe, Wrest, cook, servant to the Rt. Hon. The Earl of Kent. 1611-12/150
BIGGRAVE, see Bygrave
BIGLAND, Cornelius, Luton, barber, chirurgeon. 1679/32
BIGRAVE, see Bygrave
BILBY, Edw., Leighton Buzzard, husb. Fac. 1704/9/14
BILCLIFF, Thos., Flitton, gent. AR 1672: 1/189d
BILCOCK, Jere., Biggleswade, gardener. BwA 1823/65
BILCOCKE, Ann, Houghton Conquest. R 1511: 2/128
Edm., Houghton Conquest. 1573/127
Harry, Houghton Conquest. 1565-6/63
Hen., Silsoe. 1634-5/96
John, Houghton Conquest. R 1531: 3/43
Kath., Houghton Conquest. R 1518: 2/43
Wm., Houghton Conquest, yeo. 1613/207
BILEY, John, Kempston, clerk. 1742/36
BILL, BILLS, Eliz., Clapham, wid. R 1689-90: 1/50
Jas., Sutton. 1606/30
BILLING, BILLIN, Jn., Melchbourne, butcher. 1809/39
Joseph, Harrold, husb. 1676/23
Mary, Harrold. 1693/147
Sam., sen., Cardington, miller. 1747/66
Sam., Clifton, victualler. 1827/10
Thos., Harrold, yeo. 1671/23
Thos., Cardington, miller. A 1721/10
BILLINGTON, Alice, Leighton Buzzard. LB R 1549: 1/22d
Ben., Leighton Buzzard, matmaker. LB 1782/64
Geo., Cranfield, lab. 1733/55
Jas., Tilsworth, cordwainer. 1844/23
Jn., Flitwick, higler. 1815/42
Jn., Flitwick. A 1857/8
Robt., Billington. LB R 1540: 1/7d
Robt., Pulloxhill, dairyman. 1679/38
Susan, Harlington, wid. 1689-90/74
BILTMAS, Snowe alias Biltmas, see under Snowe
BINDELL, Simon, Northill, Upper Caldecote. R 1506: 1/96
Wm., Eyeworth. R 1529-30: 3/23
BINFIELD, Jn., Riseley, clerk. AR 1690: 1/83
BINHAM, BINGHAM, Dan., Markyate Street, yeo. 1743/24
Edw., Caddington, smith. 1737/10
Robt., Cranfield, lab. 1616/43

BINHAM, BINGHAM continued
Thos., Northill, Hatch, cooper. 1695/59
Thos., Luton, higler. 1816/2
BINION, BINNYAN, BINYON, alias Sutton, Eliz., Northill. AR 1681-2: 1/115d
Robt., Lidlington. 1836/3
Sam, Cranfield, carpenter. A 1731/48
Thos., Studham. 1664/19
Thos., Houghton Regis, yeo. A 1782/7
Thos., Houghton Regis P/IX 2 admon missing. A 1783/4
Wm., Cople, victualler. AR 1680: 1/18d
BINNS, Chris., Eversholt. 1558/274
BINSON, Keeling, Potton, blacksmith. 1833/31
see also Benson
BINYON, see Binion
BIRBY, BYRBY, BURBY, Edm., Arlesey, husb. 1584/168
Nich., Arlesey, smith. R 1545: 11/104
BIRCH, Hen., Maulden, gent. 1593-4/36
Thos., Bedford, innholder. A 1705/66
Thos., Houghton Conquest, gent. A 1723/15
BIRCHMORE, Jn., Caddington, husb. 1674/119
Ric., Farndish. R 1541: 6/100d
Ric., Caddington, yeo. 1608/20
Ric., sen., Whipsnade, yeo. 1676/144
Ric., Whipsnade, yeo. AR 1688: 1/174d
Ric., Whipsnade, yeo. A 1702/3
Thos., Caddington, yeo. 1609/177
Thos., Caddington, Mill Field, yeo. 1674/109
Thos., Caddington, Millfield, yeo. 1721/4
Wm., Caddington, yeo. 1617/209
Wm., Whipsnade, yeo. 1704/60
Wm., sen., Whipsnade, yeo. 1743/20
Wm., sen., Whipsnade, yeo. 1835/29
BIRD, BERDE, Alice, Wootton, wid. 1661-2/408
Geo., Wootton. 1655/201
Geo., Houghton Conquest, blacksmith. 1691-2/139
Hen., Heath, yeo. LB 1781/59
Hen., Billington, yeo. LB A 1812/66
Honour, Everton. A 1796/2
Hugh, Eaton Socon, lab. AR 1672: 1/62
Jas., Ampthill, keeper. 1639/37
Jas., Houghton Regis, lab. 1820/39
Jas., Houghton Regis, yeo. 1832/50
Jn., Wootton, blacksmith. 1673/43
Jn., Everton, farmer. 1808/2
Jn., Silsoe, yeo. 1818/39

BIRD, BERDE continued
Jn., Roxton, minor. A 1824/13
Mary, Heath, wid. LB 1809/44
Ric., sen., Billington, blacksmith. LB 1791/91
Ric., Billington, blacksmith. LB 1807/39a
Ric., Billington, yeo. LB 1824/26
Ric., Sandy, Beeston, farmer. 1828/6
Thos., sen., Luton. 1573-4/12
Thos., Southill, Stanford. 1651-2/39
Thos., Wrestlingworth, farmer. 1849/50
Thos., Harrold, yeo. A 1785/24
Wm., Ampthill, chandler. 1585/34
Wm., Roxton, butcher. 1812/17, I 4/218
Wm., Aspley Guise. A 1835/6
see also Birdsey
Bridge alias Bird, see under Bridge
BIRDSEY, BURDYE, Fra., Dunstable, wid. 1622-3/17
Jn., Pavenham, husb. 1615/151
Jn., Dunstable, wheelmaker. 1647/51
Jn., Wootton. AR 1683: 1/23
Jn., Lidlington, weaver. 1700/110
Nich., Lidlington, weaver. 1660-1/108
Nich., Caddington, weaver. 1687/88
Robt., Stevington, weaver. 1616/111
Robt., Odell, Gt., yeo. 1623/106
Rog., husb. R 1537: 4/93
Thos., Aspley Guise. R 1535: 4/25
Thos., Clifton, yeo. 1634-5/87
Thos., Ridgmont, weaver. 1713/75
Thos., Ridgmont, weaver. 1714/93
Thos., Leighton Buzzard, butcher. LB 1769/18
Thos., Leighton Buzzard, butcher. LB 1787/77
Wm., Lidlington, weaver. 1622/23
Wm., Leighton Buzzard, yeo. 1676/131
Wm., Markyate Street, husb. 1693-4/161
Wm., Ridgmont, yeo. 1728/3
Wm., ?Leighton Buzzard. LB A 1810/65
BIRKET, Chris., Bromham, glover. 1613-14/223
Jas., Bromham, tailor. 1618/121
BIRKHEAD, Mary, Barford, Gt., wid. of Jos., late vicar of Great Barford. 1691/113
Jos., Barford, Gt. AR 1690: 1/84
BIRRELL, BIRREALL, Nich., Cranfield, husb. R 1537: 4/86d
Wm., Cranfield. R 1546: 11/169d
see also Burrell; see also Burwell; see also Borrell

BIRT, see Burt
BISBY, Jn., Dean, Nether, yeo. 1639/128
Matthias, Bedford St. Paul. 1637-8/166
BISHOP, BYSSHOPP, Chris., sen., Pulloxhill, bricklayer. 1638-9/79
Chris., Pulloxhill, bricklayer. AR 1677-8: 1/199d
Dorothy, Toddington, wid. 1704/18
Edw., Pulloxhill, bricklayer. 1729/51
Edw., Maulden, bricklayer. 1743/60
Eliz., Flitwick, wid. 1739/59
Fra., Sandy, Girtford, baker. 1706/29
Fra., Sandy, baker. A 1714/20
Geo., Eversholt. A 1712/33
Hannah, Toddington, wid. A 1756/23
Hen., Kempston. R 1522: 2/116d
Hen., Cople, mason. 1613/169
Hen., old index "docket mislaid". A 1710/13
Hen., Pulloxhill, husb. 1748/24
Joan, sen., Barford, Gt., wid. R 1539: 6/1d
Joan, Luton, wid. 1620/62
Jn., Sandy, Girtford, baker. 1683/96
Jn., Sandy, Girtford, baker. 1701/48
Jn., jun., Sandy, Girtford. 1711-12/111
Jn., Sandy, husb. 1728/22
Jn., Oakley, yeo. 1756/31
Jn., Toddington. AR 1682: 1/164d
Jn., Toddington. A 1737/6
Jn., Carlton, yeo. A 1793/9
Jn., Toddington, yeo. 1806/9
Math., Toddington, glazier & plumber. 1732-3/12
Phillip, sen., Sandy, yeo. 1778/37
Ric., Renhold. R 1546: 11/141
Ric., Potton, innholder. 1721/58
Ric., Maulden, blacksmith. 1739-40/90
Sarah, Sandy. A 1788/9
Sus., Sandy, Girtford, wid. 1714/53
Susann., Sandy, wid. 1750/39
Thos., Elstow. R 1500: 1/21d
Wm., Biggleswade. Bw R 1546: 1/5
Wm., Pulloxhill, bricklayer. 1687-8/100
Wm., Silsoe, bricklayer. 1715/59
BITHREY, BY THE REY, Alice, Carlton, wid. R 1550: 12/110
Chas., Carlton, gent. 1721-2/71
Chas., Carlton, horsedealer. 1765/1
Chas, Carlton, gent. 1784/29
Eliz., Carlton, wid. 1799/7

BITHREY, BY THE REY continued
Gideon, Carlton, gent. 1733/15
Gideon, Carlton. 1747/11
Jn., Carlton, husb. 1630/33
Jn., Carlton, tailor. 1683-4/94
Jn., Keysoe. A 1785/8
Jn., Carlton, horsedealer. 1787/43
Jn., Bedford, hairdresser & innkeeper. 1843/48
Marg., Souldrop, wid. R 1546-7: 11/217d
Marg., Carlton, wid. 1626/82
Marg., Souldrop, wid. 1660-1/85
Ric., Carlton, yeo. 1662/76
Thos., Pertenhall, yeo. 1693-4/122
Thos., Carlton, yeo. A 1732/20
Thos., Carlton, gent. 1740-1/80
Uriah, Carlton, gent. 1747-8/70
Wm., sen., Carlton, yeo. 1652-3/112
Wm., Carlton, Moor End, yeo. 1696-7/159
Wm., Felmersham, Radwell, gent. 1779/12
Wm., sen., Carlton, yeo. 1807/11
BLACHFORD, Ric., Souldrop, yeo. 1680/18
BLACKABY, Eliz., Northill, wid. 1767/42
BLACKBURN, Octavian, Bedford St. Paul. R 1540: 6/39
Priscilla, Luton, spins. A 1722/26
Thos., sen., Ampthill, butcher. R 1548-9: 12/48
Thos., Luton, maltster. 1720-1/119
BLACKETT, BLACKED, BLACKEHED, Edw., Chalgrave, Wingfield Green, husb. 1582/124
Ovyatt alias Blackett, see Ovyatt
BLACKMAN, Robt., Everton, gent. 1605/127
BLACKNOLL, BLAKNOLL, Jn., Dunstable, husb. 1670/163
Jn., Blunham. AR 1675: 1/104
Margery, Leighton Buzzard. 1554/162
BLACKSHAW, Jos., Bedford St. Paul, victualler. A 1809/5
Mary, Bedford, wid. 1830/21
BLAIN, see Blane
BLAKELEY, Jn., Ampthill, innholder. 1757/48
BLANCHET, Wm., Oakley. A 1851/11
BLAND, Sir Jn., Odell. R 1546: 11/233d
Jn., Sharnbrook, husb. 1583-4/163
Jn., Barton P/IX2 admon missing. A 1757/17
Jn., Cardington, Harrowden, farmer. 1804/33
Luke, Battlesden, cook. 1773/42
Robt., Potton. 1625-6/132
Thos., Potton. 1668/135

BLAND continued
Wm., Bedford, victualler. 1706-7/35
BLANE, BELLAINE, BLAIN, BLAN, BLAYEN, Anth., Meppershall, Pulehanger, husb. 1672/127
Hale Robt., Sandy, Girtford, cordwainer. 1838/15
Jn., Sandy. AR 1678-9: 1/108d
Jn., Meppershall. AR 1688: 1/131
Jn., Sandy, Stratford, gardener. 1702-3/77, 1702-3/36
Jn., old index "docket mislaid". A 1710/7
Jn., Langford, dairyman. A 1746/18
Robt., Wrestlingworth, husb. 1585/28
Sarah, Sandy, wid. 1732/34
Thos., Bedford, innholder. A 1720-1/35
Thos., Sandy, gardener. 1773/4
Wm., Barton, yeo. 1738/91
BLANEY, Nehemiah, Kempston, yeo. A 1781/26
BLETHERWICK, Annes, Kempston, spins. 1620/35
BLETSOE, Ann, Irchester, Northants., spins. 1783/38
Eliz., Harrold, wid. 1757/22
Eliz., Harrold, wid. A 1787/12
Jn., Harrold, gent. 1701/36
Jn., Harrold, gent. 1724/35
Jos., Ravensden, husb. 1702/31
Jos., Ravensden, yeo. 1718/36
Robt., Harrold, gent. 1719/17
Robt., Stevington, yeo. 1745/26
Sarah, Harrold, wid. 1711/95
BLEVIS, Thos., Caddington, yeo. 1725/63
BLEWING, Lewis alias Blewing, see under Lewis
BLEWIT, Blott alias Blewit, see under Blott
Jn., Henlow. 1632/92
Nich., Southill, Broome, blacksmith. A 1715-16/39
Thos., jnr., Southill, Broome, bach. 1701/70
Thos., Sandy, horsedealer. 1816/31
Wm., Kempston, yeo. 1713/2
Wm., jnr., Sandy, victualler. 1804/43
BLICK, Pettipare alias Blick, see under Pettipare
Eliz., Leighton Buzzard, wid. 1590/158
Wm., Maulden, yeo. 1806/8
BLISS, Jos., Totternhoe, miller. A 1780/15
BLITH, see Blythe
BLOCKE, BLOKE, Anthony, Cranfield, yeo. 1577-8/68
Edith, Eaton Socon, Honeydon, spins. 1651/32
Ellen, Eaton Socon, Beggary, wid. 1616/109
Jn., Eaton Socon. 1599/97

BLOCKE, BLOKE continued
Margt., Barford. 1558/21
Ric., Cranfield. 1622/61
Thos., Barford (?Gt.) 1562/131
Wm., Potton. 1558/14
Wm., Eaton Socon, Goodwick, yeo. 1633-4/202
BLOFIELD, Edm., Flitwick. 1613-14/225
Edw. Flitwick, gent. 1667/78
Giles, Meppershall, gent. 1622/60
Jane, Eaton Socon, wid. A 1823/9
Ric., Eaton Socon, yeo. A 1798/16
BLOMELEY, Robt., Bedford St. Paul, innholder. 1625/214
BLOODWORTH, Ann, Luton, Cross Keys. 1663/53
BLOTT, BLOATT, BLOT, Ann, Ampthill, spins. 1824/32
Esther, Ampthill, spins. 1824/33
Jn., Ridgmont. R 1546: 12/39
Jn., Oakley, husb. 1604/71
Jn., Harrold, yeo. 1630/27
Jn., Mogerhanger, farmer. 1831/40
Jonathan, Melchbourne, grazier. 1840/12
Mary, Harrold, spins. 1685/98
Robt., Harrold. 1556/216
Robt., Ridgmont. 1602/34
Robt., Harrold, yeo. 1610/2
Robt., Harrold, yeo. 1610/70
Robt., Harrold. AR 1676-7: 1/40d
alias Blewitt, Wm., jnr., Harrold, husb. 1592-3/62
Wm., Harrold, yeo. 1624/35
Wm., Southill. 1658/126
Wm., Barton, collarmaker. 1781/52
Wm., Southill. AR 1683: 1/117d
BLOWES, Hen., Tempsford, gent. A 1761/29
Hen., Tempsford, gent. 1761/52
Jas., sen., Wrestlingworth. 1690/39
Jn., Eyeworth, yeo. 1719/105
Jn., sen., Caddington Green, husb. 1724/94
Jn., Tempsford, mealman. A 1759/13
Rachel, Caddington Green, wid. 1734/29
Robt., Hatley, Cockayne. 1613/209
Sar., Caddington Green, spins. 1734/24
BLUCK, Wm., Renhold. 1562/127
Wm., Renhold, (bundle 1563-5). 1562/214
BLUNDELL, Geo., Studham. 1728/89
Jn., Silsoe, Flitton. R 1501: 1/244
Jn., Turvey, yeo. 1662-3/66

BLUNDELL continued
Judith, Meppershall, wid. AR 1690: 1/133
Ric., Caddington, tilemaker. 1646/71
Ric., Luton, yeo. 1652-3/111
Thos., Meppershall. AR ?1684: 1/122d
Thos., Meppershall. 1727/52
Wm., Meppershall, yeo. 1726-7/81
Wm., sen., Potton, sweep. 1847/2
BLUNSUM, Jos., Marston, Shelton, Upper, lab. 1759/45
Sam., Cardington. 1729/88
BLUNT, Geo., Aspley Guise, lab. 1687/36
Mary, Marston. 1823/48
Sarah, Bedford St. Mary. A 1852/19
BLYTHE, BLITH, BLYTH, Alice, Mogerhanger, wid. R 1550-1: 12/142d
Jn., Blunham. 1586/89
Jn., Bolnhurst, yeo. 1619/262, I 4/113
Jn., Colmworth, lab. 1697/135
Ric., Eaton Socon, Beggary. 1628-9/18
Robt., Sandy, gardener. AR 1677: 1/107
Robt., Sandy, gardener. 1687-8/98
Thos., Keysoe. R 1523: 2/22
Thos., Mogerhanger. R 1534: 4/10d
Thos., Mogerhanger, husb. 1561/155
Thos., Blunham, husb. 1620/70
Thos., Arlesey, husb. 1728/54
Thos., Stotfold. A 1772/11
Wm., Eaton Socon. R 1508: 1/204d
Wm., Oakley, husb. 1614/95
BOARSTON(E), see Boston
BOCKNAM, see Buckingham
BODDINGTON, Alice, Turvey, wid. 1708/76
Edw., Chellington, husb. 1667/71
Edw., Felmersham, Radwell, yeo. 1755/45
Eliz., Carlton, wid. 1750/37
Geo., sen., Turvey, yeo. 1692/6
Hugh, Dunstable. R 1540: 6/32
Jn., Carlton, Carlton Hall, yeo. 1657/266
Jn., sen., Pavenham. AR 1682: 1/44
Jn., (old index "docket mislaid"). A 1708/20
Jn., Turvey, dairyman. A 1728/37
Jn., Stagsden, tailor. A 1735/25
Jn., Kempston, husb. 1777/35
Jn., Carlton, carp. 1800/48
Jonathan, Turvey. 1734/37
Mary, Turvey. 1693/93

BODDINGTON continued
Ric., Thurleigh, lab. A 1703/28
Robt., Thurleigh, lab. A 1713/26
Robt., Thurleigh, lab. A 1729/13
Robt., Carlton, yeo. A 1741/4
Robt., Carlton, blacksmith. 1768/40
Thos., jun., Turvey, yeo. 1656/85
Thos., Turvey, yeo. 1704/67
Thos., Carlton, yeo. 1713/60
Thos., Felmersham, Radwell, carp. R 1770/6
Warborrow, Turvey, wid. 1640/13
Wm., Haynes, Northwood End, butcher. 1756/19
BODGER, Ann, Yielden, wid. 1694/59
Edw., Roxton, Chawston, lab. 1781/66
Jn., Roxton, Colesden, husb. 1709/33
Jn., Roxton, farmer. A 1729/20
Jn., Roxton, Chawston, farmer. 1792/16
Jn., Sharnbrook, farmer. 1798/13
Sarah, sen., Roxton, wid. 1772/7
Wm., Roxton, Chawston, yeo. 1729/89
Wm., Eaton Socon. 1819/11
BOIVILL, see Boyvill
BOLDING, Jn., Ampthill, innholder. A 1731/53
BOLDUCK(E), see Baldock
BOLE, Wm., Lidlington. R 1513: 1/238
BOLEN, BOLLEN, Geo., Potton. 1565/2
Jn., Pirton, ?Herts. 1557/406
BOLLYE, Jas., Cople, miller. 1630/11
BOLNEY, Jn., Podington, yeo. AR 1680: 1/42
Jn., Podington, Hinwick, husb. 1706/16
Luke, Podington, yeo. A 1763/7
Mary, Podington, spins. A 1763/3
Mary, Podington, spins. 1763/5
BOLSTON, Phil., Dean, wid. 1670/185
BOLSWORTH, Jn., (old index "docket mislaid"). A 1708/15
BOLTON, BOULTON, Alexander, Bedford, gent. 1702-3/41
Anth., Bedford, grocer. 1697/31
Jn., Stagsden, yeo. R 1537-8: 5/8
Jn., Sharnbrook, vicar. 1739-40/84
Sus., Bedford, wid. 1702/5
Thos., Colmworth, husb. 1662/84
Thos., Kempston yeo. 1690/14
Wm., Cardington. R 1538: 5/15
Wm., Pavenham, yeo. 1684/87

BOND, Jn., jnr., Maulden, yeo. 1662/31
Robt., Eaton Socon, limited admon. A 1828
Wm., Pavenham, yeo. A 1788/10
Wm., Renhold, butler. A 1837/11
BONDON, Jn., Potsgrove. 1674/151
BONE, Jas., Silsoe, baker & farmer. 1831/50
Jn., Sandy, gardener. A 1824/4
BONEST, Jn., Shillington, tailor. 1667-8/108
Jn., Shillington, yeo. 1804/20
Jn., Biggleswade. Bw 1840/150
Thos., Shillington, yeo. 1677/29
Thos., Marston, yeo. 1726/94
Thos., Marston, yeo. A 1746/12
Thos., Marston, yeo. A 1800/2
BONFIELD, Edw., Eaton Socon, Honidon, lab. 1575/92
Jn., Eaton Socon, Staploe, Nr. R 1548: 12/25d
Jn., Eaton Socon, shepherd. 1648/70
Jn., Henlow. AR 1683-4: 1/120
Jn., Riseley, gent. 1740/38
Jn., Northill (P/IX2 bundle missing). A 1748/1
Jn., Riseley, farmer. 1782/18
Jn., Harrold, farmer. 1787/41
Jn., Blunham. 1836/39
Luke, Eaton Socon, Wyboston, shepherd. 1668-9/184
Luke, Eaton Socon, shepherd. 1674/116
Mary, Eaton Socon, spins. AR 1670-1: 1/60d
Mary, Northill (P/IX2 admon missing). A 1757/14, 20
Mich., Wilshamstead, miller. 1707/29
Robt., Eaton Socon, Nether Staploe, husb. 1620/56
Robt., Henlow, maltster. AR 1686: 1/127
Sam., Harrold, miller. 1830/4
Sarah, Bedford, spins. 1804/8
Wm., Ravensden, yeo. 1697/19
Wm., Clapham, victualler. A 1730/36
Wm., Riseley, yeo. A 1756/20
Wm., Riseley, farmer. 1805/8
BONHAM, Thos., sen., Carlton. R 1528-9: 3/3d
BONICK, Hen., sen., Houghton Regis, Bidwell, husb. 1771/34
Sarah, Heath, wid. 1743/8
Wm., Houghton Regis, Sewell, shepherd. 1741/48
BONNER, BONOR, Edm., Maulden. AR 1672-3: 1/190
Eliz., Caddington, wid. 1559-60/208
Eliz., Lidlington, wid. 1724/31
Hen., Luton, innholder. 1761/45
Jn., Milton Bryan. R 1544: 11/48d

BONNER, BONOR continued
Jn., Milton Bryan, husb. 1586-7/153
Jn., Pulloxhill, husb. 1629/135
Jn., Lidlington, yeo. 1653/186
Jn., sen., Flitton, carp. 1662/102
Jn., Flitton, carp. AR 1687: 1/216d
Jn., Houghton Conquest, yeo. 1707/18
Jn., Houghton Conquest. A 1729-30/54
Jn., Flitton, carp. 1737/8
Jn., Toddington, higler. 1796/38
Martha, Silsoe, wid. 1731/74
Ralph, Flitton, husb. 1654/18
Rebecca, Houghton Conquest, wid. 1737/13
Ric., Toddington, Chalton, yeo. 1611-2/182
Ric., Milton Bryan, carp. 1639/92
Thos., Toddington, husb. R 1558: 14/34d
Thos., Lidlington. 1674/176
Thos., Lidlington, yeo. 1700/112
Wm., Milton Bryan. R 1527: 11/49d
Wm., Chalgrave, Tebworth. R 1558: 14/91d
Wm., Westoning. AR 1683: 1/208d
Wm., Flitton, carp. 1686-7/84
Wm., Houghton Conquest, yeo. 1715/45
Wm., Wilshamstead, yeo. A 1721/42
BONNET, Thos., Biggleswade, victualler. Bw A 1803/46
BONNEY, Jas., Kempston, lab. A 1852/6
BONNICK, William, Leighton Buzzard. Fac. A 1741: 9/87
BONO, BONOE, Edw., Riseley. 1665/36
Eliz., Riseley, wid. 1669-70/113
Jn., Eaton Socon. AR 1691: 1/84d
Mary, Riseley, wid. 1664/8
Thos., Riseley. 1660/42
Thos., Potton, hempman. A 1756/14
Thos., Potton, flaxdresser. 1756/29
BONSKIN, Arthur alias Bonskin, see Arthur
BOOL, see Ball
BOOMER, Charles, Elstow, bricklayer. 1758/27
BOONE, BOWNE, Agnes, Dean, Nether, wid. R 1565: 16/132d
Isaac, Ravensden, lab. 1779/38
Jn., Bedford St. Cuthbert, lab. 1636/41
Lucy, Ravensden, wid. A 1780/9
Thos., Wootton, lab. 1632/46
Thos., Dean, Nether. 1663/28
Thos., Thurleigh. A 1767/14
Wm., Dean, Nether. 1626/44

BOORIGE, see Burridge
BOOT, Jn., Eaton, Ford End, weaver. 1627/176
Jn., Eaton Socon, Ford End, lab. 1671/37
Jn., sen., Eaton Socon, Eaton Ford, shoemaker. 1727/66
BORANSKYLE, Jn., Wrestlingworth, clerk. A 1730/42
BORRELL, Ric., husb. Cranfield. R 1539-40: 6/15d
Robt., Cranfield. R 1539-40: 6/8d
see also Birrell
BORNE, see Bourne
BORROWE, BORROWS, see Burrowes
BOSGROVE, Jn., Renhold, gent. 1576-7/18
BOSSARD, Math., Higham Gobion. dairyman (deed of gift) (in bundle 1710). 1708/70
see also Bosworth
BOSSINGER, Wm., Kempston, grazier. 1670/187
BOSSINGHAM, Oliv., sen., Molesworth, Hunts., yeo. 1699-1700/75
BOSTOCK, Edw., Eaton Bray, lab. 1846/4
Robt., Westoning, husb. 1558/267
BOSTON, BOARSTONE, BOWLSTON, Alice, Eaton Socon, wid. 1661/368
Ann, Eaton Socon, Wyboston, spins. 1742-3/99
Edw., Roxton, husb. A 1727-8/42
Eliz., Colmworth, wid. R 1557: 13/136
Eliz., Eaton Socon, wid. 1699/2
Eliz., Roxton, wid. A 1732/12
Fra., Barton, farmer. A 1767/7
Fra., Westoning, Samshill. 1820/32
Geo., Colmworth. 1575/106
Geo., Colmworth, yeo. 1655-6/1
Geo., Eaton Socon, Wyboston, yeo. (bundle 1669). 1667/132
Geo., Eaton Socon, (old index only, admon missing). A 1726/11
Geo., Colmworth, farmer. 1738/20
Geo., Eaton Socon, Wyboston. A 1780/10
Hen., Eaton Socon. AR 1689-90: 1/83
Jn., Eaton Socon, Wyboston, yeo. 1669/20
Jn., Eaton Socon, Wyboston, yeo. AR 1670: 1/60
Jn., Eaton Socon, Wyboston, yeo. 1670/134
Jn., Eaton Socon, cordwainer. 1737/14
Jn., Biggleswade. Bw 1798/97
Jn., Eaton Socon, Wyboston, farmer. 1816/14
Jn., Eaton Socon, Wyboston, yeo. A 1837/17
Jn., Eaton Socon, Wyboston, yeo. 1837/54
Jn., Eaton Socon, Wyboston. A 1839/7
Len., Colmworth, yeo. 1673/37
Martha, Eaton Socon, Wyboston, spins. 1701/26
Mary, Eaton Socon, Wyboston, wid. 1711/98

BOSTON, BOARSTONE, BOWLSTON continued
Mary, Eaton Socon, wid. A 1748-9/19
Mary, Gt. Barford, wid. 1788/10
Ric., Staughton, Lt., lab. 1667/77
Ric., Eaton Socon, yeo. 1699-1700/71
Ric., Goldington, lab. 1747/19
Sam., Gt. Barford, innholder. 1737-8/63
Sam., Eaton Socon, Wyboston, yeo. 1741/14
Stephen, Colmworth. 1552?/308
Thos., Blunham, smith. R 1536: 4/53d
Thos., Staughton, Lt. R 1545: 11/80
Thos., Colmworth. R 1550: 12/94
Thos., Eaton Socon, yeo. 1660/220
Thos., Eaton Socon, Wyboston, yeo. 1687/59
Thos., Colmworth, yeo. 1704/46
Thos., Eaton Socon, Wyboston, yeo. 1743/68
Thos., Eaton Socon, Wyboston, yeo. 1750/50
Thos., Southill. A 1754/10
Thos., Oakley. (P/IX2 admon missing). A 1783/25
Thos., Stevington, farmer. A 1839/13
Ursula, Oakley, wid. 1841/27
Wm., Stevington, horse courser. 1760/4
Wm., Harrold, baker. 1803/33
Wm., Oakley, farmer. A 1839/14
BOSWELL, BAWSWELL, BOSWARD, Edw., Renhold, dairyman. A 1743-4/3
Eliz., Kempston, wid. A 1706/35
Jn., Marston. R 1551: 12/173d
Jn., Stagsden, lab. 1610-11/40
Jn., Harrold, yeo. 1685/56
Mary, Renhold, wid. 1743-4/82
Thos., Stagsden, husb. 1607/101
Thos., Stagsden, lab. 1671/79
Wm., Kempston, husb. 1723/60
BOSWORTH, BOTSWORTH, Anne, Marston, wid. 1660/92
Geo., Marston, yeo. 1615-16/120
Geo., Ampthill, coachman. 1714/97
Geo., Woburn, yeo. A 1781/21
Jeremiah, Marston, yeo. 1701-2/64
Jeremiah, Marston, yeo. 1725/26
Joh., Marston Moreteyne, yeo. 1720/58
Jn., Marston, yeo. 1617-18/216
Jn., Marston, yeo. 1642/44
Jn., Marston, dairyman. 1753/21
Jn., jun., Woburn. 1781/35
Jn., Marston, yeo. 1783/51

BOSWORTH, BOTSWORTH continued
Jn., Marston, farmer. 1827/61
Margt., Bedford St. John. 1663/66
Margt., Cople, wid. 1707/78
Mary, Salford, seamstress. 1629/119
Roger, Marston, husb. 1589/74
Thos., Marston, husb. 1701/66
Thos., Marston, yeo. A 1785/18
Thos., Pulloxhill, dairyman. 1787/34
Thos., Lidlington, victualler and carpenter. 1846/48
Wm., Marston, husb. 1554/261
Wm., Marston. 1615/160
Wm., Marston, lab. A 1714-15/48
Wm., Maulden, yeo. 1749/2
Wm., Luton, barber and peruke maker. 1799/36
see also Bossard
BOTALL, Thos., Stevington, vicar. R 1539-40: 6/18d
BOTELER, see Butler
BOTLE, BOTLYE, BOTTLEY, Martha, Tingrith, wid. 1649/4
Ric., Tingrith, tailor. 1649/81
Thos., Reach. 1559-60/74
Thos., Heath, tailor. 1649/65
Wm., Reach. 1591/116
see also Bottle
BOTSWORTH, see Bosworth
BOTTE, Jn., sen., Maulden, yeo. 1695/22
BOTTERILL, Eliz., Arlesey, wid. 1743/30
Eliz., Holwell, Cadwell, wid. of Thos. 1809/47
Thos., Arlesey, husb. 1742/55
BOTTESFORD, BOTTISFORD, see Bottsford
BOTTLE, Alexander, Keysoe, farmer. 1833/44
Geo., Keysoe, farmer. 1835/10
Ric., Tempsford, innholder. A 1742/31
see also Botle; see also Bowtle
BOTTLESTONE, BOTTLESTON, Robt., Henlow, husb. 1576/4
BOTTLEY, see Botle
BOTTOMLEY, Helen, Dunstable, wid. 1612/70
BOTTOMS, Ann, Gravenhurst, wid. 1778/15
BOTTSFORD, Ann, Woburn, wid. 1761/3
Edm., Chalgrave, yeo. 1746/3
Edm., Woburn, tallow chandler. A 1752/7
Edw., Woburn, tallow chandler. 1752/15
Eliz., Milton Brian, wid. 1715/30
Hen., Chalgrave, Tebworth, ploughwright. 1709/28
Jas., Eversholt, husb. A 1727/29

BOTTSFORD continued
Jos., Heath, wheelwright. 1742/42
Jos., Luton, baker. 1782/29
Mary, Woburn, wid. 1752/16
Nich., Battlesden, lab. 1663/33
Thos., Chalgrave, Wingfield. R 1523: 2/92d
Thos., Totternhoe, priest. R 1533: 3/102
Wm., Milton Brian, cordwainer. 1715/14
BOUGHTON, BOUTGHTON, BOWGHTON, Bart., Wootton. R 1533: 3/112d
Eliz., Lidlington. 1556/187
Jn., Kempston, yeo. 1599-1600/63
Jn., Kempston. 1624/103
Jn., Roxton, singleman. 1685-6/109
Jn., Husborne Crawley, yeo. 1749/40
Ric., Eaton Socon, Devilhoe, miller. 1627/152
Ric., Thos., Husborne Crawley, The Kilns, yeo. 1847/15
Robt., Kempston, tailor. 1605/116
Robt., Colmworth, Chanels End, yeo. 1667/49
Thos., Haynes. 1568/41
Thos., Colmworth. 1616/115
Thos., Roxton, maltster. 1618/153
Thos., Houghton Conquest, husb. 1770/4
Wm., Ampthill, (P/IX2 admon missing). A 1757/18
Wm., Eaton Socon. 1570/13
Wm., Ampthill, brickmaker. 1805/40
Wm., Ampthill, brickmaker. 1852/1
see also Bowden
BOULSTRED, BOULSTROD, Felix, Bedford St. Mary, linen draper. 1666/151
Hen., Ampthill. A 1719/23
Jn., Bedford, gent. 1683-4/118
Jos., Shefford. 1691/70
Jos., Warden, (P/IX2 admon missing). A 1757/12
Margery, Warden, wid. A 1762/2
Ric., Toddington, Chalton, yeo. R 1590: 21/55d
Sarah, Shefford, spins. A 1701/14
Thos., Shefford, grocer. 1701-2/30
see also Bowstred
BOULTON, see Bolton
BOUNDY, Thos., Shelton, clerk. 1691-2/147
Wm., Roxton, Chawston. 1565/19
see also Bundy
BOURN(E), BOARNE, BOORNE, BORNE, Agnes, Haynes, wid. 1617/300
Anth., Knotting, 1657/70
Anthony, Knotting, husb. 1587-8/156
Edw., Houghton Regis, lab. AR 1671: 1/142

BOURN(E), BOARNE, BOORNE, BORNE continued
Edw., Bedford St. John, Master of the Hospital of St. John, clerk. 1713-14/56
Edw., now residing in Bedford St. Mary, vicar of Thurleigh. 1734/7
Eliz., Riseley. 1827/19
Fra., Flitton. AR 1684: 1/211
Joan, Nether Shelton, Marston, wid. 1590-1/156
Jn., Knotting. 1615/164
Jn., Knotting. 1645/22
Jn., Marston, yeo. 1663/22
Jn., sen., Riseley. 1689/57
Jn., Biggleswade, innholder. Bw 1740/32i
Ric., Bedford, mercer. 1557/251
Stephen, Knotting, grazier. 1684/19
Thos., Haynes, yeo. 1584/174
Thos., Thurleigh, yeo. 1651/20
Thos., Marston, yeo. 1668/143
Thos., Eaton Socon, lab. A 1727/32
Thos., sen., Riseley, yeo. 1728/50
Thos., Riseley, yeo. 1740/59
Thos., Riseley, grazier. 1798/28
Wm., Wootton, yeo. 1555/88
Wm., Nether Shelton, Marston, yeo., 1583/149
Wm., Marston, husb. 1657/75
Wm., Houghton Regis, Bidwell, shepherd. 1734-5/14
Win., late of St. Neots. 1743/18
Winifred, Houghton Regis, Berry Corner, wid. 1679/26
BOUSKELL, Mary, Maulden, wid. 1753/15
Thos., Bedford St. Cuthbert, pipemaker. 1709/36
alias Arthur, see under Bowskin
BOWBAR, Thos., Felmersham, clerk. A 1732/24
BOWDEN, Jn., Potsgrove. 1697/8
Jn., Harrold, grocer. 1813/13
see also Boughton
BOWDLER, Eliz., Woburn, wid. 1827/51
Geo., Woburn, grocer. 1823/42
BOWER, Jas., late Shefford now Shillington, tanner. 1804/29
Jn., Sharnbrook. R 1506: 1/97d
Ric., Sharnbrook. R 1533: 3/114d
BOWERS, Hen., Shefford, currier. 1723/73
Sam., Kempston, cordwainer. 1716/19
Thos., Eaton Socon, dairyman. AR 1680: 1/71d
Thos., Bedford. A 1741/37
BOWLER, Cath., Hockliffe, spins. 1819/36
Chas., Hockliffe. 1806/33
Eliz., Leighton Buzzard, wid. 1679-80/102

BOWLER continued
Fra., Aspley Guise, victualler. A 1778/9
Hannah, Leighton Buzzard, wid. 1748/29
Jn., Woburn, blacksmith. 1758/54
Jn., Ampthill, blacksmith. 1786/26
BOWLING, John, Tingrith. R 1532: 3/66d
BOWMAN, BOMAN, Jn., Astwick, miller. A 1722/12
Jn., Leighton Buzzard, fellmonger. LB 1737/5
BOWNE, see Boone
BOWSKIN alias Bouskell, Geo, Maulden, yeo. 1719/61
BOWSTRED, BOUSTRED, Chas., Luton, yeo. 1818/32
Debora, Hyde. 1661/330
Edw., Dunstable, maltman. R 1549: 12/57
Elizabeth, Flitwick, wife of John, gent. 1664/56
Jn., Luton. R 1523: 2/49
Margt., Bedford St. Mary, wid. AR 1670-1: 1/3d
Wm., Toddington, Chalton, yeo. 1617/208
Wm., Toddington, Chalton, yeo. 1623/189
Wm., Flitwick, dairyman. 1706/45
Wm., Caddington, husb. 1715-16/91
see also Boulstred
BOWTLE, Jas., Eyeworth, farmer. A 1752/15
see also Bottle
BOWYER, BOYER, Edm., Houghton Conquest, farmer. 1812/7
Jn., Oakley, yeo. 1851/47
Robt., Stevington, matmaker. 1788/16
Simon, Stevington, (P/IX2 admon missing). A 1757/4
Thos., Yielden, husb. 1683/41
Thos., Stevington, grocer. 1780/8
Wm., Stevington, minister. 1746/8
Christy alias Bowyer, see Christy
BOWYS (?), see Stow otherwise Bowys
BOX, Wm., Bedford, trooper. A 1727/28
BOYCE, Hen., Eversholt. A 1826/1
Wm., Kempston, carpenter. A 1840/13
BOYDEN, Geo., Sutton, yeo. A 1734/13
BOYER, see Bowyer
BOYNAN, see Bunyan
BOYVILL, BOIVILL, Eliz., Bedford St. Mary. R 1550: 12/136
BRACE, BRASE, Ann, Toddington, spins. A 1703/7
Anth., Cardington, husb. 1608-9/7
Arnold, Staughton, Lt., lab. A 1703/32
Dan., Stondon, gent. 1671-2/20
Edw., Cople, yeo. 1704 in bun. 1716/94
Eliz., Barton, wid. 1677/22

BRACE, BRASE continued
Eliz., Millbrook, spins. AR 1671: 1/188
Eliz., Bedford St. Cuthbert, wid. 1728-9/115
Geo., Tempsford, gent. A 1737/28
Jas., Cople, yeo. 1615/216
Jn., Barton, yeo. 1618/41
Jn., Millbrook, yeo. 1659/94
Mary, Cople. 1717/57
Nich., Biddenham, lab. 1582/96
Rebecca, Bedford, wid. A 1821/8
Ric., Eaton Socon, Wyboston. R 1550: 12/145
Sam., Old Warden, dairyman. AR 1684: 1/122
Sarah, Bedford, wid. 1711/72
Sarah, Bedford, spins. 1741-2/60
Thos., Barton. 1582/48
Thos., Millbrook, husb. 1626/109
Thos., Barton. 1650/111
Thos., Old Warden, Hill. 1677/11
Thos., Eaton Socon, Goodwick, yeo. 1683/63
Thos., Millbrook, yeo. 1712/57
Thos., Bedford St. Paul, shoemaker. 1726/18
Thos., Wilshamstead, yeo. 1742/48
Wm., Millbrook, yeo. 1610/142, I 4/182
Wm., Willington, husb. 1613/217
Wm., Barton, yeo. 1633/185
Wm., Cople, farmer. AR 1681: 1/19d
Wm., Barton, yeo. 1686/1
Wm., Millbrook, yeo. AR 1686: 1/216
Wm., Millbrook, yeo. 1686/27
Wm., Gt. Barford yeo. A 1749/10
BRACYER, see Brazier
BRADDEY, see Brady
BRADDOCK, Hannah, Harrold, wid. 1821/10
BRADFORD, Ann, Leighton Buzzard, wid. Fac. 1704: 9/12
Hen., Eversholt, yeo. 1737/19
Ric., Eaton Socon, Eaton Ford, yeo. 1649-50/35
BRADIN, see Bradwin
BRADLEY, BRADLYE, Ann, Bedford St. Paul, wid. 1830/2
Chas., Bedford, gent. 1840/40
Eliz., Bedford, wid. 1838/6
Jas., sen., Bedford, victualler. 1745-6/45
Jas., Bedford, grocer and tallow chandler. 1773/40
Jn., Henlow. 1609-10/132
Jn., Bedford, grocer. 1808/34
Jos., Potton, victualler. 1735/31

BRADLEY, BRADLYE continued
Richard, Toddington. R 1500: 1/11
Thos., Totternhoe, mason. 1568-9/33
Wm., Sutton, yeo. (bundle 1593). 1592/57
Wm., Bletsoe, yeo. 1669/23
Wm., Wilden, schoolmaster. 1705/68
Wm., Podington, gent. A 1716-17/3
BRADSHAW, Cornelius, Caddington, Chaul End, yeo. 1796/11
Dan., Chalgrave, Tebworth, farmer. 1841/20
Jas., Houghton Regis, clerk. 1739/13
Jn., sen., Luton, Nether Crawley, yeo. 1767/13
Jn., Caddington, Chaul End, yeo. 1787/23
Mary, Luton, spins. A 1799/10
Phillip, Dean, miller. 1828/11
Thos., Gravenhurst, Over. 1618/110
Thos., Warden, lathrender. A 1729/34
Thos., Caddington, Chaul End, yeo. 1799/47
Thos., Leighton Buzzard, late 1st Lieutenant of H.M. Ship Pearl. LB 1810/48
Thos., Caddington, farmer. A 1846/3
Wm., Caddington, Chaul End, yeo. 1784/60
BRADWELL, Jn., Ridgmont. 1651/14
Jn., Shillington, West Mills, miller. 1702/8
Thos., sen., Eversholt. R 1501: 1/27d, 28
Thos., Barton, lab. A 1716/6
BRADWIN, BRADIN, Alice, Chalgrave, Tebworth, wid. 1669/78
Jn., Studham, tailor. 1669/38
Jn., Studham, husb. 1691/82
Jn., Caddington, Woodside, gardener. 1833/5
Thos., Studham, husb. 1610/110
BRADY, BRADDY, Gilbert, Sandy. 1644/90
Thos., Sandy, scrivenor (bundle 1655). 1645/72
BRAIN, Eliz., Stevington, wid. 1803/3
Jn., Arlesey lab. 1675/32
BRAMBLE, Eliz., Southill, Broome. 1610-11/30
Ric., Southill, weaver. 1610/20
BRAMPTON, Jn., Bedford, plumber and glazier. 1723/44
BRANDE, Christian, Turvey, spins. 1730/19
Jn., Dean, husb. 1553-4/246
Jn., Dean. 1564/49
BRANDON, Hen., sen., Marston, yeo. 1781/38
Sarah, Lidlington, wife of Hen. 1769/11
Wm., Lidlington, Brogborough Park, yeo. 1769/16
BRANDRETH, Neh., Houghton Regis, esq. A 1746/30
Thoswithan, Houghton Regis, Dr. of physick. A 1752/24
BRANKLIN, BRANKLYN, Geo., sen. Bedford St. Cuthbert, husb. 1672/117

BRANKLIN, BRANKLYN continued
Thos., Tempsford. 1670/148
Thos., Bedford St. Cuthbert. AR 1685-6: 1/28d
Wm., Elstow. AR 1671: 1/4d
BRANSOME, Thos., Chalgrave, Tebworth, farmer. 1823/28
Wm., Meppershall. 1831/39
BRASE, see Brace
BRASHIER, Jas., Goldington, farmer. 1836/2
BRASIER, see BRAZIER
BRASSINTON, Wm., Leighton Buzzard, cordwainer. LB 1807/38
BRAWN(E), Hen., Bletsoe, farmer. A 1742/25
Jn., Stondon, Over. husb. 1681/24
Jn., Shillington. AR 1687: 1/30
Jn., Biggleswade. BwA 1795/41
Martha, Stagsden, wid. 1790/30
BRAY, BREY, Andr., Caddington, husb. 1617/265
Chas., Wilshamstead, West Cotton, lab. 1631-2/231
Edm., Caddington. 1622/12
Edw., Caddington, husb. 1640/119
Edw., Tempsford. AR 1682-3: 1/117d
alias Hall, Ellen, Wilshamstead. 1580/223
Emme, Elstow, wid. 1658-9/77
(?)Geoffrey, Caddington. R 1506: 1/94d
Geoff., Markyate, yeo. 1581-2/15
Geo., Clifton, tailor. 1639/47
Bray alias Hall, Giles, Biggleswade, yeo. 1557/300
Hen., Elstow, yeo. 1660/191
Isabell, Caddington, Over Woodside, wid. 1607/115
Jn., Luton, glover. 1557/295
Jn., Turvey. 1727-8/98
Jn., Husborne Crawley. 1741/43
Jonathan, Caddington, yeo. AR 1682: 1/163, 169
Jonathan, Caddington, bach. AR 1684: 1/167
Priscilla, Stevington, wid. 1694-5/84
Ric., Caddington. R 1551-2: 12/177d
Ric., Luton. 1648-9/102
Thos., Caddington, Chorley End. R 1521: 2/96
Thos., sen., Caddington Bury. R 1536: 4/58d
Thos., Caddington, husb. R 1558: 14/92
Thos., sen., Caddington, Chaul End, yeo. 1592/50
Thos., Caddington, Bunsers, yeo. 1594/27
Thos., Clifton, husb. 1630/48
Thos., Arlesey, carrier. 1662/118
Thos., Stotfold, miller. 1755/6

BRAYBROOK, Ann, Mogerhanger, wid. 1839/1
Chas., Shefford, parchment maker. 1847/18
Geo., Sandy, Girtford, gardener. 1848/2
Jn., Mogerhanger, yeo. 1822/23
Thos., Eaton Socon. A 1778/17
Thos., Bedford, lab. 1792/19
Wm., Souldrop, husb. 1623/167
Wm., Souldrop, lab. 1689/56
BRAZIER, BRACYER, BRASIER, Ann, Barton, spins. 1855/24
Edw., Bromham. R 1539: 5/35
Fra., Southill, wid. A 1728/43
Hen., Luton, yeo. 1641/215
Jas., Haynes, grazier. 1805/34
Jn., Hexton, yeo. 1789/20
Jos., Barton, yeo. 1852/4
Luke, Barton, yeo., 1705/18
Luke, Barton, gent. 1765/41
Mary, Wilshamstead, spins. 1716/90
Ric., sen., Doddington, yeo. 1727/34
Ric., Cople, victualler. A 1738-9/6
Ric., Barton, farmer. 1812/40
Sam., sen., Barton, husb. 1747/27
Sam., Barton, yeo. 1771/62
Thos., Barton, husb. 1590/152
Thos., sen., Barton, yeo. 1637/90
Thos., Barton, yeo. 1728/17
Walt., Bedford, lab. 1728-9/90
Wm., Pulloxhill, yeo. 1657/62
Wm., Toddington, dairyman. 1774/54
Wm., Barton, yeo. A 1705/33
Wm., Barton, farmer. A 1778/2
BREAD, see Breed
BREALEY, Geo., Harrold, farmer. 1803/37
BREDE, see Breed
BREDON, see Breedon
BREDSELL, Ann, (parish torn off). 1679/1
Geo., Silsoe. R 1673: 1/190d
Geo., Silsoe, yeo. 1673/40
Wm., Warden, gardener. A 1722/2
Bredsell alias Collyer, see under Collyer
BREDYMAN, (?)Thos., Ampthill. 1557/352
BREED, BREAD, BREDE, Agnes, Westoning. 1638/5
Bernard, Westoning, yeo. 1694/15
Jane, Westoning, Sampshill, wid. 1719/57
Jn., Westoning, husb. 1585/26

BREED, BREAD, BREDE continued
Jn., Flitwick, East End, yeo. 1616/116
Jn., Westoning, yeo. 1657/59
Pettit, Biggleswade, yeo. Bw 1790/85
Thos., Westoning, Sampshill, yeo. 1716/3
BREEDON, BREDON, Benj., Bedford, clothier. 1703/45
BRETT, Jn., Husborne Crawley, gent. 1705/93
Jn., Luton, farmer. 1796/15
BREWER, Langley alias Brewer, see Langley
Alice, Harrold, spins. 1610/59
Geo., Harrold. 1602/11
Hen., Tempsford, weaver. 1603-4/82
Jn., Harrold. 1584/165
Jn., Wilden, tailor. 1621/215
Jn., Cranfield, lab. 1748/21
Lydia, Toddington. A 1797/8
Mary, Harrold, wid. 1628/43
Mary, Carlton, wid. 1678/129
Robt., Toddington, Chalton, farmer. 1797/28
Thos., Harrold, husb. 1620-1/12
Thos., Lidlington, yeo. 1771/67
Walter, Harrold, husb. 1561-2/146
Wm., Harrold, lab. 1608/70
Wm., Harrold, lab. AR 1687: 1/48d
Wm., Stopsley, yeo. 1805/16
Chapman alias Brewer, see under Chapman
BREWET, Wm., Odell. R 1544: 11/19d
BRIAN, BRYAN, Hester, Ampthill, wid. 1674/96
Sar., Luton, wid. 1742/69
Thos., Aspley Guise. 1557/240
see also Bryant
BRIAR, BRYER, BRIARS, BRIERS, Edw., Staughton, Lt., yeo. 1801/4
Jn., Thurleigh, poulterer. 1724/46
Jn., Bolnhurst, yeo. 1785/3
Wm., Salford, husb. 1602/35
BRICE, Ric., Keysoe, husb. 1770/49
Wm., sen., Haynes, lab. 1730/30
BRICHENO, Wm., jun., Pertenhall, farmer. 1842/6
Wm., Pertenhall, farmer. 1844/41
BRICKETT, Eliz., Harlington, wid. A 1756/17
John, Markyate Street, yeo. 1740/89
Nath., Harlington, yeo. 1755/7
Thos., Dunstable. 1573/10
Wm., Toddington. A 1763/18

BRIDE, Edw., Houghton Conquest, yeo. 1663/68
Edw., (old index "Docket mislaid"). A 1708/36
Edw., (old index "Docket mislaid"). A 1710/6
BRIDEN, see Brydon
BRIDGE, alias Bird, Thos., Husborne Crawley, vicar. 1579/142
Wm., Leagrave, Lewsey. 1598/99
BRIDGEMAN, Wm., Luton, yeo. 1729/67
BRIDLE, see Brydall
BRIERLY, Jn., Eaton Socon, victualler. A 1744/2
BRIGGS, BRYGGS, Alice, Luton. R 1500: 1/136
Fra., Leagrave, yeo. 1674/152
Hen., Souldrop, husb. 1652/69
Hen., Campton, Stringer, carp. 1839/38
Jas., Leagrave, yeo. 1718/55
Jarvis, Tilbrook, yeo. 1743/59
Joan, (parish torn off). c1670/242
Jn., Houghton Regis. 1558-9/321
Jn., Dunstable, yeo. 1644/101
Jonas, Leagrave, Marsh yeo. 1673/33
Judith, Dunstable, wid. A 1724/46
Rebecca, Dunstable, wid. 1670-1/218
Ric., Dunstable, innholder. 1668/169
Robt., Houghton Regis, husb. 1588/25
Robt., Leagrave, husb. 1667/72
Thos., Dunstable. AR 1672: 1/143
Thos., Luton. AR 1675: 1/149d
Wm., Felmersham, shepherd. 1602/48
Wm., Colmworth. 1766/63
BRIGHT, Edw., Houghton Regis, lab. 1705/19
Jos., sen., Toddington, pig dealer. 1803/7
Wm., Ampthill, innholder. 1852/26
BRIGHTEN, Jn., Biddenham. 1632/33
BRIGHTMAN, Andrew, Woburn, lab. 1760/25
Thos., Maulden, sheepdealer. A 1845/5
Wm., Biggleswade, butcher. BwA 1758/17
BRIGNALD, Jn., Elstow, lab. 1617-18/160
BRIMLEY, Jane, Cardington, Harrowden, wid. 1825/39
Jn., Cople, 'The Hoos'. 1780/38
Jos., Willington, farmer. 1814/2
Sam., sen., Cardington, husb. 1745-6/38
Sam., Cardington, farmer. A 1771/9
Thos., Cople, yeo. 1748/48
Thos., Cardington, Harrowden, farmer. 1788/1
BRINGHURST, Isaac, Toddington, Doctor in Divinity. 1697/42
BRINKLER, Salome, Cranfield, innkeeper. A 1855/19

BRINKLEY, Eliz., Sandy, wid. 1718/63
Frances, Sandy, wife of Thos. A 1713/12
Geoff, Eversholt. AR 1671: 1/187d
Thos., Sandy, fellmonger. 1718/64
BRINKLOW, BRENCKELOW, Amelia, Aspley Guise. A 1831/13
Hen., sen., Flitwick, victualler. 1853/13
Jeff., Eaton Bray, husb. 1729/59
Jn., Sundon, husb. 1570-1/31
Jn., Milton Brian, butcher. 1639-40/149
Jn., Eaton Bray, yeo. 1683-4/108
Jn., Eversholt, yeo. 1800/22
Jn., Stanbridge, yeo. LB 1820/5
Jos., Harlington, Wood End, husb. A 1719/18
Jos., Eversholt, yeo. 1795/32
Ralph, Dunstable, butcher. 1587/99
Ric., Eaton Bray, husb. 1774/46
Ric., Flitwick, yeo. 1829/36
Robt., Eaton Bray. 1698/72
Roger, Milton Brian, yeo. 1792/14
Susannah, Hockliffe, wid. 1838/35
Wm., Toddington, Chalton. R 1546: 12/15d
BRINTON, Wm., Odell. 1554/144
BRISCOE, Jos., ("old index docket mislaid"). A 1710/1
Judith, Clifton. 1684/82
BRIST, Thos., Campton, lab. 1676/163
BRISTOW, Mary, Dunton, wid. A 1772/13
Tim., Meppershall, Polehanger, gent. 1764/15
BRITAIN, BRETEN, BRITTAIN, BRITTEN, BRITTIN, BRITTINE, BRITTYNE, BRYTTEN, Ann, Sandy, wid. AR 1688: 1/130d
Ann, Sandy. AR 1690: 1/133d
Ann, Potton (no parish given in will). 1820/8, I 4/238
Ann, Aspley Guise, wid. 1836/32
Annes, Sandy, Girtford, wid. 1602/18
Annise, Eversholt, wid. 1557/332
Baron, Sandy, gent. A 1729/21
Bartholomew, Biddenham, husb. 1580/221
Brown, Aspley Guise, carp. 1834/46
Dan., Stotfold, carp. A 1737/33
Edmund, Eversholt, husb. 1557/342
Edm., Podington, servant. 1566/70
Edw., Sandy, yeo. 1681/14
Eliz., Stotfold, wid. 1635/48
Eliz., Stagsden, spins. 1755/23
Eliz., Biggleswade. Bw 1789/82
Helen, Harlington, wid. 1615-16/108

BRITAIN, BRETEN, BRITTAIN, BRITTEN, BRITTIN, BRITTINE, BRITTYNE, BRYTTEN continued
Hen., Bedford, butcher. 1558/24
Jas., Pavenham. 1644/134
Jn., Stotfold. R 1499: 1/133
Jn., Oakley, husb. 1560/81
Jn., Harlington, lab. 1608/56
Jn., Stotfold. 1622/43
Jn., sen., Houghton Regis, husb. 1669-70/112
Jn., Houghton Regis, yeo. 1699/48
Jn., Sandy, gent. 1732/50
Jn., Turvey, yeo. 1756/54
Jn., Carlton, cordwainer. 1776/7
Jn., Chellington, farmer. 1827/35
Jos., Flitton, yeo. A 1724/26
Kitty, Aspley Guise, wid. A1855/12
Lettice, Bedford St. Paul. 1631-2/2
Mary, Houghton Regis, wid. 1707/42
Mary, Dunstable, spins. 1733/38
Mich., Henlow, millwright. 1632/44
Mich., Eaton Socon, Wyboston. 1652-3/86
Nich., Leighton Buzzard. 1579-80/218
Reg., Bedford St. Paul. 1631-2/3
Ric., Cranfield, husb. R 1533: 3/96
Ric., Biddenham. 1558/77
Ric., Knotting. 1559/173
Ric., Houghton Conquest. 1585/29
Ric., Sandy, carp. 1753/38
Ric., Stotfold, farmer. 1764/34
Ric., Biddenham, lab. A 1788/1
Ric., Northill, Brook End, yeo. 1814/15
Ric., Staughton, Lt., yeo. A 1825/12
Robt., Maulden, lab. R 1611-12: 29/1
Sam., Eaton Socon, roper. 1693-4/121
Sam., Chalgrave, Tebworth, lab. 1813/2
Simon, Bedford St. Paul, butcher. 1560/165
Thos., Tempsford. R 1528: 2/191
Thos., Sandy, Girtford. R 1533: 3/97d
Thos., Sandy, Girtford. 1558/284
Thos., Leighton Buzzard. 1561/231
Thos., Oakley, husb. 1599-1600/131
Thos., Stotfold. 1623/166
Thos., Sandy, Girtford, yeo. 1638/137
Thos., Harlington, lab. (bundle 1665). 1666/94
Thos., Thurleigh, lab. AR 1670: 1/60

BRITAIN, BRETEN, BRITTAIN, BRITTEN, BRITTIN, BRITTINE, BRITTYNE, BRYTTEN continued
Thos., Chellington, shepherd. A 1741/15
Thos., Chellington, farmer. 1803/2
Thos., Aspley Guise, yeo. 1811/22
Thos., Potton. 1818/46, I 4/230
Thos., Keysoe, farmer & grazier. 1838/37
Walt., Blunham, shepherd. 1636/32
Warine, Blunham, lab. I 1619: 4/59
Wm., Sandy, Girtford. R 1505: 1/92
Wm., Henlow. R 1534: 4/6
Wm., Knotting. 1610/116
Wm., Thurleigh. 1621/178
Wm., Houghton Regis, yeo. 1681/5
Wm., Sharnbrook. 1721/44
Wm., Wootton, chandler. 1737/5
Zaccheus, Houghton Regis, late of London, cordwainer. 1766/33
BRITCH, BRYCH, Thos., Potton. R 1500: 1/14
BRITTNELL, Sam., Eversholt, lab. 1740-1/72
Sam., Eversholt, bach. A 1741-2/30
Wm., Cranfield, yeo. 1657-8/255
Wm., Cranfield, yeo. AR 1678: 1/201d(2)
BROAD, Jn., Maulden. 1592/73
Ric., Millbrook, yeo. 1697/133
Wm., Millbrook, husb. 1599-1600/127
Wm., Millbrook, husb. 1616/64
Wm., sen., Millbrook, yeo. 1666/303
BROADFIELD, Sam., Felmersham. 1786/43
BROADHEAD, Luke, Biggleswade, yeo. Bw 1825/130
BROADLEY, BRAWDLIE, Agnes, Poddington, wid. 1616/79
BROADNECK, Jn., Woburn. A 1701/8
BROADWAY, BRODWAY, Geo., Stagsden, dairyman. 1679-80/88
alias Parsons, Harry, Westoning. 1573/115
BROCKET, Edw., Dunton, Millow, yeo. 1598/94
Edw., Dunton, Millow. 1660-1/133
Edw., sen., Dunton, yeo. 1661/291
Eliz., Limbury, wid. 1784/58
Eliz., Blunham. A 1831/1
Hen., Limbury, yeo. 1784/50
Jn., Blunham, Chalton, lab. 1847/45
BROCKIS, Edw., sen., Aspley Guise, yeo. 1700/126
Edw., Aspley Guise, husb. 1730/89
Jos., Aspley Guise, lab. A 1714-15/47
BRODWAY, see Broadway
BROGDEN, Mary Eliz., Bedford St. Peter. 1829/39

BROGRAVE, Nich., Wrestlingworth. R 1544: 11/25
BROMALD, Thos., Riseley. R 1517: 1/253
BROMFORD, Hugh, Wilshamstead, ploughwright. 1617-18/162
BROMHALL, Agnes, Stevington, wid. 1636/18
Gilbert, Melchbourne, carp. 1637/111
Jn., Stevington? 1601/81
Margt., Stevington, wid. 1666/145
Oliv., Sandy, Girtford, gent. 1663/3
Robt., Stevington, gent. 1658-9/219
see also Bromsall
BROMHAM, BROUMHAM, Eliz., Clifton, wid. 1617/240
Jn., sen., Clifton. R 1530: 3/33
Wm., Clifton, miller. 1612/45
BROMSALL, BROWNSALL, BROWNSELD, BRUMSALE, BRUNSALE,
Agnes, Sandy, Girtford, gentlewoman. 1635-6/39
Alice, Sandy, Beeston. 1610/107
Eliz., Blunham, wid. 1654/17
Eliz., Sandy, spins. 1675/11
Eliz., Bedford St. Mary, wid. A 1786/10
Geo., Blunham, tailor. 1607/94
Jane, Blunham, wid. 1613/167
Joan, Bedford St. John, spins. 1643/80
Jn., sen., Sandy, Beeston. R 1536-7: 4/76d
Jn., Blunham. 1620/96
Jn., Sandy, Beeston, yeo. 1636/31
Jn., Sandy, Girtford, yeo. 1689-90/79
Jn., Sandy, Beeston, husb. 1693-4/114
Jn., Biggleswade, grocer. A 1706/6
Ralph, Sandy, Beeston. R 1504: 1/42d
Ric., Sandy. R 1536-7: 4/88d
Robt., Sandy, Girtford, weaver. 1586/90
Robt., Sandy, yeo. 1665-6/87
Thos., Bromham. R 1513: 1/116
Thos., sen., Sandy, Beeston. R 1520-1: 2/166d
Thos., Sandy, Beeston. R 1537: 5/2
Thos., Sandy, yeo. 1560/166
Thos., Northill, Beeston, husb. 1654/159
Thos., Mogerhanger. AR 1687-8: 1/130d
Wm., Sandy, Girtford, yeo. 1674/175
Wm., Sandy, Girtford, gent. 1689-90/78
Wm., Bedford, baker & alderman. 1731/27
see also Bromhall; see also Brownsall
BROMSGROVE, Wm., Odell. 1578/81
BROOK, Mydesent, Tilsworth. R 1521-2: 2/108d

BROOKS, Adery, otherwise Brooks, Elton, Hunts. A 1789/4
Alice, Felmersham, wid. 1633-4/189
Ann, Cardington, Harrowden, wid. 1767/21
Ann, Cople, wid. 1818/4
Anne, Stevington, wid. 1621/165
Eliz., Kempston, wid. A 1716/35
Eliz., Felmersham, wid. 1722/34
Eliz., Felmersham, wid. A 1766/29
Geo., Cranfield, yeo. 1816/5
Geo., Cople, farmer. 1817/24
Hen., Meppershall, Woodhall, yeo. 1579-80/181
Hen., Carlton, husb. 1633/196
Isaac, sen., Shillington, weaver. 1776/13
Joan, Meppershall, wid. 1589/75
Jn., Turvey, husb. 1608/65
Jn., Chicksands, yeo. 1724/62
Jn., Kempston, Church End, shoemaker. 1819/39, I 4/236
Jn., Cranfield, grocer. A 1732/15
Jn., Eversholt, carpenter. A 1802/19
Lawr., Shillington, weaver. 1639/54
Ric., Felmersham. 1677/20
Ric., Clophill, husb. 1719/44
Ric., Shillington, yeo. 1792/39
Ric., Felmersham, farmer. 1818/12
Robt., Kempston. 1615/209
Steph., Clophill, butcher. 1798/39
Thos., Felmersham, lab. 1706/70
Thos., Clophill, auctioneer. 1809/22
Wm., Eaton Socon, Deviloe, lab. 1615/180
Wm., Cardington, Harrowden, yeo. 1755/5
Wm., Clophill, butcher. 1787/35
BROTHER, BROTHERS, Knight alias Brother, see Knight
Eliz., Eggington, wid. LB R 1537: 1/2d
Ric., Luton. R 1506: 1/100
Thos., Ampthill. R 1546: 11/218d
BROTHERTON, Eliz., Linslade, Bucks., wife of John, grazier. 1750/4
Jas., Sutton. 1667/38
Jas., Husborne Crawley. AR 1689-90: 1/217d
Jn., Sutton. 1614/46
Jn., Sutton, yeo. 1669/40
Jn., Husborne Crawley, cordwainer. 1803/32
Jn., Husborne Crawley, cordwainer. 1823/33
Lawr., Husborne Crawley. R 1558: 14/49
Mary, Husborne Crawley. 1829/26
Thos., jun., Husborne Crawley. 1624/86

BROTHERTON continued
Thos., Husborne Crawley, shoemaker. 1629/137
Thos., Sutton, yeo. 1670/192
Thos., Husborne Crawley, cordwainer. 1759/48
Thos., Husborne Crawley, weaver. 1782/54
BROTHWOOD, Jn., Henlow, miller. 1605-6/82
BROUGH, BROFFE, alias Forner, Nich., Bedford St. Paul, tailor. 1612-13/121
Wm., Bedford St. Paul, innholder. 1602/63
BROUGHTON, BROWTIN, Ric., Eaton Bray, blacksmith. A 1704/16
Robt., Sandy, yeo. 1714/69
Thos., Marston, lab. 1611/149
Wm., Wilshamstead. AR 1682: 1/21
BROUMHAM, see Bromham
BROWN, BROUNE, BROWNE, Collins alias Brown, see under Collins
Adam., Langford, yeo. 1615-16/136
Allen, Cardington, cordwainer. A 1780/11
Allin, Cardington, cordwainer. 1780/33
Ann, Sandy, wid. A 1728/25
Ann, Shillington, wid. 1786/15
Anne, Bedford St. Paul (bundle 1638). 1635/159
Annise, Aston Clinton, Bucks., wid. 1565/216
Chris., Melchbourne, yeo. 1660-1/226
Dan., Podington, husb. 1715-16/86
Edith, Eaton Socon, wid. 1743/36
Edw., Stotfold, weaver. 1632/28
Edw., Lt. Barford, shepherd. 1693/133
Edw., Wrestlingworth. 1696/121
Edw., Henlow, husb. 1738/82
Edw., husb. A 1712/41
Eliz., Riseley, spins. 1625-6/133
Eliz., Willington, spins. 1856/3
Eliz., Biggleswade, Stratton, wid. of Jn. Bw 1725/18
Eliz., Harrold, wid. A 1724/11
Ellen, Cardington. A 1707/31
Eunis, Eaton, weaver. 1687/48
Fra., Milton Bryan, lab. 1714/67
Fra., Maulden, victualler. 1814/45
Geo., sen., Melchbourne, husb. 1598/82
Geo., Riseley, lab. 1637/139
Geo., Eaton Bray, yeo. 1744/32
Geo., Eaton Bray, wheelwright. 1763/42
Grace, Eversholt. 1663/107
Gregory, Melchbourne, husb. 1645/42
Gregory, Melchbourne. 1674/99
Gregory, Melchbourne. AR 1674: 1/64

BROWN, BROUNE, BROWNE continued
Hannah, Dunton, spins. 1778/42
Hen., Kempston, husb. 1577/56
Hen., Sandy, Beeston, bach. 1670-1/215, 216
Hen., Harrold. A 1712/13
Hen., sen., Dunton, farmer. 1784/54
Hen., Dunton, victualler. 1801/12
Hen., Langford, farmer. 1817/20
Hen., Houghton Regis, yeo. A 1716/21
Henry, Melchbourne. 1557/337
Jas., Potton, bricklayer. A 1761/8
Jas., Milton Ernest, farmer. 1799/6
Jas., Bedford, mealman. A 1846/9
Joan, Bedford St. Cuthbert, wid. 1633/151
Jn., Knotting. R 1504: 1/41d
Jn., Melchbourne. 1538/3
Jn., Steppingley, husb. 1617/175
Jn., Bedford St. Paul, mason. I 1619/20: 4/58
Jn., Bedford. I 1619: 4/103
Jn., Bedford, carpenter. 1621-2/134
Jn., Cardington, Fenlake, tailor. 1633/170
Jn., sen., Kempston, gent. 1635-6/34
Jn., no parish given. 1648/84
Jn., Melchbourne. 1651/125
Jn., Lidlington, bricklayer. AR 1671: 1/188
Jn., Lidlington, bricklayer. 1675/20
Jn., Tempsford, husb. 1682/101
Jn., Steppingley, yeo. 1687/82
Jn., Eaton Socon, dairyman. 1704/68
Jn., Biggleswade, Stratton, dairyman. Bw A 1723/5, I
Jn., Eversholt, Tyrrells End, yeo. 1743-4/83
Jn., sen., Cardington, carp. 1749/22
Jn., Westoning, lab. 1764/60
Jn., Dunton, yeo. R 1770/20
Jn., Milton Ernest, yeo. 1782/13
Jn., Cardington, carp. 1787/22
Jn., Stotfold, farmer. 1795/33
Jn., Milton Ernest. A 1808/6
Jn., Croxton, Cambs., farmer. 1812/14
Jn., Eaton Bray, victualler, blacksmith, cutler. 1812/21
Jn., Luton, hurdlemaker. 1828/5
Jn., Dunton, farmer & publican. 1839/13
Jn., St. Albans, Herts., now Bedford. 1844/50
Jonathan, late Upwell, Cambs., now Eaton Socon, gent. 1845/5
Jos., Barton, weaver. 1716/27

BROWN, BROUNE, BROWNE continued
Jos., Shillington, cordwainer. 1761/11
Lydia, Pavenham, wid. 1793/36
Manning, Milton Ernest, farmer. 1819/37
Marger, Tillbrook, wid. 1599/152
Marian, Kempston. R 1545: 11/82
Mary, Odell, wid. 1563/78
Mary, Odell. 1636/43
Mary, Langford. A 1835/9
Mary, Farndish, wid. 1842/51
Nath., Luton, Greathampstead, husb. 1738/80
Nich., Sutton, bricklayer. 1726-7/85
Nich., Shefford, butcher. R 1776/35
Nich., Potton, bricklayer. 1845/2
Paul, Melchbourne, carp. 1681/32
Peter, Bedford St. Peter, yeo. 1849/22
Ric., Kempston. R 1568: 17/123
Ric., Campton. 1560/167
Ric., Bolnhurst. 1736/54
Ric., Podington, farmer & maltster. 1759/21
Ric., Totternhoe, victualler. R 1770/21
Ric., Cranfield. A 1757/10
Ridley, Yielden, dairyman. A 1713/38
Robt., Colmworth. 1632/64
Robt., Bedford St. Cuthbert. 1674/140
Robt., Bedford St. Cuthbert. AR 1674: 1/8
Robt., Luton, innholder. 1715/27
Robt., Willington, farmer. 1844/51
Salem, Luton. A 1786/3
Sam., Aspley Guise, baker. 1710-11/31
Sam., Harrold, cordwainer. 1771/57
Sam., Potton, weaver. R 1781/20
Samuel, Shillington, victualler. 1720/47
Sarah, Potton, wid. 1791/29
Sarah, Stony Stratford, Bucks., wid. 1824/1
Sarah, Luton, wid. A 1829/3
Sarah, Bedford, spins. 1853/39
Sarah, Silsoe. A 1755/13
Simeon, Langford, farmer. 1846/5
Susannah, Eaton Socon, wid. 1840/13
Thos., Houghton Regis. R 1530: 3/27
Thos., Bedford, fishmonger. R 1532: 3/62d
Thos., Goldington. R 1539: 5/35
alias Jennings, Thos., Potsgrove. R 1547: 12/8
Thos., Flitwick. 1606/60

BROWN, BROUNE, BROWNE continued
Thos., Thurleigh, husb. 1613/129
Thos., Cardington, Harrowden, mason. 1617/281
Thos., Bedford, brickmaker. 1644-5/113
Thos., Melchbourne. 1655-6/4
Thos., Melchbourne. 1654/23
Thos., Clifton. 1680/80
Thos., Luton, Crawley Green, gent. 1685/80
Thos., Renhold, lab. 1690/20
Thos., Renhold. AR 1690: 1/83d
Thos., Yielden. 1692/38
Thos., Bedford. 1695/43
Thos., Bedford, carrier. 1703-4/17
Thos., Flitwick, husb. 1704/58
Thos., Maulden, carp. 1713/70
Thos., Bedford St. Cuthbert, miller. 1733/21
Thos., Dunton, yeo. A 1736/14
Thos., Dunton. A 1767/17
Thos., Dunton. A 1769/31
Thos., Aspley, yeo. 1781/56
Thos., sen., Roxton, yeo. 1809/41
Thos., Dunton, Lodge Farm, farmer. 1825/2
Thos., Dunton, Church End, farmer. 1826/14
Thos., Langford, yeo. 1829/19
Thos., Sutton, farmer. 1834/38
Wm., Pertenhall. R 1505-6: 1/71
Wm., Toddington, singleman. 1559/147
Wm., Kempston. 1615/184
Wm., Melchbourne, lab. 1619/213, I 4/166
Wm., Milton Brian, lab. 1662/125
Wm., Bedford St. Cuthbert, gardener. 1667/53
Wm., Eaton Socon, Wyboston, lab. 1677-8/80
Wm., sen., Eaton Socon, weaver. 1727/101
Wm., Aspley Guise, yeo. 1761/35
Wm., Henlow, yeo. 1768/5
Wm., Dunton, farmer (bond). 1778
Wm., Sundon. A 1785/12
Wm., Bedford, haberdasher. 1797/39
Wm., sen., Westoning, lab. 1804/7
Wm., Luton, gent. 1807/37
Wm., Tilbrook, farmer. 1821/8
Wm., Dunton, farmer. 1834/25
Wm., Barton, yeo. 1836/42
Wm., Farndish, farmer. 1848/43

BROWNELL, BROWNILL, Jn., sen., Blunham. 1579/127
Jn., Cople, tailor. 1629/1
BROWNING, Ben., Cockayne Hatley, husb. 1731/58
Ben., Houghton Conquest, yeo. 1784/19
Eliz., Cockayne Hatley, wid. 1737/22
Jn., Dean, farmer. A 1737/34
Jn., Edworth, farmer. 1793/10
Jn., Tempsford, yeo. 1795/49
Jn., jun., Keysoe, farmer. 1842/18
Oliv., Biggleswade, carp. 1672-3/169
Thos., Tempsford, yeo. A 1801/8
BROWNSALL, Cicely, Roxton, wid. 1630-1/135
see also Bromsall
BROWTIN, see Broughton
BROXSON, Dan., Bedford, lab. AR 1684: 1/25
BRUCE, Jane, no parish given, ?Luton. 1606-7/12
Jn., Eaton Socon, lab. 1629/116
Jn., Wilshamstead. A 1706/44
Jn., Wilshamstead, shepherd. 1706/94
Jn., Wilshamstead, cordwainer. 1720/106
Jn., Eaton Socon, farmer. A 1729/49
Mary, Wilshamstead, wid. 1758/5
Mary, St. Neots, Hunts., wid. 1766/61
Mary, Bishop's Hatfield, midwife & wid. 1772/19
Robt., Eaton Socon, farmer. A 1722-3/36
Thos., Luton. R 1530-1: 3/38d
Thos., Wilshamstead, tailor. 1685/62
Wm., Luton, yeo. 1558/63
Wm., Luton, ?Nether Crawley. 1593/24
BRUED, Moses, Marston, servant. 1729/72
BRUGIS, Doro., Eaton Bray, wid. 1717/13
Thos., Eaton Bray, tallow chandler. 1716/57
BRUNSALE, see Bromsall
BRUNT, Thoda, Northill, spins. 1839/25
Sam., Biggleswade, Holme, farmer. Bw A 1832/73
BRUTON, Geo., Eyeworth, clerk. 1668/133
John, no place. 1553/168
BRUTY, Jn., Sutton, yeo. 1605/126, I
BRYANT, Anne, Gravenhurst, wid. 1716/47
Emma, Meppershall, wid. AR 1681: 1/114
Jeremiah, sen., Biggleswade, innholder. Bw 1777/67, I
Jn., Meppershall. AR 1678: 1/108
Jos., Eversholt, Potters End, cordwainer. 1825/33
Jos., Elstow, baker. 1837/14
Sam., Bedford St. Peter, bricklayer. A 1854/9

BRYANT continued
Thos., Gravenhurst, Over, Ion, lab. 1602/70
Thos., Leighton Buzzard. AR 1678: 1/156d
Thos., Cranfield, lab. 1687/20
Thos., Gravenhurst, Over, weaver. 1706/17
Thos., Bedford. carp. & victualler. 1819/32
see also Brian
BRYDALL, BRIDLE, Eliz., Ampthill, wid. 1771/23
Geo., Lidlington, yeo. 1716/85
BRYDON, BRIDEN, Amy, Caddington, wid. 1633/153
Dan., Markyate, wheelwright. 1674/115
Jn., Caddington. 1622/66
Jn., Toddington, Chalton, victualler. 1811/25
Kath., Husborne Crawley, wid. 1554/164
Thos., sen., Markyate Street, yeo. 1692/60
BRYER, see Briar
BUCKBY, Edm., Luton. R 1543: 6/138d
BUCKINGHAM, BOCKNAM, BUCKNAM, Eliz., Blunham, wid. 1557/298
Eliz., Flitwick, wid. 1705/75
Gabriel, Tilsworth, husb. 1699/29
Hen., parish torn off. 1670/237
Hen., Houghton Regis. 1696/109
Jas., Barton. R 1536: 4/611
Jemima, Luton, singlewoman. 1844/18
Joan, Tilsworth, wid. 1669/26
Jn., Barton. 1562/118
Jn., Tilsworth, husb. 1607/139
Jn., Harlington. 1640/101
Jn., sen., Dunstable, yeo. 1667/93
Jn., Houghton Regis, Sewell. 1669/12
Jn., Chalgrave, Wingfield, yeo. 1681/26
Jn., Chalgrave, Wingfield, yeo. 1685-6/114
Jos., Houghton Regis. A 1736/13
Judith, Eversholt, wid. A 1725/29
Luke, Totternhoe, blacksmith. 1762/17
Ric., Houghton Regis, yeo. 1684/67
Ric., Houghton Regis, Sewell, husb. 1616/139
Ric., Houghton Regis, yeo. 1679-80/104
Robt., Blunham, husb. 1554?/165
Sar., Houghton Regis, Sewell, wid. 1742/22
Sarah, Houghton Regis, wid. 1743/31
Thos., Ampthill, yeo. 1700/127
Thos., Houghton Regis, Sewell, bricklayer. 1730/6
Wm., Reach. 1586/139
Wm., Westoning, yeo. 1618/93

BUCKINGHAM, BOCKNAM, BUCKNAM continued
Wm., Harlington, husb. 1623/152
Wm., Westoning, yeo. 1640/79
BUCKLAND, Jn., Dean, Upper. 1683/16
Simon, Dean, Upper. 1710/60
BUCKLE, BUCKLES, Hen., Dunstable, painter. 1854/23
Nich., Lidlington. 1588/31
Sam., Bedford, glover. A 1702/10
Sam., Elstow. 1773/5
Thos., Cranfield, husb. 1754/42
Wm., Willington, farmer. 1828/7
BUCKLEY, Ric., Odell, yeo. A 1711/13
BUCKMASTER, ?, Totternhoe. 1577-8/217
Andrew, Eaton Bray, yeo. 1598-9/136
Ann, Chalgrave, Wingfield, wid. 1720-1/98
Ann, Houghton Regis, spins. 1761/40
Edm., Eaton, yeo. 1640/55
Edwin, Eaton Bray, gent. 1718/77
Jn., jun., Eaton, yeo. 1602/30
Jn., Caddington, Oynions, husb. 1667/58
Jn., Woburn, bodice maker. 1678/111
Jn., Eaton Bray, schoolmaster. A 1750/20
Jn., Houghton Regis, gent. 1776/15
Martin, Totternhoe, carp. 1574/30
Mary, Houghton Regis, wid. 1728/27
Mary, Houghton Regis, wid. 1782/30
Ric., Eaton Bray, yeo. R 1577-8: 19/45
Ric., Eaton, yeo. 1624/58
Thos., Totternhoe, yeo. 1609/150
Thos., Chalgrave, Wingfield, husb. 1699/24
Thos., Totternhoe, Doo Little Mill, miller. 1816/41
Wm., Chalgrave, Wingfield, husb. 1670/143
Wm., Houghton Regis, husb. 1718/35
Wm., Houghton Regis, yeo. 1760/35
BUCKNAM, see Buckingham
BUCKOKE, Thos., Turvey, clerk, minister of Turvey. 1607/79
BUDD, Ann, Bedford, wid. 1837/4
Hen., Aspley Guise, yeo. 1661/343
BUFF, Dan., Cockayne Hatley. 1695/16
BUFFIN, Hen., Heath and Reach. LB A 1767/17
BULL(E), Ann, Ecton, Northants. A 1843/14
Edw., Milton Ernest. 1649/14
Edw., Wilden, cordwainer. 1827/55
Edw., Thurleigh, farmer. AR 1685: 1/78
Edw., old index, "docket mislaid". A 1708/12

BULL(E) continued
Edw., Keysoe, lab. A 1728/44
Eliz., Cardington, wid. 1687/83
Geo., Luton, matmaker. 1763/25
Geo., Woburn. A 1811/20
Giles, Thurleigh. 1700/115
Hen., Bedford, yeo. 1759/24
Hen., sen., Wilden, yeo. 1793/31
Hen., Wilshamstead, farmer. A 1809/9
Jas., Pavenham, matmaker. 1778/23
Joan, Stagsden, wid. A 1722/29
Jn., Cardington, husb. 1556/193
Jn., Cardington, Cotton. 1576/34
Jn., Potton, lab. 1603/130
Jn., Pavenham, farmer. 1701/25
Jn., Milton Ernest, farmer. A 1759/16
Jn., Dean, Upper, farmer. 1839/14
Jos., Pavenham, matmaker. 1846/10
Marg., Bedford St. Peter. 1591-2/30
Marg., Milton Ernest. 1620/37
Mary, Wilden, wid. 1781/33
Nicholas, Cardington, Cotton End, husb. I 1618: 4/160
Peter, Woburn. 1741-2/61
Ric., Milton Ernest. R 1501: 1/26d
Ric., Keysoe. 1641/122
Ric., Renhold. 1722/23
Ric., Keysoe, miller. 1793/16
Robt., Leighton Buzzard. AR 1677: 1/198d
Robt., Shillington, yeo. A 1784/10
Sam., Bedford, gent. 1726/40
Thos., Lidlington. R 1535-6: 4/44d
Thos., Cardington. 1589/66
Thos., Potton, lab. 1597/26
Thos., Cardington, Fenlake, weaver. 1621/212
Thos., Tempsford, farmer. A 1738-9/8
Wm., Bedford St. Mary. R 1531: 3/46
Wm., Cardington, Cotton End. 1605/113
Wm., Cardington, yeo. 1616/67
Wm., Milton Ernest, lab. 1622/41
Wm., sen., Cardington. 1672/140
Wm., Toddington. AR 1682: 1/163d
Wm., Toddington. AR 1682: 1/164
Wm., Cardington, gent. 1716/51
Wm., Cardington, yeo. 1721/97
Wm., Leighton Buzzard, cordwainer. LB 1741/17

BULL(E) continued
Wm., Melchbourne, gent. 1768/9
Wm., Wilden, farmer. A 1778/3
Wm., Wilden, farmer. 1811/37, I 4/217
BULLEN, Hen., Gravenhurst, Over, lab. 1622/20
BULLOCK, Jn., Keysoe, yeo. 1646/104
Thos., Woburn, keeper to His Grace the Duke of Bedford. 1761/12
Thos., Husborne Crawley, Shorter, yeo. 1829/21
BULMER, Anth., Riseley. 1607/97
Edw., Ravensden, husb. 1619/266, I 4/108
Jn., Oakley, lab. 1624-5/106
Margery, Bletsoe. R 1558: 14/56
Thos., Keysoe. R 1500: 1/13d
Wm., Yielden, weaver. R 1638-9: 35/425
BULSTRODE, see Boulstred
BUMBERRY, see Bunberry
BUMSTEAD, Ellen, Toddington, wid. 1577/59
Ric., Aspley Guise, yeo. 1717/26
BUNBERRY, Edm., Potton, turner. 1738/53
Jn., Pulloxhill. R 1550: 12/109d
Jn., Potton, turner. 1725/10
Jos., Woburn, yeo. 1616/130
Thos., Pulloxhill. R 1544: 11/32d
Thos., Clophill, ploughwright. 1600-1/12
Thos., sen., Potton, turner. A 1763/12
Thos., sen., Potton, turner. 1763/17
Wm., Maulden. 1597/3
Wm., Arlesey, lab. 1624/64
BUNBY, Jn., Bedford St. Paul, victualler. 1749/12
Mary, Bedford. A 1736-7/23
BUNCE, Thos., Marston, shepherd. 1608/16
Thos., Totternhoe, lab. 1667/63
BUNCHER, Sarah, Ampthill, spins. 1849/47
BUNDY, BUNDYE, Agnes, Eaton Socon, Wyboston, wid. 1632/62
Ann, Roxton, wid. 1683/42
Cath., Colmworth. 1652-3/89
Jas., Roxton, husb. 1620/103
Jas., Roxton, Chawston, gent. 1624/162
Jas., Clifton, bach. 1642/29
Jas., Eaton Socon, yeo. 1653/11
Jas., Bedford, butcher. 1699/31
Jn., Eaton Socon, Wyboston. 1586/94
Jn., Roxton, yeo. 1628-9/28
Jn., Cardington, Fenlake, yeo. 1749-50/64
Marg., Roxton, Chawston, wid. 1614/44

BUNDY, BUNDYE continued
Nath., Wilshamstead, dairyman. 1688/24
Robt., Roxton, Colesden. 1592/16
Robt., Eaton Socon, Wyboston, yeo. 1648/114
Thos., Roxton. 1697/13
Thos., Eaton Socon, Wyboston. 1558/260
Thos., Roxton, husb. 1667/52
Wm., Roxton, Colesden. 1593/7
Wm., Roxton, Chawston, husb. 1611-12/180
Wm., Colmworth, lab. 1669-70/79
Wm., Stevington, farmer. A 1741/9
see also Bandy, Bendy, Boundy
BUNKER, Alice, Tingrith, wid. 1692/35
Edw., Barton, bach. AR 1679: 1/158
Jas., Ampthill, tailor. A 1819/3
Jn., Potsgrove. R 1540-1: 6/66 and 8/4d
Jn., sen., Chalgrave, Wingfield, husb. 1609/145
Jn., Tingrith, lab. 1623-4/180
Jn., Chalgrave. 1637/129
Jn., Tingrith, husb. 1687-8/65
Jn., Tingrith. AR 1689: 1/217d
Jn., Houghton Regis, Thorne, cordwainer. 1741/74
Joan, Tingrith, wid. 1625/203
Mary, Wavendon, Bucks. A 1761/26
Oliv., Tingrith, yeo. 1616/78, I
Oliv., Tingrith, husb. 1679/31
Ric., Silsoe. 1827/45
Robt., Bedford St. Mary, grocer. 1764/10
Roger, Tingrith. R 1516: 1/127
Sam., Tilsworth, farmer. 1839/11
Sarah, Marston, wid. A 1741-2/27
Thos., Chalgrave, Wingfield, baker. 1833/40
Thos., Tingrith. A 1725/4
Thos., Chalgrave, cordwainer. A 1730/17
Thos., Houghton Regis, yeo. (affidavit only). A 1833
Tim., Bedford, innholder. 1745/21
Wm., Tingrith, husb. R 1558: 14/88d
Wm., Westoning, farmer. A 1746/28
Wm., Ampthill, yeo. A 1784/21
BUNN, Alice, Luton, wid. 1763/28
Wm., Wootton, clerk. R 1683: 1/23
BUNNEY, Jn., sen., Stevington, weaver. 1608/34
Thos., Stevington, weaver. 1645/4
Wm., Stevington. 1747-8/61
BUNT, Jn., Potton, tanner. 1589/18

BUNTING, Alice, Eaton Socon, Wyboston, wid. 1584-5/269
Edith, Sandy, spins. 1843/36
Eliz., Sandy, wid. 1817/19
Jn., Sandy, mealman. A 1755/15
Jn., Sandy, yeo. A 1793/15
Thos., Eaton Socon, Wyboston. 1566?/72
Wm., Eaton Socon, Wyboston, yeo. 1584-5/270
BUNYAN, BOYNAN, Edw., Caddington. AR 1679-80: 1/158
Edw., Caddington Green, blacksmith. 1735/30
Eliz., Caddington. AR 1682-3: 1/164d
Eliz., Studham, wid. 1730/74
Hen., Chalgrave, Wingfield, yeo. 1592/83
Hen., Houghton Regis, Sewell. 1660-1/115
Hen., Milton Bryan, cordwainer. AR 1684: 1/168
Jas., Campton, carp. 1851/31
Joan, Chalgrave, Tebworth, maid. 1626/127
Joan, Totternhoe. 1660-1/116
Jn., Cranfield, bach. AR 1676: 1/195d
Jn., Bedford. AR 1688: 1/32
Jn., Bedford, brazier. 1729-30/112
Moses, Stagsden, farmer. 1794/31
Ric., Chalgrave, Tebworth. 1580-1/34
Ric., Studham, blacksmith. 1710/66
Robt., Chalgrave, Wingfield. 1579/126
Robt., Chalgrave, Tebworth, yeo. 1616/131
Thos., Elstow. R 1500: 1/209
Thos., Chalgrave. R 1545: 11/70d
Thos., Haynes. R 1545: 11/123d
Thos., Elstow, petty chapman. 1641/202
Thos., Elstow, brazier. 1675-6/74
Wm., Stanbridge. R 1537: 5/6
Wm., Stanbridge, will dated 1556 reproduced. 1594-5/93
Wm., Flitwick. 1661/285
Wm., Campton, yeo. 1825/20
Wm., Goldington. A 1701/26
BURBAGE, BURBIDGE, Deands, Addington, Bucks., wid. 1565/215
Geo., Barton, farmer. 1839/42
Thos., Woburn, innholder. 1758/42
Wm., Woburn, yeo. 1748/36
Wm., Riseley, gent. 1833/28
BURBY, see Birby
BURCOCKE, see Barcocke; see also Buckoke
BURDEN, Dan., Maulden, yeo. 1768/18
Nich., no parish given ?Eaton Socon, fletcher. 1636/2
Roger, Silsoe, fletcher. 1610/106, I

BURDEN continued
Wm., Silsoe, yeo. I 1619:4/53
Wm., Ridgmont, cordwinder. 1692/16
Wm., Clophill, husb. 1725/79
BURDER, Mary, Buckden, Staploe, Hunts. wid. A 1721/33
BURDUVS, alias Gillam, Wm., Ampthill, yeo. R 1549: 12/60
BURGE, BURGIE, Arthur, Melchbourne. AR 1680: 1/70d
Jn., Haynes, grazier. 1660/33
Jn., Ampthill, farmer. 1853/5
Jn., Dunstable (P/IX2 admon missing). A 1783/8
Lettice, Odell, wid. 1669/62
Wm., Odell, Gt., wid. 1665-6/88
Wm., Ampthill, maltster. 1841/2
BURGEN, see Burgoyne
BURGER, Mabel, Cardington, Harrowden. 1631-2/236
Thos., Cardington, Fenlake, carp. 1619-20/173, I 4/9
BURGESS, BURGIS, Anth., Arlesey, lab. 1661-2/265
Humphrey, Leighton Buzzard, yeo. 1603-4/105
Jas., Lidlington, carp. 1834/18
Jn., Toddington. R 1558: 15/9d
Jn., Eaton Socon, shepherd (bundle 1633). 1630/172
Jn., Marston. 1688/70
Jn., Melchbourne, lab. 1696/130
Jn., old index, "docket mislaid". A 1710/27
Jn., Arlesey, lab. 1715/34
Jn., old index only, bundle missing. 1717/35
Peter, Pulloxhill, weaver. 1689/65
Peter, Pulloxhill, yeo. 1758/23
Peter, Wilshamstead, aleseller. A 1776/2
Robt., Kempston. 1606-7/8
Sarah, Cranfield, wid. 1742/53
Thos., Aspley Guise, yeo. 1734/32
Tobias, Bedford St. Paul, innholder. 1676-7/184
Wm., Toddington, dairyman. 1761/20
Wm., Pulloxhill, yeo. 1777/26
BURGOYNE, BURGEN, Chas., Milton Bryan, yeo. 1781/8
Jn., Marston, victualler. A 1721/34
Jos., Flitwick, yeo. 1805/41
Ric., Flitwick, yeo. 1845/11
Sam., Flitton, Greenfield, farmer. A 1824/2
Thos., Sandy. R 1516:1/189a
Thos., Marston, yeo. A 1754/7
BURHAM, Thos., Oakley, husb. 1611/167
Wm., Oakley. 1560-1/72
BURLEIGH, see Burley

BURLETON, Robt., Potton, baker. 1750/43
BURLEY, Geo., Salford, yeo. 1692/9
Jn., Gravenhurst, Upper, Hine Farm, farmer. 1808/16, I 4/212
Mary, Maulden, wid. 1692-3/67
Mary, Cranfield, wid. 1733/9
Reg., Stagsden, yeo. 1612/124
Ric., Dunstable. 1576/43
Sarah, Gravenhurst, Upper, Ion, wid. 1813/4
Thos., Shillington, miller. 1831/13
Thos., Gravenhurst, Upper, innkeeper. 1845/18
Walt., Keysoe. 1610-11/46
Wm., Cranfield, husb. 1729/95
Wm., Gravenhurst, Upper, farmer. A 1760/12
BURLING, BURLIN, Alex., Houghton Conquest, gent. R 1535-6: 4/36
Soloman, Bedford St. Mary, joiner. 1639-40/156
Thos., Bedford St. Mary, joiner. AR 1678-9: 1/16
BURLINGTON, Mary, Potton, wid. A 1753/3
BURMER, Ric., Keysoe, husb. R 1545: 11/111d
BURN, BERNE, Eliz., Lidlington, wid. R 1527-8: 2/56d
Hen., Bedford St. Paul. R 1516-17: 1/171d, 194
Jn., Bedford, priest. R 1542-3: 6/136
Wm., Cranfield. R 1538: 5/10
BURNAGE, Eliz., Haynes, wid. A 1767/1
Richard, Henlow. R 1508: 1/118
BURNHAM, Hen., Shelton. 1774/16
Jn., Dunstable. 1582/108
Robt., no parish given. 1623/183
BURNS, Geo., Biggleswade, surgeon and apothecary. Bw 1811/110
BURR, BURGE, BURGHE, Abr., Kempston, yeo. A 1807/9
Abr., Wilshamstead, farmer. 1823/26
Abr., Wilshamstead, yeo. 1857/36
Ann, Flitton, Greenfield, wife of Jn. Ward Burr. 1837/44
Edw., Westoning, yeo. 1701/79
Edw., Westoning, yeo. 1742/86
Edw., Westoning, yeo. 1780/20
Edw., Toddington. I 1818: 4/231
Edw., Hockliffe, yeo. 1819/5
Eliz., old index "docket mislaid". A 1709/6
Eliz., Bromham, wid. A 1787/7
Ellen, Southill, Stanford, wid. 1657/257
Frances Huckle late Fra. Burr, Wilshamstead, wid. A 1788/7
Hezekiah, Houghton Regis. A 1728/16
Jane, Wootton. A 1848/15
Joan, Eaton. 1558/40

BURR, BURGE, BURGHE continued
Joan, Clophill, Beadlow, wid. 1629/145
Jn., Tilsworth, husb. R 1549: 12/59
Jn., Eaton Bray, husb. R 1551: 12/150
Jn., Toddington. 1558/308
Jn., Eaton, husb. 1612/69
Jn., Clophill, Beadlow, yeo. 1626/116
Jn., Flitwick, yeo. 1698/125
Jn., Harlington Grange, gent. 1730/53
Jn., Hockliffe, innholder. A 1732/8
Jn., Haynes, yeo. A 1741/2
Jn., Westoning, gent. 1762/36
Jn., Hockliffe. 1773/10
Jn., Kempston, farmer. 1810/13
Jn., Kempston, farmer. 1843/32
Jos., Pulloxhill, dairyman. 1708/62
Jos., Pulloxhill, dairyman. A 1741-2/29
Julian, Houghton Regis. R 1551: 12/161
Mary, Hockliffe, wid. 1755/13
Mary, Kempston, wid. A 1810/11
Math., Toddington, husb. 1630/94
Rebeccah, Wootton Pillinge, wid. 1695/40
Ric., Eaton Bray, lab. 1588/57
Ric., Southill, yeo. 1644/86
Ric., sen., Eaton Bray, yeo. 1680/60
Ric., Eaton Bray, yeo. 1712/46
Ric., Houghton Regis, late of Eaton Bray, yeo. 1760/64
Ric., Southill. AR 1689: 1/132
Roger, Shelford, vicar. 1558/330
Thos., Blunham. R 1544: 11/42
Wm., Eaton Bray. R 1530: 3/33d
Wm., sen., Streatley, Sharpenhoe, yeo. 1598/84
Wm., Odell, husb. 1599/92
Wm., Streatley, Sharpenhoe, yeo. 1622-3/21
Wm., Streatley, Sharpenhoe. 1630/19
Wm., Dunstable, carp. 1667-8/9
Wm., Streatley, Sharpenhoe, gent. 1684/33
Wm., Dunstable, carp. AR 1687: 1/173d
Wm., Streatley, yeo. A 1703/30
Wm., Pulloxhill, dairyman. 1742/29
Wm., Harlington Grange, yeo. 1761/9
Wm., Harlington Grange, dairyman and grazier, 1761/20
Wm., Harlington Grange, grazier. A 1763/1
BURRELL, Jn., Lidlington. 1556/188
see also Birrell; see also Burwell

BURRIDGE, BOORIGE, Benj., Riseley, yeo. 1658/201
Cath., Riseley. AR 1671-2: 1/61d
Eliz., Cople, wid. 1695/49
Eliz., Pulloxhill, Greenfield, spins. A 1715/1
Geo., Higham Gobion, farmer. 1802/19
Jn., Flitwick, husb. 1773/22
Mary, Bedford, wid. 1702/56
Mary, Higham Gobion, P/IX2. A 1809/1
Rebecca, Marston, wid. A 1781/20
Ric., Bromham, husb. 1602/44
Ric., Ravensden, tailor. 1640/40
Thos., Dunstable, stay bodice maker. 1759/59
Thos., Northill, Ickwell, lab. 1773/38
Wm., Pulloxhill, yeo. 1680/63
Wm., Northill, lab. A 1763/26
Wm., Millbrook, gent. 1785/1
Wm., Steppingley, farmer. A 1788/8
BURROWES, BURROWS, BORROWE, BORROWS, Ensame alias Burrowe and Ensame alias Borrowe, see under Ensame
Abr., Shillington, yeo. 1675/51
Ann, Clophill, wid. 1752/2
Barth., Eaton Bray, husb. 1806/14
Barth., Dunstable, born at Eaton Bray, lab. 1851/15
Clement, Sharnbrook, victualler. 1634-5/86
Edw., Shillington, yeo. 1660-1/79
Eliz., Eaton Bray, wid. 1814/12
Geo., Flitwick, East End, sievemaker. 1757/9
Jas., Bedford St. Mary, carman. 1839/29
Jn., Dunstable. 1746/46
Jn., Flitwick, bach., servant to Hump. Dell. 1757/10
Jn., Stotfold, yeo. 1760/58
Jn., Clophill, yeo. (monition to transmit to P.C.C., A.B.P. 1/1826). R 1822/25
Judith, Bedford, wid. 1696/90
Ric., Milton Bryan, victualler. 1841/35
Robt., Bedford, gent. A 1837/6
Sam., Clophill, builder. A 1847/17
Sam., Clophill. 1795/45
Thos., Shillington, yeo. 1657/71
Thos., Maulden. 1719/41
Thos., Clophill, victualler. 1732/37
Thos., Clophill, alehouse keeper. 1757/47
Wm., Bedford, shoemaker. 1693/102
BURT, BIRT, BYRTE, BYRTTE, Ambrose, Eversholt, yeo. 1615/186
Ann, Marston, wid. 1681/56
Ann, Lidlington, wid. 1727-8/89

BURT, BIRT, BYRTE, BYRTTE continued
Dan., Marston, husb. 1601/115
Dan., Luton, Cowridge End, gent. 1689/66
Emme, Eversholt, spins. 1665/46
Hen., Marston, lab. 1677/27
Hugh, Luton. A 1730/33
Jeremy, Carlton, innholder. 1600/61
Jn., Eversholt. R 1557: 13/107
Jn., Eversholt, yeo. 1647/54
Jn., Stagsden, yeo. AR 1685: 1/47d
Jn., Lidlington, yeo. A 1700/25
Jn., Marston, shepherd. 1700/133
Jn., Houghton Conquest, yeo. 1738-9/17
Jos., Luton, tailor. 1729/13
Judith, Lidlington, spins. 1665/33
Margt., Clophill, wid. 1589/12
Martha, Lidlington, wid. 1769/44
Martha, Chalgrave. A 1805/4
Mary, Stopsley, wid. 1705/24
Ric., Lidlington. 1743/22
Ric., parish torn off. c. 1670/222
Ric., Houghton Regis, yeo. 1851/2
Ric., Stagsden. AR 1684-5: 1/47
Robt., Bedford, P/IX2. A 1811/18
Robt., Bedford, tailor. 1811/35
Sarah, parish torn off. 1670-1/238
Sarah, Luton. A 1747/22
Sarah, Bedford, wid. 1804/9
Thos., Pulloxhill. R 1544: 11/29
Thos., Lidlington. 1617/207
Thos., Chellington, yeo. 1669/75
Thos., Cranfield, lab. 1685/2
Thos., Flitwick, yeo. 1716/4
Thos., Lidlington, victualler. 1749/33
Thos., Marston. A 1723/28
Wm., Flitton. R 1516-17?: 1/120
Wm., Kempston, carp. 1790/26
BURTON, Chris., Leighton Buzzard. 1605/136
Edw., Leighton Buzzard. 1605/136
Edw., Stotfold, yeo. 1718/76
Eliner, Stevington. 1616/82
Eliz., Hulcote, wid. 1559/162
Grace, Eyeworth, wid. A 1714/27
Hen., Felmersham. 1614/89
Jas., Eyeworth, yeo. 1759/61

BURTON continued
Jn., Bletsoe, Stoke Mill. 1567/51
Jn., sen., Podington, yeo. 1591-2/72
Jn., Bedford, cobbler. 1627/188
Jn., Rushden, Herts., yeo. 1661/395
Jn., Eyeworth, yeo. 1744/41
Jn., Eyeworth, yeo. 1750/17
Mich., Battlesden. 1718/34
Ric., Dunstable. R 1536: 4/56
Ric., Dunstable, baker. R ?1551: 12/178
Ric., Cardington, fuller. 1623/98
Ric., Eyeworth. A 1712/16
Thos., Podington. R 1529: 3/10d
Thos., Hulcote, husb. 1557/356
Thos., Felmersham. 1615/199, I
Thos., Turvey. AR 1672: 1/38
Thos., Turvey, baker. 1685/14
Wm., Podington. R 1539: 5/37
Wm., parish torn off, yeo. 1670/227
Wm., Toddington. AR 1672: 1/143d
Wm., Stotfold, baker. A 1769/24
Wm., Millbrook, yeo. 1790/24
BURWELL, Jn., Houghton Conquest, yeo. 1607/144
Simon, Houghton Conquest, yeo. 1617/246
see also Birrell; see also Burrell
BURY, see Berry
BUSBY, Jn., Chellington, cordwainer. A 1711/27
Mary, Chellington, wid. 1739/12
BUSH, Williams alias Bush, see Williams
Fra., Marston, yeo. 1718/71
Geo., Dunstable, weaver. 1606/51
Luke, Houghton Regis. 1728/97
Mary, Luton, wid. 1703/8
Ric., Dunstable. R 1530-1: 3/38
Wm., Houghton Regis. R 1529: 3/17
Wm., Blunham, Southmills, gent. 1734/42
BUSHBY, Ann, Lidlington, wid. 1685/44
Ann, Lidlington, wid. AR 1685: 1/213d
Ann, Millbrook, spins. 1722/15
Fra., Millbrook, carp. 1715-16/83
Fra., Millbrook, carp. 1773/36
Jn., Lidlington, carp. 1684/68
Jn., Lidlington, carp. 1744/7
Jn., Husborne Crawley, yeo. 1769/6
Jn., Cranfield, tailor. 1790/15

BUSHBY continued
Jn., Husborne Crawley, yeo. A 1804/2
Jn., Bedford, tailor. 1831/16
Margt., Husborne Crawley, wid. 1739/56
Ric., sen., Lidlington. 1638/144
Ric., Lidlington. AR 1680: 1/203d
Ric., Lidlington. AR 1683: 1/208d
Robt., Woburn, yeo. 1678-9/148
Sarah, Millbrook, wid. 1777/6
Thos., Mogerhanger. 1610/115
Thos., Marston, lab. 1624-5/16
Thos., Lidlington, yeo. 1655/191
Thos., Millbrook, maltster. 1655/192
Thos., Millbrook, yeo. 1698/89
Thos., Ampthill, yeo. A 1787/13
Thos., Eversholt. 1833/41
Wm., Lidlington, carp. 1609/137
Wm., Millbrook, carp. 1700-1/20
Wm., Lidlington, gardener. A 1729-30/61
BUSKIN, Arthur alias Buskin, see Arthur
Alice, Woburn. 1695/75
Hen., Lidlington. 1630-1/131
Jn., Woburn, sadler. 1687/104
Jn., Blunham, lab. A 1721/31
Jn., St. Andrew's, Holborn, late of Bedford, cooper. 1733/46
BUSSEY, Cecil, Cheston Park, ?Devon. 1632-3/209
Robt., Ampthill. 1620/60
Thos., Ampthill, gent. 1667/39
BUTCHER, BUTCHAR, Gurney alias Butcher, see Gurney;
Woolley alias Butcher, see Woolley; Sibthorpe alias Butcher, see Sibthorpe
Andrew, Aspley Guise, butcher. A 1772/7
Ann, Maulden, spins. 1836/24
Chas., Bedford. A 1738-9/2
Eliz., Clophill, wid. 1796/5
Eliz., Eversholt, Froxfield, wid. 1807/32
Fra., Toddington, Herne Farm, wid. 1834/34
Geo., Eversholt, lab. A 1813/12
Hen., Biggleswade, innholder. BwA: 1712-13/1, I
Jas., Biddenham. AR 1670-1: 1/4
Jazzard, Potton. 1638/129
Jn., Blunham, gardener. 1660/156
Jn., Woburn, yeo. 1745/6
Jn., Eversholt, baker. A 1807/10
Jn., Eversholt, baker. 1807/13
Jn., Toddington, dairyman. 1808/17

BUTCHER, BUTCHAR continued
Jn., Eversholt, baker. A 1813/14
Jn., Clophill, farmer. A 1852/1
Jos., Woburn, victualler. 1742/1
Martha, Wootton, wid. A 1767/6
Ric., Husborne Crawley, farmer. A 1805/2
Robt., Blunham, lab. 1620/97
Robt., Lidlington. 1640/110
Robt., Kempston, yeo. 1737-8/67
Robt., Wootton, butcher. A 1760/27
Sarah, Woburn, wid. 1746/2
alias Farmer, Thos., Biggleswade, Shortmead. BwR 1553: 1/4
Thos., Gt. Barford, tailor. 1663-4/94
Thos., Clophill (P/IX2 admon missing). A 1783/16
Thos., Southill, Old Rowney, farmer. 1802/35
Thos., Clophill, yeo. 1817/12
Wm., Blunham, lab. 1617/258
Wm., Carlton, lab. (bundle 1712). A 1713/48
Wm., Eversholt, baker. A 1813/13
BUTERVANT, Cath., Bedford, wid. 1691/83
Hen., Bedford, weaver. 1702/54
Thos., Bedford St. Mary, weaver. 1688/38
BUTFIELD, see Butterfield
BUTLER, BOTELER, -, Felmersham, Radwell, Moorend. R 1504: 1/163
Elisabeth, Lidlington, wid. 1557/248
Elizabeth, Lidlington (bundle 1624-5). 1623-4/1
Elizabeth, Harrold, spins. A 1712-3/8
Fowke, Bedford St. Paul, glover. 1559-60/327
Fra., Woburn, tailor. 1786/24
Geo., Stotfold. 1626-7/16
Hen., Lidlington. R 1548: 12/28d
Hen., Tempsford, lab. 1630/57
Hen., Lidlington, yeo. 1643/63
Humph., Lidlington. R 1542: 6/142d, 9/2d
Joan, Tempsford, wid. R 1525: 2/28
Jn., Potton, linen draper/shopkeeper. 1815/11, I 4/221
Jn., Tempsford. R 1501: 1/25d
Jn., Potton, husb. R 1509: 1/58d
Jn., Lidlington. R 1544: 11/31
Jn., Lidlington, husb. 1565/22
Jn., Tempsford, weaver. 1629/134
Jn., sen., Lidlington. 1638/128
Jn., Dunton. 1660/47
Jn., Lidlington, Boutton End, husb. 1678/92
Jn., sen., Potton, woolstapler and woolcomber. 1784/30

BUTLER, BOTELER continued
Jn., old index only, bundle missing. A 1717/28
Joyce, wid. no parish given, Wootton, register. 1638/3
Martha, Potton, wid. 1828/3
Mary, Lidlington, wife of Jn. 1699/44
Mary, Ridgmont. 1713/14
Ralph, Dunstable. 1560/82
Ric., Lidlington, husb. 1573-4/11
Ric., Lidlington. 1580/226
Ric., Tempsford. AR 1674: 1/101
Robt., Edworth. R 1529: 3/8d
Robt., Dunton, husb. 1636/8
Robt., sen., Wootton, Wootton Pillinge, husb. 1637/98
Robt., Wootton Pillinge, inv. only. 1641-2/192
Sam., Husborne Crawley, yeo. 1668/159
Sam., Ridgmont, wheelwright. 1741/38
Sam., Bedford, wheelwright. 1755/14
Sam., Bedford, yeo. A 1785/11
Susan, Cardington, Fenlake. 1618/45
Susan, Ampthill. A 1713/34
Thos., Salford, husb. 1582/98
Thos., Sir, Biddenham, knight. 1625-6/115
Thos., Cranfield, yeo. 1649/50
Walt., Blunham. R 1522: 2/33
Walt., Blunham. R 1546: 11/180d
Wm., Lidlington. R 1522: 2/4e
Wm., sen., Lidlington. R 1533: 3/118
Wm., Tempsford. R 1558: 14/50d
Wm., Lidlington, husb. 1604/41
Wm., Lidlington, husb. 1612/122
Wm., Wootton, yeo. 1669/90
Wm., Ridgmont, wheelwright. 1719/26
BUTMAN, Jn., Cardington, Harrowden. R 1558: 13/150d
Thos., Cardington, Harrowden. R 1542: 6/153d & 9/8
BUTT, Agnes, Elstow. R 1525: 2/37
Agnes, Westoning, wid. 1610/210
Ambrose, Westoning, Wood End, yeo. 1635-6/62
Jn., Flitwick. 1647/51
Jonas, Westoning, husb. 1625-6/139
Mary, Clophill, Beadlow, wid. 1845/41
Robt., Clophill, Beadlow, farmer. 1780/4
Robt., Clophill, Beadlow, yeo. A 1813/10
Thos., Houghton Conquest, shepherd. 1649/13
Thos., Clophill, Beadlow, husb. 1850/23
Wm., Holcote, yeo. 1633/179

BUTTER, Thos., Blunham, husb. 1573/128
BUTTERFIELD, BUTFIELD, Ann, Clophill, wid. 1688/50
Ann, Luton, wid. 1802/16
Cath., Pulloxhill, wid. 1615/214
Edw., Clophill, husb. 1723/39
Edw., Salford, gent. 1759/17
Eliz., Marston, wid. 1801/3
Eliz., Billington, wid. LB 1800/10
Hannah, Salford, spins. A 1735/30
Jas., Dunstable. A 1811/16
Jane, Houghton Regis, Thorne, wid. 1729/68
Jn., Pulloxhill, husb. 1587/120
Jn., Pulloxhill, badger. 1598-9/73
Jn., Luton, lab. 1628/59
Jn., Salford, yeo. 1670/153
Jn., Luton, lab. 1674/165
Jn., Salford, yeo. 1722/7
Jn., Salford, farmer. A 1733/21
Jn., Upper Gravenhurst, farmer. A 1744/5
Jn., sen., Luton, maltster. 1772/31
Jn., sen., Potsgrove, yeo. 1778/20
Jn., jun., Luton, maltster. 1779/44
Jn., Marston, yeo. 1785/2
Thos., Luton, Stopsley, yeo. 1722/53
Wm., sen., Caddington, Wood Side, husb. 1692/7
Wm., Dunstable, dissenting minister. A 1778/6
Wm., sen., Billington, yeo. LB 1784/70
Wm., Billington, yeo. LB 1823/19
BUTTON, Abr., Cardington, lab. 1721-2/62
Edm., Shefford, smith. A 1721/32
Eleanor, Bedford, wid. 1818/31
Eliz., Elstow. 1599/68
Eliz., Wootton. 1648-9/93
Geo., Maulden, gent. 1619/195, I 4/132
Jn., Shefford, blacksmith. A 1735-6/12
Jn., Ravensden, dairyman. A 1746/44
Thos., Bedford, ironmonger. A 1744/3
Thos., Bedford, victualler. A 1786/7
Thos., Bedford, butcher. 1811/32
Wm., Hardwick, gent. 1607/129
Wm., Shefford. AR 1685: 1/124d
BUXTON, Ann, Shefford, wid. 1693/106
BY, BYE, Jn., Colmworth. R 1525: 2/93
Jn., Potton, baker. 1630/9

BYGRAVE, BEEGRAVE, BIG(G)RAVE, Ann, Cardington, spins. 1794/25
Hannah, Eversholt, spins. 1700/95
Hannah, Cardington, wid. 1747/13
Jn., Wilden, lab. 1624/43
Jn., Stagsden, dairyman. 1728-9/121
Jn., Elstow, late Cardington, yeo. 1756/49
Jn., Southill, Ireland, lab. A 1852/8
Mary, Wilden, wid. 1641/162
Mary, Cardington, Cotton End, wid. 1727-8/92
Robt., Cardington, Cotton End. 1687-8/75
Sam., Cardington, lab. 1844/4
Thos., Barford, bach. 1661/350
Thos., sen., Cardington, Cotton End, yeo. 1725-6/73
Thos., sen., Cardington, yeo. 1747/35
Thos., Cardington, yeo. 1751/20
BYNAM, Fra., Bedford, wid., spins. 1677-8/67
BYNDELL, see Bindell
BYWAYS, Agnes, maulden. 1593/15
Mich., Aspley Guise, musician. 1601-2/150
Thos., Marston Pillinge, lab. 1717/51
BYWORTH, Joan, Riseley. R 1828-9: 3/1
Joan, Tilbrook, wid. 1598-9/115
Jn., Chalgrave, Wingfield. 1620-1/4
Jn., Tilbrook, yeo. 1559/171
Jn., Aspley Guise, weaver. 1762/18
Jn., Eaton Socon, yeo. 1776/28
Margt., Oakley. 1615-16/105
Ric., Westoning, husb. 1593/83
Renald, Westoning. 1557/334
Robt., Aspley Guise, tailor. 1670/257
Robt., Aspley Guise. AR 1677-8: 1/199

C

CADBURY, CADBERYE, Robt., St. Margarretts, St. Albans, singleman. 1576-77/222
CADDINGTON, Eliz., Edworth. R 1543: 11/9
CADGE, see Cage
CADWELL, CADWELLA, Cath., Biggleswade, wid. 1559/155
Chris., Thurleigh, husb. 1711/7
Cadwella alias Taylor, Edw., Norton, Herts. 1618/109
Edw., Bedford St. Mary, gent. 1681/33
Grace, Goldington, wid. 1700/83
Jn., Biggleswade. Bw R 1555: 1/10
Jn., Pertenhall, yeo. 1707/51

CADWELL, CADWELLA continued
Jn., (old index "docket mislaid"). A 1709/40
Lucy, Riseley, wid. 1621/191
Ric., Thurleigh, yeo. 1655/193
Robt., Thurleigh, gent. 1682-3/114
Wm., Sandy. 1567-8/19
see also Cawdell
CAGE, CADGE, Ann, (old index "mislaid docket"). A 1709/39
Ann, Sandy, Swarden, wid. 1709/86
Eliz., Sandy, wid. AR 1690-1: 1/134
Jn., Sandy, Stratford, yeo. 1725/22
Thos., Sandy, Stratford. AR 1673: 1/97d
Thos., Sandy. A 1707/9
CAGILL, Wm., sen. Sundon. R 1550: 12/89d
CAHERTY, Jn., Shefford, innholder. 1840/1
CAIN, CAINS, CANE, KANE, KAYNES, Chas., Pulloxhill, blacksmith. 1846/33
Edw., Luton, blacksmith. A 1769/16
Hannah, Luton, wid. 1739/55
Hen., Elstow, lab. 1663/13
Hen., Luton, bricklayer. 1684-5/59
Hen., Luton, bricklayer. 1734/31
Hen., Luton, bricklayer. 1741/44
Jas., Harlington, blacksmith. A 1804/9
Jas., Luton, carp. 1835/24
Jn., Warden, lab. 1700/88
Jn., Pulloxhill, yeo. 1857/8
Ric., Langford, lab. 1732/51
see also Cawne
CAINHOE, CAYNHOO, Jn., Lidlington. R 1541-2: 6/109
Peter, Cranfield, yeo. A 1708/41
Ric., Goldington. R 1535-6: 4/39d
Susan, Cranfield, wid. A 1718/85
CAKE, Hen., Eaton Bray, husb. 1573/122
CALDECOTE, see Caulcot; see also Goditot
CALEY, Simon, Ampthill, clerk. A 1703/13
CALNE, see Cawne
CALTON, Angel, Bedford St. Paul, wid. 1702-3/40
Humph., Bedford St. Paul, apothecary. 1708/66
Mary, Bletsoe, spins. 1686/5
Mary, Bletsoe, wid. 1732-1/78
Valentine, Bletsoe, clergy, rector. 1729/100
CAMBER, CAMBERS, Geo., Bedford St. Mary. 1675/3
Jere., Bromham, yeo. 1721/12

CANNON, CANNAN continued
Thos., Dean. R 1509-10: 1/63
Thos., Keysoe. R 1525: 2/182
Thos., Roxton, Colesden. 1617/181
Thos., Harrold, mercer. 1649-50/36
Swannys, Cardington, wid. 1605/115
Wm., Gt. Barford. R 1516:1/175, 189
Wm., Cardington. 1580/229
Wm., Ravensden. AR 1674: 1/65
CAPELL, Eliz., Cardington, Cotton End, wid. 1705/9
Jn., Mogerhanger, husb. 1607/119
Jn., Sandy. 1705/49
Mary, Bedford, wid. 1718/1
Thos., Sandy, Girtford, husb. 1719/20
Wm., M.A., rector of Milton Bryan. 1764/6
Wm., Milton Bryan, clerk. A 1764/1
CAPEMAN, see Capon
CAPON, CAPEMAN, Jn., Billington. 1567/66
Joan, no parish given. 1612/119
Jn., Leighton Buzzard, esq. LB 1766/4
Jn., Leighton Buzzard, gent. LB A 1818/72
Marg., wid. Ravensden. 1560-1/71
Rebecca, Lathbury, Bucks., spins. 1813/20
Thos., Billington, yeo. 1608/59
CAPP, Wm., sen., Stanbridge, yeo. LB 1795/99
Wm., sen., Stanbridge, husb. LB 1816/62, I
CAPPER, Parker alias Capper, see under Parker
CAPPERMAN, Margt., Everton, servant. 1673-4/72
CARDELL, CARDWELL, Jn., Chalgrave, Tebworth, yeo. 1632-3/10
Jn., Chalgrave, Tebworth, yeo. 1683/5
Jn., Tebworth, yeo. 1712-13/45
Robt., Chalgrave. 1584/248
Sarah, Chalgrave, Tebworth, wid. 1731/3
CARDWELL, see Cardell
CARELESS, CARLES, Ebenezer, Bedford, clothier. 1857/12
Eliz., Ampthill, spins. A 1744/8
Jn., Northill, Over Caldecote, blacksmith. 1616/73
Jn., Southill, Broome. 1661-2/261
Jn., Stotfold, miller. A 1713/1
Jn., Ampthill, apothecary. A 1738/30
Lewis, Little Staughton, husb. 1729/97
Ric., Southill, Stratford. R 1545: 11/100
CARER, Thos., Potton. 1554/184
CARESLY, Ric., rector of Toddington. 1668/152
CAREY, Geo., Woburn, farmer and brickmaker. 1783/54

CAREY continued
Margt., Kempston. 1663/48
Wm., Mogerhanger, yeo. A 1840/2
CARLES, see Careless
CARLING, Jn., Aspley Guise, victualler. 1846/8
CARLISLE, CARLILL, John, Campton. R 1505-6: 1/231
CARNELL, see Cawnell
CARPENTER, Alwen alias Carpenter, see Alwen;
Lucas alias Carpenter, see Lucas
Ann, Leighton Buzzard, Overend Green, wid. Fac. 1706: 9/21
Ann, Houghton Regis, wid. 1733/11
Eliz., Heath and Rech, wid. LB 1799/5
Harry, Totternhoe. 1569/115
alias Harris, Isabell, wid., Toddington, Herne. 1577-8/64
alias Ward, Jn., Wilden. R 1535: 4/26d
Jn., (old index only, bundle missing). A 1718/8
Jn., Houghton Regis, yeo. A 1762/13
Jn., sen., Heath and Reach, yeo. LB 1769/15
Jn., Leighton Buzzard. LB A 1790/37
Jn., Heath and Reach, yeo. LB 1828/44
Thos., Leighton Buzzard, Upper End Green, yeo. 1682/19
CARR, Edw., Dunstable, innholder. 1589/127
Jn., Millbrook, clerk. 1702/78
Jn., Flitwick, farmer and dairyman. 1823/23
Peter, Bedford, alderman. 1556/110
Thos., Eaton Socon, Beggary. 1638/70
Wm., Houghton Conquest, clerk. 1695-6/71
CARRIER, Ann, Biddenham. A 1846/4
CARRINGTON, KARENTON, Ann, Potton, wid. 1700/148
Eliz., Southill, Broome, wid. R 1613-14: 31/2
Eliz., Potton, wid. 1756/11
Fra., Toddington. 1669/42
Gerard, Dunton. R 1521-2: 2/118
Harry, Houghton Regis. 1590/147
Jn., Dunton. R 1505: 1/76
Jn., Dunton. R 1521: 1/247d
Jn., Dunton, Newtown. 1605/143
Jn., Potton, blacksmith. 1735/38
Jn., Henlow, lab. 1737/49
Jn., Potton, blacksmith. A 1748/17
Jn., Toddington, Chalton, weaver. 1628/56
Jn., Renhold, yeo. 1665/51
Jn., Southill, Broome, yeo. 1697-8/71
Jn., sen., Biggleswade, baker. 1802/5
Jn., Biggleswade, schoolmaster. Bw 1826/131

CARRINGTON continued
Margt., Houghton Regis, wid. 1608/78
Mark, Southill, Broome, singleman. 1612-13/15
Mark, Stotfold, lab. 1668-9/192
Ralph, Toddington, Chalton, husb. 1630/89
Ric., Southill, Broome, yeo. 1608/53
Robt., Dunton. R 1521: 2/114
Thos., Dunton. R 1522-3: 2/5
Thos., Toddington, Chalton, yeo. 1624/81
Thos., Southill, Broome, yeo. 1625/194
Thos., Cople, shoemaker. A 1738-9/3
Thos., Markyate Street, victualler. 1678/123
Thos., Potton, blacksmith. 1759/5
Walt., Renhold. 1645-6/57
Walt., Southill, Broome, yeo. 1661/392
Wm., Upper Gravenhurst, yeo. R 1548: 12/37
Wm., Dunstable. R 1549: 12/67d
Wm., Toddington, Chalton. 1581/11
Wm., sen., Biggleswade, baker, shopkeeper and draper. Bw 1779/71
Wm., Biggleswade, linen draper. Bw 1797/96
Wm., Biggleswade, sadler. Bw 1803/101, I
see also Charrington
CARSEY, Jn., Luton. R 1518? 1/122
CARTE, Humph., Ampthill, maltster. 1823/14
Humph., Ampthill, innholder. 1829/30
Jn., Studham, Markyate, wheelwright. I 1619: 4/105
Jn., Ampthill, plumber and glazier. 1818/21
Mary, Ampthill. A 1834/8
Mary, Ampthill, wid. 1836/8
CARTER, CARTEIR, Umney alias Carter, see under Umney
Abr., Silsoe. A 1741-2/36
Agnes, Northill, Thorncote, wid. 1638/185
Alice, Northill, Hatch, wid. 1679/13
Ben., Silsoe, innholder. 1821/13
Dan., sen., Shillington, husb. 1690/60
Dan., sen., Shillington, carp. 1740/18
Dan., Shillington, yeo. A 1761/23
Dan., Shillington, husb. 1793/11
Edw., Sandy, Beeston, husb. 1612/18
Edw., Sandy, Beeston. 1620/84
Edw., Wrestlingworth. 1700/102
Edw., Eyeworth, yeo. 1776/21
Edw., Wrestlingworth, butcher. A 1704/37
Eliz., Houghton Conquest, wid. 1677/51
Eliz., wid. Ridgmont. 1701/13

CARTER, CARTEIR continued
Eliz., Eversholt. 1717/50
Em., Kempston, wid. R 1546: 11/177d
Fra., Wootton. 1670/179
Frances, Ampthill, wid. 1716/25
Geo., Roxton, Chawston, tailor. 1663-4/98
Geo., Cople, lab. 1734/59
Grace, Roxton, Chawston. 1680-1/97
Hannah, Cardington, spins. 1836/5
Hen., Husborne Crawley. R 1533: 3/95
Hen., Dunstable. 1585/2
Humph., Shillington, husb. 1650/109
Isaac, Northill, Ickwell, yeo. 1698/153
Isaac, Northill, Ickwell, yeo. 1755/31
Jane, Upper Gravenhurst, wid. 1794/13
Jane, Silsoe, wid. 1835/18
Joan, Kempston, wid. R 1546
Joan, Shillington, wid. 1613/186
Joan, Husborne Crawley, wid. 1624/87
Jn., Husborne Crawley. R 1533: 3/113
Jn., Northill, Hatch. R 1539: 6/4
Jn., Northill, Hatch. R 1539: 6/5d
Jn., Elstow. R 1545: 11/95d
Jn., Tilsworth, singleman. 1562/105
Jn., sen., Northill, Hatch. ?1579/128
Jn., sen., Northill, Hatch. 1579/129
Jn., Leighton Buzzard. 1591/112
Jn., Northill, husb. 1597/11
Jn., Northill, Brook End. 1597/59
Jn., sen., Husborne Crawley, yeo. 1600/14
Jn., Shillington, Pegsdon, yeo. 1612/42
Jn., Northill, Hatch, yeo. 1620-1/24
Jn., Cranfield, husb. 1634/97
Jn?, Thos., Bedford St. Paul, glover/fellmonger. 1638/116, I
Jn., Chalgrave, Wingfield, tailor. 1667/91
Jn., Northill, Caldecote. 1678-9/135
Jn., Luton, clerk. 1684/79
Jn., Luton. AR 1684: 1/167d
Jn., Ampthill, clerk. 1701/27
Jn., Ampthill, gent. 1701-2/31
Jn., Upper Gravenhurst, Ion, lab. 1706/41
Jn., Clophill. 1728/103
Jn., Eversholt, yeo. 1730/50
Jn., Northill, Thorncote, yeo. 1738/47
Jn., Eaton Bray, cordwainer. 1748/59

CARTER, CARTEIR continued
Jn., Caddington, Ealey Green, yeo. 1757/3
Jn., Potsgrove, dairyman. 1768/21
Jn., Bedford St. Mary. A 1771/26
Jn., Potton, gardener. 1839/31
Jonas, Harlington, yeo. and bach. 1666/127
Jonathan, Clophill, husb. 1739/60
Jonathan, Shillington, grocer. AR 1673: 1/98
Jos., Meppershall, parish clerk. 1855/33
Kath., Harlington, wid. 1618/42
alias Omney, Laur., Sharnbrook. 1603-4/87
Marg., Marston, wid. 1624-5/11
Margt., Bletsoe, wid. 1615/228
Mary, Dunstable, wid. 1582-3/71
Mary, Clophill, wid. 1668-9/199
Mary, Shillington, wid. 1715/28
Mary, Wrestlingworth. 1715/41
Mary, Potsgrove, wid. 1774/24
Mary, alias Clark, Biggleswade. BwA 1751/16
Math., Shillington, yeo. 1611/9
Mich., Houghton Conquest. I 1619: 4/101
Mich., Upper Gravenhurst, tailor. 1696/120
Nich., Kempston. R 1528: 2/119d
Nich., Eaton Socon. 1649/69
Ric., Reach, husb. Fac. 1701: 9/1
Ric., Sundon, baker. 1766/36
Ric., Husborne Crawley, yeo. 1559/325
Ric., yeo., Husborne Crawley. 1593/67
Ric., Shefford, oatmealmaker. 1632/79
Ric., Harlington, yeo. 1649/74
Ric., Kempston, yeo. 1672/106
Ric., Harlington, East End, yeo. 1714/55
Ric., Sundon, yeo. 1739/62
Ric., Eversholt. AR 1684: 1/210
Robt., sen., Northill, Hatch. 1614/96
Robt., Husborne Crawley, carp. 1654/180
Robt., Bedford. A 1729/18
Sam., Kempston. AR 1674: 1/9d
Sam., Clophill, gent. 1738/54
Sarah, Upper Gravenhurst, wid. 1731/30
Simon, Silsoe, warrener. A 1711/26
Simon, Husborne Crawley, lab. 1806/22
Steph., Salford, dairyman. AR 1685-6: 1/214
Steven, Northill, Beeston, yeo. 1606/72

CARTER, CARTEIR continued
Susan, Northill, Beeston, wid. 1659/146
Thos., Northill, Beeston. R 1517: 1/210
Thos., Kempston. R 1544: 11/35
Thos., Tilsworth, husb. 1580/217
Thos., Husborne Crawley, husb. 1598/89
Thos., Northill, Beeston. 1612/106
Thos., Harlington, tailor. 1618/80
Thos., Studham, Markyate. I 1619: 4/91
Thos., sen., Northill, Hatch. 1627/175
Thos., sen., Kempston, gent. 1647/138
Thos., Northill, Thorncote, weaver. 1652/54
Thos., Roxton. 1663-4/99
Thos., sen., Bedford, glover. 1669/64
Thos., Northill. AR 1672: 1/95
Thos., Nether Caldecote, carp. 1679/30
Thos., Roxton, tailor. 1681/54
Thos., Kempston, gent. 1682/32
Thos., Luton, lab. 1696/89
Thos., Northill, carp. A 1715/7
Thos., Biggleswade, whipcordmaker. 1730/94
Thos., Stanbridge, yeo. LB 1736/2
Thos., Northill, lab. AR 1684: 1/121d
Thos. Arthur, Luton. A 1857/9
Wm., Kempston. R 1500-1: 1/24
Wm., Houghton Conquest, husb. 1565/20
Wm., Kempston. Admon 1569 see X 80/119
Wm., Kempston, gent. 1605/87
Wm., Marston, lab. 1618-19/14
Wm., Cranfield. 1620/83
Wm., sen., Cranfield, yeo. 1634-5/112
Wm., Cranfield, dairyman. 1663-4/81
Wm., Sandy, Beeston, yeo. AR 1670/91d
Wm., Northill. AR 1677: 1/107
Wm., Northill. AR 1681: 1/116
Wm., Ampthill, gent. 1703/1
Wm., Pulloxhill, yeo. 1719/34
Wm., Harlington, yeo. A 1722/25
Wm., Ampthill, clockmaker. 1737/31
Wm., Harlington, husb. A 1739/15
Wm., Cranfield. 1753/39
Wm., Eyeworth, yeo. A 1788/6
Wm., Biggleswade. Bw 1826/132
CARTON, Jn., Dunton, Newton, husb. 1560?/171
Jn., Sutton, husb. 1604/28

CARTWRIGHT, Edw., Lidlington. A 1726/9
Geo., Sandy. R 1543: 6/145
Hen., Bedford St. John, gent. 1578/99
Humph., Willington, yeo. 1623/198
Jn., Willington. 1645/9
Jn., Lidlington, yeo. 1698/78
Jn., Roxton, carpenter. 1757/37
Jn., Lidlington, butcher. A 1766/28
Jn., Lidlington. 1766/65
Susannah, Eaton Socon, wid. 1769/25
Thos., Roxton, yeo. 1739-40/26
Thos., Millbrook. A 1772/16
Thos., Millbrook, farmer. 1790/1
Wm., Pavenham. R 1540: 6/36d
Wm., Flitton. 1611-12/151
Wm., Biggleswade. BwA 1744/11
Wm., Biggleswade, plumber. BwA 1781/35, I
CARVELL, CARVILL, CHARVELL, Cook alias Carvell, see under Cook
Edm., Leighton Buzzard, butcher. 1600/8
Edw., Toddington, victualler. 1714/77
Edw., Holcote, dairyman. 1719/83
Edw., Toddington, butcher. 1745/13
Edw., Holcote, dairyman. A 1729/44
Edw., Holcote. A 1754/25
Jn., Toddington, butcher. 1641/199
Jn., Holcote, dairyman. A 1729/45
Mary, sen., Holcote, wid. 1723/42
Mary, Oakley, singlewoman. 1750-1/55
Wm., Holcote. 1829/37
see also Covel; see also Covill
CARVER, Abr., Bedford, basketmaker. 1818/45
Eliz., Bedford St. Peter, wid. A 1809/19
Eliz., Bedford St. Peter, Islipp, No. 19 Almshouse, Harpur St., spins. 1832/47
Sam., Keysoe, tailor. A 1712/17
Thos., Dean. 1615-16/111
Thos., Bedford, baker. 1809/16
Wm., Warden, lab. 1666/135
Wm., Sandy, lab. A 1700/23
Wm., Dunton, yeo. 1760/24
CARVILL, see Carvell
CASE, Alice, Cardington, Fenlake, wid. 1618/47
Jn., Eaton Socon, Wyboston. A 1831/12
see also Cesse; see also Chase
CASTLE, CASTELL, Jas., Stotfold, thatcher. 1633-4/199
Jn., Shillington, husb. A 1728/34

CASTLE, CASTELL continued
Mich., Eaton Socon, Devilhoe, lab. 1611-12/172
CASTLEDINE, Jn., Felmersham, mason. 1701/63
CASTLEMAN, Anne, Biggleswade, spins. Bw 1811/109
Fra., Renhold, bricklayer. 1737/56
Fra., Renhold. 1767/2
Fra., Cardington, yeo. 1837/15
Wm., Biggleswade, bricklayer. Bw 1786/78, I
CASWELL, Mary, Wavendon, Bucks., wid. A 1751/9
CATCHER, Wm., Sandy, Girtford, glover. 1576/32
CATELL, Jn., Stagsden, husb. 1573-4/5
Thos., Stagsden, lab. 1636-7/64
CATEN, see Catten
CATER, Barnard, Sandy, glover. 1625-6/136
Hen., ?Eaton. 1582/84
Joan, Sandy, wid. 1649/8
Jn., Cople, lab. 1599/142
Marg., Sandy, wid. 1578/94
Thos., Eaton ?Socon, glover. 1563/101
Wm., Southill, Stanford, tailor. 1676/160
CATHRALL, see Catterall
CATLIN, CATLING, CATLYN, Fra., Sandy, Beeston. 1612/126
Grace, Dunton, wid. 1661/374
Jas., Tilbrook, husb. 1783/19
Jas., sen., Tilbrook, farmer. 1830/26
Jn., Flitton, lab. 1601/103
Jn., Dunton, husb. 1639/19
Jn., Cople, Moxhill, dairyman. 1652/64
Jn., Potton, lab. 1668/138
Jn., Bedford, shepherd. AR 1687-8: 1/31
Nich., Goldington, lab. 1643/67
Peter, Roxton, carp. 1692-3/61
Robt., Flitwick, husb. 1625/212
Sam., Luton, husb. 1724/22
Sam., Luton, innholder. A 1715/24
Thos., Dunton. 1659/270
Thos., Tilbrook, yeo. 1729/99
Wm., Luton, shearman. 1562/115
Wm., I 1619:4/95
CATO, Jn., Ampthill, saddler. A 1842/16
CATON, CATTEN, CEATON, Ann, Flitton. AR 1691: 1/219d
Ann, Southill, Stanford, wid. 1727/25
Dan., Silsoe, yeo. 1768/23
Eliz., Flitton, Wardhedges, wid. 1667/16
Jn., Pulloxhill. R 1545: 11/121d

CATON, CATTEN, CEATON continued
Jn., Luton, yeo. 1675-6/76
Jn., Southill, Stanford, yeo. 1712-13/89
Jn., Silsoe, yeo. 1803/21
Jn., Southill, bach. A 1715/31
Math., Silsoe, yeo. 1806/24
Phillip, rector of Marston. 1683/3
Robt., Silsoe. 1625-6/161
Thos., Southill, Stanford. 1692/16
Thos., Silsoe, yeo. 1720/54
Thos., Upper Gravenhurst, Ion, yeo. 1804/12
Thos., Flitton, Studham. A 1806/15
Thos., Haynes, husb. A 1828/11
Walt., Warden. AR 1673: 1/99
Walt., sen., Warden. 1673/89
Wm., Lower Gravenhurst, yeo. 1807/20
Wm., Meppershall, husb. A 1728/10
CATTEN, see Caton
CATTERALL, CATHRALL, Ann, Luton, Dane St., wid. 1680/99
Edw., Luton, Dane St., yeo. 1736/29
Eliz., (old index, "docket mislaid"). A 1709/23
Eliz., Luton, spins. A 1741/1
alias Hookes, Geo., Luton, Crawley Green, tinplate worker. 1724-5/14
Geo., Luton, The Swan, yeo. 1645/16
Geo., Luton. A 1705/3
Jn., Luton, Dane St., farmer. AR 1674: 1/147
Jn., Luton, tanner. 1699/58
Jn., Luton, Dane St. 1702/53
Peter, Leighton Buzzard, yeo. 1608/85
alias Hooker, Peter, Luton, victualler. 1680/3
Sarah, Luton, wid. AR 1676-7: 1/152d
Thos., Shillington, yeo. 1756/57
CATTES, Wm., Roxton, Colesden. 1575/107
CAUDELL, see Cawdell
CAULCOT, Geo., Roxton, Chawston, yeo. 1741/17
Sarah, Aspley Guise, wid. 1714/17
Wm., Cranfield, dairyman. 1826/50
see also Goditot
CAUSTIN, Lawrence, Caddington, yeo. 1731/39
see also Costin
CAVE, Agnes, wife of Wm., Maulden. 1610/18
Geo., Stagsden, yeo. A 1823/6
Geo., Stagsden, yeo. A 1824/17
Geo., Stagsden, yeo. A 1825/18
Robt., Bedford, wine merchant. 1846/15

CAVE continued
Sarah, Stagsden, wid. A 1824/14
CAVINGTON, see Covington
CAVIT, Ebenezer, Pavenham, watchmaker. A 1814/11
CAWARD, see Coward
CAWDELL, CAUDELL, Edw., Shefford, cooper. 1813/5
Edw., Shefford, cooper. A 1813/5
Jn., Shillington, yeo. 1757/17
Thos., Clifton. AR 1685: 1/124d
Wm., Leighton Buzzard, accountant. LB 1826/37
see also Cadwell
CAWLEY, Math., Sandy, butcher. A 1747/18
CAWNE, CALNE, CANE, Ann, Silsoe. 1647/57
Edm., Bedford, grocer. 1687/43
Edw., Bedford St. Peter, weaver. 1641/139
Geo., Wilshamstead, lab. 1587/172
Geo., Henlow, grocer (bundle 1642). 1641/24
Geo., Henlow, grocer. 1641/154
Geo., sen., Wilshamstead, yeo. 1668-9/183
Jn., sen., Wilshamstead, yeo. 1607/116
Jn., Wilshamstead, yeo. 1662/48
Mary, Bedford, wid. 1788/31
Sibil, Bedford St. Peter, wid. 1641/156
Thos., Elstow, lab. 1615/177
Thos., Wilshamstead. AR 1672: 1/6d
Wm., Bedford St. Peter, weaver. 1638/63
Wm., Wilshamstead, yeo. 1658-9/97
Wm., Ampthill. 1682/33
Wm., Wilshamstead, yeo. 1725/54
see also Cain
CAWNELL, CARNELL, CORNELL, David, Wilshamstead. 1570/22
Simon, Wilshamstead. R 1518: 2/45d
Thos., Elstow, yeo. 1560/187
Wm., Elstow, husb. R 1549-50: 12/90d
Wm., Ridgmont. R 1555-6: 13/1
see also Cornwall
CAWOOD, see Coward
CAYNHOO, see Cainhoe
CEITH, see Keith
CESSE, Jn., Cranfield. R 1549: 12/55
see also Case; see also Chase
CHACE, see Chase
CHACKLEY, see Chalkley
CHAD, Jane, Cranfield, wid. 1739-40/87
Thos., Cranfield, lab. 1737/38

CHAD continued
see also Chat
CHADDERTON, Eliz., Carlton, wid. A 1728/15
Jos., Carlton, clerk. A 1720/12
Thos., Carlton, gent. 1735-6/18
Thos., Chellington, rector. AR 1684: 1/46
Ursula, Carlton, wid. 1754/27
Wm., Carlton. 1728/15
see also Chatterton
CHADDOCK, Barnaby, Sandy. AR 1688-9: 1/131
Ric., Leighton Buzzard. A 1743/11
CHALKLEY, CHACKLEY, CHAULKEY, Alice, Wootton. AR 1678: 1/15
Eliz., Luton, spins. 1737-8/68
Joan, Luton, wid. 1619/245, I 4/77
Jn., Luton. R 1534-5: 4/17
Jn., Sandy, Girtford. AR 1690: 1/133d
Jn., jun., Luton, yeo. 1734/48
Jonathan, Luton. 1667/24
Nich., Luton. 1684-5/60
Reinold, Wootton, yeo. 1649/1
Wm., sen., Luton, yeo. 1715/18
CHALTON, CHARLTON, Ann, Tilbrook, wid. 1713-14/39
Jas., Maulden, tawer. 1744/35
Jn., Tilbrook, gent. 1711/82
Marshall, Goldington. A 1771/13
Sam., Harrold, farmer. A 1760/14
Sam., Kempston, yeo. A 1792/5
Wm., Shefford, lab. 1723/58
Wm., Henlow. AR 1670: 1/90, 220d
CHAMBERLAIN, CHAMBERLYN, CHAMBURLEYN, Pymor alias Chamberlain see Pymor
Abraham, Whipsnade, yeo. 1726/53
alias Wakefield, Alice, Langford. 1631/183
Edm., Ravensden. R 1545-6: 11/154
Eliz., Bedford, wid. A 1766/31, 33
Eliz., no parish given. 1766/70
Fra., Riseley. A 1751/24
Geo., Wilshamstead. 1603-4/102
Geo., Bedford St. Paul. 1635/26
Geo., Cople. 1651-2/45
Godfrey, Limbury, husb. A 1756/27
Hen., sen., Dunstable, bricklayer. 1711/12
Humph., Wootton. 1647-8/9
Jacob, Kempston, blacksmith. AR 1679: 1/16
Jas., no parish given. 1692/71

CHAMBERLAIN, CHAMBERLYN, CHAMBURLEYN continued
Jas., Bedford. 1767/52
Joan, Wilshamstead. 1557/208
alias Pearce, Jn., Cardington. AR 1684: 1/24d
Jn., Silsoe, P/IX2, bundle missing. A 1747/17
Jos., Lower Gravenhurst, dairyman. 1835/37
Mary, Bedford St. Cuthbert, wid. A 1780/20
Math., Shefford, innkeeper. 1656-7/54
Phillip, Riseley, yeo. 1845/36
Ric., Bedford, blacksmith. 1770/48
Sam., Astwick. R 1689: 1/132
Sam., Biggleswade, Stratton, farmer. Bw 1776/62
Sam., Shillington, Lower Stondon, blacksmith. 1810/31
Simon, Toddington. R 1501: 1/26
Thos., Elstow. R 1508: 1/118
Thos., Oakley, Minister of the word of God at Oakley. 1617/253
Thos., Warden, dairyman. 1660/48
alias Wakefield, Thos., Henlow, lab. 1663/5
Thos., Biggleswade, Holme, dairyman. 1685/128
Thos., Leighton Buzzard, innholder. A 1750/19
Thos., Arlesey, dairyman. 1796/4
Thos., Lower Gravenhurst, husb. 1853/24
Wm., Riseley, wheelwright. 1721-2/64
CHAMBER, CHAMBERS, Halsey alias Chambers, see Halsey
Eliz., Bromham, spins. A 1848/4
Fra., parish torn off, wid. 1670/186
Jas., Potton, yeo. 1661/339
Jn., Bedford St. Mary, minister of. 1621/218
Jn., Potton, blacksmith. 1701-2/75
Jn., Potton, farmer. AR 1681-2: 1/115d
Jonathan, Clifton, yeo. 1630/42
Jonathan, Shefford, blacksmith. 1693/151
Mich., Bedford, grocer. 1715/7
Robt., Oakley, translator. 1685/75
Sybil, wid. A 1711/39
Thos., Potton. 1635/46
Thos., Northill, carp. 1637-8/161
Thos., Bedford, lab. 1829/4
Wm., Dunstable. R 1550: 12/118d
Wm., (old index, "docket mislaid"). A 1708/13
see also Camber
CHAMPERNOUNE, Chas., Marston, clerk. A 1711-12/11
CHAMPION, Robt., Eaton Socon, Beggary, lab. 1612/38
see also Campion
CHANCE, CHANNCE, Jn., Chalgrave. 1578/108

CHANCE, CHANNCE continued
Thos., Toddington, victualler. 1826/12
CHANDLER, Ann, Tempsford, wid. 1813/35
Ebenezer, Bedford, gent. 1747/29
Edw., Tempsford, farmer. A 1764/16
Eliz., Caddington, Markyate Street, wid. 1732/2
Hen., Millbrook, husb. A 1711/41
Jn., Pertenhall. R 1543: 6/168
Jn., Woburn, blacksmith. 1626/132
Jn., Northill, Beeston, husb. 1680/36
Mary, Bedford, wid. 1757/30
Percival, Leighton Buzzard, late Hollington, Soulbury, Bucks., gent. LB 1780/54
Thos., Tilbrook. R 1551: 12/164d
Thos., Thurleigh, carp. 1637-8/152
Thos., Thurleigh, yeo. 1692/46
Thos., sen., Tempsford, yeo. 1750/9
Thos., Blunham, yeo. 1767/5
Thos., Roxton, yeo. R 1770/34
Tobias, Bedford, gent. 1707/35
Wm., Northill, Caldecote, farmer. 1856/42
Wm., Sandy. A 1721/17
CHAPLIN, Edw., Henlow, lab. 1633/135
CHAPMAN, Smith alias Chapman, see under Smith
Abr., Luton, farrier. 1718/87
Abr., sen., Luton, blacksmith. 1679/19
Agnes, Bolnhurst, wid. 1613/130
Anne, Dunstable, wid. 1706/76
Bernard, Ivinghoe, gent. LBA 1816/71
alias Sheard, Bridgett, Little Staughton. 1694/35
Dan., Ampthill, yeo. 1826/30
Edw., Luton. R 1535: 4/31
Edw., jun., Oakley, farmer. 1843/46
Eliz., Colmworth, wid. 1632/91
Eliz., Bedford, wid. 1815/32
Eliz., Clophill, shopkeeper. 1830/3
Eliz., Flitwick, wid. A 1707/4a & b
Fra., Totternhoe. 1625/172
Fra., Flitton, farmer. 1783/55
Geo., Wymington, blacksmith. 1658/22
Geo., Luton. AR 1688: 1/175
Geo., Shefford, tailor. A 1729-30/69
Harry, Houghton Regis. 1592-3/9
Hen., Houghton Regis, yeo. 1627/138
Hen., Dunstable, husb. 1632/84
Hen., Luton, blacksmith. 1680/13

CHAPMAN continued
Hen., Houghton Regis, victualler. A 1752/27
Hen., Clophill, yeo. 1784/21
Hen., Wilshamstead, farmer. 1792/27
Hen., Bletsoe, farmer. 1797/43
Humph., Shillington, lab. 1638/126
Humph., Shillington, husb. 1685/59
Jas., Biggleswade, lab. Bw 1766/45
Jas., Silsoe, yeo. 1815/29
Jas., parents of Ampthill, died in East Indies. A 1831/11
Jane, Houghton Conquest, late of Clophill, wid. 1798/4
Joan, no parish given. R 1612: 30/89
Jn., Bolnhurst, lab. 1603/136
Jn., Dunstable, maltster. 1626/100
Jn., Campton, tailor. 1627/204
Jn., sen., Lidlington, yeo. 1667/120
Jn., sen., Dunton, lab. 1707/43
Jn., (old index "docket mislaid"). A 1708/9
Jn., Wymington, grazier. 1731-2/12
Jn., Dunton and Mary. A 1742/17
Jn., Dunton, yeo. 1742/35
Jn., Luton, carp. 1775/26
Jn., Clophill, yeo. 1810/41
Jn., Clophill, day labourer. 1821/2
Jos., Goldington, tailor. 1768/15
Lucy, Shillington, wid. 1639/75
Margt., Streatley, Sharpenhoe, wid. 1622-3/14
Margt., Cardington, wid. 1712-13/51
Mary, Lidlington, wid. 1657-8/16
Mary, Dunstable, wid. 1673/31
Mich., Dunstable, bricklayer. AR 1673-4: 1/147
Nich., Bedford St. Mary. R 1505: 1/102
Ric., Marston, ?drover. 1658/144
Robt., Dunstable, maltster. 1665/26
Robt., Dunstable, cordwainer. 1723/15
Russell, Colmworth, yeo. A 1797/11
Sarah, Houghton Regis, wid. 1754/52
Stephen, Luton, locksmith. 1734/57
Susannah, Luton. 1694/14
alias Shard, Thos., Eaton Socon, lab. 1620/58
alias Brewer, Thos., Toddington, lab. 1633/138
Thos., Dunstable. AR 1675-6: 1/150d
Thos., Luton, carp. AR 1679: 1/158d
Thos., Luton, carp. 1679-80/107
Thos., Luton, carp. 1726/77

CHAPMAN continued
Thos., Dunton, wheelwright. A 1733/22
Thos., Tilbrook, farmer. A 1736/8
Thos., Toddington, victualler. 1745/24
Thos., Turvey, gent. 1760/13
Thos., Dunstable, innholder. A 1814/3
Thos., Bolnhurst, farmer. 1841/1
Wm., jun., Houghton Regis, weaver. 1610-11/23
Wm., Dunstable, maltster. 1647-8/21
alias Sheard, Wm., Little Staughton, husb. 1687/18
Wm., sen., Dunstable, yeo. 1687/79
Wm., Flitwick. A 1707-8/6
Wm., Dunstable, yeo. 1716/37
Wm., Bedford St. Peter, comber and yeo. 1759/50
Wm., Odell, yeo. A 1794/4
Wm., Eversholt. 1853/49
CHAPPELL, Ben., Colmworth. 1701/17
Eliz., Luton, wid. 1673/65
Geo., Husborne Crawley, yeo. 1833/14
Jn., Kempston, corndealer. 1831/11
Mary, nee Turney, Potsgrove. A 1802/7
Nich., "of Markyate dwelling in the parish of Studham". 1557/380
Nich., Silsoe, Wrest, yeo. 1610/83, I
Rog., Eversholt, innholder. A 1784/23
Sam., Sharnbrook, farmer. 1844/28
Susan, Colmworth, wid. 1704/50
Thos., Potsgrove, yeo. 1768/29
Thos., Kempston, yeo. A 1822/13, I 4/248
Thos., jun., Holcote, yeo. 1836/1
Wm., Luton, Luton Hoo. 1661-2/274
Wm., Colmworth, yeo. 1661/297
CHARGE, Walt., Holcote. R 1543-4: 11/3
Wm., Salford. A 1560/194
CHARLES, Ben., Yielden, farmer and wheelwright. 1820/13
Isaac, Maulden, yeo. 1800/8
Jn., sen., Maulden, yeo. 1724/34
Jn., Maulden, gardener. 1763/41
Ric., Eversholt, lab. A 1735/6
Wm., Yielden, carp. 1831/12
CHARLTON, Judith, Felmersham, wid. R 1770/32
Wm., Cardington, husb. 1582/88
Wm., Carlton, farmer. 1767/50
CHARNOCKE, see Chernocke
CHARRINGTON, Joan, Toddington, Chalton, wid. 1600-1/26
Wm., Toddington, Chalton, tailor. 1609/147

CHARRINGTON continued
see also Carrington
CHARVELL, see Carvell
CHASE, Eliz., Dunton, wid. 1686/67
Fra., Luton, wid. 1847/8
Hen., Lt. Barford. 1654-5/51
Jn., Tempsford, husb. A 1706/30
Mordaunt, Milton Ernest, gent. 1648/117
Thos., Milton Ernest, gent. 1630/134
Thos., Lt. Barford. 1632/43
Thos., Lt. Barford, yeo. 1654/52
Wm., Lt. Barford. 1646/106
Wm., Dunton, lab. 1684/42
see also Case; see also Cesse
CHAT, Wm., Elstow. 1557/362
see also Chad
CHATTERTON, Geo., Wymington, clerk and parson of. 1610/114
see also Chadderton
CHELISTER, Robt., Harlington. R 1532-3: 3/86d
CHELTENHAM, Creswell, Shefford, late of Rochester, Kent, excise officer. 1740/6
CHERNIAN, Ellen, Caddington. 1563/95
CHERNOCKE, CHARNOCKE, Chris., Eversholt. 1699/17
Fra., Holcote, gent. 1708-9/82
Hen., Turvey, singleman. 1612/123
Hugh, Kempston, Bourne End, yeo. 1608/25
Jas., Eversholt, husb. 1613/202
Joan, Houghton Conquest, How End, wid. 1677-8/59
Sir Pynsent, Holcote, Bart. A 1734/9
Ric., Holcote, esq. 1615/146
Robt., Eversholt, yeo. 1638/89
Wm., Bedford, gent. 1683-4/81
Wm., Toddington. A 1755/5
CHERRY, Eliz., Dean, wid. 1721/15
Eliz., Houghton Conquest, wid. 1837/49
Geo., Upper [Over] Stondon, husb. 1749/16
Jn., Meppershall, lab. 1651-2/43
Jn., Houghton Conquest, yeo. 1812/12
Math., sen., Henlow, lab. 1640/12
Maurice, Dean, yeo. 1720/115
Thos., sen., Meppershall. 1660/163
Thos., Leighton Buzzard, lace merchant. Fac. 1704: 9/13
Thos., Shillington, yeo. 1848/26
Titus, sen., Houghton Conquest, yeo. 1831/37
Wm., Chellington. 1843/9

CHESHAM, see Chessam
CHESHIRE, Ann, Dunstable, wid. 1851/8
Eliz., Heath and Reach, wid. LB 1810/50
Jas., Heath. A 1743/14
Jas., sen., Heath, carp. LB 1810/47
Jos., Dunstable, carp. 1850/34
Phyllis, Leighton Buzzard. AR 1682: 1/163d
Ric., sen., Heath, carp. LB 1770/25
Wm., Barton, miller. 1800/18
Wm., Heath, carp. LB 1805/28
Wm., Dunstable, carp. A 1819/8
Wm., Barton, miller. A 1831/2
Wm., Dunstable, carp. 1846/42
CHESSAM, CHESHAM, CHESSUM, Eliz., Roxton, spins. 1649/15
Eliz., Maulden, spins. A 1724/31
Eliz., Wrestlingworth, wid. 1799/49
Francis, Maulden, gard. 1729/81
Hannah, Dunton, wid. 1723/54
Jas., Eaton Socon, yeo. AR 1680: 1/70d
Jas., Wrestlingworth, farmer. A 1763/5
Jn., Woburn, victualler. A 1715/27
Jn., Wrestlingworth, yeo. A 1799/3
Martha, Woburn, wid. 1707/16
Mary, Woburn, wid. and victualler. 1781/48
Ric., Roxton, tailor. 1620/116
Robt., Roxton. R 1532-3: 3/87
Thos., Eaton Socon, Wyboston. 1571/56
Thos., Eaton Socon, Wyboston, blacksmith. 1641-2/130
Thos., Eaton Socon, Wyboston, yeo. 1724/57
Thos., Wrestlingworth, yeo. A 1799/2
Thos., Markyate. R 1529-30: 3/21d
CHESSEY, Jos., Dunstable, baker. 1760/11
CHESTER, Austin, Nether Dean, yeo. 1729/75
Edw., Dunstable, baker. 1649/41
Edw., Over Gravenhurst, lon. 1664-5/72
Theodsia (old index "Docket mislaid"). A 1710/16
Thos. (alias Crosby), Haynes, aforetime London, merchant tailor. 1553/275
Thos., Eyeworth, yeo. 1670/198
Thos., Eyeworth. AR 1670: 1/91
Thos., Dunstable, baker. 1681-2/101
CHESTON, Alice, Luton, Newmill End, wid. 1601/83
CHETLOW, CHITLOW, alias Leceter, John, Bletsoe. 1556/221
Ric., Thurleigh, servant. 1620/122
CHETTLE, Jos., Thurleigh, yeo. A 1781/19
Joshua, Yielden, yeo. A 1781/19

CHEW, Wm., sen., Southill, Broom, cordwainer. 1849/36
CHEYNE, Eliz., Luton, wid. ?1715/84
Eliz., Sundon, wid. 1724/65
Robt., Luton, Bramblehanger, gent. 1630/95
Susannah, Hockliffe in Chalgrave (sic), wid. 1707-8/66
Thos., Luton, gent. 1662/30
Thos., Pertenhall, clerk. 1711/69
CHEYNEY, CHENEY, CHENY, Grace, Ampthill, wid. A 1728/8
Jn., Harrold. 1557/244
Jn., Husborne Crawley, shepherd. 1662/114
Jn., Ridgmont, lab. 1712/77
Wm., Sundon, esq. AR 1675: 1/146
Wm., Sundon. AR 1676: 1/151d
Wm., Ampthill, gent. A 1724-5/41
Wm., Luton. A 1795/14
CHICHELEY, CHICHERLY, Thos., Potton, carp. AR 1670: 1/90d
Thos., Bedford St. Mary, blacksmith. AR 1682: 1/21d
Wm., Bedford, ironmonger. A 1704/28
CHIDLEY, Ric., Leighton Buzzard, blacksmith and farrier. 1680/37
CHILD, CHILDS, CHILES, Agnes, Roxton, wid. AR 1685: 1/79d
Alice?, wid. Roxton (bundle 1556-9). 1558/13
Andrew, Dunton. 1610/51
Ann, Podington, wid. 1662/120
Ann, Roxton, Colesden, wid. 1702/6
Ann, Roxton, Colesden, wid. A 1702/7
Dinah, Roxton, spin. 1746/4
Edw., Roxton. 1666/121
Eliz., Roxton, wid. 1625/168
Fra., Maulden. 1660/31
Fra., Maulden, yeo. 1726/16
Geo., Cardington, Cotton End. c1670/217
Geo., Roxton, yeo. 1722/59
Hannah, Bletsoe, Whitwick End, wid. 1669/45
Hen., Roxton, yeo. 1706/24
Jane, Haynes, wid. 1625/181
Joan, Flitton, Fielden, wid. 1558/51
Jn., Hardwick, yeo. 1604/55
Jn., Silsoe, yeo. 1613/218
Jn., Barford. 1622/73
Jn., Barton. 1638-9/90
Jn., Roxton, Colesden, yeo. 1688-9/81
Jn., Roxton, yeo. 1698/179
Jn., Renhold, Howbury, gent. 1720/83
Jn., Barton, grocer. 1723/25
Jn., Henlow, farmer. 1764/46

CHILD, CHILDS, CHILES continued
Jn., Flitwick, yeo. 1831/49
Joyce, Marston, wid. 1719/76
Margt., Roxton, wid. 1697/32
Math., Marston Wroxhill. 1716/83
Maud, Silsoe, wid. 1614-15/9
Nich., Flitton, Fielden. 1593/13
Ralph, Shillington, lab. 1688/37
Ric., Flitton, husb. R 1551: 12/159d
Ric., Hardwicke, yeo. 1639/13
Robt., Goldington. 1564/55
Robt., Roxton, yeo. 1639/61
Robt., Roxton, yeo. 1660/52
Robt., Roxton, yeo. 1725/62
Thos., Dunton, husb. 1560/163
Thos., sen., Roxton. R 1508-9: 1/206
Thos., sen., Roxton, yeo. 1606/35
Thos., Roxton, yeo. 1612-13/7
Thos., sen., Roxton, husb. 1625/166
Thos., Bletsoe, yeo. 1656/169
Thos., Roxton, gent. 1675-6/70
Thos., Roxton, Scatsend, yeo. 1678-9/139
Thos., sen., Roxton, yeo. 1729/106
Thos., Roxton, yeo. 1767/60
Thos., Houghton Conquest, yeo. A 1776/3
Timothy, Maulden, yeo. 1686-7/82
Wm., Barton. R 1551: 12/149
Wm., Streatley, Sharpenhoe, husb. 1573/20
Wm., Roxton, lab. 1629/125
Wm., Roxton, yeo. 1639/35
Wm., Great Barford, wheelwright. 1764/56
Wm., Northill, lab. 1783/22
Wm., Henlow. A 1832/4
CHILES, see Child
CHILLINGWORTH, Giles, Kempston, lab. 1657-8/27
CHIPPERFIELD, Mary, Pulloxhill. 1814/27
CHISWICK, CHISWEEKE, Chris., Maulden, lab. 1597/17
CHITLOW, see Chetlow
CHOICE, Jn., Stotfold, yeo. 1721/9
see also Joyce
CHONGE, Edw., Felmersham. 1558-9/318
CHORLEY, Joan, Felmersham, Radwell. 1618/119
CHOWNE, Edw., Little Barford. 1634-5/119
CHRISTMAS, Agnes, Sandy, wid. 1679/69
Ann, Bedford, wid. 1777/39

CHRISTMAS continued
Edw., sen., Sandy. 1639/10
Edw., Sandy, tailor. 1662-3/74
Geo., Dunstable, barber chirurgeon. 1743/39
Hen., Halstead, Harrow, Essex, attorney's clerk, (Bedford). 1849/24
Jn., Northill, Beeston, yeo. 1706/7
Jn., Sandy, Girtford, yeo. 1739-40/83
Jn., Bedford. 1762/61
Jn., Arlesey, yeo. 1781/26
Jn., Sandy, baker. 1822/14
Maria, Sandy, wife of Thos. 1849/28
Mary, Sandy, wid. AR 1681: 1/112
Mary, Sandy, spins. 1836/28
Susan, wid. of Wm., Sandy, Beeston. 1724/32
Thos., Bromham, yeo. 1689/32
Thos., sen., Sandy, Girtford, gard. 1724/33
Thos., Blunham, weaver. A 1729/16
Wm., Sandy, husb. 1661/279
Wm., Northill, farmer. A 1723/14
Wm., Sandy, Girtford, weaver. 1736/42
Wm., sen., Sandy, baker. 1803/5
Wm., Sandy, letter carrier. 1841/28
CHRISTY, Agnes, Bedford, wid. 1633/142
Jasper, Bedford St. Paul, gent. 1624/66
Sam., Bedford, tanner. 1602/49
alias Bowyer, Thos., Bedford St. Paul. R 1568: 17/113
CHUBSEY, Thos., (old index "Docket mislaid"). A 1708/35
CHUFLEYE, see Cuffley
CHURCH, CHIRCHE, CHURCHE, Alice, Pavenham. R 1543: 11/1d
Alice, Milton Ernest, wid. 1637/39
Anth., Felmersham, baker. 1668-9/173
Anth., Stagsden, shepherd. 1801/10
Eliz., Maulden. 1774/51
Eliz., Eggington, sp. 1829
Eliz., Eggington, wid. LBA 1830/90
Fra., Felmersham. 1603/96
Geo., Sharnbrook, innholder. 1835/20
Helen, Dunstable. R 1517: 1/216
Isabella, Pavenham. R 1504: 1/40
Israel, Wymington. 1713/19
Israel, Sharnbrook, husb. 1775/20
Jn., Milton Ernest. 1581/20
Jn., Felmersham. 1599/106
Jn., Milton Ernest. 1632/27
Jn., Eaton Socon, Honeydon, lab. 1666-7/141

CHURCH, CHIRCHE, CHURCHE continued
Jn., Milton Ernest, yeo. 1673/67
Jn., Wymington, yeo. 1684/1
Jn., Luton, Otebridge, husb. 1696/135
Jn., sen., Wymington, farmer. 1698/75
Jn., Turvey. A 1703/1
Jn., Wymington, butcher. 1725-6/76
Jn., Wymington, grazier. 1747-8/57
Jn., Bedford, yeo. 1778/30
Jn., Wymington, Lodge, farmer. 1795/17
Jn., sen., Higham Gobion, Faldoe Farm, farmer and grazier. 1848/20
Levi, Kempston, butcher and victualler. 1833/29
Levi, Bedford, baker. 1845/1
Martha, Bedford St. Mary. A 1807/8
Mary, Stagsden, wid. A 1808/3
Mary, Roxton, wid. 1833/23
Nich., Stotfold. R 1509-10: 1/64d
Rebecca, Luton, Otebridge, wid. 1696/134
Ric., Dunstable, lab. A 1715/9
Ric., Bedford St. Cuthbert, lab. 1723/14
Robt., Oakley, husb. 1638/171
Robt., Felmersham, lab. 1640/77
Robt., Biddenham. AR 1689: 1/32d
Robt., Carlton, minister of the Gospel. 1721/25
Sam., sen., Goldington, mealman. 1851/19
Sarah, Riseley, wid. 1794/27
Sarah, Cranfield, wid. 1795/13
Susannah, Turvey, spins. A 1722/13
Thos., Pavenham. R 1543: 11/1
Thos., Bedford, lab. 1647/60
Thos., Wymington, yeo. 1658/188
Thos., Bedford St. Paul, innholder. 1698/118
Thos., Podington, farmer. A 1748/27
Thos., Wymington, farmer. 1774/34
Thos., wymington, farmer. 1796/9
Thos., Leighton Buzzard. LBA 1812/68
Wm., "Pavenham in the parish of Stevington". R 1521-2: 2/106
Wm., Milton Ernest. R 1528-9: 3/1
Wm., Felmersham. 1663-4/77
Wm., Lt. Barford. AR 1691: 1/134d
Wm., Bedford, yeo. A 1742/21
Wm., Woburn. 1761/41
Wm., Cranfield, yeo. 1774/40
Wm., Stevington, lab. A 1775/11
Wm., Harrold. 1815/25

CHURCHILL, Jos., Nottingham. A 1805/12
Jos., Nottingham, esq. 1805/33
CHURCHMAN, Ephraim, Turvey (P/IX2) admon missing. A 1757/16
CIRCUIT, see Cirket
CIRKET, CIRCUIT, SIRKET, Ann, Millbrook, wid. AR 1686: 1/215
Eliz., Maulden, wid. 1720/86
Fra., Millbrook, glover. 1668/142
Fra., Millbrook, dairyman. AR 1682: 1/207
Jn., Woburn, husb. 1712-13/23
Jn., Maulden, husb. 1720/14
Jn., Maulden, yeo. 1738/7
Jn., Harlington, dairyman. 1744/30
Jos., Woburn, yeo. 1758/61
Jos., Woburn, yeo. 1849/26
Mary, Meppershall, wid. A 1750/11
Ric., Woburn, yeo. 1736/23
Ric., Meppershall, dairyman. A 1722/10
Ric., Luton (P/IX2 limited admon). A 1812/6
Sam., Flitwick, dairyman. A 1731/28
Sarah, Woburn, wid. 1748/40
Wm., Millbrook, lab. 1697/1
CLAPHAM, Alice, Sandy, wid. 1660/140
CLARE, Chris., Riseley. 1619/211, I 4/137
Edw., Sharnbrook, day labourer. 1604/70
Eliz., Kempston, wid. 1647/52
Emmot, Wootton, wid. 1610/125
Fra., Kempston Hardwick, grazier. 1647/50
Jane or Joan, Felmersham, wid. 1609/68
Jn., "of Pavenham of the parish of Stevington". 1557/336
Jn., Sharnbrook, tailor. 1639/27
Jn., Stagsden. 1687/17
Jn., Stagsden, husb. 1742/11
Jn., sen., Shefford, innholder. 1748/8
Mary, Riseley, wid. 1620-1/197
Mary, Cardington, Cotton End, wid. 1753/26
Ric., Stevington. R 1543: 6/150
Ric., Sharnbrook, fuller. 1647/44
Robt., Tempsford. 1559-60/201
Robt., Pavenham. 1609/158
Robt., Harrold, husb. 1661/233
Robt., Bedford, barber chirurgeon. 1739-40/82
Robt., Pavenham, yeo. 1740-1/79
Thos., Stagsden. R 1566: 16/147
Thos., Pavenham. 1637/171
Thos., Pavenham. 1637/174

CLARE continued
Thos., Cardington, Cotton End, yeo. 1735/25
Thos., Pavenham, gent. 1795/39
CLARIDGE, Geo., Leighton Buzzard, baker. LB 1821/12
Mackaness, Yielden. 1803/1
Wm., Yielden, yeo. A 1743/6
Wm., Keysoe, farmer. 1814/38
Wm., Yielden, farmer. 1844/19
CLARK, CLARKE, CLEARKE, CLERKE, Anstill alias Clarke, see Anstill; Carter alias Clark, see Carter; Furmason alias Clarke, see Furmason; Mason alias Clarke, see Mason; Thomasin alias Clarke, see Thomasin
--, Dunstable, wid. A 1723/30
Abigail, Bedford, wid. 1705-6/86
Agnes, Eversholt, wid. 1592/46
Alex., Sandy. R 1509: 1/54
Alex., Biggleswade, wheeler. Bw 1727/27, I
Alice, Northill, wid. A 1711/17
Amos, Dunstable, victualler. 1716/40
Ann, Chalgrave, Tebworth. AR 1679-80: 1/158
Ann, Potton, wid. 1710-11/2
Ann, Bedford, publican. 1839/33
Anth., Harrold, baker. 1668/112
alias Thomasin, Barnaby, Wrestlingworth, yeo. I 1619: 4/97
Barth., Eversholt, yeo. 1612-13/57
Beatrice, Houghton Conquest, wid. 1607/102
Ben., Maulden, yeo. 1824/4
Ben., Houghton Conquest, carp. 1847/40
Bridgett, Odell, wife of Nich., husb. 1683-4/123
Cath., Bedford, wid. 1661-2/404
Cath., Harrold, wid. A 1765/16
Chris., Chalgrave, Tebworth, gent. 1683/37
Chris., Sandy, Beeston, innholder. 1802/23
Edm., Studham. R 1531: 3/41d
Edm., Luton, yeo. 1590/159
Edm., Stopsley, Scoryend, yeo. 1649/72
Edw., Wrestlingworth. 1663/74
Edw., Luton, Rinsford, yeo. 1664-5/74
Edw., Langford, farmer and dairyman. 1788/7
Eliz., Gt. Barford. R 1545: 11/71d
Eliz., Henlow, wid. 1574-5/51
Eliz., Pulloxhill, wid. 1638/190
Eliz., Arlesey, wid. A 1707/41
Eliz., Biggleswade, wid. Bw 1728/30
Eliz., Biggleswade, wid. A 1733/17
Eliz., Bedford St. Paul. A 1742/10

CLARK, CLARKE, CLEARKE, CLERKE continued
Eliz., Wymington, spins. A 1750/5
Ellen, Milton Ernest, wid. 1623/164
Ellis, Harrold, baker. AR 1673: 1/37
Ellis, Harrold, baker. A?1673: 1/38d
Fra., Lidlington, yeo. 1584-5/261
Fra., Sharnbrook, yeo. 1647/45
Fra., Wootton, Wootton Pillinge, gent. 1661-2/241
Fra., Souldrop, husb. (bundle 1663). 1662/57
Fra., Houghton Regis. wid. AR 1671-2: 1/142
Hen., Studham. R 1545: 11/65d
Hen., Stevington, husb. 1581-2/3
Hen., Potton. 1587/164
Hen., Southill, tailor. 1643/82
Hen., Langford, weaver. 1668/145
Hen., Sharnbrook. AR 1689: 1/50
Hen., sen., Woburn, innholder. 1767/61
Hen., Woburn. A 1806/12
Hen., Blunham, yeo. 1829/38
Hen., Southill, victualler. 1835/16
Humph., Potton, turner. A 1705/19
Humph., Ampthill, baker. 1813/46
Isaac, Coomworth, shoemaker. A 1729/43
Isaac, Kempston, yeo. 1838/8
Jacob, Bedford, architect. 1846/11
Jas., Luton. R 1540: 7/33
Jas., Leighton Buzzard. LBA 1774/27
Jas., Bedford St. Paul, yeo. A 1790/7
Jas., Luton, straw plait dealer. 1844/31
Jas., Northill, Thorncote, yeo. 1849/42
Jas., Leighton Buzzard, innholder and maltster. LB 1830/48
Jane, Northill, Thorncote, wid. 1794/12
Joan, Willington, wid. R 1557-8: 14/46d
Joan, Knotting, wid. 1629/132
Joan, Luton, spins. 1673-4/77
Joan, Bromham, wid. 1711/67
Jn., Oakley. R 1508-9: 1/208d
Jn., Houghton Regis. 1555/84
Jn., Lidlington. 1556/191
Jn., Lidlington. R 1558: 14/51
alias Astell, Jn., Marston, husb. 1561/184
Jn., Barford. 1568/52
Jn., Luton. 1570/26
Jn., Marston, husb. 1570-1/28
Jn., Henlow, yeo. 1600/6

CLARK, CLARKE, CLEARKE, CLERKE continued
Jn., Elstow, gent. 1609/163
Jn., Southill, blacksmith. 1611/1
Jn., Cople, lab. 1612-13/82
Jn., Southill, blacksmith. 1616/100
Jn., Pulloxhill. 1619-20/239, I 4/51
Jn., Southill, Stanford. 1620-1/10
Jn., Bedford St. John, shoemaker. 1624/94
Jn., Southill, Broome, carp. 1632-3/173
Jn., Flitton, lab. 1634-5/80
Jn., Pulloxhill, lab. 1639/49
Jn., Barton, yeo. 1660-1/114
Jn., Lidlington, yeo. 1673/49
Jn., Bedford St. Mary. AR 1674: 1/8d
Jn., Heath, yeo. Fac. 1705: 9/17
Jn., Arlesey, husb. A 1706/37
Jn., sen., Houghton Conquest, husb. 1718/41
Jn., Lidlingtpn. A 1719/5
Jn., Felmersham, husb. 1724/19
Jn., Houghton Conquest, yeo. 1730/33
Jn., Luton, husb. 1741/62
Jn., Woburn, butcher. 1750/10
Jn., Meppershall, farmer. A 1751/17
Jn., Sandy, bricklayer. 1762/43
Jn., Upper Sundon, farmer. A 1764/17
Jn., Hinwick, yeo. 1764/45
Jn., sen., Bedford St. Paul, carp. 1775/14
Jn., Haynes, carp. 1807/17
Jn., Harrold, yeo. 1818/36
Jos., Southill, blacksmith. 1633/124
Jos., Clifton, blacksmith. 1643/71
Jos., Houghton Conquest, yeo. 1739/58
Jos., Flitton, Greenfield, miller. 1830/36
Jos., Maulden. 1846/22
Joyce, Ampthill, wid. 1682/70
Judith, Luton, wid. 1846/32
Lancelot, Maulden, skinner. 1727/33
Lawr., Turvey, tailor. 1609/141
Lawr., Bedford, brandy merchant. A 1747/5
Lewis, Eaton Socon, lab. 1762/54
Lewis, Little Staughton, yeo. 1854/28
Marg., Aspley Guise, wid. 1582-3/109
Martin, Shillington, shoemaker. 1641/158
Mary, Felmersham, wid. 1726/47
Mary, Lidlington, wid. 1747/1

CLARK, CLARKE, CLEARKE, CLERKE continued
Mary, Toddington, late Stony Stratford, Bucks., wid. 1778/11
Mary, Farndish, wid. 1789/14
Mary, Leighton Buzzard, wid. LB 1799/8
Mich., Sutton, carp. 1590/181
Nich., Eaton, sawyer. 1584/250
Nich., ?Marston, yeo. ?1681/1
Oliv., Kempston, yeo. 1631-2/229
Peter, Marston Moreteyne. 1619-20/217, I 4/26
Phillip, Potsgrove. 1672/164
Rachel, Bedford, wid. 1816/6
Randall, Ampthill, sadler. AR 1681: 1/205
Rebecca, Leighton Buzzard, wid. LBA 1805/56
Ric., Dunstable, innholder. 1600/5
Ric., Henlow. 1604/30
Ric., Odell, husb. 1681-2/76
Ric., Luton, yeo. AR 1686: 1/172d
Ric., Keysoe, woodward. 1686/55
Ric., Bedford St. Mary. 1713/58
Ric., Woburn, grocer. 1846/14
Robt., Barford. 1574-5/43
alias Sumner, Robt., Sharnbrook, yeo. 1605/109
Robt., Eaton, lab. 1627/160
Robt., Sandy, Beeston, blacksmith. 1661/384
Robt., Bedford St. Paul. AR 1675: 1/10d
Robt., Potton. AR 1676-7: 1/106d
Robt., Shillington, bach. AR 1681: 1/112
Robt., Biddenham, husb. 1681/81
Robt., Sandy, Beeston. AR 1683: 1/120d
Robt., Northill. AR 1687-8: 1/130
Robt., Thurleigh, yeo. 1705/3
Robt., Heath and Reach, shepherd. 1748/1
Robt., Houghton Conquest, clerk. A 1760/13
Rog., Eggington, husb. 1558/38
Sam., Sandy, Beeston, yeo. 1669/30
Sam., Tillbrook. A 1736/7
Sara, Pulloxhill, spins. 1699/53
Sarah, Barton, spins. AR 1688: 1/174
Sarah, Lidlington, spins. 1690-1/50
Sarah, Stagsden, wid. 1714/61
Sarah, Southill, wid. 1847/41
Simon, Tempsford, husb. 1584/173
Simon, Bromham. 1729/78
Sith (sic), Elstow, wid. 1627/197
Susan, Woburn, wid. 1725/30

CLARK, CLARKE, CLEARKE, CLERKE continued
Susannah, Bedford, wid. AR 1688: 1/31d
Thos., Pulloxhill. R 1500: 1/10
Thos., Lidlington. R 1508: 1/166
Thos., Harrold, weaver. 1554/162
Thos., Eversholt. 1558/62
Thos., Marston, husb. 1558-9/294
Thos., Shillington, husb. 1584/179
Thos., Wootton. 1630/91
Thos., sen., Shillington, yeo. 1660-1/82
Thos., Shillington, yeo. 1675/24
Thos., Biddenham, yeo. 1675/54
Thos., Shillington, yeo. 1684/62
Thos., Bedford, collarmaker. A 1705/68
Thos., Biddenham, husb. A 1707/33
Thos., Stagsden, husb. 1709/59
Thos., (old index only, bundle mising). A 1717/11
Thos., Houghton Conquest, dairyman. A 1720/55
Thos., Lidlington, yeo. 1721-2/80
Thos., Riseley, poulterer. 1726/95
Thos., Biddenham, Ford End, gent. 1754/50
Thos., Houghton Conquest, Chapel End, husb. 1762/64
Thos., Sundon, shoemaker. A 1782/12
Thos., Colmworth. 1782/23
Thos., Marston, yeo. 1783/52
Thos., Salford, yeo. A 1793/14
Thos., Cranfield, Barratt, yeo. 1811/41
Thos., Biggleswade, wheelwright. Bw 1734/32a
Thos., Billington, farmer. LB 1812/58
Walt., Potton. R 1499: 1/151d
Wm., Houghton Regis. R 1515: 1/193
Wm., Lidlington. R 1543-4: 11/8d
Wm., Northill, Ickwell. R 1546-7: 11/220
Wm., Lidlington. R 1549-50: 12/87
Wm., sen., Barford, husb. 1557/246
Wm., Shillington, Nether Stondon, yeo. 1617/256
Wm., Goldington. 1619/248, I 4/69
Wm., Dunton. 1620/47
Wm., Milton Ernest, lab. 1622/26
Wm., Barton. AR 1684: 1/167
Wm., Dunstable. 1648/81
Wm., Lidlington, yeo. 1685/7
Wm., Woburn. AR 1690-1: 1/218d
Wm., Cockayne Hatley, yeo. 1691-2/128
Wm., sen., Woburn, innholder. 1714/47

CLARK, CLARKE, CLEARKE, CLERKE continued
Wm., Biggleswade, yeo. Bw 1727/25
Wm., Woburn, butcher. 1733/34
Wm., Flitton. A 1738/25
Wm., Biggleswade, yeo. 1742/27
Wm., Cardington, lab. A 1743/45
Wm., Houghton Conquest, farmer. A 1763/11
Wm., Harrold, barber. 1765/21
Wm., Houghton Conquest, How End, yeo. 1766/28
Wm., Flitton, miller. A 1802/4
Wm., Salford, husb. 1803/6
Wm., Cranfield, yeo. A 1804/11
Wm., Bedford, victualler. 1826/10
Wm., Markyate Street, late Flitton, Greenfield Mill, gent. 1831/20
Wm., Silsoe, carp. 1842/38
Wm., Luton, cordwainer. 1847/50
Wm., Bedford, formerly butcher and publican "but now out of business". 1853/33
CLARKSON, CLARKESON, Christian, Eversholt. 1553/161
CLARRETT, Ste., Sandy, Stratford, gardener. 1748/12
CLAVERS, Geo., Blunham, lab. 1729-30/109
CLAY, Alice, Sandy, wid. R 1532: 3/71
Eliz., Luton, servant to Thos. Peter. A 1574/40
Jn., Sandy, Beeston. R 1498: 1/28d
Thos., Potton. R 1505: 1/105
Thos., Sandy, Beeston. R 1528: 2/145d
Thos., Silsoe, servant. A 1625-6/142
CLAYPOLE, Wm., Roxton. R 1504-5: 1/86d
CLAYSON, Ruth, Harrold, wid. 1791/4
Uriah, sen., Harrold, mason. 1766/34
Wm., Harrold, farmer. 1803/42
see also Clearson
CLAYTON, CLEYTON, Alice, Renhold, wid. 1628/67
Ann, Sutton, wid. 1799/32
Eliz., Southill, wid. 1616-17/30
Jn., Cople, lab. 1660-1/103
Jn., Goldington, yeo. 1661/364
Jn., Tingrith. AR 1691: 1/219d
Jn., Biddenham, husb. A 1707-8/23
Jn., Sherrington, Bucks., yeo. 1818/17
Jn., Cople, yeo. R 1840/30
Matth., Milton Bryan, tailor. 1748/17
Ric., Sutton. R 1550: 12/96d
Ric., Sutton. 1630/100
Ric., Sutton, yeo. A 1790/2

CLAYTON, CLEYTON continued
Robt., Goldington, Putnoe, yeo. 1727-8/112
Robt., Goldington, yeo. A 1728/39
Thos., Willington. R 1545: 11/78
Thos., Willington, husb. 1616/114
Thos., Goldington, yeo. 1695/34
Thos., Bedford, maltster. 1727-8/96
Thos., Bedford. A 1775/16
Wm., Renhold, yeo. 1626/38
Wm., Renhold. 1668/121
see also Cleydon, Cleaton
CLEARSON, Sam., sen., Shefford, victualler. 1724/66
Sam., Shefford, maltster. 1740/56
see also Clayson
CLEATON, CLETON, Geo., Wymington, tailor. 1579/143
Jn., Sandy. AR 1675: 1/102d
Jn., Flitwick, late of Tingrith, carp. 1781/44
Math., sen., Bedford, lab. 1682/97
Nath., Riseley. 1719-20/3
Ric., ?Lidlington. 1723/70
Wm., Southill, yeo. 1612-13/61
see also Clayton
CLEMENTS, Agnes, Luton, wid. 1607/120
Anne, Aspley Guise. 1617/260
Eliz., Haynes. A 1811/11
Humph., Luton, shepherd. 1628-9/27
Jn., Roxton, husb. 1583/143
Jn., Roxton, husb. 1585/79
Jn., Wymington, husb. "now a sojourner at the Badger Inn in St. John's, Clerkenwell". 1733/59
CLEMENTSON, Sarah, Dunstable, wid. 1819/9
see also Clemson
CLEMSON, Hen., Eversholt. 1692/2
see also Clementson
CLETHERALL, Wm., Bedford St. Mary, victualler. 1593/21
CLEVELEY, Hen., Odell. AR 1684-5: 1/46d
CLEWES, CLUS, Mary, Westoning, spins. A 1766/16
CLEYDON, Wm., Eaton, lab. 1647/139
see also Clayton
CLIFTON, Geo., Bedford St. Peter, baker. 1849/45
Wm., Ampthill, carrier. 1680-1/86
CLINTON, Sam., Dunton, (old index, bundle missing). A 1745/3
CLOAD, Eleanor, Aspley Guise, wid. 1704/72
Richard, Aspley Guise, gent. 1703/24

CLOBER, CLOBARNE, Jn., Heath. 1558/45
Thos., Heath and Reach. 1590/157
Wm., sen., Heath and Reach. 1598/78
CLORIDGE, Alice, Yielden, wid. 1701-2/65
Edw., Melchbourne, dairyman. 1733/56
Hannah, Yielden, wid. 1726/35
Valentine, Yielden, husb. A 1700/20
Wm., Stagsden, lab. 1669/92
CLOTHIER, Adowne alias Clothier, see under Adowne
CLOVERS, Lewis, Blunham, lab. 1710-11/25
CLOWS, Wm., (old index, "docket mislaid"). A 1710/11
COANN, see Cowen
COAST, COST, COSTE, Eliz., Cardington, spins. A 1726/7
Rog., Wootton, Wootton Pillinge, lab. 1643/66
Sam., Cardington, Cotton End, dairyman. 1705/38
Sam., Cardington, dairyman. A 1705/5
Wm., Marston, Pillinge, lab. 1612/39, I 4/183
COATES, COTES, COTS, Ric., Potton. R 1500-11: 1/125
Thos., Dunstable, innholder. A 1825/15
Wm., sen., Husborne Crawley, farmer. A 1713/71
COATMAN, Jn., Bedford, miller. 1730/60
COBB, COBBE, Hobkins alias Cobbe, see Hobkins
Anne, wid., Felmersham. 1612/37
Dorothy, Sharnbrook, wife of Thos., esq.. 1664-5/84
Eliz., Westoning, wid. 1801/33
Jn., Sharnbrook, gent. 1648-9/92
Jn., Sharnbrook, gent. 1672/104
Jn., Sharnbrook, gent. AR 1672: 1/36d
Jn., Renhold, grazier. 1682-3/112
Joel, Potton. 1671/36
Margt., Sharnbrook, gentlewoman, wid. 1592/39
Mary, Renhold, wid. 1710/27
Mary, Bedford, wid. 1717-18/63
Paul, Souldrop, gent. 1623/175
Paul, Bedford, gent. 1700/92
Rebecca, Sharnbrook, spins. 1668/176
Sam., Langford, lab. 1825/37
?Thos., ?Sharnbrook. 1573/17. Document badly torn and neither christian name or parish appears. The above information was gleaned from the *History of the Willey Hundred* and *V.C.H.*, III, p. 91.
Thos., Sharnbrook, gent. 1625-6/116
Thos., Kempston. 1663/15
Thos., Sharnbrook, esq. 1670-1/71
Thos., Westoning, Sampshill, yeo. 1786/14
Wm., Sharnbrook. R 1522: 2/3

COBB, COBBE continued
Wm., Northill, Ickwell. R 1545-6: 11/156
Wm., Sharnbrook. 1558-9/307
Wm., sen., Felmersham, yeo. 1624/100
Wm., Ravensden, yeo. 1682/60
Wm., Sharnbrook. AR 1688-9: 1/49d
COCHING, see Cotching
COCK, Hen., Luton, Stapleford, yeo. 1673/42
Hugh, Eaton (?Bray). R 1548: 12/35
Jn., Stagsden. R 1504: 1/39d
Jn., jnr., Stagsden. R 1522: 2/20
Jn., Aspley Guise. R 1547: 12/21
Jn., Stevington, husb. 1581/44
Ralph, Biggleswade husb. 1561/60
Ric., Biggleswade (defective). A c.1550/341
Robt., Stagsden. R 1523: 2/14d
Robt., Dunton, husb. 1723/56
Sam., Bedford, gent. 1644/123
Susan, Chellington, spins. 1674/85
see also Cox; see also Cook
COCKAYNE, Marshall alias Cockayne, see Marshall
Ann, Tempsford, wid. A 1735/23
Jn., Wrestlingworth, esq. 1626/125
Jn., Cockayne Hatley, esq. 1628-9/21
Jn., Cardington, Cotton End, gent. 1702/3
Nich., Harlington, husb. 1661-2/252
Oliv., Bedford St. Mary, gent. 1648/112
Wm., "Bury Hatley". R 1527: 2/75d
COCKER, Jn., Willington, husb. 1664/27
COCKERELL, Edm., Eaton Socon, yeo. 1637-8/151
Simon, Elstow, yeo. 1624/56
COCKERTON, Gilbert, Wootton, yeo. 1792/24
COCKING, Jas., Sandy, Beeston, gard. 1852/18
Ric., Renhold, lab. 1652/76
COCKLE, Robt., Biggleswade, Stratton, blacksmith. 1672/168
Roger, Totternhoe, lab. 1602-3/79
COCKMAN, Jn., Bedford St. Mary, tiler. 1614/75
Wm., Bedford St. Paul, bricklayer. 1652-3/97
CODGBROOK, Thos., Bedford St. Mary, yeo. A 1786/5
COE, Alice, Dunton, Milloe. 1622/64
Dorothy, Souldrop, wid. 1685-6/111
COGGDELL, Agnes, Leagrave, wid. 1629/138
COIL, Alice, Bedford St. Peter Merton. R 1539: 5/32
see also Cole
COITE, see Coyte

COKE, see Cooke
COLBECK, COLBACK, Jn., Bedford St. Cuthbert, lab. 1712/76
Luce, Tempsford. R 1547: 11/245d
COLBECK, COLBACK continued
Robt., Eaton Socon, Wyboston, yeo. 1684/65
Thos., Tempsford. R 1546: 11/146
COLBREND, Thos., Southill, gent. 1668-9/191
COLE, COLL, COALE, COLES, COOLE, Fisher alias Cole, see Fisher
Ann, Turvey, wid. A 1761/27
Edm., Leighton Buzzard. 1660-1/77
Eliz., Wilden. 1635/4
Eliz., Luton, wid. 1739-40/76
Eliz., Steppingley, wid. 1746-7/48
Gerrard, Lidlington. 1646/72
Hannah, Bletsoe, wid. 1774/2
Hen., jun., Bromham, yeo. 1611-12/134
Hen., Keysoe, carp. 1694/23
Jas., Wilshamstead, farmer. 1855/21
Jeremy, Blunham, Chalton, husb. 1633/135
Joan, Lidlington, wid. R 1532: 3/76
Jn., Lidlington, lab. 1560/212
Jn., Dunstable. R 1565: 16/120d
Jn., sen., Lidlington, yeo. 1614/34
Jn., Limbury, shepherd. 1647/30
Jn., Harlington, Wood End, yeo. 1662/132
Jn., Wrestlingworth, yeo. 1680-1/89
Jn., Woburn. AR 1685: 1/212d
Jn., Luton, chirurgeon. A 1722/14
Jn., Bromham. A 1754/19
Jn., Luton, tallow chandler. 1762/37
Jn., Willington, victualler. A 1766/2
Jn., Bletsoe, victualler. A 1773/11
Jn., Willington, publican. 1816/26
Jos., Pulloxhill, farmer. A 1805/13
Margt., Lidlington, wid. 1568/124a
Martin, Turvey, blacksmith. A 1721/11
Martin, Podington, blacksmith. 1730/62
Martin, Podington, blacksmith. 1736/49
Martin, Turvey, victualler. A 1758/26
Martin, Turvey. 1786/17
Math., Woburn, collarmaker. A 1740/1
Nath., Clophill, clerk. 1662/100
Phillip, wid. (sic), Lidlington. 1637/84
Ric., Harrold, shepherd. A 1727-8/47
Robt., Moggerhanger, blacksmith. 1620/25

COLE, COLL, COALE, COLES, COOLE continued
Robt., Biggleswade. Bw R 1542: 1/2
Sam., Riseley, gent. 1746-7/49
Sarah, Willington, wid. A 1787/3
Sarah, Pulloxhill, Kitchen End. 1813/38, I 4/219
Susannah, Cople, wid. A 1784/11
Thos., Dunstable, scrivenor. 1614/72
Thos., Lidlington, yeo. 1672/156
Thos., Northill, Upper Caldecote, blacksmith. 1672-3/177
Thos., Harrold, farmer. A 1736-7/27
Thos., Cranfield, dairyman. 1750/33
Wm., Lidlington, husb. 1578/92
Wm., Lidlington. 1554/182
Wm., Ridgmont, yeo. 1620/45
Wm., Lidlington, yeo. 1657/58
Wm., Lidlington. AR 1685-6: 1/214d
Wm., Keysoe, carp. 1697/4
Wm., Yielden, yeo. 1725/9
Wm., Steppingley, tallow chandler. 1739-40/74
Wm., Cople, victualler. A 1770/15
Wm., Woburn Abbey, yeo. A 1823/1
Wm., Willington, farmer. 1834/39
see also Coil
COLEMAN, Barber, Sharnbrook, gent. R 1776/37
Chas., Aspley Guise. AR 1689: 1/217d
Christian, Kempston, wid. 1601-2/133
Dan., Higham Gobion, gent. A 1723/11
Edw., Stotfold, lab. 1660/213
Edw., Odell, publican. A 1857/7
Fra., Woburn, ironmonger. 1710/36
Fra., Aspley Guise. A 1712/10
Geo., Pavenham, lab. 1657/191
Geo., Arlesey, farmer. 1813/1
Hannah, Leighton Buzzard. Fac. A 1758: 9/71, 91
Hen., Bromham. 1661/309
Hen., Shillington, yeo. 1691/111
Hen., Shillington, yeo. 1729/71
Jas., Luton, baker. 1728/58
Jas., Luton, bricklayer. Monition to transmit to P.C.C., A.B.P. 1/1832
Jeremiah, Luton, Sourge End, yeo. 1740/45
Jn., Luton, shoemaker. 1618-9/17
Jn., Stotfold, lab. 1635-6/42
Jn., Arlesey, lab. 1638-9/103
Jn., Harrold, baker, grocer & draper. 1853/45
Jos., Houghton Regis, grocer. 1714/90

COLEMAN continued
Jos., Bedford, grocer. 1831/7
Lawr., Shillington, yeo. 1657/15
Lawr., Shillington, Pegsden, yeo. 1737/17
Mary, Bromham, wid. 1682/14
Mary, Luton, wid. 1741-2/77
Sarah, Cranfield. A 1727-8/34
Sarah, Arlesey, wid. A 1824/15
Thos., Shillington, yeo. 1568/130
Thos., Potsgrove, husb. 1580/234
Thos., Shillington. 1588/116
Thos., sen., Shillington. 1620-1/5
Thos., Shillington, yeo. 1627/166
Thos., Shillington, shoemaker. 1635/49
Thos., Shillington. AR 1675: 1/102
Thos., Shillington, yeo. 1721/70
Thos., Shillington, yeo. 1735/53
Thos., Billington, yeo. LB 1776/42
Wm., Billington, yeo. LB 1788/83
COLES, see Cole
COLEY, Ben., Wilshamstead, lab. 1838/29
Jn., Potton, husb. 1570/7
see also Colley
COLIN, see Collins
COLLETT, Ann, Husborne Crawley, wid. 1680/71
Ann, Leighton Buzzard. LBA 1758/11
Elias, Dean. A 1781/10
Elias Boswell, Dean, gent. 1844/24
Jn., sen., Husborne Crawley, yeo. 1657/106
Jn., Husborne Crawley, yeo. 1664/4
Jn., Billington, farmer. A 1748-9/24
Robt., Billington, yeo. 1751/55
COLLEY, Ellen, Clophill. A 1723/5
Ralph, Chicksands, farrier. 1685/68
Ric., Bedford, innholder. A 1777/11
see also Coley
COLLIER, see Collyer
COLLINGTON, Sarah, old index "docket mislaid". A 1710/42
COLLINS, COLLENS, COLLING, COLLINGE, COLYN
Alice, Milton Bryan, wid. R 1558: 14/48
Barwell, Cardington, clerk. 1742-3/100
Edm., Toddington. 1750/44
Edm., Toddington, gent. A 1810/25
Edw., Luton. R 1509: 1/60d
Edw., Godmanchester, Hunts., yeo. 1574/58

COLLINS, COLLENS, COLLING, COLLINGE, COLYN continued
Edw., Houghton Regis, yeo. 1663-4/96
Edw., Houghton Regis, bach. AR 1683: 1/165d
Eliz., Milton Bryan, wid. 1658/233
Eliz., Farndish, wid. 1714/35
Eliz., Stanbridge, wid. LB 1770/26
Eliz., Gt. Barford, spins. A 1777/10
Hen., Eaton, husb. 1555/92
Hen., Houghton Regis. 1576/17
Hen., Southill. 1615-16/121
Hen., Eversholt, yeo. 1743/16
Humph., Milton Bryan, yeo. 1631/186
Jn., Eaton. R 1528: 2/186
alias Brown, Jn., Kempston. R 1533: 3/112
Jn., Luton, Stapleford. R 1547-8: 12/14
Jn., Houghton Regis. 1566-7/71
Jn., jun., Eaton, husb. 1598/93
Jn., Woburn, yeo. 1619/236
Jn., Husborne Crawley, yeo. I1619/20: 4/52
Jn., Chalgrave, Tebworth, yeo. 1680/26
Jn., Houghton Regis. AR 1680: 1/159
Jn., Steppingley, lab. AR 1685: 1/213d
Jn., Chalgrave, Tebworth, yeo. 1728/38
Kath., Old Warden. 1617-18/161
Lawr., Totternhoe, lab. 1599/149
Margt., Luton. R 1544-5: 11/50
Mary, Elstow. I1619: 4/104
Mary, Chalgrave, Tebworth, wid. 1746/19
Mary, Biggleswade, spins. Bw 1763/40
Mary, Houghton Regis, wid. AR 1681: 1/161
Ric., Flitton. R 1503: 1/35d
Ric., Luton, Stapleford, widower. 1561/179
Ric., Toddington, Herne. 1564/34
Ric., Colmworth, lab. 1676/134
Ric., Leighton Buzzard, tailor. Fac. 1701: 9/2
Ric., Battlesden, yeo. 1779/45
Ric., Leighton Buzzard. LBA 1755/7
Robt., Milton Bryan, yeo. 1618/96, 97
Robt., Cople, maltster. 1662/83
Robt., Goldington, clerk. A 1749/2
Roger, Eaton Bray. R 1558: 14/88
Simon, Eversholt. 1621-2/149
Thos., Milton Bryan, parson. 1604/40
Thos., Chalgrave, Tebworth, yeo. 1607-8/158
Thos., Luton, maltman. 1610/105

COLLINS, COLLENS, COLLING, COLLINGE, COLYN
Thos., Milton Bryan, yeo. 1616/132
Thos., Luton, Stapleford. 1618/113
Thos., Woburn, yeo. 1655/13
Thos., Luton, Stapleford. 1674/81
Thos., Billington, yeo. 1682/18
Wm., Luton, Stapleford, husb. 1565-6/61
Wm., Marston, husb. 1582/110
Wm., Luton. 1583/148
Wm., sen., Turvey. 1593/16
Wm., Arlesey, lab. 1617/261
Wm., Stopsley. 1660-1/105
Wm., Totternhoe, lab. 1675-6/79
Wm., (old index "docket mislaid"). A 1710/39
Wm., Totternhoe, yeo. 1727/68
Wm., Barton, farmer. A 1729/5
Wm., Battlesden, yeo. A 1735/4
Wm., Caddington, Woodside, carp. 1743/21
Wm., Leighton Buzzard, draper and tailor. LB 1811/55
Wm., Leighton Buzzard, vict. LB 1834/56
COLLINSON, Wm., Wilden, schoolmaster. 1628/40
see also Collison
COLLIS, Agnes, Wilden, wid. 1627-8/217
Thos., Turvey, farmer. 1784/17
COLLISON, Thos., Colmworth, yeo. 1616-17/16
see also Collinson
COLLOP, Alice, Flitwick, wid. c. 1553/290
Eliz., Flitwick, wid. 1660/215
Geo., Flitwick, husb. 1593-4/32
Hen., Flitwick, gent. AR 1673-4: 1/191
Hen., Flitwick, gent. AR 1677-8: 1/199
Jn., Eversholt, gent. 1711/20
Keziah, Biggleswade. Bw 1838/149
Margt., Flitwick, wid. 1622/65
Reignold, Flitwick, gent. 1590/123
Reinald, Pulloxhill, yeo. 1606/6
Renold, sen., Flitwick. R 1546: 11/202
Reynold, Flitwick, gent. 1657-8/259
Reynolds, Flitwick, gent. 1579/182
Thos., Southill, Broome. 1719/99
COLLYER, COLLIER, COLLYAR, Bredsell alias Collyer, see under Bredsell
Bredsell, Bedford St. Paul, cordwinder. 1676-7/147
Eliz., Bedford St. Peter, wid. 1647/24
Fra., sen., Houghton Regis, husb. 1759/28

COLLYER, COLLIER, COLLYAR continued
Fra., Pulloxhill, farmer & dairyman. 1809/23
Joan, Potsgrove, wid. 1626/64
Jn., Marston. 1558/250
Jn., Marston. 1560/191
alias Bredsell, Jn., Bedford, cordwainer. AR 1676-7: 1/12d
Phil., clerk & rector of Bedford St. Peter. 1644/121
Ric., Blunham. R 1519-20: 2/147
Thos., Blunham. R 1520-1: 2/168
Thos., Leighton Buzzard. 1558/9
Thos., Marston. 1593/49
Thos., Potsgrove, grazier. 1607-8/154
Thos., Pulloxhill, yeo. 1764/18
Wm., Sandy, Stratford, yeo. 1639/62
Wm., Pirton, Herts., lab. 1673/27
Wm., Toddington, lab. 1682-3/120
Wm., Sundon, husb. 1684/63
Wm., sen., Houghton Regis, husb. 1724/11
Wm., Pulloxhill, dairyman. 1740/25
Wm., Pulloxhill, farmer. 1793/33
COLMAN, see Coleman
COLMWORTHE, Eliz., Biggleswade, Holme, wid. 1564/60
COLSON, Ann, Bedford, wid. 1719/23
Ben., Bedford, baker. 1715/1
Jas., Eaton Socon. 1798/19
COLTON, Thos., Little Paxton, Hunts., yeo. 1660/221
COLTRYTT, Margt., wid., Rushden. 1558/157
COMEDALLE, Jn., Kempston, fuller. 1556/116
COMFORT, Hen., Thurleigh, shepherd. 1657/46
COMPTON, Ann, Potton, wid. A 1705/62
Ann, Potton. 1705/67
Dorothy, Potton, spins. 1685/95
Greg., Bromham. R 1530: 3/27d
Jn., Stagsden. R 1528: 2/187d
Jn., sen., Potton, yeo. 1636-7/119
Jn., Potton, cordwainer. 1688/6
Jn., Potton, husb. 1587/105
Ralph, Maulden, yeo. 1610-11/82
Ralph, Clophill, gent. AR 1669-70: 1/186
Sybell, Stevington, wid. 1672/153
Thos., Stagsden, husb. 1590/133
Thos., Potton, cordwainer. AR 1670: 1/90
Thos., Clophill. AR 1679: 1/202d
Thos., Sutton, yeo. 1715/36
Thos., Potton, shoemaker. A 1732/21

COMPTON continued
Walt., Potton, cordwainer. A 1701-2/20
Wm., Potton, bach. 1678/132
see also Cownton
CONFIELD, Ric., Bedford, cooper. 1750-1/60
CONN, Fra., Cranfield, dairyman. 1733/33
Jeff., North Crawley, Bucks., yeo. 1731/10
CONNINGTON, CUNNINGTON, Edw., Keysoe, weaver. 1680/79
Hannah, Wilden, late Keysoe. 1842/11
Jn., jun., Keysoe, lab. 1690/55
Jn., jun., Keysoe. AR 1690: 1/83d
Jn., Eaton Socon, lab. A 1724/25
Peter, Keysoe, weaver. 1626/84
Thos., Eaton Socon, yeo. 1721/95
Thos., sen., Keysoe, yeo. 1825/30
Wm., Colmworth, yeo. 1766/11
Wm., Riseley, yeo. 1821/1
Wm., Keysoe Row, yeo. 1830/7
Wm., Keysoe, farmer. 1841/36
CONQUEST, Audrey, Houghton Conquest, wid. c.1591-2/96
Ben., son of Sir Ric., Houghton Conquest. 1695/17
Benedict, Houghton Conquest, esq. A 1733/28
Edm., Houghton Conquest, gent. R 1532: 3/57d
Eliz., Dame, wid., Houghton Conquest, The Grove. 1639-40/139
Eliz., Biggleswade, wid. straw hat manufacturer. Bw 1819/118
Etheldred, Ampthill, Ewe Green, wid. 1724/64
Geo., Biggleswade, plumber and glazier. Bw 1819/120
Jas., Biggleswade, draper. Bw 1821/125
Jn., ?Wilden (Gen. Beds. Blaydes). 1617/327
Jn., Wilden, yeo. 1701-2/72
Jn., Bedford St. Paul, butcher. 1767/32
Kenelin, Stevington, gent. 1697/140
Thos., Bedford St. Paul, Gwynne Street, late Cardington, farmer. 1848/25
Wm., Southill. R 1521: 2/179
CONSTABLE, Ralph, Biggleswade, gent.. AR 1678-9: 1/11d
Steph., Shillington, yeo. 1714/64
Thos., Maulden, yeo. 1584/246
CONSTANT, Sam, Bedford, gard. A 1839/15
CONSTANTINE, Robt., Totternhoe, husb. 1568/49
CONY, Hen., Cardington, Harrowden, weaver. 1624/24
Hugh, Potton, tallow chandler. 1572-3/86

COOCH, Hen., sen., Upper Gravenhurst, husb. 1721/24
Jn., Shillington, husb. 1658/121
Jn., Bedford St. Paul, maltster. 1733/45
Jn., Bedford, grocer. 1751/12
Robt., Kempston, lab. 1686/8
Thos., Shillington, husb. 1591/113
Wm., Bedford. A 1734/8
COOK, COOKE, COCKE, COKE, COWKE, KOK
Ainsworth alias Cooke, see Ainsworth
Alea alias Cook, see Alea
Fletcher alias Cook(e), see Fletcher
Talks alias Cook, see Talks
Agnes, Eaton Bray, wid. 1599/176
Agnes, Chalgrave, Tebworth, wid. 1638/161
Alice, Eaton Bray. R 1521: 2/89
Alice, Harlington, wid. 1598/77
Alice, Eaton, wid. 1630/41
Alice, Eaton Bray, wid. 1664/63
Alice, Leighton Buzzard, wid. Fac. 1703: 9/7
Alice, Houghton Regis, Sewell, spins. 1715/32
Ann, Kempston, wid. AR 1679: 1/16d
Ann, Kempston, wid. 1679/43
Ann, Bedford St. Cuthbert, wid. 1681/17
Ann, Toddington, wid. 1691/92
Ann, Bedford St. Paul, wid. 1758/9
Ann, Eversholt, wife of Fra. 1769/12
Anne, Bedford St. Paul, spins. 1642/25
Anthony, Bedford St. Paul, butcher. 1694/45
Edm., sen., Eaton Bray. 1588/138
Edm., Eaton, yeo. 1609-10/107
Edm., Eaton, yeo. 1641/185
Edm., jun., Eaton Bray, husb. 1684/46
Edm., Eaton Bray, yeo. 1694/18
Edm., Eaton Bray, yeo. A 1748/21
Edw., Houghton Regis. 1616/137
Edw., Higham Gobion, Gubbins Wood, dairyman. 1812/51
alias Carvell, Edw., Eversholt, blacksmith. 1733/64
Eliz., Milton Bryan, spins. 1662/89
Eliz., Eaton Bray, spins. AR 1681: 1/60d
Eliz., Eaton Bray, wid. 1683/31
Eliz., Ampthill, wid. 1837/31
Eliz., Barton, wid. 1851/5
Ellen, Milton Bryan, wid. 1580/215
Fra., Milton Bryan, yeo. 1642/12
Fra., Milton Bryan, yeo. 1702/72

COOK, COOKE, COCKE, COKE, COWKE, KOK continued
Fra., sen., Milton Bryan, gent. 1752/6
Fra., Eversholt, gent. 1795/9
Fra., Hockliffe, Fanhill, dairyman. 1812/55
Fra., Sundon, farmer. 1846/46
Geo., Eaton, yeo. 1620-1/11
Geo., sen., Wilshamstead, Cotton End, yeo. 1626/103
Geo., sen., Eaton Bray, yeo. 1658-9/183
Geo., Eaton Bray, yeo. 1683-4/119
Geo., Wilshamstead, yeo. AR 1685: 1/26d
Geo., Wilden, (citation only). 1773
Geo., Flitwick Wood, farmer. 1853/14
Geo., Biggleswade. Bw R 1546: 1/5
Gregory, Eversholt, farmer. A 1768/4
Hannah, Silsoe. A 1855/28
Helen, Oakley, wid. 1631/153
Hen., Little Staughton. 1632/82
Hen., Eaton, lab. 1637/109
Hen., Melchbourne. AR 1677: 1/67
Hugh, Eaton, yeo. 1646/70
Hugh., Eaton Bray, shepherd. R 1755/17
Isabell, Woburn Abbey, spins. 1672/149
Jas., Eaton, weaver. 1648/137
Jas., sen., ?Eaton Bray. 1684/5
Jas., Billington, yeo. LB 1792/94
Jane, Eaton, wid. 1615/145
Jane, Potsgrove, wid. 1769/28
Jn., Stotfold. R 1495: 1/151
Jn., Langford, Holme. R 1508: 1/173
Jn., Elstow. R 1509: 1/55
Jn., Bluntisham, Hunts. R 1512: 1/167
Jn., Eaton, husb. 1588-9/35
Jn., sen., Eaton, husb. 1592/49
Jn., Stotfold. 1598/85
Jn., Eaton, yeo. 1600/4
Jn., sen., Leagrave, husb. 1600/32
Jn., Clifton, gard. AR 1685: 1/125
Jn., Haynes, yeo. 1708-9/65
Jn., Northill, poulterer. 1713/33
Jn., Bedford, tanner. 1723/57
Jn., sen., Chalgrave, Tebworth, yeo. 1728/20
Jn., Ridgmont, husb. 1728-9/109
Jn., Ridgmont, yeo. 1733-4/25
Jn., Wilshamstead. 1742/46
Jn., Potsgrove, dairyman. 1743/50

COOK, COOKE, COCKE, COKE, COWKE, KOK continued
Jn., Dunstable, maltster. 1747/34
Jn., Cardington, yeo. 1771/9
Jn., Ridgmont, yeo. 1776/11
Jn., Dunstable, innholder. A 1789/10
Jn., Luton, victualler. 1802/17
Jn., Bletsoe, shopkeeper. 1830/40
Jn., Potton, sadler & harness maker. 1835/36
Jn., Lidlington, yeo. 1848/9
Jn., Toddington, plait dealer. 1853/31
Joan, Maulden, late wife of Martin. 1608/61
Joan, Stagsden, spins. AR 1678: 1/41d
Jos., Eversholt, gent. 1748/43
Jos., Ridgmont, yeo. 1766/25
Jos., Luton. A 1753/4
Julian, wid., Eyton (?Eaton). 1553/271
Luke, Bedford, maltmiller. 1619/188, I 4/116
Margt., Woburn, wid. R 1535-6: 4/50
Maria, Toddington, strawplait dealer. 1853/43
Martha Mary, wid., Flitwick. 1853/3
alias Gibbs, Mary, Eversholt, wid. A 1729-30/67
Mary, Ridgmont, wid. 1739/61
Mary, Ampthill, wid. 1750/2
Mary, Eversholt, spins. 1775/33
Mary, Steppingley, wid. 1810/50
Math., Flitwick, yeo. 1831/28
Mich., Houghton Regis, Sewell, yeo. 1630/72
Mich., Houghton Regis, Sewell, yeo. 1677/44
Newman, Leighton Buzzard, innholder. LB 1787/78
Nich., Cardington, Cotton End, yeo. 1600-1/20
Nich., Kempston, yeo. 1705-6/46
Nich., Kempston, yeo. A 1705-6/12
Ralph, Eaton, blacksmith. 1659/282
Ralph, Eaton, blacksmith. 1659/293
Rebecca, Streatley, Sharpenhoe, wid. 1854/41
Ric., Eaton Bray. R 1547: 11/235d
Ric., Wilshamstead, West Cotton. 1558/69
Ric., Eaton Bray, carp. 1562/126
Ric., Cranfield. 1571-2/58
Ric., Wilshamstead, lab. 1615/206
Ric., Cardington, Harrowden, husb. 1618/90
Ric., sen., Cranfield, yeo. 1623/130
Ric., Toddington. 1633/119
Ric., Marston, yeo. 1635/11
Ric., Chalgrave, Tebworth. 1635/20

COOK, COOKE, COCKE, COKE, COWKE, KOK continued
Ric., Cranfield. AR 1674-5: 1/193
Ric., Eaton Bray, Moore End, lab. 1682/40
Ric., Billington, yeo. Fac. 1704: 9/11
Ric., Eaton Bray, cordwainer. 1705/33
Ric., Pulloxhill. 1707/24
Ric., Billington. LBA 1753/3
Ric., sen., Steppingley, farmer & dairyman. 1814/34
Robt., Woburn Chapel. R 1535: 4/19d
Robt., Milton Bryan, yeo. 1605/101
Robt., Eaton Bray, yeo. 1659/272
Robt., Milton Bryan, yeo. 1684/100
Robt., Milton Bryan, yeo. 1687-8/103
Robt., Milton Bryan. AR 1687-8: 1/174
Robt., Houghton Regis, Sewell, yeo. 1697-8/46
Robt., Dunstable, yeo. 1718/73
Robt., Houghton Regis, Sewell, yeo. 1773/44
Robt., Steppingley, yeo. A 1826/10
Roger, Langford, husb. 1578/111
Roger, Cranfield. I 1619: 4/65
Roger, Sundon, husb. 1639-40/134
Ruth, Luton, wid. A 1825/9
Sam., Houghton Conquest, hosier. A 1727-8/50
Sam., Potton. A 1768/14
Sarah, Eaton Bray, wid. 1714-15/112
Sarah, Eggington, wid. LB 1830/50a
Stallworth, Flitwick. A 1850/14
Thos., sen., Eaton, husb. R 1551: 12/167
Thos., Toddington. 1558/268
Thos., Stanbridge, husb. 1561/182
Thos., Bedford, weaver. 1577-8/66
Thos., vicar of Salford and parson of Moulsoe, Bucks. c. 1578-9/98 & 98a
Thos., Oakley, husb. 1586-7/141
Thos., Bedford St. Cuthbert. 1617/233
Thos., Cardington, yeo. 1618/89
Thos., Elstow, yeo. 1619/260, I 4/88
Thos., Eaton, lab. 1629/131
Thos., Langford, dairyman. 1639/82
Thos., Bedford St. Cuthbert, shoemaker. 1645/114
Thos., Wilshamstead, Cotton End. 1663-4/78
Thos., sen., Langford, yeo. 1670/147
Thos., Bedford St. Paul, sadler. AR 1676: 1/12d
Thos., Bedford St. Paul, sadler. 1677/7
Thos., Ridgmont, cordwinder. 1685/50
Thos., Sandy, bach. AR 1685-6: 1/126d

COOK, COOKE, COCKE, COKE, COWKE, KOK continued
Thos., Lidlington. AR 1692: 1/220
Thos., Eaton Bray, husb. 1699/34
Thos., Bedford, butcher. 1701/37
Thos., Bedford St. Paul, glover. 1725-6/41
Thos., Lidlington. 1740/28
Thos., Cople. 1756/50
Thos., Woburn, victualler. 1764/23
Thos., Steppingley Park, yeo. 1774/60
Thos., Toddington, Herne, dairyman. 1785/13
Thos., Ampthill, innholder. 1787/45
Thos., Flitwick, yeo. 1794/21
Thos., sen., Flitwick, yeo. 1815/1
Thos., Steppingley, husb. A 1821/6
Uryan, Eaton, carp. 1614/28
Wm., Toddington. R 1518: 2/94
Wm., Milton Bryan. 1553/285
Wm., Tilsworth, husb. 1587/158
Wm., sen., Eaton Bray, bach. 1588/101
Wm., Toddington, tailor. 1612/66
Wm., Leagrave, yeo. 1644-5/114
Wm., Ridgmont, farmer. 1693/85
Wm., sen., Ridgmont, yeo. 1693/101
Wm., Eaton Bray, husb. 1707/59
Wm., Tilsworth, yeo. 1710/24
Wm., Eversholt, cordwainer. A 1712/49
Wm., Eaton Bray, shepherd. 1716/93
Wm., Bedford, tanner. 1717-18/76
Wm., Goldington, lab. A 1727/16
Wm., sen., Milton Bryan, yeo. 1771/17
Wm., Milton Bryan, yeo. 1810/32
Wm., Ampthill, yeo., late innholder. 1833/36
COOKSON, Jas., Luton, Park St., carp. 1852/10
COOLE, Jn., Riseley. R 1528: 2/134d
Robt., Potton. R 1524: 2/78
COOLIDGE, Jn., Blunham. 1731-2/49
COOLING, Dennis, Wootton, clerk. A 1711/6
COOMBES, COOMB, COOMBE, COOMBS, Ann, Bedford, wid. 1740/61
Eliz., Woburn. 1591-2/91
Jn., Bedford, limemaker. 1785/31
Jn., Bedford, limeburner. 1823/12
Margt., Bedford, spins. 1728/76
Sarah, Bedford St. Paul, wid. 1804/34
Stephen, Bedford, victualler. 1681/8
Stephen, Bedford St. Paul, victualler. 1729/8

COOMBES, COOMB, COOMBE, COOMBS continued
Wm., Bedford, butcher. 1720/77
Wm., Bedford, limemaker. 1773/3
Wm., Bedford St. Paul, yeo. A 1799/6
COOPER, COUPER, COPER, COWPER, CUPPER, Arnold alias Cooper, see Arno
Godfrey alias Cooper, see Godfrey
Smith alias Cooper, see Smith
Mrs., Eaton Bray (no date, 19th century). I 4/284
Agnes, Tempsford. R 1500: 1/10d
Alice, Clifton. 1628/58
Ambrose, Marston. 1662/40
Andrew, Toddington, yeo. 1727/14
Andrew, Ampthill, Little Park, yeo. 1760/15
Ann, Salford, wid. 1618/49
Ann, Biggleswade, Holme, wid. 1697/12
Ann, Lower Gravenhurst, wid. 1740/53
Ann, Leighton Buzzard, spins. LB 1791/89
Ann, Aspley, spins. 1794/14
Ann, Aspley Guise, spins. 1799/41
Ann, Bedford St. Paul, wid. 1835/40
Anne, Eversholt, wid. of John. R 1541: 6/115d
Anne, Potton, wid. 1617/179
Ballard, Milton Ernest, yeo. 1762/4
Barth., Dunstable. 1693/82
Ben., Henlow. 1698/151
Ben., Riseley. 1857/38
Brian, Sandy, yeo. 1741/30
Cath., Keysoe, wid. 1617/316
Christian,Bromham. wid. 1553/270
Dinah, Leighton Buzzard, Clipstone, wid. LB 1766/3
Edm., Turvey, husb. 1564/51
Edm., Wilshamstead, tailor. 1660-1/98
Edm., Wrestlingworth, yeo. 1670-1/223
Edw., Blunham. R 1501: 1/31
Edw., sen., Stanbridge, yeo. 1677/43
Edw., Stanbridge, yeo. LB 1739/11
Edw., Tilsworth, bach. 1819/27
Edw., Northill (P/IX2 admon. missing). A 1783/21
Edw., Milton Bryan, farmer. A 1784/24
Edw., Stanbridge. Fac. A 1764: 9/92
Eliz., Dunstable, spins. 1582-3/33
Eliz., Cardington, wid. 1620/119
Eliz., Bedford St. Paul, spins. 1716/44
Eliz., Toddington, Chalton, wid. 1723/76
Eliz., Tilsworth, wife of Jos. 1744/31

COOPER, COUPER, COPER, COWPER, CUPPER continued
Eliz., Aspley Guise, (P/IX2). A 1812/2
Eliz., Tilsworth, wid. 1817/27
Eliz., Langford, wid. 1851/18
Eliz., Wrestlingworth, wid. A 1720/33
Fra., Ampthill. 1624/57
Fra., Chalgrave, Tebworth, bach. 1763/29
Geo., Cardington, Harrowden, husb. 1660/56
Geo., Cardington, Harrowden, bach. 1662/20
Geo., Marston, lab. AR 1684: 1/210d
Geo., Cardington, weaver. 1695/32
Geo., Northill, Over Caldecote, yeo. 1726/49
Geo., sen., Leighton Buzzard, blacksmith. LBA 1772/24
Geo. Osborne, sen., Sandy, Beeston, cordwainer. 1834/35
Geo., Shefford, late glover "but now out of business". 1853/18
Geo., sen., Leighton Buzzard, blacksmith and farrier. LB 1841/79
Geo., Northill, yeo. A 1771/38
Groom, Tilsworth, farmer. 1843/20
Harry, Cardington, husb. 1554/173
Hen., Cardington, Harrowden, yeo. 1592/68
Hen., sen., Milton Bryan, yeo. 1715/53
Hen., Bletsoe. 1734-5/15
Hum., Henlow, carp.. 1672/158
Humph., Harrold, lab. A 1728/32
Isabel, Blunham, weaver. 1633-4/192
Jas., Southill, Broome, yeo. 1593-4/89
Jas., Campton, husb. 1662/131
Jas., Kempston, yeo. A 1801/1
Jane, Stanbridge, wid. LB 1774/37
Joan, Carlton, wid. 1583-4/140
Joan, Upper Gravenhurst, wid. 1707/11
Jn., Bedford St. Paul. R 1502: 1/32d
Jn., sen., Harrowden, husb. R 1535: 4/35d
Jn., Clophill. R 1541: 6/98
Jn., Turvey, husb. 1558/73
Jn., Oakley. 1558/85
Jn., Totternhoe (Tottyrnoll). 1558-9/305
Jn., Houghton Conquest, husb. 1573/141
Jn., Ravensden. 1576/5
Jn., Wootton. 1577/58
Jn., Tempsford, husb. 1617/314
Jn., Toddington, Chalton, lab. 1639/56
Jn., Over Gravenhurst. 1649/45
Jn., Dean, Over, lab. 1651/132
Jn., Blunham. 1661-2/262

COOPER, COUPER, COPER, COWPER, CUPPER continued
Jn., Biggleswade, Holme. AR 1686: 1/126
Jn., Marston. 1699/10
Jn., Dunstable, victualler. A 1705/43
Jn., Henlow, yeo. 1720/69
Jn., Stotfold, yeo. 1724-5/67
Jn., Chicksands, miller. 1726/46
Jn., Bedford, heelmaker. A 1731/38
Jn., Roxton, lab. A 1734-5/30
Jn., Southill, Holme Mills, miller. 1740-1/87
Jn., Potton, collar maker. 1741/15
Jn., Cople, yeo. 1761/42
Jn., Silsoe, dairyman. 1764/30
Jn., Ampthill, farmer. A 1766/30
Jn., Thurleigh. A 1768/7
Jn., Chalgrave, Tebworth, yeo. 1774/45
alias Farrer, Jn., sen., Kempston, tailor and innholder. 1782/21
Jn., sen., Sandy, Beeston, gard. 1815/12
Jn., Cople, cordwainer. 1815/16
Jos., Henlow, husb. 1675/43
Jos., sen., Chalgrave, Tebworth, husb. 1739/68
Jos., sen., Tilsworth, yeo. 1752/20
Jos., Arlesey, lab. A 1753/20
Jos., sen., Tilsworth, yeo. 1765/19
Jos., Lidlington, husb. 1783/46
Jos., sen., Tilsworth. 1793/25
Jos., Chalgrave, farmer (debtor in county Gaol). 1795/22
Jos., Wilshamstead, late of H.M. Regiment of Guards. 1838/30
Luke, old index "docket mislaid". A 1708/3
Mary, Cardington, wid. 1554/169
Mary, Odell. 1639/110
Mary, Cardington, Harrowden. 1660/35
Mary, Henlow. 1702, see ABO 2/11
Mary, Henlow, wife of Thos., yeo. 1706/87
Mary, Pulloxhill, wid. 1721/65
Mary, Odell, wid. 1726/30
alias Farrer, Mary, Kempston, wid. A 1744-5/7
Mary, Stanbridge. LBA 1761/20
Eyles formerly Cooper, Mary, Elstow. A 1800/2
Mary, Shefford, spins. 1821/11
Mary, Langford. A 1851/17
Mich., Henlow. R 1539-40: 6/16d
Nich., Cardington, Harrowden. 1564/58
Nich., Haynes, lab. 1616/123
Nich., Stagsden, lab. 1629/73

COOPER, COUPER, COPER, COWPER, CUPPER continued
Peter, Cardington, lab. 1625-6/154
Phil., Kempston. 1558-9/314
Ralph, Tempsford. 1648/71
Rebecca, Campton, wid. 1772/8
Ric., Eversholt. R 1536: 4/51
Ric., Shillington. 1558/13
Ric., Cardington, Harrowden. 1559-60/212
Ric., Houghton Conquest, yeo. 1610/131
Ric., Odell. 1614/60
Ric., Bedford, heelmaker. 1674/118
Ric., Bletsoe, innholder. A 1706/22
Ric., Toddington, Chalton, yeo. A 1719/16
Ric., Clifton, weaver. A 1721-2/49
Ric., Langford. 1780/19
Robt., Tempsford. R 1523: 2/11
Robt., Keysoe, husb. R 1544-5: 11/58d
Robt., Cardington. 1558/217
Robt., Elstow. 1578/83
Robt., Cardington, Harrowden. 1582/121
Robt., Salford, husb. 1608/51
Robt., Cardington. 1610-11/28
Robt., Blunham, lab. 1615/211
Robt., or Thos., Odell. 1637/164
Robt., Cardington, Harrowden, yeo. 1656/199
Robt., Lower Gravenhurst, farmer. 1722/26
Robt., Biggleswade, yeo. Bw 1726/22
Robt., Biggleswade, miller. Bw 1773/60
Robt., Eaton Socon, butcher. 1820/27
Sam., Oakley, husb. 1728/47
Sam., Leighton Buzzard, farrier. LB 1807/39, I
Sar., Milton Bryan, wid. 1725/15
Sar., Sandy, wid. 1759/23
Sar., Ampthill, Little Park, wid. 1769/25
Sar., Langford, wid. 1789/22
Sar., Arlesey, (P/IX2). A 1812/8
Sim., Wilden, tailor. 1724/77
Simon, Riseley. 1854/40
Steph., Luton, Crawley Green, farmer. 1840/37
Thos., Blunham. R 1517-18: 1/218
Thos., Lidlington. R 1529: 3/17
Thos., Bedford. R 1545: 11/83
Thos., Wootton, yeo. 1558/2
Thos., Carlton. 1565/11
Thos., ?Cardington. 1603/128

COOPER, COUPER, COPER, COWPER, CUPPER continued
Thos., Cardington. 1616/38
Thos., Potton, lab. 1639/40
Thos., Flitwick. 1639/109
Thos., Haynes, dairyman. 1640/99
Thos., Carlton, innkeeper. 1649/12
Thos., Luton, maltster. 1658-9/235
Thos., Toddington, gard. 1670/171
Thos., Luton. AR 1679: 1/155d
Thos., Bedford, heelmaker. 1721/59
Thos., Colmworth, Netherstead, yeo. 1723/47
Thos., Arlesey, weaver. 1728-9/77
alias Farrer, Thos., sen., Kempston, tailor. 1737/42
alias Farrer, Thos., sen., Kempston, tailor and innholder. 1742/33
Thos., Yielden, butcher. A 1760/23
Thos., Yielden, butcher. 1760/44
Thos., Milton Bryan, farmer. 1783/43
Thos., sen., Langford, farmer. 1815/24
Thos., Sandy, Beeston, gard. 1829/10
Thos., Luton, Crawley Green, farmer. 1849/12
Thos., Wilshamstead, thatcher, etc. 1854/14
Thos., Stotfold, Pooley, thatcher. 1856/15
Thos., sen., Leighton Buzzard, farmer. LB 1809/43
Urian, Cardington, weaver. 1624/47
Wm., Barton, husb. 1552/317
Wm., Blunham. 1557/279
Wm., Marston. 1557/392
Wm., Wootton. 1562-3/141
Wm., Cardington. 1582/117
Wm., Southill, Stanford, yeo. 1584-5/274
Wm., Southill, Stanford, yeo. 1593/9
Wm., Bedford St. Paul, shoemaker. 1598/141
Wm., Keysoe, husb. 1617/308
Wm., Keysoe, husb. 1617/335
Wm., Southill, Broom, yeo. 1625-6/155
Wm., Bedford. 1647/32
Wm., sen., Colmworth, bricklayer. 1654/108
Wm., sen., Colmworth, bricklayer. 1654/183
Wm., Campton, husb. AR 1670: 1/90d
Wm., Colmworth, bach. 1686/54
Wm., Shillington, servant. 1704/22
Wm., old index only, bundle missing. A 1718/34
Wm., Odell, lacebuyer. A 1720/2
Wm., Sandy, warrener. 1759/15
Wm., Lower Gravenhurst, yeo. 1759/33

COOPER, COUPER, COPER, COWPER, CUPPER continued
Wm., Leagrave, farmer. A 1772/15
Wm., Moggerhanger, yeo. 1784/34
Wm., Biggleswade, Holme, yeo. BwA 1720-1/3, I
COOTE, COOWTE, Ann, Haynes, wid. 1724-5/78
Fra., Maulden, wife of Isaac, miller. 1781/46
Isaac, Maulden, miller. 1779/26
Jn., sen., Eaton Socon, Wyboston, husb. 1720/44
Mary, Roxton, Chawston, wid. 1661-2/402
Robt., Sandy. 1575/78
Robt., Cople, husb. 1587/166
Robt., Lidlington, dairyman. 1680/6
Thos., Haynes, husb. AR 1671-2: 1/189
Thos., Marston. AR 1690-1: 1/218d
Thos., Haynes, dairyman. A 1716/27
Thos., old index only, bundle missing. A 1718/3
Thos., old index only, bundle missing. A 1718/4
Wm., Wilden, husb. 1580/238
Wm., Colmworth, yeo. 1681/3
Wm., old index "docket mislaid". A 1708/13
Wm., Roxton, lab. A 1729-30/57
COPE, Edw., Aspley Guise, gent. 1692/18
Edw., Aspley Guise. A 1712-13/44
COPPER, Thos., Kempston. 1590/21
Thos., Eaton Socon, mason. 1626/43
COPPERWHEAT, Chas., Ampthill, maltster. 1751/39
Thos., Ampthill. 1726/61
Thos., Cople, weaver. 1734/40
COPPING, COPPIN, Jn., Pulloxhill, Upberry, esq. AR 1684-5: 1/26
Jn., Pulloxhill, Upberry, esq. AR 1684-5: 1/211d
COPPLEY, COPELY, Eliz., Campton, wid. c. 1555/141
Humph., Southill, gent. 1563/21
CORBETT, Fra., Sundon, gent. AR 1672/3: 1/145
Jn., Sutton. R 1545: 11/244
Jn., Sandy, Girtford, tailor. 1578/97
Jn., Sutton, lab. 1612/33
Robt., Sutton. 1591-2/90
Robt., sen., Dean, Nether, grocer. 1834/24
Wm., Biggleswade, sadler. BwA 1806/48
CORBY, CORBE, Jn., Sundon. R 1545: 11/70
Jn., Marston. 1731/80
Margery, Sundon. 1557/264
Ric., Streatley, lab. 1574/37
Thos., Streatley, yeo. 1602/17
Thos., Yielden, blacksmith. 1799/22

COTCHING, Alice, Leighton Buzzard, wid. 1760/60
Eliz., Westoning, wid. A 1793/10
Jn., Eversholt, oatmealman. 1725/25
Jn., Eversholt, bach. A 1763/4
Judith, Eversholt, wid. A 1760/28
Len., Westoning, draper and shopkeeper. 1793/4
COTTEY, Wm., Eaton Socon, shepherd. 1640/107
Wm., Eaton Socon, shepherd. 1646/113
COTTON, Ann, Northampton, wid. (Campton, bundle 1717). 1716/38
Hen., Edworth, yeo. 1672/124
Jn., Southill, Broom. R 1500: 1/138
Jn., Southill, Broom. R 1515: 2/131d
Jn., Kempston. 1617/305
Jos., Haynes, Northwood End, yeo. 1737/4
Margt., Southill. R 1502: 1/33d
Margt., Southill, Broom, wid. 1606/39
Ric., Southill, Broome. 1557/259
Wm., Bolnhurst, clerke, parson of Bolnhurst. 1565-6/192
Wm., Maulden. R 1546: 11/210d
Wm., sen., Biggleswade, innholder. 1689/71
Wm., Shillington, lab. 1691-2/133
Wm., Sutton. 1692-3/68
Wm., Eaton Socon. 1709-10/44
COTTRELL, Mary, Woburn, servant. 1632/9
COUCH, Wm., Shillington, husb. 1641/187
COUNTON, see Cownton
COUPEES, Jn., Luton, straw hat dealer. A 1806/28
Wm., Luton, straw hat manufacturer. 1812/2
COURTIER, Marmaduke, Bedford St. Paul, maltster. AR 1690: 1/33d
Mary, Bedford, wid. 1694/54
COUSIN, COSYN, Edm., Felmersham. R 1527-8: 2/74
Jas., Eaton Socon, Eaton Ford, yeo. 1722-3/65
Jn., Tempsford, yeo. 1617/278
Mich., sen., Arlesey, lab. 1687/69
Thos., Blunham. 1660/138
Thos., Felmersham, yeo. 1567/139
Wm., Felmersham, Radwell, yeo. 1661/356
Wm., Keysoe. 1674-5/93
Wm., Radwell. 1558/257
see also Curzon
COVEL, COVELL, Wm., Riseley, yeo. 1674/87
Wm., Riseley, yeo. AR 1674: 1/64
see also Carvell, Covill
COVEN, Wm., Houghton Gildable (Conquest), clerk and parson. R 1549: 12/67
COVENTRY, Geo., Battlesden. 1664-5/82

COVERLEY, Ric., Leighton Buzzard, fellmonger. 1680/23
COVILL, Mich., Husborne Crawley, yeo. 1648/128
see also Carvell, Covel
COVINGTON, CAVINGTON, COVENTON, Agnes, Thurleigh, wid. 1631/214
Arthur, Bedford. A 1757/2
Edw., Bedford, grocer. 1683-4/79
Edw., Bedford St.Peter, dairyman. 1812/34
Geo., Eaton Socon. 1613/205
Jas., Shillington. 1801/6
Jn., Bedford St. Paul, blacksmith. 1598/87
Jn., Riseley. 1647-8/3
Jn., Thurleigh. 1652-3/109
Jos., Bedford St. Peter, lace dealer. A 1828/13
Marg., Bedford, wid. 1631/177
Ric., Keysoe, weaver. 1610/88
Ric., Pavenham. I 1619/IO: 4/13
Robt., Podington, husb. R 1558: 14/75
Sim., jnr., Bedford St. Cuthbert, thatcher. 1766/73
Thos., Harrold, clothworker. 1654/73
Wm., Turvey, blacksmith. 1662-3/67
COWARD, CAWARD, Eliz., Southill. 1564/57
Jn., Bedford St. Peter, lab. AR 1685: 1/27d
COWDEN, Thos., Toddington, yeo. 1622/51
COWEN, Jonathan, Eaton Socon, Cross Hall, yeo. 1718/84
COWLAND, Jn., Cardington, farmer. 1781/28
Jn. Jos., Wilshamstead, castrator. A 1854/4
Jos., Shillington, farmer. A 1784/15
Stephen, Cardington, Fenlake, lab. 1621/213
Wm., Cardington, yeo. A 1794/10
COWLEY, Cristian, Ampthill, spins. 1626-7/24
Edw., Elstow, yeo. 1723/26
Hen., Riseley, yeo. 1711/40
Jane, Leighton Buzzard, wid. Fac. 1718: 9/76
Jn., jun., Aspley Guise, husb. A 1714/3
Judith, Aspley Guise, wid. 1714/16
Martha, Elstow, wid. 1730/59
Robt., Blunham, husb. 1600/73
Wm., Wootton, yeo. 1617/293
Wm., Bedford (old index only, admon. missing). A 1726/10
COWNTON, COUNTON, Jeman, Kempston. ?1558/172
Jn., Stagsden, husb. 1562/128
Lewis, Stagsden, husb. 1651/24
Marion, Kempston, wid. 1554/163
Ric., Stevington, husb. 1695-6/70
see also Compton

COWPER, see Cooper
COX, COCKS, COXE, Agnes, Stevington, wid. 1619/272
Ant., Henlow, weaver. 1606/30
Ben., Flitwick, yeo. 1830/1
Ben., Flitwick, yeo. A 1830/2
Cath., Northill, wid. AR 1683: 1/118
Deb., Stevington, wid. 1674/169
Edw., Totternhoe, lab. 1714/85
Eliz., Stagsden, wid. 1558/216
Eliz., sen., Potsgrove, wid. 1726/70
Fra., Eaton, yeo. 1621/199
Fra., Potsgrove, yeo. 1693/83
Fra., Great Barford, wid. 1704/66
Fra., Heath, yeo. Fac. 1734: 9/77
Geo., sen., Stevington, yeo. 1688/39
Geo., Stevington, yeo. 1724-5/82
Hen., Kempston, yeo. 1615/193
Hen., Bromham, husb. 1670-1/219
Hen., Little Staughton, lab. 1729/63
Hen., Cranfield, lab. A 1720/58
Humph., Turvey, lab. 1611/25
Israel, Sandy, Beeston. 1604/66
Jacob, Kempston, husb. A 1707/13
Jas., Wilshamstead, yeo. A 1707/24
Jas., Willington, yeo. A 1743/17
Joan, Eaton, wid. 1602-3/77
Jn., Wymington. R 1534: 4/12
Jn., Kempston. 1625-6/135
Jn., Houghton Conquest, How End, lab. 1631/142
Jn., Stevington. 1660-1/193
Jn., Stevington, yeo. 1714/83
Jn., Stagsden, husb. 1747/2
Jn., Elstow, farmer. 1768/36
Jn., Potton, innholder. 1784/41
Jn., Millbrook, victualler. 1794/10
Jn., Kempston, lab. 1811/27
Jn., Houghton Regis, lab. 1819/2
Jn., Leighton Buzzard, china & glass warehouseman. LB 1837/63
Jn., Elstow. A 1739-40/27
Jn., Leighton Buzzard, barber. Fac. A 1751: 9/89
Jn., Stagsden, husb. A 1766/5
Jn., Houghton Regis, lab. A 1819/11
Jn., Wilshamstead, lab. A 1826/11
Jonathan, Thurleigh, husb. A 1705/57
Jos., Houghton Regis, lab. 1771/35

COX, COCKS, COXE continued
Mary, Stevington. 1663/11
Mary, Langford. A 1738/24
Mary, Cardington, Fenlake, wid. A 1807/2
Math., Stagsden, husb. 1682/55
Math., Stagsden. 1758/47
Math., Cardington. A 1748/4
Nich., Stagsden. R 1545: 11/86d
Nich., Eaton, collarmaker. 1602/31
Nich., Stagsden, lab. 1660-1/66
Peter, Bromham, lab. 1630/34
Ric., Stevington. 1558/78
Ric., Bromham, lab. 1657/6
Ric., Stevington. 1661-2/246
Ric., jun., Hockliffe, brazier. A 1735/24
Ric., Podington, cordwainer. 1838/42
Robt., Blunham, weaver. 1614/51
Sam., Luton, yeo. 1729/11
Sam., Stotfold, cordwainer. 1776/25
Sarah, Houghton Regis, wid. 1755/53
Steph., Stagsden. 1593/64
Steph., Kempston, yeo. 1700/90
Steph., Kempston, yeo. A 1700/5
Susannah, Luton, wid. 1797/19
Thos., Horton, Oxford. 1558/83
Thos., Stevington, deacon. 1614/41
Thos., Stevington, lab. 1623/133
Thos., sen., Bedford. 1639/14
Thos., Lidlington, lab. 1661-2/256
Thos., Little Staughton, lab. 1662/85
Thos., (parish torn off). 1670/228
Thos., sen., Cranfield, yeo. 1676/109
Thos., Stotfold, lab. A 1722/18
Thos., Stagsden. 1736/44
Thos., Elstow, yeo. 1751/41
Thos., Sutton, yeo. 1786/47
Thos., Great Barford, farmer. A 1736/9
Thos., Willington (P/IX2 admon. missing). A 1783/24
Whitbread, Clapham, gent. 1844/7
Wm., Marston Moreteyne. R 1509: 1/55d
Wm., Stagsden, yeo. R 1550: 12/144
Wm., Wymington, husb. R 1558: 14/77d
Wm., Chellington, lab. 1582/51
Wm., Chellington, lab. 1591/108
Wm., Henlow, weaver. 1615/218

COX, COCKS, COXE continued
Wm., Lidlington, shepherd. 1620-1/2a
Wm., Stagsden, tailor. 1637/88
Wm., (old index only, bundle missing). A 1718/10
Wm., Houghton Regis, yeo. 1750-51/63
Wm., Cardington, farmer. A 1763/2
Wm., Wheathampstead, Herts., servant. A 1770/2
Wm., Cardington, Fenlake, yeo. 1770/3
Wm., Luton, Dallow Farm, yeo. 1799/1
see also Cock
COXALL, Lawrence, Sutton, farmer. 1818/18
COYLL, see Coil
COYRYOR, see Currier
COYTE, Jn., Maulden. 1579/133
Ric., Maulden. 1560-1/65
Wm., Maulden, yeo. 1636/66
Wm., Maulden, husb. 1660/32
see also Quait
COZEN, see Cousin
CRABTREE, Alice, Potton, wid. 1618-19/25
Thos., Potton, vicar. 1618/134, I
CRACKIN, Jas., Hockliffe yeo. 1740/66
CRADDOCK, CRADOCK, Eliz., Arlesey, wid. 1715/66
Jn., Henlow, miller. A 1700/7
Jn., Bolnhurst, miller. A 1714/19
Jn., Arlesey, husb. A 1729/38
Jn., Stevington, lab. 1747/46
Robt., Kempston, hempdresser. 1743-4/79
Winifred, Kempston, wid. 1766/12
CRAFT, CRAFTS, Edw., Maulden, husb. 1728/85
Edw., Biggleswade, dairyman. AR 1678: 1/108
Eliz., Cople. 1715/33
Fran., Biggleswade, Stratton, wid. Bw 1793/90
Jn., Potton, husb. 1605-6/78
Jn., Biggleswade, Stratton, yeo. 1678/84
Jn., Bedford. AR 1680: 1/18
Ric., Bletsoe. 1611/37
Ric., Barton. A 1725/7
Ric., Bedford St. Paul, cordwainer. 1739-40/77
Ric., Stotfold, strawplait dealer. 1851/24
Thos., Bedford. 1749/36
Thos., Bedford. AR 1679: 1/16d
Thos., Bedford St. Cuthbert, tanner. AR 1685-6: 1/28d
Wm., Bedford, cordwainer. 1665-6/15
CRAIG, Alex., Haynes. A 1827/2

CRAN, see Crane
CRANE, Abr., Renhold, shepherd. 1618/88
Eliz., Wilden, wid. (bundle 1669). 1668/17
Hen., Bedford, lab. 1739-40/75
Hester, Wilshamstead, wid. 1731-2/77
Jeremy, Houghton Conquest, yeo. 1639/55
Joan, Cardington, wid. 1626/119
Joan, Roxton, spins. 1664/49
Jn., Wilden, husb. 1571/53
Jn., sen., Wilden, shepherd. 1606/66
Jn., Wilden, yeo. 1638/204
Jn., Houghton Conquest, lab. 1706/96
Robt., Wilden, lab. 1611/176
Stephen, Cardington, dairyman. 1638/36
Thos., Wilden, husb. 1583/147
Thos., Wilden, yeo. 1623-4/95
Thos., Pavenham, yeo. 1739-40/2
Thos., Wrestlingworth, carpenter. 1771/20
Wm., Blunham. 1579-80/159
Wm., Wilden, yeo. 1649-50/32
Wm., Pavenham, yeo. 1685-6/122
Wm., Wilshamstead, yeo. 1722-3/70
Wm., Wilshamstead, farmer. A 1742-3/47
CRANFIELD, CRANSFIELD, Alice, Eaton Socon, wid. A 1729-30/60
Ann, Cople, wid. 1615-16/131
Ann, Cardington, wid. 1724-5/70
Ann, Shefford, spins. 1730/31
Edw., Elstow. 1651-2/49
Edw., Elstow, lab. 1670/173
Ide, Little Barford, wid. 1631/224
Jane, Oakley, wid. 1633-4/204
Jn., Felmersham. R 1521: 2/176
Jn., Cardington, husb. R 1524: 2/63
Jn., jun., Cardington, yeo. 1616/45
Jn., Cardington, yeo. 1691/118
Jn., Shillington, blacksmith. 1735/52
Jn., Leighton Buzzard, innholder. Fac. 1736: 9/78
Jn., Cardington, blacksmith. 1741-2/75
Jn., Bedford, glazier. A 1755/8
Jonathan, Cardington, innholder. 1706/93
Jonathan, Cardington, Harrowden, yeo. 1736/8
Jonathan, Cardington, Harrowden, farmer. 1789/24
Jonathan, Cardington, farmer. A 1777/9
Mary, Cardington, wid. 1745-6/50
Robt., Eaton Socon, Goodwick, yeo. 1727-8/87

CRANFIELD, CRANSFIELD continued
Sarah, Cardington, wid. 1721/101
Thos., Shefford. 1579/179
Thos., sen., Elstow, yeo. 1613/131
Thos., Shefford, gent. 1617/199
Thos., Shefford, vintner. 1636/38
Thos., Cardington, husb. 1658-9/82
Thos., sen., cardington, lab. A 1705/21
Thos., Cardington, lab. 1710-11/28
Thos., Stevington, yeo. A 1785/29
"Widdow", Cardington. 1662/22
Wm., Cardington. 1590/124
Wm., Cardington, husb. 1641/204
Wm., Cardington, yeo. 1660-1/63
Wm., Cardington, yeo. 1660/211
Wm., Cardington, lab. 1688/48
Wm., sen., Shefford, cooper. 1701-2/46
Wm., Shefford. 1705/16
Wm., Eaton Socon. 1710-11/37
CRANSFIELD, see Cranfield
CRANWELL, Jn., Flitwick. R 1519-20: 2/151
Jn., Flitwick. 1636/30
Ric., Toddington. R 1546: 11/156d
Thos., Flitwick. R 1549-50: 12/87d
Thos., Luton. 1587/167
CRASE, Jn., Campton. R 1545: 11/66d
see also Crasse
CRASH, Baxter alias Crash see under Baxter
alias Baxter, Edw., Bedford, baker. 1619/193, I 4/130
Edw., Bedford St. Mary. AR 1682-3: 1/22
CRASLEY, Ric., (old index "docket mislaid"). A 1709/7
Robt., Luton, Stopsley, yeo. 1558/6
alias Suses, Wm., Langford, yeo. 1687/53
CRASSE, Ben., Hockliffe, fellmonger. 1731/79
Jn., Hockliffe. 1648-9/89
Jn., Harlington, Wood End, yeo. 1738/71
see also Crase, Cresse
CRAVEN, Mary, Pavenham, wid. 1632/22
Nich., Pavenham, clerk. 1626/39
CRAWE, see Crowe
CRAWLEY, Freeman alias Crawley, see Freeman
Agnes, Barton, wid. 1649/70
Alex., Bedford St. John. R 1523: 2/92
Ann, Leagrave Marsh, spins. 1663/52
Ann, Luton, Someries, spins. 1687/21

CRAWLEY continued
Ann, Potton. 1705/58
Christian, Luton, wid. 1618/96
Edw., Luton, singleman. R 1545: 11/53
Edw., Barton, yeo. 1629/144
Edw., Limbury, widower. 1665/38
Edw., Southill. AR 1676: 1/105d
Eliz., Dunstable, spins. 1732/22
Eliz., Luton, wid. 1739/15
Eliz., Luton, wid. 1740/23
Farmer, Eaton Bray, carpenter. 1734/20
Fra., Luton. AR 1676: 1/152
Fra., Milton Bryan, yeo. 1744/20
Geo., Whipsnade, farmer. 1754/24
Geo., Meppershall, yeo. A 1771/15
Humph., Milton Bryan, yeo. 1714/86
Jas., sen., Luton, cordwainer. 1721/41
Jane, Aspley Guise, wid. 1617/273
Jane, Luton, wid. 1659/124
Jane, Leighton Buzzard, wid. A 1743/24
Jeremiah, Luton. A 1799/12
Joan, Leighton Buzzard, wid. A 1750/12
Jn., Luton. R 1519: 1/22d, 126
Jn., Luton. R 1530: 3/31d
Jn., Luton, Dawn End. R 1545: 11/55
Jn., Luton. 1546/8
Jn., Luton, Downend, yeo. 1571/59
Jn., Lidlington. 1608/38
Jn., Sundon, yeo. 1610-11/21
Jn., Luton, Greathamstead. 1617/289
Jn., Luton, yeo. 1639/160
Jn., Stopsley, yeo. 1645/26
Jn., Stopsley, yeo. 1660-1/180
Jn., jun., Luton, Church Street, maltster. 1661/307
Jn., Tilsworth, husb. 1667/92
Jn., Ampthill, yeo. 1691/119
Jn., Aspley Guise. 1693/99
Jn., Pulloxhill, shoemaker. 1702/68
Jn., Pulloxhill, yeo. 1711/107
Jn., Dunstable, gent. 1728/44
Jn., Leighton Buzzard, carp. 1750/22
Jn., Edworth, yeo. 1782/32
Jn., Chalgrave, straw hat manufacturer. LBA 1814/69
Jn., Luton, butcher. 1836/23
Jn., Bedford. AR 1670: 1/1d

CRAWLEY continued
Jn., Dunstable. AR 1676: 1/152
Jn., Holwell. A 1771/20
Lawr., Aspley Guise, yeo. 1629/79
Lawr., Ampthill, baker. 1675/58
Lawr., Aspley Guise. AR 1676: 1/195(2)
Margt., Luton. 1580-1/207
Mary, Luton, wid. 1623/123
Mary, Houghton Regis, wid. 1676-7/165
Mary, Flitton, wid. 1705-6/87
Mary. LBA 1756/8
Mary, Leighton Buzzard, spins. LB 1804/15
Ric., Stopsley, yeo. 1578-9/100
Ric., Tilsworth, husb. 1582-3/70
Ric., Luton, Dunstable Lane, yeo. 1618/99
Ric., Harlington. 1639-40/145
Ric., Harlington, practitioner in physic. 1640/120
Ric., Houghton Regis, yeo. 1662/43
Ric., Westoning, yeo. 1673/19
Ric., Aspley Guise, yeo. 1674/91
Ric., Westoning, yeo. 1681/93
Ric., Luton, Crawley Green, husb. 1683/48
Ric., Arlesey, yeo. 1689/1
Ric., Lower Gravenhurst, yeo. 1721/100
Ric., Nether Gravenhurst, husb. 1751/6
Ric., Eaton Bray, carp. 1780/5
Ric., Leighton Buzzard, carp. LB 1756/27
Robt., Aspley Guise, husb. 1611/174
Robt., Luton, yeo. 1633/152
Robt., Silsoe, farrier. 1706/5
Robt., Leighton Buzzard, carp. 1742/61
Roger, Leagrave, yeo. 1598/118
Sarah, Bedford, wid. 1684/40
Susan, Dunstable. AR 1672: 1/144
Susan, Dunstable. 1672/154
Susanna, Streatley. A 1841/7
Thos., Elstow, Medbury. 1616-17/39
Thos., Luton, Danes Street, yeo. 1637-8/155
Thos., Leagrave, yeo. 1638/131
Thos., Luton, gent. 1646/74
Thos., sen., Barton, yeo. 1650-1/128
Thos., Rector of Barton. AR 1677: 1/153
Thos., Luton. AR 1686: 1/171
Thos., Milton Bryan, yeo. 1687/13
Thos., Harlington, yeo. 1707/2

CRAWLEY continued
Thos., Luton, cordwainer. 1740/43
Thos., Shefford, fellmonger. 1747/28
Thos., Chellington, butcher. 1780/45
Thos., no parish given. 1786/44
Thos., Luton, Little Bramingham, farmer. R 1827/26
Valentine, Milton Bryan, yeo. 1588/33
Wm., Luton. R 1525: 2/73
Wm., Barton. 1584/177
Wm., Luton, Greathampstead, yeo. 1591/107
Wm., sen., Luton, Sunning Lane End, yeo. 1629/108
Wm., Luton, Sondis, yeo. 1674/164
Wm., Luton, husb. 1676/133
Wm., Luton. AR 1676: 1/151d
Wm., Milton Bryan, gent. 1680/29
Wm., Cardington, Fenlake Barns, yeo. 1697/47
Wm., Southill, coachman. 1719-20/84
Wm., Kimpton, Herts., lab. 1766/31
Wm., Luton, grocer. 1810/1
Wm., Bedford, mason. 1810/10
Wm., Gravenhurst, Ion, farmer. A 1826/7
Wm., Streatley. 1830/41
CRAYFORD, Sir Wm., Ridgmont, Beckerings Park. 1636/55
CREAK, CREKE, Jas., Lidlington, farmer. A 1809/10
Jn., Shillington. R 1533: 3/106
Jn., Thurleigh. AR 1688-9: 1/82d
see also Crick
CREAMER, Dan., Eaton Socon, Cross Hall, yeo. A 1797/1
Godfrey, Pavenham. 1590/178
Jas., Pavenham, glazier. R 1639: 22/99, 35/232
Jn., Warden. 1660/40
Jn., Pavenham, matmaker. 1745/40
Thos., Colmworth, farmer. 1840/4
Wm., sen., Pavenham. 1709/3
Wm., Pavenham, husb. 1742-3/98
Wm., Eaton Socon, Topham End, yeo. 1750-1/71
Wm., Roxton, Chawston, farmer. 1799/24
CRECY, see Cresse
CREED, Cth., Bedford St. Paul, wid. A 1846/8
Cuth., Clapham, grazier. 1677/34
Ric., Leighton Buzzard. LBA 1803/54
CRESSE, CRESSEY, CRECY, Ann, Eaton Bray, wid. 1698/106
Geo., Eaton Bray, gard. 1685/27
Jas., Eaton Bray, yeo. 1737/11
Thos., Bedford St. Peter, formerly parson of Bolnhurst, "now resting". 1553/148

CRESSE, CRESSEY, CRECY continued
Valentine, Houghton Regis, clerk. 1728/84
see also Crasse
CRESWELL, Jas., Flitton. AR 1691: 1/219d
Thos., Luton, Crawley Green, gent. 1669/8
CRICK, CRIKE, Clement, Wilshamstead, yeo. c1670/229
Eliz., Woburn, spins. 1831/1
Hen., Wootton, lab. 1664/50
Jn., Wilshamstead, lab. 1638-9
Mary Ann, Ampthill, wid. 1846/21
Sam., Wilshamstead, yeo. A 1763/29
Sarah, Wilshamstead, wid. 1686/29
Wm., Ampthill, yeo. 1833/10
Wm., Ampthill, gard. 1853/54
see also Creak
CRIKE, see Crick
CRIPPS, CRIPTS, Edw., Cranfield, yeo. A 1782/16
Eliz., Dunstable. 1825/23
Jn., Cranfield. 1778/38
Jn., Cranfield, farmer. A 1822/17
Jos., Cranfield, gent., also limited admon. 1798/35
Lawr., Millbrook, grazier. 1732/9
Ric., Cranfield, Purratt, yeo. 1855/25
Sarah, Cranfield, wid. A 1803/5
Wm., Ridgmont, Segenhoe, shoemaker. 1629/120
CRIPSEY, CRIPSEE, Barnet alias Cripsey, see under Barnet
Agnes, Houghton Conquest, wid. 1632/24
David, Houghton Conquest, How End, yeo. 1658/109
alias Barnard, Thomasin, wife of Geo., Flitwick. 1661/377
alias Barnarde, Wm. I 1619: 4/87
Wm., sen., Shillington, lab. 1639/113
CRIPTS, see Cripps
CRISP, CHRISP, Judith, Souldrop, wid. of Peace. 1819/23 & A 1819/12
CRISPLEY, Barnard alias Crispley, see under Barnard
CROASLEY, see Crosley
CROCKER, see Croker
CROCKETT, Hester alias Crockett, see under Hester
CROCKFORD, CROCKSFORD, CROXFORD, Jn., Silsoe, yeo. 1849/46
Joshua, Cardington, lab. 1823/31, I 4/250
Wm., Thurleigh, Baptist minister. 1837/5
CROCKSON, CROXON, Oliv., Woburn, baker and innkeeper. 1840/44
Wm., Barton. 1584-5/257
see also Croxton
CROFT, CROFTS, Ann, Meppershall. A 1799/5
Fra., Keysoe, yeo. 1818/6

CROFT, CROFTS continued
Hen., Melchbourne, gard. 1723/12
Jn., Biggleswade, Stratton, dairyman. A 1704-5/17
Mary, Bedford, spins.. AR 1684: 1/25, 46
Mary, Biggleswade, Stratton, dairywoman. BW 1714/3B
Wm., Bedford, yeo. 1824/12
CROKER, CROCKER, Eliz., Kempston, wid. 1681-2/91
Eliz., Bedford. 1690/148
Jn., Kempston, miller. 1671/41
Jn., Bedford, maltster. 1718/31
Jn., Kempston. AR 1683: 1/24
Mary, Elstow. 1754/47
Thos., Eaton Bray, weaver. 1598/138
Thos., Tilsworth, yeo. 1611-12/152
CROMPTON, Jn., Campton, gent. 1731/44
see also Crumpton
CROOK, Jn., Maulden, yeo. 1815/22
Wm., Bromham, lab. 1743/53
CROOKEY, Geo., Hockliffe, innholder. 1785/6
Sarah, Hockliffe. A 1740/5
Sarah, Hockliffe, wid. 1787/51
CROOTE, Cath., Biggleswade, wid. 1691/127
Eliz., Dunstable, spins. A 1715/5
Geo., Westoning, shopkeeper. 1777/28
Jas., Biggleswade. AR 1688: 1/131
Jn., Biggleswade. 1698/117
Jn., Willington, yeo. A 1806/7, I 4/204
Mary, Riseley (P/IX2, admon missing). A 1783/27
Thos., Bedford, yeo. 1632/59
Thos., Southill, lab. AR 1681-2: 1/114
Thos., Renhold, yeo. 1741-2/78
see also Crout, Crotes
CROSBY, Ann, Clifton. 1849/49
Thos., Clifton, carp. 1833/8
see also Chester alias Crosby
CROSFIELD, CROSFILD, Jn., Ampthill, tilemaker. 1585/30
CROSLEY, see Crowsley
CROSON, see Crowson
CROSS, CROSSE, Hen., Meppershall, Pullinger. R 1533: 3/122
Jas., Wrestlingworth. 1556/189
Jn., Bedford. 1629/141
Nich., Warden, yeo. 1739/53
Stephen, Bletsoe, dairyman. 1703-4/18
Wm., Maulden, husb. 1599/128
CROSTHWAITE, Chas., Bedford, late Moravian minister, Riseley. 1850/8

CROTES, Ric., Dean, husb. 1557/153
see also Croote
CROUCH, CROWCHE, CROUCHE, CHRUCHE, Agnes, Sutton. 1614/29
Agnes, Husborne Crawley, wid. 1613-14/159
Alice, Barton, wid. 1605/122
Alice, Shillington, wid. 1636/12
Alice, Toddington, wid. 1756/12
Alice, Clophill, Cainho, wid. 1771/13
Amy, Westoning, wid. 1592/70
Andrew, Caddington, shepherd. 1640/25
Ann, (old index "docket mislaid"). A 1709/24
Ann, Felmersham, Radwell, wid. 1720/76
Ann, wife of Jn., Lidlington. 1803/41
Ann, Lidlington, wid. 1845/52
Annis, Westoning, wid. 1614-15/11
Chris., Potton, innholder. 1630/71
Chris., Westoning, yeo. 1705/60
Dorothy, Higham Gobion, wid. of Nich. 1738/78
Edm., Shillington, lab. 1661/342
Edw., Stotfold, yeo. 1661/327
Edw., Stotfold. AR 1685: 1/124
Edw., Felmersham, Radwell, yeo. 1708/11
Edw., Biggleswade, Holme, yeo. 1746/5
Edw., Arlesey, yeo. 1748/38
Edw., Shillington. AR 1688: 1/130d
Eliz., Salford, wid. 1583/128
Eliz., (parish torn off). 1670/205
Eliz., Luton, wid. 1714/38
Geo., Stotfold, yeo. 1689/39
Jas., Shillington, yeo. A 1701/4
Jas., Dunstable, bricklayer. 1752/30
Jas., sen., Clophill, Cainhoe. 1785/7
Jas., Clophill, Cainhoe, House Farm, yeo. 1816/19
Joan., Lidlington, wid. 1680/24
Jn., Caddington. R 1500: 1/12
Jn., Potton, yeo. 1589/11
Jn., Northill, Ickwell, yeo. 1591-2/88
Jn., Houghton Conquest, carp. 1626-7/22
Jn., Barton, yeo. 1630/2
Jn., Barton, yeo. 1643/68
Jn., (no parish given). 1659/93
Jn., Cranfield. 1670-1/235
Jn., Langford, yeo. 1671/67
Jn., Lidlington, gent. 1699/28
Jn., Shillington, tailor. 1716/8

CROUCH, CROWCHE, CROVCHE, CHRUCHE continued
Jn., Flitton, gent. 1720-1/79
Jn., Flitton, gent. 1725/61
Jn., Houghton Regis. A 1738/32
Jn., Lidlington, yeo. A 1742/34
Jn., Bedford, victualler. 1745-6/47
Jn., Houghton Regis, blacksmith. A 1781/2
Jn., Lidlington, yeo. (reg. only). R 1810/4
Jos., Ampthill, Brickhill Pastures, farmer. 1764/26
Mary, Luton, spins. 1727/95
Math., jun., Toddington, apothecary. 1748-9/68
Nich., Husborne Crawley, husb. R 1558: 14/60d
Nich., Husborne Crawley, yeo. 1624/30
Nich., Flitton. AR 1674-5: 1/192d
Nich., Barton. AR 1690: 1/177
Nich., Higham Gobion, Buckingham Hall, husb. 1726/37
Phoebe, Eaton Bray, wid. AR 1672: 1/143d
Rebecca, Houghton Conquest. 1727/37
Reynold, Husborne Crawley. 1565/10
Ric., Houghton Conquest. 1557/389
Ric., Houghton Conquest. 1570/14
Ric., Barton, alehousekeeper. 1666/148
Ric., Stotfold. AR 1686: 1/126
Ric., Stotfold, lab. 1686/43
Ric., Clifton, yeo. 1731/31
Ric., Barton, yeo. 1735-6/23
Ric., Luton, tailor. 1737-8/54
Ric., Blunham, farmer. A 1752/16
Robt., Willington. 1685/70
Robt., Barton, tailor. A 1703-4/11
Robt., Husborne Crawley, bricklayer. 1708/85
Roger, sen., Husborne Crawley. 1551?/145
Roger, Husborne Crawley, lab. (bundle 1585-7). 1571/115
Sam., Shillington, bach. A 1716-17/4
Sarah, Eversholt, wid. 1672/134
Sarah, Husborne Crawley, wid. 1719/25
Sarah, Ampthill, wid. A 1725/6
Sarah, Luton. 1739/27
Sarah, Barton, wid. A 1743/20
Susan, Dunstable, wid. 1746/25
Sybil, Shillington, wid. 1658/33
Thos., sen., Barton. R 1558: 14/67d
Thos., sen., Shillington. 1582/62
Thos., Barton, butcher. 1599-1600/129
Thos., Westoning. 1607-8/153

CROUCH, CROWCHE, CROVCHE, CHRUCHE continued
Thos., Harlington. 1649/7
Thos., Shillington, husb. 1675/41
Thos., Clophill, Beadlow, dairyman. 1680/64
Thos., sen., Shillington, yeo. 1691/68
Thos., Dunstable, victualler. 1722/69
Thos., Holwell, yeo. 1725-6/77
Thos., Barton, farmer. A 1737/37
Thos., Cardington. 1739-40/81
Thos., Podington. (P/IX2 bundle missing). A 1747/27
Thos., sen., Maulden, husb. 1750-1/54
Thos., sen., Luton, cooper. 1754/40
Thos., Maulden, yeo. 1773/15
Thos., Maulden, yeo. 1776/44
Ursula, Westoning. 1632/94
Wm., Barton, butcher. R 1559: 15/55
Wm., Husborne Crawley. 1553/295
Wm., Marston. 1557/359
Wm., Langford. 1615/139
Wm., Barton, blacksmith. 1658/43
Wm., Lidlington, yeo. 1701/12
Wm., (old index "docket mislaid"). A 1710/34
Wm., Barton, husb. 1722/14
Wm., Ampthill, maltster. 1723/55
Wm., Shillington, husb. 1743/35
Wm., Lidlington, farmer. 1813/27
CROUT, Jn., Biggleswade, New Spring, yeo. 1730/13
Thos., Sandy, Girtford, yeo. 1815/20
Wm., Biggleswade, Stratton. Bw 1760/35, I
see also Croote
CROW, CROWE, CRAWE, Agnes, Colmworth. R 1504: 1/40
Agnes, Colmworth. 1560/214
Alice, Little Staughton, wid. AR 1673: 1/63
Alice, Little Staughton, wid. 1674/84
Ann, Renhold, wid. 1699/55
Ann, Eaton Socon, wid. 1785/26
Edm., Wilden, yeo. 1646/84
Goodwin, Eaton Socon, carp. 1765/15
Hen., Keysoe, yeo. 1676/186
Jas., Eaton Socon, yeo. ?1714/31
Jas., Eaton Socon, Ford End. 1795/36
Jane, Eaton Socon. 1753/27
Jn., Colmworth. R 1500: 1/12d
Jn., sen., Little Staughton, yeo. 1655/118
Jn., Wilden, East End, yeo. 1685-6/101

CROW, CROWE, CRAWE continued
Jn., Little Staughton, yeo. 1703/46
Jn., Bolnhurst, husb. 1742/31
Mary, Bedford St. Paul. 1637/173
Mary, Eaton Socon, wid. 1703/32
Mary, Wilden, wid. A 1720/22
Ric., Eaton Socon, yeo. 1684-5/56
Ric., Eaton Socon, yeo. 1693-4/109
Thos., Colmworth. 1552/330
Thos., Little Staughton, husb. 1581/31
Thos., Renhold, blacksmith. 1690/46
Thos., Keysoe, yeo. 1720/97
Wm., Little Staughton. 1584-5/243
Wm., Elstow. 1620-1/18
Wm., Wilden, yeo. 1661/383
Wm., sen., Little Staughton, yeo. 1667/89
Wm., Wilden. yeo. 1717-18/64
see also Croy
CROWLEY, Alice, Sundon, wid. 1614-15/8
Alice, Kempston, wid. 1635/30
Edw., Aspley Guise, yeo. 1632-3/15
Fra., Roxton, Chawston. 1674/108
Gabriel, Tilsworth. 1631/170
Jn., Kempston. R 1536-7: 4/75
Jn., Shefford, poulter. 1575-6/65
Jn., Kempston, yeo. 1673/28
Ric., Salford, husb. 1583/156
Ric., Biggleswade, yeo. 1673/90
Theodore, rector of Bedford St. John, clerk. 1662/121
Thos., Elstow. 1557/377
Thos., Kempston, yeo. 1651-2/42
Wm., Wootton, husb. 1604-5/3
Wm., Kempston, yeo. 1627/179
see also Crowsley
CROWSLEY, CROASLEY, CROSLEY, Anthony alias Crosley, see under Anthony
Jn., Luton, yeo. 1669-70/111
alias Anthony, Jn., Aspley Guise, husb. 1685/28
Jn., Millbrook, husb. A 1735/20
Jn., Kempston, blacksmith. 1772/39
Jn., Kempston. A 1814/15
Jos., Shefford, sawyer. A 1817/6
alias Anthony, Mary, Toddington, Hearne, wid. 1670/224
Ric., Aspley Guise. 1660-1/117
alias Heus, Wm., (tuition bond only). 1687

CROWSLEY, CROASLEY, CROSLEY continued
Wm., Langford, farmer. 1854/29
see also Crowley
CROWSON, CROSON, Joan, Marston, wid. A 1707-8/15
Ric., Eversholt (old index, bundle missing). A 1745/4
CROWTHER, Edm., Willington. 1723/13
Edm., Bedford, innholder. A 1746/13
Sarah, Ampthill, wid. 1743/7
CROXFORD, see Crockford
CROXON, see Crockson
CROXTON, Oliv., Milton Ernest. 1648/99
see also Crockson
CROY, Ric., Wilden. R 1500: 1/17d
see also Crow
CRUMP, Geo., Elstow, lab. AR 1681: 1/20
Jn., Cardington, Harrowden, lab. 1641/193
Jn., sen., Dunstable, carp. 1827/4
Mary, Bedford St. John. 1684-5/55
CRUMPTON, Mary, Woburn, wid. 1629/103
see also Crompton
CRUTCHLEY, Jn., Milton Ernest, weaver. 1664/1
CUFFLEY, Hen., Toddington, husb. 1560-1/68
Jas., Barton. 1557/355
Robt., Barton, husb. 1604-5/12
Robt., Barton, yeo. AR 1685-6: 1/170d
Thos., Westoning, Sampshill, wid. 1649/5
CULCHETH, Ralph, Stevington. I 1589: 4/178
CULLET, Thos., Roxton, lab. 1700/85
CULLICK, CULLWICKE, Chas., Bromham. 1659/83
Geo., Wrestlingworth. 1630-1/114
Geo., Eyeworth, yeo. 1657-8/254
Hen., Sutton, miller. A 1700/22
Jn., Oakley, yeo. 1630-1/197
Jn., Eyeworth, yeo. 1639/34
Jn., Eyeworth, lab. 1714/70
Jn., Oakley. AR 1673: 1/38 (2)
Ric., Wrestlingworth. AR 1684: 1/121
Ric., Wrestlingworth, yeo. 1642-3/9
Wm., Shillington, husb. 1583/153
Wm., Willington, husb. 1739/7
CULPIN, Mich., North Crawley, husb. R 1590-1: 24/7d
CULVERHOUSE, Eliz., Eaton Bray, wid. 1728/106
Jn., Totternhoe, yeo. 1604/51
Jn., Eaton Bray, butcher. A 1703/21
Ric., Eaton Bray, butcher. A 1730/34

CULVERHOUSE continued
Ric., Leighton Buzzard. LBA 1793/43
Wm., sen., Totternhoe. 1574/33
CULWICKE, see Cullick
CUMBERLAND, Dixie, Elstow, farmer. 1811/12
Eliz., Clifton, wid. 1637/91
Eliz., Houghton Regis, spins. A 1818/2
Hen., Marston, husb. 1696-7/143
Hen., sen., Houghton Regis, yeo. 1766/13
Jn., Northill, Caldecote. I 1619: 4/76
Jn., Oakley. 1662/94
Jn., Oakley, yeo. 1703-4/54
Jn., Bedford St. Paul, innholder. 1755/2
Jos., Dunstable, shepherd. 1724/10
Joyce, wid., (later Joyce Green), Hockliffe. A 1788/3
Lawr., Odell, yeo. 1726-7/102
Lawr., Odell, yeo. A 1738-9/5
Lawr., Odell, farmer. R 1770/37
Lawr., Stevington. A 1817/3
Mary, Marston, wid. 1718/53
Ric., Toddington, Chalton, husb. 1659/89
Robt., Bedford St. Paul. A 1770/12
Sarah, Oakley, wid. 1709-10/64
Thos., Elstow, farmer. 1797/27
Thos., sen., Houghton Regis, yeo. 1826/11
Wm., Henlow, gent. 1681/2
Wm., Clifton, gent. 1711/77
Wm., sen., Odell, yeo. 1760/53
Wm., Elstow, farmer. 1783/5
Wm., Houghton Regis, yeo. 1806/28
Wm., Bedford St. Paul, cordwainer. 1833/46
Wm., Gt. Barford, blacksmith. 1847/47
CUMMING, CUMMINGS, Robt., Gt. Barford, yeo. 1801/20
CUNNINGHAM, Anna Maria, Turvey, wid. 1745/18
David, Turvey, yeo. 1690-1/33
Edw., (old index only, bundle missing). A 1718/15
Edw., Wootton, cordwainer. A 1759/8
Edw., Clophill, grocer. 1782/49
Eliz., Wootton, spins. 1775/19
Ric., Bedford St. Paul, carp. 1579-80/189
Sam., Turvey, innholder. A 1704/35
Sarah, Turvey, wid. 1772/52
Sarah, Cranfield, wid. A 1730/26
CUNNINGTON, see Connington
CUPIS, see Kippist

CUPPER, see Cooper
CURBY, see Kirby
CURD, Jn., Leighton Buzzard. Fac. 1741: 9/81
CURFEY, Ann, Lidlington, wid. 1688/51
Jn., Kempston Hardwick, dairyman. 1687/29
Thos., Lidlington, lab. 1684/24
Thos., Lidlington. AR 1684: 1/211d
Wm., Lidlington, lab. 1702/23
Wm., Lidlington, yeo. 1704/54
CURRIER, COYRYOR, Thos., Roxton. R 1504: 1/50d
CURTIS, CURTEYS, CURTICE, Edw., Toddington, carrier. 1716/20
Elinor, Toddington. AR 1690: 1/177d
Eliz., Elstow, wid. R 1550: 12/116
Eliz., Chalgrave. AR 1674: 1/148d
Eliz., (old index only, bundle missing). A 1717/27
Eliz., Bromham, wid. A 1810/21
Eliz., Northill, wid. A 1814/1
Francis, Eversholt. 1755/41
Geo., Oakley, shepherd. 1624/33
Jac., Harrold, lacemaker. AR 1684: 1/47
Jas., Northill, Ickwell, carp. 1790/9
Jas., Stagsden, yeo. 1799/46
Jn., Upper Dean, husb. 1619-20/178, I 4/12
Jn., Cockayne Hatley. 1627/164
Jn., Bletsoe. 1663-4/111
Jn., Potton. AR 1681-2: 1/115
Jn., Milton Bryan, husb. 1698/121
Jn., Flitton, husb. A 1707/26
Jn., Potton, carp. A 1715/15
Jn., Riseley, lab. 1722/8
Jn., Blunham, tailor. A 1726/25
Mercy, Blunham, wid. 1727/23
Richard, Warden, Hill. R 1499: 1/134
Ric., Thurleigh, lab. 1658/21
Ric., Eversholt, yeo. 1680/74
Robt., Wilshamstead, Cotton End, yeo. 1786/36
Sarah, Southill, wid. 1627/146
Thos., Bedford, gent. 1638-9/83
Thos., Odell. 1666/117
Thos., Biggleswade. AR 1675: 1/103d
Thos., Chalgrave, Wingfield, yeo. 1685/37
Thos., Chalgrave. A 1701/9
Thos., Henlow, miller. A 1728/17
Thos., Harlington, gardener. 1769/50
Wm., Elstow. R 1547: 11/240

CURTIS, CURTEYS, CURTICE continued
Wm., Northill, Ickwell, carp. 1739-40/78
Wm., Stagsden, yeo. 1799/26
Wm., Bedford St. Paul, lab. A 1851/2
CURTMAN, Jn., Eaton Socon. R 1544: 11/37d
CURWEN, Hen., Toddington. R 1528: 2/188d
CURZON, CURSON, Robt., Ampthill, gent. 1576/41
see also Cousin
CUSTERSON, Eben., Cardington, husb. 1771/38
Sam., Cardington, husb. 1786/27
CUTBEARD, Robt., Roxton, lab. 1638-9/99
see also Cuthbert
CUTHBERT, CUTBERT, Alice, Yielden, spins. AR 1682: 1/75
see also Cutbeard
Len., Houghton Conquest, butcher. 1761/55
Wm., Woburn, tailor. 1733-4/52
CUTLER, Wyatt alias Cutler see under Wyatt
Ann, Sundon, wid. AR 1673-4: 1/147
Jn., Toddington, Chalton, weaver. 1702/18
Jn., Studham. A 1843/12
Thos., Leighton Buzzard, gent. LB 1768/12
CUTLET, Alice, Eaton, wid. 1640/80
Cuth., Eaton Bray. R 1521: 1/246
Cuth., Eaton Bray. R 1521: 2/97
Cuth., Eaton Bray, soldier. R 1544: 11/39d
Cuth., Eaton, lab. 1620/41
Edm., Eaton Bray, yeo. 1677/41
Eliz., Eaton Bray, wid. 1721/98
Fra., Eaton, yeo. 1663-4/83
Geo., Eaton Bray, yeo. 1696/137
Jn., Eaton Bray. 1606-7/10
Jn., sen., Eaton Bray, yeo. 1663-4/84
Thos., Eaton, husb. 1608-9/9
CUTTRISS, Wm., Ridgmont. 1830/11
CYNE, see Dyne

D

DAFFARNE, DAFFERNE, Jn., Eaton Socon, locksmith. 1693/103
Martha, Eaton Socon, wid. AR 1680: 1/70
DALBORNE, Chris., Steppingley, lab. 1626/72
DALBY, DAULBEY, Anne, Shelton. 1718/46
Hen., Tempsford, grocer. 1738/12
Thos., Aspley Guise, bach. 1683-4/99
Thos., Aspley Guise. AR 1683-4: 1/120

DALBY, DAULBEY continued
Thos., Marston, shepherd. 1684/12
Wm., Shelton, yeo. 1689/19
DALDERNE, David, Dunstable, maltman. 1580/228
Robt., sen., Limbury, yeo. 1589/112
see also Daldron, Dalton
DALDRON, Humph., Limbury. R 1550: 12/105
see also Dalderne
DALE, Edw., Langford, lab. 1649/60
Jn., Bedford St. Paul, butcher. 1579-80/185
Jn., Carlton, tailor. 1645/11
Ric., Henlow, yeo. 1608/11
Robt., Potton, lab. 1692/12
Thos., Langford, husb. 1571/60
Thos., Potton, lab. 1711/8
see also Dalle
DALLAND, Alan, Higham Gobion, yeo. R 1548: 12/17d
DALLE, Thos., Sandy. R 1539: 6/4d
see also Dale, Dally
DALLY, Jas., Ampthill, gardener. A 1849/7
Mary, Stevington, wid. 1756/23
Thos., Elstow, grocer. 1730-1/15
see also Dalle
DALTON, DOLTON, DOLETON, Dalderne alias Dalton see under Dalderne
Eliz., Holcote. 1748-9/65
Hannah, Biggleswade, Sunderland, wid. Bw 1776/65
Hannah, Biggleswade, Sunderland, spins. Bw 1799/98
Jn., Sandy, lab. A 1704/26
Mary, Ridgmont, wid. A 1756/7
Ric., Silsoe, cordwainer. A 1798/15
Thos., Over Dean, butcher. 1698/109
Thos., Biggleswade, shoemaker. Bw 1841/154
Wm., Woburn. A 1736/29
Wm., Woburn, Lowleys, yeo. 1750/15
Wm., Woburn, coachmaker. 1805/25
see also Dalderne
DANAWAY, see Danoway
DANE, DAENE, Brunould, Sandy, Girtford. 1630-1/136
Chris., Shillington, lab. 1640/29
Hen., Caddington. R 1537: 5/6d
Jas., Maulden, gent. R 1543: 6/169 & 9/20
DANEY, Ric., Flitwick. 1652/75
DANIEL(S), DANYLL, Ann, Eversholt. A 1835/11
Dan., Eversholt, grazier. 1846/40
Edw., Ridgmont, Segenhoe, lab. 1602/37

DANIEL(S), DANYLL continued
 Eliz., Eversholt, wid. 1772/33
 Geo., Stevington. 1660-1/126
 Jas., Biggleswade, gardener. Bw 1840/151
 Jn., Bedford, chirurgeon. 1728/33
 Jn., sen., Eversholt, yeo. 1821/27
 Jn., Biggleswade, gardener. Bw 1857/168
 Math., Bedford, surgeon & apothecary. 1755/3
 Ric., Yielden. 1610/133
 Ric., Sandy, Stratford, gardener. 1844/38
 Thos., Yielden. 1558/72
 Thos., Eversholt, Berry End, yeo. 1758/56
 Thos., Wilshamstead, farmer. 1820/5
 Wm., Ampthill, weaver. 1624-5/17
 Wm., Silsoe, Newberry, esq. 1706/78
 Wm., Chalgrave, Tebworth, butcher & farmer. 1849/17
DANOWAY, DANAWAY, Alice, Marston Pillinge, wid. 1717/67
 Jn., Marston Moreteyne, lab. 1709/69
DARBY, Jn., Dunstable, lab. 1846/7
DARING, Thos., Sandy, Stratford, lab. 1618/38
DARLING, DERLING, Aylse, Thurleigh, wid. 1620/3
 Geo., Bedford, fellmonger. 1713/3
 Giles, Potton, fellmonger. 1708/27
 Giles, Woburn, brazier. 1731/35
 Giles, sen., Woburn, brazier. 1762/47
 Hen., Holwell, yeo. 1608/86
 Isabell, Bletsoe, wid. 1624/84
 Jn., Bromham. R 1502: 1/33
 Jn., Stevington. R 1529: 3/6
 Jn., sen., Thurleigh, husb. 1563/97
 Jn., Felmersham, husb. 1573/114
 Jn., Thurleigh, husb. 1608-9/88
 Jn., Bletsoe, husb. 1603/120
 Jn., Thurleigh, husb. A 1705/47
 Jn., sen., Chellington, farmer. 1708/33
 Jn., (no parish). 1717/37
 Margt., Stevington, wid. R 1529/30: 3/20
 Mary, Felmersham, spins. 1735/25
 Nich., Thurleigh, yeo. 1626/122
 Ric., Stevington. R 1545: 12/179d
 Ric., Potton, gent. 1717-18/85
 Sam., Keysoe (P/IX2 admon missing). A 1783/22
 Thos., Wilden, husb. R 1546: 11/135d
 Thos., Thurleigh, yeo. 1628/41
 Thos., Bletsoe, husb. 1659/274

DARLING, DERLING continued
Thos., Bletsoe, husb. A 1703/4
Wm., Thurleigh, husb. R 1543: 6/160d & 9/14d
Wm., Leighton Buzzard, brazier. LB 1770/24
DARLOW, Fra., Elstow. 1620/101
Susannah, Elstow, wid. 1692-3/73
Wm., Goldington. 1679/4
Wm., Elstow, tailor. 1684/17
Wm., Thurleigh, husb. 1803/31
DARNELL, Thos., Shelton, dairyman. A 1725/14
DARRINGTON, Eliz., Tempsford, wid. 1613-14/150
Jn., Little Barford, yeo. 1731-2/64
DARROT, Wm., Bedford St. Mary, lab. 1716-17/26
DASSON, Nich., Thurleigh (bundle 1642). 1644-5/51
DAVBYE, Wm., Houghton Conquest, lab. 1552/234
DAVEY, DAVIE, DAVY, Agnes, Maulden, wid. 1560/175
Edw., Ampthill, butcher. R 1545-6: 11/132
Ellis, Goldington. 1602/46
Ellis, Goldington. 1604/27
Hen., Ampthill. R 1506: 1/161d
Hen., Silsoe, mercer. 1611/159
Hen., Husborne Crawley, miller. 1660/27
Hen., Southill, yeo. 1670/197
Jn., Warden. R 1500: 1/10d
Jn., Ampthill, yeo. R 1548-9: 12/49d
Jn., West Hyde. 1584/170
Jn., Houghton Conquest, How End, yeo. 1660/177
Jn., Toddington, cordwinder. 1670/164
Jn., Toddington, Chalton. AR 1679: 1/157d
?Jn., Meppershall. 1690/1
Jn., sen., Husborne Crawley, fellmonger. 1702/20
Jn., Luton, wheelwright. 1705/17
Jn., Husborne Crawley, fellmonger. 1711/89
Jn., Husborne Crawley, fellmonger. ?1713/45
Judith, Wootton, wid. 1708-9/89
Lawr., Shefford, mercer. 1613-14/153
Marian, Ampthill. R 1500?: 1/9d
Mary, Cranfield. 1621/207
Mary, Silsoe, wid. 1630/74
Mary, Felmersham, spins. 1702/32
Mary, Husborne Crawley, wid. 1703/13
Matthew, Southill, yeo. 1590/174
Ric., Flitwick, husb. 1561/143
Ric., ?Sandy. 1606/64
Ric., Flitwick. 1615-16/117

DAVEY, DAVIE, DAVY continued
Robt., Maulden. 1558/251
Robt., Little Staughton. I 1587: 4/170
Thos., Dunstable. R 1518: 2/84d
Thos., Maulden, weaver. 1578/84
Thos., Silsoe, weaver. 1632/96
Thos., Flitwick, yeo. 1654-5/182
Thos., sen., Flitwick, yeo. 1680/75
Thos., Flitwick, husb. 1695/51
Thos., Felmersham, yeo. 1708/12
Thos., (old index only, bundle missing). A 1718/37
Wm., sen., Flitton. R 1506: 1/161
Wm., Willington, lab. 1636-7/53
Wm., Felmersham, yeo. 1665/75
Wm., Cranfield, mason. 1678/130
Wm., Felmersham, yeo. AR 1681-2: 1/43d
see also Davis, Davies
DAVIS, DAVIES, Ann, Colmworth, wid. 1828/45
Ben., Southill, brickmaker. A 1714/24
Crout, Arlesey, farmer. 1803/27
Geo., Bletsoe, yeo. 1617/211
Humph., Leighton Buzzard, innholder. 1749/3
Isaac, Bletsoe, grazier. 1762/25
Jas., Biddenham, Ford End, tailor. 1817/14
Jas., Arlesey, Hermitage Farm. A 1827/1, I: 4/273
Jane, Southill, spins. 1685/76
Jeremiah, Bedford St. Mary, yeo. A 1800/9
Jn., Goldington, esq. AR 1687: 1/31
Jn., Bedford, esq. 1695/5
Jn., (old index, "docket mislaid"). A 1708/7
Jn., Luton, wheelwright. 1737/48
Jn., Caddington, Onyons, farmer. 1769/18
Jn., Bedford, yeo. A 1795/1
Jn., Stopsley. 1844/20
Margt., Sandy, Girtford, wid. 1610-11/13
Martha, Cranfield, wid. 1782/27
Mary, Goldington, wid. 1721/90
Mary, Arlesey, wid. of Thos. Davies. 1833/17
Ric., Battlesden. A 1738/23
Ric., Cranfield, shopkeeper. 1782/7
Ric., Milton Ernest, yeo. 1786/3
Rob., Warden Hill, dairyman. 1680/38
Sara, Bletsoe. A 1771/12
Sarah, Woburn, wid. 1717-18/80
Sarah, Caddington, Onyons, wid. A 1769/18

DAVIS, DAVIES continued
alias Johnson, Thos., Southill, yeo. 1684/93
Thos., Felmersham, glover. 1726-7/98
Thos., Colmworth, yeo. 1806/2
Thos., Arlesey, farmer. A 1848/9
Wm., Harrold. AR 1688-9: 1/49d
Wm., Woburn, barber. A 1716/36
Wm., Woburn, butcher. 1780/41
Wm., Ampthill, innholder. 1786/4
Wm., sen., Stopsley. 1835/44
Wm., Luton, Falconers Hall, farmer. 1843/31
DAVISON, Jas., Bedford St. Peter, husb. 1634/109
Jas., Ampthill, surveyor of taxes. A 1827/11
Jn., Bedford St. Peter, cooper. 1633-4/206
Jn., Bedford St. Peter, weaver. A 1714-15/40
Jn., Luton. A 1737-8/1
Robt., Kempston, yeo. 1714/74
Sarah, Hyde Mill, wid. 1761/44
Skevington, Turvey, miller & baker. 1812/33
Wm., Turvey, farmer & watchmaker. 1845/16
Wm., Turvey, yeo. 1849/16
Wm., Turvey. A 1773/5
DAWBONE, Jn., Marston. A 1715/42
see also Dawbourne
DAWBOURNE, Jn., Lidlington, grocer. 1693/100
Mary, Marston, wid. 1739/31
Thos., Lidlington, mercer. 1640/63
Thos., Lidlington, yeo. 1713/15
see also Dawbone
DAWBY, Thos., Marston, husb. 1602/54
Roger, Marston. 1615-16/123
Eliz., Ridgmont, wid. 1615/197
DAWES, Jn., Chellington, lab. I 1619: 4/66
Judith, Bletsoe, wid. 1661/347
Thos., Leighton Buzzard. 1607/95
DAWESWORTH, Jn., Bedford St. Mary. I 1619/20: 4/32
DAWSON, Alex., Harrold, yeo. 1729/44
Ben., Keysoe. 1725-6/28
Dan., Riseley, yeo. A 1782/14
Dorothy, Harrold, wid. A 1730/29
Eliz., Clifton, wid. 1774/56
Fra., Riseley, wid. 1697/85
Gregory, Roxton, yeo. 1761/28
Hen., Goldington, miller. 1607-8/151
Hugh, Riseley, lab. A 1728/29

DAWSON continued
alias Bedford, Jane, Dunstable, wid. 1617/158
Jn., Riseley. 1669-70/105
Jn., Luton, husb. 1722-3/83
Jn., sen., Riseley, tailor. 1730/88
Jn., Leighton Buzzard, carpenter. LB 1790/88
Jn., sen., Oakley, yeo. 1841/21
Mich., Riseley, mason. 1708/20
Randall, Bletsoe, lab. AR 1672: 1/37
Robt., Ampthill, sadler. 1642/45
Roger, Dunstable, maltman. 1602/76
Roger, Lower Sundon. 1730/71
alias Bedford, Thos., Dunstable, glazier. 1613/187
Thos., Thurleigh, lab. AR 1670: 1/60
Thos., Dean, mason. 1752/68
Thos., sen., Leighton Buzzard, carpenter. LB 1761/39
Thos., jun., Leighton Buzzard, carpenter. LB 1781/55
Thos., Leighton Buzzard, carpenter. LB 1782/62
Thos., Clapham, bricklayer. 1851/42
Wm., Riseley. A 1705/65
Wm., Bedford, victualler. 1835/13
DAY, DAYSE, Agnes, Tempsford, wid. 1570-1/30
Alice, Haynes wid. AR 1678: 1/200d
Alice, Haynes, wid. (Bundle 1679). 1678/41
Alice, Luton, spins. 1737/2
Ann Maria, Pulloxhill, wid. 1777/36
Anne, Luton, Crawley Green, wid. 1605/112
Anne, Little Staughton, wid. A 1706/32
Antijua, Eaton Socon, wid. 1657-8/193
Antijua, Eaton Socon, wid. 1657-8/246
Clement, Eaton Socon, yeo. 1649/68
Edm., Westoning. R 1549: 12/70d
Edm., no parish given. 1611/31
Edw., Luton. 1564/6
Edw., Roxton, lab. 1713/30
Eleanor, Southill, wid. 1640/34
Eliz., Old Warden, wid. AR 1670-1: 1/94
Eliz., Warden, wid. 1670/139
Eliz., Houghton Conquest, wid. 1688/195
Eliz., Marston, wid. 1708/77
Eliz., Potton, wid. 1746/29
Fra., Riseley, lab. 1639/94
Fra., Ampthill, bricklayer. 1699/51
Fra., Luton, farmer. A 1737/25
Geo., Streatley, yeo. 1661/323

DAY, DAYSE continued
Geo., Luton, Wigmore Hall, farmer. 1803/26
Geo., Tempsford, yeo. A 1829/5
Grace, Bolnhurst, wid. 1642/23
Gregory, Riseley, lab. 1617/301
Helen, Bolnhurst, Woodende. 1587/161
Hen., Sundon, lab. 1575-6/67
Hen., Cople, yeo. A 1784/17
Hugh, Goldington, miller. 1604-5/7
Humph., Northill, dairyman. 1689/50
Jas., Northill, yeo. 1757/31
Joan, Potton, wid. A 1726-7/29
Jn., Souldrop. R 1505: 1/67
Jn., Little Staughton. R 1506: 1/202d
Jn., Souldrop. R 1524-5: 2/34d
Jn., sen., Tilbrook. R 1541: 6/75d
Jn., Luton, Crawley Green. R 1546: 11/182d
Jn., Tilbrook. 1557/263
Jn., Leighton Buzzard. 1559/176
Jn., sen., Luton, yeo. 1610/109
Jn., Wilshamstead, yeo. 1622-3/6
Jn., Upper Shelton, Marston, tailor. 1625-6/143
Jn., Bedford St. John. 1633-4/171
Jn., Sharnbrook, lab. 1635-6/45
Jn., Stopsley, Crawley Green, yeo. 1645/17
Jn., Luton, bach. AR 1683: 1/165d
Jn., Bedford, basketmaker. 1698/81
Jn., (old index "docket mislaid"). A 1709/33
Jn., Tilbrook, lab. 1717/84
Jn., Clophill, victualler. A 1723-4/40
Jn., Marston, bricklayer. 1724-5/79
Jn., sen., Pulloxhill, dairyman. 1729/50
Jn., Bedford, basketmaker. 1763/19
Jn., Cople, yeo. 1764/52
Jn., Biggleswade. Bw 1765/42
Jn., Haynes, yeo. 1774/17
Jn., Spaldwick, Hunts. A 1816/7a
Jn., Pertenhall, gardener. 1853/42
Jos., Eaton Socon, wid. A 1753/18
Margt., Wilshamstead, wid. 1625-6/140
Marion, Wilshamstead. 1560/188
Mary, Cople, wid. 1767/1
Oliver, Riseley. AR 1685-6/ 1/79d
Oliver, Riseley, lab. 1725/66
Paul, Melchbourne, servant to the Rt. Hon. Oliv., Lord St. John. 1622/37

DAY, DAYSE continued
Ralph, Ampthill, innholder. 1641/206
Ralph, London and Eaton Socon, citizen and carpenter. 1671/74
Rebecca, Sharnbrook, wid. A 1784/14
Ric., Westoning. R 1541: 6/87d and 8/9
Ric., Southill, husb. R 1546: 11/174d
Ric., Southill, yeo. 1589/109
Ric., Leagrave, yeo. 1667/70
Ric., Marston, bricklayer. A 1700/16
Ric., Houghton Conquest, lab. A 1719/17
Robt., Southill. 1568/43
Robt., Bolnhurst, yeo. 1627/150
Robt., Melchbourne, yeo. 1716/99
Susan, Luton, wid. 1748/35
Susan, Flitwick, spins. 1760/57
Susanna, Sharnbrook, wid. A 1715/23
Thos., Houghton Conquest, weaver. R 1542: 6/130
Thos., Luton, "Bandland". R 1566-7: 17/104
Thos., Luton, maltman. 1582/77
Thos., Southill, lab. 1597-8/44
Thos., Keysoe, yeo. 1637/172
Thos., Keysoe, yeo. 1637-8/188
Thos., Warden, dairyman. 1684/112
Thos., Tilbrook. AR 1688: 1/82
Thos., Flitton, Ward Hedges, husb. 1691-2/130
Thos., Pulloxhill, Upberry, yeo. 1706/19
Thos., Luton, yeo. 1711-12/33
Thos., Roxton, yeo. 1719/75
Thos., Northill, Nether Caldecote, yeo. 1723/66
Thos., Colmworth, victualler. A 1723/8
Thos., Shillington, Chibley, husb. 1736/41
Thos., Shillington, husb. 1739/52
Thos., Luton, carpenter. 1744/28
Thos., Ridgmont, shopkeeper. A 1779/5
Wm., Houghton Conquest, weaver. R 1535-6: 4/46d
Wm., Sundon. R 1550: 12/134d
Wm., Harlington, husb. 1557/305
Wm., sen., Bolnhurst, Wood End, husb. 1557/363
Wm., Bolnhurst. 1559/189
Wm., Westoning. 1559/198
Wm., Houghton Conquest. 1562/113
Wm., Blunham, husb. 1564/47
Wm., Tempsford, ploughwright. 1568/53
Wm., Luton. 1600/66
Wm., Tilbrook, husb. 1610/73

DAY, DAYSE continued
Wm., Southill, yeo. 1632/102
Wm., Leagrave, yeo. 1650-1/127
Wm., Pulloxhill, dairyman. A 1769/27
alias Jas., Wm., sen., Bedford. AR 1684: 1/25
Wm., sen., Tilbrook, yeo. 1690/16
Wm., Upper Dean, mason. 1700/97
Wm., Luton, grocer. 1709/11
Wm., Tempsford, gardener. 1718/8
Wm., Eaton Socon, gent. 1847/35
DAYSE, see Day
DEACON, Alex., Luton, Bramingham, yeo. 1749/47
Cornelius, Tingrith, husb. 1740/67
Fra., Tilsworth, butcher. 1743/18
Fra., Chalgrave, Tebworth, wid. 1760/32
Geo., Elstow. 1610-11/183
Hannah, Stanbridge, spins. 1758/19
Hen., Clophill, husb. 1609/189
Hen., Flitwick, East End, yeo. 1746/14
Joan, Elstow, Medbury. 1622/80
Jn., Caddington. 1617/298
Jn., Caddington. 1637-8/27
Jn., Eversholt, Rads End, yeo. 1742-3/97
Mary, Ampthill, wid. 1827/58
Mary, Eversholt, spins. 1816/12
Matthew, Limbury, yeo. 1714-15/199
Ralph, Streatley, Sharpenhoe, yeo. 1684/38
Ric., Marston, gent. R 1543: 6/164d; 9/16d
Ric., Streatley, Sharpenhoe, lab. 1582/125
Robt., Leighton Buzzard, weaver. 1612/78
Thos., Elstow, Medbury, gent. 1610-11/132
Thos., Clophill, lab. 1631/215
Thos., Clophill, yeo. 1633/140
Thos., Clophill, yeo. 1645-6/54
Thos., sen., Over Stondon, yeo. 1698/167
Thos., Flitwick, yeo. 1727/10
Thos., Toddington, tailor. A 1746/29
Thos., Luton, Bramingham, yeo. 1759/60
Thos., Leighton Buzzard. LBA 1772/24a
Thos., Tingrith, yeo. 1797/30
Timothy, Eversholt, farmer. A 1723/13
Timothy, Eversholt, poulterer. A 1723/24
Wm., Wilshamstead. R 1536-7: 4/73
Wm., Eversholt, yeo. 1727-8/103
Wm., Clophill, husb. 1630/13

DEACON continued
 Wm., Flitwick, husb. 1786/38
 Wm., Marston, farmer. 1807/38
DEAN(S), Anne, Wilden, wid. 1621-2/158
 Cicely, Colmworth. 1631/190
 Edm., Elstow, yeo. 1608/35
 Edm., Little Staughton, yeo. 1626/68
 Eleanor, Leighton Buzzard, wid. LB 1736/4
 Hen., Elstow, yeo. 1618/162
 Hen., Leighton Buzzard, yeo. Fac. 1713: 9/42
 Jn., Odell, lab. 1684-5/106
 Jn., Leighton Buzzard, grazier. Fac. 1704: 9/8
 Jn., Biggleswade, victualler. Bw 1855/164
 Marg., Colmworth, Church End, wid. 1661/238
 Ric., Colmworth, yeo. 1664/7
 Ric., Sandy, lab. 1699/4
 Robt., Melchbourne. R 1545: 11/64d
 Robt., Sandy, Girtford, lab. 1660/144
 Sarah, Sandy, wid. 1728-9/116
 Thos., Little Staughton, husb. 1615/168
 Thos., Colmworth, lab. 1645-6/50
 Thos., Colmworth, lab. 1645/51
 Thos., Leighton Buzzard. AR 1683: 1/165
 Wm., Toddington. R 1530: 3/33
 Wm., Blunham. 1660/136
 Wm., sen., Leighton Buzzard, bricklayer. LB 1738/7
DEAR, DEER, Abr., Arlesey, victualler. 1810/6
 Abr., Arlesey. 1844/3
 Ann, Holwell, Fakeswell, wid. 1826/5
 Dorothy, Wilshamstead, wid. 1670/195
 Dorothy, Wilshamstead. AR 1670: 1/2d
 Edm., Southill. 1839/28
 Edw., Arlesey, carpenter. 1687/90
 Edw., Shillington, carpenter. 1761/6
 Edw., Shillington, carpenter. A 1761/6
 Edw., Shillington, carpenter. A 1762/5
 Eliz., Biggleswade, wid. 1683/62
 Eliz., Arlesey, wid. A 1706/51
 Eliz., Langford, wid. A 1848/3
 Fra., Arlesey, yeo. AR 1672: 1/95d
 Fra., Biggleswade, carpenter. AR 1686: 1/127d
 Fra., Biggleswade, carpenter. Bw 1715/5a, I
 Geo., Southill, Broome, husb. 1639/32
 Geo., Langford, yeo. 1823/25
 Humph., Southill. AR 1684-5: 1/122d

DEAR, DEER continued
Jas., Southill, Broome. 1618-19/15
Jas., Shillington, carpenter. 1635/51
Jas., Northill, Upper Caldecote, carpenter. 1750/8
Jas., Langford, yeo. 1841/19
Joan, Southill, Broome, wid. 1610/104
Jn., Wilshamstead, blacksmith. 1630-1/117
Jn., Arlesey, yeo. 1721/36
Jn., Maulden, yeo. 1811/33
Jn., Arlesey, yeo. 1856/24
Jn., Bedford, gent. A 1700-1/40
Jn., Barton, carpenter. A 1753/6
Jos., Holwell, Fakeswell, yeo. 1810/22
Jos., Streatley, Sharpenhoe, lab. 1853/44
Mich., Arlesey, tailor. A 1720/10
Phillip, Biggleswade, grocer. 1682-3/111
Ric., Wilshamstead, husb. 1593/44
Ric., Wilshamstead, husb. (bundle 1597). 1593/47
Sar., Shillington. A 1759/17
Sar., Harlington. 1820/1
Sar., Maulden, wid. 1825/6
Soloman, Biggleswade, Stratton, yeo. Bw 1714/3a
Susanna, Arlesey, wid. A 1814/16
Thos., Wilshamstead. R 1548: 12/24d
Thos., Elstow, shepherd. 1615/141
Thos., Stotfold, yeo. 1669/6
Twydell, Shillington. 1833/18
Wm., Wilshamstead. R 1536-7: 4/77d
Wm., sen., Southill, Broome. 1631/196
Wm., Shillington, carpenter. 1644/104
Wm., Arlesey. AR 1675-6: 1/105
Wm., Southill, Broome, yeo. 1694-5/83
Wm., Barton, bach. A 1707-8/5
Wm., Arlesey, gardener. 1741/12
Wm., Northill, Upper Caldecote, carpenter. 1780/34
Wm., sen., Potton, carpenter & victualler. 1818/8
Wm., Langford, yeo. 1827/12
DEARDS, Jn., Potsgrove, yeo. 1638-9/208
DEARMAN, Math., Chalgrave, Wingfield, husb. 1649/73
Ric., Toddington (bundle 1638). 1637-8/17
Roger, Wilshamstead, dairyman. 1617/326
Susan, Toddington, wid. 1672/146
Wm., Wilshamstead, husb. 1648/20
see also Dearmer

DEARMER, DERMER, DEERMER, Agnes, Houghton Regis, wid. 1649/22
Alice, Luton. 1579/179
Edw., Caddington. R 1518: 2/26
Edw., Luton. 1562/114
Edw., Luton, maltster. 1638-9/100
Edw., Caddington, yeo. 1658/227
Geo., Wilshamstead, grazier. 1665-6/8
Hen., Wilshamstead, yeo. 1686/3
Hen., Elstow, grocer. 1696/83
Jn., Luton. R 1563: 16/89d
Jn., Pulloxhill, husb. 1578/95
Jos., Wilshamstead, yeo. 1711/59
Jos., Wilshamstead, farmer. A 1737/5
Nich., Barton, bach. 1598-9/63
Robt., Dunstable. R 1525: 2/129
Steph., Luton, apothecary. A 1707/7
Thos., Luton. 1583-4/157
Thos., Clophill, yeo. 1630/97
Thos., Caddington, grocer. AR 1684: 1/167d
Wm., Caddington, Oynions. 1672/139
Wm., Wilshamstead, yeo. 1720/63
Wm., Eaton Socon, yeo. A 1746/5
see also Dearman, Diemer
DEATON, Thos., Wymington, shepherd. 1771/29
DEBBET, Anne, Sutton, wid. 1609/170
DECESON, see Dixon
DECKERMAN, Jn., Marston. R 1543: 6/167d
see also Dickerman
DEER, see Dear
DEERY, Thos., Cardington, lab. 1630/99
DEFRAYNE, Peter, Woburn, joiner. 1613/219
Ric., Toddington. 1608/50
Thos., Woburn, collarmaker. 1624/23
DELL, Ann, Leighton Buzzard, spins. LBA 1802/52
Jas., Houghton Regis, Sewell, husb. 1697/35
Jas., Dunstable, yeo. A 1711/15
Jas., Leighton Buzzard, butcher. LB 1806/33
Ric., Eggington, yeo. LB 1819/3
DELVE, Thos., Keysoe, gent. 1639/114
DENBY, DENBIGH, Ann, Ampthill, wid. 1740/26
Edwin, Ampthill, gent. 1720/114
Jn., Lidlington, gent. 1734/58
Jn., Ampthill, gent. 1759/49
Ric., Ridgmont, gent. 1686/9
Sus., Marston Moreteyne, wid. 1717/29

DENET, see Dennitt
DENHAM, Ben., Luton, husb. A 1729/73
Jn., Ravensden, dairyman. 1705/37
Jn., North Cray, Kent (relatives at Haynes). 1763/7
Jos., Wilshamstead, farmer. A 1735/19
DENIS, see Dennis
DENNIS, DENES, DENYS, DYNNIS, DENIS, DENNYS, DINNIS, Warner alias Dennis, see Warner
Warriner alias Dennis, see Warner
Andrew, Bedford St. John, clerk. 1633/178
Edm., Little Staughton, carpenter. 1658/228
Edm., Little Staughton, carpenter. 1673/50
Edw., Bedford St. Mary. A 1771/1
Edw., Bedford, glazier. 1734/38
Edw., Renhold. 1760/21
Eliz., Woburn, wid. 1726-7/104
Eliz., Renhold, wid. A 1761/17
Eliz., Dunstable, wid. 1762/45
Geo., Sandy, Girtford, bach. 1774/13
Hen., Blunham, butcher. 1796/34
Jn., Bedford St. Peter Merton. R 1503: 1/28d, 36d
Jn., Felmersham, cordwainer. A 1705/26
Jn., Renhold, dairyman. 1751/25
Jn., Upper Gravenhurst, yeo. 1758/50
Jn., Potton. A 1835/12
Jn., Blunham, butcher. 1842/50
Len., Stagsden. 1624/39
Mark, Felmersham, shoemaker. 1835/27
Mary, Potton, wid. 1820/33
Math., sen., Kempston, gent. 1672/129
Math., Tempsford, carpenter. AR 1681-2: 1/115
Math., Woburn, blacksmith. A 1736/15
Nath., Maulden, yeo. 1784/1
Ric., Stevington. 1615-16/110
Ric., Marston Pillinge, Marston, yeo. 1678/98
alias Warner, Ric., Little Staughton, husb. 1685/40
Ric., Gt. Barford, gent. 1831/36
Robt., Flitwick, husb. 1611-2/158
Robt., Marston, gent. 1680/40
Robt., Ampthill, staymaker. 1755/42
Sam., Bedford. 1704/84
Thos., Wymington, husb. 1552/331
Thos., Upper Gravenhurst, lab. AR 1674: 1/98d
Thos., Blunham, butcher. 1802/12

DENNIS, DENES, DENYS, DYNNIS, DENIS, DENNYS, DINNIS continued
Wm., Melchbourne, husb. 1631/152
Wm., sen., Bedford St. Paul, joiner. 1663/73
Wm., Stevington, gent. 1671-2/6
Wm., Wrestlingworth. 1697/52
Wm., Millbrook. A 1704-5/20
Wm., Woburn, blacksmith. A 1715/17
Wm., Kempston, gent. 1747/67
Wm., Potton, carpenter. A 1749/16
Wm., Felmersham, cordwainer. 1760/3
DENNITT, DENET, Geo., Husborne Crawley, yeo. 1657/76
Jn., Kempston, husb. 1564/53
Mary, Kempston, wid. 1652/114
Ren., Kempston. R 1550: 12/119
Thos., Husborne Crawley, yeo. 1643/77
Wm., Kempston. R 1550-1: 12/141d
DENSHIRE, Wm., Kempston. 1749-50/54
DENTON, Anne, Barton, wid. 1609-10/134
alias Yarway, Grace, Houghton Conquest. AR 1682: 1/20d
Jeremiah, Northill, bricklayer. A 1729/12
Joan, Silsoe, wid. 1580/211
Jn., Poddington, husb. 1686/46
Jn., Marston, lab. 1764/63
Math., Barton, esq. 1640/70
Math., Ampthill, esq. 1679/22
Math., Clophill, yeo. 1834/3
Matt., Ampthill, Ewe Green, esq. (In 1706 bundle). A 1705/15
Nich., Silsoe. 1583/129
Nich., Houghton Conquest, gent. AR 1691: 1/34d
Ric., Podington, husb. 1707/93
Robt., Silsoe, yeo. 1578/113
Wm., Tingrith, carpenter. 1837/30
DENYER, Jn., Elstow, shopkeeper. 1826/1, I 4/262
Sarah, Elstow, wid. 1835/9
DERBY, see Darby
DERICK, Stramproe alias Derick, see under Stramproe
Hen., Stevington, lab. 1627/172
DERLING, see Darling
DEROMEE, Thos., Luton, yeo. 1553/276
DERRY, Thos., Heath and Reach. 1605-6/79
DESBOROUGH, Lawr., Bedford, yeo. 1768/16
Thos., Thurleigh, farmer. 1800/10
DEVELL, Ric., Markyate Street, victualler. 1605/120
DEVEREAUX, Chas., Silsoe, bricklayer. 1818/25
Wm., Bedford, yeo. 1712-13/32

DEVEREAUX continued
Wm., Arlesey. 1807/46
DEVERELL, Geo., Ampthill, yeo. 1806/7
Jos., Ampthill, butcher. 1835/22
DEVERIS, Thos., Riseley, carpenter. 1592/15
DEVEY, Wm., Potton, maltster. 1772/2
DEVIT, Martha, Bedford St. Mary, wid. 1741/31
Walt., Bedford. 1661/288
DEVONSHIRE, see Denshire
DEVYAS, Joan, Houghton Regis, Sewell. R 1543: 6/142d
DEW, Thos., Bedford, yeo. 1724/24
Thos., Bedford St. Paul, yeo. A 1725/21
DEWBERRY, Jn., Yielden, weaver. 1618/50
Jn., Riseley, innholder. 1761/32
Sam., Bedford, gent. 1721/96
Thos., Riseley, husb. A 1706/3
DEWCE, Wm., Bedford St. Mary, glazier. AR 1679: 1/17
DEWELL, DUEWELL, Jn., Upper Gravenhurst, gardener. A 1744/9
DEXTER, Eliz., Bedford, maid. 1578/118
Eliz., Turvey, wid. 1724/1
DICKASON, see Dickenson
DICKENS, see Dickins
DICKENSON, DICKASON, Geo., Carlton, weaver. 1630-1/232
Jn., Harlington, yeo. 1730/44
Jn., Bedford, lab. 1739/8
Ric., Oakley, miller. 1715/72
Thos., Carlton, weaver. 1615/217
see also Dickerson, Dixon
DICKERMAN, DECKERMAN, Alice, wid., Marston. 1624-5/107
see also Dickman
DICKERSON, Jn., Maulden, yeo. 1774/48
see also Dickenson, Dixon
DICKINS, DYCKYNS, DUKYNS, Anne, Stanbridge, wid. 1554/174
Dan., Riseley, bricklayer. 1852/21
Dinah, Northill, Thorncote, late of Potton, wid. 1796/25
Emme, Kempston, wid. 1632/45
Geo., Riseley, bricklayer. 1782/51
Gerrard, Sharnbrook, plumber and glazier. A 1851/3
Jn., Hockliffe. 1556/104
Jn., Riseley. 1669-70/125
Jn., Potton, lab. 1778/7
Jn., Bedford St. Paul. 1810/24
Mich., Ledbourne, Mentmore, Bucks., husb. 1669/13
Robt., Riseley, carpenter. 1617-18/167
Robt., Riseley, carpenter. 1670/178

DICKINS, DYCKYNS, DUKYNS continued
Robt., Nether Dean, shepherd. 1721/50
Sam., Bedford, cordwainer. 1681-2/99
Sam., Riseley, yeo. 1690/57
Sophia, Keysoe. A 1847/11
Susannah, Wilshamstead, wid. 1710/34
Thos., Stanbridge. LBR 1551-2: 1/23
Thos., Lidlington, yeo. 1722/84
Wm., Kempston, lab. 1647/33
Wm., Keysoe, yeo. A 1798/19
Wm., Riseley, yeo. A 1799/7
Wm., Riseley, miller. 1818/38
DICKMAN, Thos., Sutton, singleman. 1726/83
see also Dickerman
DICKS, see Dix
DICKSON, see Dixon
DIEMER, see Dearmer, Dearman
DIER, see Dyer
DIGBY, Jn., (old index only, bundle missing). A 1718/33
Thos., Bromham, husb. 1600/65
DILLEY, Ann, Southill, spins. AR 1683: 1/119
Eliz., Southill, wid. AR 1683: 1/120
Eliz., Biggleswade, wid. BwA 1758/18, I
Geo., Clifton, lab. 1638-9/153
Geo., Henlow, yeo. 1796/18
Geo., Southill, Broome, yeo. 1840/2
Geo., Henlow, farmer. A 1768/24
Geo., Bedford, builder. A 1847/1
Hannah, Clifton, wife of Rich. 1662/104
Jn., Clifton, husb. 1604/46
Jn., Henlow, victualler. A 1773/9
Jn., Dunton, farmer. A 1823/10
Margt., Houghton Conquest, wid. A 1763/8
Mary, Dunton, Newton, wid. 1815/19
Ric., Henlow, carrier. A 1736-7/37
Thos., Clifton, tailor. 1752/76
Thos., Southill, yeo. AR 1671: 1/93
Thos., Henlow, carrier. A 1782/26
Wm., Biggleswade. BwA 1758/19
Wm., Dunton, yeo. 1787/18
Wm., Dunton, cottager. A 1838/4
DILLINGHAM, DYLYNGHAM, Chris., Nether Dean, yeo. 1651/48
Fra., Wilden, clerk. 1625/204
Geo., Pertenhall. 1657/245
Hen., Over Dean, yeo. 1624/37

DILLINGHAM, DYLYNGHAM continued
Joan, wid., Dean. 1558/282
Jn., Over Dean, yeo. R 1541: 6/102d
Jn., sen., son and heir of Wm., Dean, yeo. R 1603-4: 26/25d
Jn., Nether Dean, yeo. 1684/37
Jn., Dean, gent. 1695/13
Jn., Shelton. 1772/16
Robt., Nether Dean. 1607/87
Sam., Upper Dean, grazier. 1788/18
Sarah, Upper Dean, wid. 1802/15
Thos., Nether Dean, husb. 1647/29
Thos., Shelton, yeo. 1706/4
Thos., Shelton, yeo. 1750-1/56
Thomasin, Over Dean, wid. 1599/72
Wm., Pertenhall, yeo. 1686/57
Wm., Odell, clerk. 1689/86
DILLINGTON, Thos., Elstow. 1557/249
DIMMOCK, DYMOCK, Charlotte, Luton, Round Green, wife of Edw. 1832/6
Eliz., Eaton Bray, wid. 1735/9
Joan, Elstow, wid. 1641/169
Jn., sen., Eaton Bray, gent. 1710/1
Jn., Eaton Bray, gent. 1720/5
Jos., Wootton, Barnet, yeo. 1825/35
Math., Bedford St. John, yeo. 1720/93
Robt., Luton, farmer & licensed victualler. 1846/31
Wm., Elstow, yeo. 1623/173
DINE, see Dyne
DINGLE, Thos., Stevington, yeo. 1718-19/86
DINNIS, see Dennis
DINSEY, Nich., Bedford St. Cuthbert, vicar. 1563/102
DISHFORD, Jn., Stanbridge, weaver. Fac. 1719: 9/57
DISNEY, DYSNAYE, Wm., Toddington, Chalton. 1557/372
DITTON, Hen., Sharnbrook, yeo. 1604/77
DIX, DIKKS, DYX, DICKS, DUKKES, Abra., Marston, locksmith.
AR 1680: 1/203d
Abra., Westoning, yeo. 1720/62
Abra., Westoning, farmer. A 1779/7
Abra., Toddington, innholder and draper. 1785/24
Alice, Over Gravenhurst, wid. 1612-3/55
Ann, Blunham, wid. A 1706-7/21
Ann, Blunham, wid. A 1750/8
Ann, Pavenham, wid. and farmer. A 1825/10, I4/261
Dorothy, Bromham, wid. 1600/55
Eliz., Toddington. A 1798/11
Eliz., Toddington. A 1798/12

DIX, DIKKS, DYX, DICKS, DUKKES continued
Eliz., Luton. A 1799/13
Isaac, Harlington, tailor. 1632/48
Isaac, Cranfield, lab. 1723-4/71
Isaac, Ampthill, carpenter. 1771/21
Jacob, Westoning, yeo. 1641/168
Joan, Aspley Guise, wid. 1656/34
Joan, Aspley Guise, wid. 1656/196
Joan, Felmersham, wid. 1679-80/91
Jn., Westoning, husb. 1624/51
Jn., Chellington, shepherd. 1677/12
Jn., Westoning, lab. 1681/67
Jn., Elstow. AR 1691: 1/34
Jn., Westoning, farmer. 1786/23
Jn., Westoning. A 1798/7
Hodgkins nee Dix, Mary, Toddington. A 1798/14
Mary, Toddington, wid. 1814/22
Roland, Westoning. 1558/242
Rowland, Westoning, husb. 1585/25
Thos., Potton. R 1499: 1/151
Thos., Blunham, farmer. 1721/91
Thos., Bedford. AR 1670: 1/1d
Thos., Blunham, husb. A 1701/29
Wm., Goldington. R 1547-8: 12/11
Wm., Bromham, yeo. 1600/54
Wm., Houghton Regis. 1617/288
Wm., Blunham, farmer. A 1747/14
Wm., Westoning, exciseman. A 1798/13
Wm., Pavenham, yeo. A 1821/11, I 4/243
Wm., Pavenham, glazier. 1839/27
Woodfield, Blunham, weaver. 1784/61
DIXEY, Edw., Roxton, Chawston, yeo. 1740/12
Hugh, Eaton Socon, Eaton Ford, butcher. 1649/66
Jane, Eaton Socon, wid. 1677-8/88
Jonathan, Biggleswade, lab. Bw 1769/50
DIXON, DECESON, Faith, Ampthill, wid. 1707/90
Jn., Woburn, dairyman. 1720/90
Marg., Horton, Northants., wid. 1657/48
Mary, Toddington, Chalton. 1641/209
Thos., Woburn chapel. R 1537-8: 5/6d
Wm., Woburn. 1622/30
Wm., sen., Riseley, mason. 1715/35
see also Dickenson; see also Dickerson
DOBSON, Fra., Luton. 1683/58
Jn., Whipsnade, gent. 1639-40/140

DOBSON continued
Wm., Sandy, Girtford, gent. 1842/39
Wm., Southill, Stanford, miller. A 1716/14
Wm., Sandy. P/IX2. A 1812/5
Wm., Sandy, Girtford, gent. A 1829/11
DOCWRA, Dorothy, Ridgmont, wid. 1712/67
DOD, Edw., sen., Totternhoe, husb. 1705/96
Edw., Totternhoe, husb. 1708/60
Jn., Melchbourne, preacher of the word of God. 1624/52
Jn., Totternhoe, tailor. 1722/3
Robt., Blunham. R 1549: 12/70
Sarah, Melchbourne. 1629/92
DODGSON, DODSON, Eliz., Bedford, wid. A 1740/19
Fra., Goldington, victualler. A 1726/30
Wm., Bedford, innholder. 1729/107
DODKYN, Todgill alias Dodky see under Todgill
DODSLEY, Wm., Husborne Crawley, lab. 1699/1
DODSON, see Dodgson
DOE, DOO, Anth., Elstow, lab. 1638/19
Anth., Elstow, lab. 1684/30
Geo., Elstow, sawyer. 1670/199
Geo., Elstow. AR 1670: 1/3
Harry, Cranfield, glover. 1565/191
Hen., Cranfield, tanner. 1639/87
Jn., (parish torn off). 1670/245
Margt., Cranfield. 1638/183
Thos., Luton, husb. A 1704/3
Timothy, Shelton. 1624/53
Wm., Cranfield. 1573/126
Wm., sen., Cranfield, yeo. 1638/203
see also Dowe
DOESITER, see Dossiter
DOGGOT, DOGGAT, DOGGETT, Abra., I 1612: 4/184
Alice, Eggington. 1615/221
Alice, Eggington. 1649/59
Edw., Whipsnade, bach. 1618/123
Edw., Leighton Buzzard, innholder. Fac. 1702: 9/6
Eliz., Hockliffe in Chalgrave *(sic)*, wid. 1712/8
Joan, Limbury, spins. R 1546: 11/184d
Jn., Marston, husb. 1575/85
Judith, Wootton, spins. 1681/75
Lyddia, Wootton, wid. 1698/155
Mary, Chalgrave, wid. 1720/27
Ric., Leighton Buzzard, tailor. Fac. 1705: 9/16
Ric., Westoning, Wood End, carpenter. 1671/38

DOGGOT, DOGGAT, DOGGETT continued
Ric., Steppingley, husb. 1719/12
Robt., Marston, husb. 1562/109
Robt., Steppingley, carpenter. 1613-14/146
Silvester, Marston, yeo. 1662-3/1
Thos., Houghton Conquest, husb. 1620/85
Thos., Westoning, Wood End, carpenter. 1670/136
Thos., Hockliffe, innholder. 1708/78
Thos., Kempston, yeo. 1776/46
Wm., Westoning, carpenter. 1617/317
Wm., Hockliffe, grocer. 1695/53
Wm., Hockliffe, butcher. 1720/6
Wm., Leighton Buzzard, tailor. LB 1761/38
DOLBY, see Dalby
DOLLY, Elinor, Milton Ernest, wid. 1628-9/7
DOLT, Margt., Hockliffe. 1617/212
Mary, Chalgrave. 1652/92
DOLTON, see Dalton
DOO, see Doe
DORMER, Jn., (old index, 'docket mislaid'). A 1708/27
DORRANT, see Durrant
DORRIDGE, DORYCHE, Wm., Barford. 1554/179
DORRINGTON, Ann, Potton, wid. AR 1688: 1/130
Jn., Elstow, tailor. 1724/99
Ralph, Biggleswade, carpenter. 1639/3
Thos., Luton, yeo. 1750/34
DOSSITER, DOESITER, DORSETER, Thos., sen., Silsoe, wheelwright. 1711/123
Thos., Kempston, cordwainer. A 1777/6
DOTTERELL, Jane, Tempsford, wid. 1767/12b
DOUGLAS, Wm., Kempston, yeo. 1824/21
Wm., Kempston, butcher. A 1772/3
DOULTON, Thos., Biggleswade, farmer. BwA 1743/9
DOVE, Jn., (parish torn off), victualler. 1686-7/77
Wm., Bedford, cordwainer. 1727/62
DOVER, Ann, Woburn, wid. 1823/49
DOVEY, Wm., Colmworth, weaver. 1709/5
DOWDSWELL, Edw., Maulden, victualler & farmer. 1839/43
DOWE, Roger, Wootton. R 1538: 5/15
see also Doe
DOWLING, Ruth, Potton, wid. 1774/37
DOWNMAN, Wm., Bedford, carpenter. 1814/30
DOWNS, Eliz., Caddington, wid. A 1746/24
Kath., Biddenham, wid. 1591/111
DRABLE, Edw., Wymington, lab. 1615-16/109

DRABLE continued
Edw., Yielden. 1616/142
Jn., Sandy, gardener. 1743/43
Ric., Yielden. 1615/187
Ric., Yielden (bundle 1665). 1666/96
Robt., Melchbourne. R 1539-40: 6/40
Robt., Yielden, lab. 1614/81
Robt., Campton, yeo. 1688/44
Thos., Willington. 1621/196
Wm., Yielden, lab. 1708/68
DRAGE, Ann, Bedford St. Mary, wid. 1738/22
Jos., Harrold, breeches maker. 1830/12
Thos., Bedford, tanner. 1645/52
Wm., (old index only, bundle missing). A 1718/12
DRAKE, Jn., Stagsden. 1667/94
DRAPER, Abr., Cople, yeo. 1763/26
Caroline, Houghton Conquest, wid. 1824/29
Dan., Shillington, husb. 1630/67
Dan., Pulloxhill. 1695/39
Hen., Eversholt. R 1540-1: 6/68d
Jn., Eversholt. 1636/24
Jn., Stevington, clerk. 1722/58
Jos., Caddington, clerk (bundle 1665). 1666/93
Phineas, Biggleswade, carpenter. 1707/82
Thos., Wilden, yeo. 1851/43
alias Rawlins, Wm., Stanbridge. 1585/128
Wm., Cople, yeo. A 1786/11
DRASERD, Thos., Totternhoe. 1634-5/81
DRAWORTH, Ellen, Bedford St. Mary. 1619-20/1a, I
DREW, Ann, Potton, wid. A 1849/4
Chas., Bedford, stonemason. 1826/39
DRINKWATER, Geo., Chalgrave, Tebworth, lab. 1723/53
Geo., Toddington, horsedealer. A 1777/8
Geo., Toddington, horse dealer & farmer. 1787/52
Geo., Toddington, miller. 1799/34
Mary, Toddington. A 1787/9
Thos., Toddington, yeo. 1830/32
DRIVER, Jn., Colmworth. R 1539: 6/2d
Jn., Shillington, husb. R 1548: 12/20
Thos., Eaton. 1558/214
DROVER, Wm., Tilsworth, yeo. A 1780/1
DRURY, Jn., Henlow, butcher. 1560/196
Richford, Langford, shoemaker. A 1737/26
DUDLEY, Ann, Harrold, spins. 1693/135
Edwin, Blunham, Chalton, farmer. 1856/23

DUDLEY continued
Eliz., Ridgmont, wife of Thos., lab. A 1744/10
Fra., Little Staughton, wid. 1853/1
Jn., Leighton Buzzard, yeo. 1678/124
Jn., sen., Stevington. 1685/57
Jn., Flitwick, husb. A 1730/9
Jos., Toddington, yeo. 1776/31
Lawr., Gt. Woolston, Bucks., husb. R 1590-1: 24/7
Mary, Toddington, wid. R 1783/42
Ric., Stevington, lab. 1732-3/55
Sam., Little Staughton, farmer. 1842/29
Wm., Kempston, farmer. 1829/9
DUEWELL, see Dewell
DUFFIN, Jn., Potton. 1829/33
DUKE, Jane. Husborne Crawley, spins. 1797/2
DUKKES, see Dix
DUNCAN, Anth., Ampthill, yeo. 1679-80/101
DUNCH, Hannah, Aspley Guise. 1752/79
DUNCOMBE, DUNKHAM, Chas., Sharnbrook, yeo. 1805/14
Cicely, Houghton Conquest, wid. 1625/193
Sir Edw., Battlesden, knight. 1637-8/165
Eliz., Ridgmont, spins. AR 1676: 1/195d
Geo., sen., Marston, yeo. 1825/22
Hen., Tiscott, Herts. R 1558: 15/15
Hen., Cranfield. 1701/15
Jas., Gt. Barford, yeo. 1816/23
Jn., Chalgrave, Tebworth. 1771/70
Kath., Chalgrave, Tebworth. 1751/54
Mary, Sundon, wid. 1701/77
Mrs., Gt. Barford. I 1816: 4/225
Ric., Westoning, lab. 1616-17/29
Ric., Harlington, husb. 1671-2/2
Thos., Harlington. AR 1675: 1/194
Thos., Houghton Regis, builder. 1856/8
Wm., jun., Sundon, yeo. 1699/45
Wm., Cranfield. A 1719/25
Wm., Houghton Regis, innkeeper. 1843/53
DUNHAM, Ann, Haynes, wid. 1778/1
Ann, Shillington, Chibley. 1822/5
Jn., Haynes, yeo. 1700/104
Jn., Ravensden, dairyman. A 1730/37
Jn., Sandy, Girtford, yeo. 1750/35
Jn., Cople, Wood End, farmer. 1794/37
Jn., Shillington, farmer. 1802/14
Jn., Cople, farmer. 1829/18

DUNHAM continued
Jn., Shillington, shoemaker. 1837/21
Nath., Wootton, yeo. A 1813/3
Ric., Langford, poulter. 1624-5/2
Sam., Cardington, farmer. A 1732-3/28
Sam., Haynes, Northwood End, yeo. 1752/42
Sam., Wilshamstead, farmer. 1814/17
Thos., Haynes, dairyman. 1761/18
Wm., Lidlington, lab. 1684/80
Wm., Haynes, yeo. 1747-8/59
Wm., sen., Shillington, yeo. A 1751/1
Wm., Cople, farmer. A 1778/18
Wm., Cople, farmer. A 1779/6
Wm., Cople, husb. (Bundle 1778). 1779/44
Wm., Shillington, farmer. 1793/17
Wm., Cople, yeo. 1819/27, I 4/234
DUNKIN, see Duncan
DUNKLEY, Ric., Harrold, lab. 1699/77
DUNLOP, Jas., Bedford, cornfactor. A 1849/9
Wm., Keysoe, farmer. A 1837/10
DUNNE, Joan, Potton, wid. 1702-3/52
DUNSTALL, Jn., Lidlington. 1557/379
Thos., Marston, husb. 1575-6/63
DUNTON, Thos., Clophill, miller, yeo. A 1784/18
DURANT, see Durrant
DURDEN, DURDENT, DURDAINE, Jn., Dunton, wheelwright. 1736/15
Ric., Eyeworth. 1619/270, I 4/102
Wm., Eyeworth. AR 1675: 1/103d
DURHAM, Fra., Bedford, wid. 1740/15
Jos., Dunstable, victualler. A 1735/1
Sar., Dunstable. A 1743/41
DURRANT, Eliz., Shelton. 1726/42
Jn., Potsgrove, dairyman. 1730/18
Ric., Dunstable, yeo. 1815/39
Thos., Shelton. 1726/43
Wm., sen., Whipsnade, husb. 1778/34
DUST, Wm., Keysoe Row, farmer. 1825/3
Wm., Blunham, wheelwright. 1852/41
DUTTON, Eliz., Steppingley, wid. 1746-7/47
Jas., Eversholt, rector. 1698-9/171
Jn., Langford, gent. 1590-1/176
Margt., Woburn, innkeeper. 1621/177
Math., Steppingley, yeo. 1719/77
Theodore, Eversholt, clerk. AR 1680: 1/204d
Rev. Wm., Sundon, vicar. 1787/12

DYCKES, see Dix
DYER, DIER, Eliz., Luton, wid. R 1549: 12/83d
Jn., Eaton Bray, husb. 1605/104
Jn., Over Gravenhurst, weaver. 1614/65
Jn., Marston, gent. 1686/71
Jn., Eaton Bray, miller. 1764/13
Mary, Eaton Bray, wid. 1783/58
Ric., Stopsley, lab. 1611/160
Ric., Luton, maltster. 1663/54
Sam., Eaton Bray, Bellowes Mill, miller and farmer. 1814/21
Thos., Woburn. AR 1683: 1/209d
Thos., Woburn. AR 1684: 1/210d
Wm., Over Gravenhurst, Ion, weaver. 1638/138
Wm., Goldington, esq. AR 1691: 1/34
DYKE, DYCKE, Hen., Goldington, vicar. R 1550: 12/132d
DYKELYFFE, see Leicester alias Dykelyffe
DYKES, see Dix
DYMOCK, see Dimmock
DYNE, DYNES, DINES, Edw. Luton. 1838/17
Eliz., Odell. A 1847/14
Jas., Eaton Socon, wheelwright. 1853/46
Jn., Houghton Regis, Thorne. 1557/285
Jn., Cardington, wheelwright. 1844/30
Jos., Totternhoe. 1616-17/32
Mich., Dunstable, husb. 1621/214
Thos., Houghton Regis. R 1509: 1/61d
Thos., Houghton Regis, Bidwell. 1592/79
Thos., Houghton Regis, Bidwell, lab. 1621/209
Wm., Houghton Regis, Thorn. 1555/145
Wm., Houghton Regis. 1604/50
Wm., Millbrook, dairyman. 1704-5/73
Wm., Houghton Regis, Sewell, lab. 1728/57
DYSON, Jeremiah Jas., Potton, clock and watchmaker. 1844/47
Martha, Milton Ernest. 1837/19

E

EADES, EADS, Eliz., Harrold, wid. 1701-2/74
Wm., Harrold. AR 1690-1: 1/50d
see also Edis
EADY, EEDEY, Robt., Pavenham, wid. 1810/5
EAGLES, Jas., Leighton Buzzard, basket maker. LB 1836/61
Susanna, Ridgmont, wid. A 1831/14
Thos., Bedford, yeo. A 1796/9
EAKINS, see Ekins

EALES, see Eeles
EALING, Jn., Eyeworth. 1638/132
see also Eling; see also Illing
EAME, EAMES, EME, Alice, Houghton Regis, wid. 1634/98
Dan., Tilsworth, yeo. 1762/16
Dan., sen., Houghton Regis, farmer. 1773/34
Edw., Shillington. 1576/48
Edw., Houghton Regis, lab. 1761/25
Eliz., Houghton Regis, wid. 1661/157
Ellen, Shillington, wid. 1580/8
Jas., Shillington, baker. 1764/49
Jas., Dunstable. A 1828/7
Jas., Stondon, farmer. 1835/12
Jn., sen., Houghton Regis. R 1543: 6/143
Jn., Houghton Regis. R 1543: 6/163d and 9/15d
Jn., Chalgrave, Tebworth, husb. 1684/88
Jn., Kempston, cordwainer. 1685/55
Jn., Kempston, cordwainer. 1717/27
Jn., Dunstable, collarmaker. 1728/24
Jn., jun., Houghton Regis, Bidwell, farmer. 1809/20
Jn., Houghton Regis, yeo. 1815/2
Jn., Leighton Buzzard (inventory only, no date). LB 1846/91
Jos., Eggington, farmer. A 1743/28
Jos., Eggington, farmer. LB 1788/82
Mary, Houghton Regis, aledrawer. 1692/40
Mary, Dunstable, wid. 1756/39
Ric., Houghton Regis, yeo. 1634/77
Robt., Totternhoe, yeo. 1758/24
Robt., Tilsworth, yeo. 1759/30
Sarah, Tilsworth, wid. 1765/9
Thos., Houghton Regis. R 1544: 6/16
Thos., Stanbridge, cordwainer. LB 1794/98
Thos., Houghton Regis, Bury Corner, yeo. 1819/3
Wm., Dunstable. 1579/150
Wm., Harlington, vicar. 1605/139
Wm., Houghton Regis, yeo. 1663/55
Wm., Dunstable, barber. A 1706/17
Wm., Dunstable, victualler. A 1707/1
Wm., Leighton Buzzard, late Gt. Brickhill, yeo. LB 1840/74
Wm., Toddington, Chalton, yeo. 1847/28
see also Hems
EARES, Ares alias Eares see Ayre
EARL, ERLE, Hen., Oakley. 1591-2/24
Jacob, Toddington, dairyman. A 1754/26
Jas., Ravensden, yeo. 1729/43

EARL, ERLE continued
Jn., Marston, yeo. 1610-11/32
Jn., Odell, yeo. A 1714/25
Mary, Over Gravenhurst, wid. 1680/83
Sarah, Toddington, wid. 1752/45
Simon, sen., Odell, grazier. 1701-2/32
Simon, sen., Toddington, dairyman. 1743/52
Steph., Bromham. 1695/52
Thos., Yielden. R ?1501: 1/26d
Thos., Thurleigh, Park End, husb. 1682/29
Thos., Lidlington, yeo. 1705-6/70
Wm., Clapham. 1668/151
Wm., Thurleigh. 1760/41
Wm., Upper Gravenhurst, lab. AR 1672: 1/95
see also Harl
EAST, EST, Harry, Marston Moreteyne. R 1506: 1/97
Jas., Southill, yeo. 1601/134
Jas., Southill. 1640/69
Jas., Bedford. AR 1684: 1/24d
Joan, Marston Moreteyne. R 1506: 1/97d
Jn., Caddington, yeo. 1672/163
Jn., Caddington, yeo. (Bundle 1679). 1678/21
Jn., Caddington. AR 1678: 1/156
Jn., Roxton, blacksmith. 1729/91
Jn., Roxton. A 1733/30
Nich., Biggleswade, tanner. 1681/36
Robt., Wilden, farmer. A 1768/10
Thos., Clapham, lab. 1838/25
EASTAFFE, Ann, Bedford St. Peter, wid. 1853/48
Emery, Bedford St. Peter, wid. 1818/34
Jas., Bedford, carpenter. 1782/45
Jas., Bedford St. Peter, cooper. 1848/15
Jonathan, Dunstable, carpenter. 1759/1
EASTFIELD, ESTFYLDE, Harry, Totternhoe. 1559/166
EASTLING, David, Bedford, innholder. 1728-9/118
EASTON, EASSON, Bathsheba, Bletsoe, wid. 1642-3/35
Hatton, Bedford, grocer. 1722/28
Jn., Little Staughton, yeo. 1713/6
Jn., Leighton Buzzard, shepherd. LB 1760/37
Mary, Little Staughton, wid. 1719/47
Wm., Nether Dean, yeo. 1593/47
see also Eston
EASTWALL, see Eastwell
EASTWELL, ESTWELL, EASTWALL, Edw., Bolnhurst. 1688/13
Edw., Cople, farmer. A 1734/26

EASTWELL, ESTWELL, EASTWALL continued
Eliz., Cople, wid. 1735-6/16
Libeus, Bedford, innholder. 1746/6
Lybbeus, Bolnhurst, millwright. 1632-3/14
Lybbeus, Wilden, miller. 1688/65
Robt., Wilden, miller. 1702/7
Thos., Little Staughton. 1645/35
EASTWICK, see Estwick
EASTWOOD, ESTWOOD, Abel, Bedford St. Cuthbert, yeo. 1792/1
Eliz., Caddington, wid. 1632/80
Martha, Arlesey. 1667/17
Paul, Woburn weaver. 1659/180
Robt., Markyate, butcher. 1583/27
EASY, Mary, Biggleswade, wid. Bw 1797/95
Robt., Biggleswade, Holme, lab. 1700/111
Thos., Biggleswade, victualler. Bw 1770/55
EATES, Thos., Bedford. 1761/29
EATON, ETUN, Chris., Luton, clerk. 1745/28
Edw., Turvey, farmer. AR 1683: 1/45
alias Trimmer, Eliz., Stotfold, wid. A 1730/13
Hen., Bromham, smith. 1583-4/132
Hen., Wootton, lab. 1629/109
Jn., Toddington, Chalton. R 1501: 1/29d
Jn., Flitwick. R 1548: 12/27d
Jn., Tilbrook, yeo. 1634-5/82
Jn., Warden. AR 1672: 1/96d
Jn., Cardington, victualler. A 1735-6/10
Jn., Nether Dean, yeo. 1824/8
Jos., Riseley, farmer. 1849/2
Math., Warden, minister. 1639-40/164
Mich., Bletsoe, blacksmith. 1668-9/180
Mich., Cardington, Fenlake, yeo. 1737/36
Oliver, Cople. AR 1686: 1/29
Ric., Leighton Buzzard. 1588/119
Ric., Stevington, farmer and blacksmith. 1845/6
Robt., Woburn. 1559/194
Sam., Nether Dean, carpenter. 1812/44
Sam., Upper Dean, carpenter. 1826/24, I 4/266
Sarah, Ampthill, wid. 1709/15
Susan, Turvey, wid. 1704-5/56
Thos., Cople, yeo. 1632-3/7
Thos., Dean, carpenter. A 1733/13
Thos., Nether Dean, carpenter. 1799/4
Thos., Upper Dean, carpenter. 1851/4
Thos., jun., Turvey, castrator. 1852/37

EATON, ETUN continued
Walt., Riseley. R 1504: 1/43
Wm., Wilshamstead. R 1527: 2/65d
alias Tryomer, Wm., Clifton, glover. 1624/82
Wm., Luton. AR 1678: 1/155
Wm., Turvey, yeo. 1682/46
Wm., Wootton, lab. 1682-3/90
Wm., Nether Dean, carpenter. 1696/131
alias Trimmer, Wm., Stotfold, fellmonger. 1714/84
Wm., Nether Dean, carpenter. 1764/40
Wm., Eaton Socon, Basmead, yeo. A 1789/5
EAVES, Edm., Barton, carpenter. 1597/24
EAVESDEN, Thos., Shefford. AR 1678-9: 1/109
EAVESTAFFE, see Evestaffe
EBB, EBBS, see Hebbes
EBDEN, Paul, Marston. 1564/46
ECCLES, Geo., Elstow, carpenter. 1636/39
Sybil, Elstow, wid. 1640/106
EDDINGSTONE, Anne, Keysoe, wid. 1727/69
EDDINS, Wm., Milton Bryan, blacksmith. A 1741/11
EDDOWS, Ann, Eaton Bray, wid. 1753/3
EDE, Jas., Dunstable. R 1507-8: 1/78d
Thos., Knotting. 1598/80
Wm., Odell. 1555/139
EDEN, EEDON, Alice, Pulloxhill, wid. 1661/354
Cath., Eaton Socon, wid. A 1760/24
Eliz., Knotting, wid. 1606-7/15
Hen., Flitton. 1601/86
Isaac, Odell, Odell End, farmer. 1769/21
Jn., Knotting, yeo. 1699/41
Jonathan, Souldrop, yeo. 1748-9/63
Jos., Souldrop, yeo. 1736/19
Jos., Souldrop, grazier. A 1738/28
Mary, Knotting, wid. of Jn. 1703-4/20
Sam., Tilbrook, grocer. 1742/6
Sam., Thurleigh, farmer. A 1779/9
Thos., Odell, farmer. 1776/48
Wm. Clark, Souldrop, cutler. A 1854/11
EDES, see Eades
EDGAR, Thos., Dunstable, innholder. 1769/33
EDGE, Math., Leighton Buzzard. LBA 1764/15
Thos., Westoning. 1597-8/43
Thos., Cranfield, lab. 1604/53
Thos., Bedford, brickmaker. 1843/15
EDGELY, Edw., Biggleswade, Stratton, farmer. Bw 1770/54, I

EDGERLY, Chas., Bedford, woolstapler. A 1737/40
EDIS, Alice, Little Staughton. A 1771/4
Mary, Little Staughton, spins. 1844/34
Robt., Little Staughton, farmer. 1807/9
see also Eades
EDITH, Jn., Riseley, lab. 1731-2/40
EDMONDSON, Robt., Cranfield. 1565/208
EDMUNDS, EDMUND, Alice, Bedford, wid. R 1548: 12/43d
Alice, Melchbourne, wid. A 1776/7
Anth., Turvey. 1622/50
Cath., Leighton Buzzard, wid. LB 1831/52
Edw., Podington, Hinwick, yeo. 1691/86
Eliz., Bedford St. Paul. 1681/88
Geo., sen., Stevington, carpenter. 1706/20
Jn., Eversholt. 1640/38
Jn., Eaton Socon, clothdrawer. 1656/29
Jn., Battlesden, bricklayer. 1692/45
Jn., Woburn, glazier. 1767/16
Mary (old index 'docket mislaid'). A 1710/12
Ric., Ravensden, weaver. 1669/74
Robt., Little Staughton, weaver. 1652/105
Roger, Eaton Socon, yeo. 1638/10
Silvester, Eaton Socon, yeo. 1685/85
Silvester, Eaton Socon, baker. A 1743/46
Susannah (old index, 'docket mislaid'). A 1710/30
Thos., Kempston, lab. 1618/102
Thos., sen., Whipsnade, yeo. 1730/105
Thos., Whipsnade, yeo. 1760/40
Thos., Melchbourne, yeo. 1771/33
Walt., Dunstable, lab. 1713/46
Wm., Melchbourne. 1681/11
Wm., Woburn. 1682/9
Wm., Melchbourne. 1713/76
Wm., Melchbourne, yeo. 1768/34
Wm., sen., Turvey, wheelwright. 1795/20
Wm., Turvey, wheelwright. A 1819/10, I 4/237
EDRICH, EDERYCH, Edm., Harlington. 1560?/230
Margt., Harlington. 1562/130
Margt., Harlington. 1563/79
EDROP, EYDROPPE, Agnes, Sandy. 1612-13/14
Ann, Northill, Thorncote, wid. A 1725/1
Edw., Northill, Thorncote, mason. 1669-70/110
Joan, Sandy, Girtford, wid. 1590/132
Math., Langford, lab. 1572-3/81
Ric., sen., Sandy, Girtford. 1610/34

EDROP, EYDROPPE continued
Ric., sen., Sandy, lab. 1621/167
EDSALL, Thos., (old index only). A 1718/24
EDWARD, EDWARDS, Alice, Turvey, wid. 1601/107
Cath., Potton, wid. 1788/20
Dorothy, Henlow, wid. 1664/64
Dorothy, Bedford, wid. 1760/2
Edw., sen., Harrold, yeo. 1658-9/221
Edw., Bedford St. John, husb. 1732/59
Edw., Harrold. AR 1681: 1/43
Eliz., Wootton, spins. 1681/82
Fra., Temspford, lab. 1675/57
Geo., Wilshamstead. 1612-13/83
Geo., Wilshamstead, Cotton End, yeo. 1619/52, I 4/63
Geo., Wilshamstead, Cotton End, yeo. 1642/43
Geo., Wilshamstead, yeo. 1655/54
Geo., Wilshamstead, yeo. 1679/76
Geo., Roxton. AR 1682-3: 1/75d
Geo., Wilshamstead, yeo. 1696-7/156
Geo., Wilshamstead, yeo. 1696-7/156
Geo., Lidlington. 1752/65
Hen., Turvey, husb. 1583/154
Hen., Turvey, husb. 1583-4/162
Hen., Marston, yeo. 1613/151
Hen., Temspford, husb. 1631/191
Jasper, Lt. Barford, esq. AR 1680: 1/111
Joan, Biddenham, wid. 1617/225
Jn., Houghton Conquest. R 1508-9: 1/206d
Jn., Wilshamstead. R 1518-9: 2/72d
Jn., Henlow. R 1529: 3/6d
Jn., Shefford, clothworker. AR 1685: 1/123d
Jn., Luton. 1725/53
Jn., Cranfield, gent. 1727/107
Jn., sen., Potton, yeo. 1765/28
Jn., Cranfield. A 1769/17
Jn., Potton, farmer. 1840/38
Josiah, Tilbrook, tailor. 1678-9/145
Josiah, sen., Tilbrook, tailor. 1716/49
Josiah, Tilbrook. 1729/40
Judah, Wilshamstead, wid. 1690-1/36
Judy, Harrold, wid. 1681-2/98
Marg., Ridgmont. 1636/18
Margery, Oakley, wid. R 1516/7: 1/171
Marrion, Milton Ernest, wid. 1628/44
Mary, Wilshamstead. AR 1682: 1/22

EDWARD, EDWARDS continued
Mary, Wilshamstead, wid. AR 1683: 1/22d
Mary, Wilshamstead. AR 1685: 1/26d
Mary, Cranfield, wid. 1728/56
Mary, Bedford, wid. A 1731/44
Peter, Shillington, yeo. 1635-6/40
Peter, Biggleswade. AR 1675: 1/103d
Peter, sen., Cranfield, yeo. 1682/8
Peter, Cranfield, gent. A 1724-5/43
Peter, jun., Cranfield, gent. A 1725/12
Ric., Wilshamstead. 1554/166
Ric., Wilshamstead. 1576/10
Ric., Arlesey, esq. (not a will but a note saying that will was proved in PCC). 1638/142
Robt., Shefford, husb. 1565/194
Robt., Milton Ernest, yeo. 1623/160
Robt., Harrold, maltster. AR 1677: 1/40, 41
Robt., gent. A 1701/12
Sarah, Steppingley, wid. 1783/18
Thos., Turvey. 1558/224
Thos., Wilshamstead. 1558/249
Thos., Bedford. I 1588: 4/174
Thos., Tempsford, husb. 1597-8/53
Thos., Wilshamstead. 1612/104
Thos., Ridgmont, husb. 1647/38
Thos., Wrestlingworth, husb. 1670/188
Thos., Clophill, yeo. 1706/50
Thos., Cranfield, yeo. 1712/9
Thos., Cockayne Hatley, yeo. 1723/83
Thos., Bedford, vintner and alderman. 1739/37
Thos., Steppingley, lab. 1776/36
Wm., Carlton, husb. R 1546: 11/143
Wm., Henlow. R 1546: 11/176
Wm., Wilshamstead, Cotton, 1558. 1563-5/210
Wm., Pertenhall, husb. 1593/11
Wm., Wilshamstead. 1666/118
Wm., Potton. AR 1685: 1/123
Wm., Bedford, lab. A 1719/1
Wm., Bedford, esq. 1758/35
Wm., Sutton, miller. 1761/15
Wm., Potton, yeo. 1764/33
Wm., Biggleswade, yeo. Bw 1806/103
EDWIN, EDWINE, Dorothy, Leighton Buzzard, wid. of Thos. LBA 1790/36
Maria, Soulbury, Bucks., wid. of Thos. LBA 1810/64
Wm., Holcote, yeo. 1618-19/3

EDY, see Eady
EELES, EALES, EELS, EEILS, Jn., Ridgmont, yeo. 1844/38
Math., Wootton. 1724/15
Ric., Old Warden Hill, husb. 1639/48
see also Heelas
EELING, see Ealing
EGLETON, Jn., Lidlington. R 1544: 11/26
EGRAM, Jas., Clophill, gent. R 1776/41
Jn., Haynes, butcher. A 1760/4
Nich., Silsoe, butcher. 1777/13
Thos., Clophill, butcher, bach. A 1776/17
see also Ingram
EKINS, Ann, Little Staughton. 1814/18
Ann, Bedford St. Paul, spins. A 1831/16
Eliz., Eaton Socon, wid. 1818/10
Grace, Oakley, wid. 1804/23
Hen., Dean, farmer. 1812/3
Jas., Bedford St. Cuthbert, shoemaker. 1749-50/67
Jn., Eaton Socon, carpenter. A 1715/30
Jn., Pertenhall, late Great Staughton, Hunts., farmer. 1827/18, I 4/269
Jn., Riseley, victualler and farmer. 1845/13
Martha, Bedford, wid. 1728/30
Mary, Riseley, wid. 1850/5
Sam., jun., Riseley, yeo. 1819/38
Thos. Barnes, Eaton Socon, tailor. 1854/35
Wm., Riseley, yeo. 1781/12
Wm., Oakley. A 1782/17
Wm., Eaton Socon, yeo. A 1816/7
Wm., sen., Riseley, yeo. 1819/15
ELBOURNE, see Albon
ELDER, ELDRE, Thos., Stagsden. 1565/7
ELDERSHAW, Jas., Woburn, clothworker. 1708/4
ELEMENT, Wm., sen., Dunstable, yeo. 1682/11
ELGER, Isaac, Bedford, innholder. 1770/52
Isaac, Bedford, carpenter. 1807/1
Mary, Bedford, wid. A 1790/10
ELIAS, see Heelas
ELING, ELYNGE, ILLING, Hen., Haynes. 1568/54
see also Ealing
ELISHA, Jn., Southill, farrier. 1712 addition
ELKERTON, Jas., Leighton Buzzard, glover. LB 1799/6
ELKINS, Jn., Eaton Socon. AR 1672: 1/62d
Jn., Eaton Socon. 1672-3/162
Jn., Eversholt, husb. 1714/80
ELL, Chas., Henlow. A 1819/9

ELL continued
Jn., Henlow, farmer. 1790/7
Thos., Eaton Socon, wheelwright. A 1777/5
Wm., Henlow, baker. A 1849/8
see also Else
ELLARD, ELLERD, Ann, Husborne Crawley, wid. 1778/43
Eliz., Cranfield, wid. 1701/43
Geo., Luton, painter and glazier. 1844/2
Jas., Ridgmont, yeo. 1681/46
Jas., Ridgmont, yeo. A 1728/42
Jas., Shefford, glazier. A 1729/28
Jas., Husborne Crawley, yeo. 1763/20
Jn., Renhold, vicar. 1798/18
Thos., Cranfield, husb. 1700/89
Wm., Meppershall, husb. 1724/68
ELLBOROUGH, Wm., Odell, blacksmith. 1693-4/124
ELLINGHAM, Arthur, sen., Stanbridge, yeo. LB 1768/11
Arthur, sen., Stanbridge, yeo. LB 1785/73
Arthur, Potsgrove, yeo. 1809/35
Christian, Flitton, Greenfield, wid. 1728/45
Cuthbert, Houghton Regis. 1567/95
Dan., Stanbridge, yeo. LB 1756/28
Dan., Eaton Bray, husb. 1781/69
Gabriel, Totternhoe, husb. A 1766/20
Gabriel, sen., Houghton Regis, farmer. 1796/3
Jane, Stanbridge, wid. of Jn. 1807/24
Jn., Leighton Buzzard, Clipstone, farmer. LB 1737/65 and affidavit LB W/V5
Jn., Stanbridge, yeo. 1750/20
Jn., Stanbridge, yeo. LB 1808/40
Mary, Stanbridge, wid. 1748/28
Ric., Leighton Buzzard. LBR 1537: 1/1
Robt., Tilsworth, husb. 1657/258
Sarah, Toddington, spins. A 1756/23
Thos., Eaton Bray. AR 1683: 1/165
Thos., Markyate Street, gent.. 1756/9
Wm., Leighton Buzzard. 1556/137
Wm., Toddington, weaver. 1741/25
Wm., Stanbridge, yeo. LB 1814/60
see also Allingham
ELLIOT, ELLIOTT, YLYOT, ELLOT, Ann, Leighton Buzzard. LB 1820/6
Ann, Riseley, wid. 1822/9
Edw., Leighton Buzzard, innholder. 1618-19/26
Geo., jun., Leighton Buzzard. AR 1679-80: 1/158d
Geo., Leighton Buzzard, innholder. Fac. 1708: 9/30
Jas., Lower Gravenhurst, yeo. 1818/22

ELLIOT, ELLIOTT, YLYOT, ELLOT continued
Jn., Limbury, husb. R 1551: 12/148
Jn., Houghton Regis, husb. 1706/83
Jn., Bedford, hempdresser. A 1764/12
Jn., Dunstable, cornfactor. 1830/20
Jn., Wilden, farmer. 1837/46
Jos., Dunstable, gent. 1799/27
Rebecca, Dunstable, wid. 1839/18
Ric., sen., Leighton Buzzard, cordwainer. 1612/74
Sarah, Dunstable, wid. 1804/6
Thos., Riseley, yeo. 1734/39
Thos., Riseley, yeo. 1774/15
Thos., Riseley, husb. 1796/41
Wm., Farndish. R 1529: 3/11d
Wm., Souldrop, lab. 1630/241
Wm., Ampthill, victualler. 1815/9
see also Hilleat; Ilatt; Elyard
ELLIS, ELLSE, ELS, ELYS, ELYCE, Alice, Wootton. R 1516-17: 1/155
Chas., sen., Goldington, yeo. 1789/25
Hannah, Ampthill, victualler. 1793/27
Isabell, Sandy. 1694/86
Jas., Ampthill, publican. 1792/42
Jas., Toddington, yeo. A 1835/2
Jn., Wootton. R 1515: 1/157
Jn., Cockayne Hatley. 1597/35
Jn., Silsoe, servant to the Earl of Kent. 1633/120
Jn., Northill, Thorncote, lab. 1727-8/106
Jos., Houghton Regis, gardener. 1770/35
Mary Ann, Bedford, spins. 1839/16
Mary Ann, Bedford, spins. A 1843/3
Rachael, Potton, wid. and "ironmongeres". 1829/11
Robt., Dunton. 1633/169
Sam., Haynes, gardener. 1742/44
Thos., Bow Brickhill, lab. R 1591: 24/8
Thos., Flamstead, Herts., husb. 1604/24
Thos., Sandy, gent. 1714/54
Thos., Potton, ironmonger and innholder. 1818/43, I 4/228
Wm., Wootton. 1553/262
Wm., Wootton. 1575/72
see also ELSE, EYLES
ELLS, see Else and Ellis
ELMER, AYLEMER, Eleanor, Shillington, wid. 1689/51
Geo., Stotfold, weaver. 1680-1/113
Jn., Shillington, carpenter. 1584-5/271
Jn., sen., Silsoe, lab. 1631/164

ELMER, AYLEMER continued
Jn., Odell. 1651/35
Jn., Shillington. 1698/94
Jn., Shillington. A 1701/16
Jn., Cople, yeo. 1781/13
Lettice, Haynes, Northwood End, wid. 1621/210
Mary, Shillington, wid. 1728/31
Ric., priest (no parish given), Shillington. R 1543-4: 11/6
Robt., Shillington. 1619/265, I 4/109
Susan, Shillington, wid. 1641/138
Thos., Haynes, yeo. 1604-5/2
Thos., Shillington. 1684/32
Thos., Shillington, gent. A 1716/16
Thos., Odell, lab. 1730/66
Wm., Haynes, Northwood End, yeo. 1638/166
Wm., Shillington, husb. A 1701/17
Wm., Flitwick. A 1722/6
ELMS, Ann, Bolnhurst. 1756/37
Thos., Felmersham, gent. R 1560: 15/124
Thos., Thurleigh, yeo. A 1784/9
ELNER, Jn., Hockliffe, 1546. 1563-5/213
ELSAME, ELSOM, Ann, Thurleigh, wid. 1710/22
Eliz., Thurleigh. 1616/65
Geo., Thurleigh, husb. 1593/48
Oliv., sen., Thurleigh, lab. 1636-7/117
Oliv., Thurleigh, lab. 1685/69
Oliv., Thurleigh, farmer. A 1721/13
Oliv., Thurleigh, shopkeeper. 1801/15
Wm., Thurleigh, weaver. 1631-2/200
see also Elson
ELSE, ELLS, ELL, EYLES, Alex., Oakley, lab. 1640-1/90
Chas., Luton, sack carrier. A 1747/12
Chas, sen., Luton, victualler. 1795/10
see also Ell; Ellis
ELSON, Ann, Riseley, wid. 1681/39
Ann, Bedford. 1705/54
Geare, Podington, Hinwick, spins. 1641/127
Hugh, Melchbourne, lab. 1708/87
Jas., Sharnbrook, lab. 1702/28
Jas., Odell. 1731-2/57
Jn., sen., Bedford, weaver. 1684/27
Jn., Thurleigh, yeo. 1704/64
Jn., Bedford, yeo. 1719/69
Jn., Thurleigh, farmer. 1722/38
Math., Sharnbrook, wid. 1665-6/103

ELSON continued
Wm., sen., Blunham, yeo. 1837/45
see also Ilson; Elsame
ELWOOD, Wm., Bromham, cordwainer. 1675/6
ELYARD, Math., Ridgmont. 1728-9/110
see also Hillyard, Elliot
EMANT, EMENT, Hen., sen., Northill. R 1675: 1/104
Hen., Northill. 1678-9/137
Jn., Northill. 1606/48
see also Emmont
EMBERTON, Margaret, Shefford, wid. 1707/1
EMBRY, Ric., Leighton Buzzard. 1612/72
Robt., Goldington. 1645/37
EME, see Eame
EMENSON, Eliz., Lt. Barford, wid. 1638/43
Joan, wid., Elstow. 1557/205
Steph., Lt. Barford (PCC). 1637/79
see also Emerson
EMERSON, Edw., Elstow. 1553/263
Edw., Bedford, husb. 1657/2,3
see also Emenson
EMERTON, Eliz., Toddington. 1741/29
Jn., Studham, husb. 1557/395
alias Emberton, Jn., Aspley Guise, lab. 1597-8/54
Jn., Stanbridge, butcher. 1685/39
Jn., Dunstable, maltster. 1693/126
Jn., Ampthill, barber. 1740-1/75
Jn., Leighton Buzzard. LBA 1763/14
Jn., Leighton Buzzard. LBA 1767/19
Jn., Stanbridge, tailor. LB 1783/66
Jos., Stanbridge, tailor. LBA 1808/59
Kath., Heath, wid. Fac. 1709: 9/32
Percival, Flitwick, husb. 1563/187
Robt., Leighton Buzzard, cordwainer. LB 1784/68
Robt., Leighton Buzzard, cordwainer. 1805/11
Steph., sen., Husborne Crawley, gardener. 1713/44
Steph., Husborne Crawley, yeo. 1733/63
Steph., Husborne Crawley, yeo. 1776/24
Thos., Husborne Crawley, yeo. 1683-4/102
Thos., Lidlington, lab. 1713-14/38
Thos., Toddington, Chalton, lab. 1717/4
Thos., Salford, cordwainer. 1810/33
Thos., Tilsworth, lab. 1847/48
Wm., sen., Steppingley, yeo. 1684-5/96
Wm., Steppingley, yeo. A 1730/6

EMERTON continued
Wm., Wootton, clockmaker. A 1790/9
Wm., Woburn, watchmaker. 1794/40
Wm., Woburn, writer. 1808/3, I 4/211
EMERY, Edith, Eaton Socon, wid. AR 1676: 1/66d
Edm., Arlesey. R 1546: 11/159
Edw., Keysoe, blacksmith. 1675/30
Edw., Eaton Socon, Wyboston. AR 1686: 1/80
Edw., Eaton Socon, Wyboston, yeo. 1731/54
Edw., Roxton, Chawston, yeo. A 1769/20
Edw., Blunham, gent. 1792/43
Edw., Cople, farmer. 1803/38
Edw., Blunham, gent. 1830 addition
Eliz., Maulden, wid. 1686/60
Eliz., Lidlington, spins. 1698/79
Geo., Eaton Socon, Wyboston, yeo. 1648/118
Geo., Lt. Barford. A 1753/2
Geo., Eaton Socon, Wyboston, farmer. 1818/30
Isaac, Potton, cordwainer. 1782/15
Jas., Eaton Socon, Wyboston. A 1839/3
Jn., Eaton Socon, yeo. 1653-4/93
Jn., Eaton Socon, Wyboston. 1672/114
Jn., Pertenhall, blacksmith. 1698/177
Jn., Lt. Barford, yeo. 1734/60
Jn., Eaton Socon, yeo. 1739/1
Jn., Wilden, farmer. A 1746-7/37
Jn., Ravensden, yeo. 1753/1
Jn., Eaton Socon, Honeydon, yeo. 1792/28
Jn., Kempston Hardwick, yeo. 1820/30
Jos., Bedford St. Peter, stationer. AR 1685: 1/27
Marg., Milton Ernest, wid. 1584-5/256
Mary, Bedford, wid. 1712/36
Mary, Eaton Socon, Wyboston, wid. 1731/65
Matthias, Blunham, lab. 1843/23
Rebecca, Bedford, wid. 1834/6
Ric., Biddenham, lab. 1608/73
Ric., Arlesey, gent. 1630/68
Ric., sen., Roxton, Chawston. 1662/90
Ric., Eaton Socon, Wyboston. 1719/32
Ric., Eaton Socon, Wyboston, yeo. 1731/71
Ric., Tempsford, farmer. A 1764/13
Ric., Eaton Socon, cordwainer. A 1770/3
Ric., sen., Biggleswade, cordwainer. Bw 1822/126
Roger, Eaton Socon, Wyboston. 1624-5/110
Sam., Potton, Woodcock, yeo. 1835/6

EMERY continued
Sarah, Ampthill, spins. 1692/17
Sarah, Eaton Socon, Wyboston, wid. 1835/47
Thos., Goldington. 1609/152
Thos., Bedford, bookseller. A 1704-5/29
Thos., Eaton Socon, Wyboston, shopkeeper. 1836/36
Thos., Potton, thatcher. 1837/1
Thos., Eaton Socon, Honeydon, farmer. 1854/21
True., Shelton, wid. 1776/5
Wm., Biddenham, yeo. 1646/78
Wm., Lt. Barford, yeo. 1747-8/55
Wm., Eaton Socon, Wyboston, yeo. 1792/29
Wm., Eaton Socon, Wyboston, yeo. 1793/2
Wm., Eaton Socon, Wyboston, farmer. 1813/34
Wm., Roxton, yeo. 1823/46, I 4/251
see also Amery
EMMETT, see Emmont
EMMONT, Mich., Battlesden, clerk. 1601/128
alias Norris, Wm., (no parish given). 1630/16
see also Emant
EMPEY, see Impey
EMPSTON, EMSON, EMENT, Eliz., Thurleigh, wid. 1724/25
Hen., sen., Northill. AR 1675: 1/104
Hen., Thurleigh, yeo. 1722/52
Joan, Totternhoe, wid. 1600/9
Jn., Thurleigh, yeo. A 1733/9
Thos., Ridgmont. R 1546: 11/206
see also Hempson
ENDERSBY, Jn., Campton, yeo. 1742/18
Jn., Houghton Conquest, yeo. 1793/6
Ric., Clifton, yeo. 1717/66
Robt., Clifton, yeo. 1806/29
Sam., jun., Houghton Conquest. A 1769/32
Sarah, Clifton, wid. 1726/82
Thos., Wrestlingworth, lab. 1683/36
Thos., Potton, clockmaker. 1741/46
ENFIELD, see Infield
ENGLAND, Chas., Keysoe. 1806/15
Jn., Bedford, baker. 1622/34
ENGLISH, YNGLYSH, Thos., Ravensden. R 1509-10: 1/63d
ENSAME, ENSHAM, ENSEHM, Agnes, Shillington, wid. 1627-8/227
Amy, Shillington, Holwell Bury, wid. 1600-1/64
Jn., Shillington, yeo. 1616/106
alias Borrowe, Jn., Haynes. 1619-20/219, I 4/36
Jn., Meppershall. 1622-3/2

ENSAME, ENSHAM, ENSEHM continued
alias Burrowes, Jn., Shillington, yeo. AR 1683: 1/118d
Martin, Shillington. R 1533: 3/105
alias Burrow, Martin, Shillington, yeo. 1630/83
Matt., Shillington. R ?1541: 6/92d
Ric., Shillington. 1615/223
alias Borrowe, Robt., Shillington, yeo. 1618/115
Robt., Shillington, lab. 1625/165
alias Burrowe, Robt., sen., Shillington, yeo. 1647-8/14
Thos., Shillington, yeo. 1598/113
Thos., Shillington, husb. 1613-14/127
Thos., Stevington, husb. 1644/122
Wm., Shillington. R 1529: 3/13
Wm., Shillington, Aspley End. 1560/218
Wm., Shillington, yeo. 1609-10/122
see also Eynsham
ENTERDUCE, ENTERDEWCE, Barber (or ?Barker) alias Enterduce, see Barber
Thos., Houghton Conquest, farmer. A 1719/24
ENTWHISTLE, Thos., Leighton Buzzard, gent. Fac. 1719: 9/62
ERLAND, see Ireland
ERRINGTON, Jn., Chellington, blacksmith. 1697-8/49
Wm., Chellington, shoemaker. 1738/64
see also Harrington
ESGOR, Bart., Woburn. R 1531-2: 3/54
see also Askew
ESSEX, Eliz., Felmersham. A 1769/11
Math., Felmersham, lab. 1728/70
Matthias, Felmersham, laceman. 1761/17
Steph., Bedford St. Paul. 1753/9
EST, see East
ESTON, Andrew, Bedford, draper. 1602/53
Jn., sen., Bedford St. Paul, gent. 1663/44
Jn., Pertenhall, rector. 1689-90/80
Jn., Bedford, esq. 1697/26
Negus, Bedford, carpenter. 1792/22
Ric., Nether Dean, yeo. 1610/175
Ric., Bedford St. Mary, carpenter. 1714/32
Thos., Nether Dean. R 1539-40: 6/9d
see also Easton
ESTWELL, see Eastwell
ESTWICK, Chris, Milton Bryan, gent. 1598/130
Eliz., Chellington, wid. 1747/43
Jn., Bletsoe, yeo. 1730/78
Marian, Milton Bryan, wid. 1600/1

ESTWICK continued
Steph., sen., Odell, yeo. 1684-5/57
Steph., Pavenham, yeo. 1738/42
Steph., Odell, yeo. A 1713/31
Steph., Bedford, victualler. A 1730/45
Steven, Odell, yeo. 1626-7/131
Thos., Wootton, yeo. 1632/20
Thos., Pavenham, horse dealer. 1767/8
Thos., Bedford, farmer. 1778/27
Thos., jun., Biddenham, yeo. 1801/7
Thos., Biddenham, farmer. 1820/29
ETHRIDGE, ETHERIDGE, Hen., sen., Sundon, yeo. 1609-10/106
Hen., Flitwick, husb. 1619/203, I 4/152
Hen., Maulden, yeo. 1627/206
Jn., Maulden. 1603/113
Jn., Flitton, yeo. 1617/297
Robt., Meppershall. 1606/62
Thos., Flitton, yeo. 1621/143
ETON, see Eaton
EUSTACE, Hen., Eaton Bray, farmer. 1854/4
EVANS, Richard alias Evans, see under Richards
Abr., Barton, husb. 1744/27
Ann Paradine, Bedford, wife of Chas. 1830/37
Cath., Ampthill, wid. 1806/35
Cath., Woburn, wid. 1819/20
Dav., Biggleswade, dissenting minister. Bw 1786/76, I
Dav., Bedford St. Mary, innholder. A 1736-7/29
Edw., Westoning, Sampshill, husb. 1693/84
Jane, Houghton Regis, Bidwell, wid. 1765/12
Jn., Leighton Buzzard. 1586/127
Jn., Husborne Crawley, lab. 1720/72
Jon., Markyate St. A 1704/10
Jos., Luton, Oatbridge, victualler. 1757/13
Jos., Souldrop, innholder. A 1781/9
Margt., Eaton Bray, wid. 1759/3
Mary, Westoning, Sampshill, wid. 1700/128
Mary, Ridgmont. A 1770/13
Mary, Ridgmont. 1770/44
Math., Langford, tailor. A 1727-8/46
Math., Houghton Regis, Bidwell, blacksmith. 1765/2
Nich., Ampthill. 1674/160
Ric., Ampthill, brickmaker. 1660/89
Sarah, Ampthill, wid. 1689/7
Thos., Lidlington, yeo. 1660/207
Thos., Ampthill, glover. 1680/4

EVANS continued
Thos., jun., Barton, sawyer. 1716/34
Thos., Barton, carpenter. 1738/37
Thos., Eaton Bray, shopkeeper. A 1756/18
Wm., Ampthill, lab. 1688/63
EVE, Wm., Shefford, gent. 1837/39
EVERARD, Elenor, Bedford St. Peter, wid. 1665-6/12
Hester, Sandy, wid. 1700/146
Jos., Sandy, Beeston Green. 1678/131
Nich., Northill, yeo. A 1730/16
Ric., Totternhoe, yeo. 1704/1
Thos., Sandy, clerk. 1673/26
see also Everitt
EVERED, Jn., Toddington, Chalton, husb. 1573/138
Ric., Luton, maltman. 1556/85
see also Everitt
EVERITT, EVERHEAD, Alice, Sandy, Beeston, wid. 1613-14/135
Eliz., Meppershall. 1630/20
Fra., Toddington, yeo. 1626/114
Geo., Toddington. 1618/91
Geo., Bedford, woolbuyer. 1850/38
Jn., Luton, yeo. R 1549: 12/71
Jn., Sandy, Beeston, husb. 1599-1600/170
Jn., Toddington. 1604/65
Jn., Henlow. AR 1676: 1/105d
Jn., Henlow, lab. 1676/127
Marg., Sandy, Beeston, wid. 1599/120
Margt., Arlesey, wid. 1639/46
Mary, Luton. A 1779/8
Mary, Luton, wid. 1797/4
Mary, Luton. A 1797/15
Ric., Totternhoe, yeo. 1636/56
Ric., Colmworth, Nether Stead, yeo. 1774/50
Robt., Sandy. 1597-8/25
Sam., Ampthill, miller. 1764/27
Sam., Sandy, a minor. A 1797/13
Thos., Sandy, Beeston. R 1541: 6/99d
Thos., Totternhoe, yeo. 1623/172
Walter, Sandy. R 1506: 1/98d
Wm., Sandy, gardener. AR 1685: 1/125
Wm., Luton, yeo. AR 1688-9: 1/175d
Wm., Sandy, minor. A 1797/14
Wm., Luton, journeyman draper. 1820/37
see also Everard and Evered
EVERTON, Wm., Eaton. 1554/161

EVESDEN, see Eavesden
EVESTAFFE, Jn., Caddington. AR 1671: 1/141d
Jn., Leighton Buzzard, yeo. LB 1791/93
Ric., Heath, gardener. LB 1804/17
Sarah, Heath, wid. LB 1809/46
Wm., Westoning, husb. 1696-7/142
EWE, Jn., Houghton Regis, husb. 1558/259
EWER, Edw., Dunstable, victualler. A 1707/32
Jn., Luton, gent. A 1723/4
Maud., Luton, wid. 1626-7/26
Sarah, Luton, wid. A 1730-1/46
see also Hewer
EXTON, Fra., Woburn, gent. 1767/65
Geo., Bedford, late Riseley, gent. 1841/29
Peter, Ampthill, woollen draper. 1749/8
see also Hexton
EYLER, Robt., Harrold, lab. 1693/127
EYLES, EYELES, Jn., Wootton. R 1516-7: 1/213
Jn., Oakley, lab. 1753/22
Jn., Carlton, yeo. 1781/59
Jn., Sharnbrook, butcher. 1807/8
Jn., Sharnbrook, yeo. 1810/12
Marshall, Carlton, farmer. 1826/31
Mary, Elstow, nee Cooper. A 1800/2
Phoebe, Sharnbrook, wid. 1800/29
Skevington, Elstow, yeo. 1852/36
Wm., Odell, farmer. 1738/67
Wm., Harrold, farmer. 1786/33
see also Else, Ellis
EYNSHAM, AYNSHAM, Jn., Shillington, Chyble. R 1501: 1/27
Jn., Shillington. R 1515: 2/132
Jn., Shillington. 1556/128
see also Ensame
EYRE, EYER, EYRES, Augustine, Colmworth, lab. 1581/32
Jn., Biddenham. R 1520: 2/167
Jn., Kempston. 1557/315
Mary, Blunham, wid. of Ben. late of Aston, North. 1811/18
Thos., Blunham, farmer. 1834/29
see also Ayre, Ayres, Hare, Hares
EYTCHES, Wm., Riseley, P/IX2. A 1812/12
EYTE, Sarah, Eaton Socon, wid. 1816/11
Thos., Eaton Socon, yeo. 1803/24

F

FABIAN, Wm., Flitwick, husb. R 1563: 16/75
FACER, Math., Houghton Conquest, farmer. 1799/36
FADLET, Abigail, Willington, spins. 1692/30
Anne, Willington, wid. 1620/69
Basel, Cople, Wood End, spins. 1694/19
Geo., Willington, yeo. 1615/212
Sarah, Kempston, wid. 1656/209
Thos., Willington. 1686/40
see also Fallet, Farthlet
FAGE, Eliz., Clifton, wid. 1616-17/25
Geo., Clifton, clerk. 1569-70/126
Hen., Sandy. A 1706/43
Jn., Tempsford. R 1500: 1/14d
Thos., Tempsford. R 1509: 1/57d, 207
Thos., Clapham, husb. 1546/78
Thos., Southill, Stanford, yeo. 1681/89
Thos., Southill, Stanford, yeo. 1721/16
Thos., Southill, Stanford, farmer. 1772/26
Wm., Roxton, Chawston, husb. R 1543: 6/170
see also Fagg
FAGG, Eliz., Upper Gravenhurst, wid. 1731/6
see also Fage
FAINE, see Fanne
FAIRCLOUGH, Eliz., Bedford, wid. A 1670: 1/2
Eliz., Bedford, wid. 1670/189
Lawr., Renhold, gent. 1667-8/101
FAIREY, FAYREY, FAYRE, FAIRY, FAREY, FEWRY, Ann, Toddington, wid. 1676/108
Ann, Bedford, wid. A 1721-2/51
Edm., Flitwick, husb. 1617-18/222
Edm., Flitwick, yeo. 1660/50
Edm., Flitwick, yeo. 1675/81
Edm., Flitwick, yeo. A 1728/11
Edw., Flitwick, yeo. 1752/21
Edw., sen., Flitwick, yeo. 1808/29
Edw., Flitwick, yeo. 1824/38
Eliz., Toddington, wid. 1636/9
Geo., Wilden, lab. AR 1680: 1/71
Hen., Shefford. R 1522: 2/6
Hen., Holcote, yeo. (Bundle 1597). 1596/60
Hen., Holcote, yeo. 1597-8/52
Jane, Lower Dean. 1705/83
Jn., Wootton. 1554/151

FAIREY, FAYREY, FAYRE, FAIRY, FAREY, FEWRY
Jn., Wootton. 1554/171
Jn., Holcote, husb. 1556/107
Jn., Holcote, husb. 1556/109
Jn., Holcote, husb. 1556/197
Jn., Holcote, husb. 1556/219
Jn., Flitwick, Denell End, yeo. 1582/75
Jn., Flitwick, yeo. 1635-6/19
Jn., Flitwick, yeo. 1676-7/183
Jn., Gt. Barford, lab. 1749/37
Jn., Woburn, carpenter. 1752/71
Jn., Carlton, blacksmith. 1771/48
Jn., Potsgrove, yeo. A 1798/5
Jn., Dunstable, bricklayer. A 1806/17
Jn., Harrold, innholder. A 1834/6
Jos., Keysoe, weaver. 1740/2
Kath., Renhold, wid. 1617/156
Mary, Renhold. 1626/74
Mary, Edworth, wid. 1758/17
Nich., Silsoe, gardener. 1638/156
Oliver, Harrold, carpenter. 1734/27
Oliver, Harrold, carpenter. 1766/20
Peter, Edworth, yeo. 1691/141
Peter, Dean, lab. A 1716/7
Ric., Holcote, husb. 1556/231
Ric., Dean, weaver. 1651/5
Ric., Dean, weaver. 1652/95
Ric., Biddenham, carpenter. A 1772/4
Robt., Harrold, carpenter. 1682-3/113
Robt., Moggerhanger. 1688/16
Sam., Upper Dean, weaver. 1707/40
Sam., Dean, weaver. 1720/121
Sam., sen., Upper Dean. 1779/22
Sam., Upper Dean, yeo. 1798/24
Sarah, Harrold, wid. 1849/51
Thos., Flitton. R 1524: 2/54
Thos., Elstow. R 1537: 4/95d
Thos., Over Dean, weaver. 1624/97
Thos., Thurleigh, husb. A 1711/66
Thos., Harrold, a minor. A 1852/3
Wm., Salford, husb. 1592/52
Wm., Toddington. AR 1674: 1/148d
FAIRFORD, Robt., Toddington, yeo. R 1550-51: 12/140
FALDO, FALDOE, FAULDO, Abr., Harrold, vicar. 1696/99
Barth., Sutton. 1641/163

FALDO, FALDOE, FAULDO continued
David, Biddenham, gent. 1640/1
Eliz., Maulden, wid. R 1549: 12/68d
Eliz., Southwark, Middx., late of Bedford, wid. 1729-30/125
Eliz., Flitton, wid. 1811/9
Jn. and Joan, Maulden. R 1501: 1/40d
Jn., Sutton, gent. 1580/233
Jn., Goldington, gent. 1622/42
Jn., sen., Oakley, gent. 1625-6/150
Jn., Oakley, gent. 1650-51/123
Jn., Bedford, gent. 1681-2/106
Jn., Bedford, gent. AR 1681-2: 1/20
Jn., sen., Bedford, tanner. 1720/37
Jn., Bedford, gent. 1765/35
Lucy, Biddenham, wid. 1701-2/67
Luke, Bedford St. Paul, apothecary. 1629/93
Margt., Oakley, wid., gentlewoman. 1632/114
Mary, Bedford St. Mary, wid. 1771/43
Mary, Bedford St. Paul. AR 1676: 1/11d
Math., Bedford St. Paul, apothecary. AR 1678: 1/15d
Nich., Biddenham. R 1536: 4/65d
Osbert, Oakley. AR 1687: 1/49
Paul, Bedford, clerk. 1714/103
Peter, Bedford, coal merchant. A 1735-6/14
Rachel, Hockliffe, wid. 1690/9
Ric., Maulden, yeo. R 1541: 6/75
Robt., Biddenham. R 1537-8: 5/5d
Robt., Oakley, gent. AR 1682: 1/44d
Robt., Oakley, gent. 1703-4/76
Thos., Bedford, glover. 1625/162
Thos., Oakley, gent. 1628/38
Thos., Shefford, clockmaker. A 1729/39
Thos., Bedford St. Cuthbert. 1764/48
Wm., Oakley. R 1543: 6/158
Wm., Bromham, husb. 1563/77
Wm., sen., Bedford, gent. 1644/100
Wm., Bedford, alderman, gent. 1665/31
Wm., sen., Bedford, alderman. 1693/132
Wm., Harlington, husb. 1714/66
Wm., Bedford, tanner, 1715. 1714/123
Wm., Bedford, gent., alderman. 1718/13
Wm., Bedford, merchant. 1734-5/67
Wm., Lidlington, farmer. A 1778/8
Wm., Bedford St. Mary. A 1804/19
Wm., Lidlington. A 1829/2

FALDO, FALDOE, FAULDO continued
see also Faulder
FALDOR, see Faulder
FALL, FAWLE, FALLE, Thos., Flitton, vicar. 1601/79
Wm., Henlow. R 1538: 5/22d
FALLET, Robt., Felmersham, Radwell. R 1542: 6/131
see also Fadlet; Farthlet
FANCH, Isaac, Kempston, farmer. 1766/1
Jn., Kempston, yeo. 1756/32
see also Finch, Faunch
FANE, FAN, Edw., Elstow. R 1529-30: 3/23
Jn., Sandy, farmer. 1843/40
Peter, sen., Woburn, butcher. 1819/7
Thos., Ampthill, Little Park, grazier and farmer. 1809/19
Thos., Bedford, late Shefford, grocer. 1847/12
Thos., Flitwick, farmer. 1847/34
Wm., Elstow. R ?1529: 3/15
Wm., Flitwick, tanner. 1808/5
FANNE, PHANNE, FAINE, Edw., Elstow. 1607/140
Eliz., Potton, wid. 1634-5/104
Eliz., Woburn. A 1798/10
Jn., Henlow, husb. 1568/102
Jn., Wilshamstead, bach. 1619/189, I 4/114
Jn., Potton, tailor. 1662/105
Michael, Potton, carpenter. 1617/310
Robt., Moggerhanger. AR 1670: 1/90d
Robt., Henlow, carpenter. 1681/29
Thos., Silsoe, innholder. A 1750/13
Thos., Sandy, farmer. A 1839/10
Wm., sen., Flitwick, tanner. 1782/33
Wm., Langford, woolman. 1590-1/126
see also Fane
FARLOW, Wm., Eaton Socon. A 1754/3
FARMER, FERMER, Beard alias Farmer, see under Beard
Butcher alias Farmer, see Butcher
Edm., Streatley, Sharpenhoe. 1626/79
Edw., Barton, yeo. 1704-5/90
Geo., sen., Chiltern Green, husb. 1657/40
Hannah, Ampthill. A 1837/8
Jas., Harlington, yeo. 1718/67
Jas., Harlington, grocer. 1743-4/85
Jn., Cople. 1630/43
Jn., Sutton. 1664/14
Jn., Steppingley, yeo. 1695/48
Jn., Steppingley, yeo. 1719. 1720/56

FARMER, FERMER continued
Jn., Steppingley, dairyman and bricklayer. 1742/26
Jn., Upper Gravenhurst. A 1771/31
Nich., Sutton. R 1558: 14/80
Robt., Steppingley, yeo. 1742/12
Simon, Sutton, yeo. (PCC) 1639-40/137
Steven, Bletsoe. 1641/160
Thos., Sutton, yeo. 1643-4/89
FARNELL, Ann, Eversholt, wid. 1657/53
Ben., Ridgmont, bach. AR 1683: 1/209d
Chas., Ampthill, grocer. 1773/35
Chas., Bedford, brazier. 1804/14
Jn., sen., Eversholt, Wakes, yeo. 1638/155
Jn., Eversholt, Wakes, yeo. 1661/345
Mary, Ampthill, wid. 1709/77
Ric., Lidlington. 1628-9/13
Ric., Maulden, blacksmith. 1688/67
Ric., Ampthill, blacksmith. 1693/112
Ric., Bedford, brazier. 1788/34
Robt., Ampthill, grocer. 1751/26
Thos., Ridgmont, Segenhoe, yeo. 1630/92
Thos., Ridgmont, wheelwright. AR 1677-8: 1/199d
Thos., Ridgmont, Lyefield, wheelwright. 1707-8/73
Wm., Ampthill, brazier. 1830/34
FARNLEY, Hen., Tempsford. 1633/116
FARR, FARRE, Ben., Stevington, grocer. 1722/49
Ben., Eaton Socon, Duloe, yeo. 1752/51
Ben., Wilshamstead, husb. 1764/5
Edm., Clophill, yeo. 1621/204
Edw., Clophill, husb. ?1654-5/21
Edw., Clophill, husb. 1654-5/109
Edw., Husborne Crawley, yeo. 1668/149
Edw., Barton, weaver. A 1720/24
Geo., Aspley Guise, yeo. 1758/55
Hester, Stevington, spins. 1740/31
Jas., Haynes, hogman. A 1761/10
Jeremiah, Shefford, victualler. AR 1671: 1/92d
Jn., Aspley Guise. R 1551: 12/170
Jn., Henlow, lab. AR 1671: 1/92d
Jn., Blunham, grocer. 1693/156
Jn., Marston, dairyman. 1727/4
Jn., Marston, butcher. A 1742/30
Jn., Luton, Kingsbourne Green, victualler. 1807/13
Jn., Aspley Guise, carpenter. 1821/28
Jos., Eaton Socon, Ford End, yeo. 1754/26

FARR, FARRE continued
Jos., Eaton Socon, yeo. 1827/28
Jos., Haynes, butcher. 1840/3
Jos., Temspford, farmer. A 1736/19
Jos., Roxton, Colesden, yeo. A 1791/2
Mary, Husborne Crawley, wid. 1668/148
Mary, Salford, wid. 1747/65
Mich., Arlesey, husb. 1640/76
Roger, Lidlington. 1638-9/91
Roger, Marston. 1750/41
Roger, Marston, yeo. A 1712/23
Susannah, Marston, wid. 1748/7
Thos., Haynes, yeo. 1687/34
Thos., Sandy. AR 1670: 1/91
Wm., Aspley Guise. 1617/200
Wm., sen., Aspley Guise. 1617/225
Wm., Shefford, innholder. 1660-1/78
Wm., Aspley Guise, husb. 1665/74
Wm., Haynes, yeo. 1683-4/84
Wm., Aspley Guise, yeo. 1712/82
Wm., Blunham, husb. A 1728-9/50
Wm., Marston, dairyman and farmer. 1728-9/117
Wm., Leighton Buzzard, innholder. 1742/20
Wm., Luton, Kingston Green, victualler. 1836/31
FARRER, Cooper alias Farrer, see under Cooper
Eliz., Flitwick, wid. 1774/62
Hannah, Riseley, wid. A 1827/15
Hannah, Riseley, wid. 1828/28
Jn., sen., Flitwick, East End, yeo. 1850/3
Jos., Riseley, yeo. 1817/28
Martha, Harrold, wid. 1625/198
Ralph, Harrold. 1627/205
Thos., Riseley, farmer. 1853/19
Wm., Haynes, schoolmaster. A 1766/21
Wm., Haynes, schoolmaster and yeo. 1766/42
Wm., Shillington, farmer. A 1801/9
Wm., Flitwick. A 1811/21
Wm., Bedford St. Mary, publican. A 1827/10
FARRINGTON, Jn., Sandy, Beeston, bach. AR 1686-7: 1/128d
Thos., Biggleswade, yeo. Bw 1791/87
FARROW, Jos., no parish given. 1826/27
Thos., Pertenhall. R 1511: 2/127
Wm., Langford, lab. 1743/70
FARTHLET, Jn., Stotfold. 1602/29
see also Fadlett, Fallet

FAULDER, FALDOR. Eliz., Lidlington, wid. 1816/33
Fra., Woburn, butcher. 1738/65
Jn., Marston, yeo. 1812/1
see also Faldo
FAULKNER, Eliz., Carlton, wid. 1848/54
Jn., Keysoe Row, farmer. 1805/36
Wm., Carlton, yeo. 1832/12
Wm., Toddington, maltster. 1856/2
FAUNCH, Jn., Bedford St. John. A 1771/10
Sarah, Woburn, late Milton Bryan, wid. 1856/10
Wm., Milton Bryan, shopkeeper. 1848/51
see also Fanch
FAVEL, Chris., Wilshamstead, carpenter. 1670/158
Eleanor, Shefford, wid. 1786/34
Fra., Pertenhall, wid. of Rev. Geo., late rector of Finningley, Notts. 1779/32
Geo., Blunham, husb. A 1714/22
Geo., Wilshamstead, carpenter. 1672/116
Geo., sen., Wilshamstead, carpenter. 1676/128
Geo., Gt. Barford, yeo. AR 1682: 1/22d
Geo., Gt. Barford, yeo AR 1682: 1/75
Geo., Gt. Barford, yeo. 1682/103
Geo., Wilshamstead, carpenter. 1695-6/64
Geo., Gt. Barford, gent. 1718/16
Geo., Renhold. 1725/32
Huin, Milbrook, joiner. 1666/133
Jn., Blunham, yeo. 1648-9/90
Jn., Wilshamstead, lab. A 1741/38
Jn., Shefford, plumber and glazier. 1785/44
Jn., Wilden, farmer. 1851/13
Margt., Gt. Barford, spins. 1792/18
Patrick, Thurleigh, farmer. 1852/23
Ric., Wilshamstead, carpenter. 1650/102
Robt., Gt. Barford, yeo. 1654/176
Roger, Barford, yeo. 1612/79
Roger, Barford, yeo. ?1630/6
Roger, Gt. Barford. AR 1675-6: 1/66
Thos., Wilden, yeo. 1720/34
Thos., Wilden, lab. A 1731/39
Walt., Shefford, maltster. 1709-10/55
Wm., Renhold, husb. 1658/163
Wm., Barton, yeo. 1671/69
Wm., Colmworth, husb. 1712/79
see also Fevel
FAWN, Geo., Bedford, lace merchant. A 1829/7
FAYSANT, see Pheasant

FEARY, see Fairey
FEASY, Jos., Kempston, farmer. A 1832/1
see also Fessey
FECKMAN, Able, Turvey. 1648/69
FEEDOM, Robt., Over Dean, lab. 1599/121
FEHEWE, Nich., Wilden. 1579-80/122
FEILD, see Field
FELCE, FELSE, FELLS, FELTS, Agnes, wid., Ampthill. 1605/92
alias Fox, Chris., Over Dean, yeo. 1603/97
Eliz., Harlington, wid. 1747/43
Jas., sen., Biddenham, farmer, baker and shopkeeper. 1852/25
Jn., Toddington, gent. 1701/49
Ric., Stagsden, husb. 1585/31
Ric., Harlington, yeo. 1707/22
Ric., Harlington, farmer and dairyman. 1753/33
Robt., sen., Harlington, yeo. 1735/11
Thos., Oakley. 1564/37
Thos., Dunstable, yeo. 1703/10
Wm., Harlington, lab. 1783/3
FELL, Fra., Toddington, cordwainer. AR 1672: 1/144
Hen., Little Staughton, lab. 1657/69
Hen., Little Staughton, cordwainer. 1724/97
Hen., Little Staughton, farmer. 1746/7
Joan, Ampthill. AR 1681-2: 1/206
Jn., Heath and Reach, dairyman. A 1734-5/32
Jn., Harrold. A 1749/23
Susannah, (old index, 'Docket mislaid'). A 1710/38
Thos., Dunstable, yeo. A 1703/5
Wm., Little Staughton, husb. 1634-5/85
Wm., Little Staughton, victualler. A 1704-5/23
see also Felce
FELPTS, see Phelps
FENCE, Ric., Renhold, dairyman. R 1681: 1/73
FENDALL, Hen., London, citizen and draper. R 1558: 14/58d
see also Fennell
FENN, Ann, Clophill, wid. 1700/119
Edw., Toddington, yeo. 1606-7/2, I
Fra., Clophill, tailor. 1676/113
Fra., Billington, yeo. Fac. 1705: 9/18
Jn., Bedford, gent. 1705-6/57
Mary, Sundon. 1827/25
Robt., Bedford. 1637/123
Robt., Sundon, yeo. A 1808/4
Sam., Bedford, haberdasher. 1681-2/80
Sam., Clophill, tailor. 1696-7/150

FENN continued
Sar., Bedford St. Paul, wid. 1717/28
Thos., Bedford, upholsterer. A 1735-6/11
Thos., Eaton Bray, husb. 1756/52
Wm., Bedford St. Paul, gent. AR 1679: 1/17
FENNEL, Geo., Shefford, cordwainer. 1726/60
Lambert, Harrold, lab. 1703-4/23
Lambert, Oakley, yeo. 1710/56
Martha, Campton. A 1814/2
Math., Shelton, yeo. 1750-1/72
Robt., Potton, gardener. 1756/28
see also Fendall
FENNER, Jn. sen., Ampthill, butcher. 1648/116
Wm., Flitton, butcher. 1665/53
FENNIMORE, Thos., Roxton, Chawston. R 1542: 6/117
FENNY, Alice, Henlow, spins. 1737-8/52
FENSHAM, see Fensome
FENSOME, FENSHAM, Costin late Fensham, see Costin
Agnes, Chalgrave, Wingfield, wid. 1616/77
Alse, Toddington, wid. 1669/82
Ann, Toddington, wid. 1684-5/104
Ben., Upper Sundon, yeo. 1730/37
Edm., Toddington, carpenter. 1586/82
Edw., Toddington, weaver. 1683/4
Eliz., Toddington, Chalton. A 1788/12
Fra., Bedford, blacksmith. A 1724/13
Fra., Ampthill, blacksmith. A 1727/6
Geo., Chalgrave, Wingfield, husb. 1598-9/117
Geo., Totternhoe. 1635/67
Geo., Maulden, yeo. 1660/30
Geo., Totternhoe, yeo. 1695/3
Geo., sen., Upper Sundon. 1729/56
Geo., Stotfold, farmer. A 1746/19
Geo., sen., Sundon, farmer. 1759/63
Geo., Sundon, victualler. 1786/12
Hen., Toddington, butcher. A 1703-4/24
Humph., Chalgrave, husb. 1604/67
Humph., Wootton, gent. 1745/23
Jas., Toddington, victualler. 1855/26
Jn., Dunstable, smith. R 1545: 11/88
Jn., Toddington, lab. R 1549-50: 12/85d
Jn., Toddington, lab. 1618-19/1
Jn., Toddington, carpenter. 1631/181
Jn., Stotfold, yeo. 1746/30
Jn., Colmworth. 1765/3

FENSOME, FENSHAM continued
Jn., Chalgrave, Tebworth, husb. 1824/24
Mary, Sundon, wid. 1740/14
Mary, Dunstable, wid. 1746/31
Mary Ann, Toddington, Chalton. A 1852/10
Math., Sundon, lab. 1739/64
Ric., Chalgrave, Wingfield. 1615/191
Ric., Toddington. 1660-1/184
Ric., Toddington, butcher. A 1752/9
Ric., Houghton Regis, Bidwell, yeo. 1827/16
Robt., Eversholt, yeo. 1695/76
Sam., Bletsoe, yeo. A 1782/10
Thos., Wootton, husb. 1714/101
Thos., Sundon, lab. A 1740/14
Thos., Bolnhurst, farmer. A 1751/4
Wm., Toddington. R 1545: 11/107
Wm., Arlesey, lab. 1623/127
Wm., Totternhoe, husb. 1637-8/158
Wm., Sundon. 1741-2/65
Wm., Toddington, Chalton, farmer. 1838/5
see also Fincham
FENTHAM, see Ventham
FENTMAN, see Venteman
FENTON, Thos., (old index 'Docket missing'). A 1709/15
see also Phentham
FERMAN, see Firman
FERNLEY, FERNLY, Hen., Tempsford. 1663/6
Hen., (old index 'Docket mislaid'). A 1710/8
Mary, Milbrook, wid. 1688/35
Thos., Tempsford. 1618/125
FERRIAN, Wm., Shillington, miller. 1630/69
FERRIS, FERREYS, Barth., Kempston, gent. 1628/31
Jas., Gt. Barford, lab. 1728-9/122
FESAND, see Pheasant
FESSEY, FEASEY, Eliz., Lidlington, wid. 1776/32
?Hen., Husborne Crawley. R 1558: 14/39d
Jarvise, Lidlington, yeo. 1768/20
Thos., Southill, Broome, lab. 1638/61
Thos., Southill, bach. 1662/6
see also Feasy
FETCH, Ann, Thurleigh, spins. AR 1681: 1/72
FEVELL, Hewine, Barton, carpenter. 1617-18/217
see also Favel
FEVER, Wm., Harrold, yeo., late of Kimbolton, butcher. 1837/6
FICKIES, see Vickies

FIDON, Mary, Kempston. 1715/50
FIELD, FYLDE, FELDS, Abr., Kempston, lab. 1667/43
Abr., Kempston, woodward. A 1722/23
Agnes, Potton, wid. 1608/72
Agnes, Barford, wid. 1614/99
Anth., Clifton. 1640/20
Barnaby, Luton, maltster. 1612/29
Barth., Barton, yeo. 1606/45
Benj., Cranfield, yeo. 1660/37
Dan., Bedford, grocer. 1722-3/64
Edm., Stopsley, husb. R 1545: 11/89d
Edw., Shefford, husb. 1604/60
Edw., Luton, Crawley Green, husb. 1662/79
Eliz., Luton, spins. 1588/61
Eliz., Cranfield, wid. 1699/36
Eliz., Barton. A 1811/9
Ellen, Barton, wid. 1558/64
Ellen, Lilley, Herts., wid. 1619-20/227
Ellen, Luton, wid. I 1619-20: 4/43
Eustace, Marston, lab. 1599/67
Geo., Luton, maltman. 1560/200
Harry, Bedford St. Peter. 1564/56
Hen., Barford. 1606/13
Hen., Maulden, husb. 1646/92
Jas., Luton, watchmaker. 1814/6
Jn., Stopsley, husb. 1593/50
Jn., Studham, wid. 1608/19
Jn., Luton, yeo. 1610/86
Jn., Shefford, yeo. 1630/82
Jn., Bedford, woollen draper. 1665-6/14
Jn., Northill, husb. A 1705/44
Jn., Renhold, dairyman. 1710/55
Jn., Flitton. 1711/120
Jn., Biggleswade, yeo. Bw 1715/3c, I
Jn., Luton, tanner. 1722/37
Jn., Barton Hill, victualler. 1753/13
Jn., Clifton, farmer. 1760/9
Jn., Bedford, late of Oakley. 1807/48
Jn., sen., Clifton, gent. 1810/54
Jn., Shillington, Pegsdon, yeo. 1817/32
Jn., Shillington, Lower Stondon, lab. 1824/9
Jos., Langford, farmer. 1772/21
Jos., Cranfield, gent. A 1742/26
Jos., Temspford, merchant. A 1766/15
Lawr., Barton, husb. 1583-4/160

FIELD, FYLDE, FELDS continued
Lawr., Haynes, Northwood End. 1640-1/94
Margt., Barton, wid. 1585-6/15
Margt., Meppershall, wid. A 1754/15
Marshall, Cranfield, lab. 1793/14
Mary, Shillington, Aspley Bury, wid. 1652/83
Mary, Temspford, wid. 1789/5
Mary, Aspley Guise. AR 1691-2: 1/220
Math., Luton, butcher. 1812/22
Nich., Battlesden. 1557/230
Nich., Shefford, yeo. 1690/64
Nich., Shefford. AR 1690: 1/133d
Nich., Haynes, yeo. 1697/58
Phillip, Barton, yeo. 1685/81
Phillip, Barton, yeo. 1735-6/19
Ric., Maulden. R 1515: 1/193
Ric., Barton. R 1529: 3/16
Ric., Leighton Buzzard, husb. 1599/62
Ric., sen., Barford, husb. 1610/130
Ric., Luton, lab. 1627-8/155
Ric., Sundon, husb. 1637/82
Ric., Shillington, alehousekeeper. 1638/120
Ric., parish torn off. c. 1670/249
Robt., Leighton Buzzard. 1592-3/60
Robt., Studham, yeo. 1621/170
Robt., sen., Luton, maltster. 1667-8/7
Robt., Lidlington, yeo. 1705/15
Robt., Shillington, yeo. 1739/33
Robt., Lidlington. A 1741/22
Roger, Barford. 1661/360
Sam., Luton, shopkeeper. 1815/3
Sarah, Barton, spins. AR 1676-7: 1/152d
Susan, Renhold, wid. 1744/36
Susannah, Shillington, Lower Stondon, wid. 1832/25
Thos., Higham Gobion. 1583/146
Thos., Harlington, Bunce Green. 1593-4/2
Thos., Haynes, yeo. 1605/103
Thos., Over Gravenhurst, Ion, yeo. 1629/107
Thos., Shillington, innholder. 1662/77
Thos., Barton, yeo. AR 1672: 1/144
Thos., sen., Gt. Barford, gent. 1674-5/149
Thos., Shillington, innholder. 1675/31
Thos., Renhold, yeo. 1704-5/25
Thos., Maulden, yeo. 1717/32
Thos., Cranfield, yeo. 1718/72

FIELD, FYLDE, FELDS continued
Thos., Bedford, gent. 1722-3/72
Thos., Bedford, lab. A 1737/16
Thos., Barton, yeo. 1743/47
Thos., jun., Bedford, farmer. 1749/28
Thos., Tempsford, yeo. 1771/4
Thos., Tempsford, merchant. 1779/13
Thos., Shillington, farmer. A 1818/12
Tim., Cranfield, laceman. 1716/100
Wm., Lt. Barford. R 1508-9: 1/207d
Wm., Renhold, husb. R 1531: 3/45
Wm., Goldington. R 1543: 6/179d
Wm., Dunstable. R 1545-6: 11/81d
Wm., Houghton Regis, Thorn. R 1548: 12/28
Wm., Studham. 1574/34
Wm., Cranfield, shepherd. 1622/58
Wm., jun., Goldington, yeo. 1661/380
Wm., Over Gravenhurst, Ion, yeo. 1668/129
Wm., Barton, innholder. 1689/41
Wm., Cranfield, bonelacemaker. 1689/93
Wm., Cranfield, yeo. 1694/1
Wm., Dunstable. 1703/38
Wm., Stotfold, gent. A 1711/71
Wm., Stotfold, gent. 1713/74
Wm., Salford, tailor. 1714/94
Wm., Lidlington, weaver. 1721-2/81
Wm., Ravensden. 1722/13
Wm., Gt. Barford, bricklayer. A 1742-3/43
Wm., Barton, yeo. 1745/10
Wm., Cranfield, yeo. 1750/27
Wm., Wootton, yeo. A 1795/7
FIELDEN, Jn., Yielden. 1640/36
FIELDING, Ric., Yielden, husb. 1600/42
FIFIELD, Fra., Pavenham, shepherd. 1645/23
FILDE, see Field
FILLER, Ann, Barton, wid. 1699/56
Austin, Barton. 1574/60
Eliz., (old index only, bundle missing). A 1718/28
Mary, Silsoe, spins. A 1728/23
Nich., Barton, husb. 1633/126
Ric., Aspley, servant. 1615/213
Sarah, Barton, spins. 1683/32
Wm., Barton, yeo. 1613/160
Wm., Barton, grocer. A 1704/4
Wm., Barton, yeo. 1727/63

FILPOT, see Philpott
FINALL, see Fynall
FINCH, FYNCH, Agnes, Flitton, wid. of Jas. R 1547: 12/14d
Alice, Clapham, wid. 1627/202
Ann, Tempsford, wid. 1649/40
Ann, Southill, wid. AR 1672: 1/96
Cath., Northill, Over Caldecote. 1638/44
Eliz., Dunstable, wid. 1607/123
Hen., Biggleswade, yeo. 1565/193
Hen., Meppershall, yeo. 1602/74
Hen., Potton, lab. 1739-40/92
Hen., Warden, victualler. A 1761/2
Humph., Goldington, yeo. 1783/50
Jas., Flitton and Bedford St. Paul. R 1546: 11/161
Jeff., Flitton. R 1536: 4/79
Jn., Flitton, Greenfield. 1657/52
Jn., Eaton Bray, yeo. 1704-5/35
Jn., Millbrook, yeo. 1713/34
Jn., Eversholt, lab. 1728/13
Jn., Barton, lab. AR 1670: 1/140
Martha, Bedford. 1672/145
Ric., Dunstable, citizen and merchant tailor of London, bach. 1640-1/85
Rog., Luton, singingman. 1558/47
Thos., sen., Dunstable, yeo. R 1558: 14/85d
Thos., Clophill. 1576/16
Thos., sen., Dunstable, draper. 1586-7/180
Thos., Ampthill, yeo. 1778/13
Thos., Bedford, clothes salesman. 1830/24
Thos., Southill, gent. AR 1684-5: 1/122d
Thos., Southill, gent. A 1721/47
Wm., Clapham, lab. 1625/123
Wm., Warden, lab. A 1725/23
Wm., Old Warden, yeo. A 1782/9
Wm., Turvey, farmer, butcher and innkeeper. 1843/56
see also Fanch
FINCHAM, Wm., Eyeworth, yeo. 1653/88
see also Fensome
FINCHER, Jas., Tilsworth, yeo. 1617/311
FIND, FINND, Jn., Willington, husb. 1578/80
FINDING, FINDIN, Ben., Sundon, yeo. 1736-7/26
Eliz., Riseley. A 1703/18
Jn., Riseley, tailor. 1639-40/148
Jn., Riseley, cordwainer. A 1703/17
Thos., Riseley, cordwinder. 1676/185
Thos., Riseley, cordwainer. AR 1682: 1/67

FINDING, FINDIN continued
Wm., Oakley, husb. 1660/93
Wm., Elstow, lab. A 1776/11
FINDLAY, FINDLEY, Jn., Ampthill, gent. 1747-8/71
Jn., Ampthill, gent. A 1809/6
Wm., Ampthill, gent. 1750/42
FINEY, see Finney
FINNE, Ann, Marston, Marston Pillinge, spins. 1676/156
FINNEY, FINEY, Jn., Silsoe, yeo. 1752/64
Jonathan, sen., Podington, husb. 1715/15
Russell, Silsoe, Newberry, farmer. 1784/33
Thos., Henlow. 1818/5
FIPPS, see Phipps
FIRBY, Sarah, Bedford St. Paul, wid. 1714/22
FIRMAN, Geo., Biggleswade, Holme, lab. 1631/166
Jn., Leighton Buzzard, wheelwright. Fac. 1713: 9/43
Mary, Lidlington, wid. 1655/101
Robt., Bletsoe. 1713/5
Wm., Eversholt, yeo. 1663-4/103
Wm., Battlesden, yeo. 1697/132
FIRMARY, see Furmary
FIRTH, FURTH, Cath., sen., Leighton Buzzard, wid. LB 1766/5
Eliz., Leighton Buzzard, wid. Fac. 1720: 9/64
Mich., Felmersham, clerk. 1756/14
Ralph, Eversholt. R 1541: 6/100
Wm., Leighton Buzzard. LBA 1785/33
see also Furtho
FISH, FYCHE, FITCH, FYSHE, Agnes, Riseley, wid. (Deed of Gift). 1640/42
Dorothy, Eaton Socon, Ford End, wid. AR 1679: 1/68d
Hen., Riseley. 1679/40
Jn., Riseley. R 1501: 1/31d
Jn., Westoning, excise officer. 1790/20
Robt., Riseley. R 1538: 5/23
Thos., sen., Riseley, yeo. 1630/29
Thos., Eaton, tailor. 1641-2/191
Wm., Riseley, husb. 1562/121
Wm., Southill, esq. 1628/32
see also Fisher
FISHER, FYSSHER, Stokes alias Fisher, see under Stokes
-, Stevington. R 1500-1: 1/24
Abr., Colmworth, cottager. A 1739-40/2
Abr., Keysoe Row, farmer. 1790/5
Agnes, Potton, wid. R 1532: 3/69d
Agnes, Tempsford. R 1546: 11/220d
alias Pope, Agnes, Sandy, wid. 1576/29

FISHER, FYSSHER continued
Anne, Barford, wid. 1617/336
Edw., Sandy. 1614/52
alias Cole, Edw., Potton, lab. 1642/39
Edw., Toddington, yeo. 1730/25
Edw., Little Staughton, yeo. 1787/10
Eliz., Wilden, wid. 1658/216
Eliz., Cranfield, wid. 1662/58
Eliz., Studham, wid. 1674/132
Eliz., Southill, wid. A 1733/6
Eliz., Toddington, wid. A 1733/20
Fra., Northill. 1557/384
Fra., Sandy, wid. 1636/35
Giles, ?Moggerhanger. 1698/127
Hen., Barford, husb. 1592/37
Hen., Northill, Ickwell. 1610/77
Hen., Moggerhanger, husb. 1612/117
Hen., Flitwick, yeo. AR 1685: 1/212d
Hen., Higham Gobion, dairyman. A 1719/20
Jasper, rector of Wilden. 1650/104
Joan, wid., Barford. 1576-7/9
Jn., Tempsford. R 1500: 1/17
Jn., Pavenham. R 1518: 1/240
Jn., Goldington. R 1519: 1/242
Jn., Gt. Barford. R 1540: 6/36
Jn., Northill, Caldecote. R 1549: 12/76d
Jn., Willington, husb. R 1558: 14/79
Jn., Carlton. 1565/207
Jn., Langford. 1580-1/4
Jn., Farndish, husb. 1585/38
Jn., Sandy, Girtford, husb. 1589/73
Jn., Wootton, husb. 1631/212
Jn., Stotfold, glover. 1662-3/72
Jn., Flitwick. 1663-4/104
Jn., Potton, yeo. 1674/170
Jn., Wootton. 1690/40
Jn., Eaton Socon, baker. 1778/2
Jn., Maulden, gardener. A 1808/20
Leonard, Colmworth, husb. 1702/15
Marg., Maulden, wid. 1625/210
Margt., Edworth. R 1536: 4/60d
Mary, Potton. AR 1674: 1/101d
Mary, Colmworth, wid. 1767/59
Mary, Hockliffe. A 1744/11
Mat., Tilbrook, husb. 1617/201

FISHER, FYSSHER continued
Nath., Studham, yeo. 1676/107
Ralph, Goldington, yeo. 1619-20/215, I 4/27
Ric., Stevington. R 1522: 2/48
Ric., Potton, yeo. R 1530: 3/32d
Ric., Lidlington, yeo. 1604/62
Ric., Milton Ernest, yeo. 1619-20/243, I 4/47
Ric., Sandy, weaver. 1667/116
Ric., Podington, Hinwick, yeo. 1691/103
Ric., Shillington, Wattershires, servant. 1710/5
Ric., Colmworth, farmer. A 1746/3
Ric., Eaton Socon, Wyboston, yeo. 1833/2
Robt., Lt. Barford. R 1541? 6/92
Robt., Blunham. 1616/56
Robt., Northill, Nether Caldecote, lab. 1675/18
Sarah, Keysoe, wid. A 1806/25, I 4/203
Sarah, Bedford, wid. 1841/7
Thos., Gt. Barford. 1557/344
Thos., Carlton, husb. 1558/74
Thos., Moggerhanger. 1558/233
Thos., sen., Moggerhanger. 1558/287
Thos., Blunham. 1560/80
Thos., Oakley. (Bundle 1563-5). 1560/211
Thos., Moggerhanger, husb. R 1567: 17/3d
Thos., Tempsford. 1590/134
Thos., Stotfold, lab. 1612-13/8
Thos., Maulden. 1615/196
Thos., Keysoe. 1618/39
Thos., jun., Keysoe. 1618/154
Thos., Blunham, husb. 1636/33
Thos., Bedford St. Paul, lab. 1640/37
Thos., Blunham, husb. 1649/3
Thos., Biggleswade, innholder. 1706/22
Thos., Toddington, blacksmith. 1713/32
Thos., Colmworth, yeo. 1731/32
Thos., Southill, Broom, lab. 1732-3/53
Thos., and Eliz., Southill. A 1734/31
Thos., Kempston, victualler. A 1769/4
Thos., Millbrook, yeo. 1818/49
Thos., Moggerhanger, victualler. 1840/41
Walt., Biggleswade. 1567/20
Walt., Potton, baker. 1609/149
Walt., Eyeworth, husb. 1657/253
Walt., Langford, lab. 1671-2/16
Wm., Biddenham. 1561/117

FISHER, FYSSHER continued
Wm., Barford. 1572/84
Wm., Pulloxhill, yeo. 1638/175
Wm., Dunton, husb. 1669/94
Wm., Hockliffe, cordwainer. 1698/126
Wm., Eaton Socon, Beggary, dairyman. 1701/34
Wm., Millbrook, fellmonger. A 1705/30
Wm., Millbrook, fellmonger. 1705/90
Wm., Hockliffe, cordwainer. 1707/49
Wm., Millbrook, fellmonger. 1721/3
Wm., Pulloxhill, grazier. A 1723/12
Wm., Eaton Socon. 1739/66
Wm., Pulloxhill, Kitchen End, grazier. 1742/68
Wm., Eaton Socon, thatcher. A 1749-50/21
Wm., Hockliffe, cordwainer and victualler. 1791/8
Wm., Blunham, carpenter. 1792/34
Wm., Northill, Ickwell, farmer. 1797/23
see also Fish
FITCH, FYCHE, see Fish
FITTON, Chas., Eaton Socon, Wyboston, husb. 1673/23
Cornelius, Sutton, yeo. 1668/139
Jn., Clifton. 1725/5
Jn., Clifton. A 1731-2/10
Jn., Clifton. 1750/24
Wm., Tempsford. 1700/149
FITZ, Simon, Aspley Guise. R 1544: 11/43
FITZACKERLEY, VAZACKERLY, Nich., Stotfold. 1571/43
FITZGEOFFREY, Anne, Bedford St. Mary, wid. 1627/161
Cicely, Felmersham, wid. 1664/40
Eliz., Thurleigh. R 1532: 3/80
Geo., Gt. Barford, Creakers, late of Rowney, esq. 1616/52
Gerrard, Barford, gent. 1610/75
Jn., Gt. Barford, Creakers, esq. R 1535: 4/34d
Jn., Felmersham, gent. 1661-2/398
Jn., Bedford, gent. 1673/111
Margt., Bromham, wid. 1603-4/83
Oliv., Thurleigh, gent. 1598-9/122
Thos., Wilshamstead, gent. 1612/21
FITZHUGH, FITZHUE, Eliz., Wilden. AR 1676: 1/66
Geo., Wilden. AR 1672: 1/62
Hen., Bedford, gent. 1632/51
Jn., Barford. 1579/183
Jn., Gt. Barford. (Old index only, admon. missing). A 1726/16
Nich., Wilden, gent. 1575/80
Robt., Wilden, gent. 1712-13/29

FITZHUGH, FITZHUE continued
Thos., Bedford, maltster. 1640/118
Wm., Bedford, maltster. 1633/155
FLANDERS, FLAUNDERS, Eliz., Wilshamstead, wid. 1761/39
Jn., Wilshamstead, husb. 1753/5
Phill., Roxton, shepherd. A 1758/3
Ric., Colmworth. R 1543: 6/177d
Ric., Colmworth. 1605/121
Robt., Keysoe, Keysoe Row, carpenter. 1781/68
Sus., Roxton, Chawston, wid. 1855/31
Thos., Little Staughton, carpenter. 1794/18
Wm., Little Staughton, lab. AR 1671: 1/61
Wm., Colmworth, lab. A 1739/11
FLANINGHAM, Mary, Toddington, wid. 1699/21
FLAWNE, Eliz., Marston, wid. 1617-18/223
Jn., Wymington, husb. R 1546-7: 11/232d
Jn., Ampthill, shoemaker. 1629/88
Jn., Pulloxhill, locksmith. 1640/18
Jn., Flitton, Ward Hedges. 1662-3/62
Jn., Clapham, farmer. A 1736-7/26
Thos., Wymington. R 1534: 4/6
Thos., Eaton Socon, blacksmith. A 1815/12
FLECKNAR, see Fleckney
FLECKNEY, FLECKNAR, Hen., Pulloxhill, husb. 1741-2/63
Jos., Riseley, farmer. 1762/8
Ric., Eaton Socon, yeo. 1771/12
FLEET, FLIT, Jn., Chalgrave, yeo. A 1760/19
FLEMING, FLEMENS, FLEMONS, Jn., Dunton. 1660-1/58
Jn., Bedford, victualler. 1823/40
Jos., Leighton Buzzard, miller. 1743/9
Jos., Leighton Buzzard, miller. LB 1793/96
Mary, Leighton Buzzard, wid. LB 1809/41
Mary, Leighton Buzzard, wid. LBA 1828/87
Ric., Leighton Buzzard, miller. LB 1768/14
Ric., Leighton Buzzard, baker. LB 1779/52
Sarah, Leighton Buzzard, The Mill, wid. LB 1775/39
Wm., Bedford St. Cuthbert, clerk. 1794/19
FLETCHER, Edw., Houghton Regis. 1616/134, I
Geo., Biggleswade, gent.. Bw 1770/53, I
Humph., Silsoe, gent. 1751/14
Jas., Toddington, farmer and grazier. 1812/48
Jeamsing (sic), Roxton, Colesden. 1634-5/118
Jos., Luton, Chiltern Green, yeo. 1744/34
alias Cook, Ric., sen., Northill. R 1525: 2/61
Ric., Shillington, butcher. 1638/122

FLETCHER continued
Ric., Renhold, yeo. 1668-9/185
Ric., Clifton, tailor. 1734/25
Robt., Bedford St. Mary, cordwainer. 1788/2
Sarah, Harrold. AR 1690: 1/50d
alias Cooke, Thos., Northill, husb. 1587-8/100
Thos., Haynes, joiner. 1637/144
Thos., Bedford St. Paul. AR 1678: 1/15d
Thos., Harrold, Harrold Park, yeo. 1693-4/128
Thos., Harrold Park, gent. 1720/120
Thos., Marston, yeo. A 1808/1
Wm., Harrold, Harrold Park, keeper. 1687/74
Wm., Marston, farmer. 1796/32
FLINDALL, Edw., Dunstable, carpenter. AR 1673: 1/146d
Sam., (old index "Docket mislaid"). A 1708/4
Thos., Clophill, farmer. A 1752/8
FLINDELL, Eliz., Dunstable, wid. 1721/85
Eliz., Clophill. 1733/40
Hannah, Clophill, wid. 1758/48
Jn., Dunstable, yeo. 1670/204
Mary, Clophill, wid. 1741/19
Robt., sen., Dunstable, carpenter. 1690/17
Sam., Clophill, husb. 1736/9
FLINDEN, Ric., Luton. R 1541: 6/84d
FLINDERS, Geo., Shefford. R 1533: 3/109
Jn., Luton, tanner. 1618/118
Mich., Blunham, wid. 1640/74
Robt., Wootton, yeo. 1626/10
FLINT, FLYNTE, Pateman alias Flint, see Pateman
Anne, Bedford, wid. 1714/116
Eliz., Blunham, wid. 1630-1/113
Eliz., Dean. 1760/54
Hen., Shillington, Nether Stondon. 1662-3/60
Jas., Warden, farmer. 1813/28
Jn., Shillington, Watershires, yeo. 1701/19
Jn., sen., Shillington, husb. 1720/22
Jn., Over Stondon, husb. 1742/24
Lewis, Holwell. 1739/9
Lewis, Shillington, tailor. 1831/27
Mary, Bedford St. Paul, wid. 1687/44
Ric., Bedford St. Paul, glover. 1560/216
Ric., (parish torn off), butcher. 1670/184
Ric., Bedford, butcher. AR 1680-1: 1/18d
Ric., Bedford, barber. 1714/128
Ric., Riseley, gent. 1724/16

FLINT, FLYNTE continued
Thos., Lidlington, husb. A 1716/33
Thos., Shillington, Chibley, yeo. 1774/18
Wm., Shillington, husb. 1767/7
FLINTHAM, Eliz., Tilbrook, wid. 1776/6
FLOOD, FLUDE, Geo. Hen., Bedford St. Paul, currier and leather seller. 1850/31
Jn., Bedford St. Paul, whitesmith. 1848/37
Thos., Renhold, farmer. A 1813/16
FLOWER, FLOWERS, Edw., Eaton Socon, husb. 1724-5/102
Jn., Flitwick. 1555/125b
Robt., Southill, butcher. AR 1681: 1/113d
Wm., Ampthill, bricklayer. A 1734/3
FLOYD, Ann, Wootton, wid. A 1703/25
Geo., Wootton, dairyman. 1703/55
Rebecca, Tingrith, spins. AR 1679: 1/202d
FOBBYGE, Wm., Eaton Socon. 1568/46
see also Fobeck, Folbeck, Folbigg
FOBECK, FOBACK, Bridget, Bedford, wid. 1623/164
Luke, Bolnhurst, carpenter. 1732/68
see also Fobbyge, Folbeck, Folbigg, Fulbeck
FODERY, Jane, Bolnhurst, wid. 1757/32
Wm., Bolnhurst. 1757/25
FOLBECK, Walt., Keysoe, husb. R 1548: 12/19
see also Fobeck, Folbigg, Fobbyge
FOLBIGG, Eliz., Keysoe, wid. 1631/163
Hen., Keysoe. 1746/41
Sam., Eaton Socon, Duloe, yeo. 1813/11
Simon, Keysoe, farmer. 1768/7
Simon, Keysoe, yeo. A 1787/11
Thos., sen., Dunton, husb. 1722/51
Thos., Dunton, yeo. 1784/3
Wm., Keysoe, husb. 1617/186
see also Fobeck, Fobbyge, Folbeck
FOLL, Jn., Greatworth, Northants, (Toddington), yeo. 1812/56
FOLWELL, Wm., Toddington, grocer. A 1823/13
FONTAINE, FONTEYNE, Jn., Leighton. 1552/298
see also Fountaine
FOOKES, see Foulkes
FOOT, FOTE, FOOTE, Chris., sen., Gt. Barford, carpenter. 1669/97
Ellen, Eaton, wid. 1661/357
Fra., Turvey, husb. 1687/52
Jas., Gt. Barford, bach. AR 1682: 1/75
Jn., Turvey, carpenter. 1693/146
Thos., Tempsford, husb. 1568/40

FOOT, FOTE, FOOTE continued
Walt., Hockliffe, clerk. A 1750/14
FORD, FURDE, FOARDE, Ann, Eversholt, wid. 1702/12
Edw., Clifton. 1726/20
Hen., Eversholt, husb. 1678/125
Hen., Eversholt. A 1712/46
Hen., Eversholt. A 1739/19
Jas., Goldington, clockmaker. 1697/24
Jas., Wilshamstead, grazier. 1837/20
Jn., Holcote. 1623/158
Jn., Clophill, Beadlow, dairyman. 1678-9/147
Jn., Wootton, yeo. 1719-20/104
Jn., Stotfold, husb. 1751/10
Jn., Roxton, Colesden, farmer. 1838/50
Jn., Clophill, Beadlow, dairyman. AR 1678-9: 1/201
Jn., Eversholt, lab. A 1706/9
Mary, Kempston, wid. 1703/31
Nich., Hockliffe. R 1545: 11/127d
Randolph, Bletsoe, farrier. 1625/186
Rebecca, Wootton. (Old index, bundle missing). A 1745/5
Ric., Wootton. A 1769/9
Ric., Cranfield, yeo. 1804/51
Sam. (Old index only, bundle missing). A 1718/14
Simon, Bedford St. Peter. 1564-5/30
Susannah, Southill, Holme Mills, spins. 1692/21
Susannah, Wootton, wid. 1720/25
Thos., Houghton Regis. 1559/179
Thos., Shillington, lab. 1624/93
Thos., Kempston Hardwick, husb. 1694-5/87
Wm., Bedford St. Paul. 1557/294
Wm., sen., Stotfold, yeo. 1637-8/163
Wm., Shillington, husb. 1644-5/112
Wm., Stotfold, yeo. 1661/333
FORDHAM, Sarah, Biggleswade, Holme Green, wid. 1844/39
Thos., Biggleswade, Holme. Bw 1844/156
FORDYMELL, Ric., Wilshamstead. R 1536: 4/53
FOREMAN, Ben., Kempston, lab. 1626-7/130
Thos., Marston, bach. 1681/21
Wm., Wavendon, Bucks., priest. R 1558: 15/2
FORFEIT, Robt., Marston, dairyman. 1714/2
Robt., Marston, dairyman. 1735/34
FORFITT, Eliz. (Old index only, bundle missing). A 1717/17
FORNER, Brough alias Forner, see under Brough
FORRESTER, Sophia, Biggleswade. BwA 1849/76

FORSTER, Tim., Bedford, gent. 1831/46
Wm., Northill, Upper Caldecot, thatcher. 1770/43
FORTESCUE, see Foscue
FORTH, Margt., (alias Preston), Bedford St. Peter, wid. 1552/318
FORTUNE, Geo., Odell, late Pavenham, lab. 1698-9/159
Wm., Eaton Socon, innholder. 1711/78
FOSCOTT, see Foskett
FOSCROFT, Alex., Wrestlingworth, parson. R 1559: 13/156d
FOSCUE, Marg., Sandy, wid. 1617/283
Thos., Eaton Bray, lab. 1780/49
FOSKETT, FOSCOTT, Eliz., Potton, wid. 1767/54
Fra., Potton, yeo. A 1762/8
Fra., Potton, yeo. 1762/11
Joan, wid., Bedford St. Mary. 1620/114
Jos., Pertenhall, lab. A 1711/54
Margt., Bedford St. Peter, spins. 1630-1/107
Ric., Biddenham, husb. 1553/286
Robt., Bedford, glover. 1614/102
Robt., Potton, cordwainer. 1709/57
Thos. (Old index only, bundle missing). A 1717/7
Thos., Potton, yeo. 1759/16
Thos., Cople, shopkeeper. 1843/3
FOSS, FOSSE, see Fossey
FOSSEY, FOSSY, FOSS, VOSSE, Dan, jun., Dunstable, grocer. 1717/17
Edm., Caddington, husb. 1635/32
Edw., Southill, Rowney, gent. 1697/139
Eme, Houghton Regis, wid. R 1532-3: 3/82d
Jas., sen., Houghton Regis, husb. 1623-4/147
Jas., sen., Houghton Regis, bach., yeo. 1639/108
Jas., Chalgrave, Tebworth, yeo. 1684/71
Jas., Chalgrave, Tebworth. AR 1692: 1/177d
Jas., Houghton Regis, farmer. 1820/18
Joan, Houghton Regis, wid. 1652-3/103
Jn., Leighton Buzzard, lab. Fac. 1716:9/52
Jn., Dunstable, bach. A 1743/19
Jn., Arlesey, farmer. 1809/15
Prudence, Hockliffe, wid. 1682/44
Sam., Houghton Regis, yeo. 1756/13
Sam., Woburn, late Luton, Lewsey, gent. 1827/44
Thos., Toddington, poulter. 1617/250
Thos., sen., Houghton Regis, Bidwell, yeo. 1638-9/147
Thos., Houghton Regis, yeo. A 1802/13
Wm., Houghton Regis. R 1524: 2/54d
Wm., Milton Bryan. 1554?/237
Wm., Houghton Regis, Bidwell. 1601/93

FOSSEY, FOSSY, FOSS, VOSSE continued
Wm., Chalgrave, Tebworth, yeo. 1670/159
Wm., Toddington, Chalton, yeo. 1670/191
Wm., jun., Dunstable, tallow chandler. 1687/31
Wm., Houghton Regis. AR 1689-90: 1/176d
Wm., Caddington, Zouches, yeo. 1725/48
Wm., Toddington, Chalton, gent. 1741/11
Wm., sen., Dunstable, draper. 1764/64
Wm., Houghton Regis, gent. 1801/11
Wm., Dunstable. P/IX2. A 1812/4
Wm., Shillington, Apsley End, yeo. 1816/9
Wm., Shillington, Apsley End, yeo. 1826/17
FOSTER, Agnes, Haynes, wid. 1599/133
Ann, Biggleswade, wid. Bw 1724/16
Barbara, Gt. Barford, spins. 1733/57
Ben., Cranfield, Hickman, wheelwright. 1840/16
Ben., Cranfield, Hickman, innkeeper. 1856/30
Chas., Cardington, Harrowden, gent. 1669/14
Dan., Wrestlingworth, yeo. 1724/17
Dorothy, Ampthill, wid. 1728/96
Edm., Cardington, Harrowden. 1608/66
Edw., Northill, Ickwell, farmer. A 1843/7
Eliz., Luton, wid. 1645/44
Fra., Leighton Buzzard, apothecary. LB 1781/60
Geo., Cardington? 1604/29
Geo., Millbrook, yeo. 1680/28
Geo., Barton, yeo. 1682/31
Grace, Leighton Buzzard, wid. Fac. 1715: 9/48
Hen., Cardington, yeo. 1605/123
Hen., Cardington, gent. 1624-5/4
Hen., Ampthill, cordwainer. 1674/155
Jas., Chalgrave, lab. A 1786/9
Jas., Bedford St. Paul. A 1808/5
Jn., Clifton. R 1527: 2/52
Jn., Pulloxhill. 1584/268
Jn., Luton, carpenter. 1638/124
Jn., Kempston. 1648/83
Jn., sen., Cardington, gent. 1658-9/206
Jn., Cardington, Harrowden. 1667/44
Jn., Edworth, yeo. 1699/20
Jn., Sandy, Beeston, wheelwright. 1760/51
Jn., Woburn, schoolmaster. 1787/13
Jn., Holwell, yeo. 1830/8
Jn., Odell, Stagsden, wheelwright. 1840/6
Jos., Cranfield, carpenter. A 1855/29

FOSTER continued
Margt., Woburn, wid. 1667/20
Martha, Cardington, Harrowden. 1669/15
Mary, Sandy, Beeston, wid. 1769/9
Mary, Northill. P/IX2. A 1812/1
Miles, Bedford St. Paul, cutler. 1579/179a
Miles, Ampthill, cordwainer. 1710/7
Nich., Hawnes. 1628-9/14
Rebecca, Cardington, Harrowden. AR 1671: 1/4d
Rebeccah, Cardington, Harrowden, wid. 1669/93
Robt., Dunstable, musician. R 1562-3: 16/57
Roland, Cardington, Eastcotts, gent. 1646/79
Sam., Houghton Regis, grocer and general shopkeeper. 1852/42
Sam., Biggleswade, baker. Bw 1720/9
Sus., Cranfield, wid.: affidavit 1843/16
Susannah, Cranfield, wid. 1845/23
Thos., Clifton, husb. 1567-8/119
Thos., Cardington, yeo. 1617/252
Thos., Campton, draper. 1638-9/96
Thos., Cardington, Cotton End, gent. 1647/40
Thos., Cardington, Cotton End, gent. 1661-2/242
Thos., Luton, tailor. 1683-4/124, I
Thos., Leighton Buzzard, grocer. Fac. 1712: 9/36
Thos., sen., Luton, cooper. 1831/17
Wm., Clifton, yeo. 1586-7/137
Wm., Biggleswade, Holme, lab. 1598-9/101
Wm., Cardington, Cotton End, gent. 1642-3/28
Wm., Dunton, Milloe, lab. 1681/37
Wm., Bedford, esq. 1688-9/82
Wm., Biggleswade, poulterer. Bw 1719/8
FOSTON, Margt., Dunton, Millow, wid. R 1540: 6/51d
FOTHERGILL, Jn., Eaton Socon, Bushmead, yeo. 1672/96
FOULKES, FOWKS, FOLXE, FOWX, Agnes, Wootton, wid. 1648/78
Alice, Wootton, wid. 1696/157
Edm., Woburn, gent. 1706/47
Hen., sen., Wootton, yeo. 1650/119
Hen., Wootton, yeo. 1672-3/175
Hen., jun., Wootton, yeo. AR 1672-3: 1/7d
Hen., Ampthill, gent. 1689/18
Hen., Stagsden, butcher. A 1785/15
Hugh, Elstow, yeo. 1694-5/101
Jn. R 1516: 1/196d
Jn., sen., Wootton, husb. 1558/158
Jn., Over Dean, husb. 1564/48
Joan, Bedford, wid. 1637-8/167

FOULKES, FOWKS, FOLXE, FOWX continued
Joan, Cranfield. 1664/10
Lewis, Wootton, yeo. 1675/62
Mathey, Wootton, wid. 1626/37
Ric., Wootton, farmer. 1729/41
Ric., Wootton, victualler. 1778/21
Ric., Houghton Conquest. A 1773/10
Robt., Tingrith. A 1706/11
Sarah, London, Bedford Row, spins. A 1804/14
Susannah, Stagsden, wid. 1787/36
Thos., sen., Wootton, husb. 1587-8/108
Thos., Wootton. 1614/74
Thos., Dunstable, gent. A 1778/7
Thos., Husborne Crawley, yeo. 1827/24
Wm., Dean, husb. R 1541-2: 6/121d
Wm., Ampthill, barber. A 1716/22
Wm., Husborne Crawley. A 1837/13
see also Vauxe, Fookes, Fowkes
FOULSTONE, Geo., Podington. 1753/30
FOUND, Geo., Blunham, blacksmith. 1687/84
Giles, Northill, Nether Caldecote, yeo. 1681/18
Giles, Biggleswade, bach. A 1705-6/16
Jn., sen., Moggerhanger, yeo. 1660/135
Jn., Blunham, bach. A 1705-6/15
Robt., Sandy, Beeston, husb. 1615/150
Thos., Cardington, Harrowden. 1672-3/171
see also Fownes
FOUNTAIN(E), Abra., Whipsnade, yeo. A 1806/21
Christian, Lidlington. 1609/162
Edw., Lidlington, lab. 1682/49
Edw., Lidlington. AR 1682: 1/208
Eliz., Sharnbrook, spins. 1834/1
Fra., Lidlington, husb. 1660/173
Jas., Cranfield, farmer. A 1850/13
Jn., Eversholt, yeo. 1665/79
Jn., Cardington, tailor. A 1711-12/20
Jn., Millbrook, cordwainer. 1726/44
Jn., Eaton Bray, cordwainer. A 1780/18
Jn., sen., Eaton Bray, cordwainer. 1780/48
Jn., Sharnbrook, collarmaker. 1809/46
Jn., sen., Eaton Bray, victualler and cordwainer. 1816/30
Jn., sen., Eaton Bray, yeo. 1840/21
Jos., Sharnbrook, sadler. 1835/8
Margt., wife of Thos., yeo., Eaton Bray. 1664/62
Mark, Leighton Buzzard, yeo. A 1747/21

FOUNTAIN(E) continued
formerly Rudd, Mary, Kempston. A 1746/49
Nich., Houghton Regis. R 1533: 3/93
Robt., Lidlington. 1604/75
Robt., Millbrook, dairyman. AR 1686-7: 1/216
Robt., Bolnhurst, dairyman. A 1705/29
Robt., Bolnhurst, dairyman. 1705/89
Thos., Kempston. 1635/50
Thos., Kempston, gent. 1635-6/33
Thos., Eaton Bray, schoolmaster. 1765/16
Wm., Lidlington, yeo. 1622/56
Wm., Millbrook, yeo. 1679/60
see also Fontaine
FOWBRIDGE, Jn., Knotting. R 1505: 1/98d
FOWKS, see Foulkes
FOWLER, Fowler, afterwards Turner, see Turner,
Smith alias Fowler, see Smith
Ann, Billington, wid. 1802/18
Ann, Toddington, wid. A 1837/2
Ann, Henlow, spins. 1848/41
Anne, Oakley, wid. A 1746/27
Dan., Bedford, butcher. A 1720/19
Edw., Meppershall How, farmer. 1754/4
Eliz., Marston. 1763/14
Eliz., Toddington. A 1797/7
Fra., Henlow, yeo. A 1785/23
Fra., Meppershall, farmer. 1789/4
Geo., Shillington, yeo. 1687-8/66
Geo., Meppershall, Woodhall, yeo. 1716-17/9
Geo., Toddington, yeo. 1792/15
Geo., Luton, gent. A 1758/23
Geo., Billington, yeo. LB 1823/21, I
Jacob, Harrold, yeo. 1763/15
Jane, Luton. A 1763/22
Jas., (old index only, bundle missing). A 1718/7
Jas., Toddington, dairyman. 1819/4
Jeremiah, Silsoe, yeo. 1705/2
Joan, Yielden. R 1544: 11/45d
Jn., Kempston. 1613/214
Jn., Milton Bryan, lab. 1622/74
Jn., Wilden, yeo. 1652-3/106
Jn., Thurleigh, yeo. 1661/358
Jn., Bromham, grocer. 1718/78
Jn., Tilsworth, shopkeeper. 1764/2
Jn., Toddington, yeo. 1816/8

FOWLER continued
Jn., Toddington. A 1818/8
Judith, Oakley. 1702/22
Judith, Oakley, wid. A 1702/9
Lawr., Barford, yeo. 1638-9/108
Levi, Bedford, gent. 1831/18
Margt., Shillington, wid. 1623/171
Margt., Meppershall, wid. 1754/7
Mary, Dunstable, wid. 1694/28
Mary, Luton, spins. 1723-4/80
Mary, a minor, Houghton Regis, spins. A 1808/22
Percival, Leighton Buzzard. 1560/75
Phillip, sen., Toddington, Chalton, yeo. 1800/7
Ric., Tilsworth, lab. 1667-8/99
Robt., Holwell. 1560/222
Robt., Maulden, miller. 1620/61
Robt., Shillington, yeo. AR 1675-6: 1/104d
Robt., Maulden, husb. 1759/7
Sam., Blunham, clerk. A 1704-5/32
Sarah, Shillington, wid. A 1729/47
Sarah, Shillington, spins. 1738/70
Thos., Shillington, yeo. 1613/194
Thos., sen., Shillington, blacksmith. 1657/14
Thos., Wootton, yeo. 1663/20
Thos., Shillington, blacksmith. 1704/63
Thos., sen., Shillington, yeo. 1716/45
Thos., Southill, Stanford, husb. 1721/33
Thos., sen., Houghton Regis, Thorn, yeo. 1767/49
Thos., Houghton Regis, farmer. A 1776/16
Thos., Houghton Regis, Thorn, cutter. 1803/35
Wm., Hockliffe, husb. 1570/17
Wm., Shillington, Chibley, yeo. 1661/369
Wm., Meppershall, Woodhall, gent. 1680/81
Wm., Shillington, blacksmith. 1684/92
Wm., Eaton Bray, lab. 1702/63
Wm., sen., Flitton, Cainhoe, gent. 1706/1
Wm., Shillington, yeo. A 1725/26
FOWNES, Sarah, Bedford St. Peter, spins. 1748/16
see also Found
FOX, Felce alias Fox see under Felce
Abr., Ridgmont, victualler. 1838/33
Alice, Haynes, spins. 1660/41
Ben., Leighton Buzzard, yeo. LB 1761/41
Chas., Silsoe, barber. 1753/8
Chris., Tilbrook, yeo. 1655-6/127

FOX continued
Chris., Tilbrook. AR 1683: 1/76
Chris., Upper Dean, gent. 1689-90/90
Chris., Tilbrook, yeo. 1705/43
Chris., Nether Dean, yeo. 1729/18
Chris., Dean. 1772/42
Eliz., Eaton, wid. R 1519: 1/188
Eliz., Leighton Buzzard, wid. LB 1772/31
Eliz., Toddington, victualler. A 1761/11
Ellen, Wootton, wid. R 1549: 12/47d
Fra., Wilshamstead, spins. 1660/44
Fra., Bedford St. Paul. AR 1672: 1/7
Geoff., Elstow. 1709/70
Hen., Reach. 1562/108
Hen., Elstow. 1592-3/5
Jn., sen., Kempston. R 1532: 3/58d
Jn., Clophill. 1552/316
Jn., Kempston, husb. 1582/87
Jn., Tilbrook, yeo. 1673-4/69
Jn., Dean, gent. A 1719-20/32
Jn., Luton, tailor. A 1731/18
Jn., Elstow, carpenter. 1756/16
Jn., Dean. A 1770/17
Jn., Elstow, carpenter. 1785/10
Jn., Leighton Buzzard, maltster. LB 1800/9
Jn., Cardington, carpenter. 1805/39
Jn., Dean. A 1808/8
Jos., sen., Ampthill, Ewe Green, woadman. 1740/29
Jos., Toddington, dairyman. 1771/40
Judith, Bedford, wid. A 1766/22
Judith, Bedford. A 1810/10
Mary, Houghton Regis. 1717/56
Mary, Dean. A 1786/6
Mihill, Toddington, Chalton, yeo. 1660-1/113
Robt., Felmersham, Radwell, husb. 1600/45
Robt., Wootton Pillinge, husb. 1640/6
Robt., Upper Dean. 1717/55
Sam., Bedford St. Mary, tanner. A 1713-14/35
Sam., Ampthill, barber and peruke maker. 1736/20
Sarah, Bedford St. Paul, spins. 1799/13
Sophia, Bedford St. Peter, wid. A 1820/3
Steph., Toddington, victualler. A 1750/4
Thos., Wootton. R 1537: 4/83
Thos., Kempston. R 1549-50: 12/85
Thos., Kempston, husb. 1593/8

FOX continued
Thos., Milton Ernest, lab. 1601/102
Thos., Barton. 1601-2/151
Thos., Wilshamstead, weaver. 1660/45
Thos., Felmersham, Radwell, lab. 1661-2/239
Thos., Haynes. 1669/28
Thos., Luton, yeo. 1726/57
Thos., Pertenhall. 1729-30/127
Thos., Toddington, yeo. 1789/18
Thos., Nether Dean, gent. 1798/14
Thos., Dean, farmer. 1806/37
Wm., Chalgrave, Wingfield. 1629/136
Wm., (no parish given). 1638/16
Wm., Elstow, lab. 1644/135
Wm., Toddington. AR 1680: 1/159d
Wm., Southill, maltster. 1730/8
FOXEN, Edw., Toddington, yeo. 1720/51
Edw., Toddington, yeo. 1819/29
Hen., Toddington, yeo. 1827/31
Jn., Barton, farmer. 1823/16
Mary, Toddington, wid. 1794/35
Ric., Toddington, yeo. 1826/15
Robt., Dunstable, yeo. 1679/37
Robt., Dunstable, victualler. 1730/64
Robt., Markyate Street, butcher. 1760/22
Thos., Dunstable, butcher. 1665/47
Thos., Dunstable, butcher. 1702-3/42
Thos., Eaton Bray, yeo. 1767/28
Thos., sen., Toddington, yeo. 1768/36
Thos., sen., Toddington, farmer. 1781/49
Wm., sen., Toddington, farmer. 1838/45
FOXLEY, FOXLEE, Jos., Aspley Guise. 1809/11
Thos., Leagrave, wheelwright. 1826/40
Thos., Woburn, carpenter. 1839/32
FOXON, Mary, Dunstable, infant. AR 1671-2: 1/142
Thos., Toddington, yeo. A 1806/16
FRAIL, Wm., Husborne Crawley, tailor. 1674/120
FRANCE, Gload alias Globe, Westoning, servant. A 1729/13
Sam., Cranfield, butcher. A 1701/6
FRANCH, Ric., Odell. R 1537: 4/97d
see also French
FRANCIS, FRANCES, FRANNCES, Alice, Renhold, wid. 1830/45
David, Bedford St. Mary, bricklayer. 1850/29
Edw., Renhold, schoolmaster. 1759/42
Eliz., Houghton Regis, wid., spins. 1700/109

FRANCIS, FRANCES, FRANNCES continued
Eliz., Cranfield, wid. 1756/22
Geo., Northill, Ickwell, bricklayer. R 1770/1
Geo., Bedford, bricklayer and victualler. 1840/22
Geo., Biggleswade, bricklayer. Bw 1853/163
Joan, Wootton. R 1505: 1/88
Jn., Langford, clerk. 1623/134
Jn., Luton, tanner. 1682/61
Jn., Arlesey, bricklayer. A 1734/24
Jn., Cranfield, maltster. 1738/27
Jn., Northill, Ickwell, bricklayer. 1752/77
Jn., Renhold, schoolmaster. A 1830/6
Jn., Bedford, builder. 1852/2
Jonathan, Biggleswade. AR 1686-7: 1/128
Mary, Potton, wid. 1672/144
Mary (Sarah), Potton. AR 1672: 1/94d
Mary Ann, Bedford, wid. 1844/17
Rebecca, Bedford, wid. A 1842/10
Ric., Westoning. 1612-13/9
Ric., Westoning, Wood End, husb. 1651/8
Sarah, Woburn, wid. 1854/38
Thos., Wootton. R 1505: 1/88
Thos., Roxton. 1552/321
Thos., Henlow, bricklayer. 1727-8/86
Thos., Henlow, bricklayer. 1730/81
Wm., Bedford St. Mary. 1557/150
Wm., Bedford St. Mary. 1557/272
Wm., Ravensden. 1608/26
Wm., Houghton Regis, lab. 1682/39
Wm., Eyeworth. 1696-7/151
Wm., sen., Keysoe. 1712-13/72
Wm., Thurleigh, husb. A 1713/36
Wm., Houghton Regis, cordwainer. 1722/19
Wm., Shillington, carpenter. 1827/8
Wm., Bedford, builder. 1848/35
Wm., Bedford, bankers clerk. 1857/31
FRANK(S), FRANCKE, Ann, Bedford, wid. 1736/53
Barbary, Eaton Socon, Wyboston, wid. 1708/56
Edw., Eaton Socon, Wyboston, yeo. 1824/15
Eliz., Eaton Socon. 1734/52
Joan, Moggerhanger, spins. 1618/131
Jn., Eaton Socon, Wyboston, husb. 1633-4/193
Jn., Eaton Socon, Wyboston, yeo. 1682-3/108
Jn., Eaton Socon, Wyboston, leyman. 1727-8/88
Jn., Tilbrook, shepherd. 1737/15

FRANK(S), FRANCKE continued
Jn., Eaton Socon, wheelwright. 1768/47
Jn., Eaton Socon, Wyboston, yeo. 1771/26
Livett, Potton. A 1815/1
Ric., Moggerhanger, yeo. 1637-8/149
Ric., Eaton Socon, Wyboston, yeo. 1674/101
Ric., Eaton Socon, Nether Staploe, yeo. 1691-2/143
Robt., Tempsford, husb. 1733/23
Thos., Sandy, yeo. 1622-3/24
Thos., Eaton Socon, husb. 1635/24
Thos., Eaton Socon, wid. AR 1680: 1/70d
Thos., sen., Eaton Socon, carpenter. 1720/110
Thos., Eaton Socon, carpenter. 1744/24
Thos., Sutton, yeo. 1746/11
Wm., Sandy. 1557/255
Wm., Eaton Socon, Wyboston. 1573/130
Wm., Eaton Socon, Wyboston, yeo. 1608-9/97
Wm., Eaton Socon, Nether Staploe, dairyman. 1636/6
Wm., Moggerhanger, yeo. 1638/179
Wm., Bedford St. Paul, gent. 1751/15
FRANKLAND, Wm., Potton, husb. 1609/99
FRANKLIN, FRANCKLEYN, FRANCKLIN, Alice, Harrold, wid. 1564/50
Alice, Marston, wid. R 1558: 14/52
Amy, Eversholt, wid. 1745/8
Andrew, Billington, tailor. 1682/64
Ann, Harrold, wid. 1738/57
Bridgett, Potton, wid. 1617/182, I: 4/186
Chas., Potton, surgeon & apothecary. 1806/23
Edw., Kempston. 1661-2/254
Edw., Higham Gobion, dairyman. 1731/41
Edw., Sutton, gardener. A 1766/12
Eliz., Thurleigh. R 1544: 11/34
Eliz., Bedford St. Mary, wid. A 1701/38
Garrard, Marston, yeo. 1683/22
Geo., Stanbridge, yeo. 1606/56
Geo., Bromham, yeo. 1667/18
Hen., Billington. 1574/148
Hen., Houghton Conquest, lab. 1639/28
Hen., Cranfield, yeo. 1662-3/59
Hen., Lidlington, yeo. 1669/36
Hen., Bromham, yeo. AR 1685: 1/48
Hen., Lidlington, yeo. 1770/54
Hen., Clophill, late of Wilshamstead, farmer & grazier. 1834/23
Jas., shepherd. R 1517-8: 2/143
Jas., Eaton Socon, tailor. 1668/118

FRANKLIN, FRANCKLEYN, FRANCKLIN continued
Jas., Eversholt, yeo. 1721/92
Jas., Ampthill, sadler. 1736/28
Jn., Marston, sen. R 1530: 3/30
Jn., Aspley Guise. R 1536: 4/62
Jn., Wootton. R 1547: 11/229d
Jn., Lidlington. 1556/108
Jn., Marston, Wood End, yeo. 1584/172
Jn., Lidlington, husb. 1601-2/146
Jn., Cranfield. 1660/164
Jn., Lidlington, yeo. 1671/56
Jn., Bedford, gent. AR 1687-8: 1/31d
Jn., sen., Bedford St. Paul, woolcomber. 1724-5/71
Jn., Bedford St. Mary, grocer. 1737-8/62
Jn., Maulden, husb. 1747/20
Jn., Barton, butcher. A 1763/23
Jos., sen., Southill, Shefford Mill, miller. 1719/92
Juliana, Leighton Buzzard, wid. LB 1823/17
Margt., Lidlington, spins. 1613/137
Margt., Clapham, wid. (Bundle 1633). 1634-5/208
Mary, Bromham, wid. 1677/63
Mary, Bedford St. Mary, wid. 1719/35
Mary, Bedford St. Mary, spins. 1740/19
Math., Lidlington, yeo. 1713-14/36
Nich., (old index "Docket mislaid"). A 1708/16
Ric., Marston. R 1533: 3/92d
Ric., Wootton. 1652/79
Robt., Marston, husb. 1557/275
Robt., Marston Moreteyne. I 1587: 4/168
Robt., Harrold, yeo. 1668/196
Robt., Bedford St. Mary, tanner. 1700-1/140
Robt., Carlton, lab. 1713/68
Robt., Heath and Reach, yeo. LB 1757/32
Sam., Kempston, yeo. A 1767/10
Sam., Kempston, yeo. 1767/42A
Sarah, Lidlington, wid. 1717/41
Thos., sen., Marston, husb. 1582/68
Thos., Bromham, yeo. 1647/66
Thos., Flitwick. 1674/172
Thos., Marston, yeo. 1708/37
Thos., Langford, yeo. 1709-10/63
Thos., (old index only, bundle missing). A 1717/33
Thos., Bedford. A 1811/12
Wm., Thurleigh. R 1558-9: 15/142d
Wm., sen., Bromham, husb. 1608-9/92

FRANKLIN, FRANCKLEYN, FRANCKLIN continued
Wm., Bromham, carpenter. 1625/185
Wm., sen., Bromham, husb. 1631-2/139
Wm., Lidlington, husb. 1643/76
Wm., Bromham, yeo. 1646/91
Wm., Eaton, yeo. 1653-4/95
Wm., Woburn, Woburn Lodge, gent. 1706-7/67
Wm., Toddington, lab. 1720/75
Wm., Lidlington, yeo. A 1798/4
Wm., sen., Marston, farmer & dairyman. 1837/50
Wm., Bedford, tailor & draper. 1847/11
FRAY(E), Jas., Luton, husb. A 1706/10
Wm., Meppershall. 1559-60/210
see also Frey
FRAZER, Andrew, Potton, bookseller & stationer. 1842/45
FREELOVE, FRELOUE, Agnes, Chellington, wid. 1567/90
Geo., Chellington, husb. 1570/12
Joan, Bedford, wid. 1696/91
Jn., Flitwick. 1631-2/160
Jn., Flitton, yeo. 1691/71
Jos., Kempston, yeo. A 1799/9
Math., Steppingley, yeo. AR 1673: 1/190
Math., Flitwick, husb. 1727/13
Nich., Steppingley, husb. 1632/31
Sam., Bedford, barber. 1704/42
Thos., Felmersham. 1554/163
Thos., Steppingley. 1556/223
Thos., Bedford St. Cuthbert, lab. 1611/143
Thos., Wootton, lab. 1623/120
Thos., Houghton Conquest, yeo. 1660/169
Thos., Wilshamstead. AR 1670: 1/1
Thos., Flitwick, East End, yeo. 1675/1
Thos., Streatley, Sharpenhoe Grange, husb. 1755/30
Wm., Wootton, wid. 1641/181
Wm., Bedford, gardener. A 1715/22
Wm., (no parish). 1716/89
FREEMAN, Abr., (old index, "docket mislaid"). A 1709/14
Agnes, Podington, wid. 1617/325
Alice, sen., Stotfold, wid. 1669-70/128
Alice, Stotfold, wid. 1681/79
Alice, Stotfold, wid. AR 1681: 1/115d
Cath., Haynes, wid. & victualler. 1830/17
David, Luton, farmer. A 1734/28
Deborah, Toddington. A 1831/7
Dinah, Sandy, wid. 1792/36

FREEMAN continued
Edw., Stotfold, gent. 1618/168, I 4/188
Edw., Sandy, Girtford. 1710/45
Eliz., Lt. Barford, wid. 1749/15
Estwick Wm., Stotfold, gent. 1687/80
Fra., Toddington, millwright. 1787/38
Geo., Luton, Ashwell Bridge, farmer. 1826/2
alias Crawley, Hannah, Limbury. AR 1670: 1/140d
Hannah, Stotfold. 1688/45
Hannah, Stotfold, wid. AR 1688: 1/131
Hen., Dean. R 1529-30: 3/22
Isaac, Biscot. 1686/6
Isaac, Limbury. 1698/76
Jane, Hockliffe, wid. 1663/71
Jas., Stotfold, lab. 1664/34
Jas., Toddington, millwright. 1815/8
Joan, Dunton. 1616/112
Jn., Wilden, lab. 1585/9
Jn., Leagrave, yeo. 1684/34
Jn., Dean, clerk 1689/2
Jn., Stotfold, tailor. 1692/59
Jn., Podington, Hinwick, lab. 1700/114
Jn., Stotfold, shepherd. 1727/21
Jn., Woburn, gent. 1784/44
Jn., sen., Toddington, millwright. 1834/20
Jos., Luton, miller. A 1845/2
Jos., sen., Houghton Regis, miller, baker & farmer. 1847/7
Jos., sen., Houghton Regis, miller. 1857/3
Luce, Bedford St. Paul, wid. 1618/129
Margt., Tempsford, wid. 1616/75
Mary, Sandy, wid. 1813/43
Mich., Stotfold, shepherd. A 1716/30
Moses, Haynes, victualler. 1824/18
Nich., Husborne Crawley, carpenter. 1763/18
Phoebe, Leagrave, wid. 1732/27
Ric., Cranfield, dairyman. 1661/308
Ric., Luton, Biscot, husb. 1729/77
Robt., Dunton. 1607/80
Robt., Nether Dean, lab. 1641/140
Sarah, Cople, wid. A 1855/9
Simon, Biscot, yeo. 1659/294
Susan, Stotfold. 1631/146
Thos., Stotfold, miller. 1611-12/136
Thos., Biscot, yeo. 1651/7
Thos., Dean, husb. 1651/11

FREEMAN continued
Thos., Limbury. AR 1674: 1/148
Thos., Stotfold, grocer. 1678-9/119
Thos., Luton, Lewsey, yeo. 1717-8/83
alias Thompson, Wm., Eaton Socon, lab. 1561/181
Wm., Stotfold, miller. 1586/133
Wm. 1593/35
Wm., Stotfold, gent. 1680-1/110
Wm., Wootton. 1620/128
Wm., Ampthill, surgeon & physician. 1707/50
Wm., Sandy, gardener. A 1713/25
Wm., Sandy, carpenter. 1779/23
Wm., Luton, P/IX2. A 1812/10
Wm., Cardington, affidavit only. A 1828
FREER, Eliz.,Pertenhall, wid. 1812/15
Geo., Pertenhall, farmer. 1797/34
Jn., sen., Salford. R 1540: 6/40
FREESTONE, FRYSTONE, Thos., Toddington, chaplain. R 1505: 1/49d
FREETH, see Frith
FRENCH, David, Podington, P/IX2. A 1812/9
Eliz., Eversholt, wid. 1812/43
Fred., Podington, Hinwick, gent. 1830/19
Hannah, Hinwick, spins. 1719/19
Jane, Dunstable, spins. 1743/77
Jn., Salford, bricklayer. 1690/13
Julian, Stoke Poges, Bucks., wid. R 1558: 15/1
Lucy, Podington, Hinwick, wid. 1825/1
Robt., Maulden, bricklayer. A 1808/9
Wm., Eversholt, farmer. A 1781/11
Wm., Eversholt, bach. A 1815/16
Wm., Maulden, yeo. 1856/22
see also Franch
FRESHWATER, Hannah, Thurleigh, wid. 1817/11
Jn., Gt. Barford, carpenter. 1737-8/53
Jn., Gt. Barford, carpenter. A 1742/11
Jn., Blunham, Chalton, yeo. A 1822/6
Jn., Gt. Barford, baker. 1835/42
Jn., Gt. Barford, carpenter. 1849/19
Mary, Bedford St. Mary, spins. 1852/40
Paul, Roxton, farmer. 1775/22
Robt., Wootton Pillinge, lab. 1663/67
Robt., Little Staughton, carpenter. A 1743/23
Robt., Eaton Socon, Eaton Ford, carpenter. 1767/35
Sam., Bedford St. Paul, builder. 1856/35
Thos., Gt. Barford, late farmer. 1833/47

FRESHWATER continued
Wm., Gt. Barford, farmer. 1780/40
Wm., Gt. Barford, farmer. 1797/42
FREY, Thos., Lidlington. R 1550-1: 12/145d
see also Fraye
FRINT, Fra., Oakley. 1662/126
FRISBY, Jn., Potton. R 1530: 3/36
Law., Pavenham. 1607/93
FRITH, FREYTH, FREETH, FRYTH, Jn., Luton, linen draper. 1769/45
Jn., Luton, ironmonger. 1812/47
Jos., Luton, ironmonger. 1826/51
Nich., Studham. AR 1677: 1/153d
Thos., Leighton Buzzard. 1564/2
FRITWELL, Sutton alias Fritwell see Sutton
Thos., Woburn, shoemaker. 1671/58
FROST, Edw., Podington. 1840/10
Jn., Cranfield. 1556/202
Jn., Cranfield, husb. 1557/350
Wm., Podington, farmer. 1850/47
FROUNT, FRONT, Jn., Colmworth. R 1529: 3/13d
Thos., Riseley. R 1520: 2/156d
FRUD, Anne, Eaton Socon, Nether Staploe. 1661-2/251
FRUIT, FRUYTE, Wm., Cranfield, yeo. 1649/23
Wm., Cranfield, yeo. 1658/224
FRUYTE, see Fruit
FRY, Eliz., Husborne Crawley, wid. 1738/72
Fra., Woburn, gent. A 1707/2
Jn., Woburn, apothecary. 1711/73
FRYER, Alice, Harrold, wid. 1650/117
Jane, Biggleswade. AR 1679-80: 1/110
Jn., Bedford St. Mary, barber. ?1685/38
Jn., Bolnhurst. AR 1690-1: 1/84
Thos., Willington, innholder. 1686-7/78
Thos., Willington, victualler. AR 1686-7: 1/30
FULBECK, Wm., Goldington, dairyman. AR 1685: 1/27
see also Fobeck
FULFOR, FULFAR, FULLFARRE, FULPHER, FULLFAIRE
Anne, Potton, wid. 1733/67
Jn., Barford, tailor. 1635/16
Jn., Barford, tailor. 1636/44
Jn., Gt. Barford, innholder. A 1724/9
Margt., Gt. Barford, wid. AR 1675: 1/65
Reuben, Cardington, farmer. 1793/32
Thos., Gt. Barford. AR 1690: 1/83d

FULFOR, FULFAR, FULLFARRE, FULPHER, FULLFAIRE continued
Thos., Gt. Barford, tailor. 1726/33
Wm., Potton, tailor. A 1731/47
FULLER, Abr., Harrold, lab. A 1737/30
Agnes, Chellington. R 1536: 4/69
Agnes, Cranfield. R 1545-6: 11/152d
Agnes, Barton, wid. 1572/82
Ann, Chellington, wid. 1634/128
Ann, Tempsford, wid. 1688/11
Dor., Biggleswade. BwA 1813/51
Edw., Luton, lab. 1646/68
Eliz., Houghton Regis, wid. 1628-9/29
Geo., Sandy, gent. 1703-4/21
Jas., Campton. A 1713/30
Jn., Lidlington. 1560-1/77
Jn., Eaton. 1563/104
Jn., Chellington, husb. 1593-4/30
Jn., Toddington, husb. 1610/112
Jn., Cranfield. 1620-1/1
Jn., Biggleswade, miller. AR 1684-5: 1/123
Jn., Leighton Buzzard. Fac. A 1741: 9/68, 86
Jn., Biggleswade. BwA 1813/54
Jn., Wilden, farmer. 1852/11
Ric., Temspford, lab. A 1705/59
Roger, Eaton Bray. R 1558: 14/93
Thos., Toddington, husb. 1573/118
Thos., Toddington. 1620/63
Thos., Houghton Conquest. 1647-8/6
Thos., Arlesey. 1667/41
Thos., Wymington, carpenter. 1685-6/100
Thos., Wilshamstead, yeo. 1703/64
Thos., Leighton Buzzard, hempdresser. 1749-50/57
Thos., Harrold, cooper. 1771/58
Thos., Tempsford, lab. A 1705/60
Wm., Cranfield. R 1518: 1/128
Wm., Chellington. R 1535: 4/23d
Wm., Arlesey, husb. 1621-2/132
Wm., Wilden, yeo. 1830/46
FULLFARRE, see Fulfor
FULLWOOD, Geo., Henlow, butcher. 1780/15
FULPHER, see Fulfor
FUNDE, Jn., Willington, husb. R 1578: 19/57
FURMAN, see Firman
FURMARY, Wm., Leighton Buzzard, innholder. 1747/23
FURMASON, alias Clarke, Wm., Harlington, husb. 1614/64

FURNESS, Harriet, Bedford, spins. 1838/47
Jn., Dunstable, innholder. 1760/18
Mary, Wilshamstead, spins. A 1736/1
Ric., Wilshamstead, carpenter. A 1737/24
Ric., Dunstable, yeo. A 1810/24
FURNIVAL, Jas., Bedford, yeo. A 1798/3
Thos., Bedford. Sergt. Maj. in Beds. militia. A 1800/5
FURR, Ben., Clifton, yeo. 1843/42
Ralph, Aspley Guise, farmer. A 1749/5
FURTHOWE, Robt., Potton. R 1518: 1/129
see also Firth
FURZE, Eliz., Lidlington, wid. 1836/19
Jn., Lidlington, victualler. 1814/7
Jn., Bedford, schoolmaster. 1847/4
FYCHE, see Fish
FYNALL, FINALL, Jane, Steppingley, wid. 1675-6/80
Sandar?, Kempston. 1557/316
Wm., Kempston. R 1534: 4/15d
Wm., jun., Marston. 1660/165
FYNSON, see Vincent
FYTZ, see Fitz

G

GABRIEL, Ric., Kempston, lab. 1690/12
GADBURY, Margt., Eyeworth, wid. 1630-1/122
Ric., Eyeworth, gent. 1624/55
Ric., sen., Totternhoe, ploughwright. 1684/29
Ric., sen., Eaton Bray, Totternhoe, yeo. 1709/30
Ric., Dunstable, husb. 1742/28
GADLINGSTOCK, Hen., Dunstable, maltster. 1664/43
Hester, Dunstable, wid. 1677/37
GADSBY, Thos., Shelton. 1766/64
GADSDEN, Eliz., Eaton Bray. 1825/26
Geoff., Eaton Bray, baker. 1809/25
Geoff., Eaton Bray, yeo. 1826/38
Jn., Eaton Bray, yeo. A 1826/19
Ric., sen., Eaton Bray, dairyman & farmer. 1810/18
GAILING, Jn., Pavenham, stonecutter. A 1728/22
GALE, GAYLE, Alice, Oakley, wid. C. 1558/277
Alice, Oakley, wid. (bundle 1566-[?9]). 1558/2
Ann, Bedford, wid. (bundle 1656). 1658/155
Barth., Silsoe, Wrest. 1684/51

GALE, GAYLE continued
Edm., Oakley, yeo. 1638/47
Edw., Stevington, husb. 1593/23
Edw., Northill, Ickwell. 1625-6/138
Edw., Oakley, gent. 1680-1/92
Edw., Woburn, yeo. 1687/46
Eliz., Ampthill, wid. 1814/28
Eve., Toddington, wid. & draper. A 1765/6
Hen., Little Staughton, clerk. 1639/63
Joan, Oakley, wid. R 1544-5: 11/63
Jn., Oakley. R 1540: 6/47
Jn., Oakley. R 1544-5: 11/61
Jn., Goldington, husb. 1574/36
Jn., Tempsford, collarmaker. 1576-7/15
Jn., sen., Thurleigh, husb. 1589/133
Jn., Oakley. 1616/53
Jn., Goldington. 1648/136
Jn., jun., Bedford St. Paul, tailor. 1651/44
Jn., Clapham. AR 1676-7: 1/40d
Jn., Cardington, grocer. 1683/34
Jn., Wilshamstead, yeo. 1685-6/120
Jn., Thurleigh. 1687/58
Jn., Clapham, husb. A 1720/40
Jn., Thurleigh. 1818/40, I 4/227
Jos., Colmworth, yeo. 1754/8
Kath., Oakley, wid. 1617/269
Marg., Bedford St. Mary, wid. 1650/89
Mary, Elstow, wid. 1632/77
Matthew, Milton Ernest, lab. 1616/60
Oliver, Oakley, lab. 1629/100
Ric., Stevington. AR 1678: 1/41d
Ric., Bedford, carrier. A 1706/38
Robt., Goldington, husb. 1563/105
Robt., Oakley, yeo. 1619-20/240, I 4/50
Robt., Goldington. 1639/25
Robt., Goldington, Newnham. 1667/14
Robt., Wootton, farmer. AR 1683: 1/23
Robt., Oakley, gent. A 1723-4/41
Simon, Oakley, yeo. 1655-6/205
Simon, Oakley, clerk. 1712/88
Simon, Oakley, farmer. A 1754/19
Symon, Oakley. 1557/399
Thos., Thurleigh. R 1544-5: 11/48
Thos., Roxton. R 1546: 11/182
Thos., Tempsford. 1573-4/144

GALE, GAYLE continued
Thos., Kempston, husb. 1615/203
Thos., Riseley. 1616/110
Thos., Clapham, lab. 1634/101
Thos., Houghton Conquest, yeo. 1652/81
Thos., Thurleigh, Cross End, dairyman. 1660-1/69
Thos., Goldington, Putnoe, yeo. 1665/68
Thos., Clapham, farmer. A 1725/22
Thos., Toddington, draper. A 1762/11
Thos., Ampthill, brazier. 1793/29
Wm., Goldington, husb. 1584/182
see also Gall, Gell, Jeyles
GALL, Edw., Cranfield, husb. 1602/26
see also Gale, Gell
GALLAWAY, Edm., Great Staughton, Perry, Hunts. R 1526: 2/59
GALLIGAN, Nich., Cople. 1616/104, I
GAMBLE, Constance, Pulloxhill, wid. 1612/48
Geo., Flitton, gent. 1647/67
Jn., Pulloxhill, yeo. 1599/177
Jn., Lt. Barford, clerk. 1764/4
Oliv., Flitton, yeo. 1639/1
Ric., Pulloxhill, yeo. 1581/38
Ric., Pulloxhill, yeo. 1649/77
Thos., Pulloxhill, gent. 1692/32
Thos., Clifton, cordwainer. 1713/20
Wm., Pulloxhill, yeo. 1601-2/139
GAMBY, Jn., Southill, dissenting minister. 1802/28
Jn., Barton, blacksmith. 1821/22
GAMMAN, Wm., Riseley. R 1509: 1/59
GANFORD, Wm., Bromham. AR 1675: 1/39
GANTT, Robt., Bedford St. Peter. 1557/376
GARDEN, Jas., sojourner at Biddenham. 1727-8/99
GARDINER, GARDNER, Alice, Stagsden, wid. 1663-4/108
Annise, Stagsden. 1558/19
Christ., Oakley, yeo. 1607/81
Eliz., Leighton Buzzard, wid. LB 1761/42
Eliz., Biggleswade, wid. Bw 1820/121
Jn., Felmersham. R 1513: 1/223d
Jn., Colmworth. R 1529-30: 3/23d
Jn., Dean. R 1544: 11/45d
Jn., Stevington. 1554/152
Jn., Stagsden. R 1558: 11/71d
Jn., Stagsden, husb. 1582/112
Jn., jun., Kempston, lab. 1682/25
Mary, Shillington, Stondon, wid. 1639/15

GARDINER, GARDNER continued
Mary, Maulden, wid. 1681/86
Matt., Blunham. I 1587: 4/171
Phillip, Biscot, yeo. (bundle 1630-1). 1628/75
Ric., Leighton Buzzard. LBA 1793/44
Robt., sen., Blunham, husb. 1614-15/21
Robt., Northill, Ickwell, lab. 1676/145
Robt., Sandy, yeo. 1731/81
Thos., Ampthill. R 1544: 11/19
Thos., Kempston, lab. 1663/50
Thos., Tempsford, farmer. A 1733/24
Wm., Great Gravenhurst, priest & curate. 1558/285
Wm., Kempston, yeo. 1626/11
GARLAND, Edw., Woburn. R 1560: 15/126d
Jn., Woburn, gent. 1576/45
GARNER, Edm., Sandy, Beeston, yeo. 1670/200
Edm., Biggleswade, gardener. Bw 1830/139
Eliz., Wootton, wid. 1712-13/25
Geo., Barton, bach. & lab. 1758/14
Hen., sen., Stagsden, husb. 1651/33
Jas., Shillington. A 1855/20
Jn., Stagsden, lab. 1637-8/176
Jn., sen., Kempston Hardwick, victualler. 1740/57
Jn., sen., Old Warden, farmer. 1749/20
Jn., sen., Old Warden, farmer. 1787/37
Jn., Kempston, shepherd. A 1721/21
Jn., Kempston, victualler. A 1759/22
Jn., Bedford St. Paul, victualler. A 1805/6
Jn., Warden, woodman. A 1844/6
Lawr., Lidlington. 1755/12
Mary, Warden, wid. & farmer. 1751/49
Mary, Kempston Hardwick, wid. 1774/44
Ric., Leagrave. A 1712/18
Robt., Leagrave, yeo. 1739/48
Wm., Stagsden, husb. 1654/117B
Wm., Wootton, dairyman. 1718-19/66
Wm., Clophill. A 1829/14
Wm., Warden, carpenter. A 1844/5
GARNET, Alice, Eaton Socon, Wyboston, wid. 1706/3
Jn., Eaton Socon, yeo. A 1705/31
Rice, Leighton Buzzard, innholder. 1608-9/4
Wm., Dunstable, late of Southwark, St. John, baker. 1754/22
see also Jarnet

GARRETT, JERRAT, Agnes, Bedford St. Mary. 1557/381
Ann, Nether Dean. 1685/20a
Billing, Cardington, farmer. A 1744/14
Eliz., Cardington, Cotton End, wid. 1682/67
Geo., Luton, shepherd. AR 1683-4: 1/166
Geo., Henlow, miller. A 1741/18
Hester, Flitwick, wid. 1702/71
Jas., Wilshamstead, yeo. 1787/44
Jn., Bedford. 1559/188
Jn., Oakley, lab. 1627/229
Jn., Nether Dean. AR 1685: 1/79
Jn., Nether Dean. 1685/20
Jn., Eyeworth, yeo. 1777/14
Jn., Roxton, yeo. 1798/29
Jn., Blunham, blacksmith. 1803/22
Jos., Wilshamstead, yeo. 1796/21
Judith, Shillington, wid. 1726/65
Ric., Cardington. 1723/10
Robt., Cardington, Somerfield, dairyman. 1697-8/64
Seth., Willington. 1732/1
Thos., Henlow, stringer. 1556/120
Thos., Luton, Bramblehanger, lab. 1634/99
Thos., Flitwick, yeo. 1695/27
Thos., Cardington, yeo. 1815/33
Wm., Westoning, husb. 1592-3/1
Wm., Cardington, Cotton End. 1659/154
Wm., Ampthill, mercer. 1664/57
Wm., Cardington, apothecary. 1752/7
Wm., Bedford. 1827/13
see also Gerrard
GARSIDE, Ben., Leighton Buzzard, victualler. LB 1846/90
GARY, see Gery
GASCOIGNE, Dorothy, Bedford, wid. 1717/77
Geo., Bedford, victualler. 1715/31
Hen., Clophill, singleman. 1728/309
Jn., Bedford St. Mary, miller. 1612/86
Jn., Ampthill. A 1856/8
Jonathan, Stevington, yeo. 1740/5
Mary, Stevington, wid. A 1746/31
Pearce, Northill. AR 1679-80: 1/110
Ric., Little Staughton, yeo. 1633/164
Robt., sen., Bedford, miller. 1640/81
alias Gaskin, Thos., Bromham, yeo. 1762/59
Wm., Bedford St. John, bricklayer. 1799/42
see also Gaskin

GAZELEY continued
Sarah, Dunstable, spins. 1701/3
Thos., Whipsnade, husb. 1688/55
Thos., Shillington, Lower Stondon, farmer. 1848/1
see also Gastley
GEALING, Wm., Pavenham, stonemason. 1813/19
GEARY, see Gery
GEDDING, Jn., Wootton. R 1505: 1/101d
Jn., Bedford. R 1546: 11/188
Ric., Bedford St. Peter Merton. R 1546-7: 11/232
Thos., Bedford St. Peter. 1557/321
Wm., Odell. R 1539: 5/39
GEDGELL, Edw., Beeston, Sandy, yeo. 1630-1/108
Thos., Campton. 1638-9/81
see also Jiggles, see also Jegell
GEE, Agnes, Bedford St. Paul. 1569-70/111
Chas., Eaton Socon. 1741/41
Eliz., Eaton Socon, Crosshall, wid. 1764/58
Eliz., Wilshamstead. 1797/24
Geo., Flitton, Warhedges, husb. 1613/174
Geo., Flitwick. 1635-6/56
Jn., Meppershall. 1567/18
Mich., Silsoe, lab. 1638-9/92
Nath., Silsoe. A 1832/10
Robt., Barford. 1629/112
Wm., Steppingley, husb. 1624/92
Wm., sen., Steppingley, yeo. 1667/68
Wm., jun., Steppingley, husb. 1669-70/101
see also Guy
GEFFORD, see Gifford
GELIEN, Math., Woburn. A 1753/17
see also Julian, see also Gillian
GELL, Alice, Sharnbrook. A 1827/3
Hen., Yielden. 1555/114
Jn., Yielden, yeo. 1634-5/135
Jn., sen., Yielden, lab. 1669/67
Jn., Yielden, yeo. 1673/62
Jn., Yielden. AR 1688: 1/81d
Jn., Yielden, farmer. A 1721/57
Jn., Riseley, late of Sharnbrook, farmer. 1838/11
Judith, Riseley, wid. 1714/111
Lawr., Thurleigh, yeo. A 1823/4
Lucy, Bedford, spins. 1855/22
Margt., Tilbrook, wid. 1639/93
Ric., Yielden. 1557/288

GELL continued
Ric., Kempston, yeo. 1617/304
Ric., Yielden, maltster. 1731/59
Ric., Bedford, grocer and tallow chandler. 1738-9/33
Ric., Tempsford, farmer. 1839/17
Ric., Bedford St. Mary, baker. A 1853/9
Ric., Sharnbrook, farmer. A 1856/1
Thos., sen., Yielden, husb. 1593/62
Thos., Yielden. 1606/68
Thos., Yielden. 1609-10/121
Thos., Riseley, lab. 1616/145
Thos., Yielden, husb. 1652/59
Thos., Yielden. 1700/91
Thos., Riseley, lab. 1725/70
Thos., Thurleigh, farmer. 1729-30/103
Thos., Thurleigh, farmer. A 1734/33
Thos., sen., Tempsford, yeo. 1814/39
Wm., Shelton, yeo. 1662/14
Wm., Riseley, wid. 1701-2/69
see also Gale; Gall
GELLIS, see Jellis
GENEWAY, Wm., Gransden, Cambs., late Wrestlingworth, yeo. 1683/72
GENNINGS, see Jennings
GENTLE, Luce, Wilden, wid. 1665/65
GEOFFREY, GEFFROYE, Jn., Odell. 1554/183
see also Jeffrey
GEORGE, GORDGE, GORGE, Ann, Leighton Buzzard, wid. LB 1763/46
Ann, Keysoe. 1847/13
Cuthbert, Eaton Bray, husb. 1626/56
Edw., Tempsford, innholder. 1820/44
Eliz., Riseley, wid. 1807/36
Hen., Eaton Bray. R 1547: 11/238
Jas., Kempston, farmer. 1848/11
Jn., Eaton, lab. 1563/89
Jn., Eaton. 1598-9/88
Jn., Luton, husb. 1640/46
Jn., sen., Eaton Bray, yeo. 1660/216
Jn., Eaton Bray, yeo. 1685-6/91
Jn., Eyeworth, yeo. 1707/44
Jn., Leighton Buzzard, innholder. 1750/40
Jn., Wyboston. (P/IX2 admon missing). A 1783/11
Martin, Bedford St. Paul, yeo. A 1798/8
Martin, Keysoe Row, yeo. 1819/21
Mary, Eaton Bray, wid. 1676-7/169
Matt., Tempsford, victualler. 1771/42

GEORGE, GORDGE, GORGE continued
Robt., Eaton Socon, Wyboston. A 1786/4
Robt., Bedford, tailor. 1790/11
Robt., Bedford St. Paul, farmer. A 1818/9
Simon, Riseley, farmer. 1801/18
Thos., Eaton. 1562/102
Thos., Eyeworth, yeo. A 1725/13
Thos., Keysoe, farmer. 1838/38
Wm., Wrestlingworth, farmer. A 1774/7
GERALD, GERROLE, Ric., Eversholt, turner. 1616/62
GERMAIN, Geo., Studham (old index only, admon missing). A 1726/15
GERMAN, Agnes, Leighton Buzzard, wid. LBR 1540: 1/8
Margery, Totternhoe. R 1542: 6/118d
Ric., Potton. 1557/388
see also Jarman, Jermyn
GERRARD, Jn., Bedford. 1559/188
see also Garrett
GERROLE, see Gerald
GERY, GEARY, GEREY, GERE, Agnes, Wymington, wid. 1615-16/135
Agnes, Turvey, wid. 1711-12/94
Eleanor, Bushmead Priory, wid. 1796/10
Eliz., Sharnbrook, wid. 1592/66
Hen., Houghton Regis, Puddle Hill, shepherd. 1750/64
Jn., Sharnbrook. R 1529: 3/13d
Jn., Sharnbrook. 1553/284
Jn., sen., Sharnbrook, yeo. 1629/8
Jn., Milton Ernest. AR 1672: 1/36d
Jn., Milton Ernest, yeo. 1672/98
Jn., sen., Caddington, Chaul End, yeo. 1734/45
Jn., Ridgmont, yeo. 1835/3
Jn., Eaton Socon, farmer. A 1743/43
Lawr., jun., Sharnbrook. 1568/48
Lawr., Milton Ernest, yeo. 1661-2/270
Mary, Milton Ernest, spins. 1668/172
Math., Turvey. AR 1691: 1/51
Ric., Potton. 1603/126
Ric., Bushmead. 1638
Thos., Sharnbrook. R 1538: 5/21
Thos., Sharnbrook, lab. 1613-14/144
Thos., Eversholt, yro. 1705/95
Thos., Bedford St. Paul, combmaker. A 1714-15/40
Thos., Eaton Socon, Wade, Bushmead. A 1829/6
Wm., sen., Sharnbrook. R 1499: 1/134
Wm., Sharnbrook. R 1519-20: 2/149
Wm., Sharnbrook, husb. 1561/144

GERY, GEARY, GEREY, GERE continued
Wm., Sharnbrook, husb. 1600/51
Wm., Potton, yeo. 1601/94
Wm., Sharnbrook, yeo. 1639/64
Wm., (no parish given). 1689/30
GEVE, see Jeeve
GIAT, Hen., Bromham, yeo. 1587-9/119
GIBBARD, Ann, Sharnbrook, wid. 1806/20
Robt., Toddington, innholder. 1823/17
GIBBONS, GIBBINS, Bailey alias Gibbons, see under Bailey
Jas., Warden. 1669/47
Jn., Tempsford, glover. 1670/210
Mary, Sundon, late Toddington, Chalton, wid. 1830/31
Robt., Milton Ernest, farmer. 1815/23
Sarah, Pulloxhill, wid. 1840/27
Thos., sen., Tingrith, yeo. 1804/5
Thos., Pulloxhill, yeo. 1814/33
GIBBS, Cook alias Gibbs, see Cook
Edw., Eversholt, yeo. 1611-12/139
Edw., Eversholt, Froxfield. 1633/134
Edw., Milton Bryan. 1728/81
Edw., Milton Bryan, yeo. A 1743/10
Edw., Luton, farmer. A 1751/7
Eliz., Eversholt, Froxfield, wid. 1626-7/27
Geo., Milton Bryan, yeo. A 1725/28
Jn., Eversholt. 1558/273
Jn., Eversholt, yeo. 1598/178
Jn., Eversholt, yeo. (bundle 1600). 1598/108
Jn., Tempsford, shepherd. 1609/156
Jn., Eggington, lab. 1742/39
Mary, Milton Bryan, wid. A 1754/23
Ric., Lidlington. AR 1683-4: 1/210
Sam., Bedford. 1661/338
Thos., sen., Bedford, cooper. 1602/16
Thos., Bedford, gent. 1661-2/243
GIBSON, GEBSON, Ann, Kempston, wid. 1776/18
Hen., Ridgmont, yeo. 1663-4/88
Hen., Ridgmont, husb. 1676/101
Jane, Bedford St. Peter, wid. R 1530-1: 3/38
Jn., Westoning, lab. 1616/93
Jn., Kempston, blacksmith. 1751/29
Marg., Husborne Crawley, wid. 1557/367
Mich., citizen and merchant taylor of London (to be buried in the churchyard of Eversholt). 1615-16/130
Robt., Westoning, yeo. 1660/91

GIBSON, GEBSON continued
Thos., Kempston, blacksmith. 1693/145
Thos., Kempston, blacksmith. 1776/2
GIDDENS, see Giddings
GIDDINGS, Cath., Clapham. 1625/124
Eliz., Clapham, spins. 1630-1/112
Fra., Blunham, husb. 1637/92
Gabriel, Silsoe, wheelwright. 1677/5
Geo., Dunstable, plumber and glazier. 1847/32
Harriett, Dunstable. A 1853/16
Joan, Henlow, wid. 1618/117
Jn., Odell, lab. 1578/102
Jn., Clapham, husb. 1620/125
Jn., Henlow, wheelwright. 1641-2/205
Jn., Clifton, wheelwright. 1762/40
Jn., Bedford, bricklayer. A 1712/15
Jn., Streatley. A 1731-2/22
Mary, Shefford, spins. 1719/56
Mary, Eaton Socon, wid. of Thos. 1786/11
Mary, Silsoe, wid. AR 1677: 1/197d
Mich., Clapham, husb. 1615/225
Oliver, Turvey. 1593/42
Ric., Flitton. 1674/80
Roger, Turvey. 1600-1/76
Thos., Sandy, yeo. 1658-9/220
Thos., Silsoe, wheelwright. 1677/30
Thos., Silsoe, wheelwright. AR 1677: 1/197d
Thos., Silsoe, wheelwright. 1718-19/59
Thos., Silsoe, wheelwright. 1762/31
Thos., Eaton Socon, yeo. A 1782/11
Wm., Keysoe, husb. 1630-1/104
Wm., Shefford, grocer. 1721-2/72
Wm., Barton, shepherd. 1729/31
Wm., Shillington. A 1770/1
Wm., Silsoe, wheelwright. 1830/5
Wm., Dunstable, plumber and glazier. 1844/46
Wm., Eaton Socon, Duloe, victualler A 1842/14
GIFFORD, Frances, Bedford St. Paul, wid. 1615-16/125
Jn., Luton, tailor. 1607-8/165
Jn., Bedford. 1655/165
Jn., Bedford. 1656/26
Sam., Cardington, yeo. 1802/22
Sam., Bedford. 1827/11
GIGGELL, Jn., Meppershall. I 1619: 4/147
GILBEE, see Gilby

GILBERT, Ben., Meppershall, blacksmith. 1766/60
Edith, Pavenham. 1607/85
Geo., Ampthill. R 1524:2/18d
Jas. Eames, Cardington, Cotton End, poulterer. 1856/37
Jn., Stagsden. 1623/105
Jn., Gt. Barford, tailor. 1788/38
Jn., Potton, yeo. 1809/30, I 4/214
Jn. Franklin, Wilshamstead, wid. 1855/37
Jos., Potton, maltster. A 1740/17
Jos., Potton. A 1837/12
Mary, Pavenham, spins. AR 1686-7: 1/48
Mary, Leighton Buzzard, wid. LBA 1819/75
Rachel, Pertenhall, wid. 1713/43
Ric., Pavenham, husb. 1669-70/114
Ric., Pavenham, yeo. 1696/88
Ric., Pavenham, yeo. A 1704-5/33
Ric., Pavenham, victualler. A 1742-3/41
Thos., Luton, innholder. 1666/115
Thos., sen., Pavenham, yeo. 1673/35
Thos., (old index "docket mislaid"). A 1709/16
Thos., (no parish given). 1713-14/59
Thos., Keysoe, yeo. A 1719-20/34
Thos., Wilden, bach. 1752/13
Wm., Pavenham, husb. 1617/244
Wm., Pavenham, yeo. 1656-7/194
Wm., Dunstable, vict. 1745/30
Wm., Leighton Buzzard, miller. LB 1817/67
see also Gilbord
GILBORD, GILBORE, Thos., Blunham. 1708/58
see also Gilbert
GILBY, Edw., Tingrith. 1552/309
Robt., Hockliffe, shopkeeper. 1732/10
GILES, GYLLS, Agnes, Bletsoe, spins. 1638/30
Eliz., Ravensden, wid. 1798/31
Isaac, Kempston, tailor. 1665/77
Jas., Henlow, husb. 1692/10
Jn., Bletsoe, yeo. 1671-2/22
Jn., Wilden, yeo. A 1781/7
Mary, Oakley, wid. A 1711/55
Wm., Heath. R 1567: 17/11
GILGRIST, Thos., Leighton Buzzard. 1607/126
GILHAM, see Gillham
GILL, GILLES, GYLL, GYLLS, Alvery, Woburn, yeo. 1684/85
Jn., Wootton. R 1516-17: 1/213
Jn., Luton. R 1540: 5/53d, 8/5

GILL, GILLES, GYLL, GYLLS continued
Jn., sen., Kempston. 1572/90
Jn., Odell, husb. 1610-11/44
Jn., Bedford St. John, carp. 1623/201
Jn., Gt. Barford, lab. 1646/105
Jn., Goldington. 1661/417
Jn., Gt. Barford, lab. 1698/84
Lawr., Barford, lab. 1612/111
Sophia, Dunstable, spins. 1836/49
Thos., Kempston. 1555/100
Wm., Wilshamstead, lab. 1623/200
Wm., Gt. Barford, collarmaker. 1660-1/102
Wm., Gt. Barford. A 1700-1/28
Wm., Sandy, Girtford, yeo. 1736-7/37
Wm., Sandy, Girtford, yeo. 1783/25
GILLIAN, see Gelian, see also Julian
GILLAM, see Gillham
GILLETT, GILLAT, GILLET, Edm., Eaton Socon, Staploe. R 1545: 11/113
Geo., Cranfield, husb. 1689/47
Jn., Eaton Socon, Nether Staploe, lab. AR 1670: 1/60
Thos., Eaton Socon, Nether Staploe. 1617/285
GILLHAM, GILHAM, GILLAM, Burdu(v)s alias Gillam, see Burduvs
Grubbe alias Gillam, see Grubbe
Ann, Luton, wid. 1663/45
Jn., Luton, blacksmith. 1723/40
Ric., Eaton Socon, Honeydon. 1679/74
Susannah, Bedford, spins. 1832/31
Wm., sen., Luton, brazier. 1658/213
Wm., Luton, locksmith. 1693/157
GILLIONS, GYLIUNS, Christian, Northill. R 1508: 1/196
GILLMAN, GYLMYN, Ambrose, Milton Ernest, yeo. 1622/38
Ann, Wilden, wid. 1703-4/69
Barth., Sutton, yeo. 1617/332
David, Potton. 1562/112
Eliz., Milton Ernest, wid. 1599/74
Eliz., Hockliffe, wid. 1855/45
Joan, Southill, wid. 1647/27
Mich., sen., Hockliffe, gent. 1844/9
Robt., Southill, bach. 1647/26
Thos., Milton Ernest. R 1506: 1/82
Thos., Sutton. 1572-3/77
Thos., Milton Ernest. 1603/124
Thos., Flitwick, Denil End, lab. 1750/12
Wm., Milton Ernest, husb. 1587/162
Wm., Thurleigh. 1610/62

GILLMAN, GYLMYN continued
Wm., Southill, warrener. 1661/334
Wm., Thurleigh. 1690/58
Wm., Southill, lab. A 1723/2
Wm., Southill. A 1725/2
Wm., Flitton. A 1826/13
GILLNIS, Jn., Maulden. R 1691-2: 1/220
GILNEY, Nich., Southill, lab. 1627-8/222
Thos., Southill, husb. 1609-10/129
GILPIN, Esther, Chalgrave, wid. A 1735-6/15
Jn., Carlton, yeo. A 1794/2
Math., Hockliffe, innholder. 1734/2
Robt., Hockliffe, bachelor in divinity. 1641-2/189
Robt., Hockliffe, gent. 1716/28
GILSON, GYLSON, Robt., Potton, husb. 1555/135
GIMBIRDE, Ric., Wilden, servant. 1620/118
GININGS, see Jennings
GINN, Jemima, Keysoe, wid. 1826/8
Jn., Bedford, staymaker. A 1756/21
Thos., Marston, lab. 1741/27
Thos., Wootton, cordwainer. A 1767/13
GINNINGS, Thos., Wootton. AR 1691: 1/34
GIPS, see Jeps
GIRDIER, Wm., Sandy. 1570/3
GIRTON, Alice, Cranfield, wid. 1704/41
Jn., sen., Cranfield, yeo. 1631/147
Jn., sen., Cranfield, yeo. 1687/37
Jn., Cranfield, yeo. A 1701/1
Nich., Cranfield, glover. 1614/57
Thos., Biggleswade, Holme, bach. AR 1684: 1/122
GISTE, see Guest
GLADMAN, alias Green, Adam, Studham, butcher. 1765/17
alias Green, Eliz., Toddington, wid. 1736/17
Jn., Toddington, husb. 1749/17
alias Green, Sarah, Studham, wid. 1768/42
Thos., Studham, butcher. 1672/155
Thos., Studham, butcher. 1720/124
Thos., Toddington, husb. A 1720/51
GLADWIN, GLADWEN, Robt., Leighton Buzzard. 1585/145
GLANFIELD, alias Neville, Ric., Baldock, Herts., yeo. 1623-4/135
GLASBROOKE, Nich., Stotfold. 1630-1/126
GLASCOCKE, Andrew, Bromham, gent. 1657/66
Margt., Bromham, wid. 1657/67
GLEN, John, Eaton Socon, Wyboston, husb. 1561/122

GLENISTER, Edw., Luton, shopkeeper and lab. 1802/29
Jn., Southill, East End, yeo. 1657-8/7
Wm., son of Wm., Stotfold, yeo. 1676/157
Wm., Shillington, Nether Stondon, yeo. 1690/28
GLIDEWELL, Jn., Cranfield, fuller. 1640/17
Wm., Eaton Bray, husb. 1787/8
GLINISTER, see Glenister
GLOUCESTER, Workman alias Gloucester, see Workman
GLOVER, Smith alias Glover, see Smith
Agnes, Dunstable, wid. 1623-4/199
Ed., Bedford St. Cuthbert. I 1619-20: 4/16
Eliz., Dunstable, wid. 1621/194
Eliz., Odell, wid. 1673/53
Faith, Eversholt, wid. 1713/55
Gertrude, Bletsoe, spins. 1625-6/131
Jn., Wilshamstead, husb. 1660/205
Jn., Sandy. AR 1675: 1/104d
Mary, Markyate Street, wid. 1764/53
Ric., Maulden, lab. 1612/47
Ric., Thurleigh, yeo. 1659/271
Robt., Bromham, husb. 1579/173
Thos., Clophill, farmer. AR 1682: 1/207d
Thos., Pertenhall. 1719-20/90
Thos., Sandy, Girtford, yeo. 1729-30/115
Thos., Wilshamstead, lab. 1838/39
Tobias, Eversholt, tanner. 1681/70
Wm., Husborne Crawley. 1610/128
Wm., sen., Studham, innholder. 1692/43
Wm., Markyate Street, yeo. 1755/29
GLYN, alias Linnis, Jn., Maulden, grocer. 1743/27
GOARE, see Gore
GOBBEY, GOBEY, Robt., Lidlington, carpenter. 1771/50
GOBBY, Eliz., Leagrave, wid. A 1805/10
GODDARD, Belinda, Goldington, wid. A 1843/2
Edith, Carlton. c1670/203
Eliz., Elstow, wid. A 1729-30/62
Geo., Renhold, blacksmith. 1736-7/36
Geo., Goldington, blacksmith. 1795/26
Jn., Elstow, blacksmith. A 1725/10
Math., Little Staughton, yeo. 1738/45
Robt., Goldington, blacksmith. A 1762/20
Thos., Little Staughton, lab. A 1729/25
Vincent, Carlton, gent. 1698/154
Wm., Goldington, blacksmith. 1843/7

GODFREY, alias Cooper, Agnes, Bedford St. Paul. 1600-1/24
Ambrose, Kempston, dairyman. 1771/59
Ann, Silsoe, wid. 1664/58
Eliz., Silsoe, wid. 1707/12
Geo., Ridgmont, Segenhoe, "Norwoode". 1577/73
Geo., Westoning, innholder. 1675-6/77
Geo., Toddington, yeo. 1805/21
Hen., Totternhoe, husb. 1569/128
Hen., Silsoe, grocer. 1681-2/102
Hen., Silsoe, grocer. 1730/16
Jeremiah, Houghton Regis, Thorne, yeo. 1796/31
Jn., Houghton Regis, Sewell, yeo. 1584/183
alias Cooper, Jn., Sharnbrook, husb. 1616/66
Jn., Silsoe, yeo. 1656/40
Jn., Silsoe, yeo. 1683/82
Jn., Silsoe, grocer. A 1705/56
Jn., Harrold, gent. A 1766/13
Jn., Harrold. 1766/26
Jn., Potton, yeo. AR 1672: 1/94d
Mary, Biggleswade. A 1766/24
Oliver, Eaton Socon. AR 1681: 1/73
Rhoda, Westoning, Samshill, wid. 1787/47
alias Cooper, Robt., Stagsden, yeo. 1634-5/131
alias Cooper, Thos., Luton. 1553/272
Thos., Luton. R 1546: 11/161d
alias Cooper, Thos., Silsoe, innholder. 1674/127
Wm., Luton. R 1518: 1/112
Wm., Potsgrove, husb. 1586-7/147
Wm., Podington, lab. 1634/132
Wm., Harlington, Wood End, yeo. 1719/16
Wm., Westoning, Sampshill, dairyman. A 1781/18
Wm., Westoning, Samshill, dairyman. 1781/32
Wm., Houghton Conquest, farmer. 1809/11
Wm., Pulloxhill, yeo. 1829/6
Young, Campton. 1762/41
GODITOT, Hen., Wootton. R 1522: 1/251
see also Caldecote; Cawlcot
GODWARD, Wm., (no parish given). 1637/83
GOFF, GOUGH, Jn., Turvey, farmer. A 1758/14
Jn., sen., Harrold, yeo. A 1840/10
GOFFE, Thos., Harrold Park, farmer. 1812/32
see also Gough
GOGEUN, see Gudgin
GOLD, Wm., Bedford, priest. R 1504? 1/52

GOLDING, GOLDIN, Ann, Stagsden. 1729/53
Edw., Stagsden, lab. 1727/7
Eliz., Roxton, wid. 1776/42
Jn., Eversholt, lab. 1731/70
Jn., Roxton. A 1768/29
Mary, wid. 1846/34
Miller, Biddenham, gent. 1843/49
GOLDINGTON, Thos., Houghton Conquest. R 1518: 1/234
GOLDSMITH, GOULDSMITH, Abr., Barton. AR 1672: 1/143
Abr., Barton, yeo. 1702-3/49
Chris., Campton, yeo. 1614/231
Chris., Barton. 1641/184
Dan., Campton, clerk. 1685/87
Dan., Luton, currier. 1740/10
Edw., Bedford St. Mary. 1616/144
Edw., Flitton, Greenfield, husb. 1620/43
Eliz., Flitton, Greenfield. 1627/187
Eliz., Toddington, wid. 1685/25
Fra., Shefford, wid. 1648-9/98
Hen., sen., Eversholt. 1699/63
Jane, Barton, wid. 1703/9
Jn., Campton. 1639/73
Jn., Aspley Guise, gardener. A 1729/35
Lydia, Toddington, Chalton, wid. 1741-2/87
Matthew, Flitton, Greenfield. 1571/54
Nathan., Toddington, Chalton, gent. 1741/84
Peter, Shillington, carpenter. 1700/125
Peter, Shillington, carpenter. 1726/78
Ric., Westoning, yeo. 1637/122
Ric., Campton, yeo. 1640/14
Ric., Luton, grocer. AR 1688: 1/175d
Ric., Barton, yeo. 1707/70
Thos., Houghton Conquest, yeo. 1581/10
Thos., Shillington, carpenter. 1664/89
Thos., Toddington, Chalton, gent. 1674/174
Thos., Toddington, Chalton, gent. 1723/11
Wm., Barton, tailor. 1599/143
Wm., Barton, lab. 1615/148
Wm., Higham Gobion, Faldo. 1623/126
Wm., Shefford, tanner. 1638-9/102
Wm., Campton, clerk. 1667/12
GOLSTON, Jn., Stagsden. R 1522: 2/138
GOOD, GOODES, GOODS, Agnes, Bedford, wid., late wife of Thos. Rolittle
R 1532: 3/60d
Annes, Toddington, wid. 1588-9/85

GOOD, GOODES, GOODS continued
Ben., Ampthill, warrener and dealer in hardware. 1765/23
Ben., Toddington, innholder. 1774/21
Fra., Bedford, baker. A 1743/49
Geo., Odell, husb. (bundle 1701). A 1700/39
Jas., Carlton, blacksmith. 1849/11
Jn., Bedford, innholder. A 1723/17
Nich., Stotfold, shepherd (bundle 1665). 1666/100
Robt., Tilbrook. R 1538-9: 5/28d
Robt., Stotfold, carpenter. 1615/220
Robt., Ridgmont, cordwainer. 1783/44
Robt., Biggleswade, ginger bread baker. BwA 1788/37
Thos., Caddington, ("old index", bundle missing). A 1745/7
Thos., Bedford, grocer. A 1755/1
Wm., Biggleswade, gent. 1672/170
see also Goud
GOODDALL, GOODALE, Smith alias Goodall, see Smith
Alex., Whipsnade, yeo. 1651/38
Alex., sen., Markyate Street, yeo. 1722/81
Alex., Markyate Street, baker. 1763/10
Jn., Bedford, gent. 1632/100
Jn., Bedford, gent. A 1711/4
Martha, Caddington, wid. AR 1678: 1/155d
Nich., Shillington, blacksmith. 1721/38
Peter, Houghton Regis, Thorne. 1663-4/100
Ric., Bedford St. Mary. 1554/165
Ric., Upper Gravenhurst, lab. 1637/75
Robt., Bedford St. Mary, miller. 1574/45
Thos., Shillington, husb. 1625/28
Thos., Shillington, blacksmith. 1665/43
Wm., Houghton Conquest, blacksmith. 1650/107
Wm., Shillington, blacksmith. 1602/60
Wm., Shillington, blacksmith. 1747-8/60
Wm., Upper Gravenhurst, farmer. 1855/19
GOODCHEAP, Jn., Campton, husb. 1605/114
see also Goodship
GOODCHILD, Ann, Little Staughton. A 1713/8
Jn., Little Staughton, yeo. 1705/22
Owen, Little Staughton, yeo. 1768/10
THos., Little Staughton, husb. A 1705/63
GOODEY, see Goody
GOODFELLOW, Geo., Eaton Socon, Brickerfield, gent. 1638/73
GOODING, GOODEN, GUDINE, (torn), Flitton. 1571/76
Ann, Everton, spins. 1687/98a
Eliz., Flitton, Greenfield, wid. 1721/87

GOODING, GOODEN, GUDINE continued
Jane, Wootton, wid. A 1786/14
Nathan., Wootton, dairyman. 1776/39
Ric., Barton, husb. 1670/144
Robt., Cardington, lab. 1635/23
Robt., Lidlington, carpenter. 1689/29
Thos., Cardington, Harrowden, lab. 1626/41
Thos., Everton, bach. 1682/82
Thos., Everton. AR 1682: 1/117d
Wm., Bedford, bach. 1597-8/31
Wm., Sandy, Beeston, blacksmith. 1613-14/154
Wm., Houghton Conquest, husb. 1682-3/117
see also Goodwin
GOODLIFFE, Ann, Little Staughton, wid. 1830/13, I 4/280
Edw., Eaton Socon, Duloe, farmer. 1791/28
Eliz., Little Staughton, wid. 1844/21
Eliz., Little Staughton, wid. 1845/49
Jn., Eaton Socon. A 1738-9/10
Jos., Little Staughton, farmer. 1813/14
Mary, Eaton Socon, Upper Staploe, wid. 1766/56
Mary, Eaton Socon, Duloe, wid. 1820/47
Mich., Eaton Socon, Over Staploe, yeo. 1740/16
Wm., Eaton Socon, Duloe, yeo. 1783/29
GOODMAN, Anne, Millbrook, wid. 1714/117
Ben., Cardington, lab. 1710/48
Ben., Goldington, lab. 1713/69
Edw., Caddington, lab. 1604/43
Geo., Leighton Buzzard, Grange Mill, miller. LB 1789/84
Geo., Leighton Buzzard. LBA 1792/40
Hen., Thurleigh, lab. 1626-7/32
Hen., Lidlington, innholder and dealer in hogs. 1761/30
Hen., Cranfield, farmer. 1800/23
Jas., Biggleswade, publican. Bw 1795/94
Joanna, Salford, wid. A 1819/2
Jn., sen., Colmworth, yeo. 1612/88
Jn., Millbrook, yeo. 1712/26
Jn., Lidlington, yeo. 1741/34
Jn., Barton, farmer. 1784/25
Jn., Husborne Crawley, gent. 1802/38
Jn., Steppingley, farmer. A 1846/11
Martha, Bedford, wid. 1709/72
Mary, Lidlington, wid. 1771/55
Mary, Eversholt, Froxfield, wid. 1801/37
Mary, Flitwick, wid. A 1829/12
Mary, Steppingley, wid. A 1843/10

GOODMAN continued
Math., Clophill yeo. 1763/8
Math., Clophill, yeo. A 1817/2
Mich., Millbrook, yeo. A 1703/26
Mich., Maulden, cordwainer. 1787/15
Ric., Colmworth, yeo. 1638/76
Ric., Eaton Socon, Basmey, gent. 1660/204
Ric., Flitwick, miller. 1776/12
Ric., Flitwick, miller. 1832/46
Ric., Wymington, farmer. AR 1688: 1/49
Ric., Flitwick, yeo. A 1813/24
Ric., Flitwick, yeo. A 1845/3
Robt., Dunstable. A 1765/11
Susannah, Dunstable. A 1771/28
Thos., Holcote, yeo. 1812/25
Thos., Woburn, shoemaker. 1823/19
Thos., Bedford St. Paul. 1835/23
Thos., Salford, miller. 1836/25
Thos., Biggleswade, farmer. Bw 1791/88
Thos., Leighton Buzzard, Grange Mill, miller. LB 1836/58
Wm., Southill, Stanford. R 1598: 24/21d
Wm., Sharnbrook, lab. 1616/26
Wm., Lidlington, yeo. A 1729/41
Wm., Husborne Crawley, shopkeeper. 1796/29
Wm., Salford, miller. A 1809/17
Wm., Woburn, yeo. 1813/10
Wm., Barton, publican and timber merchant. 1840/42
Wm., Cranfield, lab. 1848/24
GOODRICH, Ric., Luton. R 1518-19: 2/122
GOODRID, Fra., Cranfield, yeo. 1773/27
Thos., Cranfield. A 1833/1
GOODSHIP, Jn., Campton. 1637/127
Sarah, Wilshamstead, wid. 1707/30
see also Goodcheap
GOODSOLE, Jas., Leighton Buzzard, hempdresser. Fac. 1719: 9/56
GOODSON, Geo., Little Staughton. 1591-2/93
Mich., Eaton Socon, Devilhoe, husb. 1612/184
Ric., (parish torn off), yeo. 1636-7/52
Thos., Eaton Socon, gent. 1648/73
Thos., Eaton Socon, Duloe. AR 1672-3: 1/63
GOODSPEED, Jn., Stanbridge, yeo. 1769/16
GOODWIN, GOODWINE, Ann, Eaton Socon, spins. 1764/51
Eliz., Houghton Conquest, wid. 1702-3/76
Jac., Souldrop, yeo. AR 1670-1: 1/36
Jacob, Souldrop. 1670-1/240

GOODWIN, GOODWINE continued
Jn., Flitton, Greenfield, yeo. I 1619: 4/83
Jn., Eaton Socon, innholder. AR 1682: 1/73d
Jn., Eaton Socon, yeo. 1708/72
Jn., Eaton Socon, gent. 1742/94
Mary, Luton, wid. 1625-6/159
Ric., Shefford, plumber. A 1744/12
Ric., Shefford, plumber and glazier. A 1767/9
Sam., Eaton Socon, Staploe. 1618/106
Sam., Tilbrook, lab. A 1725/24
Steven, West Hyde, Otebridge, husb. 1647/56
Thos., Kempston. R 1513: 1/238d
Thos., Flitton, Worthing. R 1527-8: 2/19
Thos., Flitwick, lab. 1673/39
Thos., Luton, Chiltern Green, yeo. 1695/19
Thos., Maulden, victualler. A 1732/19
Thos., Harlington, miller. 1755/18
Wm., Flitton, Greenfield. 1559/310
Wm., Luton. 1625/177
Wm., Bedford, dyer. 1628/9
Wm., Flitton, Greenfield, yeo. 1694-5/73
see also Gooding
GOODY, Alice, Goldington. 1630/243, I 4/199
Eliz., Stagsden, wid. 1618/43
Eliz., Warden, wid. 1660/166
Joan, Kempston, wid. 1610/76
Jn., Kempston. 1561/49
Robt., Kempston. I 1587-8: 4/177
Robt., Stagsden, lab. 1624/29
Thos., Warden. 1620/74
Thos., Goldington. 1727/32
GOOSEY, Jn., Podington, farmer. 1849/29
Wm., sen., Podington, baker. 1803/43
Wm., Podington, farmer and baker. 1844/36
GORDGE, see George
GORDON, Ann, Ampthill, spins. A 1797/2
Wm., Houghton Conquest, dairyman and farmer. 1802/31
see also Corden
GORE, GOARE, Agnes, Keysoe. 1612/113
Alice, Chicksands, wid. 1613/179
Eatton, Stotfold, lab. A 1739-40/3
Eleanor, Tilbrook, wid. 1688/9
Eliz., Eaton Socon, Topham, wid. 1668-9/188
Geo., Southill, Stanford, butcher. 1686/23
Geo., Southill, woollen draper? [*lanionis*]. R 1686: 1/128

GORE, GOARE continued
Geo., Blunham, Chalton, farmer. A 1714/37
Gilbert, Shelton. 1616/148
Griffen, Melchbourne, husb. 1599/71
Hen., Eaton Socon, Beggary, dairyman. 1682/10
Jane, Eaton Socon, Honeydon, wid. 1677/17
Joan, Honeydon, wid. 1552/312
Jn., Eaton Socon, Honeydon. R 1531: 3/50d
Jn., Keysoe, husb. R 1548: 12/40d
Jn., Keysoe, husb. 1611/168
Jn., Keysoe, husb. 1638/182
Jn., Yielden, carpenter. 1707/37
Jn., Melchbourne, bach. 1723-4/4
Jn., Shelton, carpenter. 1728/62
Robt., Henlow, butcher. 1700/98
Thos., Melchbourne, husb. 1608/42
Thos., Eaton Socon, yeo. 1664/65
Thos., Melchbourne, yeo. 1672/105
Wm., sen., Eaton Socon, Honeydon, yeo. 1634/116
Wm., Stotfold, butcher. 1683-4/126
Wm., Melchbourne, dairyman. 1731/69
see also Core, see also Gower
GOREHAM, Eliz., Woburn, wid. 1708/1
Reynold, Lathbury, Bucks., yeo. 1704/78
GORING, Geo., Houghton Regis. AR 1679: 1/156d
Geo., Houghton Regis, Thorne, yeo. 1698/110
Mary, Houghton Regis, Thorne, wid. 1704/52
GOSBELL, Ric., sen., Houghton Regis, Thorne, yeo. 1720/70
Robt., Caddington, yeo. 1727/29
GOSLEY, Eliz., Woburn, wid. 1625-6/117
GOSS, GOSSE, Ann, Riseley, wid. 1744-5/43
Eliz., Cardington, Harrowden, wid. 1602/1
Eliz., Riseley, wid. 1771/28
Fra. Mary, Stanbridge, wid. LB 1842/82
Hen., Cardington, Harrowden, lab. 1593/76
Hen., Cardington, Fenlake. 1705/59
Jane, Stanbridge, wid. LBA 1809/60
Jn., jun., Cardington, Harrowden, shepherd. 1643/74
Jn., Cardington, Harrowden, lab. 1689/4
Jn., Cardington, Fenlake, lab. 1697/10
Jn., Keysoe, yeo. 1848/12
Jos., Cranfield, miller. 1839/24
Math., Ampthill. 1799/52
Ric., Chalgrave, Tebworth, cordwainer. 1779/7
Ric., Stanbridge, cordwainer and victualler. LB 1805/26

GOSS, GOSSE continued
Thos., Cardington, lab. 1729-30/117
Thos., Sharnbrook, dairyman. A 1744/15
Thos., Stanbridge, victualler. LB 1841/76
Wm., Cardington, Harrowden, lab. 1633-4/200
Wm., Sandy, Stratford, yeo. A 1793/5
GOST(E)LOW, Mary, Woburn, wid. A 1799/8
GOSTLOE, Edm., Little Staughton, yeo. c1587/170
Fred., Millbrook, gent. 1832/14
Jas., sen., Dunstable, farmer. 1826/7
Jas., Dunstable, farmer. 1830/28
Jn., Woburn, innholder. 1792/8
Thos., Dunstable, farmer. 1838/46
GOSTWICK, GOSTICK, Jn., Willington, gent. 1558/279
Jn., Willington, esq. 1583/134
Mary, Bedford St. Mary. A 1769/23
Robt., Willington, chaplain. R 1541: 6/104d
Robt., Warden, gent. R 1561: 14/29
Robt., Marston, gent. 1604/34
Wm., Houghton Conquest, shopkeeper. 1847/53
GOSWELL, Thos., Chicksands, yeo. 1637/101
GOTHER, Paul, Tingrith, parson, clerk. 1601/104
GOTHERD, GODTHARD, Mary, Pertenhall, wid. 1710/69
Thos., Little Staughton, yeo. 1737/57
GOTHORNE, Jn., Riseley, shepherd 1730/40
GOTOBED, Alice, Langford, wid. 1618-19/30
GOUD, Hen., Harlington, lab. 1665/6
Wm., Bedford St. Paul, butcher. 1685-6/113
see also Good
GOUGE, Wm., Leighton Buzzard, chandler. 1573/149
GOUGH, see Jenkin alias Gough
see also Goffe
GOUNTER, Mary, Blunham, gentlewoman. 1658-9/136
GOWER, Paul, Marston, lab. 1706/34
see also Gore
GOWLER, Jn., Eaton Socon, brickmaker. 1707-8/83
Hannah, "old index but missing". A 1714/1
GRACE, Jas., Pulloxhill, yeo. A 1779/10
Mary, wife of Jn., Cranfield. 1777/25
Sarah, Pulloxhill, wid. 1792/20
GRAHAM, Jeremiah, Goldington, miller. 1765/4
GRAINGER, GRANGER, Chris, jun., Toddington, lab. 1679/55
Chris., jun., Toddington. AR 1679: 1/157d
Jn., Kempston. 1561/159
Sarah, Shillington, wid. 1711-12/84

GRAMAT, see Grummett
GRANBOROUGH, Frances, Husborne Crawley, wid. 1809/21
Wm., Husborne Crawley, baker. A 1760/6
Wm., Husborne Crawley, yeo. 1773/51
Wm., Husborne Crawley, yeo. 1795/4
Wm., Woburn, lace-dealer: limited admon. A 1840
GRANGE, Ric., Cranfield, gent. 1683-4/127
Robt., Dunstable, yeo. 1684-5/114
GRANSDEN, Jonathan, Little Staughton, lab. 1732/71
Mary, Little Staughton, wid. 1753/11
Wm., Little Staughton, farmer. A 1741/10
GRANT, GRAUNT, Cath., Houghton Regis. R 1537-8: 4/96d
Eliz., Goldington. 1624/34
Jas., Dunstable, currier. A 1706/18
Jn., Toddington. R 1533: 3/99d
Jn., Wootton, shepherd. 1639/68
Jn., Goldington. 1644-5/111
Jn., Bedford St. Paul. AR 1671-2: 1/5d
Jn., Goldington. A 1739/31
Jn., Ravensden, farmer. A 1778/14
Jn., Great Barford, yeo. 1817/6
Jn., Bolnhurst, wheelwright. 1842/27
Mary, Blunham, wid. 1766/67
Nath., Chellington, yeo. 1810/55
Sarah, (old index "Docket mislaid"). A 1709/27
Thos., Dean. R 1500: 1/13
Thos., Goldington, yeo. 1649/48
Wm., sen., Goldington. 1639/86
Wm., Goldington, Newenham, yeo. 1660/55
Wm., Goldington, lab. 1674/117
Wm., Goldington. AR 1689: 1/32d
Wm., Blunham, yeo. 1763/39
Wm., Little Staughton. 1783/37
GRASHOPPE, Jn., Cranfield, yeo. 1658-9/211
Thos., Cranfield, husb. 1617/236
GRASLEY, Mary, Marston, wid. 1762/1
Thos., Marston, yeo. 1750/14
Wm., Marston, Pillinge, yeo. 1757/45
GRAUNT, see Grant
GRAVES, GREAVES, GREYVES, Alice, Leighton Buzzard, wid. 1600/2
Eliz., Eaton Socon. A 1731/26
Robt., Leighton Buzzard. 1578/223
Wm., Eaton Socon, Nether Staploe. 1690-1/53
GRAVESTOCK, Jas., Langford, yeo. 1836/9
GRAVIDGE, Hen., Dunstable. 1672/103

GRAY, GREY, Alice, Goldington. R 1505: 1/103d
Alice, Dunstable, wid. 1623/194
Barb., Eaton Socon, wid. 1610-11/42
Dan., Wilshamstead, yeo. (register only). 1812/11
Edm., Dean, clerk and parson. R 1540: 6/22d
Edw., Goldington, lab. 1658/217
Edw., Harrold, wheelwright. 1743-4/78
Fra., Riseley, lab. 1694/24
Geo., Harrold, blacksmith. AR 1680-1: 1/42d
Geo., Eaton Socon. AR 1689-90: 1/83
Geo., Luton, carpenter. 1837/42
Jas., Upper Stondon, yeo. 1848/53
Joan, Northill, Caldecote, wife of Wm. 1612-13/103
Jere., Ampthill, yeo. 1720/67
Jn., Northill. R 1500: 1/15
Jn., Goldington. R 1500: 1/19
Jn., Eaton Socon. R 1528: 2/138d
Jn., Eaton Socon. R 1540: 6/44d
Jn., Colmworth. 1566/74
Jn., Flitwick. 1586/3
Jn., Eaton Socon, Over Staploe, husb. 1603-4/108
Jn., Wymington, husb. 1604/54
Jn., sen., Pertenhall, gent. 1618-19/7
Jn., (old index only, bundle missing). A 1718/22
Jn., Bedford, millwright. A 1719/13
Jn., Potton, barber. A 1730/39
Jn., sen., Edworth, farmer. 1755/37
Jn., Edworth, farmer. 1776/20
Jn., Felmersham, gent. 1813/41
Jn., Great Staughton, Bushmead, farmer. 1822/13
Jos., Wymington, yeo. A 1702/17
Jos., Clifton, husb. 1710-11/64
Judith, Oakley, spins. 1664/46
Margt., Dunstable, spins. 1627/153
Margt., Roxton, wid. 1632-3/13
Mary, Bedford St. Mary. A 1855/4
Mary Ann, Eaton Socon, spins. A 1845/9
Mich., Houghton Regis, husb. 1560/195
Owen, Little Staughton, plumber and glazier. A 1850/7
Ralph, Kempston. 1658/20
Reynold, Kempston, esq. R 1533-4: 2/193d
Ric., Nether Gravenhurst, parson. 1553/289
Ric., Goldington. 1560/189
Ric., Goldington. 1560/192
Ric., Stotfold, tailor. 1609-10/135

GRAY, GREY continued
Ric., Tingrith. AR 1690: 1/218
Ric., Shefford, cordwainer. A 1719/30
Ric., Southill, Stanford, lab. 1749-50/55
Robt., sen., Eaton Socon, Over Staploe, yeo. 1603/92
Robt., sen., Eaton Socon, Over Staploe, husb. 1608-9/87
Robt., Moggerhanger, lab. 1617-18/170
Robt., Luton, husb. 1630/37
Robt., Eaton Socon, Honeydon. 1637/126
Robt., Eaton Socon, Over Staploe, ploughwright. 1651/37
Robt., Eaton Socon, yeo. 1705/7
Sam., Wootton, yeo. 1651/17
Sam., Eaton Socon, yeo. 1712/33
Sybell, Pertenhall, wid. 1662/36
Theophilius, Silsoe, esq. 1679/114
Thos., Cople, esq. R 1506: 1/93
Thos., Southill. R 1533: 3/114d
Thos., refers to Blunham, gent. 1552/302
Thos., Moggerhanger, husb. 1601-2/152
Thos., Blunham, Southill Mills. 1624/45
Thos., Wootton, farrier. AR 1686: 1/29d
Thos., (old index "docket mislaid"). A 1709/31
Wm., Eaton Socon, Over Staploe. R 1535-6: 4/27d
Wm., Langford. R 1543: 6/151 and 9/6d
Wm., Stotfold, lab. 1582/122
Wm., Tilbrook, yeo. 1602/12
Wm., Northill, Caldecote, weaver. 1612/125
Wm., Marston, Pillinge, yeo. 1717/31
Wm., Luton, carpenter. 1834/22
Zachariah, Colmworth, yeo. 1793/19
Zachary, Houghton Conquest, rector. 1767/27
GRAZIER, Alice, Houghton Regis, wid. 1623-4/136
GRAZELEY, Thos., Stotfold, farmer. A 1748/11
GREATBATCH, Thos., Carlton, clerk. 1684/49
GREEN, GRANE, GRENE, Gladman alias Green, see Gladman
Harper alias Green, see Harper
Abr., sen., Shillington, Chibley End, farmer. 1694/34
Agnes, Leighton Buzzard, wid. 1608/43
Ann, Shillington, spins. A 1737/18
Anne, Eversholt, wid. 1658/172
Anne, Southill, Broom, wid. R 1841/38 (monition to transmit to PCC, ABP1/1841)
Dorothy, Shillington, wid. 1742/15
Huchins, Dorothy, late Dorothy Green, Felmersham. A 1789/3
Edm., Carlton, yeo. 1639/95

GREEN, GRANE, GRENE continued
Edm., Husborne Crawley, woollen draper. 1696/140
Edm., Bedford, draper. 1723-4/82
Edw., Warden, Hill. R 1545: 11/108
Edw., Arlesey. 1586/124
Edw., Stopsley, yeo. 1736/16
Edw., Southill, Rowney, farmer. 1761/56
Edw., Southill, Rowney, farmer. 1779/18
Eleanor, Bedford, wid. 1811/20
Eliz., Toddington. R 1543: 6/157 and 9/9d
Eliz., Dunton, wid. 1599/135
Eliz., Husborne Crawley, wid. 1659-60/92
Eliz., Woburn, wid. 1711/36
Eliz., Leighton Buzzard, wid. LB 1774/36
Eliz., Dunton. Bw 1835/146
Eliz., Clifton, spins. 1854/19
Ellen, Silsoe. 1769/7
Foster, sen., Maulden, yeo. 1722/21
Foster, Flitwick, Denel End, yeo. 1731/15
Gabriel, Carlton, cordwainer. 1711-12/97
Geo., Elstow, wheelwright. 1609/153
Geo., Elstow, yeo. 1686/15
Geo., Elstow. AR 1688: 1/32(2)
Hannah, Haynes, wid. A 1855/2
Hen., Leighton Buzzard. 1548/15
Hen., Husborne Crawley, weaver. 1661/378
Hen., Eversholt, yeo. 1711/110
Hen., Cardington, husb. A 1728-9/48
Hester, Flitwick, Denel End, wid. 1742/3
Jacob, Millbrook, shopkeeper. 1772/41
Jas., Luton. 1558/56
Jane, Langford, wid. 1699/66
Jn., Luton, husb. R 1535: 4/30
Jn., Husborne Crawley. R 1558: 13/148d
Jn., Shillington. R 1559: 13/159
Jn., Langford. 1564/35
Jn., Husborne Crawley, weaver. 1605-6/96
Jn., Shillington, oatmealmaker. 1614/26
Jn., Langford, husb. 1614-15/15
Jn., Bletsoe, servant. 1627/135
Jn., sen., Langford, husb. 1647-8/13
Jn., Husborne Crawley, tailor. 1648-9/101
Jn., sen., St. Neots, Hunts., baker. 1657/74
Jn., Haynes, shepherd. 1680/12
alias Harper, Jn., Biddenham, lab. 1681/47

GREEN, GRANE, GRENE continued
Jn., Silsoe, yeo. 1682-3/104
Jn., sen., Shillington, lab. 1695/8
Jn., Shillington, Lower Stondon, yeo. 1707/69
Jn., Husborne Crawley, fellmonger and Sarah his wife. A 1711/67
Jn., Kempston. 1722-3/74
Jn., Arlesey, yeo. 1758/6
Jn., Northill, farmer. A 1765/4
Jn., Shefford, mealman and baker. 1810/23
Jn., Totternhoe, dairyman. 1820/3
Jn., Ampthill, publican. 1822/6
Jn., Bedford, merchant. 1831/5
Jn., Melchbourne, carpenter. A 1831/15
Jn., Bolnhurst, farmer. A 1842/1
Jn., Bedford, dyer. 1843/22
Jn., Bedford, carpenter. 1849/5
Jn., Northill, cordwainer "but now out of business". 1854/8
Jos., Eaton Socon, grocer and tallow chandler. 1776/29
Joyce, late Joyce Cumberland, Hockliffe, wid. A 1788/3
Manastee, Eaton Socon, yeo. 1714-15/131
Margt., Shillington, wid. 1658-9/236
Martin, Shillington, lab. 1639-40/133
Mary, Bedford, wid. 1623-4/102
alias Harper, Mary, Sharnbrook, wid. 1639/84
Mary, Langford, wid. 1719-20/5
Mary, Cardington, Cotton End, wid. A 1775/23
Mary, Podington. A 1790/1
Math., Over Gravenhurst. 1618/146
Math., Lidlington, butcher. A 1764/8
Nich., Houghton Conquest, How End, husb. 1631/144
Phillip, Leighton Buzzard. 1598/81
Ralph, Fenny Stratford, Bucks., glover. R 1589: 21/54d
Remington, Woburn, woollen draper. 1706/55
Ric., Shillington. R 1504: 1/45
Ric., sen., Hyde, Chiltern Green. 1558/81
Ric., Shillington. 1584-5/273
Ric., Dunton. 1619/197, I 4/126
Ric., Warden, lab. 1658/90
Ric., Clophill, yeo. 1658/157
Ric., Leighton Buzzard, miller. LB 1741/13
Ric., Battlesden. A 1855/1
Robt., Shillington, yeo. 1602/64
Robt., Bedford, baker. 1607/166
Robt., Dunton. 1627/169
Robt., Shillington, Chibley, yeo. 1635-6/57

GREEN, GRANE, GRENE continued
Robt., Langford, yeo. 1664-5/76
Robt., Langford, yeo. 1688/27
Robt., Dean, lab. A 1720/11
Sam., Caddington, farmer. 1817/31
Sarah, Haynes, spins. 1754/6
Sarah, Clifton, wid. 1852/47
Soloman, Husborne Crawley, carpenter. 1661/301
Thos., Barton. R 1508: 1/169
Thos., Dunstable, smith. R 1533: 3/97
Thos., Marston. 1559/312
Thos., Elstow. 1620-1/19
Thos., Husborne Crawley, tailor. 1645/38
Thos., Houghton Conquest, How End, yeo. 1675/16
Thos., Biggleswade, Stratton. AR 1681: 1/114d
Thos., sen., Potton, baker. 1709/67
Thos., Langford, mercer. 1711/18
Thos., Wymington. 1711/71
Thos., Wymington, lab. A 1714/53
Thos., Chellington. 1716/65
Thos., Stotfold. A 1728-9/47
Thos., Shillington, yeo. A 1728-9/55
Thos., Northill, Ickwell, lab. 1746/15
Thos., Ampthill. 1795/2
Thos., Dunstable, innholder. 1834/15
Thos., Dean, farmer. A 1749/8
Thos., Pavenham. A 1769/6
Thos., Pavenham, yeo. A 1787/14
Thos., Southill, Stanford, yeo. A 1853/1
Warner, Shefford, butcher. 1853/53
Wm., Dunstable. R 1533: 3/102d
Wm., Biddenham. 1552/307
Wm., Leighton Buzzard, innholder. 1589/132
Wm., Westoning, Sampshill. 1623/181
Wm., Langford, shepherd. 1634-5/121
Wm., Oakley, Reynes, yeo. 1650/87
Wm., Langford, yeo. 1691/105
Wm., Henlow. 1699/9
Wm., (no parish given). 1715-16/92
Wm., Henlow, farmer. A 1744/13
Wm., Chicksands, farmer. A 1751/8
Wm., Biggleswade, common victualler. Bw 1766/44, I
Wm., Arlesey, yeo. A 1786/13
Wm., Luton, innholder. 1793/24
Wm., Clifton, yeo. A 1806/11

GREEN, GRANE, GRENE continued
Wm., Shefford, baker. 1826/53
Wm., Bolnhurst, farmer. A 1827/12
Wm., Shefford, spirit merchant. 1838/31
Wm., Haynes. A 1854/7
Wm., Bedford. (P/IX2 only). A 1856/7
GREENHILL, Wm., Biggleswade, Stratton, husb. 1561/61
GREENHOOD, Bernard, Cranfield, carpenter. 1825/18
GREENING, Jas., London, (Riseley), apothecary. 1774/12
GREENLEAF, Agnes, Blunham, wid. 1597-8/30
Jas., Eaton Socon. R 1525: 2/29
GREENOUGH, Wm., Aspley Guise, clerk and parson. 1633/143
GREENWICH, Jn., Maulden. 1580-1/214
GREENWOOD, Chris., Lidlington, husb. 1618/143
Eliz., Pulloxhill, Greenfield, wid. 1637/104
Jas., Pulloxhill, yeo. 1612-13/224
Ralph, Cranfield, husb. 1668/132
Ric., no parish given. 1680/9
Robt., jun., Steppingley, yeo. 1683-4/89
Susannah, Bedford, wid. 1701/40
Thos., Flitwick, husb. 1618-19/24
Wm., Steppingley. 1575/108
GREGGS, GREGG, Hen., Langford. 1685/83
Jn., Pavenham, gent. 1724/42
Jn., Pavenham, yeo. A 1802/14
GREGORY, Tompkins alias Gregory, see Tompkins
Ambrose, Eversholt, yeo. 1587/171
Ambrose, sen., Eversholt, yeo. 1615/143
Ambrose, Eversholt, yeo. 1641/198
Ambrose, Eversholt, Radsend, yeo. 1664/21
Ambrose, sen., Eversholt, yeo. 1674/158
Ambrose, Eversholt, yeo. 1681/61
Ann, Barton, wid. 1730/5
Ann, Thurleigh, wife of Peter, yeo. 1734/61
Cath., Woburn. 1714/52
Cath., Ridgmont, wife of Jn., gent.. 1730-1/61
Edw., Dunstable. R 1549: 12/58d
Edw., Flitwick, husb. 1645/25
Edw., Shillington. AR 1672: 1/95
Edw., Shillington. 1711-12/81
Edw., Shillington, yeo. 1735/50
Edw., Biggleswade, surgeon. BwA 1795/42
Eliz., Eversholt, wid. 1620-1/6
Eliz., Melchbourne. 1814/43
Emma, Luton. A 1850/15

GREGORY continued
Fra., Eversholt, yeo. A 1727/4
Fra., Eversholt, dealer. A 1752/6
Geo., Eversholt. 1557/282
Geo., sen., Eversholt, yeo. 1626/106
Geo., Eversholt, yeo. 1657/200
Geo., Eversholt, yeo. 1659/251
Geo., Eversholt, gent. 1711/117
Geo., Wootton, yeo. 1778/5
Grace, Ampthill, wid. 1727/100
Hen., Goldington. 1641-2/203
Isabel, Eversholt, wid. 1660-1/188
Jas., Shillington, Pegsdon, yeo. R 1547: 11/244
Jas., Shillington. 1609/167
Jas., Shillington, tailor. 1629/80
Jas., Kempston, yeo. 1661/394
Jas., Eversholt. A 1721/40
Jn., Bolnhurst, husb. 1610-11/45
Jn., Eversholt, yeo. 1649/11
Jn., Eversholt, yeo. ?1660/146
Jn., Eversholt, yeo. 1660/147a
Jn., Eversholt, yeo. 1666-7/139
Jn., Sundon, yeo. 1684/50
Jn., Eversholt. 1685/15
Jn., Eversholt, Potters End, yeo. 1700/81
Jn., Little Staughton, yeo. A 1703/6
Jn., Thurleigh, yeo. 1704-5/19
Jn., Barton, weaver. 1727/38
Jn., Stagsden, butcher. A 1761/21
Jn., Stagsden, butcher. A 1765/23
Jn., Eversholt, Bury End, gent. 1766/58
Jn., Stagsden, farmer. 1788/25
Jn., Eversholt, gent. (also limited admon). 1794/4
Jn., Shillington, Pegsdon, yeo. 1816/43
Jn., Eversholt, yeo. A 1834/1
Jn., Eversholt. A 1855/6
Jos., Toddington, Chalton, yeo. 1804/38
Jos., Leighton Buzzard, baker. Fac. 1702: 9/4
Mary, Thurleigh, wid. A 1712/7
Mary, Sharnbrook, wid. A 1734/7
Mary, Shillington, Pegsdon, wid. of Rich. 1744/3
Mary, Shillington, Pegsdon, wid. 1812/16
Mary, Eversholt, wid. 1823/45
Mary, Milton Bryan, spins. A 1847/5
Ric., Thurleigh, yeo. 1658-9/78

GREGORY continued
Ric., (parish illegible), bach. 1669/129
Ric., Eversholt, yeo. 1680/61
Ric., sen., Shillington, Pegsdon, yeo. 1697/23
Ric., Sundon, lab. A 1713/29
Ric., Shillington, Pegsdon, husb. 1721/20
Ric., Eversholt, gent. 1728/37
Ric., Shillington, Pegsdon, farmer. 1729/83
Ric., Shillington, Pegsdon End, tanner. 1765/18
Ric., Shillington, Pegsdon, yeo. 1807/18
Robt., Biggleswade, bricklayer. 1680-1/82
Sarah, Eversholt, spins. A 1737/43
Susan, Leighton Buzzard, wid. 1749/1
Thos., Barton, husb. 1588/87
alias Redhead, Thos., Langford. 1625-6/157
Thos., Lidlington. 1645-6/60
Thos., Whipsnade, yeo. 1701/81
Thos., Sundon, yeo. 1728/23
Thos., Sharnbrook, farmer. A 1731/45
Thos., Shillington, farmer. A 1760/18
Thos., Felmersham, farmer. 1771/15
Thos., Toddington, schoolmaster. 1816/28
Tobias, Eversholt, yeo. 1711/114
Wm., Eversholt. R 1500-1: 1/23d
Wm., sen., Eversholt. R 1546: 11/170d
Wm., Eversholt, Witsend, husb. 1559/177
Wm., Pulloxhill, husb. 1575/81
Wm., Eversholt, bach. 1592/11
Wm., Pulloxhill. 1607-8/155
Wm., Maulden. 1609/166
Wm., Eversholt, Bury End. 1634/94
Wm., sen., Eversholt, yeo. 1638-9/149
Wm., sen., Eversholt, yeo. 1659/292
Wm., Eversholt. 1670-1/246
Wm., Barton, weaver. 1688/64
Wm., Thurleigh. 1699/11
Wm., sen., Shillington, Pegsdon, yeo. 1708/36
Wm., Eversholt, gent. 1711-12/57
Wm., Ampthill, innholder. A 1723/27
Wm., Shillington. A 1747/9
Wm., Stotfold, farmer. 1780/11
Wm., Luton, farmer. R 1835/2 (monition to transmit to PCC, ABP1/1840)
GRENDON, Jn., Oakley, lab. 1622-3/35
Robt., Oakley, lab. 1635/65
Wm., Felmersham. R 1504-5: 1/49d

GRITCHFIELD, Edw., Luton, Farley. 1720/122
GROMANT, GROMONT, see Grummett
GROOM, GROME, Abr., Eaton Bray, wheelwright. 1772/43
Ben., Chalgrave, Wingfield. 1711-12/31
Ben., sen., Houghton Regis, tailor (reg. only). 1755/1
Dan., Chalgrave, Wingfield, tailor. 1680/66
Edw., Chalgrave. AR 1681: 1/160d
Eliz., Chalgrave, Tebworth. 1564-5/28
Eliz., Eaton Bray, wid. 1784/51
Geo., Harlington, yeo. 1696/82
Hen., Tilsworth, husb. R 1545: 11/98d
Humph., (no parish given). 1651/120
Jn., Chalgrave, gent. A 1763/21
Jn., Chalgrave, Tebworth. 1584/252
Jn., Battlesden, husb. 1592/13
Jn., Chalgrave, Wingfield, tailor. 1648/76
Jn., Eaton Bray, yeo. 1663-4/82
Jn., sen., Dunstable, yeo. 1685/67
Jn., Dunstable, cooper. 1748/69
Jn., Dunstable, cooper. 1786/32
Mary, Houghton Regis, wid. 1733/13
Mary, Dunstable, wid. 1798/16
Nath., Dunstable, esq. A 1742/18
Nich., Hockliffe. R 1546: 11/163d
Nich., Chalgrave, Wingfield, lab. 1619-20/216, I 4/30
Ric., Hockliffe. R 1535: 4/18
Ric., Dunstable. A 1734/16
Ric., Dunstable, maltster. 1734/28
Robt., (no parish given). 1636/11
Stephen, Battlesden. 1559/186
Susanna, Stopsley, wid. 1699-1700/69
Thos., Tebworth. 1552/282
Thos., Tilsworth, husb. 1562-3/99
Thos., Nether Dean. 1641/178
Thos., Eaton Bray, yeo. 1705/99
Thos., old index "Docket mislaid". A 1709/18
Thos., sen., Dunstable, gent. (bundle 1725). 1724-5/1
Wm., Hockliffe. R 1545: 11/108d
Wm., Hockliffe. 1569/123
Wm., Houghton Regis. 1612-13/60
Wm., Dunstable, maltster. 1706/44
Wm., Houghton Regis, shepherd. A 1727/13
Wm., Eaton Bray, wheelwright. 1793/26
Wm., Eaton Bray, wheelwright. 1830/16
GROSS, Edw., Stevington, husb. 1638/21

GROVE, GROVES, Ann, Bedford, spins. 1799/14
Edward, Toddington, husb. 1554/253
Margt., wid., Woburn. 1574-5/39
Mary, Barton, wid. A 1758/22
Sam., Bedford, gardener. A 1749/6
Wm., Southill. 1679/92
GROVER, Jn., Leagrave, yeo. A 1712/11
GRUBBE, Law., Clophill, lab. 1611/164
alias Gillam, Ric., Langford, lab. 1625-6/128
Thos., Cranfield, parson of. 1652/108
GRUE, see Grew
GRUMMETT, GRAMAT, GROMANT, GROMONT, GRUMANT
Eliz., Bedford, wid. A 1809/13
Eliz., Bedford, wid. 1809/17
Hen., Barton, servant. 1618-19/13
Jn., Maulden. 1557/313
Jn., Clophill, weaver. 1606-7/17
Limby, Bedford, carpenter. 1790/6
Thos., Clophill. R 1543: 11/7d
Thos., sen., Cranfield, shoemaker. 1663/4
Wm., Cranfield, cordwainer. A 1702/37
GRUNDINE, Alice, Flitton. 1586-7/151
GRUNDON, Chris., Odell, husb. A 1703-4/22
Eliz., Oakley, wid. of Thos. 1660-1/128
Jane, Turvey, wid. 1711/99
Jn., Odell. 1628-9/2
Jn., Shillington, lab. 1711-12/108
Phillip, Oakley, yeo. 1683/13
Robt., Turvey, husb. A 1712/40
Thos., Oakley, tailor. 1662-3/65
Thos., Odell, bach. A 1703-4/23
Thos., Oakley, yeo. 1704/47
see also Grendon
GRYMSON, Lawrence, Shefford. I 1619: 4/119
GUARIGUES, Ric., Ampthill, gent. A 1746/15
GU(OO)DGIN, GUGEON, GOGEUN, Anna Maria, Haynes, wid. A 1809/20
Eliz., Toddington. A 1855/15
Jn., Haynes. R 1501: 1/34
Jn., Pulloxhill, dairyman. 1784/11
Jn., Maulden, yeo. 1788/19
Jn., Haynes, farmer. A 1835/10
Jn., Cople, farmer and victualler. 1835/15
Jos., Pulloxhill, dairyman. 1805/29
Mary, Bletsoe. 1663-4/105
Mary, Pulloxhill, wid. 1785/8

GUDGIN, GUGEON, GOODGIN, GOGEUN continued
Oliver, Bletsoe. 1628-9/17
Ric., Maulden, yeo. A 1790/5
Thos., Wilshamstead, lab. 1607/99
Thos., Houghton Conquest, farmer. 1833/37
Thos., Holwell, Snailwell, lab. 1834/5
Wm., sen., Shillington, Pegsdon, farmer. 1779/47
GUESS, see Guest
GUEST, GISTE, GUESS, Daniel, Ravensden, clerk. 1626/65, 65a
Jn., Leighton Buzzard, husb. 1608/63
Jn., Bedford, lab. 1727/50
GUIDOT, Robt., Bedford St. John, clerk. AR 1677: 1/14d
GULLIVER, Clement, Turvey, almsman. 1615/202
GUN, Phillip, Woburn, bricklayer. 1746/10
Thos., Roxton. 1557/335
GUNTHORPE, Sam., Biggleswade, innholder. Bw 1740/32g
GURNEY, Alice, Goldington, wid. 1665/21
Ann, Henlow, spins. 1850/42
Dan., Tilsworth, husb. 1666/109
Edm., Houghton Regis. 1582-3/104
Edw., Tilsworth, yeo. 1688-9/60
Edw., Chalgrave, yeo. 1758/41
alias Butcher, Eliz., Keysoe, wid. 1592/18
Eliz., Kempston, wid. 1731/4
Eliz., Leighton Buzzard, spins. LB 1736/1
Fra., Bedford, wid. 1728/14
Fra., Pavenham, miller. 1750/51
Fra., Henlow, farmer. A 1804/7
Fra., Henlow, farmer. A 1837/3
Geo., Oakley. 1563/63
Geo., Millbrook, grazier. 1712/90
Geo., Ampthill, draper. 1775/7
Hen., Leighton Buzzard, Eggington, husb. 1559/339
Hen., Potsgrove, grazier. 1741/88
Hen., Wootton, butcher. A 1736/33
Joan, Tilsworth, wid. AR 1670: 1/90d
Joan, Tilsworth, wid. AR 1670: 1/140d
Jn., Husborne Crawley, gent. 1710/77
Jn., Kempston, yeo. A 1716/12
Jn., Husborne Crawley, Crawley Mills, miller. 1761/31
Jn., Willington, blacksmith. 1814/23
Jn., Willington. A 1836/16
Jn., Shillington, farmer. A 1837/15
Jos., Ampthill. 1828/19
Jos., Leighton Buzzard, yeo. LB 1806/34, I

GURNEY continued
Jos., Houghton Conquest. A 1772/9
Judith, Ampthill, wid. A 1761/20
Lawr., Goldington, yeo. 1665/22
Leonard, Goldington, ploughwright. 1616/146
Margt., Leighton Buzzard, wid. 1607/142
Martha, Pavenham, wid. 1758/20
Mary, Goldington, wid. 1665/4
Mary, Chalgrave. A 1774/5
Mary, Westoning, wid. 1774/31
Ric., Houghton Regis, yeo. 1581/25
Ric., Eversholt, yeo. 1720/15
Ric., Southill. AR 1683: 1/119
Sam., Keysoe Bury, farmer. 1779/4
Thos., sen., Millbrook, yeo. 1557/290
Thos., Dean, yeo. 1635/6
Thos., Toddington, miller. 1661-2/401
Thos., Bromham, miller. AR 1688: 1/49
Thos., Studham, yeo. 1691/87
Thos., Shillington, miller. AR 1705 (addition)
Thos., Kempston, yeo. 1705-6/94
Thos., Milton Ernest, miller. A 1707/27
Thos., Wootton, yeo. A 1722/19
Thos., Kempston, yeo. 1728-9/87
Thos., Clophill. A 1741-2/26
Thos., Steppingley, lab. A 1764/14
Thos., Great Barford. A 1836/4
Thos., Husborne Crawley, tailor and beer retailer. 1842/4
Thos., Henlow, farmer. A 1846/1
Wm., Dunton. 1606-7/4
Wm., Marston, lab. 1627/232
Wm., Eaton Bray, blacksmith. 1846/3
GURNISH, Jn., Tilsworth, yeo. 1671/54, AR 1671/141d
GURREY, GURRE, GUREY, Ann, Bolnhurst, wid. 1727/44
Jn., Little Staughton, yeo. 1839/23
Jn., Lidlington, yeo. 1843/17
Jos., Lidlington. 1852/35
Mary, Bolnhurst, wid. 1708/15
Mary, Eaton Socon. A 1770/18
Ric., Bolnhurst, blacksmith. 1677/47
Sam., Bolnhurst, gent. 1719/24
Thos., Dean, husb. R 1546: 11/150d
Thos., Eaton Socon, yeo. 1769/4
Thos., Eaton Socon. A 1770/19
Wm., Stanbridge. 1558/252

GUTTERIDGE, Ann, Luton, wid. A 1712/19
Charlotte, Luton. A 1811/3
Dan., Luton, maltster. 1699/57
Dan., Luton, yeo. A 1823/3
Eliz., Luton, wid. 1738/88
Jn., Luton, maltster. 1685/24
Jn., Blunham, grocer and shopkeeper. 1795/8
Jos., Luton. A 1714-15/46
Jos., Luton, Dollar Farme, farmer. 1821/38
Jos., Luton, Donkey Hall, bricklayer. 1842/31
Martha, Luton. A 1844/3
Mary, Blunham, wid. and shopkeeper. 1802/10
Mary, Bedford St. Peter, wid. 1855/13
Math., Luton, Dallow, yeo. 1729/23
Math., Luton, grocer. 1829/7
Ric., Luton, yeo. 1699-1700/67
Ric., Luton, Dallow, yeo. 1709/54
Ric., Dunstable, gent. 1752/59
Ric., jun., Houghton Regis, farmer. 1831/26
Robt., Tilsworth, husb. 1748/55
Ruth, Luton, wid. 1803/28
Sarah, Luton, wid. A 1715/2
Sarah, Luton, wid. 1810/37
Sarah, Luton, spins. 1811/3
Sarah, Luton, wid. 1836/30
Sarah, Whipsnade. A 1839/2
Thos., Toddington, shoemaker. 1650-1/134
Thos., Luton, innholder. 1751/51
GUY, GIE, Jn., Steppingley (?Gee). 1610/117
Rose, Tempsford, wid. 1714/14
see also Gee
GWYNNE, Geo., Silsoe, yeo. 1712/34
Hen., Silsoe, joiner. A 1746/10
Hen., Chicksands, lab. A 1839/9
Thos., Silsoe, yeo. 1697/43
GYPPS, see Jepps

H

HABRAHAM, see Abraham
HACKE, Jn., Eaton Bray, miller. 1719-20/82
Jn., sen., Hockliffe, dairyman. 1779/11
HACKETT, Martha, Houghton Conquest, spins. 1687/64
HACKLET, HACLET, Audryan, Bedford, servant. 1578/149
HACKTON, John, Odell. R 1533: 3/110

HADDEN, HAYDON, ADDENDES, Marian, Dunstable, wid. 1599/174
Robt., Dunstable, baker. 1597-8/61
Thos., Dunstable, baker. 1606/53
see also Adeane and Adowne
HADDOCK, HADDUCK. Edw., Barton, yeo. 1667-8/10
Marie, Bedford, wid. 1624/62
Walt., Tempsford. 1694-5/90
HADFIELD, see Hatfield
HADLAND, see Headland
HADLY, Mary, Bedford St. Paul, wid. 1645/24
Robt., Bedford St. Mary, fletcher. 1613/190
HADNAM, Thos., Wrestlingworth. R 1532: 3/66
HADNOTT, Wm., Leighton Buzzard, blacksmith. LB 1776/41
HAFFORD, Wm., Great Barford. 1689-90/84
HAGAR, Margt., Ampthill, wid. 1831/32
see also Ager
HAGGAS, HAGGUS, HAGGEST, alias Hills, Alice, Henlow. AR 1680: 1/110d
Anne, Henlow, wid. 1670/137
Eliz., Henlow, wid. of Wm. 1661-2/264
Jn., Henlow, bach. AR 1673: 1/97d
Jn., Henlow, bach. AR 1673: 1/37
Jn., Henlow, bach. AR 1674: 1/101
Ric., Southill, lab. 1573/124
Robt., Henlow, yeo. AR 1672: 1/94
Robt., Henlow, yeo. 1653/87
Thos., Henlow, husb. 1573/120
Thos., Maulden. 1614/103
Thos., Maulden, husb. (bundle). 1614/153
Wm., Henlow. AR 1674: 1/100d
see also Aggs and Agglets
HAGGATT, Sam., Eaton Socon, Ford End, lab. 1629/77
HAGGER, Jos., Luton, brazier. A 1830/10
HAILEY, ALEY, ALEE, Geo., Arlesey, gent. 1751/46
Geo., Shefford, surgeon. 1760/61
Geo., Shefford, surgeon. A 1816/5
see also Hale
HAILSTONE, AYLSTON, Kath., Elstow. R 1503: 1/38d
Wm., Elstow. R 1502: 1/39
HALCOCK, see Alcock
HALE, HAYLL, HAYLE, Agnes, Marston. R 1546: 11/134
Alice, Clapham, wid. 1651/19
Ann, Biggleswade, Stratton, wid. 1677-8/76
Avice, Roxton, wid. AR 1689: 1/82
Ben., Silsoe. 1632/90
Dan., Barton, husb. 1632/98

HALE, HAYLL, HAYLE continued
Eliz., Pulloxhill, wid. 1728/43
Ellen, Biggleswade, wid. AR 1690: 1/133d
Hen., Shillington, gent. 1630-1/118
Joan, Shillington, Pegsdon. 1560/111
Jn., Streatley, yeo. 1670/230
Jn., Barton, yeo. 1717-18/74
Jn., Lidlington. 1718/11
Jn., Elstow, carpenter. 1724/50
Lawr., Wootton. 1617-18/227
Lawr., Biggleswade, yeo. AR 1679-80: 1/110
Mary, Tingrith, wid. 1672-3/44
Ric., Barton, husb. 1556/215
Ric., Roxton, clerk. AR 1684: 1/77
Ric., jun., Roxton. AR 1689: 1/82d
Thos., Barton. 1559/146
Thos., Clapham. 1639/116
Thos., Everton. 1682/22
Thos., Maulden, lab. 1686/50
Thos., Wymington. AR 1690: 1/84
Wm., sen., Marston Moreteyne, yeo. R 1530: 3/12
Wm., Barton. 1557/312
Wm., Harrold, yeo. 1589-90/126
Wm., Over Gravenhurst, Ion, yeo. 1621-2/151
Wm., Biggleswade, grocer. AR 1685: 1/125
Wm., Haynes, cordwainer. AR 1685: 1/312d
Wm., Colmworth, lab. 1689-90/87
Wm., Everton, gent. 1713/66
see also Hall; Hailey; Alee
HALFHEAD, Alice, Oakley, wid. 1630/198
Thos., Keysoe, yeo. 1659/278
Thos., Keysoe, yeo. 1659/291
Thos., Markyate St., carpenter. 1856/41
Wm., Cardington, Pork Lane, yeo. 1682/68
Wm., Northill, Caldecote, yeo. 1692/24
Wm., Markyate St., carpenter. 1841/22
HALFHIDE, Jas., Potton. 1577-8/72
Sarah, Potton, wid. 1708/29
Thos., Odell, yeo. 1724/40
HALFORD, Jane, Blunham, wid. 1725-6/88
see also Alford
HALFPENNY, Jn., (no parish given). 1627/173
Aubeny, Abney, alias Halfpenny, Wm., Clophill, yeo. 1845/42
see also Aburney
HALKOC, see Alcocke

HALL, HALLE, HAWLE, Bray alias Hall, see Bray
Agnes, Ridgmont, wid. 1794/33
Ann, Bedford St. John. 1769/15
Anth., Clophill, whipcordmaker. 1561/53
Barnard, Toddington, carpenter. 1581/22
Chris., Bletsoe, husb. 1557/343
Dav., Wrestlingworth, shepherd. 1669-70/106
Edw., Aspley Guise, clerk. 1718/27
Eliz., Bedford St. Paul. 1559/328
Eliz., Clophill, wid. 1640/52
Eliz., Milton Bryan, wid. 1747/62
Eliz., Biggleswade. BwA 1790/38
Eliz., Ridgmont. A 1843/6
Eliz. & Thos., Potton, spins. and bach. A 1856/5 & 6
Fra., Milton Bryan, yeo. 1749/39
Fra., sen., Toddington, farrier. 1803/11
Geo., Holcote, lab. 1709/27
Geo., Toddington, blacksmith. 1747/50
Geo., Bedford, sadler. A 1841/5
Hen., Cardington, Fenlake, lab. 1616-17/21
Humph., Eaton Socon, yeo. 1822/4
Joan, Barton. 1588/122
Joan, Harrold, wid. 1617/267
Jn., Flitton. R 1506: 1/96
Jn., Bolnhurst. R 1535: 4/26
Jn., Harrold. R 1539-40: 6/20
Jn., Billington. 1554/175
Jn., Maulden. 1584/242
Jn., Arlesey, weaver. 1605/135
Jn., sen., Harrold. 1606/74
Jn., sen., Potton, baker. 1619/252, I 4/64
Jn., Keysoe. 1622/28
Jn., Whipsnade. 1624-5/12
Jn., Clophill, lab. 1669-70/122
Jn., Keysoe, yeo. 1681/53
Jn., Keysoe. AR 1686: 1/80
Jn., Biggleswade, carpenter. 1694-5/6
Jn., Knotting, yeo. 1710/14
Jn., London, St. Catherine Creed, confectioner. 1718/28
Jos., Knotting, Fox. 1771/32
Jos., Bedford, gentleman's servant. 1847/42
Kath., Thurleigh. 1660/194
Mary, Cranfield, wid. 1788/9
Percival, Podington. 1557/256
Reg., Harrold. R 1539: 5/40

HALL, HALLE, HAWLE continued
Ric., Leighton Buzzard. 1558/28
Ric., Bolnhurst. 1558/289
Ric., Riseley. 1558-9/316
Ric., Biggleswade, Stratton, yeo. 1655/179
Ric., Biggleswade, Stratton, yeo. 1683-4/120
Ric., Eaton Socon, yeo. 1780/27
Robt., Yielden, husb. 1616-17/34
Robt., Henlow, farmer. 1766/71
Roger, Hulcote, parson. 1576/22
Sam., Flitton, dairyman. 1694/53
Sam., Eaton Socon. A 1811/6
Sarah, Luton, spins. 1842/24
Sarah, Dunstable. A 1857/3
Thos., Harrold. R 1539: 5/39
Thos., Barton, carpenter. 1593/3
Thos., Bolnhurst, tailor. 1623/87
Thos., Bolnhurst, tailor. 1623/139
Thos., Husborne Crawley, yeo. 1633/197
Thos., sen., Upper Gravenhurst, lon. 1683-4/121
Thos., Odell. 1686/51
Thos., Potton, yeo. 1695/41
Thos., Toddington, farmer. 1717/23
Thos., Milton Bryan, dairyman. 1731/82
Thos., Southill, shepherd. 1748/6
Thos., Knotting, yeo. 1766/54
Thos., Biggleswade, draper. BW 1783/74
Warren, Potton, brazier. A 1755/9
Wm., Keysoe. R 1543-4: 11/5
Wm., Pulloxhill. 1557/235
Wm., Keysoe, husb. 1574-5/23
Wm., Yielden, husb. 1575/66
Wm., Arlesey, yeo. 1645/5
Wm., Houghton Regis, Sewell. 1648/107
Wm., Cranfield, dairyman. A 1724/32
Wm., Bedford, lab. A 1728/41
Wm., Cranfield, dairyman. 1738-9/30
Wm., Southill, lab. 1767/68
Wm., Milton Bryan, yeo. 1772/30
Wm., Haynes, shopkeeper. 1777/9
Wm., Holcote, yeo. A 1787/8
Wm., sen., Eaton Socon, maltster and butcher. 1810/30
see also Hale
HALLAM, Margt., Wootton, wid. R 1512-3: 1/132
HALLINGWORTH, see Hollingsworth; see also Hallworth

HALLWORTH, Chas., Maulden, miller. 1854/10
Eliz., Pulloxhill, wid. 1851/22
James, Marston, farmer. A 1795/9
Margt., Lidlington, wid. 1797/7
Phillip, Maulden, victualler. 1849/14
Wm., Milton Bryan, shepherd. 1724-5/5
see also Hollingsworth
HALSEY, Edm., Caddington. AR 1675: 1/150
alias Chambers, Edm., Caddington, Cantloes alias Cantletts, yeo. 1631/221
Edm., Studham, Clements End, weaver. 1676/138
Edm., Studham, yeo. 1684/6
Ephraim, Caddington. AR 1675: 1/150
alias Chamber, Hen., Caddington. 1604/39
alias Chamber, Hen., sen., Caddington, yeo. 1607-8/157
Hen., West Hyde, yeo. 1652/66
Jn., Biddenham, singleman. R 1550: 12/108d
alias Chambers, Jn., Dunstable, yeo. 1559/172
Jn., Toddington, Chalton, husb. 1667-8/104
alias Chamber, Jn., Luton, carpenter. 1717/54
Thos., Caddington, Chaul End, yeo. 1659/281
Thos., Caddington, yeo. 1675/13
Thos., Leighton Buzzard, baker. Fac. 1719: 9/55
Thos., Markyate, victualler. 1782/10
Wm., Biddenham, husb. R 1547: 11/247d
alias Chambers, Wm., sen., Caddington, husb. 1622-3/19
Wm., Caddington, farmer. AR 1673: 1/145d
alias Chambers, Wm., Houghton Regis. AR 1689: 1/176d
HALWAY, see Alway
HAMANT, Wm., Bedford St. Paul. R 1543: 6/159 and 9/12
HAMERTON, Steph., Sandy. R 1518-9: 2/141
HAMILTON, Wm., sen., Hardwick, gent. R 1546: 11/173
HAMLETEN, see Hamilton
HAMMOND, HAMONT, Eliz., (no parish given). 1635/74
Eliz., Bedford, spins. 1709/23
Ric., Bedford, tailor. 1702/26
Robt., Marston. 1616/149
Thos., Cardington, shepherd. I 1619/20: 4/46
see also Awmont, see also Hamant
HAMONT, see Hammond
HAMP, see Ampes
HAMPTON, Joan, Chellington, wid. 1557/284
Thos., Biggleswade. AR 1682: 1/117
HANBY, Thos., Billington, yeo. LB 1779/49
HANCE, Stone alias Hance, see Stone

HANCOCK, Abr., Sharnbrook, maltster. A 1734/27
Isaac, Sharnbrook, blacksmith. 1759/43
Jn., sen., Bedford, pewterer. 1663/9
Jn., Ampthill, glazier. 1731-2/84
Pensey, Eversholt, clerk. A 1746/25
Dr. Ralph, Blunham, rector. A 1742/12
Robt., Willington, yeo. 1664-5/78
Thos., Ampthill. A 1719/26
Walt., Willington, gent. 1723/46
Wm., Willington. 1694-5/71
HANDCOMB, see Handscombe
HANDFORDE, Hugh, Podington, Hinwick, husb. 1564/43
HANDLEY, Andr., Wrestlingworth, husb. 1680-1/106
James, Wrestlingworth, bach. A 1733/7
Jn., Wrestlingworth. 1638/181
Ric., Wrestlingworth, lab. 1637-8/153
HANDS, Rachael, Bedford, wid. 1828/10
Ric., Cranfield, farmer. 1821/26
HANERON, see Haveron
HANGAR, HENGER, Alice, Clapham, wid. 1660/218
Jn., Souldrop, husb. R 1547: 11/231d
Ric., Souldrop, clerk. 1558/158
Ric., sen., Souldrop, yeo. 1613/201
Robt., Souldrop, husb. 1605/108
Robt., Souldrop, yeo. 1706/21
Thos., Souldrop, husb. 1562-3/98
Thos., Barton, yeo. 1639/2
Thos., Bletsoe, yeo. 1730/92
Wm., Souldrop, yeo. 1641/183
see also Anger
HANGER, Jn., Souldrop, lab. 1734/8
Jn., Ampthill, baker. A 1769/19
Thos., Flitwick, yeo. 1767/26
Wm., Felmersham, Radwell, yeo. 1813/25
HANING, Agnes, Wilshamstead. 1631/245
HANKIN(S), Cornelius alias Hankin, see Cornelius
Jn., Carlton. 1741/56
Sarah, Carlton, wid. A 1743-4/5
HANNAH, Jn., Carlton. 1754/56
Jn., Stagsden, farmer. 1779/21
Wm., Felmersham, shopkeeper. 1772/34
Wm., Stagsden, yeo. A 1787/5
HANNELL, HANWELL, Ann, Bromham, wid., innholder. A 1754/12
Anne, Heath, wid. Fac. 1719: 9/60
Edw., Heath, yeo. Fac. 1711: 9/34

HANNELL, HANWELL continued
Edw., Hockliffe, yeo. 1738-9/10
Edw., Lidlington, yeo. 1741/1
Edw., Woburn, carpenter. 1826/46
Eliz., Hockliffe, wid. 1760/31
Eliz., Leighton Buzzard, wid. LBA 1767/16
Eliz., Salford, spins. 1819/8
Jas., Hockliffe, carpenter. A 1761/5
Mich., Woburn, carpenter. 1817/9
Paul, Kempston. 1746/39
Shem, Bedford. 1691/131
Thos., Leighton Buzzard, yeo. LB 1765/23
Thos., Leighton Buzzard, Clipstone, gent. LB 1770/23
Wm., Houghton Regis, blacksmith. 1612/51
Wm., Lidlington, gent. 1758/33
HANSCOMBE, Ann, Moggerhanger, wid. 1679/2
Anthony, Shefford, innholder. 1641/218
Cath., Meppershall, wid. A 1700/17
Edw., Shillington. 1624/59
Edw., Woburn. 1812/13
Fra., Wootton, husb. 1628/62
Fra., Wootton, husb. 1672-3/181
Jas., Shillington, yeo. 1660-1/100
Jas., Shillington. 1691/107
Jas., Shillington, gent. A 1701/35
Jas., sen., Clifton, gent. 1781/67
Jeremy, Meppershall, yeo. 1698/102
Joan, wid. (no parish given). 1588-9/115
Jn., Shefford, poulter. 1576/20
Jn., Tempsford, husb. 1674/86
Jn., sen., Shillington, husb. 1718/37
Jn., Husborne Crawley, sawyer. 1731/83
Jn., Aspley Guise, yeo. 1824/19
Luther, Holwell, yeo. 1656/198
Madeline, Clifton, wid. 1637-8/147
Margery, Marston, wid. 1589/131
Martha, Ampthill, alehouse keeper. 1783/16
Mary, Shillington, wid. 1650/99
Mary, Shillington, spins. A 1762/1
Math., Holwell, yeo. 1592/34
Math., Over Stondon, husb. 1667/40
Math., Potton, shoemaker. 1674/128
Math., Shillington, yeo. 1720/102
Ric., Holwell. 1569/117
Robt., Holwell. 1573/133

HARCOCK, Sim., Stevington, 1718/10
see also Alcock
HARDEN, Agnes, Heath, wid. A 1742/24
Eliz., Dean, wid. 1778/2
John, Dunton. 1617/259, I
Thos., Dean, husb. 1768/24
see also Harding, Arden, Hardon
HARDING, Bayes alias Harding, see Bayes
Alice, Husborne Crawley, wid. R 1533: 4/1
Anne, Keysoe, wid. 1657-8/265
Eliz., Bedford St. Leonard, wid. 1612/116
Eliz., Henlow. 1643/59
Hugh, Bedford St. John, St. Leonard, yeo. 1604/31
Jn., Harlington, Wood End. R 1523: 2/8
Jn., sen., Aspley Guise. R 1530: 3/35
Jn., Eaton. 1599/69
Jn., Bedford St. Leonard, yeo. 1607-8/150
Jn., Henlow. 1643/53, I 4/289
Jn., Stotfold, lab. A 1707/22
Lewis, Northill, esq. 1617/195
Mary, Cople, wid. 1813/18
Mary, Bedford St. Paul, wid. 1696/93
Math., Streatley, yeo. 1626/96
Math., Flitwick, Denel End, yeo. 1630/15
Math., Moggerhanger, carpenter. A 1712/1
Nich., Streatley. R 1545-6: 11/155d
Nich., Streatley. 1632-3/11
Ric., Leagrave, husb. R 1559: 15/56d
Ric., Toddington, Chalton, lab. 1638/34
Ric., Maulden, tailor. 1639/67
Robt., sen., Streatley, husb. 1588/84
Robt., Cople, lab. 1665-6/85
Robt., Moggerhanger, dairyman. 1690-1/54
Sarah, Bedford, spins. 1854/9
Steph., Cople, yeo. 1739-40/89
Thos., Houghton Regis. R 1540: 6/24
Thos., Streatley, husb. 1560/164
Thos., sen., Streatley, yeo. 1603/89
Thos., Milton Bryan, yeo. 1630/66
Thos., Westoning, Sampsill. 1639/23
Thos., Bedford, yeo. 1641/142
Thos., Wootton, yeo. 1661-2/406
Thos., Bedford, collarmaker. 1688-9/57
Thos., Cople. 1698/107
Thos., Cople, thatcher. 1800/14

HARDING continued
Wm., Streatley. R 1536-7: 4/78d
Wm., Chalgrave. 1572/87
Wm., Elstow, yeo. 1638/163
Wm., Harlington. 1641/219
Wm., Southill, Stanford. 1743/12
see also Arden, Harden, Hardon
HARDON, Jn., Northill, Ickwell, husb. 1597-8/2
Jn., Dunton. 1617/259
see also Arden, Harden, Harding
HARDWICK, Edw., Felmersham, Radwell. 1714/3
Fran., Clapham, bach. 1610-11/38
Jas., Stagsden, tailor. 1757/29
Jos., Carlton, tailor. 1738/8
Martin, Dunstable (2 copies). 1553/146
Nich., Sharnbrook. R 1505?: 1/70
Robt., Marston, victualler and farmer. 1839/7
Thos., Stagsden, lab. 1726/39
Thos., Ridgmont, servant to the Duke of Bedford. 1781/58
Thos., Ridgmont, clockmaker. 1824/22
Wm., Houghton Regis. R 1550: 12/104
Wm., Marston, yeo. 1706/51
Wm., Little Staughton. 1752/74
Wm., Cranfield, yeo. 1798/8
HARDY, Cath., Toddington, wid. of Key. 1837/12
Hen., Harrold, butcher. R 1537: 5/10d
John, Bedford, fishmonger. R 1537-8: 5/9
Key, sen., Toddington, farmer. 1829/31
HARE, HARES, Agnes., Shillington, wid. 1593/52
Agnes, Shillington, spins. 1620/109
Ann, Shillington, wid. 1693-4/123
Charles, Flitton, yeo. 1625/164
Eliz., Shillington, spins. 1696/138
Enoch, Upper Gravenhurst, yeo. 1819/19
Geoff., Ampthill, bricklayer. AR 1682: 1/207d
Hen., Stagsden, cottager. 1733/47
Hen., Upper Gravenhurst, farmer and innkeeper. 1847/24
Jn., Dean, weaver. 1579/153
Jn., Shillington, Nether Stondon. 1580/218
Jn., Shillington. 1593/82
Luke, Wilshamstead, cordwainer. 1638/40
Martin, Shillington, carpenter. 1669/69
Math., Shillington, carpenter. 1635/70
Peter, Shillington. 1665-6/91
Ric., Shillington, Nether Stondon. 1608/81

HARPER continued
Ric., Eaton Socon, Wyboston, fisherman. A 1781/6
Robt., Bromham. R 1539: 5/31d
Rog., Bedford St. Paul. 1620/33
Sam., Goldington, farmer. 1837/35
Soloman, Carlton, lab. A 1777/12
Thos., Biddenham. R 1520: 2/162d
Thos., Biddenham, husb. 1614/59
Thos., Elstow, joiner. 1642/37
Thos., Roxton, Chalston, lab. 1676/175
Thos., Eaton Socon, Wyboston, fisherman. 1685/86
Thos., Northill. AR 1689: 1/132
Thos., Carlton, shepherd. 1725/18
Wm., Maulden, smith. R 1543: 11/2
Wm., Bletsoe, husb. R 1558: 14/53d
Wm., sen., Potton, yeo. 1670/225
Wm., Eaton Socon, Honidon, lab. 1675/93
Wm., Sharnbrook. AR 1689: 1/50
Wm., sen., Potton, cooper. 1707/54
Wm., Potton, yeo. 1708-9/55
Wm., Biggleswade, baker. BwA 1817/59
Harper alias Green, Wm., Biddenham. 1573/142
HARRATT, Jane, Bolnhurst, wid. 1808/1
HARRIAT, Agnes, Totternhoe. 1576/21
Jn., Totternhoe, husb. 1569/120
alias Simont, Thos., Northill, Over Caldecote. R 1568-9: 17/114d
HARRIMAN, Thos., Luton, victualler. 1766/5
HARRINGTON, Anth., Bedford, cooper. 1697/66
see also Errington
HARRIS, Carpenter alias Harris, see Carpenter
West alias Harris, see West
Able, Tilsworth, yeo. 1726/75
Alice, Podington, wid. AR 1678: 1/41d
Ann, Toddington, wid. 1665/69
Ben., Stotfold, husb. 1722/6
Chas., Clophill, brickmaker. 1740-1/92
Dan., Woburn, whitesmith. 1739-40/86
Dorcas, Luton, wid. 1752/1
Edw., Stopsley, lab. 1852/28
Eliz., Milton Bryan, wid. 1661/362
Eliz., Bedford St. Paul, wid. 1751/1
Geo., Pertenhall. 1579/141
Geo., ?Eaton Socon, Ford. 1686/2
Geo., Husborne Crawley, farmer and carman. 1853/9
Hannah, Biddenham, wid. 1752/62

HARRIS continued
Harry, Ridgmont, Segenhoe. 1559/183
Hen., Luton, yeo. 1741/49
Hugh, sen., Markyate Street, yeo. 1613/185, I
James, Leighton Buzzard. 1600/18
Jane, Shelton, wid. 1849/25
Joan, Pertenhall, wid. 1579-80/157
Joan, Toddington, wid. 1665/29
Jn., Milton Bryan. R 1538: 5/26
Jn., Leighton Buzzard. 1559/168
Jn., Totternhoe. 1620/110
Jn., Maulden, lab. 1626/96
Jn., Totternhoe. 1627/140
Jn., Toddington, yeo. 1661/390
Jn., Campton, blacksmith. AR 1670: 1/91
Jn., Campton, cordwinder. 1679/35
Jn., Biggleswade, gardener. Bw 1713/1, I
Jn., Toddington, yeo. 1727/2
Jn., Shefford, grocer and tallow chandler. 1741/15
Jn., Leighton Buzzard. LBA 1758/10
Jn., Bedford, gent. 1773/7
Jn., Husborne Crawley, carpenter. 1830/44
Jos., Wymington, lab. 1703/40
Jos., Woburn. 1735/5
Jos., Woburn, yeo. 1797/15
Len., Woburn, gardener. 1667-8/5
Margery, Podington, spinster. AR 1681: 1/43
Mary, Bedford, late of Biddenham, wid. 1737/55
Mary, Flitwick, Dennell End, wid. 1787/17
Mary Ann, Bedford St. Paul, Tavistock Street. 1855/29
Ric., Northill, Upper Caldecote, yeo. A 1795/5
Ric., Milton Bryan, husb. 1603/123
Ric., Odell, mason. 1617/284
alias Stevens, Robt., Tingrith, husb. 1636/23
Robt., Potsgrove. 1670/176
Robt., Bedford, baker. A 1738/16
Sam., Renhold, shepherd. 1750/5
Sam., Husborne Crawley, farmer. 1848/22
Sarah, Toddington, spins. 1741/8
Sarah, Woburn, spins. A 1797/3
Thos., Eynsbury, Hunts., bach. 1634-5/95
Thos., Milton Bryan, husb. 1652/55
Thos., Eaton Socon, barber chirurgeon. AR 1673: 1/63
Thos., Eaton Socon. AR 1682: 1/74d
Thos., Eaton Socon, Ford End, victualler. 1683/71

HARRIS continued
Thos., Warden, yeo. 1716/68
Thos., (old index only, bundle missing). A 1717/12
Thos., sen., Wymington, husb. 1718/18
Thos., Biddenham, yeo. 1745-51
Thos., Houghton Regis, poulterer. A 1766/23
Thos., Southill, blacksmith. 1827/37, I 4/270
Thos., Wilden, farmer. 1851/39
Wm., Studham, warriner. 1602/75
Wm., Cardington, lab. 1621/140
Wm., Podington, husb. 1658/214
Wm., Milton Bryan, yeo. 1675/23
Wm., Flitton, clerk. AR 1688: 1/214d
Wm., Milton Bryan, yeo. 1696/107
Wm., Biddenham, yeo. 1727-8/108
Wm., Colmworth, yeo. A 1762/4
Wm., Bedford, baker. 1785/33
Wm., Bedford St. Paul, baker. 1788/37
Wm., Leighton Buzzard, yeo. LB 1824/27
Wm., Leighton Buzzard, yeo. LBA 1824/84b
Wm., Stotfold, farmer. 1856/33
see also Arris
HARRISON, HARISON, HARRYSON, HARESON, Agnes, Houghton Conquest, wid. 1660/142
Chris., Stotfold, smith. R 1559: 15/57
Clement, Eaton Socon, Nether Staploe, yeo. 1598-9/96
Edw., Stotfold, husb. 1623/185
Eliz., Roxton, Colesden, Grange, wid. 1720/41
Eliz., Pavenham, wid. 1770/42
Geo., Leighton Buzzard. 1558/246
Joan, Nether Gravenhurst, spinster. 1606-7/1
Joan, Maulden, wid. 1618-19/35
Jn., Cople, weaver. 1632/58
Jn., Bedford St. Paul, yeo. 1653/3
Jn., Roxton, husb. 1704/65
Jn., Turvey, farmer. 1740/37
Jn., Roxton, esq.. (P/IX2, bundle missing). A 1747/28
Jn., Turvey, husb. 1750/48
Jos., Chellington, glover. A 1716-17/2
Mary, Southill. A 1805/1
Ric., Battlesden. 1560/203
Ric., Odell, glover. 1692-3/65
Ric., Odell, mason. A 1731/17
Ric., Sharnbrook, glover. 1714-15/124
Robt., Northill. R 1500: 1/16d

HARRISON, HARISON, HARRYSON, HARESON continued
Robt., Houghton Conquest, tailor. 1547/17
Robt., Luton, loader. 1638/28
Robt., Odell, mason. 1705/55
Roger, Stanbridge, lab. 1605/148
Sam., Pavenham, victualler. 1820/46
Sarah, Odell, wid. 1739-40/73
Sarah, Toddington, wid. 1772/13
Steph., Cranfield, victualler. 1772/35
Steph., Pavenham, grocer and matmaker. 1799/18
Thos., Warden, lab. 1640/48
Thos., Pavenham, mason. 1756/51
Thos., Harrold, mason. 1786/31
Thos., sen., Pavenham, mason. 1792/12
Thos., Pavenham, yeo. 1832/3
Wm., Blunham, husb. 1564/66
Wm., Houghton Conquest, lab. 1638/41
Wm., Toddington, leather clogg maker. A 1768/23
Wm., Pavenham, matmaker. 1787/3
HARROLD, Mary, Shillington, wid. 1737/7
Robt., Ampthill, yeo. 1654/187
HARROWDEN, HARRADINE, Edm., Warden, carpenter. 1660/26
Hugh, Biggleswade. BwR 1546: 1/4d
Isaac, Sandy, yeo. (reg. only). 1798/3
Ric., Potton, carpenter. A 1716/29
Stev., Moggerhanger. 1674-5/145
Thos., Southill, yeo. 1691/67
see also Horrodine
HARROWER, Jn., Milton Ernest, husb. 1634/89
HARSTON, Phoebe, Wilby, Northants., wid. 1638/51
HART, Eliz., Milton Ernest, wid. 1732-3/42
Geo., Kempston, butcher. 1850/30
James, Kempston, yeo. 1815/27
Joan, Elstow. 1619/182
Jn., Milton Ernest. AR 1676: 1/40
Jn., Kempston, shopkeeper. 1825/17
Jos., Bedford St. Paul, shoemaker. 1852/43
Mark, Gt. Barford, yeo. 1784/49
Martha, Cockayne Hatley, wid. 1850/4
Mary, Leighton Buzzard, wid. A 1751/10
Rebecca, Leighton Buzzard, wid. 1856/1
Ric., Bedford St. Cuthbert, shopkeeper. 1852/13
Robt., Haynes, cordwainer. 1841/15
Thos., Colmworth. 1685-6/124
Thos., Great Barford, shepherd. A 1702/16

HART continued
Thos., Gt. Barford. 1702/38
Thos., Milton Ernest (index only, admon. missing). 1726/19
Thos., Eaton Socon, yeo. 1809/33
Thos., Gt. Barford, yeo. A 1826/9
Thos., Riseley, yeo. 1851/6
Wm., Tilbrook. AR 1691-2: 1/84d
Wm., Lidlington, husb. A 1711/24
Wm., Eaton Socon, Wyboston, carpenter. A 1720/6
Wm., Colmworth, yeo. A 1725-6/32
Wm. Barns, Bedford, coach porter. 1846/23
Wm., Leighton Buzzard, shepherd. LB 1841/80
HARTING, Wm., Leighton Buzzard, shopkeeper. LB 1776/43
HARTOP, Ben., Thurleigh. 1851/33
Jn., Bolnhurst, Mavorn Farm, farmer. 1837/59
Thos., Keysoe, husb. A 1753/14
Thos., Keysoe, (P/IX 2, admon missing). A 1757/9
Thos., Keysoe, farmer. A 1780/5
HARTWELL, Eliz., Odell, wid. A 1720/21
Geo., Cranfield. AR 1690: 1/218d
Jas., Milton Ernest, victualler. 1782/50
Joan, Cranfield, wid. 1724/44
Jn., Bedford St. Peter, Brickhill, husb. 1691/80
Joshua, Cranfield. 1709/26
Joshua, Cranfield, grocer. 1714/92
Mary, Harrold, wid. 1681/7
Math., Leagrave. AR 1679: 1/157
Nich., Cranfield. 1632/156
Oswald, Odell, lab. 1614/63
Ralph, Luton. AR 1684: 1/166
Ric., Woburn, cordwainer. 1688/1
Ric., Cranfield, yeo. 1740/1
Robt., Upper Sundon, yeo. 1758/52
Sam., Harrold, lab. 1781/31
Thos., Billington. 1567/82
Thos., Harrold, yeo. 1729/2
Wm., Leighton Buzzard (bundle 1575). 1576-7/147
Wm., Bedford St. Mary, husb. 1685/84
HARTY, Harting alias Harty, see Harting
HARUE, see Harvey
HARVEY, HARUE, HERVY , ?, jun., Roxton, Chawston, lab. 1565/18
Chris., Eyeworth, yeo. 1675/26
Eliz., Thurleigh, spins. 1681/10
Eliz., Dunton, wid. 1687/60
Eliz., Dunton, wid. AR 1687: 1/129d

HARVEY, HARUE, HERVY continued
Jas., Bedford St. Paul, doctor in physick. 1711-12/47
Jn., Roxton, Chawston, lab. 1565/18
Jn., Harrold, fuller. 1591-2/22
Jn., Bedford St. Mary, glover. 1609/112
Jn., Thurleigh, esq. 1622/25
Jn., Thurleigh, gent. 1663-4/93
Jn., Wilden, dairyman. AR 1678: 1/68d
Jn., Bedford, lab. A 1705/41
Jn., Thurleigh, esq. 1716/54
Jn., Luton, gardener. A 1720/20
Jn., Harrold, carpenter. 1731/60
Judith, Ickwell, wife of Wm., gent.. 1740-1/70
Mary, Shillington, wid. 1667/15
Peter, Dunton, Millow, husb. 1589/69
Peter, Eyeworth, yeo. 1683/18
Ric., Bedford. 1589/83
Ric., Husborne Crawley, vicar. 1623/195
Ric., Wilden, husb. 1658/25
Sam., Dunton, lab. 1679/51
Sarah, Bedford, wid. 1728/78
Thos., Oakley, husb. 1617/203
Thos., Bedford St. Mary, glover. 1625/213
Thos., Warden, lab. 1662/41
Thos., Oakley, yeo. A 1700/11
Thos., Ampthill, grocer. 1708/88
Thos., Elstow, victualler. 1786/48
Wm., Oakley, husb. (Bundle 1660). 1659-60/195
Wm., Shillington, yeo. 1662-3/63
Wm., Toddington, innholder. A 1700/8
Wm., Toddington, innholder. 1700/101
Wm., Oakley, yeo. 1712/81
Wm., Elstow, victualler and pig dealer. 1811/11; I 4/286
HARWAR, Jn., Milton Ernest. 1588/100
Thos., Wilshamstead, vicar. 1558/243
Wm., sen., Milton Ernest. AR 1532: 3/63
HARWOOD, HAWODE, Alice, Sutton, wid. 1593/46
Edw., Shefford, glazier and plumber. 1756/10
Geo., Clifton, wheelwright. A 1840/3
Jn., Willington. 1715/24
Jn., Sandy, Beeston, gardener. 1815/6; I 4/220
Marg., Haynes, wid. 1576/39
Sarah, Willington, wid. A 1720/32
Thos., Sutton. 1581/12
Wm., Little Staughton, shepherd. 1616/68

HARWOOD, HAWODE continued
Wm., Clifton, wheelwright. A 1826/12
see also Hayward
HASCLEDINE, see Hasledene
HASEBERRY, Wm., Odell. 1679-80/83
HASELGROVE, Thos., Luton, stonemason. 1848/13
HASELWOOD, see Hazelwood
HASLEDEN, Margt., Stagsden. R 1551: 12/173
HASLEDENE, HASLEDINE, HASCLEDINE, HAZELDEAN
Ben., Goldington, esq. 1677/0
Ben., Goldington, gent. 1697/146
Cath., Goldington, wid. 1694/61
Doro., Potton, spins. 1737/12
Eliz., Goldington, gentlewoman. 1642/16
Eliz., Bedford, wid. 1700/75a
Jn., Marston, tailor. 1705/4
Jn., Bedford St. Paul, farmer. A 1826/4
Margt., Goldington, wid. 1641/172
Mary, Haynes. 1687/7
Paul, Houghton Conquest, yeo. 1673/41
Robt., Goldington, esq. AR 1682: 1/21d
Robt., jun., Goldington, gent. 1632/67
Robt., Bedford, gent. 1742-3/103
Thos., Marston, tailor. 1671/39
Wm., Goldington, gent. 1581/24
Wm., Colmworth. 1610-11/39
see also Hazelton
HASLEWOOD, see Hazelwood
HASTER, Ann, Millbrook, wid. 1683/101
Eliz., Kempston, wid. 1658/215
Hen., Bromham, shepherd. 1619/201; I 4/154
Jn., Totternhoe. 1611/10
see also Hester
HASTON, Robt., Markyate. R 1545: 11/79d
see also Astin; see also Ashton
HATCH, Wm., Luton, Stapleford, yeo. 1601-2/137
HATCHET, Reynold, Toddington, gent.. AR 1670: 1/141
Wm., Sutton. R 1538: 5/24d
HATFIELD, Edith, Dunstable, wid. AR 1671-2: 1/142d
Eliz., Dunstable, spins. 1719/98
Ric., Dunstable. AR 1672: 1/142
HATHAM, HATTHAM, HATTAM, Edw., Caddington, 1584/166
Edw., Heath, farmer. A 1750/18
Thos., Markyate. R 1535: 4/31d

HATLEY, Chris., Goldington, Putternhoe. 1576/37
Edw., Bedford St. Peter, lab. 1607/138
Godfrey, Cople. R 1549: 12/64d
Ric., Clifton, gent.. (Bundle 1667) 1666/1
Thos., Cople. R 1533: 3/98d
see also Attlee
HATRED, Eleanor, Dunstable, wid. 1740/54
Thos., Dunstable, farmer. 1730/41
HATTER, Margt., Dunstable, wid. 1731/48
Wm., Dunstable, innholder. 1719-20/97
HATTON, Eliz., Woburn, wid. A 1711/22
Hen., Woburn, dairyman. 1752/19
Jn., Woburn, victualler. 1776/3
Jonas, Harlington, yeo. 1636/27
Mary, Woburn, Apesfield, wid. 1759/53
Rebeccah, Woburn, wid. 1777/21
Ric., Harlington, lab. 1566-7/17
Ric., Harlington, lab. 1567/85
Wm., Blunham, miller. 1857/23
HAUGHTON, see Houghton
HAUPMAN, Lewis, Bedford St. Peter, cordwainer. 1804/30
HAVELYFFE, Thos., Caddington. 1560/200
HAVERON, ?HANERON, Wm., Sharnbrook. R 1531-2: 3/52
HAVITT, Jn., Eaton Socon, blacksmith. 1667/29
HAWATT, Eliz., Eaton Socon, spins. A 1716-17/1
HAWDLEY, see Audley
HAWES, Alice, Stanbridge. 1552/310
Hen., Astwick, parson. R 1534/4 loose between pages 48d and 49
Jn., Tempsford, yeo. R 1504: 1/43d
Jn., Caddington, husb. 1565/4b
Jn., Sundon, bricklayer. 1636/26
Letitia, Bedford. 1639/7
Mary, Northill, Over Caldecote, wid. 1663/112
Mary, Bedford, wid. 1745/5
Robt., Bedford, gent. 1626-7/225 (proved Prerogative Court of Canterbury)
Thos., Sharnbrook, lab. 1638/196
Thos., Ampthill, victualler. A 1720/38
HAWGOOD, Mary, Leighton Buzzard, spins. LB 1825/32
Mary, Leighton Buzzard, spins. LB 1830/49
HAWIKEY, Ed., Luton, gent. 1573/143 (doc. torn. Surname ex endorsement).
HAWKES, Alice, wid. ?1694/102 (badly torn, all information ex previous index)
Anne, Goldington, wid. 1623-4/92
Easey, Thurleigh, lab. A 1785/20
Eliz., Thurleigh, wid. A 1795/12
Geo., Podington, lab. 1679/18

HAWKES continued
Jn., Elstow, gent. c. 1670/220
Jn., Elstow, gent. AR 1671: 1/4
Jn., Bedford, gent. 1681/105
Jn., Thurleigh. 1811/19
Jn., Luton, bricklayer. 1818/14
Jos., Luton, bricklayer. 1831/8
Mary, Bedford, wid. 1718/70
Paul, Carlton, husb. 1691/81
Ric., Luton, lab. A 1715/8
Sarah, Totternhoe, wid. A 1803/2
Thos., Lidlington, yeo. 1616-17/4
HAWKINS, Quarry formerly Hawkins, see Quarry
?, ?Dunstable. 1559?/272
Alice, Houghton Regis. 1560/193
Alice, Dunstable, wid. 1697/25
Ann, Southill, Broom. A 1840/14
Cath., Bedford St. John, wid. AR 1678: 1/15d
Edm., Eaton, yeo. 1640/27
Edw., Marston, dairyman. 1647/35
Edw., Bedford, tailor. 1659-60/277
Edw., Eaton Bray, yeo. 1669/10
Eliz., Wilshamstead, wid. A 1728-9/53
Eliza, Flitton, yeo. 1676-7/176
Eustace, Northill, Thorncote. R 1512: 1/21
Fra., Fielden. 1799/37
Geo., Melchbourne. 1640/9
Geo., Bedford St. Mary, woollen draper. AR 1676: 1/12
Geo., Luton, husb. A 1701-2/42
Geoff., Marston, yeo. 1850/45
Hen., Tilsworth, husb. 1619-20/233
Hen., Houghton Regis. 1629/87
Hen., Thurleigh, lab. 1733/6
Jas., Leighton Buzzard. LBA 1767/18
Jeptha, Eaton Bray, carpenter. 1716/22
Jn., Houghton Regis. R 1521: 2/87
Jn., Houghton Regis. R 1551: 12/153
Jn., Northill, Thorncote, husb. 1561/152
Jn., Houghton Regis. 1563/94
Jn., Hockliffe, bach. 1582-3/116
Jn., Tilbrook, husb. 1589/72
Jn., Eaton Socon, Wyboston, lab. 1615/159
Jn., Houghton Regis. 1656/121
Jn., sen., Houghton Regis, yeo. 1689/25
Jn. Sanderson, Goldington, gent. 1718/24

HAWKINS continued
Jn., Tilbrook, yeo. (bundle 1719). 1720/37
Jn., Milton Ernest, vicar. 1721/48
Jn., Steppingley, yeo. 1738/11
Jn., sen., Houghton Regis, farmer. 1740/51
Jn., Luton. P/IX 2. A 1812/11
Jn., Luton, maltster. A 1817/4
Jn., sen., Bolnhurst, farmer. 1845/39
Marian, Houghton Regis, wid. 1545: 11/115d
Mary, Clifton, wid. 1741-2/73
Nich., Melchbourne. R 1509-10: 1/64d
Oliv., Tilbrook, husb. 1680/78
Rebecca, Ampthill, wid. (regis. only) 1779/16
Ric., Houghton Regis, Sewell. 1563/91
Ric., Renhold, yeo. 1586/91
Ric., Northill. 1588/86
Ric., Northill. 1588/88
Ric., Tilsworth, yeo. 1649/57
Ric., Streatley, yeo. 1694/52
Ric., Streatley, yeo. 1718/21
Ric., Streatley, farmer. 1741-2/72
Ric., Ampthill, grocer. 1765/14
Robt., Houghton Regis. 1579-80/169
Robt., Houghton Regis, husb. 1610/91
Robt., Knotting, clerk. 1664-5/88
Robt., Houghton Regis, Bidwell, weaver. 1710/73
Robt., Goldington, clerk. 1715/13
Robt., Chalgrave, Winfield, yeo. 1729/32
Sus., Eaton Bray, wid. 1743/5
Thos., Tilsworth. 1582-3/119
Thos., Houghton Regis, yeo. 1601/153
Thos., Houghton Regis, the Willows, yeo. 1629-30/140
Thos., Bedford St. Paul. 1632/17
Thos., sen., Woburn, butcher. 1665/34
Thos., Ampthill, butcher. AR 1671: 1/187d
Thos., Dunstable, tailor. AR 1680: 1/160
Thos., East Hyde, husb. 1680/94
Thos., Southill, tailor. 1720/32
Thos., Houghton Regis, yeo. 1730/52
Thos., Luton, maltster. 1748/31
Wm., Wilshamstead, farmer. A 1728/4
Wm., Tilsworth, husb. R 1545: 11/74d
Wm., Houghton Regis, husb. 1587-8/101
Wm., Houghton Regis, Sewell, husb. 1618/40
Wm., Tilbrook, husb. 1652/93

HAWKINS continued
Wm., Houghton Regis, Berry Corner, lab. 1671/26
Wm., Houghton Regis, Thorne, bricklayer. 1704/61
Wm., sen., Eaton Bray, husb. 1728/55
HAWLEY, Thos., Kempston, yeo. 1810/25
HAWSEY, Geo., Kempston, yeo. 1591/100
HAWSHEDE, Simon, Leighton Buzzard, mercer. 1558/229
HAWTHORN(E), HEYTHORN, Nich., Eversholt, woodward. 1664/53
Robt., Pulloxhill. R 1524: 2/24
Sarah, Bedford, wid. 1726/5
Steph., Stevington. 1694-5/97
Steph., Renhold, husb. 1705-6/88
Wm., Holcote, yeo. 1664/26
HAWTREY, Ed., Luton, gent. 1573/143 (Document torn. Surname taken from endorsement)
HAXBY, Thos., Potton, clerk. 1693/140
HAYCOCK, Edw., Chalgrave. AR 1678: 1/155
Wm., Pavenham, yeo. 1686/59
HAYDON, Jas., Luton, husb. A 1766/6
Joan, Leighton Buzzard. LBAR 1537: 1/4
Mich., Westoning, Wood End, yeo. 1788/22
Ric., Luton, New Mill End, yeo. 1778/6
Sam., sen., Luton, New Mill End, farmer. 1813/7
Wm., Leagrave, lab. 1841/37
see also Hadden, Adean, Addendes, Adown, Hayton
HAYES, HAYS, HEYE, HEIS, Ben., Bedford, innholder. 1744/14
Eliz., Elstow. 1560/207
Fra., Campton, spins. A 1758/7
Geo., Campton, dairyman. 1739/24
Margt., Bedford. 1553/279
Philip, Northill, Upper Caldecote, herdsman. 1663/113
Thos., Bedford. 1708/64
Jn., Upper Gravenhurst, minister. 1711/25
Thos., Sharnbrook, carpenter. A 1731/31
Wm., Elstow. 1560/228
Wm., Harrold, lab. 1773/26
HAYNES, HANES, HEYNES, Simpson alias Haynes, see under Simpson
Adam, Little Staughton, mason. 1663/40
Edw., Renhold, yeo. 1610/124
Edw., Riseley, lab. 1642/38
Edw., Bolnhurst, shepherd. 1712/41
Edw., Sharnbrook, Colmworth, lab. 1757/38
Eliz., Dean, wid. A 1711/68
Eliz., Meppershall, wid. 1797/45
Eliz., late Whittlebury, Northants. (Mentions son at Toddington). 1843/33

HAYNES, HANES, HEYNES continued
alias Peterson, Fra., Clifton. 1643/70
Fra., Bolnhurst, yeo. 1655/133
Gilbert, Bedford, innkeeper. 1818/9
Grace, Biddenham. 1652/96
Hen., Biddenham, yeo. 1642/32
Hen., Biddenham, yeo. 1713/49
Hen., Keysoe, yeo. A 1732-3/32
Hen., Woburn, blacksmith. 1839/9
Jn., Riseley, lab. 1632/21
Jn., Bedford, gardener. 1680-1/108
Jn., Kempston, yeo. 1723/62
Jn., Nether Dean, weaver. 1745/12
Margt., Bedford, wid. 1724/56
Peter, Lidlington, miller. A 1714/11
Phil., Silsoe, yeo. 1640/64
Ric., Bolnhurst, lab. 1619/204; I 4/146
Robt., Bolnhurst, husb. 1593/54
Robt., Sutton, husb. 1632-3/16
Robt., Lidlington, farmer. AR 1685: 1/212d
Robt., Colmworth, blacksmith. 1679-80/89
Robt., Blunham, yeo. 1830/38
Sam., Nether Dean, weaver. 1753/20
Sarah, Kempston, wid. A 1734/25
Simon, Bolnhurst, yeo. 1680/67
Steph., Oakley. AR 1691-2: 1/51
Steph., Cranfield, yeo. A 1755/2
Stev., Biddenham, yeo. 1673/75
Thos., sen., Bolnhurst, husb. 1617-18/220
Thos., Carlton, yeo. 1667/85
Thos., Keysoe, yeo. 1693/79
Thos., Stagsden, husb. 1719/64
Thos., Biggleswade, lab. Bw 1759/34
Walt., Renhold, yeo. 1632-3/4
Wm., Milton Bryan, husb. 1573/121
Wm., Cranfield, lab. 1698/129
Wm., Bedford, cordwainer. 1701/39
Wm., Yielden, innholder. A 1733/1
Wm., Wootton, yeo. 1800/24
Wm., Kempston, blacksmith. 1823/11
Wm., Woburn, Shefford, bricklayer, but now "out of business". 1854/25
See also Heyne
HAYTON, Wm., sen., Ivinghoe, esq. LBA 1818/73
see also Haydon

HAYWARD, HAWARD, Eliz., Marston, wid. 1711/113
Geo., Bedford, yeo. 1694/33
Jn., sen., Podington. R 1516-7: 1/254d
Jn., Henlow. R 1541-2: 6/111d
Jn., Marston, carpenter. 1711/112
Mary, Luton, wid. 1624/104
Mary, Pavenham, wid. 1632-3/39
Mary, Leighton Buzzard, wid. LBA 1771/21
Oliver, Maulden. 1560/219
Rebeccah, Sutton, wid. 1686/20
Robt., Caddington, yeo. 1618-19/32
Thos., Pavenham, husb. 1573/3
Thos., Sutton, yeo. 1623-4/91
Wm., Dunstable. R 1518: 2/83
Wm., Houghton Regis. 1532: 3/65d
Wm., Bedford, butcher. 1723/28
see also Howard; Harwood; Heward
HAZELDEAN, see Hasledene
HAZELTON alias Whaddon, Jn., Silsoe, shepherd. 1632/86
see also Hazeldean
HAZELWOOD, Jn., Wrestlingworth. AR 1674: 1/99d
Ric., Langford. BwR 1552-3: 1/7d
Ric., Langford, husb. 1618-19/31
Ric., Henlow. 1646/95
Wm., Biggleswade, Holme. 1582-3/105
HEAD, Ann, Chalgrave, wid. 1675/42
Judith, Chalgrave, Tebworth, wid. 1677-8/79
Luke, Lidlington, husb. 1616/150
Luke, Woburn, whitetanner. 1639/17
Ric., Chalgrave, Tebworth. 1584/266
Ric., Chalgrave. 1663-4/80
Wm., Chalgrave, Tebworth. R 1558: 14/87
HEADING, HEDDING Math., Eaton Socon, bricklayer. 1721-2/75
Wm., Eaton Socon, Wyboston, farmer. 1820/2
Wm., Eaton Socon, Wyboston, surveyor of the North Road. 1849/1
Wm., sen.,Old Warden, farmer. A 1847/7
see also Headling
HEADLAND, Wm., Woburn, yeo. 1597/55
HEADLING, HEDLING, Jn., Potton. 1641/137
Jn., Cardington, Fenlake, lab. 1661/385
Jn., Cardington, Harrowden, husb. 1682/15
Jos., Wilshamstead, tailor. 1692-3/56
Ric., Wilshamstead, grazier. 1638/68
Thos., Potton, lab. 1686/66
Wm., Cardington, Fenlake, husb. 1634-5/123

HEADLING, HEDLING continued
Wm., Fenlake, lab. 1677-8/58
see also Heading
HEALE, HELE, Robt., Leighton Buzzard, yeo. LB 1741/14
HEALEY, Geo., Billington, lab. A 1842/97
Jos., Bedford, victualler. 1782/6
Martha, Leighton Buzzard, spins. LB 1795/100
Susannah, Leighton Buzzard, spins. 1839/71
Thos., Leighton Buzzard. A 1809/62
see also Hely
HEARD, see Herd
HEASE, Thos., Carlton, lab. 1689/55
HEATH, HETHE, Edw., Dunstable, yeo. 1664/42
Geo., Flitton, Greenfield, yeo. 1693-4/120
Gregory, Luton, Newmill End, husb. 1706/53
Jn., Pulloxhill, yeo. A 1779/11
Jn., Flitton, carpenter. 1760/23
Jn., jun., Bedford, miller. 1842/26
Robt., Clophill. 1662/88
Thos., Dunstable. 1601/120
Trustrum, Clophill, brickmaker. 1660/28
Wm., Whipsnade. 1558?/241
Wm., Lidlington, yeo. 1600/28
HEATHFIELD, Jas., Campton, yeo. 1853/37
Jn., Campton, lab. 1826/26
HEATHWAITE, Edw., Bedford, innholder. A 1711-12/36
HEATLEY, Thos., Riseley, tanner. AR 1558-9: 13/154d
HEBBS, HEBBES, HEBBYS, Agnes, Battlesden, wid. 1637/81
Edm., Chalgrave, Wingfield, husb. 1620/44
Hen., Chalgrave, Tebworth. R 1545: 11/106
Hen., Houghton Regis, lab. 1661-2/411
Hen., sen., Chalgrave, Wingfield, yeo. 1662/55
Hen., Chalgrave, Wingfield, yeo. 1662/123
Jn., Sundon, yeo. 1582/53
Jn., Hockliffe, carpenter. 1620/108
Jn., Lidlington. 1632-3/32
Jn., Hockliffe, cordwainer. 1732/3
Mary, Woburn, wid. AR 1674-5: 1/192d
Mary, Woburn. 1700/118
Ric., Tilsworth. R 1505: 1/85
Ric., Sandy. 1553?/264
Ric., Tilsworth. 1575/82
Ric., Hockliffe, lab. 1611-2/146
Ric., Leighton Buzzard, yeo. 1611-12/184
Ric., Wrestlingworth, tailor. 1638/52

HEMING, HEMMING, HEMYNG, HEMMEN continued
Jn., Biggleswade, Holme, yeo. 1686/64
Jn., Biggleswade, Holme. 1694/17
Jn., Edworth, yeo. 1726/92
Jn., Biggleswade, Holme, yeo. 1730/27
Judith, Astwick, wid. 1738/60
Mary, Lidlington, wid. 1818/23
Ric., Langford, yeo. 1620/100
Ric., Langford. 1687/6
Robt., Arlesey. R 1537: 5/12
Robt., Langford, husb. 1614/73
Thos., Langford, husb. 1615-16/134
Thos., Edworth, bach. 1696/81
Wm., Langford. 1617/196
Wm., Lidlington, dairyman. 1812/58
HEMMEN, see Heming
HEMPSON, Jn., Wootton, cordwainer. 1730-1/95
see also Empston
HEMPSTOCK, Hen., Turvey, lab. 1615-16/227
HEMS, Wm., Bromham. R 1545: 11/112d
see also Eame, Eames, Ampes
HENDERSON, Thos., Luton, carpenter. A 1825/8
HENE, Wm., sen., Little Staughton, husb. 1557/331
HENGER, see Hangar
HENISEEDE, see Hennessy
HENLEY, Jas., Cardington, miller. 1606-7/14
Jn., Holwell, clerk. 1636-7/112
Thos., Eaton Bray, farmer. 1816/20
Wm., Markyate Street, yeo. and maltster. 1790/32
Wm., Markyate Street, maltster. 1797/41
HENMAN, David, Bromham, farmer. 1855/15
Sarah, Bow Brickhill, Bucks. wid. 1802/6
Wm., Bromham, yeo. 1847/9
see also Hensman
HENNESSY, HENISEEDE, Jn., Eaton Socon, Ford End, mason. 1642/30
HENSHAW, Thos., Biggleswade. BwA 1829/70
HENSMAN, HENCEMAN, HENCHMAN, Ben., Bedford. A 1742-3/45
Chris., Totternhoe. R 1549: 12/53d
Eliz., Biddenham. A 1719/8
Eliz., Harrold, wid. 1747/16
Fra., Dunstable, innholder. 1650/105
Geo., Bedford, peruke maker. 1742/79
Isabell, Totternhoe, wid. 1600/62
Jn., Odell, husb. 1669/80
Jn., Bedford St. Paul, collarmaker. 1694/5

HENSMAN, HENCEMAN, HENCHMAN continued
Jn., Odell, farmer. 1745/43
Jn., Flitwick, victualler and wheelwright. 1834/43
Mark, Bedford, gent. A 1747/2
Mich., Carlton, victualler. A 1725-6/34
Rachael, Bedford, wid. A 1779/12
Ric., Bedford, butcher. 1849/13
Robt., Lidlington, husb. A 1813/19
Sam., Bedford, oilman. A 1735/3
Sarah, Carlton (P/IX 2 admon. missing) A 1783/20
Thos., Totternhoe, tailor. 1598/110
Thos., Eaton. 1624-5/13
Thos., Cranfield, yeo. 1650/140
Thos., Harrold. AR 1676: 1/40
Thos., Wootton, grocer. 1684/14
Thos., Totternhoe. A 1719-20/40
Thos., Bromham, dairyman. 1752/9
Thos., Carlton, victualler and yeo. 1772/36
Thos., Aspley Guise, yeo. 1789/19
Thos., Carlton, victualler. A 1821/17
Wm., Totternhoe. R 1510: 2/125d
Wm., Totternhoe. 1560/210
Wm., Tempsford, Lambcourt End. 1610/81
Wm., Odell, yeo. 1728/88
Wm., Ridgmont, baker (reg. only). 1770/5
Wm., Bedford St. Paul, mealman. A 1806/5
Wm., Bedford, staymaker. (Limited admon) A 1843/17
see also Henman
HENSON, Fra., Odell, lab. 1614-15/12
Grace, Odell, wid. 1614-15/5
Jn., Keysoe, shepherd. 1694-5/82
Mary, Maulden, wid. 1785/28
Ric., Tempsford, Lampit End, husb. 1578/105
Robt., Sharnbrook, vicar. 1573/113
Wm., Tempsford, Lambcourt End. 1610/81
Wm., Ampthill, yeo. A 1796/13
Wm., Ampthill, carpenter. A 1831/20
HEPPLEWHITE, HEBULWHERE, Giles, Shillington, weaver. R 1504: 1/205
HERBERT, Pirton alias Herbert, see Pirton
Fra., Milton Bryan, wid. 1731/85
Geo., Totternhoe, carpenter. A 1742/15
Geo., Totternhoe. (Old index only, bundle missing). 1745/8
Jn., Riseley, gear layer. 1699/30
Jn., Kempston. 1728/95
Mary, Cranfield, wid. 1732/62

HERBERT continued
Nich., Milton Bryan, lab. A 1711/40
Ralph, Totternhoe, yeo. 1704/30
Susannah, Kempston, spins. A 1736/5
Thos., Wilshamstead, lab. 1643/69
Thos., Eaton Bray, schoolmaster. 1668/162
Thos., Cranfield, tailor. A 1723-4/42
Wm., Melchbourne, gent. 1685/125
Wm., Houghton Regis, yeo. 1782/34
see also Harbert
HERBREW, Edw., Milton Bryan, carpenter. 1728/59
HERD, HEARD, Hen., Melchbourne, yeo. 1668/156
HERMITAGE, ARMITAGE, Wm., Sandy, cooper. 1699/7
HERNE, HEARN, Steph., Bedford St. Paul. 1715/29
Thos., Bedford, Beasley, stay and truss maker. 1843/28
HERRING, HEARRINGE, Jn., Bedford, innholder. 1609/114
Thos., Little Staughton, husb. 1572-3/85
Thos., Bolnhurst, husb. 1630/63
Wm., Little Staughton, husb. 1575/139
Wm., Bolnhurst, yeo. 1637-8/24
Wm., Little Staughton, yeo. 1639-40/158
Wm., Little Staughton, husb. 1659/273
HESTER, alias Crockett, Jn., Bedford St. Paul, bach. 1682-3/118, AR 1682-3: 1/23
Thos., Bedford St. Paul, Silver Street, chimney sweep and earthenware dealer. 1847/52
see also Haster
HEWARD, Jas., Roxton, Chawston, lab. 1612/50
Jn., Sutton, yeo. 1666/125
Jn., Turvey, metalman. AR 1681: 1/42d
Thos., Eaton, carpenter. 1660-1/111
Thos., Marston, yeo. 1688/14
see also Hayward, Howard, Hewett
HEWER, Wm., Luton, husb. R 1529: 3/5
see also Ewer
HEWETT, HEWET, HEWITT, HUET, Alex., Bedford St. Cuthbert, husb. 1560/208
Emma, Riseley, wid. 1704/39
Hen., Bedford St. Mary. AR 1674: 1/8
Jn., Knotting. 1605-6/97
Jn., Eaton Bray, yeo. 1700-1/145
Jn., Eaton Socon, ironmonger. 1704/89
Nich., Yielden. 1555/138
Robt., Ampthill, gent. 1559/311

HEWETT, HEWET, HEWITT, HUET continued
Robt., Tempsford, yeo. 1775/28
Thos., Bedford. 1558/240
Thos., (parish torn off). c 1670/221
Thos., Eaton Socon, baker. 1831/44
Walt., Melchbourne. 1558/65
Wm., Tilsworth. R 1500-1?: 1/25d
Wm., Melchbourne, husb. 1590-1/136
Wm., Melchbourne, husb. 1608/49
Wm., Milbrook, esq. 1622-3/32
Wm., Odell, husb. 1668/147
Wm., Eaton Bray, miller. 1721/1
Wm., Eaton Socon, baker. 1835/6
see also Heward
HEWINGS, Margt., Dunstable, wid. 1759/51
see also Huggins
HEWKINS, Sarah, Bedford St. Mary, wid. 1758/3
HEWLETT, HULET, Chas., Felmersham, Moor End, yeo. 1687-8/97
Chas., Pavenham, lab. A 1810/13
Hen., Turvey, carpenter. 1683/38
Jas., Oakley, baker. 1836/48
Jn., Turvey, bailiff to Mrs Brands. 1739-40/4
Jn., Thurleigh, lab. A 1713/23
Mary, Felmersham, Radwell, wid. 1754/10
Mary, Felmersham, wid. A 1820/10
Nathan, Bedford, carpenter. 1825/10
Steph., Pavenham, grocer. A 1857/5
Thos., Harrold, tailor. 1697/21
Thos., Felmersham, yeo. 1787/14
Thos., Pavenham, miller. A 1808/11
Wm., Turvey, carpenter. 1625/188
Wm., Harrold. 1639-40/117
Wm., Felmersham, farmer. A 1743/12
Wm., Felmersham, yeo. 1801/17
Wm., Oakley, fisherman. 1838/20
HEWMAN, Anne, Shillington, wid. 1628-9/22
HEXTON, Rogers alias Hexton, see under Rogers
see also Exton
HEY, Nich., Toddington, 'porcionar' [i.e. parcener] and parson of Broughton, Bucks. 1553/269
HEYCOCK, See Haycock
HEYDON, see Haydon
HEYNE, Jn., Bolnhurst. 1557/401
Ric., Bolnhurst. 1556/113
Thos., Keysoe, husb. R 1558: 14/143d

HEYNE continued
see also Haynes
HEYTHORN, see Hawthorn
HIBBS, see Ibbs
HICHE, HYCHE, HITCH, Augustine, Kempston, Hardwick. 1559/333
Ellen, Kempston, wid. R 1549: 12/52
Jn., sen., Kempston. R 1541: 6/72
Jn., sen., Kempston, Hardwick. R 1548: 12/35d
Roger, Kempston. R 1550: 12/137d
Roger, Kempston. 1550/25
Thos., Sutton. R 1504: 1/49
Thos., Ampthill. R 1504-5: 1/68
Thos., Bedford St. Paul. R 1520: 2/161d
Wm., Kempston, Hardwick. 1586-7/125
HICKLEFIELD, Andr., Colmworth. 1720/10
HICKMAN, Cath., Cardington, spins. 1727-8/73
Edw., Leighton Buzzard, oatmealmaker. 1679-80/105
Eliz., Leighton Buzzard. LB AR 1544: 1/10d
Eliz., Cardington, spins. 1745/15
Eliz., Cardington, wid. A 1790/12
Humph., Lidlington, yeo. 1626/66
Humph., Lidlington, gent. 1657/171
Jn., Southill, Stanford. R 1532-3: 3/83d
Jn., Eggington. 1558/228
Jn., Leighton Buzzard, bricklayer. LB 1767/9
Jn., Cardington, yeo. A 1785/9
Jn., Dunstable, shepherd. 1829/17
Jn., sen., Cardington, yeo. 1847/36
Jonathan, Markyate Street, bricklayer. 1792/5
Jos., sen., Felmersham, Radwell. 1787/30
Mary, Cardington. 1733/49
Mary, Uppingham, Rutland, wife of Wm. Beaumont Chase, property at Cranfield and elsewhere in Beds. 1793/38
Ric., Lidlington, oatmealmaker. 1663-4/102
Ric., Hockliffe, yeo. 1819/30
Robt., Eggington. 1609/164
Thos., Campton, husb. 1602/71
Thos., Cardington, dairyman. A 1706/31
Thos., Marston, dairyman. A 1711/19
Thos., Cardington, yeo. 1719/10
Thos., Cardington, farmer. A 1733/8
Thos., Markyate Street, bricklayer. 1804/16
Wm., Leighton Buzzard. LB AR 1554: 1/24
Wm., Leighton Buzzard. 1554/160
Wm., Leighton Buzzard. AR 1675: 1/193d

HICKMAN continued
Wm., jun., Lidlington, yeo. 1691/145
Wm., Lidlington, yeo. 1695/62
see also Higman
HICKS, HYXE, HIX, Eliz., Potsgrove, wid. A 1727/3
Eliz., Long Sutton, Lincs. A 1792/6
Geo., Husborne Crawley, yeo. 1714-15/50
Geo., Shefford, surgeon. 1805/3
Geo., Toddington, Denbigh. 1828/1
Jn., Eaton Socon, periwigmaker. 1774/49
Jn., Cranfield, lacemaker. A 1712/53
Jonathan, Potsgrove. AR 1688: 1/174d
Ric., (no place). 1558/86
Robt., Potton, clerk. 1746/12
Robt., Toddington, Denbigh, surgeon. A 1814/4
HICKSON, Amy, Dunstable, wid. 1672/147
Edw., Markyate Street, blacksmith. 1765/27
Jos., Langford, farrier. 1807/43
Jos., Langford. 1821/7
Math., Dunstable, yeo. 1644/55
Thos., sen., Markyate St., blacksmith. 1728/107
see also Higson
HICKTON, Jas., Bedford St. Paul, Hassett Street, Chelsea pensioner and registrar of births and deaths. 1857/4
HIDE, see Hyde
HIGBID, HYCKBED, Geo., sen., Whipsnade, yeo. 1721/2
Jn., Cardington. R 1558: 14/55d
Ric., Caddington, Chawl End. R 1538: 5/16
Thos., Leighton Buzzard, barber. A 1748-9/25
Wm., Studham, yeo. 1720/12
Wm., Leighton Buzzard, maltster. LB 1741/15
HIGBY, HIGBEE, Eliz., jun., Eaton Socon. A 1705/10
Geo., Whipsnade. AR 1684: 1/167
Wm., Leighton Buzzard. AR 1677: 1/197
HIGDEN, Ric., Luton, Thrale End, husb. 1710/19
HIGGINBOTTOM, HICKENBOTTOM, Jn., Leighton Buzzard, gardener. 1816/63
HIGGINS, Barth., Salford, farmer. 1857/40
Ellen, Ampthill. 1647/48
Jn., Marston, yeo. 1648/104
Jn., Kempston, yeo. 1723/50
Jn., Luton, plumber and glazier. A 1837/1
Mary Ann, Bedford. A 1831/4
Rebecca, Aspley Guise, wid. 1707/36
Sarah, Kempston, wid. 1746/20

HIGGINS continued
Thos., Kempston, laceman. 1693/111
HIGGS, Dugliss, Bedford St. Peter, spins. 1704/10
Geo., Dunstable, bricklayer. 1761/24
Jn., Bedford St. Peter, lab. AR 1684: 1/24d
Ric., Dunstable, bricklayer. 1827/46
Thos., Bedford St. Paul. 1638-9/101
Thos., Dunstable, builder. A 1848/17
Wm., Westoning. A 1854/5
HIGH, Wm., Pidley, Hunts. R 1512: 1/178
see also Hyde
HIGHAM, Ambrose, Maulden, Limbersey, husb. 1761/50
Sam., Tingrith, lab. 1793/23
Thos., Silsoe, husb. 1741/68
Thos., Maulden, yeo. 1794/42
HIGHWAY, see Heeway
HIGHT, Sam., Colmworth, farmer. A 1849/10
HIGMAN, HYGMAN, Thos., Potton. R 1505: 1/107
see also Hickman
HIGSON, Eliz., Shefford, wid. A 1791/11
Thos., Cardington, yeo. 1708-9/50
see also Hickson
HILL, HILLS, Haggis alias Hills, see Haggis; Shaw alias Hill, see Shaw
Abigail, Kempston, wid. 1705/26
Agnes, Lidlington, wid. 1677/45
Alice, Blunham. R 1538-9: 5/37d
Alice, Cranfield, wid. A 1739/16
Ann, Tingrith, publican. A 1845/10
Charlotte, Bedford, wid. 1811/29
Christian, (parish not given), wid. 1618-19/12
Edw., Eaton Socon. 1554?/228
Edw., Maulden, yeo. 1575/84
Edw., Silsoe. 1584/258
Edw., sen., Clophill, yeo. 1684/84
Edw., Clophill. AR 1684: 1/210d
Edw., Maulden. 1702/2
Edw., Clifton, innholder. 1739/38
Edw., Clophill
Eliz., Silsoe, wid. 1614/32
Eliz., Maulden, wid. 1661/298
Eliz., Barton, wid. 1672/108
Eliz., Barton, wid. AR 1672: 1/143
Eliz., Clophill, spins. AR 1688: 1/217
Ellen, Lidlington. 1609/180
Ephraim, Bedford St. Paul, yeo. or peruke maker. A 1792/3

HILL, HILLS continued
Fra., Bedford, spins. 1760/45
Geo., Wootton, shoemaker. 1632/56
Geo., Silsoe, wid. 1612/40
Geo., Bletsoe. 1636/46
Hen., Wootton, yeo. 1650/122
Hen., Luton, husb. 1658/60
Hen., Wootton, yeo. 1720/68
Hen., Barton, husb. 1749/11
Humph., Tingrith, clerk. 1637-8/159
Jn., Lidlington. R 1500: 1/22d
Jn., Barton, husb. 1538/4
Jn., Studham. R 1540-1: 6/63d
Jn., Silsoe. R 1546: 11/196d
Jn., Turvey. R 1558: 14/74d
Jn., Houghton Conquest. 1559/161
Jn., Silsoe, gent. 1607-8/146
Jn., Goldington, lab. 1613-14/156
Jn., sen., Wootton, yeo. 1624/61
Jn., Arlesey, husb. 1625/209
Jn., Cople. 1627/137
Jn., Southill, Stanford Bury, gent. 1642/49
Jn., Wootton, yeo. 1648/120
Jn., Wootton, yeo. 1697-8/65
Jn., Biggleswade, cordwainer. A 1705/36
Jn., Blunham, miller. A 1711-12/31
Jn., Maulden, husb. 1717/1
Jn., Wootton, gent. A 1724/21
Jn., Langford, blacksmith. 1729/19
Jn., Ampthill, grocer. 1730/83
Jn., Wootton, yeo. A 1731/4
Jn., Flitton, dairyman. 1743/33
Jn., Silsoe, farmer. A 1778/12
Jn., Bedford, blacksmith. 1780/18
Jn., Riseley, farmer. 1797/6
Jn., Keysoe, farmer. 1803/19
Jn., Luton, publican. 1821/41
Jn., Wootton, shoemaker. A 1827/13
Jos., Maulden, dairyman. 1704/85
Jos., Wootton, grocer. 1712/5
Jos., Clophill, victualler. 1731/37
Jos., Potsgrove, farmer. 1856/19
Margt., Sharnbook, wid. 1612/101
Margy., Blunham. R 1540: 6/27d
Martha, Ampthill, spins. 1639-40/121

HILL, HILLS continued
Mary, Wootton, spins. 1661-2/407
Mary, Riseley, wid. 1692/44
Mary, Holcote, wid. 1728/102
Math., Wootton, yeo. 1724-5/15
Math., Colmworth, farmer. 1738-9/38
Mich., sen., Bedford. 1744-5/42
Phillip, Felmersham, gent. A 1737/13
Reg., Silsoe, gent. 1622-3/18
Ric., Blunham. R 1538-9: 5/29
Ric., Luton. R 1545: 11/52d
Ric., Luton. 1556/94
Ric., Souldrop, lab. 1628/45
Ric., sen., Maulden, yeo. 1639-40/146
Ric., Maulden, yeo. 1675/27
Ric., Shillington. AR 1676: 1/106
Robt., sen., Eaton Socon, Staploe, husb. 1579-80/158
Robt., Tempsford. 1630-1/106
Robt., Potton, blacksmith. A 1744/17
Robt., Cranfield, yeo. 1767/36
Robt., Cranfield, farmer. 1790/12
Robt., Luton, carpenter. 1820/40
Ruth., Luton, spins. A 1826/23
Sam., Shillington, farmer. A 1847/10
Sighe, Wootton, wid. 1650/116
Susan, Wootton, wid. 1708/18
Susanna, Langford, wid. A 1745/18
Temperance, Wootton, spins. 1822/24
Thos., Lidlington. R 1504: 1/3d
Thos., Lidlington, yeo. 1574-5/46
Thos., Willington, husb. 1614/38
Thos., Eaton Socon, Nether Staploe. 1616-17/8
Thos., sen., Wootton. ?1647/37
Thos., Silsoe, cordwinder. 1669-70/123
Thos., Woburn. AR 1676: 1/196
Thos., Lidlington, gent. 1696/114
Thos., Woburn, husb. A 1720/25
Thos., Barton, butcher. A 1721/6
Thos., Wootton, cordwainer. 1726/50
Thos., Dunstable, clerk. 1754/23
Thos., Luton, blacksmith. 1774/29
Thos., Bedford, bricklayer. 1811/7
Thos., Pertenhall, woolcomber. 1831/38
Thos., Upper Gravenhurst, White Hall Farm, farmer. 1857/30
Walt., Thurleigh, yeo. 1605/88

HILL, HILLS continued
Wm., Studham. 1577/76
Wm., Wootton, yeo. 1611/163
Wm., Barton, blacksmith. 1656-7/204
Wm., sen., Wootton, yeo. 1686-7/83
Wm., sen., Wootton, yeo. 1689/72
Wm., Campton, clerk. 1702-3/60
Wm., Keysoe, dairyman. A 1705/27
Wm., Clophill, yeo. A 1707/35
Wm., Bedford St. Mary, innholder. 1773/46
Wm., Bedford. A 1809/15
Wm., Bedford St. Peter, High Street, grocer. 1857/33
HILLEAT, Jn., Clapham, lab. 1672/150
Lewis, Bedford St. Peter, maltster. 1708/63
Robt., Oakley, lab. 1662/75
see also Elliott
HILLERSDEN, HILSDEN, HILSDON, Eliz., Luton, wid. 1723/78
Eliz., Dunstable, spins. 1828/14
Jos., Chalgrave, farmer. A 1781/5
Thos., Battlesden, yeo. 1570/19
Wm., Elstow, esq. 1725/24
HILLIARD, see Hillyard
HILLIER, Hen., Salford. 1672/138
Joan, Salford, wid. 1693-4/7
Jn., Cranfield, miller. 1648/74
Jn., Meppershall, lab. 1749/41
see also Hillyard
HILLS, see Hill
HILLYARD, HILLIARD, Jn., Clapham. AR 1685: 1/48
Jn. Hearns, Toddington, yeo. 1736/11
Jos., Bedford, gardener. 1848/44
Mary, Eaton Bray, wid. 1736/32
Thos., Marston, yeo. 1711/74
see also Hillier, Elyard
HILSDEN, see Hillersden
HILSLEY, see Ilsley
HILSON, Sam., Little Staughton, lab. A 1833/2
HILTON, Fra., sen., Oakley, yeo. 1772/4
Fra., Pavenham, yeo. A 1800/10
Fra., Oakley, farmer. 1841/32
Jas., Wootton, farmer. 1852/15
Jn., Oakley, farmer. 1786/22
Judith, Twyford, Bucks. 1557/297
HIND, HINDS, HINDE, HINDES, HYNDE, Beatrice, Roxton, Chawston, wid. 1609/191

HIND, HINDS, HINDE, HINDES, HYNDE continued
Eliz., Odell. 1640/67
Eliz., Westoning, wid. A 1851/1
Eliz., Bedford, Gadsby Street, wid. 1854/39
Geo., Wilden, lab. 1603/119
Jas., Langford, Holme, yeo. 1601-2/138
Jas., Podington, plasterer. A 1769/25
Jn., Bletsoe. R 1520-1: 2/165d
Jn., Hockliffe, dairyman. 1800/17
Jn., Wootton, yeo. 1804/3
Jn., Bedford, plumber, glazier and painter. 1843/4
Phillip, Houghton Conquest. 1593/75
Ric., Westoning, shopkeeper. 1831/47
Robt., Northill. 1583/152
Sarah, Bedford, wid. 1851/34
Thos., husb. R 1551: 12/163
Thos., Odell. 1579/148
Thos., Bletsoe, husb. 1586/86
Thos., Sundon. AR 1679: 1/155d
Thos., Bedford St. Cuthbert. AR 1685: 1/27d
Thos., Bedford St. Cuthbert, plumber. 1843/5
Wm., Carlton. R 1543: 6/171
see also Hine, Hines
HINE, HINES, Ann, Odell. 1828/26
Chas., Shefford, glazier and plumber. 1780/47
Geo., Odell, yeo. 1772/38
Jn., sen., Higham Gobion, yeo. 1793/7
Jn., Potton, grocer. 1806/17
Ric., Biggleswade, lab. Bw 1767/47
Roger, Dunstable. 1590/135
Sarah, Upper Gravenhurst, wid. 1770/57
Sarah, Silsoe, wid. 1828/41
Sarah, Potton, spins. 1838/10
Steph., Carlton, grocer. A 1732/1
Thos., Carlton. R 1513-4: 1/200
Thos., Shefford, peruke maker and yeo. A 1785/27
Wm., Over Gravenhurst, victualler and dairyman. A 1750-1/25
Wm., Bletsoe, shopkeeper. 1735/26
Wm., Odell, yeo. 1759/55
Wm., Bedford, innholder. 1797/16
see also Hind
HINKLEY, Chris., Maulden, lab. 1708/59
HINKSLEY, Jn., Woburn (old index, bundle missing). A 1745/11
HINSON, Jn., Luton. A 1813/21
Jos., Potton, solicitor. A 1807/3

HINTON, HYNTON, Ann, Langford, wid. 1591/162
Jn., Steppingley. R 1541: 6/97d
Jn., Langford. R 1547: 12/1d
Jn., Stotfold. 1617-18/228
Ric., Shillington, gardener. 1735/12
Thos., Langford. 1589/129
Wm., Stotfold. 1607/106
HINXLEY, see Hinksley
HIPPON, Nich., Westoning. 1610/15
HIPSLEY, Martha, Sutton, wid. 1663/8
HIPWELL, Ann, (old index, "Docket mislaid") A 1710/23
Anth., Pavenham, lab. 1656/195
Dan., Pavenham, matmaker. 1818/26
Geo., Pertenhall. 1624/49
Geo., Tilbrook, husb. R 1637-8: 35/495
Gregory, Eaton Socon, Honeydon, carpenter. 1750/58
Jn., jun., Pavenham, blacksmith. 1660/168
Jn., Sharnbrook, yeo. 1713/8
Jn., Pavenham, matmaker. 1750/6
Jn., Sharnbrook, yeo. 1770/19
Mary, Sharnbrook, wid. 1728/12
Reb., Bedford St. Mary, spins. 1755/57
Thos., Colmworth, husb. 1684/45
Thos., Sharnbrook, yeo. 1687/28
Thos., sen., Pavenham, matmaker. 1748/45
Thos., Pavenham, matmaker. 1764/33
Wm., Pavenham, matmaker. 1795/35
Wm., Pavenham, matting manufacturer. 1852/27
HIRST, see Hurst
HITCH, see Hiche
HITCHCOCK, Isaac, Flitton, yeo. AR 1678-9: 1/201
Jas., Leighton Buzzard, husb. LB AR 1549: 1/21
Joel, Northill, Hatch, yeo. 1698/158
Jn., Luton, Crawley Green. AR 1685: 1/170
Jn., Elstow, yeo. 1703/43
Jn., Northill, Thorncote. 1734-5/65
Wm., Westoning, yeo. 1687/89
HOARE, HOORE, Jas., Shillington. 1621-2/157
Joan, Bedford St. Peter, wid. 1674/102
Joan, Bedford St. Peter. AR 1674: 1/8d
Ric., Shillington, lab. 1617/319
Wm., Tingrith, clerk. 1742/5
HOBBS, HOBBE, Dan., jun., Sundon, yeo. 1690/38
Dan., Sundon. 1713/7
Dor., Eaton Bray, wid. A 1704/9

HOBBS, HOBBE continued
Eliz., Cardington, wid. 1726/59
Eliz., Sundon, wid. A 1704/1
Faith, Eaton Bray, wid. 1678/114
Hen., Eaton, yeo. 1660-1/112
Hen., Totternhoe, yeo. 1678/151
Hen., Flitwick, lab. A 1763/30
Hen., Flitwick, yeo. A 1839/5
Jas., Flitwick, farmer. 1853/4
Jn., Houghton Regis. 1616/61
Jn., Totternhoe, lab. 1662/119
Jn., Totternhoe, weaver. 1701-2/57
Jn., Henlow, gent. 1713-4/57
Jn., Marston, yeo. 1729/93
Jn., Cranfield, yeo. 1783/17
Jos., Colmworth, clerk. 1717/47
Math., Bedford, gent. 1695/77
Ric., Flitwick. 1609/113
Ric., Toddington. A 1785/14
Sar., Totternhoe, wid. 1685-6/104
Thos., Eaton Bray. A 1700/27
Thos., Flitwick. A 1844/11
Thos., Toddington, cooper. 1845/22
Wm., Sundon, yeo. 1704/6
Wm., sen., Toddington, butcher. 1791/20
HOBCRAFT, Wm., Eversholt, cordwainer. 1743/34
see also Hopcraft
HOBKINS, alias Sherle, Jn., Sutton. R 1561: 55
alias Cobbe, Nich., Ridgmont. R 1550: 12/135
Ric., (no parish given). R 1549-50: 12/86d
see also Hopkins
HOBSON, Jn., Felmersham, Radwell, lab. AR 1670: 1/35
Thos., Sutton. R 1519: 1/242d
Wm., Tilbrook. AR 1688: 1/81d
HOCAM, see Hookam
HOCKELL, see Huckle
HOCKETT, Han., Bedford, wid. A 1726/20
Sus., Wilshamstead, St. Macutes, wid. 1678-9/150
Wm., Potsgrove, farmer. AR 1671: 1/141d
Wm., Bedford, innholder. A 1724/6
HOCKLEY, Thos., Roxton. 1678/117
HODDLE, see Hodle
HODDEN, Thos., Haynes. 1636-7/59
HODGE, HODGES, Joan, Upper Gravenhurst, wid. 1689/48
Jn., Farndish, yeo. 1686/56

HODGE, HODGES continued
Mark, Potton, wheelwright. A 1706/28
Ric., Maulden, schoolmaster. 1622/68
Rose, Maulden, wid. 1625/196
Thos., Millbrook, carpenter. 1572/83
Thos., Potton, wheelwright. 1704/36
Wm., Gravenhurst. 1660-1/80
HODGISON, Hudson alias Hodgison, see under Hudson
Jas., Flitwick. 1733/42
Jn., Luton, Thrales End, blacksmith. 1663/114
HODGKINS, Dan., (no parish given). 1669-70/108
Eliz., Flitton, wid. 1631/244
Jn., Eaton Socon, lab. 1741/79
Mary, nee Dix, Toddington. A 1798/14
Mary, Bedford St. Paul, wid. 1842/36
Paradine, Bedford, staymaker. 1831/34
Thos., Melchbourne, smith. 1610/49
Thos., Bedford, cooper. 1836/10
Wm., Flitton, Greenfield, husb. 1621/198
Wm., Flitton, shepherd. 1630-1/128
HODGSON, HODSON, Jas., Kempston, wheelwright. A 1768/13
Jas., Kempston, wheelwright. A 1782/2
Mary, Flitwick. A 1739/24
HODLE, Fra., Southill, Stanford, wid. 1709/66
Jn., Southill, husb. 1706/58
Mary, Elstow, wid. 1630/61
Stephen, Elstow. 1609/104
Wm., Elstow, husb. 1638/57
Wm., Elstow, lab. 1682/13
see also Odell
HODSON, see Hodgson, see also Hudson
HOGAN, Eliz., Dunstable, spins. 1726-7/82
Nath., Whipsnade, rector. 1678/113
HOGETT, Eliz., Northill, wife of Jn., clerk. 1673/46
HOGG, Em., Billington, wid. 1557/301
Joan, Billington. 1558/231
Jn., Billington. 1558/31
Jn., Billington. 1567/83
Jn., Chalgrave, Wingfield, husb. 1708/71
Mary, Houghton Regis, wid. A 1724/10
Ric., Billington. LB AR 1545: 1/16
Thos., Billington. 1578/226
Thos., Billington, singleman. 1612/75
Wm., Billington, yeo. 1678/108
Wm., Houghton Regis, Sewell, yeo. 1713/25

HOGSDEN, HOGGISDEN, Ric., Roxton, Chawston. R 1543: 6/175d
HOIGHT, Fra., Stagsden, yeo. 1742/65
Jn., Stagsden, yeo. 1729/82
Robt., Odell. R 1539-40: 6/13d
HOLBORN, HOLBEN, Ann, Eyeworth, wid. 1805/38
Robt., Eyeworth, farmer. 1835/17
Thos., sen., Eyeworth, farmer. 1788/35
see also Albany
HOLCOTE, Thos., (no parish given). R 1543: 6/167
HOLCROFT, Jn., Goldington. 1667/37
HOLDAM, Geo., Marston, husb. 1783/53
Jn., Ampthill. 1762/65
see also Oldham
HOLDEN, Wright alias Holden, see Wright
Hen., Dunton. 1560/169
Jn., Bedford, yeo. 1612/115
Ric., Felmersham, clerk. 1682/20
Wm. (no parish given). 1582/114
HOLDER, HOULDER, Geo., Houghton Conquest, How End, husb. 1583/139
Hen., Marston. 1589/108
HOLDESTAKE, see Holdstock
HOLDING, Thos., Haynes, yeo. 1651/18
HOLDINGSWORTH, see Hollingworth
HOLDSBROOKE, Thos., Houghton Conquest. 1572/71
HOLDSTOCK, HOLDESTAKE, HOLSTOCK, Jn., Houghton Conquest, parson. 1569/106
Jn., sen., Kempston Hardwick. 1633/187
Jn., Tingrith. 1639/22
Jn., Thurleigh. 1700/116
Jos., Bedford, victualler. A 1728/30
Robt., Elstow. 1688-9/5
Robt., Elstow. 1689/5
Wm., Houghton Conquest husb. 1613/189
Wm., Elstow, matmaker. 1692-3/64
Wm., Maulden, husb. 1710/15
Wm., Streatley, blacksmith. 1839/19
HOLIDAY, Luke, Dunton. 1627/170
Robt. (no parish given). 1632/168
HOLLAND, Jn., Tilbrook, husb. 1674/107
Reynold, Leighton Buzzard. 1586-7/130
Thos., Tilbrook, farmer. AR 1673-4: 1/63d
Thos., sen., Leighton Buzzard, lab. LB 1809/42
Wm., Leighton Buzzard. 1574/151
Wm., Tilbrook, yeo. 1679/71
Wm., Tilbrook. AR 1679: 1/69

HOLLAND continued
Wm., Leighton Buzzard, weaver. LB 1741/19
see also Hulland
HOLLICK, Jn., Cranfield, lab. A 1725/15
HOLLILEY, Chris., Clifton, gent. A 1705/28
HOLLIMAN, Jn., Luton, weaver. 1734/46
see also Holman, Holloman
HOLLINGSWORTH, Jane, Eversholt, spins. 1738/3
Jas., Ampthill. A 1811/8
Jn., Leighton Buzzard. AR 1675: 1/193d
Jn., Woburn, cooper. 1708/35
Math., Ridgmont, cooper. 1697/9
Robt., Clophill. 1622/39
Thos., Ampthill, cooper. 1699/50
Thos., Ampthill. 1722-3/71
Thos., Ridgmont, cooper. 1723/59
Thos., sen., Ampthill, cooper. 1760/17
Thos., Ridgmont, cooper. 1776/1
Thos., Ridgmont, cooper. A 1776/1
Thos., Ampthill, cooper. A 1808/2
see also Hallworth, see also Hollingworth
HOLLINGWORTH, Thos., Ampthill, maltster and cooper. 1790/4
HOLLIS, Jn., Toddington, yeo. 1794/7
Jn., sen., Pertenhall. 1812/4
Sar., Toddington. A 1793/12
Thos., Toddington, farmer. A 1794/8
Wm., sen., Toddington, Fancote, farmer. 1780/35
Wm., Toddington, Chalton, farmer. 1785/46
Wm., Tilbrook, farmer. 1843/35
HOLLIT, Edw., Maulden, yeo. 1787/16
HOLLOMAN, Thos., Cardington, Eastcotts, cottager. 1823/11
see also Holman, Holliman
HOLLOWAY, Cath., Bedford, wid. 1750/7
David, Bedford, carrier. A 1742/2
Edw., Cranfield. 1752/10
Wm., Colmworth, yeo. 1777/37
see also Alloway
HOLMAN, alias Homan, Wm., sen., Husborne Crawley, yeo. 1611/171
see also Holliman, Holloman, see also Allman
HOLMES, HOMES, Abra., Stopsley, yeo. 1662/56
Ann, Stopsley, wid. 1708-9/34
Eliz., Kempston, wid. 1733-4/26
Ezekiah, Woburn, coachman. 1742/57
Joan, wid. 1592-3/10
Jn., Sandy. R 1529-30: 3/21

HOLMES, HOMES continued
Jn., Leighton Buzzard. 1579-80/219
Jn., Eaton Bray. 1853/47
Thos., Stopsley, weaver. 1707/71
Wm. A 1710/26
HOLT, Barnard, Sundon, butcher. 1702/16
Barnard, Sundon. A 1702/8
Edw., Dunstable, carpenter. 1747/37
Fra., Houghton Regis, yeo. A 1719/15
Jane, Houghton Regis, wid. 1767/28
Joan, Dunstable, wid. AR 1680: 1/159d
Jos., Houghton Regis, Caldecote. A 1741/6
Wm., Houghton Regis, yeo. 1755/8
Wm., Totternhoe, farmer. 1821/24
HOLTON, Thos., Cranfield, dairyman. 1779/9
HOMAN, Holman alias Homan, see Holman
HOMER, Wm., Houghton Regis, blacksmith. 1660-1/110
HOMES, see Holmes
HOMNEY, see Umney
HONER, see Honour
HONEYBONE, HONEYBUN, Edw., Cardington, lab. 1710/26
Geo., Shefford, wheelwright. A 1733/25
Geo., Campton, farmer. 1787/54
HONEYLOVE, Thos., sen., Bedford, cordwainer. 1709/14
HONOUR, HONER, Ann, Wootton, wid. 1659/95
Edw., Barton. 1668/119
Eme, Ampthill, wid. 1668/167
Eliz., Harlington, wid. 1601/122
Eve, Reach, wid. of Wm. Fac. 1709: 9/33
Fra., Harlington, carpenter. 1657-8/56
Hen., Woburn, lab. 1629/3
Hen., Tilsworth, husb. 1668/131
Hen., Stanbridge, yeo. Fac. 1715: 9/47
Jane, Toddington, spins. 1662/8
Jn., Eaton Bray. R 1545: 11/91d
Jn., Harlington, husb. 1598-9/98
Jn., Leighton Buzzard, yeo. Fac. 1706: 9/22
Jn., Shillington, gent. A 1716/17
Jos., Shillington, lab. 1715/77
Jos., Clifton, yeo. 1726/79
Marian, Eaton Bray, wid. of Jn. R 1545: 11/90d
Mary, Bedford, wid. 1695/74
Mary, Leighton Buzzard, wid. Fac. 1719: 9/58
Mary, Shillington, Holwell Bury, wid. 1727-8/72
Ric., Eaton. 1639/8

HONOUR, HONER continued
Rich. A 1709/11
Robt., Dunstable, shoemaker. 1582-3/72
Robt., Potsgrove, husb. 1582/89
Thos., Stanbridge, husb. 1565/1
Thos., Potsgrove, yeo. 1614/71
Thos., jun., Toddington, yeo. 1664-5/85
Thos., Warden Street, husb. 1675/52
Thos., Goldington, Putnoe, yeo. 1694/74
Wm., Milton Bryan, husb. 1573/121
Wm., Potsgrove, yeo. 1615/142
Wm., Woburn. (Bundle 1670). 1664/251
Wm., Shillington, Holwell Bury, yeo. 1754/25
Wm., Holwell, yeo. 1798/1
HOOD, Jn., Leighton Buzzard, yeo. LB 1833/57
Ric., Chellington, yeo. 1695-6/66
HOOK, HOOKS, Searle alias Hooks, see Searle
Catterall alias Hookes, see Catterall
Chris., Cople, late of Sutton, yeo. 1714/5
HOOKAM, HOCAM, Eliz., Renhold, wid. 1638/58
Jn., Renhold, husb. 1610/72
Jn., Renhold, yeo. 1680-1/85
Jn., Ravensden, Ravensden Grange, yeo. 1724/2
Mich., Renhold, lab. 1633/150
Wm., Renhold, husb. 1604/36
Wm., Moggerhanger, dairyman. 1638/168
HOOKER, Catterall alias Hooker, see Catterall
Blanch, Sandy, wid. A 1741/5
Eliz. A 1709/19
Jnthn., Sandy, clerk. 1723/36
Nath., Sandy, gent. A 1714/34
Thos., Chicksands. AR 1673-4: 1/99
Thos., Chicksands. 1674-5/163
HOOKS, see Hook
HOOSE, see House
HOOSON, Jos., Sharnbrook, farmer. 1850/50
see also Housden
HOOTON, Ralph, Bromham. 1646/89
Wm., Stevington, lab. 1616/80
HOPCRAFT, Eliz., Bedford St. Mary, spins. 1711/122
Ric., Flitwick, lab. A 1738/17
see also Hobcraft
HOPKINS, OPKYNS, Searle alias Hopkins, see Searle
Ann, Leighton Buzzard, wid. LB 1828/42
Barnard, Stevington, yeo. 1667/25

HOPKINS, OPKYNS continued
Cecily, Dunton, Millow. R 1499: 1/150d
Constance, Ampthill. R 1545-6: 11/155
Edm., Silsoe, gent. 1671/40
alias Janes, Eliz., Eaton Bray, spins. 1736/4
Fra., Luton. 1729/30
Fra., Luton, wid. 1745/19
Jas., Leighton Buzzard, grocer. LBA 1807/57
alias Cobb, Jn., Toddington, lab. 1624-5/32
Jn., Flitwick, Preacher of the word of God. 1645/32
Jn., Toddington. 1682/89
Jn., Riseley, husb. A 1706/26
Jn., Clophill, dairyman. A 1721/1
Jn., Toddington, blacksmith. A 1836/9
Jnthn., Clophill, Beadlow, yeo. 1728/66
Jos., Leighton Buzzard, butcher. LB 1790/86
Mary, Dunstable, wid. 1736/14
Mary, Barton, wid. 1773/20
alias Cobb, Nich., Toddington, yeo. 1709/24
Parnell, Pulloxhill, wid. 1657/242
Ric., Sandy, lab. 1613/220
alias Searle, Ric., Sandy, tailor. 1615/205
Ric., Melchbourne, husb. 1785/39
Robt., Wrestlingworth, weaver. 1564/59
Sam., Pulloxhill, Minister and public preacher of the holy word of God. 1657/47
Sam., Luton, grocer. A 1729/31
Sam., Luton, tallow chandler. A 1736/12
Sam., Leighton Buzzard, farmer and gardener. LB 1843/84
Sar., Clophill, Beadlow, wid. 1721/108
alias Searle, Thos., Dunton, Millow. R 1521: 2/100d
alias Cobbe, Thos., Toddington, lab. 1624/68
Thos., Keysoe, shepherd. 1649/56
Thos., Toddington, yeo. 1696/110
Wm., Ridgmont, Segenhoe. 1561/129
alias Cobb, Wm., Ridgmont, Segenhoe, yeo. 1604/21
Wm., Stagsden. 1627/194
Wm., Flitton, Cainhoe, gent. 1678/90
Wm., Clophill, Cainhoe, gent. AR 1678: 1/199d
Wm., Clophill, Beadlow, yeo. 1707-8/47
see also Hobkins
HOPKINSON, Wm., Chicksands. R 1523: 2/21d
HORLEY, Edw., Toddington, innholder and farmer. 1758/13
Edw., Toddington, husb. A 1806/22
Harry, Toddington, Red Hill, farmer. 1850/36
Walter, Potton, yeo. R 1550: 12/117

HORN, HORNE, Bernard, sen., Totternhoe, yeo. 1726/93
Edw., Kempston, carpenter. 1607/107
Edw., sen., Clophill, farmer. 1809/43
Edw., Pulloxhill, farmer and dairyman. 1823/18
Eliz., Luton. A 1850/16
Eliz., Bedford St. Paul, wid. A 1852/11a
Jas., Totternhoe, carpenter. 1659/279
Jas., Clophill Warren, farmer. 1835/7
Jas., Clophill, New Inn, victualler. 1846/27
Jn., Totternhoe, carpenter. 1679/24
Jn., Luton, wheelwright. 1702/67
Jn., Totternhoe, tailor. 1756/43
Jn., Clophill, horse dealer. 1794/6
Jos., Clophill, yeo. 1820/35
Robt., Cranfield, lab. 1637/105
Thos., Dunstable, shoemaker. 1618/116
Thos., Wilshamstead, late Toddington, yeo. 1847/57
Wm., Houghton Regis, Bidwell, lab. 1745/3
HORNBUCKLE, Ann, Bedford St. Peter, wid. 1696-7/115
Eliz., Bedford, wid. 1726-7/12
Eliz., Bedford, wid. A 1742/39
Eliz., Beford, spins. 1792/32
Jn. A 1717/14
Thos., Bedford St. Peter. 1692/4
Thos., Bedford St. Peter, millwright. 1734/56
Thos., Bedford, millwright. 1784/40
Thos., Bedford St. John. A 1803/3
Wm., Bedford, millwright. A 1713/20
HORNER, David, Eversholt, yeo. 1746/17
HORNSBY, Edm., Roxton, Colesden, yeo. 1765/7
Thos., Wymington. 1697/16
alias Paul, Wm., Harrold. 1611/34
HORRODINE, Robt., Stotfold, lab. 1631/172
see also Harrowden
HORSEHEAD, see Hawshede
HORSEMAN, Shelley alias Horseman, see Shelley
HORSEPOOL, Fra., Pulloxhill, yeo. 1829/27
HORSEWRIGHT, Jn., Cardington. R 1540: 6/33d
HORSFORD, Wm., Melchbourne, lab. A 1713/13
HORSLEY, Charles, Thurleigh, yeo. 1623/114
Clement, Sutton, husb. 1639/9
Oliver, Campton, yeo. 1581/35
HORTH, Jn., Cople, victualler. A 1810/2
HORWOOD, Wm. Summers, Leighton Buzzard. LBA 1790/34
HOSPITAL, see Aspital

HOTT, Thos., Husborne Crawley, yeo. 1632/87
HOUGHILL, Robt., Willington, clerk. 1648/126
HOUGHTON, HAUGHTON, HORTON, HOATTON, HOWTON,
Adam, Felmersham, yeo. 1675/35
Adam, Hockliffe, clerk. A 1713/14
Adam, Hockliffe, clerk. A 1743/18
Dorcas, Eversholt, wid. A 1707/34
Eliz., Stagsden, wid. AR 1670: 1/35
Eliz., Bedford, wid. A 1759/1
Eliz., sen., Billington, wid. LB 1807/35
Eliz., Stagsden, wid. A 1760/3
Eliz., Eversholt, wid. A 1761/25
Ezekiel, Eversholt, husb. 1699/33
Geo., Stevington. AR 1672: 1/36d
Geo., Stevington. AR 1684: 1/46d
Jas., Eggington, Clipstone, shepherd. 1786/8
Jn., Eaton Bray, vicar. 1626/55
Jn., Felmersham, minor. AR 1670-1: 1/35d
Jn., Whipsnade, husb. 1726/54
Jn., Clophill, miller. 1837/2
Mary, Sandy, Girtford, lab. 1642/5
Mary, Felmersham. AR 1671: 1/36
Mary, Aspley Guise wid. 1798/20
Michael, Kempston, yeo. 1709/2
Rebecca, Hockliffe, wid. A 1744/16
Ric., Biddenham. 1573/136
Ric., Woburn, yeo. AR 1671: 1/188
Robt., sen., Great Billington, husb. 1742/38
Robt., sen., Billington, yeo. LB 1802/13
Sarah, Kempston, wid. 1717/49
Sarah, Newport Pagnell, Bucks., spins. 1776/26
Sarah, Shillington, wid. 1799/20
Susannah, Felmersham, minor. AR 1670-1: 1/35d
Thos., Sandy, Girtford, lab. 1635-6/143
Thos., Stevington, lab. 1661/158
Thos., Salford, husb. 1716/17
Thos., Bedford, yeo. 1772/45
Thos., Totternhoe. 1832/20
Wm., Kempston. 1575/91
Wm., Podington, husb. 1658-9/205
Wm., Eversholt, yeo. 1686-7/86
Wm., Eversholt, Berry End, husb. 1743/61
Wm., Salford. A 1756/5
Wm., Harrold, victualler. 1777/18
Wm., Colmworth farmer. 1842/8

HOUGHTON, HAUGHTON, HORTON, HOATTON, HOWTON continued
see also Hooton
HOUSDEN, HOUSON, Smith alias Housden, see Smith
Eliz., Flitwick, wid. 1702/19
Jn., Elstow, bach. 1640/39
Jn., sen., Flitwick, yeo. 1694/25
Jn., Westoning, blacksmith. 1713/41
Jn., Flitwick, yeo. 1772/18
Jn., Sandy, Girtford, grocer and gardener. 1831/42
Thos., Flitwick, East End, shepherd. 1645/41
Thos., Clophill, yeo. 1657/244
Thos., Flitwick, yeo. 1715/73
Wm., Biggleswade, gardener. A 1854/79
see also Hooson
HOUSE, see Howes
HOUSON, see Housden
HOWARD, Ann, Stotfold, wid. 1850/9
Eliz., Bedford St. Paul, wid. 1741/47
Hen., Streatley, Sharpenhoe. 1686/7
Hen., Dunstable, bricklayer. 1706/75
Israel, Dean. (P/IX 2, admon. missing) A 1757/15
Jas., Bedford. R 1770/30
Jas., Elstow, yeo. A 1785/1
Joan, Wilden, wid. 1629/98
Jn., Nether Shelton, carpenter, Marston. 1727/80
Jn., Caddington, yeo. A 1734/29
Jn., Markyate Street, schoolmaster. 1741/26
Jn., Bedford, butcher and alderman. 1776/30
Jn., Eaton Bray, cordwainer. 1796/14
Jn., Bedford, tripe seller. 1820/10
Jn. Moore, Bedford, Priory Farm. 1830/30
Marg., Bedford, wid. 1787/40
Mary, Bedford, wid. 1773/37
Paradine, Bedford St. Paul, butcher. 1767/51
Sam., Lidlington. AR 1690: 1/217d
Sar., Northill, Upper Caldecote, wid. 1747/63
Thos., Eaton Bray, husb. 1727/18
Thos., Marston, farmer. A 1750/124
Thos., Studham, victualler. 1779/37
Thos., Bedford, innholder. 1784/8
Wm., Bedford, butcher. 1737/28
Wm., Northill, Upper Caldecote, farmer. 1746/27
see also Hayward, see also Heward
HOWDEN, Wright alias Howden, see Wright
Thos., Biddenham. R 1508: 1/169d

HOWE, HOW, HOWES, HOWSE, HOOSE, HOUSE, HOWEST, HOUST
Agnes, Houghton Regis. R 1544: 11/15
Amy, Shefford, wid. A 1797/16
Andrew, Meppershall, lab. A 1761/18
Anthony, Leighton Buzzard. 1590/168
Barth., Stopsley, yeo. 1677/9
Cath., Stopsley, wid. 1784/39
Dan., Caddington, yeo. 1724/54
Edw., Marston, lab. 1646/96
Eliz., Haynes wid. 1625-6/156
Eliz., Stopsley, wid. 1686-7/91
Eliz., Wilden, wid. 1694/57
Eliz., Luton, wid. 1727/36
Fra., Husborne Crawley. AR 1677: 1/198d
Fra., Husborne Crawley, husb. 1677/56
Fra., Stopsley, Mixhill, yeo. 1722/68
Fra., Luton, tailor. 1748-9/60
Fra., Houghton Regis, barber and peruke maker. 1750/26
Hen., Houghton Regis, husb. 1603/138
Hen., Houghton Regis, husb. (bundle 1660) 1642/210
Hen., sen., Houghton Regis, husb. 1644-5/109
Hen., Limbury, lab. 1661/325
Hen., Totternhoe, yeo. 1666/111
Hen., Houghton Regis. AR 1671-2: 1/142d
Hen., Houghton Regis, husb. 1741/42
Hen., Houghton Regis, Sewell, husb. 1747/69
Jas., Houghton Regis, Bidwell. AR 1684: 1/168d
Jas., Houghton Regis, Bidwell, yeo. 1684/74
Jas., Ampthill, plumber, glazier and painter. 1850/52
Jas., Maulden, lace dealer. 1850/53
Joan, Aspley Guise, wid. 1607-8/149
Jn., Houghton Regis. R 1503: 1/36
Jn., Houghton Regis. R 1505: 1/101
Jn., Chalgrave, Tebworth, husb. 1630/53
Jn., Maulden, lab. 1653/132
Jn., Caddington, Chaul End. 1659/283
Jn., Leighton Buzzard (old index, bundle missing). A 1745/10
Jn., Luton. 1756/44
Jn., Luton, draper. 1769/20
Jn., Biggleswade, yeo. Bw 1809/106
Jos., Turvey, shopkeeper. 1742/56
Lettice, Luton wid. 1725/31
Marg., Chalgrave, Tebworth, wid. 1651/10
Mary, Turvey. (P/IX 2, bundle missing) A 1748/5
Mary, Flitton, Wardhedges, wid. 1815/28

HOWE, HOW, HOWES, HOWSE, HOOSE, HOUSE, HOWEST, HOUST cont.
Mary, Luton wid. 1832/5
Ric., Houghton Regis. R 1542-3: 6/138
Ric., Aspley Guise, husb. 1602/23
Ric., Caddington. 1615/153
Ric., Luton, victualler. 1822/21
Robt., Totternhoe. R 1544-5: 11/50d
Robt., Leighton Buzzard lab. 1593/66
Robt., Houghton Conquest, lab. A 1705/14
Robt., Totternhoe, yeo. 1661-2/413
Robt., Totternhoe, yeo. 1666/132
Roger, Pulloxhill, yeo. 1757/19
Spencer, Bedford St. Paul, cordwainer. A 1806/23
Thos., Houghton Regis, Sewell. R 1546: 11/144d
Thos., Houghton Regis, Sewell. R 1546: 11/168d
Thos., Houghton Regis, husb. 1614-5/1
Thos., Houghton Regis. 1617/274
alias Smith, Thos., Shillington. 1622/57
Thos., Luton, Cowridge End, yeo. 1664/47
Thos., sen., Luton, Cowridge End, yeo. 1670/193
Thos., Luton. AR 1688: 1/175d
Thos., Toddington, victualler. 1710/43
Thos., Luton, lab. A 1732/10
Thos., Aspley Guise, gent. A 1749-50/25
Thos., Luton, Pound Green, yeo. 1774/30
Timothy, Houghton Regis, lab. 1689/37
Wm., sen., Stopsley, Cowridge End, yeo. 1629/146
Wm., sen., Houghton Regis, yeo. 1669-70/104
Wm., Dunstable, victualler. AR 1683-4: 1/166
Wm., sen., Stopsley, yeo. 1685/48
Wm., Houghton Regis, yeo. 1696/122
Wm., Luton, Cowridge End, yeo. 1706/46
Wm., Houghton Regis, yeo. 1732/7
Wm., Aspley Guise, Briggins, surgeon. A 1804/18
Wm., Pavenham, lab. 1844/5
Wm., Luton, baker. 1847/29
HOWELL, Joan, Chalgrave, Tebworth, wid. 1586/96
HOWEN, Thos., Bedford, gent. 1722/9
HOWERS, Hen., Nether Dean. 1558/280
HOWETT, Eliz., Blunham. 1663/7
Jn., Eaton Socon, weaver. 1627/154
HOWKINS, Ann, Roxton, Colesden, wid. 1824/3
Ann, Thurleigh, spins. A 1848/11
Jn., sen., Ravensden, farmer. 1841/25
Jn., Thurleigh, farmer. A 1844/1

HOWKINS continued
Lettice, Thurleigh, wid. 1848/17
Sarah Jane, Thurleigh, spins. A 1848/10
Thos., Eaton Socon, Wyboston, farmer. 1828/30
Wm., Eaton Socon, yeo. 1726/8
Wm., Colmworth, farmer. A 1760/11
Wm., Roxton, Colesden, carpenter. 1804/47
Wm., Thurleigh, husb. 1833/48
HOWMAN, HOUGHMAN, HOMAN, Jn., Woburn. 1564-5/25
Jn., Leighton Buzzard, baker. A 1748/10
Robt., Bolnhurst, husb. A 1707/25
Wm., Felmersham. R 1546: 11/219d
HOWSE, see Howe
HOWSON, Edw., Flitwick, lab. AR 1679: 1/202
Wm., Lidlington, vicar. R 1517: 2/39
HOYE, Audley alias Hoye, see Audley
HOYT, see Hoight
HUBBARD, Fra., Willington, yeo. 1689/62
Thos., Blunham, maltster. A 1743/35
Wm., Moggerhanger, farmer. A 1778/1
HUBBINS, Ann, Toddington, wid. 1793/5
Benj., Marston, Nether Shelton, husb. 1686/19
Benj., Toddington, carpenter. 1764/3
Edw., Chalgrave, Tebworth. AR 1684: 1/168
Edw., Chalgrave, Tebworth. 1684/53
Lydia, Luton, wid. 1812/9
Mary, Dunstable, wid. 1781/7
Rebeccah, Shelton, Marston, wid. 1723/6
Ric., Kempston, yeo. 1670/194
Robt., Cranfield, lab. A 1728/28
Thos., Kempston, parish clerk. 1706/18
Thos., sen., Toddington. 1774/58
HUCKINGS, Jn., Lidlington. 1771/64
HUCKLE, HOKYLL, HOCKELL, HUCKELL, HUCKULL, Agnes, Henlow, wid. R 1539: 6/10d
Dorcan, Biggleswade, spins. Bw 1850/159
Edith, Millbrook, wid. 1635-6/53
Edw., Millbrook, husb. 1680/15
Ellen, Ampthill, wid. 1582/58
Ellen, Biggleswade, wid. 1679/106
Fra., Millbrook, lab. 1667-8/105
Fra., Woburn, yeo. 1726/21
Frances, late Fra. Burr, Wilshamstead, wid. A 1788/7
Geo., Cardington, husb. 1597/39
Geo., Cardington, Harrowden, weaver. 1641/188

HUCKLE, HOKYLL, HOCKELL, HUCKELL, HUCKULL continued
Geo., Cardington, weaver. 1707/80
Geo., Cardington, husb. 1746/16
Geo., Cranfield, yeo. A 1805/9
Hen., Blunham, Chalton, yeo. 1657/256
Hen., Blunham, Chalton. 1709/68
Jn., sen., Henlow. R 1529: 3/10
Jn., Henlow. R 1541-2: 6/112
Jn., Cardington. 1633/160
Jn., Woburn, yeo. 1662/27
Jn., Millbrook, yeo. 1683-4/107
Jn., Blunham, yeo. 1685/58
Jn., Sandy, Girtford. 1706/89
Marg., Blunham, Chalton, wid. 1668/193
Mary, Shillington, Lower Stondon, wid. 1821/35
Ric., Barford, husb. 1570/5
Ric., Biggleswade, bricklayer. Bw 1795/93
Robt., Cardington. 1557/265
Robt., Millbrook, shepherd. 1635-6/52
Robt., Blunham, South Mills, yeo. 1674/154
Robt., Great Barford. A 1743/22
Roger, Henlow. R 1543: 6/178d
Sobriety, Cardington. 1660-1/70
Thos., Herseley [?Arlesey]. R 1508: 1/4
Thos., Tempsford. AR 1677: 1/108
Thos., Tempsford. 1677/54
Walter, Sutton. R 1543: 6/154 and 9/9
Wm., Barford, trauntor [carrier]. 1567/135
Wm., Cardington, yeo. 1602/56
Wm., Eaton Socon, Nether Staploe, lab. 1620/68
Wm., Cardington, yeo. 1772/51
HUDD, Jane, Leighton Buzzard, wid. 1675-6/72
HUDNALL, Jos., Houghton Regis, Sewell, yeo. 1727/48
Jos., Totternhoe, husb. 1781/43
HUDSON, Alice, Great Brickhill, Bucks., wid. 1732/33
Gabriel, Lidlington, dairyman. A 1716/32
Gabriel, Kempston, farmer. 1759/66
Hen., Kempston, husb. A 1743/31
Jas., Bedford St. Mary. 1780/13
Jn., Kempston, yeo. 1701/42
Jn., Pulloxhill, carpenter. A 1704/22
Jn., Bedford, tinsmith. 1747/30
Jn., Marston, yeo. 1767/62
alias Hodgeson, Margery, wid., Bedford St. Paul. 1584-5/264
Mary, Dunstable, wid. 1704/71

HUDSON continued
Mary, Kempston. 1715/39
Mary, Marston, wid. 1768/41
Moses, Podington, Hinwick, shepherd. 1766/9
alias Hodgeson, Percival, Bedford St. Paul, barber. 1575/76
Ric., Bedford St. Paul. 1579/134
Steph., Wootton, yeo. 1750/18
Thos., Oakley, fuller. 1592/36
Thos., Shillington, Cadwell, lab. 1677/25
Wm., Maulden. 1660/94
HUGGINS, HUGINGS, HUGHINS, Chas., Woburn, surgeon. 1752/11
Edm., Woburn. A 1762/15
Fra., Woburn. A 1762/16
Geo., Woburn, surgeon. A 1753/16
Jn., Haynes, lab. 1707/33
Ric., Southill, bricklayer. 1716/64
Thos., Dunstable, bricklayer. 1740-1/91
see also Hewings
HUGHES, HEWES, HEUS, Sherle alias Hughes, see Sherle; Shorley alias Hughes, see Shorley; Welsh alias Hughes, see Welsh
Abraham, Langford, butcher. 1729/85
Ann, Wootton, wid. 1817/33
Nath., Eaton Socon, gardener. 1728/105
Norman, Wootton, yeo. 1795/24
Thos., Little Staughton, husb. 1576/36
Wm., Bedford, victualler. 1723-4/3
Wm., Langford. 1767/40
Wm., Biggleswade, butcher. 1821/29
HUGHINGS, see Hewings
HULATE, see Hewlett
HULL, Dor., Eaton Socon, spins. A 1810/15
Dor., Eaton Socon, Wyboston. 1810/26
Geo., Colmworth, carpenter. 1732/63
Hen., Stondon. 1845/26
Janet, Stondon, spins. 1832/24
Jn., Kempston Hardwick. 1561/154
Jn., Bedford St. Peter. 1567/21
Jn., Sutton. 1687/101
Jn., Henlow, lab. A 1727/26
Jn., Renhold, farmer. 1740/64
Joel, Renhold, husb. 1719-20/89
Jos., Renhold. 1707/76
Jos., Renhold, farmer. 1783/61
Lucy, Tempsford, spins. A 1841/11
Mary, Billington, wid. A 1743/44

HULL continued
Mary, Leighton Buzzard, wid. LB 1753/21
Nich., Clophill, butcher. 1699-1700/72
Ric., Henlow. AR 1675-6: 1/105
Robt., Bedford St. Paul. R 1537-8: 5/4d
Robt., Sutton, yeo. 1690/5
Robt., Thurleigh, dairyman. A 1723/23
Sam., Langford, smith. A 1843/8
Thos., Blunham. R 1537: 4/94
Thos., Wilshamstead, musician. 1678-9/146
Thos., sen., Leighton Buzzard, yeo. 1742/13
Thos., Wootton. 1771/44
Thos., Maulden, butcher. A 1772/6
Thos., Billington, lab. LBA 1819/81
Thos., Maulden, yeo. 1828/4
Wm., Salford. R 1558: 14/49d
Wm., Cardington, Cotton End. 1636-7/58
Wm., Luton, baker. AR 1689: 1/176
Wm., Kempston, yeo. 1762/20
HULLAND, Robt., Tilbrook, husb. 1559-60/334
Wm., Tilbrook. 1694/82
see also Holland
HULSE, Len., Upper Stondon, singleman. 1603/91
HUMBERSTONE, UMBERSTONE, Chas., Upper Gravenhurst. 1828/42
Jas., Upper Gravenhurst, yeo. 1800/49
Jane, Clifton, wid. A 1721-2/50
Jn., Gravenhurst. 1828/43
Laur., Ampthill, surgeon. A 1827/16
Lawr., Ampthill, yeo. A 1796/7
Math., Clifton, gardener. 1713/61
Robt., Biggleswade, publican. Bw 1856/166
Thos., Clophill, brickmaker. 1766/15
Thos., Clophill, brickmaker. A 1785/3
Thos., Gravenhurst, yeo. 1811/38
HUMBLE, HUMBLES, Thos., Leighton Buzzard, gardener. LB 1811/56
HUMBLEY, Eliz., Cople, wid. 1821/15
Jn., Cople, yeo. 1801/21
HUMPHREY, HUMFREY, HUMPHRIES, Edw., Henlow. R 1541-2: 6/113
Geo., Luton, carpenter. 1856/29
Jas., Ampthill, mealman. 1799/52
Jn., Moggerhanger, husb. 1632/53
Jn., Moggerhanger, husb. 1645/126
Jn., Blunham, farmer. AR 1682: 1/116
Jos., Luton, blacksmith. 1714/91
Margt., Northill. 1761/46

HUMPHREY, HUMFREY, HUMPHRIES continued
Margt., Moggerhanger, wid. AR 1681: 1/115d
Mile, Northill. (P/IX 2 admon. missing) A 1782/5
Wm., Luton. 1605/86
Wm., Shefford, yeo. 1627/147
Wm., Moggerhanger, yeo. 1681/103
Wm., Houghton Regis, baker. 1852/22
HUNS, Thos., Northill, carpenter. A 1704/25
Thos., Northill, yeo. A 1723/31
HUNT, HUNTE, Alex., Tempsford, gent. 1593/33
Alice, Roxton, Chawston, wid. of Thos. 1559-60/340
Alice, Stotfold, wid. 1716/82
Ann, Roxton, wid. of Roger, Chalston, esq. 1694/99
Ann, Biggleswade, wid. (reg. only) 1823/8
Anne, Biggleswade, wid. Bw 1821/124
Dor., Houghton Conquest, wid. 1641/122
Edw., Roxton, Chawston, clerk. 1557/261
Edw., Wilden, farmer. A 1740/3
Edw., Biggleswade, waggoner. BwA 1725/7, I
Eliz., Roxton, wid. R 1520: 2/157d
Ellen, Wrestlingworth, spins. 1667/102
Fra., Bedford, clerk. A 1738-9/7
Geo., Carlton. 1764/9
Hen., Woburn, husb. R 1549: 12/50d
Hen., Lidlington, husb. 1605/132
Hen., Lidlington. 1640/60
Hen., Woburn, gent. [Letter attached describes him as a poor servant of the Duke of Bedford]. 1663/66
Hen., Westoning, clerk. 1710-11/61
Humph., Stotfold, lab. 1608-9/3
Jeremiah, Arlesey, husb. 1692/25
Jn., Stotfold. R 1546: 11/181d
Jn., Farndish, husb. R 1550: 12/95d
Jn., Sharnbrook, gent. 1557/346
Jn., Sandy, Girtford. 1565/189
Jn., Sandy, Girtford. 1565/190
Jn., Cardington, Fenlake, lab. 1616-17/36
Jn., Thurleigh. 1671/86
Jn., Henlow. AR 1675: 1/102d
Jn., Thurleigh. AR 1676: 1/66d
Jn., Biggleswade, gardener. BwA 1813/52
Marg., Langford, Holme, wid. 1618-19/33
Mary, Biggleswade, spins. BwA 1826/67
Robt. 1554/186
Robt., Houghton Regis, victualler. 1830/39

HUNT, HUNTE continued
Thos., Roxton, Chawston, gent. R 1546: 11/208
Thos., Roxton, Chawston. 1554/185
Thos., Southill, Stanford, yeo. 1591/122
Thos., Roxton, Chawston, gent. 1669-70/100
Thos., Flitwick, lab. 1682/7
Thos., Pertenhall, carpenter. 1693/96
Thos., Millbrook, blacksmith. 1720-21/103
Wm., Maulden, husb. 1574-5/27
Wm., Chellington, husb. 1609-10/120
Wm., Luton, lab. A 1828/1
Wm., Biggleswade, gardener. BwA 1826/68
HUNTER, Jn., Shillington. R 1504: 1/45d
Jn., Pertenhall. 1570/4
Ric., Colmworth, clerk. 1628/39
Wm., Stotfold. R 1538-9: 5/27
HURDLE, Wm., Woburn, gent. A 1827/6
HURNDALL, Jn., Aspley Guise. R 1529-30: 3/18d
HURST, HIRST, Alice, Arlesey, wid. 1632/71
Anna Frances, Bedford, wid. 1785/23
Dan., Shefford, bach. AR 1670: 1/90d
Edw., Marston, yeo. 1677/6
Eliz., Luton, spins. 1745/7
Hen., Henlow, yeo. 1570/41
Isaac, Bedford, innholder. A 1702-3/39
Isaac, Bedford, innholder. A 1754/14
Jas., Shefford, tanner. 1651/22
Jas., Shefford, lab. A 1714/29
Jn., Henlow, maltster. 1721-2/79
Jn., Henlow, yeo. 1727/47
Jn., Sandy, Girtford, yeo. 1729-30/128
Jonathan, Toddington, Herne, late Harlington, yeo. 1812/42
Thos., Barton, collarmaker. 1727/70
Thos., Great Barford. A 1743/25
Thos., Harlington (old index, bundle missing). A 1745/9
Wm., Langford, tailor. 1589/107
Wm., Chicksands yeo. 1691/117
HUSSEY, Jane, Flitton. 1612/102
Thos., Westoning, gent. 1605-6/95
HUSTLER, Jos., Ampthill, gent. A 1738-9/11
HUSTWHAT, HUSTWAIT, Hen., Over Dean, cordwinder. 1679-80/113
Phillip, Tempsford, yeo. 1816/37
HUTCHINS, Dorothy, late Green, Felmersham. A 1789/3
HUTCHINSON, Dan., Tempsford, blacksmith. 1724-5/74
Jn., Felmersham, clerk. 1792/30

HUTCHINSON continued
Wm., Ampthill, butcher. A 1723/16
HUTTON, Cath., Aspley Guise. 1759/13
Eliz., Aspley Guise. A 1829/8
Hen., Cranfield. AR 1690: 1/18d
Hen., Husborne Crawley, yeo. 1764/19
Jn., Gravenhurst, rector. R 1505: 1/87d
Jn., Luton. 1609/161
Jn., Marston. A 1700/14
Jos., Aspley Guise, gent.. 1759/14
Jos., Aspley Guise, gent. and wid. Cath. A 1759/9
Jos., Aspley Guise, yeo. 1822/2
Mary, Bromham, wid. 1664/22
Mich., Aspley Guise. Inventory only. 1807, I 4/206
Thos., Cranfield, yeo. 1687/57
HYCKBED, see Higbid
HYDE, HYE, HIDE, Agnes, Caddington, wid. 1638/125
Ann, Clophill. 1825/2
Ann, Biggleswade, servant. Bw 1831/140
Ann, Biggleswade, wid. BwA 1835/74
Chancellor, Biggleswade, cooper. Bw 1820/123
Jas., Flitwick, miller. 1624/71
Jas., Warden, farmer. 1724/27
Jn., Luton, husb. (bundle 1564-5). 1549/209
Jn., Studham. 1590/148
Jn., sen., Sharnbrook, husb. 1645/27
Jn., Stevington, shoemaker. 1781/22
Jn., Biggleswade, maltster. Bw 1791/86
Jonathan, Pulloxhill. 1789/6
Nich., Sharnbrook, husb. 1573-4/131
Ric., Leighton Buzzard, Leighton Mills. 1603/101
Ric., Caddington, yeo. 1625/149
Ric., Kempston, yeo. 1684/95
Ric., Biggleswade. BwA 1813/55
Sarah, Biggleswade, spins. Bw 1771/57
Thos., Stotfold, jobber. 1857/19
Wm., Sharnbrook, lab. 1669/25
Wm., Sharnbrook, bach. AR 1689: 1/49d
Wm., Sharnbrook, maltster. 1696/104
Wm., Radwell, Herts., yeo. 1764/37
Wm., Biggleswade, cooper. Bw 1769/51
Wm., Stevington, victualler. 1818/47
see also High

I

IBBOTT, YBBOT, Bart., Pertenhall. R 1531: 3/51
Eliz., Pertenhall, wid. AR 1680: 1/70
Jas., Shefford. 1789/7
Jn., Pertenhall. R 1524: 2/35
Jn., sen., Pertenhall, husb. 1621-2/155
Jn., Pertenhall, yeo. 1663/10
Jn., Warden, lab. 1664/23
Jn., Pertenhall, yeo. 1718-9/30
Thos., Melchbourne. 1593/20
Walt., Pertenhall. 1650/93
Wm., Melchbourne. R 1545-6: 11/154d
Wm., Melchbourne, lab. 1586/92
Wm., Bedford, gent. 1816/27
IBBS, Jos., Shefford, farmer and maltster. 1843/34
Martha, Shefford, wid. 1856/39
see also Hebbs
ILATT, YLATT, Robt., Limbury, husb. 1558/219
see also Elliott
ILEY, Eliz., Bedford St. Mary, wid. 1738/85
Wm., Bedford St. Mary, locksmith. 1713/27
ILIGER, Jn., Bletsoe, yeo. 1561-2/137
ILLGER, Thos., Northill, yeo. AR 1680-1: 1/111
ILLING, Jn., Houghton Regis, Sewell, lab. 1711-12/101
see also Ealing, Eling
ILLSON, Frances, Odell, wid. (bundle 1668). 1634/173
Wm., Sharnbrook, matmaker. 1661/289
see also Elson
ILSLEY, Wm., Sandy, Beeston, yeo. 1832/1
IMPEY, Ben., Pulloxhill. R 1770/16
Cath., Marston, wid. A 1713/15
Constance, Bedford, wid. 1849/32
Godfrey, Battlesden. AR 1674: 1/148
Godfrey, Battlesden. AR 1688: 1/174d
Hannah, Bedford, wid. 1752/57
Jane, Pulloxhill, late of Barton, spins. 1761/48
Jn., sen., Milton Bryan, yeo. 1689/75
Jn., Arlesey, husb. 1720/16
Jn., Houghton Conquest, husb. 1720/123
Jn., Shefford, brazier. 1828/39
Jos., Barton, grocer. A 1764/5
Ric., sen., Marston, Wroxhill, husb. 1638/65
Ric., Marston, Nether Shelton, bach. 1650/94
Ric., Marston, yeo. 1660/192

INGRAM continued
Sarah, Leighton Buzzard, wid. LB 1826/35
Uriah, Thurleigh, yeo. 1661/294
Wm., Leighton Buzzard, yeo. 1811/21
Wm., Bedford, gent. 1841/18
see also Egram
INGREY, INGERY, Jn., Tempsford, tailor. AR 1678: 1/108d
Mary, Tempsford, spins. 1682-3/109
Peter, Tempsford, dairyman. AR 1672: 1/94d
Wm., Potton. 1710/9
INKERSOL, see Ingersoll
INKLE, Alice, Cardington, Harrowden. 1662/122
INNS, Reg., Eversholt, grazier. A 1854/10
Thos., Milton Bryan, butcher. A 1822/7
INSKIP, INSKEPE, Ann, Southill, Broom, wid. A 1714-15/42
Anne, Kempston, wid. 1635-6/43
Edw., Warden, farmer. A 1744/20
Eliz., Caldecote, wid. A 1843/5
Geo., Southill, Broome. 1698/87
Geo., Southill. A 1721-2/54
Geo., Southill, yeo. A 1724/45
Hen., Old Warden, husb. 1773/21
Jn., Maulden, farmer. A 1778/5
Jos., Southill, Stanford, tailor. 1808/13
Mary, Southill, Stanford, wid. 1726/38
Mary, Southill, spins. 1760/26
Nich., Southill, yeo. A 1706/29
Thos., Southill, Broome, yeo. 1661/197
Thos., Southill, Gastlings, yeo. 1681/31
Thos., Southill, Stanford, yeo. 1698/144
Thos., Langford. 1726/99
Thos., Bromham, yeo. 1794/30
Thos., Old Warden, farmer. 1809/1
Thos., Shefford, watchmaker. 1850/6
INWARDS, see Inwoods
INWIN, see Unwin
INWOODS, INWOOD, INWARDS, Cath., Hockliffe, wid. A 1815/14
Jn., Aspley Guise, carpenter. A 1796/5
Mary, Luton, wid. 1850/26
Ric., Hockliffe, dairyman. 1744/15
Ric., Chalgrave, Tebworth, farmer. 1791/11
Wm., Eaton Bray, blacksmith. 1759/56
Wm., Hockliffe, yeo. A 1802/17
IREDALE, Thos., Woburn, cooper. 1796/40
Woodell, Hemel Hempstead, Herts., late Leighton Buzzard, yeo. LB 1805/22

IRELAND, YRLAND, Fra., Woburn, gardener. 1704/51
Fra., jun., Woburn, gardener. 1705/64
Fra., Woburn, gardener. A 1711/72
Godoon [sic], Roxton, Chawston, lab. 1640/61
Jarviss, Bedford, victualler. 1738/89
Jn., Chicksands. R 1538: 5/23
Jn., Woburn, maltster. R 1770/14
Jos., Eversholt, carrier. 1697/142
Jos., Woburn, cabinet maker. A 1848/1
formerly Stanton, Sarah, Bedford. A 1737/27
Thos., Woburn, gardener. 1700/129
Thos., sen., Woburn, yeo. 1722/78
Thos., Dunstable, gardener. 1757/34
Thos., Woburn, lab. 1758/26
Wm., Roxton. 1623/107
Wm., Roxton, Chawston, lab. 1708/3
Wm., Luton, cordwainer. 1740/46
Wm., Woburn, horse dealer. 1757/23
IREMONGER, see Ironmonger
IRESON, Chris., Bedford, lab. 1672/167
Chris., Bedford. AR 1672: 1/7
IRONMONGER, EYRNMONGER, IORMONGER, IREMONGER,
Hen., Totternhoe. 1626/52
Jn., Totternhoe. 1558-9/313
Judith, Totternhoe, spins. 1708/86
Ric., Totternhoe, gent. AR 1686: 1/171d
Thos., Totternhoe, freemason. 1685/16
Thos., Totternhoe. AR 1686: 1/171d
Wm., Ampthill, gent. 1665/32
Wm., (parish torn off) gent. 1676/129
IRONS, Eliz., Luton. A 1779/13
Jn., (old index only, bundle missing). A 1718/16
Jn., Luton, husb. 1752/14
Jn., Barton, late Pulloxhill. 1846/18
Robt., Woburn, yeo. 1686/53
Wm., Woburn, Horsemore, yeo. 1715/44
Wm., Heath and Reach, straw plait dealer. LBA 1819/79
ISAAC, ISAACS, Ann, Bedford, wid. 1676/112
Edw., Bedford, blacksmith. AR 1673: 1/7d
Robt., Clifton, husb. R 1547: 11/226
Sophia, Luton, spins. 1857/42
Thos., Henlow, husb. 1593/39
ISHERWOOD, Fra., Southill, wid. 1847/46
Robt., Southill. 1828/29, I 4/276
ISITT, ISATE, Fra., Bedford St. Mary, butcher. 1857/34

ISITT, ISATE continued
Jn., Bedford, farmer. 1854/37
Jn., Clophill, baker. 1857/17
Nich., Eaton Socon, myllenar. 1559-60/336
ISLIP(P), ISLOP, Eliz., Melchbourne, wid. A 1739/21
Ellen, Ravensden, wid. A 1728/27
Fra., Bletsoe, butcher. 1660/160
Jn., Melchbourne. 1659/287
Jn., Harrold, weaver. 1661/319
Jn., Oakley, yeo. 1689/26
Jn., Hatley Cockayne, yeo. 1691/90
Jn., Ravensden, victualler. 1757/27
Jn., Swineshead, Hunts. A 1810/7
Jn., Pertenhall, gent. 1839/34
Rebecca, Knotting, wid. 1810/42
Ric., Bletsoe, grazier. A 1736-7/39
Ric., Knotting, yeo. A 1809/8
Thos., sen., Harrold, weaver. 1635-6/44
Thos., Farndish, yeo. 1694/37
Thos., Elstow, lab. A 1705-6/58
Thos., Farndish, yeo. 1722/36
Wm., Melchbourne, gent. 1738-9/94
IVE, Wm., Chalgrave, Tebworth. R 1528: 2/188
IVES, Ann, Eversholt. 1722/50
Blanche, Stotfold, wid. 1670/208
Geo., Odell, farmer. A 1735/16
Jn., Carlton, yeo. A 1796/12
Robt., Colmworth, lab. A 1715/25
Wm., ("Docket mislaid", old index) A 1708/14
IVIT, Wm., Bedford St. Paul, lab. A 1751/19
IVORY, IVEREY, Alice, Tingrith, wid. 1670/213
Alice, Sundon. c.1670/234
Edw., Shillington, yeo. 1639-40/131
Eliz., Sutton, wid. 1705/11
Eliz., Houghton Regis. A 1713-14/18
Jn., Langford. 1579/139
Jn., Eversholt, yeo. (bundle 1665) 1666-7/105
Jn., Bedford St. John, yeo. 1685/94
Jn., Sundon, yeo. 1695/6
Jn., Bedford St. John, carpenter. 1719-20/86
Mary, Kempston, wid. 1660-1/62
Mary, Kempston. 1660/229
Peter, Clifton, husb. 1699/13
Ric., (no parish given). 1617/262
Robt., Shillington, Feaks Well. 1632/99

IVORY, IVEREY continued
Rog., Luton. 1569/107
Thos., Luton. 1562/110
Wm., Sundon, yeo. 1660/219
Wm., Biggleswade, Holme. BwR 1540: 1/1
IZZARD, IZAD, Geo., Thurleigh. A 1722-3/40
Joan, Woburn, wid. 1552/296
Jn., Thurleigh, yeo. A 1720/25
Jn., Thurleigh, minor. A 1721/46
Michael, Woburn. 1552/313

J

JACKSON, Agnes, Biggleswade. 1565/198
Chris., Henlow. 1727/64
Edw., Warden, steward. A 1825/7
Eliz., Kempston, wid. 1827/5
Helen, Eaton Bray, wid. 1677/42
Hester, St. Martin in the Fields, Middx., spins. 1649-50/115
Jas., Luton, cordwainer. A 1805/11
Jas., Dunstable, publican. A 1810/14
Jeremy, Whipsnade, carpenter. 1639-40/147
Joan, Bedford, wid. 1619-20/170, I 4/14
Joan, Ridgmont. 1621-2/133
Jn., Southill. AR 1674-5: 1/102
Jn., Southill, Broome, bach. AR 1683: 1/118
Jn., Luton, bricklayer. 1729/96
Josiah, Potton, innholder. A 1720/16
Oliver, Stagsden, Howard. 1726-7/96
Ric., Dunstable. R 1537-8: 5/9d
Ric., Ridgmont, husb. (inventory only) 1619, I 4/120
Ric., Leighton Buzzard. A 1743/13
Robt., Stagsden. 1606/73
Robt., Eaton Socon, Bushmead. A 1720/34
Robt., Kempston, yeo. 1810/53
Sarah, Bedford, wid. 1856/27
Thos., Milton Ernest, weaver. 1605/130
Thos., Maulden, lab. A 1734-5/20
Wm., Leighton Buzzard, brandy merchant. A 1819/74
JACOB, Jn., Henlow, stringer. R 1545: 11/102d
Jn., sen., Shillington, gardener. 1749/52
Wm., Henlow. R 1533-4: 3/122d
JACQUES, JAQUES, JACK, JACKS, Edw., Luton, yeo. AR 1687: 1/174
Joyce, Elstow, wid. 1609/108
Marg., Elstow, wid. 1653/115

JACQUES, JAQUES, JACK, JACKS continued
Robt., Luton, yeo. 1610/118
Thos., Stopsley. R 1547: 11/238d
Thos., Luton. 1559/154
Thos., Luton, draper, bach. AR 1671: 1/142
Thos., Stopsley, yeo. 1676/142
JAKEMAN, Jane, Cardington, wid. 1674/166
JAMES, alias Aspin, Edw., Yielden, poulterer. 1614/78
Humph., Stoke Hammond, Bucks. ?1560/332
Jeremiah, Flitwick, farmer. 1846/43
Jn., (no parish given), farmer. 1716-17/7
Jn., Tilbrook, yeo. A 1722-3/35
Jn., Over Dean, yeo. 1801/6
Jonathan, Bedford, lab. 1835/19
Jos., Kempston, West End. 1849/34
Math., Eversholt, Talbot, farmer. 1831/2
Oliver, Northill, Over Caldecote, lab. 1724-5/6
Robt., Eaton, husb. 1623-4/150
Sam., Yielden, shepherd. 1808/11
Susan, Tilbrook, wid. 1719/49
Thos., Tilbrook, farmer. A 1741-2/28
Thos., Wilshamstead, victualler. A 1762/14
alias Day, Wm., sen., Bedford. AR 1684: 1/25
Wm., Sutton, tailor. 1703/57
Wm., Bedford, carpenter. A 1734/12
Wm., Earls Barton, Northants, husb., Stevington. 1747/15
Wm., Bletsoe, yeo. 1805/19
JANE, alias Hopkins, Wm., Eggington, husb. Fac. 1712: 9/38
JANES, Hopkins alias Janes, see Hopkins
Ann, Milton Bryan, wid. 1754/18
Bartle, Houghton Regis. 1849/15
Hen., Wilshamstead, miller. 1648/105
Joshua, sen., Hockliffe, butcher. 1807/27
Thos., Tilsworth, yeo. 1695/10
Wm., sen., Milton Bryan, yeo. 1735/36
Wm., Milton Bryan, yeo. 1760/39
Wm., Eaton Bray, mealman. 1856/31
JARMAN, Sarah, Studham, wid. gentlewoman. 1743/37
see also German, Jermyn
JARNET, Sarah, Harlington, spins. 1743-4/81
see also Garnet
JARRATT, Wm., Woburn, gardener. 1724-5/95
JARVIS, JHARVYS, JARVICE, Anne, Ridgmont, wid. 1620/77
Annis, Kempston, wid. 1661-2/405
Edw., Langford, husb. 1756/5

JARVIS, JHARVYS, JARVICE continued
Hen., Meppershall, cook. 1613-4/140
Roland, Flitwick, lab. 1684/16
Rowland, Flitwick, chapman. AR 1685-6: 1/214
Steph., Ravensden. AR 1679: 1/69
Steph., sen., Kempston, yeo. 1686/69
Thos., Eaton Socon, Staploe. R 1559: 13/160
Thos., Eaton Socon, Duloe. R 1559: 13/161d
Thos., Ridgmont, lab. 1622/84
Thos., Goldington. 1660-1/224
Thos., Bedford, draper. 1677-8/77
Wm., Eaton Socon, Begwary. Inventory only. 1587, I 4/169
Wm., sen., Ridgmont. 1558/293
Wm., Ridgmont, husb. 1597/56
Wm., Eaton Socon, Beggary. 1614-15/10
Wm., Eaton Socon, Over Staploe. 1617/193
Wm., Roxton, Chawston, yeo. 1655/207
Wm., Woburn, tailor. 1696/111
Wm., Ridgmont, clothworker. 1706/90
JAYES, JEYSE, Geo., Felmersham, husb. 1640/68
Hen., Felmersham, yeo. 1578/88
Jn., Cardington, lab. 1619/210, I 4/138
Mark, Kempston, lab. 1632/55
Thos., Eaton Socon, Wyboston, yeo. 1585/22
Thos., Kempston. 1680-1/96
Wm., Colmworth (189). 1624/5
Wm., Kempston, lab. 1651-2/50
Wm., Colmworth. AR 1676: 1/66
Wm., Colmworth, yeo. 1679/47
JEAKINS, Alice, Blunham, wid. 1660/152
Jn., Eaton Socon, gent.. 1685/6
Jn., Blunham, shearman. 1706/8
Jos., Langford, farmer. A 1743/33
Mabel, Eaton Socon, wid. 1685/1
Steph., Eaton Socon, yeo. AR 1685: 1/78d
Steven, Eaton Socon, yeo. 1685/3
Thos., Blunham, shearman. 1669/22
Thos., Blunham, Chalton, yeo. 1707/4
JEANKINS, see Jenkins
JEBB, JEBE, Thos., Arlesey. R 1508/9: 1/205d
JEEVE, JEEVES, Edm., Marston, blacksmith. 1743-4/74
Hen., Sandy, Girtford, gardener. 1847/58
Jn., Henlow. 1638/115
Jn., Millbrook, husb. 1725/17
Jn., Blunham, lab. 1814/11

JEEVE, JEEVES continued
Percival, Arlesey. 1572/78
Robt., Astwick. 1632/113
Robt., Tempsford. 1694/2
Thos., Eyeworth, clerk. 1607-8/159
Thos., Henlow, lab. 1618/142
Thos., Sandy, Girtford, gardener. 1804/42
Thos., Felmersham, Radwell. A 1834/2
Thos., Sandy, Stratford, gardener. A 1840/16
Thos., Sandy, Stratford, gardener. 1840/18
Wm., sen., Sandy, yeo. and gardener. 1789/15
Wm., Sandy, Stratford End, gardener. 1816/36
Wm., Sandy, gardener. 1833/50
JEFFERSON, Edw., Southill, Stanford, innholder. 1722-3/73
Jn., Leighton Buzzard. LBR 1546-7: 1/18
Margt., Sandy, wid. 1681/49
Wm., Henlow. 1791/17
JEFFEREY, JEFFREY, JEFF(E)RIES, Page alias Jeffries, see Page
Ben., Thurleigh, farmer. 1831/23
Ben., Thurleigh. 1832/48
Ben., Ravensden, lab. A 1840/7
Eaton, Harrold, clockmaker. 1827/6
Edw., Bedford, yeo. 1816/34
Eliz., Kempston, wid. 1814/9
Jn., Turvey, Pixhill, yeo. R 1538: 5/11
Jn., Dunstable. R 1544: 11/12d
Ric., Lidlington, bach. 1588-9/114
Robt., sen., Turvey, yeo. A 1705/53
Robt., (old index "docket mislaid"). A 1708/10
Robt., Turvey, (old index, bundle missing). A 1745/12
Robt., Thurleigh. 1827/6
Robt., Thurleigh, late Cople, gent. 1841/26
Roger, Studham, vicar. R 1540: 6/62
Roger, Turvey, tailor. 1618-19/18
Sarah, Thurleigh, wid. 1848/34
Sharman, Bedford St. Cuthbert, lab. 1784/24
Steph., Turvey, husb. 1750/21
Thos., Bedford St. Paul, cutler. 1562-3/96
Thos., Northill, Ickwell, wheelwright. A 1727/19
Thos., Bromham, innholder. 1791/31
Thos., Kempston, grocer. 1810/20
Thos., Bolnhurst, farmer. 1850/46
Wm., Biddenham, yeo. 1691/75
Wm., Biddenham, victualler. A 1736/4
Wm., Great Barford, yeo. 1855/42

JOHNSON continued
Simon, Blunham, yeo. 1636/37
Steven, Oakley. 1633/154
Susan, Wilden, wid. 1706-7/60
Thos., esq., (old index "Docket mislaid"). A 1710/36
Wm., Haynes, lab. 1599/139
Wm., Biddenham, gent. 1623-4/138
Wm., Blunham, mercer. 1631/216
Wm., Toddington, innholder. 1641-2/132
Wm., Northill. AR 1682: 1/117
Wm., Streatley, husb. 1684/39
Wm., Melchbourne, grazier. A 1724/7
Wm., Melchbourne, grazier. A 1734-5/19
Wm., Bedford St. Paul, lab. 1756/6
Wm., Shefford, plumber and glazier. 1800/4
JOLLY, Jellias alias Jolly, see Jellis
JOLYS, Thomas, Ampthill. R 1506: 1/10
JONES, Agnes, Oakley. 1557/314
Beverley, Cardington, Fenlake, lab. 1750-1/66
Christian, Lidlington, wid. 1666/147
David, Barford. 1563?/204
David, Bedford, lab. A 1724/4
Edm., Luton, gent. 1689/20
Edm., Eversholt, gent., d. 1783, limited admon. A 1824
Edw., Ravensden, yeo. 1739-40/3
Edw., sen., Bedford, cordwainer. 1821/30
Eliz., Steppingley, wid. 1733/14
Eliz., Bedford, wid. A 1836/8
Eliz., Bedford St. Mary, wid. 1786/7
Fra., Houghton Conquest, How End, yeo. 1673/52
Geo., Houghton Regis, husb. 1681/43
Geo., Kempston, yeo. 1698/101
(ap Jones) Hen., Bromham, yeo. 1613/177
Hugh, Haynes. 1616-17/17
Isaac, Ampthill, musician in the Beds. Militia. 1800/32
Jacob, Stevington, baker. 1821/6
Joan, Steppingley, wid. 1639-40/150
Jn., jnr., Felmersham. 1553/156
Jn., Wymington, husb. 1585/20
Jn., Thurleigh. 1610/60
Jn., Bedford, tailor [Prerog. C. of Canterbury]. 1628-9/1a
Jn., (parish torn off). 1670/206
Jn., Steppingley, tailor. 1716/95
Jn., sen., Ampthill, hempdresser. 1737/41
Jn., Thurleigh, farmer. A 1744/19

JONES continued
Jn., Cople, ciderman. A 1746/11
Jn., Bedford, perukemaker. 1779/2
Jn. Tewis, Bedford, carpenter. 1837/3
Margt., Bolnhurst, wid. 1655/206
Martha, (old index only, bundle missing). A 1717/23
Mary, Ampthill, wid. A 1759/1
Math., Willington, blacksmith. 1705/30
Ric., Woburn. AR 1691: 1/219d
Robt., Steppingley, schoolmaster. 1716/24
Robt., Ampthill, victualler. A 1751/18
Robt., Kempston, yeo. AR 1685: 1/27
Sarah, Bedford, wid. 1846/44
Thos., Ravensden. A 1731/37
Wm., Battlesden, lab. 1616/46
Wm., sen., Kempston, blacksmith. AR 1680: 1/18
Wm., Battlesden. 1693/160
Wm., Roxton, lab. 1699/61
Wm., Willington, blacksmith. 1711-12/43
Wm., Bedford, yeo. 1734-5/62
Wm., Willington, blacksmith. A 1704/31
Wm., Bedford St. Mary, draper. A 1722/30
Wm., Blunham, Chalton, farmer. A 1735: 16/38
Wm., Ravensden, lab. 1743/1
Wm., Ampthill, cutler. 1785/38
Wm., Bedford, shepherd. 1844/15
see also Johns
JORDAN, JORDON, JORDAIN, JORDAYNE, Alice, Elstow, wid. 1603/81
Anne, Riseley, wid. A 1731/14
Barth., Kempston. R 1516-7: 1/254
Chris., Ampthill, smith. R 1536: 4/52
Edw., Luton. AR 1690: 1/177
Hugh, Riseley, weaver. 1691/74
Jn., Kempston. R 1519: 1/176
Jn., Eversholt. R 1540-1: 6/61
Jn., Keysoe, yeo. 1693/80
Jn., sen., Bedford, innholder and farmer. 1814/42
Jonathan, Campton, lab. 1827/2
Jos., Bedford, blacksmith. 1852/3
Robt., Marston. R 1504: 1/42d
Robt., Keysoe, lab. 1638/174
Thos., Stagsden. 1566/67
Thos., (old index only, bundle missing). A 1717/2
Thos., (old index only, bundle missing). A 1717/22
Wm., Elstow. 1555/149

JORDAN, JORDON, JORDAIN, JORDAYNE continued
Wm., Pertenhall, blacksmith. 1777/38
JOY, JOYE, Smith alias Joye, see Smith
Edm., Renhold. 1605/142
Geo., Steppingley. 1556/200
Joan, Steppingley. 1557/358
Jn., sen., Renhold, Salpho Bury. R 1521: 2/175d
Jn., Renhold, Salpho Bury, yeo. R 1556: 13/14d
Jn., Bedford St. Peter. 1627-8/213
Mary, Southill, Broom, spins. 1735-6/20
Ric., Renhold, Salphobury. 1560-1/69a
Ric., Bedford, gent. 1627/196
Ric., Great Barford. 1672/100
Robt., Cople, carpenter. A 1727-8/39
Thos., Bedford. R 1505-6: 1/82d
Thos., Goldington. 1732/69
Wm., Bedford. R 1503: 1/37d
Wm., Renhold, Salphobury, yeo. 1586-7/134
Wm., Renhold. 1623/129
Wm., Bedford, gent. 1696/95
see also Joyce
JOYCE, JOYES, Beatrice, Shillington, Pegsdon, wid. 1660-1/107
Edm., Wilden, tailor. 1621/161
Hannah, Cardington, wid. 1767/10
Hen., Cardington, Harrowden, farmer. 1745/36
Jn., Renhold, farmer. 1846/20
Jos., Gt. Barford, Birchfield Farm. 1853/28
Sam., Kempston. A 1857/11
Thos., Astwick, yeo. 1629/94
Thos., Carlton, lab. 1695/57
Thos., Roxton, Chawston. 1714/4
Thos., Flitton, grocer. A 1728/31
Thos., Eaton Socon, carpenter. 1769/5
Wm., Eaton Socon, dairyman. A 1734-5/22
Wm., Roxton, yeo. 1758/1
Wm., Stanbridge, shepherd. LBA 1828/85
see also Joye, Choice
JUCE, see Jewse
JUDD, JUDDE, Eliz., Milton Bryan, (fragment only). 1638/4
Harry, Colmworth. 1561/51
Jn., Colmworth, husb. 1581/19
Lawr., Colmworth. R 1531: 3/51
Ric., Colmworth, yeo. 1664/15
Robt., Blunham, farmer and maltster. 1849/20
Theophilus, Milton Bryan, clerk. A 1711/9

JUDD, JUDDE continued
Thos., Cardington. R 1504: 1/45d
Thos., Elstow. R 1540: 6/27
Thos., sen., Colmworth, husb. 1576/24
Thos., Colmworth, yeo. 1602/45
Thos., Colmworth, yeo. 1664/9
Thos., Colmworth, yeo. 1699/64
Wm., Milton Bryan. 1609/178
JUDGGE, Wm., Cranfield, lab., inventory only. 1619: I 4/140
JUDKIN, Eliz., Leighton Buzzard, spins. A 1776/19
Thos., Stagsden, clerk. 1652/100
JUFFS, Jas., Houghton Conquest, farmer. 1857/14
JUGGENS, Geo., Cranfield, roper. 1637/106
Robt., sen., Cranfield. 1617/224 I
Thos., Wootton, (bundle 1665). 1666/96
Wm., Cranfield, husb. 1652/90
Wm., Wootton, dairyman. 1719-20/106
JULES, Jn., Kempston. R 1559: 14/90d
JULIAN, alias Taylor, Thos., sen., Lidlington, mercer. R 1540: 6/29d
see also Gelian
JURY, Alice, Over Gravenhurst, wid. 1629/76
Edm., Henlow, yeo. 1631/206
JUSTICE, Thos., Biddenham, miller. 1676-7/179
Wm., Bromham. 1792/31

K

KADLEY, Jn., Maulden. R 1533: 3/125
KAGERILL, Mat., Tempsford, shearman. 1616/83
KAIRSLY, see Caresly
KANE, see Cain
KANNE, see Cain
KAY, Beatrice, Woburn, wid. (P.C.C.) 1642/1
KAYNES, see Cain, Cains
KEALE, see Keel
KEANINGE, Thos., Sundon, lab. 1621/164
KEATING, Walt., Warden, gardener. 1697/131
see also Keeton
KEBLE, KEEBLE, Jn., Northill, Nether Caldecote, husb. 1593/41
Sarah, Hockliffe, wife of Thos., blacksmith. 1731/11
Thos., Hockliffe, blacksmith. 1700/142
KEDLEY, Edw., Maulden. 1562/238
KEEBLE, see Keble
KEECH, Ann, Sharnbrook, wid. 1736-7/47
Ebenezer, Aspley Guise, Pigs Park, yeo. 1791/13

KEECH continued
Isaac, Stevington, farmer. 1852/31
Jeremiah, Nether Dean, lab. 1775/10
Jn., Milton Bryan, farmer. A 1759/18
Mary, Biggleswade. R 1807/30
Ric., Sharnbrook, yeo. 1725/69
Tim., Stevington, parish clerk. 1791/15
Tim., Stevington. 1853/29
KEEL, KEALE, Jn., Kempston, farmer. A 1729/36
Thos., Elstow, farmer. A 1729/15
Wm., Cardington. 1588/95
KEELING, KEALING, KELING, KELYNG, Antemenelli, Campton, clerk. 1726/27
Eliz., Potton. 1684-5/118
Jas., Haynes, husb. 1631/237
Jas., Dunton, lab. 1685/63
Jn., Potton, fellmonger. 1706/39
Jn., Potton, fellmonger. 1706/52
Jn., Sutton, yeo. 1736-7/25
Mary, Campton, wid. 1734/21
Philip, Dunton, sawyer. 1667/45
Ric., Haynes. 1616/42
Sarah, Warden, wid. A 1701/37
Wm., Wilden, lab. 1671-2/19
KEEN(S), KENE, KEIN, Ambrose, Ampthill, locksmith. 1708/32
Eliz., Leighton Buzzard, spins. LB 1772/30
Fra., Cranfield, husb. 1712/54
Fra., Totternhoe, wid. A 1784/1
Jn., sen., Dunstable, yeo. 1795/11
Jon., Sutton, Fuzzen House. 1751/30
Mary, Ampthill, wid. 1716/55
Mary, Berkhamstead, Herts., spins. LB 1770/21
Ric., Milton Ernest, vicar. R 1539: 5/38d
Sam., Stagsden. 1698-9/164
Sar., Caddington, Woodside, wid. 1813/31
Thos., Marston. 1672/111
Thos., Stagsden, yeo. A 1711-12/59
Thos., Dunstable, cordwainer. 1850/12
Wm., Caddington, Woodside, yeo. 1844/13
KEENORD, Ann, Keysoe, wid. AR 1689-90: 1/83
Jas., Wrestlingworth, farmer. A 1743/9
Ric., Roxton, yeo. A 1729/30
KEEP, Ann, Bedford St. Mary, spins. A 1826/2
Edw., Sandy, lab. 1763/40
Jn., Marston. 1719-20/93

KEEP continued
Jn., sen., Marston, husb. 1761/10
Jos., Sandy, Girtford, tailor. 1832/34
Thos., Marston, yeo. 1746/38
KEETON, Ann, Cardington, late Tempsford, wid. 1826/54
Wm., Tempsford, innholder. 1804/37
see also Keating
KEFFORD, KEFORDE, K(E)IFFORD, Anthony, Astwick, yeo. 1643-4/119
Eliz., Roxton, spins. 1721/102
Eliz., Roxton, Chawston, wid. 1727-8/111
Jn., sen., Wrestlingworth, yeo. 1653/175
Mary, Cople, wid. 1752/47
Nich., Wrestlingworth. 1604/26
Ric., Wrestlingworth, yeo. 1680/62
Ric., sen., Roxton, Chawston, yeo. 1717-18/70
Ric., Eaton Socon, Wyboston, farmer. 1785/35
Ric., Elstow, yeo. 1802/34
Robt., Sandy, (inventory only). 1619 I 4/55
Robt., Roxton. 1688/52
Robt., Whipsnade. 1690/63
Robt., Roxton, Chawston, yeo. 1734-5/10
Sarah, Wrestlingworth, wid. 1681-2/83
Thos., Wrestlingworth, yeo. 1716/72
Thos., Potton, lab. 1803/20
Wm., Sutton, lab. 1573/7
Wm., Cople, yeo. 1746/35
see also Kyford
KEIGLE, KEYGLE, Fra., Thurleigh. 1620/49
Jn., Toddington, Chalton, yeo. 1815-16/133
KEIN, see Keens
KEITH, CEITH, Wm., Astwick. 1556/119
KELING, see Keeling
KELKE, Edw., Cople, tailor. 1616/118 I
KELLOWE, Ben., Ampthill, gardener. 1629/81
Jonas, Maulden, poulter. 1635/72
KELLY, KELE, Cuthbert, Stanbridge, singleman. 1559/165
KELSON, Wm., Thurleigh, lab. 1663-4/86
KELYNG, see Keeling
KEMMENT, Mark, Bedford, yeo. A 1797/10
KEMP, Jas., Langford, farmer. 1841/11
Thos., Dunstable, victualler. A 1715/26
KEMPSON, see Kemson
KEMPTON, Jn., Ampthill, gardener. 1724/8
KEMSHEAD, Mary, Riseley, wid. 1778/10
Stephen, Wymington, farmer and grazier. 1769/22

KEMSON, KEMPSON, Eliz., Maulden, wid. A 1839/18
Jas., Shillington, yeo. 1835/31
Jn., Ridgmont, lab. 1728/41
Jn., sen., Flitwick, Ruxox, yeo. 1811/24
Jn., Shillington, yeo. 1817/10
Peter, Flitwick, Ruxox, yeo., A 1851/8
Thos., Shillington, yeo. 1845/21
KENDALL, Ann, Wilshamstead, wid. 1741-2/70
Edw., Wilshamstead. 1760/6
Geo., Wrestlingworth, clerk. A 1826/15
Jas., Wilshamstead, shopkeeper. 1797/11
Jn., (no parish given). R 1556: 13/40
Jn., Pertenhall, husb. 1586/149
Jn., Wilshamstead, blacksmith. 1781/55
Jn., Wilshamstead, yeo. A 1785/6
Math., Felmersham, lab. A 1736/11
Thos., Bedford, carpenter. 1608/83
Thos., Wilshamstead. A 1737/44
Thos., Wilshamstead, yeo. 1807/12
Wm., Odell, farmer. 1857/7
KENDRO, Ric., Sundon. 1558/49
KENNAN, Jn., Shelton. 1597/10
KENNETT, Ric., Sutton, bach. AR 1671: 1/92
KENNING(S), Jn., Toddington, lab. 1625/180
Thos., Bedford, collarmaker. 1812/53
KENT, Ann, Barton, wid. AR 1676: 1/152
Ann, Cople, wid. A 1706/27
Eliz., Cranfield, wid. 1712/68
Geo., Campton. 1812/39
Jn., Sharnbrook. R 1531-2: 3/52d
Jn., Clophill, yeo. AR 1680: 1/204
Jn., Cranfield, lab. A 1712/39
Jn., Cranfield, lab. 1714/30
Jos., Wymington, farmer. 1761/51
Mary Eliz., Flitton. 1856/21
Math., Silsoe. AR 1674: 1/191d
Math., Silsoe, gent. 1678/155
Nich., (no parish). 1561/148
Rebecca, Henlow, spins. 1712/38
Ric., Ridgmont, Segenhoe. 1603-4/85
Ric., Husborne Crawley. 1660-1/120
Ric., Husborne Crawley. A 1753/10
Robt., Holcote, yeo. 1584-5/253
Thos., (no parish). 1558/295
Thos., Haynes. 1578-9/114

KENT continued
Thos., Wootton, husb. 1602/66
Thos., sen., Ridgmont, Lyefield, gent. 1684/48
Thos., Cardington, Cotton End, dairyman. 1703/30
Thos., Ridgmont, gent. 1729/1
"Umfra", Felmersham. R 1544: 11/27d
Wm., Clapham. R 1527: 2/67
Wm., Wootton. 1557/267
KENWORTHY, Jn., Bedford, carpenter. 1809/9
KENYGALL, Thos., Northill. R 1500: 1/15
KERSOTTE, Geo., Bedford, pewterer. 1559-60/213
KETTLE, Hen., Husborne Crawley, yeo. 1632-3/115
KEY, Dan., Tempsford, yeo. 1801/34
Geo., Eaton Socon, Upper Staploe, yeo. 1731/86
Jn., Blunham, yeo. 1714/96
KEYES, Ric., Bedford, draper. 1557/274
KEYFHOE, Mary, Clophill, wid. 1614/88
KIDD, KID, Chas., Bletsoe, husb. A 1751/11
Edw., Bedford. AR 1675: 1/10
Jn., Elstow, gent. 1643-4/124
Jn., Bedford, periwigmaker. 1715/26
Mary, Bedford, wid. A 1733/15
Sarah, Bletsoe, wid. 1762/35
Susan, Maulden, wid. 1659/85
KIDGELL, Thos., Toddington, Herne, dairyman. 1689/15
Thos., Little Staughton, gent. 1726-7/97
KIDGER, Ann, Sundon, wid. A 1741/19
Jn., Sundon, lab. 1720/64
KIDMAN, Jas., Eaton Socon, Dallow, yeo. 1762/10
Simon, Northill. A 1759/15
Thos., Bedford, esq. 1840/19
KIFFORD, see Kefford
KIGHTLEY, Jas., Husborne Crawley. A 1773/2
Jn., Nether Dean, yeo. 1708/23
Jn., Houghton Conquest, farmer. A 1732-3/27
Jos., Dean. A 1713/5
KILBY, KYLBE, KYLBEE, Agnes, wid., Luton. R 1546: 11/163
Jn., Maulden, bricklayer. AR 1586: 1/215d
Jn., Potton, mason. A 1706/34
Jn., Millbrook, yeo. 1570-1/21
Jn., Luton, Thrales End, yeo. 1618/132
Jn., (parish torn off), bricklayer. 1683/7
Jn., Langford, dairyman. 1728/99
Jn., Luton, Newmilland, yeo. 1733/31
Jos., Ampthill, grocer. 1727/78